VICTORIAN LITERATURE
AND CULTURE

Volume 22

ADVISORY BOARD

VICTORIAN LITERATURE AND CULTURE

Volume 22

EDITORS

JOHN MAYNARD
ADRIENNE AUSLANDER MUNICH

Associate Editor: Sandra Donaldson
Managing Editor: Abigail Burnham Bloom

Review Editor: Winifred Hughes
Assistant Review Editor: Susan Katz

Special Effects Editor: Jeffrey Spear
Assistant Special Effects Editor: Pearl Hochstadt

AMS PRESS
1994

Copyright © 1995 by AMS Press, Inc.

ISSN 1060-1503

Series ISBN 0-404-64200-4

Vol. 22 ISBN 0-404-64222-5

Library of Congress Catalog Card Number: 73-80684

For current subscription information or back orders for volumes 1–21, write to AMS Press, Inc., 56 East 13th Street, New York, NY 10003, USA.

VICTORIAN LITERATURE AND CULTURE is a publication of the Browning Institute, Inc., a nonprofit organization. It is published through the generous support of New York University, the State University of New York at Stony Brook, and the University of North Dakota. The editors gratefully acknowledge our indebtedness to our editorial assistants Lisa Golmitz, Martha Heller, Catherine Pavlish, and Mary Sullivan.

Manuscripts and editorial correspondence can be addressed to either editor:
Adrienne Munich, Department of English, SUNY/Stony Brook, Stony Brook, NY 11794 (516 632 9176; fax: 516 632 6265).
John Maynard, Department of English, NYU, 19 University Pl., Rm. 235, N.Y., NY 10003 (212 998 8835; fax: 212 995 4019).

Please submit two copies of manuscripts; articles should be double-spaced throughout and follow the new MLA style (with a list of Works Cited at the conclusion). Chapters of books submitted for the *Works in Progress* section may follow the author's chosen style in the book project.

Correspondence concerning review essays should be addressed to Winifred Hughes, 50 Wheatsheaf Lane, Princeton, NJ 08540 (609 921 1489).

Suggestions for reprints of Victorian materials, texts or illustrations, should be addressed to Jeffrey Spear, Department of English, NYU, 19 University Pl., Rm. 200, N.Y., NY 10003 (212 998 8820; fax: 212 995 4019).

Manufactured in the United States of America

CONTENTS

WORKS IN PROGRESS

REVIEW ESSAYS

BROWNING BIBLIOGRAPHY

ILLUSTRATIONS

VEILED WOMEN, THE LAW OF COVERTURE, AND WILKIE COLLINS'S *THE WOMAN IN WHITE*

By Lenora Ledwon

IN NINETEENTH-CENTURY ENGLAND, women's bodies were the habitual sites of intrusive legal regulation. From birth to death, women faced legal disqualifications and disadvantages in areas such as the regulation of venereal disease, voting rights, divorce, wife abuse, child custody, child support, and property law. But the most persistent and basic deprivation women faced occurred through coverture, the loss of legal identity associated with marriage. Wilkie Collins uses coverture as the central paradigm of *The Woman in White*; coverture becomes a metonymic pattern with which to explore the issue of loss of feminine identity.[1] Using three primary triads — 1. Percival-Laura-Anne, 2. Count Fosco-Countess Fosco-Marian, and 3. Walter-Percival-Fosco — to match the tripartite structure of coverture, Collins critiques a legal system that erases feminine identity. But what begins as a radical critique of women's loss of identity under coverture finally falls back into complacency, reinforcing the ideological assumption that law should work differently for men than for women.

Blackstone, in his *Commentaries on the Laws of England*, writes that, according to the law of coverture, "the very being or legal existence of the woman is suspended during marriage" (1:430).[2] The husband's legal identity "covers" the wife, so that in the typology of the common law the husband and wife are one, and the husband is the one. Once a woman marries, she becomes nonexistent in the eyes of the law. Without separate legal existence, the married woman becomes veiled, ghostly and unknowable. She is cut adrift from privilege and power, losing her name and becoming unnameable. The veiled or covered woman not only haunts the legal system but haunts the social order, challenging that order to name her.

In *The Woman in White*, Laura Fairlie's marriage renders her blank. (The woman in white, on one level of signification, is a woman in a wedding dress.) Once married, Laura loses her property, her social position, and her very identity. Her husband stages her "death" and has her incarcerated in an insane

1

asylum under the name and identity of another woman. Thus, marriage not only is the symbolic "civil death" or loss of legal existence but also the very particular and personal loss of freedom, home, property, and social status. Laura is not the only character subject to loss of identity. As is the case with coverture, in which a wife's existence is subsumed in the husband's, *all* major characters in *Woman in White* are subject to threatened loss of identity.

The coverture formula operates along the lines of Husband + Wife = HusbandPlus. Those who are "covered" play the Lacanian role of veiled phallus, that is, they are objects of desire but cannot be desiring subjects. And their absorption by another results in the empowerment and creation of a new, third legal entity, with greater legal rights and privileges, the HusbandPlus. This threat of being "covered" by another is played out in a series of triadic power struggles. However, while Collins begins by attacking the common law of coverture, his imagination at last succumbs to the status quo, reinforcing the idea that law works differently for men than for women.

Law fails both men and women in the text, but it fails women in a different manner than it fails men. Laura, Anne, and even Marian are assimilated *by* the law. Walter *assimilates* the discourse of the law. There are disturbing signs that when the hero uses the principles of law for his own ends (to convince the reader of the truth) he learns to fill the patriarchal role all too easily. Walter uses the tactics and the very words of the tyrannical husband and even is mistaken for Sir Percival. Walter, like Laura, changes identity under the influence of coverture. However, what is waiting to "cover" him is not the blankness of nonexistence but the confining mask of the oppressor.

Before exploring the ways Collins utilizes coverture as a paradigm in *Woman in White*, it is helpful first to consider background information on the legal fiction of coverture and, second, to take into account Collins's personal interest in the law and legal issues.

Common Law of Coverture

"ENGLAND IS THE LAND of domestic happiness," remarks Count Fosco, the titanic villain of *Woman in White* (594). The Count's statement is tempered by the fact that it is part of his written criminal confession, revealing a husband's plot to deprive his wife of identity and exposing England as a land of profound domestic *un*happiness. This domestic unhappiness is tied to a legal fiction so firmly entrenched in English law that it took more than a quarter of a century of acrimonious parliamentary debates before even a partial correction was effected.[3] That legal fiction is the law of coverture.

Legal theorist Lon L. Fuller notes that the legal fiction represents the pathology of the law. When all goes well and established legal rules encompass neatly the social life they are intended to regulate, there is little occasion for fictions. . . . Only when legal reasoning falters and reaches out clumsily for help do we realize what a complex undertaking the law is. (viii)

Legal fictions can include such concepts as (1) constructive notice (in which a purchaser is said to have notice of a mortgage duly recorded, even if he or she did not have actual notice), (2) the doctrine of attractive nuisance (in which the owner is alleged to have invited children to visit his or her premises, including children of whose existence he or she is unaware), (3) the identification of a corporation as a legal person with rights and duties, as well as (4) the treatment of husband and wife as one (Fuller 12–13, 24, 33–34). Such concepts are not easily classifiable as true of false (Morris Cohen, qtd. in Fuller ix). And it is this uneasy, fantastic quality of legal fictions, in which one element (the legal fiction) oscillates between two poles of meaning (truth and falsity), that is so appealing to a sensation novelist such as Collins.

There is something disturbing and unsettling in legal fictions. As in Tzvetan Todorov's definition of the "fantastic" as the border between the uncanny and the marvelous, legal fictions seem to hover between truth and fiction. Todorov, in *The Fantastic*, identifies the "pure" fantastic as that work which sustains ambiguity completely (43–44). Like the pure ambiguity in Henry James's *The Turn of the Screw* (is there a supernatural explanation or a realistic explanation?), the ambiguity in legal fictions seems complete. Does the legal fiction belong in the realm of truth or falsity? "Legal" would seem to be aligned with truth, while "fiction" suggests falsity. The legal fiction vibrates between realms in a particularly dense, complex tautology. Collins's penchant for an intricate synthesis of Gothic, social criticism, and mystery is well-served by the legal fiction's ambiguity.

Additionally, his thematic use of the legal fiction of coverture allows Collins to explore the popularized links between women's rights and sensationalism. The inequities of coverture formed much of the basis for agitation for reform of married women's property law. During parliamentary debates concerning married women's property rights, Lord Westbury commented that the Married Women's Property Bill, "seemed to have sprung from the sensationalism of the day, which delighted in extravagancies, and sought to carry them even into the amendment of the law" (Holcombe 174). Westbury went on to state that passage of the Bill would mean, "an entire subversion of domestic rule which had prevailed in this country for more than 1,000 years" (Holcombe 174). What was so dangerous or extravagant about extending property rights to married women? The answer is that such legal changes chipped away at the doctrine of coverture and threatened the Victorian ideals of separate spheres and a family in which the wife was the angel in the house and the husband the breadwinner doing daily battle in the harsh and profaning world of business. The sensation novel (including *Woman in White*) often invested part of its energies in this chipping away at long-cherished notions of women's proper status and position. One way in which *Woman in White* carries out its own subversive critique is by extravagantly insisting on the injustices of coverture.

The essence of the doctrine of coverture lies in the suspension of a woman's legal existence upon marriage. According to the English common law, once a woman married, her legal existence was displaced, or "covered," by her husband. As Blackstone explains,

> By marriage the very being or legal existence of a woman is suspended, or at least it is incorporated or consolidated into that of the husband, under whose wing, protection and cover she performs everything, and she is therefore called in our law a feme covert; is said to be covert-baron, or under the protection and influence of her husband, her baron, or lord; and her condition during marriage is called her coverture. (1:430)

A wife has no separate legal existence apart from her husband. In fact, Blackstone comments that the reason a husband cannot contract with his own wife is that "the grant would be to suppose her separate existence; and to covenant with her, would be only [for the husband] to covenant with himself" (1:430).

This principle of identity between husband and wife imposed severe limitations on the rights and duties of a married woman, granted additional power and property rights to the husband at the expense of the wife, and in many ways made the wife the property of her husband. For example, upon marriage, a woman: lost all personal property to her husband; lost all right to any income from her real property; had to forfeit any wages or earnings during marriage to her husband; could not sue or be sued in her own name; could not sign a contract alone; and could not make a will by herself (Shanley 8). Additionally, the husband had the right to "physically correct" his wife (i.e., to beat her), had an absolute right to child custody, and could enforce the return of a runaway wife (Shanley 9).

Volume I of Blackstone's *Commentaries* is titled "Of the Rights of Persons." In this volume, Blackstone identifies the three great relations of private life as 1) master and servant, 2) husband and wife, and 3) parent and child. This grouping of binary pairs suggests that in each relationship there will be one who controls and one who is under control. As master is to servant, as parent is to child, so is husband to wife. However, while a servant can leave his or her employment, and while a child will grow into majority, a wife remains a wife and subject to the disabilities of coverture. (Divorce for most women during much of the nineteenth century was hardly a practical option. The divorce laws improved slightly over time, but only to the extent that divorce for women went from being practically impossible to being highly impractical.)

Significantly, *single* women in general had much the same property rights as men (although they did not have the right to vote). As Lee Holcombe notes, "It was not the fact of being female but the status of wife that entailed severe legal disabilities" (4). In fact, the only other persons who similarly lacked legal existence were children, idiots, and felons, as noted by Frances Power Cobbe in her 1868 article, "Criminals, Idiots, Women and Minors: Is the Classification Sound?" (Shanley 58). Children and idiots were presumed mentally incapable of legal obligations, and felons were presumed to forfeit legal rights because of their criminal actions. Married women, presumably, did not lose mental competence upon marriage, nor was marriage a crime for which only wives rather than husbands were held liable. (Cobbe poses the question a visitor from another planet might ask — "Why is the property of the woman who commits Murder, and the property of the woman who commits Matrimony, dealt with alike by your law?" [Shanley 58].) Some other justification was needed for the legal fiction of coverture.

The most common justification for perpetuating the inequities of coverture was that a woman needed protection — from the world, from business, which was presumed to profane, and from men other than her husband. (The possibility that a wife might require protection from an unscrupulous husband was not a matter of concern for the common law.) Blackstone suggests that women should be content with their position, for "even the disabilities, which the wife lies under, are for the most part intended for her protection and benefit. So great a favourite is the female sex of the laws of England" (1:433). The implicit, if disregarded, question must then become, who protects women from their protectors?

Lady Caroline Norton, involved in one of the most famous divorce cases of the nineteenth century, raised precisely this point in a series of pamphlets protesting the injustice of the common law. In her *A Letter to the Queen on Lord Chancellor Cranworth's Marriage and Divorce Bill*, she argued that women will never receive justice because legislators cannot

> succeed in acting on the legal fiction that married women are "non-existent," and man and wife are still "one," in cases of alienation, separation, and enmity, when they are about as much "one" as those ingenious twisted groups of animal death we sometimes see in sculpture; one creature wild to resist, and the other fierce to destroy. (*Selected Writings* 28)

The fiction of legal unity of husband and wife allows for only one will in marriage — the husband's.

Suffering and Identity under Coverture

LIKE THE HEROINES OF many ninteenth-century novels, including Laura Fairlie in *Woman in White*, Lady Caroline Norton suffered under the misogyny of the law. In her *Letter to the Queen*, she wrote that she "learned the English law respecting women, piecemeal, by suffering from every one of its defects of protection," adding, "My husband is a lawyer; and he has taught it to me by exercising over my tormented and restless life every quirk and quibble of its tyranny" (*Selected Writings* 62, 145). There is "scarcely any result of this anomalous position," she declared, "that I have not learned by personal and grievous experience . . .", (*English Laws* 158). Unable to bring suit for libel as a married woman (because only her husband had such a legal right), she concluded, "I was 'non-existent,' except for the purpose of suffering, as far as the law was concerned; it could oppress, but never help me" (*English Laws* 160).

The reality of coverture, according to Caroline Norton, was that wives found their legal rights and duties absorbed by their husbands. Norton insisted on her own existence, but the legal system offered no support for her position. Therefore, in order to claim an independent voice, she resorted to writing the series of pamphlets which now serve as a personal record of one woman's lived experience of coverture. Significantly, as Mary Poovey notes, in establishing a speaking identity, Norton presented herself in the mode of a fictionalized persecuted heroine. According to Poovey, Norton was "reappropriating the identity of a wronged woman by casting herself as the victim in a familiar Victorian genre, the melodrama" (Poovey 66).[4] Suffering is the way of life for the heroine of melodrama as well as for the victimized wife under coverture. But can suffering ever be seen as empowering? And what are the dangers inherent in that view?

Florence Nightingale, in her *Cassandra*, finds an ambivalent empowerment latent in women's suffering. Suffering is preferable to a state of dull stupefaction, she insists. Suffering proves one exists. And for the disenfranchised, suffering may become a curious instrument of change. Nightingale writes, "Give us back our suffering, we cry to Heaven in our hearts — suffering rather than indifferentism: for out of nothing comes nothing. But out of suffering may come the cure" (208).

Cassandra also contains Nightingale's well-known statement that, "The next Christ will perhaps be a female Christ" (230). There is a hint here of the notion of woman's special capacity for suffering, combined with the concept of redemption through sacrifice, leading to a kind of existential masochism. "I suffer, therefore, I am."

Suffering marks the unlined feminine face. And suffering becomes the quintessence of femininity. Sarah Ellis, in *The Daughters of England*, notes that women are more susceptible to both pain and pleasure than men (3). Roland Barthes, in "The Face of Garbo," links the power of Garbo's screen image to Garbo's almost transcendent capacity for suffering, a moment in screen history "where the flesh gives rise to mystical feelings of perdition" (56). Significantly, in the film Barthes discusses (*Queen Christina*), Garbo wears white, mask-like makeup. Thus, she, too, is an image of a woman in white, a woman waiting to be marked by suffering.

Initially, Laura is a more perfect woman in white than Anne, because she is less "marked" than Anne. (She also is the first woman in white, because Mrs. Fairlie notes in her letter that she dressed Anne in Laura's old white frocks and white hats [69].) Laura is smoother and more blank than Anne. Walter notes that Laura's transparent eyes and smooth purity of skin differ from Anne's troubled face (105). Even Laura's writing is more ephemeral than Anne's. Unlike Anne's warning note to Laura that nearly succeeds in halting Laura's engagement and throws the Fairlie household into domestic turmoil, Laura's writing is written in the sand: "Wind and wave had long since smoothed out the trace of her which she had left in those marks in the sand" (124). And it is this blankness that makes Laura the perfect object for marking through suffering. Angela Carter, in *The Sadeian Woman*, compares Marilyn Monroe and de Sade's Justine and reaches the chilling conclusion that "both have huge, appealing, eloquent eyes, the open windows of the soul; their dazzling fair skins are of such a delicate texture that they look as if they will bruise at a touch, carrying the exciting stigmata of sexual violence for a long time, and that is why gentlemen prefer blondes" (63). Carter adds that, "Marilyn/Justine has a childlike candour and trust and there is a faint touch of melancholy about her that has been produced by this trust, which is always absolute and always betrayed" (63).

Both Anne Catherick and Laura Fairlie are pale, fair victims whose function lies primarily in their suffering and the betrayal of their trust. (Walter finds "the key" to Laura's character in "that generous *trust* in others which, in her nature, grew innocently out of the sense of her own truth" [63, emphasis added].) This is not to say that Anne and Laura are the same type of "Good Bad Girl" as Marilyn/Justine. Anne and Laura lack the eroticism of Marilyn/Justine. However, if "blondness is a state of ambivalent grace" (Carter 65), then both fair women (Anne and Laura) qualify for that state of grace through their existence as vehicles of suffering. In the early phases of the text, while Anne's suffering is immediately apparent in the marks on her face, Laura's is yet to be made visible.

Woman in White subtly suggests that feminine suffering may become empowering, even if only momentarily or inadequately. After Laura returns from her honeymoon, Marian notes with surprise that suffering has brought to the surface a hidden strength in Laura: "Through all the years of our close intimacy this passive force in her character had been hidden from me — hidden even from herself, till love found it, and suffering called it forth" (173).

However, existential masochism does not empower the feminine so much as it reinforces an entrenched phallocentric legal system. Lacan's essay "The signification of the phallus" is helpful in understanding this point. For Lacan, the phallus is not a physical organ but a signifier of power (*the* signifier of all signifiers). That which is exchanged in society is that which has the value of the phallus. Typically for Lacan, men desire to *possess* the phallus (and thus become subjects), and women *are* the phallus (and thus become objects). In order to become a subject in language, according to Lacan, one must become masculine by possessing the phallus. Sexual identity is based either on having or being the phallus. If you possess the phallus, you are a subject. If you are the phallus, you are Other, feminine, and an object.

The phallus as the ultimate signifier plays its role veiled, and so femininity is defined by masquerade. The feminine role is to masquerade as symbol or icon. But something Lacan fails to ask is, if femininity is a masquerade, is masculinity equally a masquerade? Collins suggests the answer is "yes." The male characters in *Woman in White* constantly battle to control the economy of masquerade, to negotiate desire by taking on the mask or role of masculine subject.

Covered women are non-subjects, objects under the law, while the men who possess them are legal subjects. This goes a long way toward explaining the recurring image of the "woman in white," the woman "covered" in the symbolic color of marriage, who in several instances even appears veiled. Both Anne Catherick and Laura Fairlie are "covered" (and erased) by the legalistic machinations of Sir Percival, and both play the role of veiled phallus, the object of desire but never the desiring subject. Percival needs both of these covered, veiled women, for they empower him. Just as the veiled phallus is the necessary object of masculine empowerment, coverture empowers the husband, creating a HusbandPlus from the rights and duties of husband + wife.

Collins and the Law

WILKIE COLLINS ENTERED LINCOLN'S INN in 1846 at the age of 22 and was called to the Bar in 1851 (Ellis, *Wilkie Collins* 8). Like Bram Stoker, he was a lawyer who chose not to practice law. The law and legal issues were nevertheless recurring themes in many of his novels. For example, *No Name* (1862) revolves around legal questions of legitimacy, inheritance, and marriage. *The Moonstone* (1868) centers on an inheritance. *Man and Wife* (1870) addresses Irish and Scottish marriage laws and the English law of married women's property. *The Law and the Lady* (1875) deals with the unusual Scottish verdict of "Not Proven." And two of his works, *The Dead Secret* (1857) and *The Woman in White* (1860), had a basis in real-life legal cases.[5]

The law permeates *Woman in White*. Narrative structure, plot, imagery, and theme all are driven by the mechanisms of the law. In his Preface to the Second Edition, Collins is careful to note that he makes correct presentation of legal points (ix). He assures the reader that an experienced solicitor assisted him with legal matters in the text and adds that, "The 'law' in this book has been discussed, since its publication, by more than one competent tribunal, and has been decided to be sound" (ix–x). (The quotation marks around "law" suggest a heightened sensitivity to the close ontological relationship between law and Law — that is, between fictionalized law in the novel and the created social fiction that is Law.)

From the outset of the text, Collins incorporates legal procedure into his narrative technique.[6] He begins with the hearsay rule, a rule governing evidentiary exclusions. In the Preamble to the text, the speaker (who is Walter Hartright) asserts that "no circumstance of importance, from the beginning to the end of the disclosure, shall be related on hearsay evidence" (18). This use of the hearsay rule accounts for the much-commented upon narrative structure (the text consists of a series of narratives by different witnesses). Theoretically, each narrator will testify only to what he or she knows by firsthand evidence. Actually, the hearsay rule is not strictly followed. Not the least of the problems is that Walter actually acts as a master narrator, rearranging, editing, and acting as both advocate and witness. Walter purposely suppresses and alters part of Pesca's narrative, as a "necessary" concealment from the reader (570). Also, Walter at one point decides to present the story of Marian and Laura slightly revised, in "brief, plain, studiously simple abstract," because their actual words and story were "often interrupted, often inevitably confused" (413). Thus, the particularity of the women's voices is lost, and Walter "covers" their story by imposing a linear, logocentric speech over lived female experience.

In his use of law in the text, Collins sets up a continual tension between Law and Truth, suggesting that the two are mutually exclusive. Walter complains that the law is the servant of the long purse and indicts the law as corrupt and inadequate. However, although Walter criticizes the law, he applies legal standards of evidence to his narration. His object ("to present the truth always in its most direct and most intelligible aspect" 18–19) also is an object of the law. Thus, from the outset, Collins sets in motion an implicit irritant, a riddle that tugs and teases the framework of the text. The structure should ensure truth, but it is based on a system asserted to be inadequate. This opening tension continues throughout the text, so that the reader sees a constant undercutting of legal methods and a criticism of law, combined with self-serving use of the law's techniques of proof. This tension encourages a sceptical reading of the text.

"It is the great beauty of the Law," says Lawyer Gilmore, "that it can dispute any human statement, made under any circumstances, and reduced to any form" (139). In this respect, Collins sets up legal inquiry as a hermeneutics of suspicion — a hermeneutics practiced by most of the major characters and a hermeneutic directive for the reader. ("As the Judge might once have heard it, so the Reader shall hear it now" [18].) If the law can dispute any statement, then there can be no final truth, no comforting foundation to any story, no point at which to rest. The groud can always be cut out from under you.

The implicit difficulty with such a hermeneutics is that it may be warping, distorting, and cynicizing. Marian, for example, worries that her constant suspicious state distorts her perception of reality. (Considering how to safeguard her writing materials, Marian thinks, "*Distorted by the suspicion which had now become a part of myself*, even such trifles as these looked too dangerous to be trusted without a guard . . ." [305, emphasis added].) But such distorting scepticism is the only way to survive. In the world of the text, the innocent and the naîve suffer, and only those who maintain an attitude of constant suspicion will prevail. Even lawyers are not exempt from succumbing to naîveté. Lawyer Gilmore chides Walter for being suspicious of Sir Percival, saying,

> I am an old man, and I take the practical view. You are a young man, and you take the romantic view. Let us not dispute about our views. I live professionally in an atmosphere of disputation, Mr. Hartright, and I am only too glad to escape from it, as I am escaping here. (126)

Ironically, there is no escape. The "romantic view," which sees devious plots and schemes everywhere, *is* in actuality the "practical view." Life in fact proves to be saturated with dangerous intrigues. The only effective negotiation of life is to sustain the legal hermeneutic of scepticism.

Triads and The Woman in White[7]

THE DOUBLE IS A COMMON (and much written about) motif in the nineteenth-century novel. Significantly, *Woman in White* focuses not on doubles but on triads. Less stable, less "perfect" a relationship than the double, the triad allows for complex, shifting, and dangerous slippages of identity.

Close analysis of the text discloses a remarkably high number of triads. *The Woman in White*'s triads include: three half-sisters (Anne, Marian, and Laura), three lead male characters (Walter, Percival, and Fosco), three "good guys" (Laura, Walter, and Marian), three members of the mysterious Italian Brotherhood (Pesca, Fosco, and the man with the scar), three living members of the Hartright family (Walter, his mother, and his sister), three wives with absent husbands (Mrs. Catherick, Mrs. Fairlie, and Mrs. Clements), and the romantic triangle of the Count and his two loves (the Countess and Marian), to name a few. Also, origins are established as romantic triads. So, for example, Anne's origins are based in a romantic triangle involving Philip Fairlie, his legal wife, and Mrs. Catherick. And Marian's ties to Laura are based in the triad of Mr. Halcombe (her father), Mrs. Fairlie (her and Laura's mother), and Mr. Fairlie (Marian's stepfather). Collins sets up metaphysical triads, such as the previously discussed relationship between Law, Truth, and Falsity. And there are three versions of the written word (the marriage register) that lead to Walter's discovery of Percival's secret — the original marriage register, the altered original, and the copy of the true original.

The triad's significance rests on the unique difficulty of establishing and maintaining identity. The three-part form allows a shifting emphasis on who is to be the center (i.e., on who will cover the others, and on who will be covered or effaced). Similarly, coverture can be perceived as a three part system represented by the formula, "Husband + Wife = HusbandPlus." The law, represented by the plus sign, has a unique metamorphosing quality, so that the resulting entity (the HusbandPlus) is something different and more powerful than either the man or the woman. The HusbandPlus has additional powers and responsibilities, particularly relating to his wife's property, which he did not have before marriage. At the same time, the wife loses power and becomes invisible in the eyes of the law. This new entity, the HusbandPlus, is the result of the absorption of one entity by another, with a transformation taking place in which both are radically altered (one disappears, the other gains added power and presence). Typically, the one most subordinated or absorbed is the one in the feminine position. This accords with the legal subordination of the feminine under the common law of coverture.

The subordination of the feminine also can be understood in light of Zillah Eisenstein's recent identification of the law as "engendered," so that, "structured through the multiple oppositional layerings embedded in the dualism of man/woman, it [the law] is not able to move beyond the male referent as the standard for sex equality" (Eisenstein 42). Or, as Mary Poovey explains,

> The most basic opposition established by civil and property law in nineteenth-century Britain, and therefore the opposition both protected by and crucial to the developing state, was the opposition between subjects — those people considered able to determine and act on their own interests, hence capable of binding themselves by contract — and nonsubjects, who were not considered responsible and therefore not so bound. To the latter — children, orphans under guardianship, lunatics, and married women — the law (and increasingly the state) extended its protection in lieu of awarding rights. (Poovey 75)

This distinction between subjects and non-subjects applies to married women's property law in nineteenth-century Britain. However, whereas Eisenstein and Poovey consider the matter in light of the problems caused by dual, binary oppositions (man/woman or subject/non-subject), I would suggest that a three-part analysis offers additional understanding of the complex process of coverture.

The law looks at the married pair and sees the man. Under coverture, the husband inscribes the structure of his personality on the marriage as a whole. By deconstructing the law, the novel reacquaints the reader with the psychological origins of this paradigm. As in Jung's doctrine of the anima, the male subordinates the feminine in himself. And what is maintained in the individual male on the microcosmic scale is maintained in patriarchal law on the macrocosmic level. The engine that drives the narrative is this constant struggle for supremacy of will — who is to cover, and who is to be covered? Whose identity will prevail? And how will the "winner" be altered from his or her original state?

Three triads in the text deserve particular attention as examples of how the text critiques the law of coverture only to fall back into complacency and reinforce the legal status quo. First is the triad of Percival, Laura, and Anne. Second is the romantic triangle of Count Fosco, the Countess, and Marian, in which the Count serves as the supreme example of covering agent, obliterating those in his path. (Some of the most scathing condemnations of coverture emerge in this triad.) Third, the triad of Count Fosco, Sir Percival, and Walter is a three-way power struggle in which the victor wins the privilege of "covering" Laura. In this triad, the text reinforces the notion that a happy ending comes about through "good" coverture.

Percival-Laura-Anne

THE FIRST TRIAD is the most visible, manifest, and distinct illustration of the text's critique of coverture. Percival, in his role as HusbandPlus, has absorbed and acquired both his wife's property and the use of Anne's identity. When he plots to convert Anne into Laura, Anne becomes a substitute wife liable to be covered and absorbed. Anne, in the role of "covered" wife, is buried in Laura's grave, under the inscription, "Sacred to the memory of Laura, Lady Glyde" (410). Thus, her dead body is literally covered by the name of the husband. Laura and Anne, linked by physical, familial, and spiritual bonds, are stand-ins for the wife of the coverture formula. When combined and interchanged by the machinations of the villains, they create and empower the HusbandPlus that is Percival.

Percival's secret, like the secret underlying coverture, is not so much a sexual secret as a property secret.[8] He is not really entitled to the rank and property of a Baronet, and he needs to marry Laura for her money. Nearly all the characters in the text assume that Percival's secret (and any secret, for that matter) is a sexual secret. Walter wonders if Percival seduced Anne and thinks Anne's misfortune might be "the too common and too customary motive that has led many a woman to interpose anonymous hindrances of the marriage of the man who has ruined her" (108). The scandal of Mrs. Catherick's secret is that people presume she had an adulterous affair with Sir Percival (464). ("Was this common, too common, story of a man's treachery and a woman's frailty the key to a secret which had been the life-long terror of Sir Percival Glyde?" [466].) And Lawyer Gilmore misinterprets the meaning of the anonymous letter concerning

Percival and decides, "Things of this sort happen constantly in my experience. Anonymous letters — unfortunate woman — sad state of society. . . . [T]he case itself is, most unhappily, common — common" (125). Gilmore does not even bother to speak in complete sentences but uses an intellectual shorthand that operates in terms of "Secret = Sex." In fact, a more accurate equation would be, "Secret = Property."

The plot against Laura does not involve a sexual threat but rather a threat to identity and property. As Percival says of Laura, "I believe in nothing about her but her money" (332). In fact, there are strong hints in the text that Laura remains virginal after her marriage. Count Fosco wonders whether Percival and Laura might have children who will have a claim on Laura's estate. (Laura's future children already have been cheated out of an inheritance by the marriage settlement.) Percival tells the Count that children are "not in the least likely . . ." (328). Thus, not only are Laura's children cheated, Laura is cheated of children. Laura's lack of existence under coverture is so severe and so complete, she is not even allowed the "privilege" of being a vehicle of reproduction. (She remains white/virginal until Walter marries her and the text rewards them with a male heir.)

Perhaps an additional hint at Laura's lack of sexual function is that she is treated as if she were a child. In fact, she is equated with each of Frances Power Cobbe's categories of the disenfranchised—children, idiots, and felons. Treated as a child with no will of her own, Laura is incarcerated in an insane asylum and accused of criminally impersonating herself. (She tells Percival she will sign a legal document, "if you will only treat me as a responsible being" [250]; he is not willing to do so.) After her incarceration, Laura becomes, "socially, morally, legally — dead" (412).

But Laura's absorption is not enough. Percival needs the other veiled woman/ veiled phallus in order to empower himself as HusbandPlus. And Anne seems less naïve than Laura concerning the implications of coverture. Anne's warning letter to Laura, based on a dream-vision, is a moment when the woman's gaze is a weapon protecting her sister/herself from the dangers of coverture.

Anne dreams of Laura as veiled phallus, an object of desire, in a "beautiful white silk dress" and "long white lace veil" (88). In her dream, Anne's tears become two rays of light which illuminate Percival's inner self and which thrust asunder Percival and Laura. After this separation of husband and wife, "the clergyman looked for the marriage-service in vain; it was gone out of the book, and he shut up the leaves, and put it from him in despair" (89).

Also in her warning letter, Anne refers Laura to several Biblical citations dealing with dreams and prophecies. Most significant is the reference to Daniel iv. This Scriptural passage concerns Nebuchadnezzar's dream of impending madness ("let his mind be changed from a man's, and let a beast's mind be given to him"). This foreshadows Laura's fate under coverture. Not only will she lose her legal status, the same as would a lunatic, but Laura actually will be imprisoned in an insane asylum as one of the results of her marriage to Percival. That imprisonment affects Laura's mind, so that she for a while is partially unbalanced. A significant portion of her mind, in fact, is rendered a blank because of her imprisonment. Such is the nullifying effect of coverture for women.

Percival needs both Anne and Laura to empower him. He can become the HusbandPlus only by acquiring the veiled, covered women in white who are the veiled phallus. It is significant that Percival never seems satisfied with phallic objects he acquires but always wants to absorb more. One of Percival's compulsive habits is cutting and making new walking sticks. ("He has filled the house with walking-sticks of his own making, not one of which he ever takes up for a second time. When they have been once used his interest in them is all exhausted and he thinks of nothing but going on and making more" [234].) He constantly is attempting to acquire the phallus, never being satisfied with whatever privilege and power he gains. In Lacanian terms, desire always outstrips whatever you find to fill your loss. Collins uses Percival's dissatisfaction to further undermine the patriarchal assertion of power.

Count Fosco-Countess Fosco-Marian

EARLY IN MARIAN'S NARRATIVE, she writes that Count Fosco is, among other things, a skilled chemist who has discovered a method of petrifying the body after death (225), an apt description of the Countess's transformation after her "civil death" by marriage to the Count. While the Countess used to be an advocate of women's rights and a fiery, irascible woman, after her marriage she is frozen up, petrified. "Never have I beheld such a change produced in a woman by her marriage," comments Marian, adding that she fears the Countess's "present state of suppression may have sealed up something dangerous in her nature, which used to evaporate harmlessly in the freedom of her former life" (220, 221).

The enormously fat Count Fosco stands as a supreme example of the HusbandPlus. His fatness metonymically suggests he absorbs all around him. Like a psychic vampire, he drains those around him of will and identity. In particular, he already has absorbed his wife, and he wishes to absorb Marian.

Echoing the law of coverture, he asserts that he and his wife, "have but one opinion between us, and that opinion is mine" (246). It is not accidental that one of the operas Fosco is most fond of singing (and the one he sings to prevent Marian from leaving the room) is Rossini's *Moses the Lawgiver* (316). Fosco is more than comfortable under the Law of the Father and a happy proponent of the law of coverture. Additionally, he manipulates the law and legal tecniques to his advantage. He even acts the lawyerly role by posing hypothetical situations to Percival concerning the possibility of Laura's death (328).

Interestingly, Fosco has so absorbed his wife's essence that her very corporeality seems in question. If his fatness is an insistence on gross corporeality, her thinness and paleness (she has very white hands, and her skin is so pale it looks chalky [220]) qualify her as another woman in white, disappearing into insubstantiality. In fact, Marian comments that no one now sees the "female skeleton" supporting the woman's frame, because after her marriage, the Countess is always modestly dressed. It is as if her very bones have been absorbed by her husband: "Nobody (putting her husband out of the question, of course) now sees in her, what everybody once saw — I mean the structure of the female skeleton, in the upper regions of the collar-bones and shoulder-blades" (220).

Besides absorbing and transforming her, the Count treats his wife as if she were a child or an idiot, and involves her in his criminal activities as an accomplice. He feeds her sugarplums, placing them into her mouth as if she were one of his many small pets, and he rules her with the phallic power (both legal and sexual) which he possesses — "The rod of iron with which he rules her never appears in company — it is a private rod, and is always kept upstairs" (226).

The Count's instructions to Percival concerning how to govern a wife further evidence his complete disdain for women. He equates women with children or animals, stating that one must never accept provocation at a woman's hands: "It holds with animals, it holds with children, and it holds with women, who are nothing but children grown. Quiet resolution is the one quality the animals, the children, and the women all fail in" (324–25).

Fosco's equating of women with animals is exemplified by his sermon on the economics of marriage in which he "transforms" a pet mouse into a respectable lady:

> Come here, my jolly little mouse! Hey! presto! pass! I transform you, for the time being, into a respectable lady. Stop there, in the palm of my great big hand, my dear, and listen. (239–40)

Fosco trains and manipulates his pets in much the same way he manipulates all those around him, particularly his wife. He holds her in the palm of his hand. But he desires to absorb and control Marian, as well.

Marian confesses early on that the Count has a strange, hypnotic attraction for her. She writes,

> He looks like a man who could tame anything. If he had married a tigress, instead of a woman, he would have tamed the tigress. If he had married *me*, I should have made his cigarettes as his wife does — I should have held my tongue when he looked at me, as she holds hers. (221)

But Marian is not so easily absorbed as the Countess. She is fiercely resistant to the Count's charms and she matches wits with the Count throughout her narrative. She symbolically (and very practically) divests herself of encumbering feminine clothing in order to eavesdrop on a crucial conversation between the Count and Percival (321). In fact, if she were not stricken with illness from her exposure to the cold night rain, Marian could have subverted the plot against Laura.

The Count does succeed in covering Marian through the symbolic rape that is the reading of her private journal. He absorbs her discourse and makes it his own, adding a "Postscript By A Sincere Friend" to her journal. The next time we see Marian, she has become a veiled, marked woman. She raises her veil, and Walter notes of her face,

> Changed, changed as if years had passed over it! The eyes large and wild, and looking at me with a strange terror in them. The face worn and wasted piteously. Pain and fear and grief written on her as with a brand. (409)

The hand that has "written" these lines on Marian's face is the same hand that inscribed her diary — Fosco's.

In the Count's written confession, he notes in passing that he has "absorbed" several women, including Anne Catherick. His use of this particular term highlights his nature as HusbandPlus, as one who is empowered by the possession of the veiled phallus.

Finally, in a passage where Collins as veiled plotter almost reveals himself in the heat of the moment, Fosco answers the question concerning the secret of Countess Fosco's devotion to him. Fosco begins by asserting that a man of his historical merit always has "a woman in the background self-immolated on the altar of his life" (607). Then, in a passage dripping with hidden authorial irony, Fosco expostulates on the condition of married women in England:

> But I remember that I am writing in England, I remember that I was married in England, and I ask if a woman's marriage obligations in this country provide for her private opinion of her husband's principles? No! They charge her unreservedly to love, honour, and obey him. That is exactly what my wife has done. I stand here on a supreme moral elevation, and I loftily assert her accurate performance of her conjugal duties. Silence, Calumny! Your sympathy, wives of England, for Madame Fosco! (608–09)

Fosco's final ironic call for sympathy *from* the wives of England also is Collins's sincere call for sympathy *for* the wives of England, who suffer under the law of coverture.

Walter-Percival-Fosco

WHILE THE PREVIOUS TWO triads suggest the text's critique of the system of coverture, this final triad represents a drawing back or relapse into complacency. In this last struggle for identity, a power game in which two will *become* the veiled phallus and only one will *possess* the phallus, Walter begins in the feminine position and ends as the HusbandPlus.

Walter begins his narrative in the feminine position of passivity ("The small pulse of the life within me, and the great heart of the city around me, seemed to be sinking in unison, languidly and more languidly, with the sinking sun" [20].) One of his first acts is the maternal action of "birth" (he saves Pesca from drowning, bringing Pesca's fetus-like body up from the womb of the ocean) (22). And Walter as yet has no distinct sense of self, and so is in danger of being covered. Several times, he notes a blurring of self, as when after meeting Anne, he states, "I was abruptly *recalled to myself*" (40, emphasis added), as if he was in danger of losing himself.

However, early on in his meetings with Laura, Walter advises her to cover her head with a white handkerchief (67). This foreshadows Walter's role as covering Husband-Plus. And he describes Laura as an angel and a child but not as a woman (76). This, too, suggests his potential for filling the patriarchal role in which the husband exists at the expense of the wife's existence. Also, after confronting Anne in the churchyard, he frightens her by mention of Sir Percival. Anne says, "You know too much — I'm afraid you will always frighten me now" (114). Anne seems to recognize something the reader may not yet appreciate — Walter's affinity with the patriarchy. Walter has similarities to Percival. He manipulates Anne (112) and frightens her by his suggestion of patriarchal power. However, these are as yet only hints of the patriarchal role, and Walter must change from feminized to masculinized hero before he can compete for position as HusbandPlus.

When Marian tells Walter of Laura's engagement to Percival, he turns white, exhibiting a physical affinity with the covered woman in white. Marian's response to Walter's emotionalism is, "Don't shrink under it like a woman. Tear it out; trample it under foot like a man!" (81). Walter outwardly recovers self-control, but he still possesses an inward affinity with the helpless heroine.

Throughout the text, Walter is afraid of being covered. Early on, while still a feminized hero, Walter reluctantly conceals himself. When he hides near Mrs. Fairlie's grave, he does so with "a natural reluctance to conceal myself" (101). At a later point, after he has returned from his rites of passage into manhood, Walter refuses to disguise himself. Even though a disguise would be in order, Walter decides, "there was something so repellent to me in the idea — something so meanly like the common herd of spies and informers in the mere act of

adopting a disguise — that I dismissed the question from consideration. . . ."
He adds, "in my own character I was resolved to continue to the end" (479).

What is so threatening to Walter about taking on a disguise? Precisely the
possibility that he might lose his identity. As Walter proudly notes near the end
of his narrative, "I have disguised nothing relating to myself in these pages"
(577). And a point against Percival and Fosco in the battle for identity is the
fact that both have disguised themselves. Percival hides the fact that he is not
entitled to the name and title of Baronet. Fosco's true identity never is revealed,
and Walter speculates that Fosco may have gone so far in his disguise as to alter
his body (by becoming immensely fat) (574–75).

After Walter's return from perilous adventures abroad, it is clear that he has
undergone a sea change. He left in defeat, the lovelorn, feminized hero, but
returns masculinized and full of purpose. His first battle of identities is with
Percival.

At Laura's tombstone, it is Percival's name that disturbs Walter most. He
wants "nothing of earthly vileness to force its way between her spirit and mine"
(409). Percival's identity covers Laura at this point in the narrative, and this
bothers Walter.

Walter determines to fight for Laura, "to win the way back for her to her place
in the world of living beings" (412). Significantly, this description resonates with
the husbandly goal of Orpheus trying to win Eurydice back from the grave. And
Walter sounds more and more like the possessive, covering husband in his
description of Laura. He asserts something very much like ownership rights,
saying, "She was *mine* at last! *Mine* to support, to protect, to cherish, to restore.
Mine to love and honour as father and brother both. *Mine* to vindicate . . ."
(413, emphasis added). However, since Percival legally is Laura's husband,
Walter determines to engage with him in battle (a battle of identity). He says
that, "the struggle was now narrowed to a trial of strength between myself and
Sir Percival Glyde" (452).

In his battle with Percival, Walter slowly begins to usurp and absorb aspects
of Percival's identity as strong, tyrannical husband. For example, Percival uses
the rhetoric of the villain of melodrama: "I'll crush your obstinacy," he tells
Laura, "I'll wring it out of you" (313); and Walter, during his meeting with
Mrs. Catherick, expresses a desire to "crush" Sir Percival (485).

The name "Walter" is listed in the marriage register above the forged entry
of Percival's parents, suggesting Walter's affinity both with Percival and with
the concept of marriage (497). Walter exults in the discovery of Percival's secret,
knowing that disclosure will "deprive him, at one blow of the name, the rank,
the estate, the whole social existence that he had usurped" (506). Walter considers doing to Percival what Percival did to Laura, thus empowering Walter and
feminizing Percival. Shortly after, Percival's servant mistakes Walter for Percival in the dark (510).

When Percival dies in the fire, Walter stands by "looking, looking, looking into the burning room" (515). What is he looking for so intently? It is as if Percival were destroyed not by the flames but by Walter's annihilating gaze. When the coroner's jury tries to settle the issue of the identity of the deceased, Walter lies and denies knowing Percival. Walter refuses to identify Percival, refuses to grant him identity.

Walter then moves to absorb completely Percival's role of husband, using legal rationalization in his argument: "In our present position I have no claim on her which society sanctions, which the law allows, to strengthen me in resisting him [Fosco], and in protecting her. . . . If I am to fight our cause with the Count, strong in the consciousness of Laura's safety, I must fight it for my Wife" (555). While awaiting Laura's answer to his marriage proposal, Walter's mind is "a blank" (558). In fact, his identity as HusbandPlus will not be secure until he both marries her and defeats Fosco.

Count Fosco proves a significant covering threat. Walter finds the Count's sexuality threatening, commenting on "the horrible freshness and cheerfulness and vitality of the man" (563). Boys and women stare at Fosco's "great size, his fine black clothes, and his large cane with the gold knob to it" (543). Fosco threatens Walter by referring to the great length of his sword (586). Walter decides, "One of us must be master of the situation . . ." (575).

Just as Walter absorbs Percival's rhetoric and role as husband, so he also absorbs portions of the Count's identity, even feeling a moment of union with the Count. "At that final moment I thought with his mind, I felt with his fingers . . ." (582). Doing battle with the Count, Walter wins.

In the covering role of HusbandPlus, Walter reads aloud the narrative (in which he is master narrator and arranger) to the villagers, and introduces Laura as his wife. The text rewards Walter with a son, who is heir to Limmeridge.[9]

Most significantly, Walter has managed to begin and end the narrative, as well as to arrange and edit individual stories. He has inscribed his personality on the text in much the way the HusbandPlus inscribes his personality on the marriage. Walter also notes, in a casual aside near the end of the text, that he has assigned false names to all the characters. Thus, Walter succeeds in covering *everyone's* identity. This covering activity combined with the complacency of the happy ending of marriage, serves to reinforce the status quo. The moral seems to be that coverture is bad with a bad husband but right and proper with a good husband. Collins may after all be paralyzed by metaphor. The final victim of coverture is the novel itself, covered over by the paternalistic law it attempts to critique.

The "good coverture" ending, however, does not completely negate the earlier radical critique. Collins's sympathetic treatment of feminine loss of identity under coverture plants the seed of that sensational extravagancy — the suggestion that married women are entitled to a separate legal existence.

Self is a slippery thing, needing a terrible effort of will to maintain. It is a particularly difficult thing to hold on to under the law of coverture. Using coverture as a metonymic pattern to explore the loss of self, Collins creates a radical critique of married women's lack of legal identity. Although the text finally retreats into the status quo, Fosco's ironic call for sympathy for Madame Fosco also is Collins's sincere and sympathetic depiction of the plight of loss of feminine identity and his exposure of the legal fiction that is coverture.

Walter F. George School of Law, Mercer University

NOTES

1. Identity is one of Collins's favorite themes. So, for example, in *Armadale*, the plot revolves around which of two Allan Armadales is entitled to the name and identity. In *No Name*, Magdalen Vanstone assumes a series of false disguises in order to correct the injustice of her lack of identity. (She is discovered to be illegitimate and thus loses her identity as her parents' daughter and heir.) And in *The Moonstone*, of course, the mystery centers on the identity of the thief.
2. Blackstone's *Commentaries* were the primary reference work for women's legal position throughout most of the nineteenth century.
3. Women's legal rights, particularly in the areas of divorce and married women's property rights, were major issues of debate and political agitation in the nineteenth century. For one of the most thorough analyses of nineteenth-century married women's property law, see Holcombe. For an excellent recent work on Victorian women's legal rights and concerns, including property law, infanticide, child custody, and wife abuse, see Shanley. Perkin provides a good comprehensive analysis of women and marriage in Victorian England, and Stave is a more technical legal and historical analysis of the subject of married women's property.
4. Poovey emphasizes that circumstances forced Caroline Norton not only to play the role of injured heroine but also to play the role of her own heroic avenger (67). However, as Poovey notes, Norton never was comfortable in this dual role, preferring to emphasize the point that the law should force husbands to provide for their wives, because the law was meant to protect the weak.
5. The best general overview of Collins's use of the law is in MacEachen. For a discussion of inheritance and *The Moonstone*, see Smith. For a discussion of the American murder trial on which Collins based *The Dead Alive*, see Ashley. Finally, the article which first identified the real-life source for Collins's *Woman in White* was Hyder's.
6. As Dorothy Sayers notes of Collins, "one cannot mistake the distinctively legal attitude of mind which permeates all his work" (55). What that attitude might be is a combination of analytical skills and scepticism, that "dissective property" Dickens complained of as more Collins's than any of Collins's characters (*Letters of Charles Dickens* 2: 110). Dougald B. MacEachen finds that Collins exhibits a lawyerly detail in plotting, a generally favorable view of the legal profession in his novels, an accurate use of legal knowledge (concerning trials, wills, settlements, etc.) and a zeal for legalistic reform (121–23).
7. Before entering into an analysis of *The Woman in White* itself, it is useful to situate the novel in terms of its importance both to Collins and to literary critics. The

importance of *Woman in White* to Collins is clear from his orders for the inscription on his own tombstone — "Author of *The Woman in White* and other works of fiction" (S. M. Ellis 53). The novel's importance to critics has grown steadily in the twentieth century, so that, although *The Moonstone* has traditionally been given first place by Collins's critics (partly because it is a forerunner of detective fiction), *Woman in White* is receiving increasing attention from Feminist Critics and New Historians. The following articles suggest the scope of interest among critics of social and/or historical issues: Knoepflmacher, Meckier, and Leavy. Feminist studies include O'Neil and Tamar Heller. Additionally, critics are interested in the novel in terms of its place in Sensation Fiction, Kendrick; Reader Response Criticism and Detective Fiction, Hennelly; and Gay Studies, Miller. My own interests center on both the feminist and legal-historical fields, and I hope in this essay to combine the two fields in a new way, exploring the feminist implications of the symbiotic relations between law and literature.

8. It is not always easy to disentangle the sexual secret from the property secret. Property secrets can be thought of as sexualized to the extent that laws governing inheritance regulate sexual conduct. It is the sexual irregularity of his parents (they are not married) that invalidates Percival's legal claim to property. However, the point here is that characters in the text *expect* the existence of sexual secrets but exhibit a real blindness toward secret legalistic improprieties. Collins's point is that patriarchal legal improprieties (such as the very law of coverture) are just as scandalous as sexual improprieties, albeit less noticed.

9. Although Limmeridge comes through Laura's inheritance, she is only the ostensible owner. Once again, the masculinist bias of the law will leave control of the property to her husband.

WORKS CITED

Ashley, Robert. "Wilkie Collins and a Vermont Murder Trial." *New England Quarterly* 21.3 (September 1948): 368–73.

Barthes, Roland. "The Face of Garbo." *Mythologies.* 1957. Trans. Annette Lavers. New York: Hill and Wang, 1972. 56–57.

Blackstone, William. *Commentaries on the Laws of England: A Facsimile of the First Edition of 1765–1769.* 4 vols. Chicago: U of Chicago P, 1979.

Carter, Angela. *The Sadeian Woman and the Ideology of Pornography.* New York: Pantheon Books, 1978.

Collins, Wilkie. *The Woman in White.* 2nd ed. New York: Signet, 1985.

Dickens, Charles. *Letters of Charles Dickens.* 2nd ed. 3 vols. London: Chapman and Hall, 1880.

Eisenstein, Zillah R. *The Female Body and the Law.* Berkeley: U of California P, 1988.

Ellis, S. M. *Wilkie Collins, Le Fanu and Others.* London: Constable, 1951.

Ellis, Sarah. *The Daughters of England: Their Position in Society, Character and Responsibilities.* London: Fisher, 1842.

Fuller, Lon L. *Legal Fictions.* Stanford: Stanford UP, 1967.

Heller, Tamar. *Dead Secrets: Wilkie Collins and the Female Gothic.* New Haven: Yale UP, 1992.

Hennelly, Mark M., Jr. "Reading Detection in *The Woman in White.*" *Texas Studies in Literature and Language* 22.4 (1980): 449–67.

Holcombe, Lee. *Wives and Property: Reform of the Married Women's Property Law in Nineteenth-Century England.* Toronto: U of Toronto P, 1983.

Hyder, Clyde K. "Wilkie Collins and *The Woman in White.*" *PMLA* 54 (1939): 297–303.

Kendrick, Walter M. "The Sensationalism of *The Woman in White.*" *Nineteenth-Century Fiction* 32.1 (1977): 18–35.

Knoepflmacher, U. C. "The Counterworld of Victorian Fiction and *The Woman in White.*" *The Worlds of Victorian Fiction.* Ed. Jerome H. Buckley. Cambridge: Harvard UP, 1975. 351–69.

Lacan, Jacques. *Écrits: A Selection.* 1966. Trans. Alan Sheridan. New York: Norton, 1977.

Leavy, Barbara Fass. "Wilkie Collins's Cinderella: The History of Psychology and *The Woman in White.*" *Dickens Studies Annual* 10 (1982): 91–141.

MacEachen, Dougald B. "Wilkie Collins and British Law." *Nineteenth-Century Fiction* 5 (1950–51): 121–39.

Meckier, Jerome. "Wilkie Collins's *The Woman in White*: Providence Against the Evils of Propriety." *Journal of British Studies* 22:1 (1982): 104–26.

Miller, D. A. "Cage aux folles: Sensation and Gender in Wilkie Collins's *The Woman in White.*" *Representations* 14 (1986): 107–36.

Norton, Caroline. *English Laws for Women in the Nineteenth Century: Caroline Norton's Defense.* Chicago: Academy Chicago, 1982. Originally published: *English Laws For Women in the Nineteenth Century.* London, 1854.

Norton, Caroline. *Selected Writings of Caroline Norton.* Intro. and notes by James O. Hoge and Jane Marcus. Delmar, New York: Scholars' Facsimiles and Reprints, 1978.

Nightingale, Florence. *Cassandra and Other Selections From Suggestions For Thought.* Ed. Mary Poovey. New York: NYU Press, 1992.

O'Neil, Philip. *Wilkie Collins: Women, Property and Propriety.* Totowa, NJ: Barnes & Noble, 1988.

Perkin, Joan. *Women and Marriage in Nineteenth-Century England.* Chicago: Lyceum Books, 1989.

Poovey, Mary. *Uneven Developments: The Ideological Work of Gender in Mid-Victorian England.* Chicago: U of Chicago P, 1988.

Sayers, Dorothy L. *Wilkie Collins: A Critical and Biographical Study.* Ed. E. R. Gregory. Toledo: Friends of the University of Toledo Libraries, 1977.

Shanley, Mary Lyndon. *Feminism, Marriage, and the Law in Victorian England, 1850–1895.* Princeton: Princeton UP, 1989.

Smith, Muriel. " 'Everything to My Wife': The Inheritance Theme in *The Moonstone* and *Sense and Sensibility.*" *Wilkie Collins Society Journal* 7 (1987): 13–18.

Staves, Susan. *Married Women's Separate Property in England, 1660–1833.* Cambridge: Harvard UP, 1990.

Todorov, Tzvetan. *The Fantastic: A Structural Approach To A Literary Genre.* 1970. Trans. Richard Howard. Ithaca: Cornell UP, 1975.

UNCLE TOM IN ENGLAND

By Audrey Fisch

IN SEPTEMBER 1852, *Uncle Tom in England* was published anonymously in England.[1] This self-described "Echo, or Sequel" (iii) to Harriet Beecher Stowe's *Uncle Tom's Cabin* rode Stowe's coat-tails and capitalized on the general British interest in American "Uncle Tom."[2] Like *Uncle Tom's Cabin*, *Uncle Tom in England* was intended to mobilize British public opinion[3] against American slavery.[4] Unlike *Uncle Tom's Cabin*, however, *Uncle Tom in England* yokes together political situations on both sides of the Atlantic in order to conjoin abolitionism with Chartism, the working class reform movement. The novel exists as a new hybrid transnational phenomenon, without precedent in compounding and synthesizing the discourse of *American* slavery with *British* political rhetoric about the worker.[5]

This novel tells one particular story about British interest in American slavery. First, the novel maps dominant middle-class values onto its black characters, bolstering a middle-class vision of class which conflates birth and virtue with social value and a vision of working class education as a means of social control. Next, by re-writing history, particularly by recasting Chartism as a movement directed only at working class self-improvement and not at political or social change, the novel produces and celebrates unthreatening middle-class versions of Chartism and American abolitionism, versions which pose no threat to the British social and political status quo. The combination within the novel of these constructions of the two reform movements results not in the imagining of a unified trans-Atlantic fight against "universal" injustice but instead in an eruption of British nationalism.[6] Thus the examination of American slavery and the imagined combination of abolitionism and Chartism becomes finally an opportunity to assuage, through trans-Atlantic comparison and competition, any British anxieties about Chartism and about its treatment of its own "white" slaves, and to bolster England's national status in the emerging global field.[7]

By its appropriation of black/slave experience and of the abolitionist campaign for the cultural profit of the British middle class, the novel re-enacts larger political structures. In particular, it stages a literary version of a cultural trafficking in black bodies and black experience for the purpose of producing a powerful

23

cultural narrative of English national superiority.[8] Moreover, this fictional response to the transnational event of the black American abolitionist campaign in England of the eighteen-fifties is representative of the politics underlying much of the Victorian interest in that campaign.[9]

* * *

FROM THE BEGINNING, *Uncle Tom in England* is awkward about its purpose. The subtitle of *Uncle Tom in England*, "A Proof that Black's White," is argumentative, clumsy, and deliberately paradoxical.[10] This awkwardness no doubt stems from the fact that the novel's ostensible if ambiguous purpose — to prove "black's white" — specifically goes against the grain of Victorian common sense. Few among nineteenth-century Victorians would have accepted the idea that blacks are or deserve to be the political, social, cultural, or moral equals of whites;[11] furthermore, the publication of the novel in 1852 places it within a period during which attitudes about race and ethnicity in England were undergoing a radical reconfiguration which would culminate in the imperialism of the turn of the century.[12] In this sense, then, the paradox of the phrase "A Proof that Black's White" figures the difficult task of *Uncle Tom in England*.

Uncle Tom in England begins on the coast of Africa, where two children of Gucongo, an African chief, are being sold, with 500 other men, women, and children, as war prizes, to slavers who will transport the group, on a slave ship, into American slavery. Named Marossi and Rosetta by the slave ship's captain, these children arrive, after a gruelling journey, in Charleston, where they are bought by George Harris. Harris (previously known to readers of Stowe's *Uncle Tom's Cabin* as the basically kind but financially embarrassed owner of George and Eliza) is here an "altered man" (16), no longer sympathetic to his slaves, who buys, along with Marossi and Rosetta, a middle-aged slave named Tom in order to introduce "a new discipline" (16) to his plantation in Kentucky. On Harris's plantation, this Tom, the protagonist of *Uncle Tom in England* (a different character from Stowe's Tom but also called "Uncle Tom"), discovers that his long-lost wife, Susan, is also Harris's slave. Later, their daughter Emmeline (a character identified as Stowe's beautiful innocent with whom Cassie escapes from Simon Legree), comes to rescue her long-lost parents with the aid of a kind Quaker family, the Hanaways. Marossi, Rosetta, and Susan escape to the Hanaways, but Tom is caught at the last minute.

Tom is tried and sentenced to death for escaping and for helping other slaves to escape; Emmeline, meanwhile, dies of grief and worry. A great outcry is raised, particularly from England, over Tom's trial and sentence, and as a result Tom goes unpunished and is bought out of slavery. Tom, Susan, Marossi, and Rosetta now go to England, both to escape any danger and to work to influence public opinion in England against American slavery. In England, Tom and Susan meet Chartists and converse with many English people about "white slaves and black slaves" (116). They decide that "we must make common cause and help each other!" (120): that the black American slave and the white British slave must join forces in peaceful attempts to promote change. Finally, Thomas, the Hanaway's son, marries Rosetta. The two move to Canada and are praised by the Quaker Hanaways since "every such act of amalgamation contributes to break down the prejudice of the separate races" (123). Marossi goes to Africa as a missionary.

Uncle Tom in England is stocked with the conventions of writing about slavery: scenes of slave life, the thrill of escape, and standard discussions of the injustices of the slave system. Yet the commonplace tropes about slavery and the novel's abolitionist politics are unexpectedly (for a novel about slavery) supplanted[13] and undermined by concerns about class, concerns which serve to bolster the ideology of the Victorian middle class.[14]

In the initial pages of the novel, Rosetta and Marossi are brought onto the slave ship and scrutinized. The novel's interest, even obsession, lies not with issues of race but with the class identity of these two African children, concentrating at length on the ways in which the two distinguish themselves both from the other black slaves aboard the slave-ship and from the rough and unmannered white working class and black crew who man the ship.

First, Rosetta and Marossi are distinguished as physically superior: "likely little ones [who] will fetch well in the market . . . being pretty, and sleek" (8–9). Likewise, they are avid and capable students, particularly of physical feats: "they could climb up the ropes, and perform dexterous gymnastics upon the deck" (11).

The superiority of the children is stressed as well in the narrative's emphasis on the love and care they show for each other, "always holding each other's hands, and often embracing lovingly, and whispering words which none understood but themselves" (11). Here, the narrative domesticates the savage otherness of the children, translating their gestures into a language of Victorian domestic affection, in order to demonstrate their virtue.[15]

Just as it stresses their physical superiority and domestic virtue, the novel makes a case for the children's social superiority. Self-segregated from the other (future) slaves, the children congregate instead with the (free) sailors. They entertain the men with their clever and "interesting ways"; they "imitate[d] the songs and sayings of the sailors [and] caused a great deal of merriment" (11). In particular, they gravitate toward the Captain, whose class superiority is marked both by his rank as Captain (although of a slave ship) and by the standardized diction of his speech. (The mates, in comparison, speak in dialect such as "I calkilate"[7].) The Captain, "having little else to employ his time," leisure time here a marker of his own class superiority, "takes to the children" and devotes "a portion of [his time] to teaching [them] various odd pranks" (11).

The slave ship thus becomes a microcosm of Victorian society. The slaves and the working-class crew jockey for position beneath the ship's middle-class bureaucracy, all of whom are controlled by the absent aristocratic ship-owner. Rosetta and Marossi's social discomfort on the ship, their instinctive kinship with the ship's Captain, as well as their physical superiority and domestic virtue, signal their high position among the classes represented on the ship and assure them a superior class position in England. All of this is shored up by Rosetta and Marossi's birth: they are the children of an African chief; as such, the children represent not ordinary Africans but an aristocracy among the savages.

The novel's concerns with the children's physical appearance, their internal virtue, and their lineage reflect Victorian class ideologies. On the one hand, the narrative subscribes to the tradition of the noble savage, the belief that, untainted by the disease of civilization and the corruptions of culture, the (African) savage represents humanity at its best.[16] Their natural physical grace and skill, their natural domestic affection, as well as their natural gravitation to the ship's social elite are all corollaries of the children's uncultivated nobility. This discourse, however, implies that all black Africans, if uncorrupted by contact with white civilization, might fall within the social category of the middle class. Perhaps to contain such an implication, the novel dramatizes not only the children's natural noble savage superiority but also their social difference, as children of an African chief, from other black Africans. Pre-figured by their birth, the children's social superiority is confirmed finally by their internal virtue as demonstrated by their domestic affection.[17]

However, the translation of the children's savage otherness as domestic affection, as well as the valuation of their physical attributes and birth as tokens of superiority never entirely expunge the children's otherness. If their class superiority is based on their superior birth to an African king, presumably some measure of recognition of cultural difference, the children's superiority is still measured according to racially coded Victorian stereotypes about blacks and Africans. "Pretty" and "sleek," they are figured as an eroticized animal Other whose value is measured by the ability to please, via song, dance, and athletic feats. In other words, the mapping of Rosetta and Marossi by the novel as socially superior here is not without its racial residue; the Victorian terms of class do not seamlessly overlay contemporary ideologies of racial difference.

This racial residue is revealed as well in the novel's ending. The children deserve to achieve the novelistic "happy ending" because they possess not only the natural superiority of the noble savage, coupled with their good birth, but also the clear signs of internal virtue and value. As if race has no consequence, the novel proceeds toward that "happy ending," presumably on the assumption that Rosetta and Marossi's class will outweigh the harsh conditions of life to which their racial identity might have confined them.

But Rosetta and Marossi's reward, if predicted by and predicated on middle-class ideology, is achieved at the expense of any racial identity. Married to a white man and living in England, Rosetta's racial difference is effectively erased. Educated in England to perform the imperialist work of a missionary, Marossi returns to Africa, not to be a part of his race, but to transform Africa and his race as he has been transformed. In other words, though Rosetta and Marossi are rewarded by virtue of their class, the racial difference which marks their social identities cannot be accommodated within the novel's "happy ending."

Considered historically, it is not surprising that racism and class bias are implicit in the working out of the logic of the novel. No argument is made, as we are led to expect from the novel's title, against conventions of racial difference or of black inferiority. Indeed, if the novel can be seen as a protest against slavery at all, it is against the oppression of those blacks, like Rosetta and Marossi, whose innocence of civilization along with their good birth and internal virtue make them socially acceptable. Others, who by their lower birth and inferior actions place themselves in the class of the oppressed, actually justify their own oppression.[18] Rather than condemn measures of human worth contingent on race or class, the novel, operating within a middle-class ideology, perpetuates the idea that physical and moral value are class determined.

If Rosetta and Marossi do not deserve the violent upheaval and displacement of the slave trade and slavery, Tom and Susan, identified with the white British working class, might deserve oppression, according to the terms of the novel, because of their low birth and inferior actions.[19] And while Rosetta and Marossi's reward is ensured by their innocence, birth, and virtue, the novel witnesses Tom and Susan's struggle to attain the social superiority that Rosetta and Marossi "naturally" possess, their struggle to attain their own degree of class, all to obtain the privilege of their own "happy ending." This struggle is defined by and participates in the middle-class Victorian discourse of working class education and self-improvement.

For the middle class in mid-Victorian England, according to Dorothy Thompson, "anyone who is not educated is not anything. Literacy is the test of humanity" (241). The working class, by and large uneducated, at least by the standards of the middle class, were in this sense less than human.[20] Education became, "between the forties and the eighties, a trump card in . . . class competition" (Best 150). An explosion of working class education by mid-century was met with a concomitant obsession, on the part of the middle class, with the education of the poor. This obsession often took the form of philanthropic concern: education was touted as the key to the spiritual uplifting and social mobility of the working class. For the middle class, however, working class education was also a question of social control. As Richard Johnson writes, the

Victorian obsession with the education of the poor is best understood as a concern
about authority, about power, about the assertion (or the re-assertion?) of control
[and an] attempt to determine, through the capture of educational means, the
patterns of thought, sentiment and behavior of the working class. (119)

"Provided education," education provided and advocated by the middle class
for the working class, was an attempt "to raise a new race of working people —
respectful, cheerful, hard-working, loyal, pacific, and religious" (119). It is
this education, touted as the medium for class improvement and mobility and
manipulated for the social control of the working class, that defines Tom and
Susan's struggle.[21]

Susan educated herself; she tells Tom: "I have 'The Life of Franklin,' 'The
Life of Washington,' a part of Milton's works, some of 'Shakspere's,' [sic] the
'Life of William Penn,' the 'Life of Howard,' the 'Life of Gustavus Vasa,' [sic]
the 'Narratives' of 'Pennington,' of 'Douglass,' and of 'Phillis Wheatley.' "[22]
This literature has, as Susan says, "Taught me to know myself" (30).

Knowing herself, Susan's "mission," as she explains to Tom, is to "teach
you to speak well and correctly," to transform Tom through the process of
education so that he too may "know" himself. That Susan terms Tom's course
of study a "mission" implies that Tom is a "savage" who must be saved by
the intervening missionary. Tom, internalizing this judgment, "didn't like Susie
to discover defects in him," but Susan reminds him, "He that humbleth himself
shall be exalted" after which "he was in an extremely good mood, and adopted
her as his teacher" (30). By the end of the novel Tom and the children all speak
standard English (at the novel's start, the children know no English and Tom
speaks in dialect such as "I only know dat dey came by de great ship" [15]).
They have been transformed, and each can now reap the rewards of his or her
newly achieved station. Education, whether secular or spiritual, becomes the
key not just to the salvation of the soul but to class and social mobility.

The overlay of this middle-class discourse of education onto the story of black
American slaves is complicated by the fact that knowledge as power is also a
trope common to the genre of slave narratives, where texts might literally contain
the keys to freedom. In this novel, Susan says that she "looked for encouragement to the examples of Pennington, Douglass, Cuffe [sic], Garnet, Bayley,[23]
and others of whom she had heard and read, and she resolved that she would
succeed, in the struggle [for freedom], or die in the attempt." What we might
today call a "black canon" provides Susan with "examples" and "encouragement." As well, Susan's "Life of Washington" provides her with "a map of
the United States [and] knowledge of the country through which she must pass,
and the distance she would have to travel" (41). A "white canon," in other
words, provides for Susan both literal and metaphorical maps of white culture
and thus a degree of access to white entitlement and power. For Susan, the

struggle to acquire education is thoroughly intertwined with the struggle to acquire freedom from slavery.

The acquisition of knowledge, particularly literacy, is often represented in the slave narrative as a scene of figurative emancipation and psychological empowerment after which the journey toward physical emancipation begins.[24] For example, Frederick Douglass in his *Narrative of the Life of Frederick Douglass* (1845) discusses how a kind mistress begins to teach him to read and write. "Mistress," Douglass writes, "in teaching me the alphabet, had given me the *inch*, and no precaution could prevent me from taking the *ell*" (53; emphasis in original). Douglass associated reading with his own desire for freedom and with the possibility of freedom. In the very next paragraph, he writes,

> the thought of being *a slave for life* began to bear heavily upon my heart. Just about this time, I got hold of a book entitled "The Columbian Orator." Every opportunity I got, I used to read this book. Among much of other interesting matter, I found in it a dialogue between a master and his slave. . . . In this dialogue, the whole argument in [sic] behalf of slavery was brought forward by the master, all of which was disposed of by the slave. The slave was made to say some very smart as well as impressive things in reply to his master — things which had the desired though unexpected effect; for the conversation resulted in the voluntary emancipation of the slave on the part of the master. (54; emphasis in original)

This particular reading material, as well as his education generally, helps Douglass to articulate his discontent. This articulation, in turn, forms a part of his journey towards freedom.

This trope of empowerment through education is duplicated in the novel:

> Under Susan's influence, Tom's heart became enlarged, and his mind developed. *He was no longer a slave though in fetters.* . . . It is astonishing how rapidly truth takes root, when its seeds are cast upon a soil rich with the elements of productiveness, yet long left neglected and uncultivated. Every new truth which entered Tom's mind . . . produced a rich harvest for the struggle in which Tom subsequently engaged. His very words, in course of time, became refined, his manners less harsh and mechanical. (40–41; emphasis added)

Tom's education, detailed as "Susan's influence" and as a "harvest" of the mind, figuratively and psychologically frees him from slavery: "He was no longer a slave, though in fetters." Furthermore, his education prefigures the literal freedom Tom will shortly attain.

Marossi also experiences a moment of figurative and psychological emancipation through education.[25] One night, he overhears Susan and Tom discussing issues surrounding the sins of slavery and of seeking freedom, whether by violence or by peaceful means. Susan asks Tom, "do you not think [the slave]

would be bound, in his duty to his God and to himself, to seek his freedom . . . to insist upon his right by every peaceful means?'' (47). To this Marossi replies from his bed, *"That I do . . . I have been asleep*, but I am AWAKE
NOW!'' (47; emphasis in original). The educated slave awakens from the unhealthy sleep of slavery, a state of helpless ignorance and passivity; the journey
to freedom begins.

Marossi's language of conversion here must be understood in the context of
Pilgrim's Progress. Like Bunyan's Christian, Marossi has been awakened to
the fact that he has been spiritually unaware. Bunyan's conversion narrative,
as taken up by the mid-century Victorians, represents not merely the spiritual
conversion but the social progress of the hero.[26] Marossi's re-awakening reinvig-
orates him spiritually but, more importantly, it revives his internal virtue, restores
and confirms his class status.

Just as Rosetta and Marossi proceed toward the ''happy ending'' their class
assures, the plot acquiesces to provide Susan and Tom with the respective rewards their self-improvement and self-education merit. They both escape from
slavery to live happily in England where, the novel tells us, ''Uncle Tom and
Susan fulfilled a sphere of immense usefulness in the advocacy of the abolition
of slavery'' (123). However, while education allows a degree of mobility, Tom
and Susan can never move beyond their sphere; they are still workers but now
''useful'' workers, in the dignified fight against slavery. Like their white working
class counterparts, Tom and Susan cannot achieve unlimited social mobility
through education.

Furthermore, the application of dominant middle-class values about education
to the lives of Tom and Susan, even with the existence of a correlative value
for education within American black slave culture as recorded in the slave
narrative, denies the specificity of Tom and Susan's racial subjectivity. In particular, education, represented in the novel as self-improvement which enables
limited class mobility and freedom from slavery, is the locus of a basic contradiction.

The education Tom acquires dictates a devaluation of his intellectual and
emotional past. Before the education which ''enlarged'' his heart, his heart was
smaller and his mind was ''rich soil'' that had been ''long left neglected and
uncultivated'' (40–41). There is little indication within the novel that Tom's
heart and mind might have been not neglected but differently cultivated and that
the new cultivation might involve some loss, that Tom comes from a different,
but genuine, culture.[27]

This loss is briefly suggested, however, when Tom and Susan are first reunited
in the novel:

> Tom perceived, in the course of this conversation, that during his separation from
> his wife, a great deal of refinement had been acquired by her; she had become, in

fact, the greatest lady he ever knew, and had picked up such a lot of learning that he could scarcely understand her at times. (27)

Education, associated here with refinement and that which makes Susan into a "lady" and allows her to "know" herself, is the source of alienation between husband and wife. Like Susan, Tom, too, is forced, upon acquiring "refinement" through education (that is, standard English), to leave behind his devalued heritage of slave culture and his language.[28] Overlaying dominant middle-class values about the "light" of education onto a narrative about black slaves may "raise up a new race of working people" (Johnson 119) but it does so at the expense of their racial identities.

* * *

UNCLE TOM IN ENGLAND THUS follows the pattern of many Victorian novels: a tribute to and validation of the values of the middle class. Inevitably, embedded as it is in Victorian culture, the novel (roughly) translates American slavery into the native discourse of British class. More than an inevitable translation, however, this novel also engages in a deliberate act of cultural appropriation. Using slavery as a popular background, writing from the moral high ground of the anti-slavery movement, and manipulating the powerful rhetoric of abolition, the novel cleverly promotes a conservative agenda about class.[29]

This appropriation of slavery to fulfill its conservative class agenda is witnessed in the novel's alignment of the slave with the white British working class. Comparing his ignorance with that of the seventeenth-century white British working class, Susan tells Tom that when Milton wrote, "knowledge was not so diffused as now, and there were people in England who knew as little of truth, as our unfortunate race now does" (46). Placing the issue of British class oppression in the distant past, as if all such oppression were far distant, Susan explains that black American slaves are like this distant British working class: "we are in the same position as those ignorant people, from whom the rulers of the olden time would have excluded the light" (46).

But all such oppression in England was not far distant; if not "excluded from the light," mid-Victorian England had its share of men and women who were "ignorant" of the "light" and the "truth." In "Signs of the Times," Thomas Carlyle bemoans this ignorance of virtue as one of the repercussions of the Industrial Age:

By our skill in Mechanism, it has come to pass, that in the management of external things we excel all other ages; while in whatever respects the pure moral nature, in true dignity of soul and character, we are perhaps inferior to most civilized ages. (35)

While Carlyle does not overtly single out the working class, his comparison of Victorian society with past societies (and, implicitly, with other mid-nineteenth-century nations) and his location of a "moral" inferiority of "soul and character" caused by industrialization identifies the working class as his target.

Carlyle's solution to this problem of inferiority in the working class resembles Susan's "mission" to overcome the "defect" of the slave: self-improvement not social reform. As posed by Carlyle, the task is "To reform a world," but he hastens to add that "to reform a nation, no wise man will undertake; and all but foolish men know, that the only solid, though far slower reformation, is what each begins and perfects on *himself*" (44; emphasis in original). For Carlyle, as for Susan, the British worker, like Tom, should look to self-education. Physical emancipation, however, promised (or pre-figured) by education in the context of the slave narrative, presupposes in the context of British society a radical re-organization of the Victorian world both unfathomable to Carlyle and unintended within the vision of social control undergirding education here.

In other words, if the novel figures the social transformation of the slave through education and self-improvement, such a parallel transformation of the British worker was unimaginable in Victorian society beyond the abstract "slower reformation" (44) of the individual worker. Yet the novel pursues its mapping of race and class as if the transformations of worker and slave were parallel, as if both needed only education to begin the self-improvement that leads to freedom, and as if Chartism and abolitionism both embraced only individual self-fulfillment. In this spurious pursuit, the second half of the novel turns away from the individual stories of Tom, Susan, and the African children and away from the radical change available to the slave through education and self-improvement to a re-writing and distortion of the late working-class reform movement as a Carlylean movement aimed only at slow, individual "reformation" (I will return to the issue of the novel's resuscitation of an already collapsed Chartism).

For the novel, Chartists can be divided into two categories: those who advocate physical force and those moral force.[30] But, as Preston William Slosson writes, there exists "no clear line of demarcation between the two types of method or between the men who inclined to the one or the other." Of the difference, Slosson writes that "The moral force Chartists believed that they could carry the Charter by means of public meetings, agitation, petitions and direct or indirect influence at the polls. The physical force Chartists held that sooner or later an armed insurrection would be necessary to force the government to yield" (83). Viewed through the novel's distorting lens, however, physical force Chartism represents the danger of violent anarchy through the irresponsible actions of unenlightened men whereas moral force Chartism represents middle-class values such as the self-education and self-improvement of the working man.[31] These representations take the form of two characters: William Clarke, a moral force

Chartist, who stands opposed and superior, not just politically but morally, to Richard ("Dick") Boreas, a physical force Chartist.

Dick Boreas is described as an "idle" "drunken man" who might work more if he applied himself but who instead indulges his vices and beats his wife (115).[32] Dick complains that he has not had any work and that he and his family are starving. He argues that this misery justfies his, and by extension any, unlawful actions against the government:

> Ain't I justified in fighting? — ain't I justified in stealing? — ain't I justified in doing anything to get food and clothing for myself and those who look to me for help? What matters it to me if the hinstitutions of the country, as they calls 'em, fall to pieces? We can't live upon hinstitutions, and constitutions, and them d——d things; it's our rights as we wants — it's the Charter — to let us manage our own affairs, and not let 'em tax us and grind us in the way they do. (114)

Violence, according to Dick, is morally acceptable when the institutions of society, such as Parliament, have become so grossly unjust that they "grind" the people.[33]

But the odds in this novel are stacked against Dick and the version of physical force Chartism which he represents. His indictments of the ruling class (here both the aristocracy and the burgeoning middle class) and of British institutions as the corrupt machines of that class are dismissed out of hand within the novel because of the presentation of Dick as one of the "unenlightened." Dick's colloquial language, for example, is not presented as a native, culturally-different dialect but as flawed mispronunciation; hence Dick himself is belittled by the novel. Dick's specific misnaming of "hinstitutions" stands as a general signal of his ignorance of and inability to understand or critique institutions. (Dick's partial illiteracy here stands in contrast with Tom and Susan's labored achievement and with Rosetta and Marossi's "natural" acquisition of standard written English. Dick has neither the good birth nor internal virtue of Marossi and Rosetta nor the education of Susan and Tom. Thus, within the middle-class terms of the novel, Dick and his argument ought to be dismissed.)

In contrast to Dick Boreas and the drunken, uneducated, and irresponsible advocates of the version of physical force Chartism presented in the novel, William Clarke serves as representative of the model working class and of moral (and morally superior) force Chartism.[34] Unlike the unemployed Dick Boreas, Clarke is introduced to the reader as "an intelligent mechanic" (115).[35] Gone is the parodic language of the people; Clarke speaks in formal, "rational" language. While Richard Boreas owns the nickname "Dick"[36] and the unusual, unflattering Boreas[37] (with its connotations that Dick is a bore and an ass), William Clarke remains respectfully addressed as William.

Winning the endorsement of the novel over Dick Boreas, William Clarke's beliefs in self-education and self-improvement for the working man are advanced, whereas Boreas's proposal of violence against "hinstitutions" is dismissed. Like Boreas, Clarke argues that England's institutions are to blame for the social discontent among the lower classes, but, unlike Boreas, Clarke sees these institutions as necessary and benevolent, if temporarily malfunctioning. He explains to Tom and Susan that "much of this evil [the discontent that provokes physical force Chartism] arises not so much from political as from social misgovernment." English "good institutions" have become "enfeebled," and Clarke proposes that "an enlightened system of education . . . would suffice to enlighten the minds of the whole of these degraded creatures, or as many of them as are capable of, or willing to receive it" (116). Finally for Clarke, it is not so much that the institutions of society are to blame for the existing social problems but that the working classes have never been properly "enlightened."

Just as Tom's literal freedom was a nearly automatic consequence of the intellectual freedom which was concomitant with his education, so too the novel, by way of Clarke, suggests that the "gates of liberty will fly open of their own accord" for the working classes. In agreement with Carlyle and Susan, Clarke insists that the solution lies in self-improvement: the working class need to "acquire the power of governing themselves" (115). Using the self-improvement of Tom and Susan and their escape from slavery as its background, the novel plays out its conservative agenda, arguing that it is not the institutions of the country (such as a rigidly hierarchical class structure) which stand in the way of a person's freedom but his or her own ignorance and, by extension, lack of internal virtue.

Clarke's argument here labels the working class as not only "degraded" but responsible for their own degradation and concedes that education will "enlighten" and "relieve" only some of the working class, "as many of them as are capable of, or willing to receive it" (116). Recall here that the novel's protest against slavery was launched only for those black slaves like Marossi, Rosetta, Tom, and Susan, who because of good birth and internal virtue or because of education and enlightenment "are capable of, or willing to receive" freedom. In both cases, the novel insists from its middle-class point of view that only those who educate themselves (together of course with those who are born enlightened) deserve freedom from oppression (which is to say, deserve a job and food). The oppression of the "degraded" class, with and without black skin, will persist; it is the inevitable result of their unenlightened state.

The danger, as represented by Dick and physical force Chartism, is that violent revolution might topple the institutions of society and give power to this mass of unelevated, unenlightened, and improperly educated people. "[W]hat have violent revolutions ever done?" Clarke asks.

> What have they done in France — do they enjoy liberty there? No. And you will
> find that in proportion to the revolutions by force, which occur in any country, so

do the liberties of the people decline. These fighting Chartists destroy our chances of success. They are, as a body, people defective of habits and opinions. (115)

Given its representative, Dick, a drunken, uneducated, wife-beater, and its members, men who lack good 'habits and opinions,'' men who "cannot govern [themselves]'' (115), let alone the nation, physical force Chartism is finally discredited by its association within the novel with the bogeyman of Victorian England — the French Revolution.[38]

Dick Boreas's argument that oppression justifies violence would have been no more acceptable to middle-class Victorians even within the context of abolitionism. Middle-class mid-Victorian England was wary of the use of violence even in the fight against slavery. The *Times*, for example, while it recognizes the "stain" of slavery, warns that violence in the cause of abolition may produce Arnoldian "anarchy and confusion" (97): "Hate begets hate, and a war of races secures the rapid deterioration and decline of all the combatants. We may well shrink before rashly inviting so bloody and disastrous a conflict.''[39] The non-violent escape of a few deserving individuals, such as Tom, Susan, and the children, is acceptable; more radical, large scale social upheaval portends, for the *Times*, an undesirable "war of races.''

Reactions to the bloody insurrection of John Brown at Harper's Ferry (1859) demonstrate the same middle-class antipathy toward the use of violence. For example, the less conservative *Anti-Slavery Reporter* must construct a precarious argument in order to support Brown's use of violence.

> He (Brown) went there for the purpose of conducting such persons in the Southern States as the cruel laws had kept ignorant of the honourable means of gaining their liberty into a state of freedom; but there was no use disguising the fact that he was prepared to defend himself, even to blood, if any attempt were made to prevent the success of his enterprise. . . . John Brown went not as an insurgent against peaceable men, but against an armed band of insurgents. Blood was there already — blood, drop by drop wrung from the hearts of poor defenseless people, deprived of every means of freedom. He interfered; he saw a strong man in the act of beating out the brains of a weak man, and he interposed himself between. (16)

Notice here that sanction of Brown's use of violence to overthrow the institution of slavery comes with an insistence that violence preceded Brown, that armed conflict was already in place in the United States, hence that Brown was not initiating "mad" anarchy but merely reacting to it. It is the slaveholders, "an armed band of insurgents," who are portrayed as the rash and the violent. Further, the *Reporter* characterizes Brown's endeavor not as social upheaval, not as the overthrow of the institution of slavery, but as an attempt to gain for a few "poor defenseless people" the chance of "gaining their liberty into a state of freedom," an attempt to help "a weak man" who is being unjustly beaten by "a strong man." Only by downplaying Brown's attacks on the institution of slavery and by constructing Brown's attack as an attempt to restore peace and order can the *Reporter* condone his violent insurrection.

Pitting physical force Chartism, constructed as violently and politically irresponsible, against moral force Chartism, constructed, like John Brown, as rational and peaceable, the novel ensures support only for reform made, as Arnold put it, "by due course of law" (97). With physical force Chartism dismissed, the novel can safely endorse its version of moral force Chartism, a version of Chartism which poses no threat to the social and political status quo.

* * *

WHY DOES THE NOVEL PICK a fight with physical force Chartism when the entire Chartist movement, by the time of the publication of this novel in 1852, is, if not dead, then on its last legs?[40] In particular, why does the author revivify Chartism by giving character to physical and moral force Chartism, replaying a contest between the two that is, by 1852, moot?

The answer, I believe, is that the novel, like many of the industrial novels written after the demise of Chartism, wants to celebrate and glorify England, in particular, England's management of its own reform movement.[41] In the face of the 1848 revolutions in Europe and with what the British perceived as the time bomb of slavery steadily ticking in the United States, a resuscitated depiction of Chartism, caricatured and hamstrung within the revisionist outlook of the novel, allows England (and constructs for the British) a degree of pride and nostalgia over England's superior handling (in contrast to those other nations) of its domestic reform problems.[42]

A re-writing of the history of Chartism allows for the depiction of moral force Chartism as a movement for self-enlightenment and self-education, as a movement basically at peace with the class structure of society. De-emphasizing the crucial goal of all Chartists — universal male suffrage — the novel can suggest that moral force Chartism, indeed all of the Chartism that ever really made sense and was not simply the irrational whim of drunken uneducated men, was not defeated. Hence the novel can suggest that Chartism's goals — here written as self-enlightenment and self-education — have blended peacefully into the values of mainstream Victorian society. The defeat and disappearance of physical force Chartism, whose goals could not be blended into Victorian society, is justified by its depiction as a misguided upstart movement doomed by its internal anarchy and confusion and by the incompetence of its unenlightened (alcoholic, wife-beating, lazy) members. The rewriting of Chartism in this novel also erases any picture of a Chartist movement squelched by those in power and thus serves to enforce an idea of an enlightened England, leader among nations in peacefully acceding to social change and promoting justice.[43]

That the abolition of slavery is not the agenda for this novel explains the restrained, abrogated discussion we get of the novel's seemingly provocative subtitle — "A Proof that Black's White":

> The intention of this work has been to show, in the words of its title, "that Black's White." By this is meant that there is no natural disqualification of the black population, which should deprive them of the right to enjoy equal political and social privileges with ourselves; or, in the words of Uncle Tom, in his defence, it has been attempted to prove that "as far as our colored brethren have had the advantages of education and of civilization, they have been as peaceful, as orderly, as devout, as those of fairer skin." (123; original quotation marks)

While the passage effaces racial difference, the phrase "no natural disqualification" effectively sidesteps the issue of racial equality. It states neither that the "black population" is equal to the white population nor that they have any potential, vis-à-vis education and civilization, to be so. Rather, it back-handedly demands, through a string of negatives — "*no* natural *dis*qualification of the black population, which should *deprive* them of the right" (my emphasis) — political and social privileges for blacks.

It is crucial that the passage speaks of "privileges" in this instance and not of rights. "Education" and "civilization," here, are the "natural qualifications" for the political and social "privileges" of society. And this holds true for black slaves as well as for the British white underclass. Those without the benefits of "education" and "civilization" (such as Dick Boreas or the slaves whom Tom and Susan left behind on George Harris's farm) may be deprived of social privileges, such as a job or, in the case of slaves, of freedom. The black and white "slaves" who manage to acquire the "advantages of education and civilization" deserve privileges. The unstated connection between black and white in the contraction "black's white" is that the white working class are no more "naturally" qualified for the "privileges" of society than are black slaves. "Education" and "civilization," not skin color, determine social status.

With a rhetorical sleight of hand which exposes the fiction of the novel's abolitionist agenda and of its representation of Chartism, the connection between black and white takes another form. William Clarke insists, first, that the campaign to abolish American slavery is connected to, rather than in competition with, Chartism, and second, that abolition must take precedence over Chartism.[44] Clarke says:

> We have . . . our grievances. Where is the country that has not? But this I believe, — that we have more real liberty in England than is enjoyed in any other kingdom in the world. But we can't make much advance while what are called the enlightened governments maintain such oppressions as they do. What do our opponents tell us here? "Why," say they, "look to America; there they have your vaunted charter, and there are three million of slaves bowed to the very dust." I

consider, therefore, that a very important step to reform in our kingdom would be
the abolition of slavery by the republic of America. (115)

Clarke's argument is that abolition is "a step to reform in our kingdom," a
stage in the fight for Chartism. Clarke here suggests a hierarchy of reform
agendas: (1) abolition of American slavery, (2) domestic reform such as Chartism. This relationship between, and the prioritizing of, the two reform movements is based not on some sense that the cause of the "white slave" and the
cause of the black slave are linked but rather on the relation between "enlightened governments."

England and the United States both consider themselves "enlightened governments." Under this rubric of national chauvinism comes a moral and political
charge: England and America set the standards of reform and have certain leadership responsibilities towards the rest of the world. In general, the novel insists
that "Reciprocal influences prevail between nations as among individuals —
and one nation may determine the conduct of another nation as effectually as
one man may exercise suasion upon the mind of his fellow." England, for
example, having lit the "flame" of the Anti-Corn Law League "lights up a
kindred element in European nations. . . . the eyes of Europe have been upon
England during the recent struggle, and her example has extended its influence
wherever misgovernment exists" (125).

On the other hand, the United States, having lit the "flame" of British Chartism with its "vaunted" American charter, has failed to shine its beacon of light
onto England because the stain of slavery blocks that light.[45] England might
"look to America," to America's accomplishment of the charter, but the accomplishment can only be seen in the context of the "three million of slaves bowed
to the very dust." Thus the charter appears specious since, even without a
charter, England claims "more real liberty" than anywhere else. England does
not look up to the American charter for guidance, it looks down on that charter,
scorning the "American constitution [as] the greatest anomaly in the world"
(120). Despite the so-called advance of the charter, America still permits slavery.

America has failed to enlighten the world, and England is among "the nations
throughout the world" for which American slavery is proving a "stumbling
block" (123). This is, after all, why Clarke prioritizes the fight against America
slavery. With the stumbling block of the contradiction of the existence of slavery
in a nation which has a charter, England cannot achieve Chartist reform.

But the proposition that American reform must be primary, that the contradiction of America's lack of freedom hinders British reform, suggests that influence
in the "kinship" of "enlightened governments" flows from the United States
to England. In the example of the Anti-Corn Law League, influences flow in
one direction: from England to the rest of Europe. With the abolition of slavery,
influences also flow from England: having abolished colonial slavery, England

sends its influence on such matters to the United States which takes the lesson from its superior and goes to work on the reform. Indeed, the novel, written and originally published in England but subsequently sent to and published in America and presuming to advocate the abolition of slavery, offers itself as an example of just such an influence, a literary beacon sent with moral and political purpose from the enlightened government of England to America.

But are we really to believe that England, this center of influence, the most superior of the "enlightened governments" (as evidenced in its abolition of slavery), cannot accomplish Chartist reform without the influence of American reform? Why would England look to America at all, let alone allow the instance of the failed charter in America to stand in the way of reform in England? Are we to believe that in this instance (alone) England "look[s] to" the influences and leadership of the United States, using the American charter to set an example for British Chartism?

The reversal of the trans-Atlantic power relations in this instance is convenient for undermining the urgency and the reputability of Chartist reforms, but it is ultimately unconvincing. For all the while the United States is accorded this particular role of leadership in the instance of American slavery, the novel firmly insists that England is the *real* leader among nations. The critique of the American charter, after all, as a "vaunted charter" is a critique of American nationalism and an attempt to reaffirm British superiority. It forms part of a series of taunts running through the novel focused specifically on the icons of American nationalism, particularly the American flag, in which British nationalism is constructed and affirmed against the model of the United States. When the slave ship carrying Marossi and Rosetta arrives in the United States, the novel records, "At length the ship arrived in the harbor of Charleston"; the novel emphasizes the irony of this injustice with a sarcastic juxtaposition, "the American flag of stars and stripes floating at its mainmast!" (11). Through abolition, the stars and stripes of the American flag have taken on symbolic resonances at variance with liberty, justice, or freedom: the stars symbolize that to which only the white man may aspire while the stripes represent floggings, written upon the black man's back.[46] Likewise, Tom's trial, in which he protests the injustice of the laws and of the system which is condemning him for seeking his and his family's freedom, a scene of "vaunted" but specious American justice, is ironically entitled "The Stripes and Stars of America." Later, Thomas Hanaway writes that he and Rosetta have decided to live in the "the *United State* in Canada" (122; emphasis in original). Canada here becomes the true "United State"; it unites a people together and unites them with their liberties. Each of the "vaunted" tokens of American liberty and freedom, in these examples, turns out to be as specious as the charter.

A number of other passages work as both obloquies to the United States and accolades to England. For example, at the auction at which Tom is sold to

George Harris, the auctioneer announces that Tom is a Christian. The novel queries sarcastically, "What think you, Christian reader, would the repetition of this qualification have enhanced the value of the lot? 'Going — a *Christian* — for four hundred dollars!' Who, on *this* side of the Atlantic, will bid another fifty?" (16; emphasis in original). While Americans bid for and barter in human flesh, the novel confidently asserts the difference across the Atlantic. No British citizen, the passage presumes, would add fifty to the count.

With each of America's vaunted advances (such as the charter) and symbols of advancement (such as the American flag) debunked since none represent, according to the novel, real advances in liberty, the British citizen can feel superior to his or her American counterpart. Likewise, the narrative voice of the novel asserts, the British citizen need not feel any national inferiority based on the comparatively large size of the United States:

> The Yankee . . . looks upon this little island . . . and taunts us with wanting elbow room. There is one thing, we confess, we cannot find room for her, and that is slavery — traffic in human bodies to the sacrifice of human souls. And from our hearts we deplore the humiliating fact that so vast a country as America — a country boasting of free institutions, and having a constitution in which the rights of mankind are nobly asserted, should be stained by so foul a spot, her name a byeword [sic] among nations, a reproach upon the tongues of honest men! (17)

Rather than representing its superiority to England, the size of the United States and its relative advances in freedom, such as the Bill of Rights and the Constitution, come to represent instead the meagerness of the United States. Little England, with its ancient monarchic institutions, without the benefit of grand size and the grand institutions of freedom, is made to look that much the better in contrast.

The novel praises England on still other counts. England "has already heard and heeded the voice of slaves, and struck off their shackles!" (94); the fact that England eliminated the slave trade (1807) and colonial slavery (1833/1838) is a commonly cited source of national pride. Tom praises England as "a truly Christian land [with] a peculiarly Christian people" (110). Furthermore, England is represented as a land free of color prejudice. As Susan tells Tom, "Phillis Wheatley was a poor negress. . . . she went to England, a beautiful country, where there are people of great minds and noble hearts, and where men and women are not bought and sold, and there she was treated as a child of God without reference to the color of her skin" (30). Likewise, we see the entire family treated with kindness and respect in England, conversing with rich and poor without remark upon their complexion.

In all of these comparisons between England and a belittled United States, we see England constructing itself as the true leader among nations. Yet the very examples the novel uses expose the contradictions within this tidy national facade. The novel's self-congratulations that in England, "we cannot find room for . . . slavery — traffic in human bodies to the sacrifice of human souls" (27) flies in the face of several decades of criticism of the treatment of women and child laborers and of the working class generally. It flies in the face of criticism that has given a name to that treatment: white slavery; by 1850, the "slavery of the working class" had become the dominant term around which the plight of the condition of the working class was debated.[47] Elsewhere, when insisting that "there is no natural disqualification of the black population, which should deprive them of the right to enjoy equal political and social privileges with ourselves" (123), the novel placidly creates an England, "ourselves," in which all enjoy political and social privileges, an England which bears little resemblance to reality.[48]

In the aftermath of Chartism and the hungry forties, 1852 found England in the process of reconstructing itself as a glorious nation in an age of Progress: "It was the age of exuberance, of wealth, of invention and audacity. . . . It was all part of Progress, and Progress was identical with the spirit of the age" (ffrench 5).[49] The novel's politically contorted act of constructing this vision of a glorious England against the example of a besieged America may be seen as part of this process.

* * *

BETWEEN 1850 AND 1860, BLACK Americans active in the struggle to abolish American slavery journeyed to England. These black men and women lectured on their life experiences, circulated slave narratives, displayed enormous panoramas depicting scenes of American slavery, and revealed personal scars and the instruments of torture used in slavery. All these were consumed by the British population. The black American abolitionist campaign in England, a phenomenon grounded in the politics of abolition but infused with the energy of popular appeal, was an event with enormous possibilities for change. But what was at stake in British interest in American slavery?

Uncle Tom in England: Or, A Proof that Black's White suggests some answers; it provides a glimpse into the meanings American abolition took on for Victorians. A national cultural autobiography, the novel appropriates the black American abolitionist campaign to pursue a middle-class politics. Against the example of America and American slavery, *Uncle Tom in England* constructs an English nation of stability, order, and slow progress in which middle-class values are secure.

Jersey City State College

NOTES

1. All references to *Uncle Tom in England* are from the London edition of the novel. Several British and American editions of *Uncle Tom in England* were published.The editions vary in terms of title page illustrations and title page marginalia, but the texts of all editions seem to be identical. The American edition states on its title page that it is published "from an advance copy from England." A German translation of the novel exists, entitled, *Onkel Tom in England. Fortsetzung von Onkel Tom's Hütte*. The German edition was incorrectly attributed to Thomas Clarkson, probably because "Sclaverei und der Schlavenhandel," an excerpt translated from one of his works, appears in volume 2 of the edition.

   A version of this paper was presented at the London Seminar for Nineteenth Century Studies at Birkbeck College and at the University of Southampton. I am grateful to audiences at both universities for helpful comments and to Isobel Armstrong and Ken Hirschkop for making the respective arrangements. For patient reading and criticism of this essay, I am thankful to Catherine Hall, Claire Berardini, Elise Lemire, Kate Ellis, John Gillis, George Levine, Donald Gibson, Richard Blackett, and Mark Flynn.

2. This essay forms a part of a book-length project entitled "Uncle Tom in England: American Abolition and the Construction of English Identity," which examines the general interest exhibited by the British in the eighteen-fifties for the black American abolitionist campaign and the ideological consequences of that interest for Victorian society. This interest is witnessed not just by British consumption of Stowe's "Uncle Tom" but also by the circulation of American slave narratives and by the visits and popularity of ex-slaves and free-born black Americans on the abolitionist lecture circuit throughout England. For discussion of the black American abolitionist campaign in England, see Blackett, *Building* and *Beating*. For a survey of some of the primary texts in the field, see also, Ripley and Taylor. For more general discussion of the history of black people and of black slaves in England, see Fryer, Shyllon, and Scobie. The background on England's own anti-slavery campaign is much larger; see Rice, Temperley, Klingberg, Craton, and Walvin. For an examination of the trans-atlantic nature of anti-slavery, see Bolt.

3. For example, the novel closes with an exacting injunction that its audience (purportedly all of England) sign and send an address to America (a kind of national petition): "the united declaration of THREE MILLIONS of men, women, and youths of Great Britain against the enslavement of the negro race . . . Will not every man assert the right of his fellow-man — every woman the right of her fellow-woman — to freedom?" (126).

4. An understanding of the circulation of these texts is important to any discussion of their (popular and/or political) influence. I discuss the British circulation and reception of Stowe's novel at length elsewhere but, basically, her text set new records for sales. Wilson states that the novel sold 165,000 copies in England in its first year of circulation (419). Lorimer estimates the number of sales for the novel in the United Kingdom and the British Empire at one and a half million (82). The precise circulation of *Uncle Tom in England*, however, is difficult to document. The title page of a later American edition of *Uncle Tom in England* declares this new novel "A Book Selling Equal to 'Uncle Tom's Cabin' " and informs perusers "60,000 Copies Sold — Tenth Edition" (from New York: A. D. Failing edition in the New York Historical Society). Such advertisements do not typically present exact

historical evidence. However, the boasted figure of 60,000 copies compares favorably with Altick's estimate that "Throughout the [nineteenth] century, the ordinary circulating-library novel seldom had an edition of more than a thousand or 1,250 copies" (*Common* 264). Compare also the circulating figures for cheap editions (six shillings), which were sold in huge quantities. Altick gives the example of "Marie Corelli's *The Master Christian* [which] had a pre-publication printing of 75,000 copies" (*Common* 313).

Uncle Tom in England also seems to have received its fair share of reviews (not all of high praise), indicating a degree of circulation and visibility. For example, *The Athenaeum* on October 2, 1852, notices the novel, calling its existence "the inevitable imitation to which [the success of *Uncle Tom's Cabin*] gives birth." The review finds *Uncle Tom in England* "an echo [of *Uncle Tom's Cabin*] of the faintest. The volume, pitch, and quality of the original voice are all lost, — and nothing remains but a travestie of names and characters." The notice concludes by marking the writer's "boast" of completing the novel in "seven days and nights" with the following sarcasm: "We should rather he had taken more time — and done better." *The Spectator*, also notices the new novel, although the brief review eschews the savaging of the text above and merely notices its anti-Chartist politics: "A sort of sequel to *Uncle Tom*; the freed negro, after sundry adventures, being brought to England; and some hits made at Chartism."

Altogether, given these parameters, it seems reasonable to conclude that, although it never had the circulation of *Uncle Tom's Cabin* and although 60,000 copies may not be an accurate estimate of circulation, *Uncle Tom in England* circulated widely.

5. The comparison of worker and slave in political rhetoric has a long and tempestuous history in Britain; see Gallagher, pages 3–36. What is unusual about this text is the transnational tenor of the comparison, *American* slaves with *British* workers. In terms of British mid-century imaginative writing, only a small body of work focusing specifically on *American* slavery exists (in contrast to the larger sampling of British work dealing with colonial slavery). Frances Trollope's earlier *The Life and Adventures of Jonathan Jefferson Whitlaw; Or, Scenes on the Mississippi* (1836) which was republished under the title *Lynch Law; Or, The Life and Adventures of Jonathan Jefferson Whitlaw* (1857) is a notable exception here. In terms of popular and magazine writing, a great deal of incidental writing can be found on the subject of American slavery, varying from narratives of escape, narratives of slave life, narratives of the slave auction, narratives of the slave trade and journeys on the slave ship, as well as a variety of short poems and short fiction on these subjects. For example, *Howitt's Journal* (1847) includes an article entitled "An American Slave in London" by Elihu Burritt telling of an American slave's escape from "The land of the free and the home of the brave" to England. *Chamber's Edinburgh Journal* (1858) includes an unsigned article, "The Domestic Institution," reprinted from the *New York Tribune*, describing a slave auction in Savannah. *Blackwoods Magazine* (1860) includes a review of one of the many English narratives about a journey to America, Laurence Oliphant's *Rambles at Random in the Southern States*, which is discussed at length, amid many brief but polemical anecdotes about American slaves. It is within this sampling of British writing about and interest in American slavery that *Uncle Tom in England* can be understood as a rarity.

6. Given the nationalist foundation of the colonial anti-slavery movement and the frequency with which the British stressed their virtue at having initiated the world anti-slavery movement, it is not surprising to find British popular rhetoric about anti-slavery, as this novel evidences, turning to American slavery as further ammunition

for the construction of a superior Englishness. Of the association of the colonial anti-slavery movement with British nationalism, Hall writes, the rhetoric of anti-slavery "expressed what it should mean to be English." When England took up the cause of colonial slavery, recognizing it as a "great national crime" (27), the rhetoric makes clear that as much of this taking up was about the construction of an image of a nation which could rise above pecuniary interest, face its past, and make appropriate reparations as it was about colonial slavery. The existence of British slavery, as Ferguson emphasizes in a discussion of Hannah More's "Slavery, A Poem," is seen as "primarily a blemish on the national character that throws Britain's supposed reputation as a land of freedom and goodness into disrepute" (9). For further discussion of the way in which the colonial anti-slavery movement participated in the ongoing construction of an English national identity, see Blackburn (esp. 443–46), Turner, Turley, and Temperley (*White*).

Of course, the construction of this English reputation for freedom and goodness, especially apropos the abolition of colonial slavery, has been widely disputed by a variety of historians of the anti-slavery movement. While still a contested issue among historians, the idea that slavery in the colonies was abolished as a result of humanitarianism is disputed by those who argue that British colonial abolitionism resulted in part from the fact that colonial slavery had grown economically unprofitable, see James and E. Williams.

7. See Hall, esp. Chapter 9, "Missionary Stories," for a discussion of how England's anti-slavery as well as its industrial, economic, and political "developments" contributed to what she calls a "morbid celebration of Englishness": the development of an English national identity which was white, male, and middle class, and which refused the recognition "that Englishness is an ethnicity" (205–06).

8. For a brilliant discussion of this process of appropriation or, as she terms it, "colonial exploitation," within Charlotte Brontë's *Jane Eyre*, see Meyer.

9. See my "Uncle Tom in England: The Black American Abolitionist Campaign, 1852–1861."

10. Contrasting the subtitle of *Uncle Tom's Cabin*—"Life Among the Lowly" — with that of *Uncle Tom in England*—"A Proof that Black's White" — makes clear the differences between the two books' agendas. Stowe's subtitle is descriptive, offering the novel as a depiction of "life" among a particular group, "the lowly." Without implicating the novel in any argument or controversy (which might require "A Proof"), the subtitle strikes an "objective" and genial tone. The melodic and alliterative qualities of "Life Among the Lowly" work to confirm the relative simplicity of the novel's agenda. All of which is not to understate the complexity of Stowe's novel, as discussed in, for example, Tompkins (122–46), Zwarg, essays by Elizabeth Ammons and Dorothy Berkson in Ammons, and Brown. See also Fisher (esp. 87–127, in which he discusses Stowe's original subtitle for the novel, the "man that was a thing").

Today the subtitle of *Uncle Tom's Cabin* is sometimes suppressed from current editions of the novel. For example, in the 1981 Bantam Classics edition of *Uncle Tom's Cabin* and in the introduction to that edition by Alfred Kazin, the subtitle "Life Among the Lowly" is nowhere mentioned. Clearly slaves had a low social position and, hence, were forced to humble or "lower" themselves to others. But according to the OED, "lowly" had acquired another set of more prejudicial meanings by 1852: "low in growth" and "low in character," "mean" as in "His name was never stained with any lowly act." Presumably, the condescending and thus racist overtones of the subtitle are an embarrassment in a book now lauded as an American classic.

11. This is despite the popularity of the "Am I Not a Man and a Brother?" abolitionist slogan which asserts kinship between blacks and whites. For discussion of the anti-slavery slogans, "Am I Not a Friend and a Brother?" and its feminist counterpart, "Am I Not a Woman and a Sister?" in the American context, see Yellin (esp. 3–28). For a larger discussion of British opinions on race, see Lorimer, Bolt (*Victorian*), Stepan, and Hall (*White*).

12. As Lorimer writes, this period "saw the birth of scientific racism and a change in English racial attitudes from the humanitarian response of the early nineteenth century to the racialism of the imperialist era at the close of the Victorian age" (13). In regard to the question of Victorian attitudes toward race, Lorimer writes: "the question, 'does a black man equal a white man?' had little meaning in an age when few thought all white men deserved equality" (15). Lorimer's implication here is that questions of racism and racial equality cannot be thought about apart from questions of class equality (or inequality). See also Brantlinger, who explores the imperialist ideology of mid-century imaginative writing at the roots of the jingoist imperialism of the late Victorian and Edwardian periods.

13. By suggesting that concerns of class supplant concerns of race in the novel, I do not mean to reassert that old notion that class is an essential and all-consuming category or that class is the sole or dominant ideology in Victorian society. While issues of class seem to be foremost in the novel, the discourses of race and class remain in an angry dialogue throughout; race is thoroughly intertwined in the novel's obsession with class.

14. It is crucial to understand the novel's preoccupation with class as a part of a larger ideological shift in which the middle class was struggling with self-definition. As Morris writes, "In the early decades of the nineteenth century, marginalization by class was still a new and harsh experience; it only became the dominant form of social relation with the seizure and consolidation of hegemonic power by the middle class which brought into being the Victorian social formation" (5). As the dominant form of social relation, and following the disruption of the French Revolution for the aristocracy and for aristocratic values, the middle class defined itself against the corruption of the aristocracy by asserting the importance of "inner worth" (8) or internal virtue: "the moral virtues of enterprise, diligence, and thrifty sobriety" (6). At the same time as these internal virtues distinguished the middle class from the corrupt aristocracy, the middle class also defined themselves against the working class. To "define and justify bourgeois hegemony," the "myth of divine and economic causation . . . proved to be . . . efficacious" under which "prosperity and respectability were held to be the inevitable outward signs and consequences of inner moral worth" (8). See also Davidoff and Hall.

15. The African language the children speak to each other remains outside the comprehension of the narrator and unrepresented within the narrative. However, within the context of an ostensibly trans-cultural language of affection and the larger context of class superiority, this otherness is forgotten as the narrative represents their "savage" tongue to the reader as domestic affection.

16. The most obvious example of this paradigm of the noble savage in English literature is Aphra Behn's *Oroonoko*. For discussion of the complications in *Oroonoko*, see Spengemann and Ferguson (27–49). See also Yarborough's discussion the discourse of the noble savage in connection with *Uncle Tom's Cabin*. Yarborough argues that Stowe subscribes to a "romantic racialist . . . conception of African personality [which] held that the black was a 'natural Christian' whose soft emotionalism and gentle passivity were destined to temper the harshness of Anglo-Saxon culture" (64).

17. Note here that the children's noble birth does not serve as the sole, sufficient indicator of their class. See here McKeon's discussion of the ideological traditions on which the novel was the based, including romance idealism and naive empiricism.

18. Note that this "blaming the victim" is the consequence of the application of the ideology of the middle class to non-middle-class subjects. As Morris writes, "If prosperity and respectability were held to be the inevitable outward signs and consequences of inner moral worth, then it followed that those who failed in the competitive struggle to make a living and succeed were morally unfit" (8).

19. In *Uncle Tom's Cabin*, lighter skinned blacks are the superiors (intellectually, morally, and socially) of darker skinned black characters. This narrative economy is the logical consequence both of Stowe's racism and of the ideology of (nineteenth-century American) society generally, in which white blood was thought to improve the African. For a fuller discussion of the politics of skin-color in *Uncle Tom's Cabin*, see Yarborough.

In contrast, within the narrative economy of *Uncle Tom in England*, the "whiter" mulattoes, Tom and Susan are identified as intellectually and socially inferior to Rosetta and Marossi, the full black children, who are, in turn, more fully rewarded within the narrative. *Uncle Tom in England* seems to participate in a discourse of contagion, in which the mixture of white and black blood comes to represent the corruption and contamination of the unnatural institution of slavery. For a discussion of the discourse of contagion in the Victorian context, see Meyer.

20. The working classes had their own traditions of education — in trades, in oral culture, and in popular culture — not considered of value by middle-class standards; see E. Thompson. For a larger discussion of working class education, and of the way in the working class both absorbed and disrupted dominant middle class values about education, see D. Thompson.

21. See also Goldstrom on working class education.

22. Gustavus Vasa, or Olaudah Equiano, *The Interesting Narrative of the Life of Olaudah Equiano, or Gustavus Vasa, the African Written by Himself* (1789). J. W. C. Pennington, *The Fugitive Blacksmith*. Frederick Douglass, *Narrative of the Life of Frederick Douglass, an American Slave*. Phillis Wheatley was an American slave and poet whose first book, *Poems on Various Subjects, Religious and Moral*, was published in London in 1773.

23. Pennington, Douglass, and Henry Highland Garnet were all American ex-slaves. William Cuffee was a British free-born black who was involved with Chartism. Solomon Bayley is the author of *A Narrative of Some Remarkable Incidents in the Life of Solomon Bayley*.

24. For discussion of the relationship between freedom and literacy in the slave narrative, see Smith, especially her discussion of Douglass (20–28). For further complications of the black slave's relationship to white culture, via literacy and access to the white man's texts, see Gates (127–69).

25. Neither Rosetta nor Susan undergoes this process. Presumably the bonds of gender, especially of marriage (and both Susan and Rosetta marry), undercut the imagination of total freedom for women, even outside slavery. See Yellin's discussion of the importance of gender to the slave narrative's "quest for freedom and literacy" (*Incidents* xxvi).

26. Dickens, for example, takes up Bunyan's tradition in *Dombey and Son*. Tainted by middle-class commerce, Dombey has lost his internal virtue: he hits his daughter, he ignores his wife. Dickens's novel witnesses Dombey's re-education; Dombey must be jolted out of his mercantile sleep in order to recover spiritual but also class

awareness. For a further discussion of the way in which *Pilgrim's Progress* was taken up by the Victorians as part of the discourse of class, see Qualls.

27. Even within the "enlightened" discussions of abolitionists, "black culture" would never have been recognized or figured as anything of value, as anything other than savage barbarism which ought to be "developed" into the "civilization" of white culture.

28. The coercion of dominant culture here is not predicated on the racial subject of the novel; the same conflict gets written in class terms in many Victorian novels. Dickens's *Great Expectations* is an interrogation and critique of this very process.

29. This appropriation of abolition for a middle class political agenda conflates the range of conservative and radical agendas historically present within the ranks of British abolitionists. For a discussion of one abolitionist whose attitudes on issues of class in Britain reflected neither the hypocrisy nor the political machinations often perceived behind "telescopic philanthropy," see Tyrrell (esp. 85–134). For a thorough discussion of the range of relations between English abolitionism and working class radicalism as well as of the political range within the abolitionist movement, see Turley, Hollis, and Fladeland.

30. Roughly, moral force Chartists advocated self-education, self-improvement, and self-enlightenment in pursuit of the goals of equality and suffrage for the working classes. Physical force Chartists, in contrast, were willing to advocate violence in the hopes of pressuring the middle and upper classes to accede to their demands. Both groups sought, primarily between 1837 and 1848, adoption of the "People's Charter."

31. The novel is also misleading in its representation of self-improvement and self-education among Chartists as a thorough submersion in middle-class values and ideas. As Dorothy Thompson writes, Chartists "had in many cases proposals for change and improvement which did not involve the abadonment of cherished customs, and above all did not involve the total relinquishment of control over their own work and environment" (111). Further, Chartists were often "preserving customs and institutions which were under attack by the forces [the middle class, for example] making for conformity and respectability in early Victorian Britain" (117).

32. This description of Dick is in keeping with middle-class observations of Chartists and of the working class more generally. Dorothy Thompson remarks, "To the middle-class observer what predominates is the drunkenness, brutality and lack of formal moral education." Certainly the working class noticed these things in each other, but self-improvement working-class style was more in the form of "temperance, and even more, radical politics" (246).

33. Dick Boreas, in his condemnation of the "hinstitutions," may have been thinking of the 1845 General Enclosure Act which, instead of preserving peasant properties and creating legitimate peasant ownership of land, allowed the enclosure of common (read peasant farmed) land. Obviously, this law was a blow to the peasant farmer and was among the many causes for the general deterioration of peasant culture and life. Dickens's *Hard Times* (1854) may be considered a similar attack on "hinstitutions." As Raymond Williams puts it, "Public commissions, Blue Books, Parliamentary legislation — all these, in the world of *Hard Times* — are Gradgrindery" (106).

34. Dorothy Thompson explains that "even the most sympathetic members of the middle class only empathised with a small selected part of the working class" (251). In the novel's approval of the exceptional Clarke (and not of Boreas, Chartism, or the working class generally), we see this process of selection at work.

35. It is difficult on the basis of the term "mechanic" to determine precisely what kind of trade Clarke worked in (D. Thompson 201). It is interesting to note, however,

that mechanics, because of "the comparative rarity of their skills . . . were not as likely to be permanently excluded from employment in their trades as members of overstocked trades like weavers, shoemakers and tailors. Mechanics, therefore, who were active in the high point of Chartism, even those who served terms of imprisonment, were probably able to get work again" (D. Thompson 200). The novel's choice of trades for Clarke may be an attempt to justify his particular political views. It is clear, however, Clarke's politics do not accurately represent the convictions of Chartist mechanics.

36. As far as I can tell, in the mid-nineteenth century, the nickname "Dick" contained no reference to Richard's genitals. "Dick" did however connote the generic man, as in "Tom, Dick, or Harry: any three (or more) representatives of the populace taken at random" (OED). Dick Boreas, in other words, stands as the novel's representation of the average, unenlightened working man.

37. Boreas in Latin is North wind, commonly associated with destruction and barbarism. In this sense, the name may also be meant as a slighting reference to the preeminent Chartist newspaper, Feargus O'Connor's *Northern Star*.

38. See Gregory, Prickett, Scott. In "The Function of Criticism at the Present Time" (1860), Arnold writes of the French Revolution as "the greatest, the most animating event in history," but he complains that "the mania [in France] for giving an immediate and political and practical application to all these fine ideas of the reason was fatal" (525).

39. The *Times* was regularly critical of both the earlier colonial abolition movement in England and of American abolition. Yet its antipathy to the use of violence in the fight for the abolition of slavery must be seen as part of the paper's attempt to have it both ways: to abhor slavery and to criticize attempts to abolish slavery. See Hall's discussion of the paper's sympathy for colonial slavery (esp. 271–72), and see Fulton's discussion of the *Times* as an anti-abolitionist paper. See also Crawford.

40. Dorothy Thompson writes that "As a mass movement . . . Chartism declined rapidly after 1848" (299). "[T]he better economic climate which accompanied and followed the Great Exhibition of 1851, the increasing stability of Britain's major industries in that period and the organisations which these conditions allowed to develop among the new industrial workforce," according to Thompson, "account for [Chartism's] decline and death" (330). "[A]lthough it took a decade to die," Thompson observes, "it persisted only as a marginal force in British social history in those years" (329). Cole writes that "After 1848 Chartism was merely a residue" (22).

41. See R. Williams's discussion of the industrial novels (99–119).

42. Disturbances in Ireland were, among the 1848 revolutions, disturbances which threatened English national identity (if not English material politics) far more than revolution in more distant Europe. For discussion of the 1848 rebellion in Ireland, see Boyce (esp. 170–174). It is perhaps surprising that the novel does not address the question of Ireland and of the relation of the Irish to the "glorious" England constructed by the novel. For a general discussion of the history of racial discourse about the Irish, see Gibbons; see also Curtis and Lebow for a discussion of the racial coding of the Irish specifically within the Victorian period.

43. Historians continue to argue about the reasons for the decline of Chartism, see D. Thompson (330–39). But they do not argue about the effectiveness of police action and the violence of the British legal system in squelching the movement. An examination of the Newport Rising alone, with the violence shown by police against Chartists leaving 22 dead and the injustice shown by the government sentencing three to death for their actions in uprising, makes clear that those in power certainly

did their best to squelch Chartism. For further discussion of the Newport Rising, see D. Thompson (77–87).

44. This represents another historical distortion on the part of the novel. American abolition and Chartism had, generally, a tense and charged relation towards each other. For a discussion of the historical competition between anti-slavery and domestic reform in England, see Gallagher (3–36); see also Fladeland.

45. For a discussion of white working class and black suffrage under the "charter" of nineteenth-century America, see Roediger (55–60).

46. See, for example, the following reading of the American flag in *The Christian Weekly News*: "The stripes on the American flag are truly more significant than the stars, unless the latter are intended to indicate how ill-starred the subjects of the stripes" (Rev. of *Slave Life*). See also Wright's assertion that "When 'Uncle Tom's Cabin' was first published, the whole of England was thrilled with enthusiastic indignation. We pointed in angry scorn at the stars and stripes, and told the Americans that their national flag was the symbol of their shame; the white man might aspire to the stars, while for the poor black man there was no reward but stripes" (2–3).

47. See Gallagher (3–36). Examples of the application of the term "slavery" to the condition of the working class abound in British literature, Kingsley's *Alton Locke* (1850), for example, and Dickens's *Oliver Twist*. The near universality of comparisons between the slavery of the working class and that of American slaves seems to have prompted response to such comparisons in many slave narratives; see Harriet Jacobs, for example (184).

See also two attempts by British writers to re-direct sympathy for American slavery back toward the British poor: Coatsworth and Rymer.

48. The side of English social life not represented in *Uncle Tom in England* is vividly represented in the Chartist John C. Cobden's *The White Slaves of England* (1853).

49. The Crystal Palace might be taken as the paradigmatic moment in this national reconstruction. Altick describes the "virtual legend" of the Great Exhibition and comments that it served as "an occasion for national pride and momentary class reconciliation" (*Shows* 456).

WORKS CITED

Altick, Richard D. *The English Common Reader: A Social History of the Mass Reading Public 1800–1900*. Chicago: U of Chicago P, 1957.

———. *The Shows of London*. Cambridge, MA: Harvard UP, 1978.

Ammons, Elizabeth. *Critical Essays on Harriet Beecher Stowe*. Boston: G. K. Hall, 1980.

———. "Heroines in *Uncle Tom's Cabin*." Ammons, *Critical* 152–65.

Anti-Slavery Reporter 8.1 (Jan. 1860): 16.

Arnold, Matthew. "The Function of Criticism at the Present Time." *Victorian Poetry and Poetics*. Ed. Walter E. Houghton and G. Robert Stange. Boston: Houghton Mifflin, 1968. 522–35.

——— *Culture and Anarchy*. Ed. J. Dover Wilson. Cambridge: Cambridge P, 1932.

Berkson, Dorothy. "Millennial Politics and the Feminine Fiction of Harriet Beecher Stowe." Ammons, *Critical* 244–58.

Best, Geoffrey. *Mid-Victorian Britain: 1851–1875*. New York: Shocken Books, 1972.

Blackburn, Robin. *The Overthrow of Colonial Slavery, 1776–1848*. London: Verso, 1988.

Blackett, R. J. M. *Beating Against the Barriers: The Lives of Six Nineteenth-Century Afro-Americans*. Ithaca: Cornell UP, 1986.

———. *Building an Antislavery Wall: Black Americans in the Atlantic Abolitionist Movement, 1830–1860*. Ithaca: Cornell UP, 1983.

Bolt, Christine. *The Anti-Slavery Movement and Reconstruction: A Study in Anglo-American Co-operation 1833–77*. New York: Oxford UP, 1969.

———. *Victorian Attitudes to Race*. London: Routledge and K. Paul, 1971.

Boyce, D. George. *Nationalism in Ireland*. Baltimore: Johns Hopkins UP, 1982.

Brantlinger, Patrick. *Rule of Darkness: British Literature and Imperialism, 1830–1914*. Ithaca: Cornell UP, 1988.

Brown, Gillian. "Getting in the Kitchen with Dinah: Domestic Politics in *Uncle Tom's Cabin*." *American Quarterly* 36.4 (Fall 1984): 503–23.

Burritt, Elihu. "An American Slave in London." *Howitt's Journal* 1 (1847): 147–49.

Carlyle, Thomas. *Selected Works, reminiscences and letters*. Cambridge, MA: Harvard UP, 1970.

Cobden, John C. *The White Slaves of England*. Buffalo, NY: Derby, Orton and Mulligan, 1853.

Cole, G. D. H. *Chartist Portraits*. London: Macmillan, 1941.

Coatsworth, J. *Slavery in England, Or A Picture of the Many Hardships Endured by Our Fellow Countrymen in their Several Stations of Life*. London: E. Marlborough, 1860.

Craton, Michael. *Sinews of Empire: A Short History of British Slavery*. Garden City, NY: Anchor Books, 1974.

Crawford, Martin. *The Anglo-American Crisis of the Mid-Nineteenth Century: The Times and America, 1850–1862*. Athens: U of Georgia P, 1987.

Curtis, L. Perry, Jr. *Apes and Angels: The Irishman in Victorian Caricature*. Washington: Smithsonian Institution P, 1971.

———. *Anglo-Saxons and Celts: A Study of Anti-Irish Prejudice in Victorian England*. Bridgeport: U of Bridgeport, 1968.

Davidoff, Leonore, and Catherine Hall. *Family Fortunes: Men and women of the English middle class, 1780–1850*. Chicago: U of Chicago P, 1987.

Dickens, Charles. *Great Expectations*. New York: Penguin Books, 1982.

———. *Oliver Twist*. New York: Oxford UP, 1982.

"Domestic Institution, The." *Chamber's Edinburgh Journal* 31 (1858): 269–71.

Douglass, Frederick. *Narrative of the Life of Frederick Douglass: An American Slave*. New York: Signet, 1968.

Ferguson, Moira. *Subject to Others: British Women Writers and Colonial Slavery, 1670–1834*. New York: Routledge, 1992.

ffrench, Yvonne. *The Great Exhibition: 1851*. London: Harvill P, 1950.

Fisch, Audrey A. "Uncle Tom in England: The Black American Abolitionist Campaign, 1852–1861." Diss. Rutgers University, 1993.

Fisher, Philip. *Hard Facts: Setting and Form in the American Novel*. New York: Oxford UP, 1985.

Fladeland, Betty. *Abolitionists and Working-Class Problems in the Age of Industrialization*. Baton Rouge: Louisiana State UP, 1984.

———. " 'Our Cause being One and the Same': Abolitionists and Chartism." *Slavery and British Society: 1776–1846*. Ed. James Walvin. London: Macmillan, 1982. 69–99.

Fryer, Peter. *Staying Power: The History of Black People in Britain*. London: Pluto P, 1984.

Fulton, Richard D. " 'Now Only the *Times* is on Our Side': The London Times and America before the Civil War." *Victorian Review* 16.1 (Summer 1990): 48–58.

Gallagher, Catherine. *The Industrial Reformation of English Fiction: Social Discourse and Narrative Form, 1832–1867.* Chicago: U of Chicago P, 1985.

Gates, Henry Louis, Jr. *The Signifying Monkey: A Theory of Afro-American Literary Criticism.* New York: Oxford UP, 1988.

Gibbons, Luke. "Race Against Time: Racial Discourse and Irish History." *The Oxford Literary Review* 13.1–2 (1991): 95–117.

Goldstrom, J. M. "The content of education and the socialization of the working-class child 1830–1860." *Popular Education in the nineteenth century.* Ed. Phillip McCann. London: Methuen, 1977. 93–110.

Gregory, Allene. *The French Revolution and the English Novel.* Port Washington, NY: Kennikat P, 1915.

Hall, Catherine. *White, Male and Middle Class: Explorations in Feminism and History.* New York: Routledge, 1992.

Hollis, Patricia. "Anti-Slavery and British working-class radicalism in the years of reform." *Anti-Slavery, Religion, and Reform: Essays in Memory of Roger Anstey.* Ed. Christine Bolt and Seymour Drescher. Hamden, CT: Archon Books, 1980. 294–315.

Jacobs, Harriet A. (Linda Brent). *Incidents in the Life of a Slave Girl: Written by herself.* Cambridge, MA: Harvard UP, 1987.

James, C. L. R. *The Black Jacobins: Toussaint L'Ouverture and the San Domingo Revolution.* New York: Vintage, 1963.

Jones, Gareth Stedman. *Languages of Class: Studies in English Working Class History, 1832–1982.* New York: Cambridge UP, 1983.

Kingsley, Charles. *Alton Locke: Tailor and Poet.* New York: Oxford UP, 1983.

Klingberg, Frank J. *The Anti-Slavery Movement in England: A Study in English Humanitarianism.* Hamden, CT: Archon, 1968.

Lebow, Richard Ned. *White Britain and Black Ireland: The Influence of Stereotypes on Colonial Policy.* Philadelphia: Institute for the Study of Human Issues, 1976.

Lorimer, Douglas A. *Colour, Class and the Victorians: English attitudes to the Negro in the mid-nineteenth century.* London: Leicester UP, 1978.

McKeon, Michael. *The Origins of the English Novel, 1600–1740.* Baltimore: Johns Hopkins UP, 1987.

Meyer, Susan L. "Colonialism and the Figurative Strategy of *Jane Eyre.*" *Victorian Studies* 34.1 (Winter 1990): 247–68.

Morris, Pam. *Dickens's Class Consciousness: A Marginal View.* New York: St. Martin's P, 1991.

Onkel Tom in England. Fortsetzung von Onkel Tom's Hütte. Leipzig: O. Wigond, 1853.

Prickett, Stephen. *England and the French Revolution.* Hourdsmills, England: Macmillan Education, 1989.

Qualls, Barry. *The Secular Pilgrims of Victorian Fiction: The novel as a book of life.* New York: Cambridge UP, 1982.

Rev. of *Rambles at Random in the Southern States*, by Laurence Oliphant. *Blackwood's Magazine* 87 (Jan. 1860): 103–16.

Rev. of *Slave Life in Georgia*, by John Brown. *The Christian Weekly News* 6 March 1855:156.

Rev. of *Uncle Tom in England. The Athenaeum* 2 Oct. 1852 (no. 1301): 1056.

Rev. of *Uncle Tom in England. The Spectator* 18 Sept. 1852 (no. 1264): 904.

Rice, Duncan C. *The Scots Abolitionists, 1833–1861.* Baton Rouge: Louisiana State UP, 1981.

Ripley, C. Peter, ed. *The Black abolitionist papers*. Vol. 2. *The British Isles, 1830–1865*. Chapel Hill: U of North Carolina P, 1985.

Roediger, David R. *The Wages of Whiteness: Race and the Making of the American Working Class*. New York: Verso, 1991.

Rymer, James. *The White Slave: A Romance for the Nineteenth Century*. London: E. Lloyd, 1844.

Scobie, Edward. *Black Britannia: A History of Blacks in Britain*. Chicago: Johnson, 1972.

Scott, Iain Robertson. " 'Things As They Are': the Literary Response to the French Revolution 1789–1815." *Britain and the French Revolution, 1789–1815*. Ed. H. T. Dickinson. New York: St. Martin's P, 1989. 229–49.

Shyllon, F. O. *Black Slaves in Britain*. New York: Oxford UP, 1974.

Slosson, Preston William. *The Decline of the Chartist Movement*. New York: Columbia UP, 1916. Rpt. New York: AMS, 1968.

Smith, Valerie. *Self-Discovery and Authority in Afro-American Narrative*. Cambridge: Harvard UP, 1987.

Spengemann, William C. "The Earliest American Novel: Aphra Behn's *Oroonoko*." *Nineteenth Century Fiction* 38.4 (March 1984): 384–414.

Stepan, Nancy. *The Idea of Race in Science: Great Britain, 1800–1960*. Hamden, CT: Archon Books, 1982.

Stowe, Harriet Beecher. *Uncle Tom's Cabin*. New York: Bantam Books, 1981.

Taylor, Clare. *British and American Abolitionists. An Episode in Transatlantic Understanding*. Edinburgh: Edinburgh UP, 1974.

Temperley, Howard. *British Antislavery, 1833–1870*. Columbia: U of South Carolina P, 1972.

———. *White Dreams, Black Africa: The Antislavery Expedition to the River Niger, 1841–1842*. New Haven: Yale UP, 1991.

Thompson, Dorothy. *The Chartists: Popular Politics in the Industrial Revolution*. New York: Pantheon Books, 1984.

Thompson, E. P. *The Making of the English Working Class*. New York: Penguin Books, 1963.

Tompkins, Jane. *Sensational Designs: The Cultural Works of American Fiction, 1790–1860*. New York: Oxford UP, 1985.

Trollope, Frances. *The Life and Adventures of Jonathan Jefferson Whitlaw; Or, Scenes on the Mississippi*. London: Richard Bentley, 1836.

———. *Lynch Law: Or, The Life and Adventures of Jonathan Jefferson Whitlaw*. London: Ward and Lock, 1857.

Turley, David. *The Culture of English Antislavery, 1780–1860*. New York: Routledge, 1991.

Turner, Mary. *Slaves and Missionaries: The Disintegration of Jamaican Slave Society, 1787–1834*. Urbana: U of Illinois P, 1982.

Tyrrell, Alex. *Joseph Sturge and the Moral Radical Party in early Victorian Britain*. London: Christopher Helm, 1987.

Uncle Tom in England; Or, A Proof that Black's White. London: Houlston and Stoneman; New York: A. D. Failing, 1852.

"Uncle Tom's Cabin." *The Times* 3 Sept. 1852: 5.

Walvin, James. *England, Slaves, and Freedom, 1776–1838*. Jackson: UP of Mississippi, 1986.

Williams, Eric. *Capitalism and Slavery*. New York: Russell and Russell, 1961.

Williams, Raymond. *Culture and Society, 1780–1950*. New York: Penguin Books, 1962.

Wilson, Forrest. *Crusader in Crinoline: The Life of Harriet Beecher Stowe*. Philadelphia: J. B. Lippincott, 1941.

Wright, John P. *An Historical Parallel between the Anti-Vivisection Movement in England and the Anti-Slavery Movement in America*. (Publication information unknown, held at Dr. Williams Library, London, England, c. 1854).

Yarborough, Richard. "Strategies of Black Characterization in *Uncle Tom's Cabin* and the Early Afro-American Novel." *New Essays on Uncle Tom's Cabin*. Ed. Eric J. Sundquist. New York: Cambridge UP, 1986. 45–84.

Yellin, Jean Fagan. *Women and Sisters: The Antislavery Feminists in American Culture*. New Haven: Yale UP, 1989.

———, ed. *Incidents in the Life of a Slave Girl: Written by Herself; By Harriet A. Jacobs*. Cambridge, MA: Harvard UP, 1987.

Zwarg, Christina. "Fathering and Blackface in *Uncle Tom's Cabin*." *Novel: A Forum on Fiction* 22.3 (Spring 1989): 274–87.

ELIZABETH BARRETT BROWNING'S HEBRAIC CONVERSIONS: FEMINISM AND CHRISTIAN TYPOLOGY IN *AURORA LEIGH*

By Cynthia Scheinberg

> then, surprised
> By a sudden sense of vision and of tune,
> You feel as conquerors though you did not fight,
> And you and Israel's other singing girls,
> Ay, Miriam with them, sing the song you choose.
>
> —*Aurora Leigh*

Miriam, called a prophetess, appears after the passage of the Red sea as heading the women of Israel in that responsive song in which the glorious deliverance was celebrated (Exodus xv. 20, 21). The next occasion in which she is mentioned presents a dark contrast to that earlier day of joy. Miriam, by whom the Lord had spoken, and whom he had sent before his people unites with Aaron in jealous murmuring against Moses. Her sin is immediately visited with frightful punishment. She is struck with leprosy; and Aaron as the priest has to look on his accomplice, and officially pronounce her unclean; and consequently for seven days, till healed and cleansed by the mercy of God, she is excluded from the camp (Numbers xii; Deut. xxiv. 9). It must have read an impressive lesson to Israel that God will by no means spare the guilty—*The Treasury of Bible Knowledge*, 1870.

THE MOMENT IN WHICH AURORA claims Miriam as the mother of women's "song" in *Aurora Leigh* is a moment of great triumph, both in terms of the epic's narrative structure, as well as in terms of Aurora's personal development as poet/narrator. "Happy and unafraid of solitude" (3.169), Aurora has set herself up as an independent woman writer in London. When she likens herself and other women writers to Miriam and "Israel's other singing girls" (3.202), she invokes the Hebraic type for female, prophetic agency — and she invokes literary and theological authority for women writers.

55

But to invoke this particular image of Miriam is to tell only half of Miriam's story. As Ayre's Treasury of Bible Knowledge (1870) points out all too clearly, Miriam's moment of religious agency and leadership is short-lived. Indeed, God and the patriarchs of Israel condemned Miriam, striking her with leprosy and ejecting her from the Israelite community. The language of The Treasury, "plain, popular information . . . for general readers" (xiv), casts Miriam's demise as a moral lesson about the "guilty" who challenge patriarchal authority. Though she and Aaron share in the crime of false prophecy against Moses, it is Miriam who bears the immediate brunt of their punishment, a punishment that is enacted significantly upon her body and her rights as a member of the community. Miriam's fall is a far one: from divine poet to unclean woman, and her contradictory function in this interpretation of history becomes for us a paradigm for how women poets act, interact, and are acted upon in religious communities.

Although Miriam's biblical experiences serve as a central organizing narrative in Aurora Leigh, Barrett Browning does not make any mention of Miriam's ultimate fate in Jewish history. I do not think this is because she did not know the end of the story; indeed, her knowledge of the Hebrew scriptures was exhaustive, in part because she read them in Hebrew.[1] Barrett Browning's allusions to and transformation of Miriam's narrative throughout Aurora Leigh respond to a deep anxiety that Victorian Christian culture had towards not only Jews and Hebrew history but also towards vocal, intellectual, poetic women. While Barrett Browning's very complex idealization of the Hebrew woman is crucial to her development of an authoritative female poetic identity, the identification with the Hebraic also threatens the establishment of Christian transcendence at the end of the poem. Barrett Browning's goals of authorizing women's poetry and imagining new kinds of heterosexual and Christian relationships require a complicated narrative of conversions: Aurora must be "converted" to the transcendent state of Christian wife while still maintaining her poetic voice; Romney, as her male counterpart, must be converted from a dominant, patriarchal oppressor to a "true" Christian husband. Emphasizing the central role the Hebraic and conversion strategies play in Barrett Browning's epic enables feminist readers to understand that this poem both challenges and submits to dominant discourses of gender and religion.[2]

In Victorian Types, Victorian Shadows, George Landow has suggested that Barrett Browning "founds a theory of the arts upon typology" (6), and Landow uses Aurora Leigh as a paradigm for Victorian typological practice. While correctly noting the central role typology plays in the poem, Landow's study does not explore the relation between the poem's feminist and typological missions. By reading typologically through a feminist lens, a number of contradictions in these practices become evident, contradictions that are constantly at play throughout the poem. In *Aurora Leigh*, Christian typological practice and feminist poetics collide, leaving Barrett Browning a very complicated task of extricating Christian transcendence from a narrative that is overtly concerned with sexual difference. In this reading of *Aurora Leigh*, I argue that Barrett Browning elides the discourses of Christian typology and sexual difference in order to affirm women's experience while simultaneously maintaining that women can speak with universal Christian poetic authority.

In nineteenth-century women's poetry, the adoption of a Christian voice offered women a way to assert a "transcendent" poetic voice, a voice that did not call attention to gender difference but rather emphasized its ability to speak of the "universal" Christian experience.[3] Unlike women, it could be argued, Christians can speak for everyone, because Christian salvation is supposedly not dependent on conditions of gender and ethnicity. However, if a poet also wanted to find a way to speak her particular difference — whether as Jew or woman (or both) — then adopting the position of the Christian speaker posed a potential problem, since such a transcendent voice, in its conventional construction, erases sexual difference.[4] Barrett Browning, especially in her earlier poems like "A Drama of Exile" and "The Seraphim," positioned her voice as one with Christian authority; the goal she sets for herself in *Aurora Leigh* is to maintain that authority while also speaking as a woman, and it is Miriam who provides a legitimate Biblical precedent for a female poet. In this epic poem Barrett Browning tries to engage with the discourse of sexual difference as well as maintain a universal Christian stance; she images Aurora as the Hebraic Miriam in order to establish an authoritative figure of challenge to Christian patriarchy, but it is only by converting this Hebraic figure by the end of the epic that Barrett Browning can emerge with acceptable Christian closure.

Invocations of Miriam are made repeatedly in *Aurora Leigh*, signaling Barrett Browning's replacement of Eve as the paradigm for female experience in the Hebrew Scriptures.[5] Barrett Browning had attempted in her earlier books of poetry to find precedents for female poetic agency in the figures Eve and Mary. But her use of these female figures as models of poetic authority proved somewhat limited, in part because the weight of the culturally imbedded representations of these women: Eve as the primary example of women's intellectual and linguistic naivete, Mary as the silent suffering Pietà.[6] In many ways, Miriam solves the problem that Eve and Mary could not: Miriam's status as singer and prophet creates a legitimized model of female poetic authority. The use of Hebrew scriptural women corresponds with a renewed interest in typology in the Victorian era; just as male theologians and writers like Cardinal Newman, Henry Hart Milman, and Matthew Arnold made repeated references to "the Hebraic" and Hebrew Scripture, Jewish and Christian women poets used Hebraic scriptural women in a number of different ways to legitimate their own literary authority.[7]

The most common form of Christian typology interprets the Hebrew scriptures from a Christian point of view; the Hebrew type gains its significance in its relation to or prefigurement of an antitype, namely events, people, or concepts from Christ's life and gospels. Of course, the talmudic tradition in Judaism had always concerned itself with the interpretation of Hebrew Scripture for the use of the present community, so it is important to see that the act of interpreting Hebrew scriptural event is not what distinguishes Christian typology as a practice. What is different in a specifically Christian practice is that the Hebraic event, figure, or idea is wrenched from its literary and historical context in Hebrew scripture and read within a completely different hermeneutic frame, that of Christian revelation. Imbedded within Christian typological practice, therefore, is the assumption that hermeneutic frames are changeable and transferrable across religious histories and doctrines. Likewise, Christian conversion also assumes that an individual can choose or change his/her religious hermeneutic, an idea made clearer by comparing Christian and Jewish doctrine on conversion. Whereas being Christian is not dependent on one's ethnic identity, in Judaism, one is a Jew through dual ethnic and religious heritage — birth, not conversion, generally determines whether one is a Jew. Even Jews who ostensibly convert to other religions remain Jews in Jewish law, and there is no reconversion process that they must undergo to re-enter the Jewish covenant with God; being Jewish is a religious condition, but it is also an ethnic, familial condition.[8]

This idea that interpretative frames are mutable is at the heart of the difference between Jewish and Christian doctrine. As Rosemary Radford Ruether writes,

> Christianity confront[s] Judaism with a demand for a conversionist relation to its own past that abrogate[s] that past, in the sense that the past itself no longer provide[s] a covenant of salvation. Christianity [does] not ask Judaism merely to extend itself in continuity with its past, but to abrogate itself by substituting one covenantal principle from the past for another provided by Jesus. (80)

Ruether's emphasis on "abrogation" is crucial here, for the term makes explicit the rupture, break, and annulment of the Jewish covenant that Christian typology insists upon; though the notion of a Judeo-Christian tradition is based upon the idea that Christianity and Judaism are connected doctrinally, Ruether's description reminds us that Judaism and Christianity are based on completely different relationships to the Godhead, completely different notions of that covenant, and thus completely different hermeneutic codes. From a dominant Christian perspective, the hermeneutic of Christianity offers a "transcendent" interpretative frame in which to place Hebrew history. But of course Jews do not acknowledge that "transcendent frame," since Judaism does not recognize Jesus as the messiah. More importantly, it is not just that Christianity asserts the possibility of reading Jewish history from a Christian perspective; the typological impulse goes further in insisting that Hebrew history has no independent significance without the larger context of Christianity. Thus, typology sets up a relationship between Hebrew history and Christianity that might be termed "significance through relationship"; in such a relationship, the ongoing nature of Jewish history as well as the presence of actual Jews are erased.

This typological assumption of "significance through relationship" has an implicit connection to discourses surrounding gender in the nineteenth century, a discourse that Barrett Browning invokes throughout *Aurora Leigh*. The contemporary "moral sphere" arguments for women's influence claimed women had importance only through their effect on sons and husbands.[9] Likewise, until the Married Women's Property Acts (1870, 1882), women's property was "absorbed" into the estate of her husband; thus, both in terms of economic and moral agency, female identity was constructed as significant only through intercourse with men. The feminist challenge throughout *Aurora Leigh* works to recast this notion of female significance onto women themselves, going so far as to assert that Aurora can effect political and social change through her own poetic voice and through simultaneous attention to the domestic and public spheres of Victorian life.

The feminist impulse in *Aurora Leigh* insists that the experiences of women matter in themselves, and throughout this epic Barrett Browning foregrounds the domestic and physical realities of women's lives. For example, Marian's oppression by patriarchy is explicitly described in terms of the physical effects it has on her body; her rape is named as such, rather than alluded to in universalized terms of oppression. Likewise, Lady Waldemar's body is described in searing terms, emphasizing the corrupt nature of her social and sexual practice. Finally, Aurora herself works to learn the importance of the life of her body, and its sexual desire, in relation to the life of her intellect; even as she strives to enter the public world of literature and politics, she learns to remember her "private" life as well.[10]

But if one is interested in asserting a Christian vision while simultaneously exploring issues of sexual difference and woman's material experience — thus refuting the claim of "significance through relationship" — the assumptions underlying Christian typology become problematic. That is, the idealization of Hebrew scriptural women as independent heroic agents works in terms of the poem's feminist appeal, but it contradicts the assertion of Hebraic deficiency which is at the heart of Christian typology. What is fascinating about the poem is that it is remarkably self-conscious about its own typological practice; there is subtext running throughout the epic on what might be considered "correct" and "incorrect" typology, as Aurora tries to recast the role of women in Christian culture. Barrett Browning needs Miriam as a figure of Biblically-sanctioned poetic authority for women and so uses typology to invoke her, but the contradictions typology poses for a Christian feminist, as outlined above, insist that she

re-evaluate typology, or re-evaluate feminist practice, or both, as I argue. Likewise, her investment in the marriage plot that will unite Romney and Aurora in
the perfect Christian union also makes problematic her feminist claims, as other
critics have suggested.[11] By carefully charting Barrett Browning's typology and
feminism in *Aurora Leigh*, we can see how contradictory this identification with
Hebraic figures can be for a woman writer. Barrett Browning defuses this threat
by "converting" the more dangerous elements of her feminism into acceptable
Christian closure.

Casa Guidi Windows (1851), the book published prior to *Aurora Leigh*, offers
Barrett Browning's first reference to Miriam as a symbol for female poetic
identity, and this reference also suggests Barrett Browning's possible resistance
to conventional Christian typology. In Part 1, the speaker suggests that moral
(and poetic) progress relies on the cumulative work of successive men and
generations, "[h]ow step by step was worn, / As each man gained on each
securely" (300–01). She illustrates this idea as follows:

> Because old Jubal blew into delight
> The souls of men with clear-piped melodies,
> If youthful Asaph were content at most
> To draw from Jubal's grave, with listening eyes,
> Traditionary music's floating ghost
> Into the grass grown silence, were it wise?
> And was't not wiser, Jubal's breath being lost,
> That Miriam clashed her cymbals to surprise
> The sun between her white arms flung apart
> With new glad golden sounds? that David's strings
> O'erflowed his hand with music from his heart?
> So harmony grows full from many springs
> And happy accident turns holy art. (1. 307–19)[12]

This chronological recounting of Hebrew scriptural "singers" (and musicians)
offers a new evolutionary vision of poetic history: Jubal and Asaph are both
figures connected to musical instruments and song in the Hebrew scripture (Gen.
4:21 and 1 Chron. 6:39). Barrett Browning suggests that these individual "singers" become significant as each successive singer builds on the song of his/her
predecessors. The fact that Judaism recognizes female prophets enables Barrett
Browning's construction of male and female poetic heritage in this passage. And
while issues of gender are implicit but not central concerns in *Casa Guidi
Windows*, the inclusion of male and female singers in this list signals Barrett
Browning's growing interest in finding authoritative scriptural precedents for
poetic women.

Significantly, Barrett Browning resists the conventional Christian typological
gesture that would situate these Hebraic figures in relation to the Christian
narrative. Barrett Browning maintains Jubal, David, and Miriam's existence in

Hebrew history; their significance is asserted in terms of their historical connection to each other and in terms of what such a cooperative notion of song
can teach her readers about historical links in poetic practice. By resisting the
typological interpretation from the "transcendent" assumptions of Christianity,
Barrett Browning is able to make her point that poetic history is cumulative and
evolutionary and that women have played a significant part in that history. If
she had made the conventional move to connect these figures to Christian narrative, the radical nature of her gender claims would be erased, since there are no
female counterparts for Miriam in Christianity.

When we turn to Barrett Browning's next allusion to Miriam, which occurs
in Book 2 of *Aurora Leigh*, Barrett Browning's typological practice seems to
have shifted. It is Romney who speaks of Miriam first in *Aurora Leigh*; through
his initially misguided character, Barrett Browning initiates her self-conscious
exploration of how typology might mean differently for men and women. Romney's patriarchal Christian view of Miriam is a vision significantly revised from
that of Miriam in *Casa Guidi Windows* "clash[ing] her cymbals to surprise / The
sun between her white arms flung apart / With new glad golden sounds. . . ." In
Aurora Leigh, Romney denigrates both poetry and women, saying to Aurora:

> Who has time,
> An hour's time . . . think! . . . to sit upon a bank
> And hear the cymbal tinkle in white hands!
> When Egypt's slain, I say, let Miriam sing!—
> Before . . . where's Moses? (2. 168–72)

Romney minimizes Miriam's significance, transforming the cymbals' "clash"
to a mere "tinkle," just as the forceful synecdoche of "white arms flung apart"
is reduced to "white hands."[13] And this diminution symbolizes a larger typological point: in Romney's eyes, "Egypt" is a symbol for the "captive" state of
Victorian culture. His typology suggests that the historical event of the defeat
of Egypt exists only as analogue for the still "enslaved" condition of England;
Romney thus erases the significance of the actual (scriptural) historical defeat
of Egypt. Romney's point in this allusion is twofold, designed to claim that a
woman cannot be a significant poet because she cannot speak to "universal"
male experience and that likewise, for Romney, Jewish history has no significance outside of a Christian typological code.

This first conversation about Miriam and Moses (which is also ostensibly
about the possibility of Aurora and Romney marrying) suggests that Romney
and Aurora each have completely different interpretations of the Biblical narrative. Their argument begins the lengthy discussion of gender roles in both Hebrew history and contemporary Victorian society that makes up the first half of
Book 2. Aurora goes on to extend Romney's initial allusion to Miriam and

Moses, also questioning Romney's own aspirations to Moses' role. She transforms his question "Where's Moses?" from a repudiation of women poets into
a comment on Moses' humble beginnings.

> Ah, exactly that.
> Where's Moses?—is a Moses to be found?
> You'll seek him vainly in the bulrushes,
> While I in vain touch cymbals. Yet concede,
> Such sounding brass has done some actual good. (2. 172–76)

What Aurora does in this passage is to galvanize other aspects of the Mosaic
narrative that include Miriam as a central figure. There is no Moses to be found
in contemporary life; he remains hidden in the "bulrushes," and her reference
to Moses' infancy reminds the listener/reader of the primary moment of his
"saving" in Biblical tradition, which was enacted by women—indeed, probably
by Miriam herself.[14] Aurora's image calls on the figure of Moses at his most
vulnerable and compares it to an image of Miriam, singing at her most powerful
moment; her figure insists that poetry and women have the ability to create
significant social and moral good.

   In citing the "vain" search in the bulrushes, Aurora also makes a pun about
the motives behind typological comparison: Romney's male vanity, she implies,
motivates his desire to model the contemporary savior on a Hebraic man. This
notion of Romney's vanity — indeed his hubris in believing he can be the Moses
for the century — suggests the potential moral danger in typological comparisons
that do not recognize that in a Christian hermeneutic Moses must be a type for
Christ, not for a mere human reformer like Romney. Aurora's response suggests
that this initial argument between Romney and Aurora is about two issues:
their potential marriage and "correct" typological comparison. For Romney,
typology allows him to cast himself as a potential Moses (in his penchant for
explicit social action) as he simultaneously casts Moses' sister as a minor figure.
From Aurora's point of view, however, incorrect typology exposes Romney's
vanity, while her feminist typological vision allows her to claim the significance
of Miriam's role as poet. What is increasingly clear in this first interchange
between the epic's two main characters is that they do not share an interpretative
code which would allow consensus.

   Besides his misguided attempt to serve as Moses' antitype, Romney's other
main flaw is his misinterpretation of women, as signalled by his misreading of
Miriam's song. For it turns out that Romney's argument for a marriage in which
woman is "helpmeet" to man hinges on denying to women the ability to emulate
or symbolize the Christian antitype. He tells Aurora:

> Women as you are,
> Mere women, personal and passionate,

> You give us doting mothers and chaste wives.
> Sublime Madonnas, and enduring saints!
> We get no Christ from you,—and verily
> We shall not get a poet, in my mind. (2. 220–25)

Romney's "We get no Christ from you" is Barrett Browning's clearest articulation of a male bias in standard typological interpretation. This statement makes it evident that, since the aim of most conventional typology centers on finding a correlation to Christ's life, women are inevitably excluded from this goal because of their sexual difference from Christ. But Romney once again exhibits his misunderstanding of typological significance; it is not the human individual who provides "a Christ" — indeed, this is almost blasphemy; rather, there can only be emulation of Christ's example. His statement implies that men can provide a "Christ," and so just as he "vainly" turned to Moses as the "type" for his own Christian action above, he also rejects the possibility that women's roles in society can be modelled on Christ, since the only available figures of women in Christian narrative, in his mind, are the Madonna, saints, mothers, and wives. There is an implicit contradiction in Romney's reasoning (and a pun from Barrett Browning) in the use of the term "get," since a "Madonna" did "get" a Christ according to Christian doctrine. But for Romney, "getting a Christ" refers to finding the man who will become the savior of England; his desire to be the next Christ limits his ability to see the mythic origins of Jesus in Mary's body.[15] Romney's words assert a link between Christian agency, gender, and poetry; just as "we get no Christ" from women, so will we "get no poets." Romney assumes that a poet must be able to transcend the "personal and passionate," which mark women's expression for him. What the poem must resolve, then, in terms of Barrett Browning's larger project of articulating a Christian, female poetic identity, is how to construct an authoritative female identity that has a distinct agency within Christianity without wrongly aspiring to be Christ. Romney's accusation is exactly what Aurora must challenge; her dilemma is how to find an authoritative voice as a Christian that is also as "personal and passionate" as a woman.

Romney's speech makes plain the patriarchal role delegated to women in Christian history, and they are exactly those roles which Aurora refuses to adopt throughout the poem. In revising the image of female identity, Aurora continues to use Miriam to force a radical departure from conventional Christian concepts of women. Aurora's affinity for Miriam clearly rejects the idea that she takes "sublime Madonnas," "doting mothers," and "chaste wives" as her models, since Miriam was neither mother, nor wife, nor, indeed, "sublime" in her eventual uprising against Moses.[16] Thus, by claiming Miriam specifically as her personal point of Hebraic reference, Aurora finds a biblical figure whose model includes an element of poetic agency and a degree of independence from male dominance. To make Miriam's importance clearer, Aurora refuses comparison to another, perhaps less autonomous, Hebraic female figure.

> Why sir, you are married long ago.
> You have a wife already whom you love,
> Your social theory. Bless you both, I say.
> For my part, I am scarcely meek enough
> To be the handmaid of a lawful spouse.
> Do I look a Hagar, think you? (2. 408–13)

In rejecting Romney's marriage proposal, Aurora also rejects typological comparison to Hagar, whose experiences could be interpreted as oppressive within Hebrew polygamy. Aurora's rhetorical question articulates her resistance to being cast in a role like Hagar's and, in so doing, allows her to refuse certain standard roles of martyrdom that have functioned as paradigms of women's roles in Christian culture. By claiming Miriam, not Hagar, for her self-identification, Aurora casts herself as prophetess as opposed to "handmaid" or "wife." Implicitly, she also points to Marian's role as a Hagar, a surrogate wife to Romney, and, later, a seeming "handmaid" to Aurora.

It is Romney who first introduced the figure of Miriam into the poem, and he does so, as we saw above, to voice denial of her significance in the Exodus narrative, as well as implicitly to suggest himself as a Mosaic successor. To him, Miriam is a mere "tinkler" on the cymbals. But in Book 3, Aurora reclaims the figure of Miriam at the exact moment in which she is most independent from Romney, recasting his derisive use of Miriam into her most triumphant image of the contemporary female poet. In discussing how urban life suits a poet's purposes, Aurora explains:

> No one sings,
> Descending Sinai: on Parnassus mount,
> You take a mule to climb, and not a muse,
> Except in fable and figure: forests chant
> Their anthems to themselves, and leave you dumb.
> But sit in London, at the day's decline,
> And view the city perish in the mist
> Like Pharaoh's armaments in the deep Red Sea, —
> The chariots, horsemen, footmen, all the host,
> Sucked down and choked to silence — then, surprised
> By a sudden sense of vision and of tune,
> You feel as conquerors though you did not fight,
> And you and Israel's other singing girls,
> Ay, Miriam with them, sing the song you choose. (3. 190–203)

This apocalyptic passage is at the heart of Barrett Browning's ideas about poetic production, and it represents the culmination of her inclusion of the Hebraic into her feminist poetics. Pointing to the two central traditions of literary and theological authority — Moses' transcription of God's word on Sinai and the classical source of poetic inspiration, Mt. Parnassus — Aurora suggests that they do not symbolize the sort of poetic inspiration she seeks. Or rather, Aurora debunks the myth of these moments of inspiration. When Moses "descends" Sinai, he has just conversed with God and thus is the prophet of divine word, but this interaction has not resulted in his own poetic production; rather, he carries the tablet "written by the finger of God" — not his own finger. Similarly, the female "muses" of classical poetry exist not in "fable and figure"; the truth of climbing Parnassus is that one needs a "mule" because it is hard work. Aurora also rejects the claim that nature can be a poetic source; for her, nature has its own language, which is not available for human use. Finally, having rejected the conventional models of poetic inspiration, Aurora locates true poetry within human culture. What is striking about her comparison to "Israel's singing girls" is that their "song" is born out of a moment of intense social and political conflict, which the simile compares to a vision of the city. Further, the moment of Miriam's song is a moment of worship and praise to God; this particular Biblical moment combines political triumph with divine praise, thus locating the poetic as simultaneously religious, de-naturalized, and female. The poet is related to the position of women in the idea that s/he "did not fight" — poets and women, that is, even when outside direct physical action, are nevertheless of central importance to society through their acts of prophetic vision and inspiration to a community.[17]

Thus, in the middle of her autobiographical narrative, Aurora positions herself as a Hebrew woman, singing as a prophet and in full possession of creative agency. But this self-proclaimed "novel poem" has certain demands for narrative closure that impinge upon the figures that have been established at this point. The use of the two types, Miriam and Moses, will not really provide the figurative closure the poem seeks, since to carry Miriam's mythic narrative to conclusion would place her as Moses' antagonistic sister as well as an unclean woman expelled from the Hebrew camp. The poem must also bridge the differences in Romney's and Aurora's interpretations of the Bible, healing Romney's diseased vision of himself as a Mosaic successor, while simultaneously showing Aurora the potential joys of Christian marriage. Thus, as the poem moves toward closure in Books 8 and 9, Barrett Browning must revise Miriam's narrative in order to contain the threat that Miriam (and women poets) pose to Christian patriarchy. Likewise, she produces a revised Romney, who becomes the Christian husband who can accept the idea of a poetic wife. The three goals of this poem, authorizing female experience, asserting women's poetic authority, and imagining new Christian heterosexual relationships, come into conflict. Barrett Browning's strategy to resolve these contradictions hinges on the idea of conversion, in order that the threatening Hebraic woman can be refigured as a Christian.

Likewise, Romney must also be converted from his incorrect relationships to the Hebraic and to women.

Miriam is explicitly invoked once more by Romney, in Book 8, to signal his changed opinion of Aurora and her work.

> Oh, deserved,
> Deserved! that I, who verily had not learnt
> God's lesson half, attaining as a dunce
> To obliterate good words with fractious thumbs
> And cheat myself of the context — I should push
> Aside, with male ferocious impudence,
> The world's Aurora who had conned her part
> On the other side the leaf! ignore her so,
> Because she was a woman and a queen,
> And had no beard to bristle through her song, —
> My teacher, who has taught me with a book,
> My Miriam, whose sweet mouth, when nearly drowned
> I still heard singing on the shore! (8. 323–34)

Romney understands not only Aurora's poetic contributions but also his own sexism in his previous refusal to grant her poetic authority. He attributes his previous "blindness" to "male ferocious impudence" and understands how he had imagined maleness — figured as a "beard" — as a prerequisite to song. But the most interesting moment of his figure comes at its conclusion, when Romney positions himself as "nearly drowned" while Aurora/Miriam is "singing on the shore." With the enjambment on "nearly drowned," Barrett Browning casts Romney as an Egyptian, an oppressor, hearing the victorious song of Miriam and the Israelites right before he drowns. The text thus makes an intrinsic connection between the position of the Jews in Egypt and the position of women and oppressed groups in England, since the Christian male and Egyptian soldiers are equated metaphorically in opposition to Miriam on the shore. The lines also provide another more radical possibility as Romney suggests that Miriam reached the shore before he, figured as Moses, did: she saved him with her singing, and so Miriam is figured as the true leader of the Jews at that moment. The invocation of the Miriam and Moses figures alludes to Aurora's and Romney's earlier discussion of gender roles in Book 2, while also typologically figuring women poets as analogues to the Biblical Jews. What has changed is that Romney now is able to see the significance of Miriam's contribution as female poet.

But if these figures of Romney as oppressor and Aurora as Miriam were maintained, there could be no "new" heterosexual Christian union at the end of the poem. In part, Barrett Browning deals with the problem of Romney's male oppression by literally blinding him, a deformation which mirrors his own understanding of his previous flaw. This blindness complicates Romney's complete identification with Moses, who, as the poem has reminded us, ends his life in a moment of vision on Pisgah.[18] But one element of Romney's speech resists his complete renunciation of his prior authority: he refers to Aurora as "my Miriam." Romney's possessive metaphor makes new claims on Aurora; as "his" Miriam, she is literally possessed and absorbed into male, Christian history. Typologically Romney's "my" lifts the Miriam narrative out of its position in Hebraic history, and so this moment in the poem also reclaims Christian typology: Romney has finally learned the correct way to possess Aurora and Hebrew history. Barrett Browning elides the discourses of sexual difference and typology in order to reposition Aurora in relation to her feminist claims.

Romney's final figuring of Aurora as "[his] Miriam" enables Barrett Browning to equate Jewish oppression and female oppression and also to position Jewish types within the larger appropriative context of Christian history. But Romney remains a strangely ambiguous figure at this moment in the poem, a possible lover, "brother," or oppressor in the system of typological metaphor Barrett Browning has established. As the poem moves toward closure, it works to resolve Romney's ambivalent position, as well as to contain the "Hebraic" context in which Aurora repeatedly has been invoked. The following passage, describing Romney in his converted state ("converted" in terms of his understanding of Miriam's Hebraic importance), works to link Romney with the Hebraic figuration that has marked Aurora's identity throughout the poem.

> And then calm, equal, smooth with weights of joy,
> His voice rose, as some chief musician's song
> Amid the old Jewish temple's Selah-pause,
> And bade me mark how we two met at last
> Upon this moon-bathed promontory of earth,
> To give up much on each side, then, take all. (9. 843–48)

Aurora's comparison of Romney's voice to that of the chief musician once again locates the source of song in Hebrew culture. This passage figuratively joins Romney to Aurora as they both do work that requires a religious, inspired "voice." The reference to the "Selah-pause" displays Barrett Browning's sophisticated knowledge of Hebrew terms, the "Selah-pause" being alternatively interpreted as the moment in the service when the voice is raised up in response to the instruments or as a moment when there is a pause in the voice that directs the instruments. But even more interestingly, the 1870 *Treasury of Bible Knowledge* suggests that the pause would occur "where very warm emotions would have been expressed," just as they have been in the text of the poem (Ayre 809). Finally, this reference also refers to the practice of actual "old Jew[s]," rather than abstracted biblical "Hebrews," and so implicitly points to the ongoing nature of Jewish practice.

This acknowledgment of actual Jewish practice, as well as the comparison of Romney to a cantor, however, could be a potentially dangerous admission for

such a typologically charged text, since it is the continuing presence of uncon-
verted Jews that is a standard sign in Christianity that God's kingdom is not yet
achieved on earth. Thus, as Barrett Browning reconciles the lovers, she also
transforms this union into a moment of Christian revelation, necessitating that
Romney's Jewish voice of the cantor be converted as it gradually begins to
speak Christian doctrine.

> "Beloved" it sang, "we must be here to work;
> And men who work, can only work for men,
> And, not to work in vain, must comprehend
> Humanity, and, so work humanely,
> And raise men's bodies still by raising souls,
> As God did, first."
> "But stand upon the earth,"
> I said, "to raise them, — (this is human too;
> There's nothing high which has not first been low;
> My humbleness, said One, has made me great!)
> As God did, last."
> "And work all silently,
> And simply," he returned, "as God does all;
> Distort our nature never, for our work,
> Nor count our right hands stronger for being hoofs.
> The man most man, with tenderest human hands,
> Works best for men, — as God in Nazareth." (9. 849–63)

The "voice" is referred to in the abstract, as Aurora describes how "it sang"
to her; this abstraction enacts the distance needed to erase the threatening image
of Romney in "an old Jewish temple." More importantly, "the voice" makes
frequent ambiguous reference to God, as one who "raise[d] men's bodies still
by raising souls." Aurora's voice joins in this passage, uniting their two voices
in prophecy of future Christian work. Romney then makes the final pointed
allusion to "God in Nazareth," significantly refiguring God as Jesus. The possession of the Jews is completed in this passage, as the figure of the "Jewish"
cantor is recast as a Christian, speaking with his Miriam who has also been
appropriated into a Christian epistemology.

Finally, in line 950, Aurora cries "My Romney," enacting the final conversion of the poem. She claims him, accepts him possessively just as he had
claimed her as "my Miriam." It is significant that she does not say "My
Moses," avoiding the comparison between Romney and Moses that had been
Romney's downfall. Her resistance to typological comparison here signals that,
while she and Romney have come to a clear understanding, Aurora still operates
in a different kind of typological hermeneutic. Her possession of Romney signals
her own revision of gender roles in Christian heterosexuality, while also ce-
menting the idea that Romney has been converted into an acceptance of Aurora.

Indeed, Romney has just described the effect her book has had on him; reading her text has been a central factor in his conversion narrative. The figure of Miriam is central, then, not only for how it authorizes Aurora's poetic identity but also for how the figure finally teaches Romney a new covenantal relationship to Moses, Christianity, and woman. Woman is no longer mere "wifely hand maid" to Romney but rather the poet/prophet who will enable the communication of his Christian vision to those "at the bottom" of Pisgah.

Barrett Browning establishes conventional closure by rewriting Miriam's narrative so that it can be a source not only for women's poetry but also for refiguring heterosexual union. In the first part of the poem, standard typological practice is both invoked and criticized; in particular, Romney is presented as a misguided typologist (or Christian) and a sexist, while Aurora seeks to reeducate him in both areas by pointing to Miriam's example. But as the "novel-poem" seeks a traditional comic ending of marriage, the initial identifications with and idealizations of Hebraic figures are gradually converted into their Christian significance.[19] While her initial use of Miriam asserts a radical and feminist understanding of typology (as the Hebrew female prophets and singers legitimate the idea of woman poet), Barrett Browning eventually "converts" her own "Hebrew" characters in order to satisfy the demands of her larger Christian narrative. The generic demands of narrative closure, her feminist concern to claim woman's poetic identity, and her Christian affiliation all converge in the second half of *Aurora Leigh* and allow us to see how genre conventions, feminist poetics, and religious identity have inseparable influences on each other in this text.

By focusing on *Aurora Leigh's* use of Hebrew history and Hebraic figures, we can understand Barrett Browning's creation of a female figure who is both radical and conservative, one who seeks to challenge the sexual politics of her moment while nevertheless reclaiming the Christian ideology that supported Victorian separate spheres.[20] What feminist critics have ignored in reading *Aurora Leigh* is the text's explicit concern with typology (just as typology-centered readings like Landow's have ignored the poem's feminist impulses). Assuming the poem to be conventional in its religious doctrine, critics overlook Barrett Browning's careful exploration of feminist practice within a particular religious hermeneutic. It is because the Hebrew scriptures provide figures of women that stand as agents, prophets, and speakers that Christian women writers like Barrett Browning could use these figures as sanctioned sources of female agency. Yet as Barrett Browning's conversionary maneuvers at the end of *Aurora Leigh* suggest, the Christian woman's identification with the Hebraic woman was fraught with contradiction, since any typological construction of Hebraic identity would necessarily construct the Hebraic woman as "lacking," even as the Christian woman tried to figure Hebraic women as "complete" in their achieved prophetic status. Indeed, the desire to find a complete Christian identity necessitated the rejection of even the possibility that Jewish/Hebraic identity could ever be complete in itself. Thus, the idealization of the Hebraic woman completely unravels the assumptions of Jewish/Hebraic lack upon which Christian typology is based. Barrett Browning solves this problem by imbedding her Hebraic female figure in a larger discourse of heterosexual marriage in which (in *Aurora Leigh*) *both* male and female characters must undergo a sort of conversion. Indeed, it is Barrett Browning's critique of the idea that woman is significant only in relation to a man that allows her to imagine this dual conversion process. For Barrett Browning, typology resolves the tensions of sexual difference and religious difference simultaneously, so that she can assert the possiblity of a Christian, female heroic identity at the end of *Aurora Leigh*.

Mills College

NOTES

1. See Mermin on Barrett Browning's study of Hebrew (*Origins*, 19, 47).
2. This issue of whether the feminist politics of *Aurora Leigh* are radical or conservative is at the heart of the critical debate surrounding this text, though few critics include an extended discussion of religion in their feminist approach (with the exception of Dorothy Mermin and Helen Cooper). See Blake, Case, Cooper, David, Friedman, Gelpi, Kaplan, Mermin, Stone, and Zonana.
3. See Mermin, *Origins*, and Cooper on how Christianity provided a viable position from which women poets could speak. The "transcendent" voice of the Christian poet is also related to the issue of finding lyric universality, especially in a poetic tradition that assumes Christianity to be normative; for two discussions of lyric universality, see Adorno and Rorty.
4. In other chapters of this project, I explore these issues of poetic voice in relation to Christina Rossetti and the Anglo-Jewish women poets Grace Aguilar (1816–47) and Amy Levy (1861–89).
5. See Cooper's book for a discussion of the centrality of Eve figures in Barrett Browning's work.
6. See Smith, chap. 2, for an excellent discussion of Eve's relationship to language and public discourse.
7. Nor is the use of Hebraic women unusual for Christian women writers; the women of Hebrew Scripture fascinate women poets like Christina Rossetti, Felicia Hemans, and Alice Meynell, perhaps because these female characters are often agents of theological and political reform within Hebrew history. This examination of women writers' use of typology becomes even more interesting when we include women of differing religious backgrounds; Grace Aguilar, for example, writing as a Jewish woman, constructed very different notions of gender identity that are also based on female figures from Hebrew history. Aguilar's *Women of Israel* (1845) examines Hebrew scriptural women from a Jewish perspective.
8. For more on Christian typology from both Jewish and Christian perspectives see Charity, Cohen, Frei, Landow, Josipovici, Miner, and Ruether.
9. The influential "moral sphere" argument made popular by writers like Sarah Stickney Ellis (*The Women of England*, 1838) and Sarah Lewis (*Woman's Mission*, 1839)

asserted that women had moral superiority to men, and that their role in Christian culture was to use this moral and spiritual superiority to guide and influence their husbands and sons; see also Davidoff and Hall, Taylor, and Levine.

10. I am in debt to Joyce Zonana for suggesting that in this way Aurora represents a "complete" poetic self.

11. See David, and Mermin, *Elizabeth Barrett Browning*.

12. This and all subsequent references to Barrett Browning's poetry are from *The Poetical Works of Elizabeth Barrett Browning* (New York: Macmillan, 1903).

13. The emphasis on "whiteness" here is a fascinating repression of Miriam's Semitic skin.

14. It is often surmised that it is Miriam, referred to only as "Moses' sister" in Exodus 2:4–8, who really enables his adoption by Pharaoh's daughter. See Plaut (388).

15. Barrett Browning explicitly explores this issue of Mary's agency in bearing Christ in her dramatic monologue "The Virgin Mary to the Child Jesus."

16. There is some scriptural evidence that Miriam married; however, she stands out from other Biblical female prophets in not being immediately identified as "wife of" in the first mention of her name.

17. Aurora's assertion that she and the other "girls . . . sing the song [they] choose" claims Miriam's authorial relation to her words, rather than suggesting they are a derivation of Moses' earlier song, the Shirah. Most English translations of Miriam's song are an exact replica of Moses' earlier words, and Hebrew scholarship offers two interpretations of the relationship between Miriam's and Moses' songs. In his commentary on the Torah, Plaut suggests some earlier authorial source for her song, making her a "performer" (many interpretations also stress her role as a "dancer") rather than an original poet (487). It is unclear whether Barrett Browning had access to such information, but her inclusion of Miriam singing the song she chooses asserts choice, agency, and creativity into the Miriam narrative.

18. In Book 5, Sir Blaise compares Romney to Moses "getting to the top of Pisgah hill"; he goes on to make the connection to his flawed vision by asserting that "Leigh . . . is scarce advanced to see as far as this" (5. 730, 734).

19. For an excellent discussion of how conversion works as a narrative figure, see Ragussis; for more on linguistic conversion see Gilman.

20. Nor surprisingly, the evaluation of this poem as radical or conservative has been at the heart of current critical debate. Readers like Cora Kaplan assert that we can read the poem "as contributing to a feminist theory of art which argues that women's language, precisely because it has been suppressed by patriarchal societies, re-enters discourse with a shattering revolutionary force" (11). This reading makes implicit the identification of Aurora with Miriam, challenging the patriarchal control of language; Aurora's identification with Miriam suggests that women can make prophetic claims to authority and song in Hebrew history, an authority which Barrett Browning transfers metaphorically onto Aurora and into Victorian culture.

Other readings of the poem find this a text that finally "submits" to partriarchal ideology. For Deirdre David, the conflation of Aurora's sexual identity with her poetic creativity impinges upon the poem's more radical assertions about women's poetic authority, and so the poem is read as "a coherent expression of Barrett Browning's conservative political views, with which her sexual politics are consistently coherent" (98). David's reading acknowledges the anxiety about poetic, theological women that the second half of *Aurora Leigh* seeks to mediate through conversion strategies. I argue that *Aurora Leigh* both challenges and submits to dominant ideological positions for women through a figure of conversion.

WORKS CITED

Adorno, Theodor W. "Lyric Poetry and Society." *Telos* 20 (1974): 56–71.

Ayre, Reverend John. *The Treasury of Bible Knowledge*. London: Longman Green, 1870.

Blake, Kathleen. "Elizabeth Barrett Browning and Wordsworth: The Romantic Poet as a Woman." *Victorian Poetry* 24 (1986): 387–98.

Browning, Elizabeth Barrett. *The Poetical Works of Elizabeth Barrett Browning*. New York: Macmillan, 1903.

Case, Alison. "Gender and Narration in *Aurora Leigh*." *Victorian Poetry* 29 (1991): 17–32.

Charity, A. C. *Events and Their Afterlife: The Dialectic of Typology in the Bible and Dante*. Cambridge: Cambridge UP, 1966.

Cohen, Arthur. *The Myth of the Judeo-Christian Tradition*. New York: Harper and Row, 1970.

Cooper, Helen. *Elizabeth Barrett Browning, Woman & Artist*. Chapel Hill: U of North Carolina P, 1988.

David, Deirdre. *Intellectual Women and Victorian Patriarchy: Harriet Martineau, Elizabeth Barrett Browning, George Eliot*. Ithaca: Cornell UP, 1987.

Davidoff, Leonore, and Catherine Hall. *Family Fortunes: Men and Women of the English Middle Class, 1780–1850*. Chicago: U of Chicago P, 1987.

Frei, Hans W. *The Eclipse of Biblical Narrative*. New Haven: Yale UP, 1974.

Friedman, Susan Stanford. "Gender and Genre Anxiety: Elizabeth Barrett Browning and H. D. as Epic Poets." *Tulsa Studies in Women's Literature* 5 (1986): 203–28.

Gelpi, Barbara Charlesworth. "*Aurora Leigh*: The Vocation of the Woman Poet." *Victorian Poetry* 19 (1981): 35–48.

Gilman, Sander L. *Jewish Self-Hatred*. Baltimore: Johns Hopkins UP, 1986.

Josipovici, Gabriel. *The Book of God: A Response to the Bible*. New Haven: Yale UP, 1988.

Kaplan, Cora. Introduction. *Aurora Leigh and Other Poems*. London: The Women's P, 1978.

Landow, George. *Victorian Types, Victorian Shadows*. London: Routledge Kegan Paul, 1980.

Levine, Philippa. *Victorian Feminism: 1850–1900*. Tallahassee: Florida State UP, 1987.

Mermin, Dorothy. *Elizabeth Barrett Browning: The Origins of a New Poetry*. Chicago: U of Chicago Press, 1989.

———. "The Damsel, the Knight, and the Victorian Woman Poet." *Critical Inquiry* 13 (1986): 64–80.

Miner, Earl, ed. *Literary Uses of Typology*. Princeton: Princeton UP, 1977.

Plaut, W. Gunther, ed. *The Torah: A Modern Commentary*. New York: Union of American Hebrew Congregations, 1981.

Ragussis, Michael. "Representation, Conversion, and Literary Form: *Harrington* and the Novel of Jewish Identity." *Critical Inquiry* 16 (Autumn 1989): 113–43.

Rorty, Richard. "Chapter 2: The Contingency of Selfhood." *Contingency, Irony and Solidarity*. Cambridge: Cambridge UP, 1979. 23–43.

Ruether, Rosemary Radford. *Faith and Fratricide: The Theological Roots of Anti-Semitism*. New York: Seabury Press, 1974.

Smith, Sidonie. *A Poetics of Women's Autobiography*. Bloomington: Indiana UP, 1987.

Stone, Marjorie. "Genre Subversion and Gender Inversion: *The Princess* and *Aurora Leigh*." *Victorian Poetry* 25 (1987): 101–27.

Taylor, Barbara. *Eve and the New Jerusalem: Socialism and Feminism in the Nineteenth Century*. New York: Pantheon, 1983.

Zonana, Joyce. "The Embodied Muse: Elizabeth Barrett Browning's *Aurora Leigh* and Feminist Poetics." *Tulsa Studies in Women's Literature* 8 (1989): 241–62.

DIS-MEMBRANCE OF THINGS PAST: RE-VISION OF WORDSWORTHIAN RETROSPECTION IN *JANE EYRE* AND *VILLETTE*

By Ruth D. Johnston

THE FUNCTION OF ROMANTIC and Gothic elements to qualify the conventions of realistic representation in Charlotte Brontë's fiction has long been recognized. And a number of such discussions conflate the Gothic and Romantic.[1] But in this essay I will uphold this distinction and focus on the revision of Words-worthian narrative paradigms in *Jane Eyre* and *Villette*. In so doing I wish to shift critical attention from thematic concerns (realized on the level of the story through the use of Gothic machinery) to the meaning-making process (repre-sented on the level of narration as a particular structure of retrospection).[2]

Not that I wish to mininize the importance of Gothic conventions by associat-ing them with narrative "content" or "surface," for it is precisely on this level that they operate to oppose the Romantic conception of imagination as transcendent, as an order of awareness autonomous from sensation and the natural world. The Gothic literalizes the power of the imagination to shape the perceived world by presenting subjective states as part of the physical world of objects (Homans 259). The Gothic mode compels a reconsideration of the ontological status of psychic phenomena by rendering them accessible to percep-tion in the form of mirror images, dreams, apparitions, telepathic calls.

This external projection of psychic phenomena correlates with an attention to surfaces in Gothic characterization, which unsettles the surface/depth opposition that privileges depth in support of a psychological notion of identity. As Eve Sedgwick argues, what is all too often dismissed as "flatness" is rather a concep-tion of human character based on a different set of priorities, among them a concern for (and uncertainty about) the boundaries of the self (256). The Gothic manifests its obsession with the threat to autonomy posed by the instability of the periphery through doubling. Hence the association of the Gothic with the

73

uncanny. (A major portion of Freud's essay "The 'Uncanny' " is devoted to a discussion of the theme of the Double and its inherent ambiguity.)

There is no question about Charlotte Brontë's engagement with the Gothic. At the same time, it is noteworthy that she does *not* employ the kind of narrative structure usually associated with the Gothic. The frequent recourse to spatial metaphor to describe Gothic narrative — the concentric arrangement of tales said to be like a Chinese nest of boxes, one inside another — suggests an epistemology that assumes the priority of perception/space/the single moment over temporality.[3] In fact, Gothic narrative obliterates time insofar as its labyrinthine arrangements blur the distinction between story and narration, which depends upon a temporal separation. The proliferation of tellers who are simultaneously characters produces a jumble of perspectives which resists the kind of consensus that a single point of view achieves through retrospection in Romantic narrative. Within this two-dimensional context, seeing is believing, and identity is established through perception (for example, likeness made visible when two faces are juxtaposed [Sedgwick 263]). It is just this Gothic over-valuation of perception that Brontë critiques by situating her Gothic conventions in an explicitly retrospective narrative context, the autobiographical, which insists upon the importance of time for the comprehension of psychic phenomena.

Now it is precisely this concern with temporality that aligns Romantic narrative with realism even as it accounts for the difference between them. For both realism and Romanticism are supported by an empirical epistemology that conceives of time as a continuous and consistent medium extending into infinity. This temporal definition in turn underpins the empirical notion of identity as consistent over duration. However, to conceive of identity as emerging over time means that there is necessarily a gap separating the initial perception or experience of an object from its comprehension or identification. And the existence of this temporal gap contradicts the definition of time as consistent and continuous. Realistic narrative procedures (including the use of past tense and omniscient narration) operate to conceal this central contradiction.

In Romantic narrative, on the other hand, the temporal separation between experience and knowledge is a fundamental theme. Herein resides its capacity to call into question empirical notions of time and identity. However, this critique exists in conflict with defensive strategies that cover up the recognition of this temporal predicament. Thus Romanticism can be regarded as a qualified commitment to realistic/empirical premises, which in turn explains why autobiography is its basic narrative mode. Considered as a rhetorical form (and *not* as a transcription, whether factual or fictional, of the author's life), autobiography is particularly suited to express the conflict central to Romanticism. In the first place, it is distinguished by the "identity" of person between protagonist and narrator, which enables it to foreground the relation between the experiencing self and the writing self, the very issue of subjectivity. Secondly, its retrospective structure, which explicitly depends on the narrator's memory with all its fallibilities and limitations, problematizes the access to past experience, the very foundation of knowledge. In other words, the use of Romantic autobiographical forms in Brontë's novels constitutes a critique of the epistemological assumptions of the Gothic mode on the one hand and of realism on the other.[4]

I will argue further that the displacement of the epistemological model which underpins the Gothic by that of Romantic narrative is inextricably bound up with an abiding concern with the inscription of sexual difference in the narrative discourse. This last claim will seem paradoxical — initially: although gender and genre are not intrinsically linked, the Gothic mode has been practiced predominantly by women, Romantic poetry predominantly by men. Moreover, Gothic literalization opposes the transcendence of the Romantic imagination by approaching the mind/body, depth/surface, subject/object polarities from the subordinate positions traditionally associated with the feminine in our culture.

But as Margaret Homans points out, for this very reason the Gothic represents the underside of the Romantic tradition. Ultimately, an opposition that operates through sheer reversal leaves intact the terms of the binary logic that organizes our culture in favor of the masculine model. Insofar as the Gothic continues to align the feminine with the literal and material, it risks repeating the Romantic gesture of consigning the woman to the status of children, idiots, leech gatherers, and vagrants destined to be "Rolled round in earth's diurnal course, / With rocks, and stones, and trees" (Homans 258–59).[5]

Given that the Romantic and Gothic traditions are bipolar opposites, it follows that to substitute the premise of temporal continuity (the support of the Romantic notion of identity expressed in the dictum "The child is father of the man") for perception (the ground of knowledge and guarantee of identity in the Gothic) merely perpetuates the same process of meaning, including its sexual specificity. For this reason, Brontë does not merely adapt, she radically transforms Wordsworthian narrative paradigms. More precisely, through the formal manipulation of retrospective structures, she calls into question the continuity of time that ultimately ensures the reconciliation of different vantage points in Romantic narrative and undermines its critique of empiricism. For the significance of temporality in Brontë's novels does not reside in its replacement of perception as an organizing principle, but in its subversion of the very idea of such a principle, its radical discontinuity.

Thus in *Jane Eyre* and *Villette* Gothic anxiety (engendered by the question of the real or imaginary status of a phenomenon) is displaced by an epistemological crisis which precludes any answer to this question. The crisis is precipitated by the realization that experience has a complex diachronic structure which makes it impossible to locate the uncanny or any other psychic phenomenon in a solitary moment or in a single, material event. Because the question regarding the real or imaginary status of a phenomenon cannot be answered, it is transformed into an interrogation of the foundations of meaning and identity in this epistemological model. For this reason, Freud's discussion of *das Unheimliche* (the uncanny), which is frequently used to theorize the affective power of the Gothic mode, has only limited applicability to the concerns of this essay.[6] Far more pertinent to the kind of temporality I wish to explore in the textual analyses which follow is Freud's concept of *Nachträglichkeit* (translated as "deferred action"). The term refers to the deferred reworking or revision of psychic material and thus to a complex temporal logic that defies narrativization in the form of a neat chronological disposition of events. One of the fullest elaborations of this notion appears as part of Freud's seduction theory in the 1895 "Project for a Scientific Psychology," where it describes the temporal structure of trauma.

Freud resorted to a theory of seduction as *proton pseudos* ("primal deceit") because he could not establish seduction as an event.[7] The theory does not invoke "bad faith and simulation" on the part of hysterics. Rather, the term *proton pseudos* refers to a fundamental duplicity or "a kind of objective lie inscribed in the facts" of which hysterics are above all the first victims (Laplanche 34). The case of a hysteric called Emma illustrates this duplicity. Freud's analysis reveals that her phobia of entering shops alone results from the conjunction of two scenes because the event as such escapes consciousness, and only the memory excites the affect. When Emma was eight, she was twice assaulted by a shopkeeper who grabbed at her genitals through her clothes. However, at this time she was too young to understand the sexual significance of his actions. At the age of twelve, she entered a shop alone and saw two shop assistants laughing, perhaps at her clothes. This banal, non-sexual detail of resemblance activated the memory of the grinning shopkeeper's assault, which she now understood for the first time because of the onset of puberty. Freud writes, "The recollection aroused (what the event when it occurred could certainly not have done) a sexual release, which turned into anxiety," which in turn instituted a repression of the earlier scene and symptom formation (*Origins* 411).[8]

The notion of deferred action thus suspends trauma in the difference between two events as well as two registers of meaning: perception and consciousness. That is to say in the unconscious, which, according to Lacan, "must . . . be apprehended in its experience of rupture, between perception and consciousness, in that non-temporal locus . . . which forces us to posit . . . the idea of another locality, another space, another scene, *the between perception and consciousness*" (*Fundamental Concepts* 56; emphasis in original). Consequently, neither "event" exists as a simple experience. The later event is a palimpsest, a memory overlaid with an incident which somewhat resembles that memory. The earlier event, although "pre-sexual" with respect to the subject, is not bereft of sexual meaning per se: it marks the subject's inscription in a pre-existing sexual/cultural order, which means that this initial event is itself a complex structure.[9] Moreover, since the earlier scene is subject to repression right after the sexual release activated by the second scenario, it leaves only memory traces, which thereafter can never be reproduced in the form of a recollection, but only as a reconstruction.

Freud thus assumes a psychical apparatus structured through the repeated revision of a memory. This process of stratification renders any linear conception of causality untenable because the "originary scene" can never be empirically verified.[10] Despite its chronological placement, it is the after-effect or inference of an interpretive process. Thus *Nachträglichkeit* subverts the very idea of cause as original event or primal scene.

One last point: in subsequent texts Freud detaches the function of trauma from the hysteria scenario and generalizes its application. In his 1925 description of the castration scenario, for instance, deferred action structures only the little boy's interpretation of sexual difference: "he begins by showing irresolution and lack of interest" in the perception of the girl's anatomical difference; "he sees nothing or disavows what he has seen." Later, after "some threat of castration has obtained a hold upon him," the memory "arouses a terrible storm of emotion in him," and he retroactively interprets the girl's difference as *her* castration. In the process the earlier scene — the initial uncertainty of his perception — is repressed ("Some Psychical Consequences" 252).

In this scenario the little girl serves two functions. First of all, she confirms the boy's displacement of castration onto her, even though this interpretation means that she curiously disregards her own difference. She thereby confirms the boy's wholeness and integrity. Secondly, inasmuch as her corroboration takes the form of an immediate perception ("she makes her judgement and her decision in a flash. She has seen it and knows that she is without it and wants to have it" [252]), it reenforces the repression of the uncertainty of perception. It reinstates perception as the ground of knowledge.

But what is perhaps most curious about the scenario is that Freud, like the boy and the girl, also locates castration in the girl's anatomy. He repeats their failure to acknowledge castration as a trauma, suspended in the gap between experience (the initial "irresolution" of perception) and understanding (the interpretation of sexual difference). Like the little boy, he thereby disavows the implication of castration for himself. In this scenario, then, deferred action makes no (sexual) difference. For all — girl, boy, Freud/narrator — see the same *thing*.[11]

Against this assimilation of the temporality of trauma to the masculine model, which works to erase sexual difference, the readings below will demonstrate that the instances of deferred action, while not sexually delimited, remain sexually inflected. The (sexual) difference is a function of the text's relation to this temporality and causality. That is to say, the retroactive construction of meaning also informs Wordsworth's poems. (Indeed, his definition of poetry as "emotions recollected in tranquility'' can be regarded as an early formulation of this temporality.) Yet Wordsworth's narratives, like Freud's castration scenario, simultaneously stage a defense against the indeterminacy implicit in the concept through the apparent mastery of the past. The chief means for muting the operation of deferred action is the device of superimposition, which is used to present the past as the negative/subordinate of the present and to imply the continuity of time and of one consciousness with another. Brontë's novels, on the other hand, revise Wordsworth's narrative procedures in the interest of exposing the operation of this complex temporality and its corollary, the indeterminacy of origin or cause. What is at stake in these diverse strategies is the possibility of the construction of a feminine subject.

* * *

IN *Jane Eyre* BRONTË'S qualification of realistic narrative conventions by systematically imitating *and* exaggerating Wordsworthian autobiographical procedures is especially evident in both Gateshead episodes.[12]

Brontë's narrative of childhood in the opening Gateshead section, which is virtually without precedent in the history of fiction, is akin to Wordsworth's procedure and conforms to the empirical notion of identity insofar as the narrative superimposes two consciousnesses, creating the illusion of continuity between present and past selves. Accordingly, much of the action is described from the child's vantage point in an attempt to recreate past experience. For example, the description of Jane's interview with Brocklehurst reproduces the child's perception through the careful presentation of physical detail from her eye view and the verbal echoes of Little Red Ridinghood's description of the wolf. At first Jane must *look up* at Brocklehurst, who resembles ''a black pillar.'' Next, standing in front of a seated Brocklehurst, she remarks, ''What a face he had, now that it was almost on a level with mine! what a great nose! and what a great mouth! and what large prominent teeth!'' (33–34; ch. 4).

Superimposed upon this child's perspective, the mature narrator's consciousness performs several functions. First, it articulates emotions beyond the child's power to express. For instance, little Jane can only vaguely explain how Mrs. Reed is destroying her chances for future success and contentment by informing Brocklehurst that Jane is a liar: ''I felt, though I could not have expressed the feeling, that she was sowing aversion and unkindness along my future path'' (36; ch. 4). The narrator also supplements the child's judgments of some of the characters who appear in this section. Referring to Mr. Lloyd's eyes, the narrator comments, ''I daresay I should think them shrewd now'' (22; ch. 3). And the mature voice interjects a more moderate evaluation of Mrs. Reed than young Jane's, explaining that Mrs. Reed believed that she had kept her promise to her husband (14; ch. 2). Finally, the mature narrator judges her younger self as well by directly commenting on her immaturity and identifying her faults. For example, the mature voice refers to young Jane's "undeveloped understanding and imperfect feelings" (5; ch. 1) and interprets the vision in the red-room.

Furthermore, as in "Tintern Abbey," pure perception of the sensory object in itself exists at neither of the two superimposed moments. But the reason is different, and the difference is most significant. Recall that Wordsworth's speaker cannot recapture his past experience upon his return to the banks of the Wye: he in fact states, "I cannot paint / What then I was" (lines 76–77); he then proceeds to superimpose two later representations — a memory ("the picture of the mind," [62]) and, "with many recognitions dim and faint" (60), a revival of that picture in the present — which superimposition creates the illusion of continuity in consciousness. The creation of that illusion marks Wordsworth's investment in an empirical rationalization of different selves even as his poem explicitly puts in question the possibility of a reconciliation with one's past self.

In *Jane Eyre*, estrangement from pure sensory perception is not aligned with the discontinuity between past and present selves in precisely the same way. For the echoes of Red Ridinghood and other literary references in this section identify the fictional sources of the forms which already shape young Jane's perception at ten years old and imply that there is no past self that exists outside of representation/language. Wordsworth's text, on the other hand, posits a self which he cannot paint and which exists prior to "the picture of the mind." It therefore demonstrates only that consciousness cannot manifest itself outside of language, which is not the same as putting in doubt the pre-linguistic existence of the self. Moreover, the famous spots of time posit an autonomous mode of awareness beyond consciousness, an atemporal, non-spatial order of experience, described in "Tintern Abbey" as a bodily sleep which suspends all sensation and permits direct access to a non-empirical, transcendent source of knowledge (lines 38–49). In short, Wordsworth's procedures can be made to accommodate the priority of (sexual) identity to language. Brontë's conception of even Jane's past self as an "effect" of language, in contrast, implicitly defines (sexual) identity as a relation to language, hence knowledge.

In a world where representation has no outside (either in the form of pure sensory perception or transcendent imagination), the only viable differential left for the discrimination of identity is time. The next Gateshead episode elaborates the consequences of grounding identity in time by pushing Wordsworthian forms to the limit; it measures the radical insufficiency of such a representation.

The entire episode of Jane's revisit can be considered a rupture because it is inserted precisely in the middle of the Thornfield section and of her entire history. Like the narrative of childhood, Jane's second visit to (or re-vision of) the primal scene at Gateshead also creates a Wordsworthian situation. Its circular plot imitates the shape of autobiographical poems like "Tintern Abbey," and many

Wordsworthian devices express both Jane's sense of continuity and distance from her past. First, like the speaker in Wordsworth's poem, she begins by precisely pinpointing the time: she reaches the lodge at Gateshead on the first of May at five in the afternoon (283; ch. 21). Secondly, she observes many things that have remained the same. Bessie addresses Jane "quite in her old, peremptory tones" and relieves her of her outdoor garments just as she used to undress her when a child (284). Jane also observes that all the furniture and books at the hall look "just as [they] did on the morning [Jane] was first introduced to Mr. Brocklehurst" (285). Thirdly, Jane's relation to Bessie's children, Robert and Jane, recalls the transformation of the speaker's sister into a vision of his former self at the end of "Tintern Abbey": "Old times crowded fast back on me as I watched [Bessie] bustling about . . . giving little Robert or Jane an occasional tap or push, just as she used to give me in former days" (284; ch. 21). Finally, despite the unaltered state in which she finds Gateshead, Jane, like Wordsworth's speaker, senses a difference in herself. Treading the well remembered path up to the hall she observes,

> I still felt as a wanderer on the face of the earth: but I experienced firmer trust in myself and my own powers, and less withering dread of oppression. The gaping wound of my wrongs, too, was now quite healed; and the flame of resentment extinguished. (285; ch. 21)

Jane remarks that she no longer feels bitterness and hatred towards Mrs. Reed, only "a sort of ruth for her great sufferings, and a strong yearning to forget and forgive all injuries" (288–89). Thus, as in Wordsworth's text, "the still, sad music of humanity" (line 92) displaces the unbridled passions of her former self. In short, her return to Gateshead measures Jane's growth.

The first signal that Wordsworthian forms are pushed to the extreme in this section is the proliferation of superimposed consciousnesses. A whole series rather than simply two superimposed consciousnesses chart Jane's transformation. Jane, here eighteen years old, evaluates a younger Jane, age ten, but is in turn judged by the narrator, Jane at age thirty. Moreover, the Jane who revisits Gateshead compares herself not only to the child she was nine years before but also to the Jane of just a year ago:

> It had heretofore been my habit always to shrink from arrogance: received as I had been to-day, I should, a year ago, have resolved to quit Gateshead the very next morning; now, it was disclosed to me all at once, that that would be a foolish plan. (288; ch. 21)

Such a complex superimposition of interpenetrating consciousnesses does not merely provide a sensitive instrument for measuring the discrepancies within Jane's development; it also reveals that Jane's more mature perceptions are subject to further revision. For instance, the text clearly describes Jane at the time of this visit to Gateshead as only relatively more mature. For however much improved she may be at this stage in her life, Jane's pleasure at the prospect of returning to Thornfield and Rochester is described by a still older Jane (at the time of the writing) as youthfully headstrong and blind (305; ch. 22). The comment suggests that if Jane's psychological development is incomplete at eighteen, so may it be at the age of thirty, which is, after all, a very young age for an autobiographer. Thus the essentially open-ended structure of autobiographical narrative is underscored by her youth, and the ending is much more overtly recognized as provisional than in Wordsworth's poem.[13]

The multiplicity of superimposed consciousnesses in this return to Gateshead may hint at the sophistication of the temporal structure in this novel, but the extent of its complexity emerges only with a recognition that the episode is not a flashback (a memory within a memory) but an actual return to the scene, which entails a reintroduction of characters.[14] On the one hand, the reintroduction of characters as a substitute for a flashback permits Brontë to preserve a straightforward chronological arrangement on the surface, consistent with the ordinary calendar time we all subscribe to. On the other hand, a reintroduction of characters generates more overlapping time levels than a flashback because each character stands in a different relation to the past and future; each consciousness has a distinct retrospective structure. Insofar as their individual rhythms fail to coincide and their temporal structures to harmonize, this multiplicity undermines the homogeneity of the temporal medium and its corollary, the continuity of one consciousness with another, both of which are basic tenets of empiricism. (In this connection, contrast the second superimposition in "Tintern Abbey" [lines 117–22], which does posit continuity of consciousness between the speaker and his sister. The representation of the past as his sister thus disavows the earlier acknowledgement of the irreducible difference of past experience; it is a gesture made in the absence of an omniscient narrator to express that faith in continuity and the extension of the system beyond the scope of the text that is endemic to realism/empiricism.)

More specifically, each of the Reeds conceives of time differently. Georgiana, for instance, cannot relate to the present:

> It was strange she never once adverted either to her mother's illness, or her brother's death, or the present gloomy state of the family prospects. Her mind seemed wholly taken up with reminiscences of past gaiety, and aspirations after dissipations to come. (293; ch. 21)

In contrast, each day for Eliza is the same. She follows a rigid routine of "clockwork regularity" (294), the repetitiveness of which obliterates distinctions between past, present, and future. Eliza awaits her mother's death to sever all ties with the past. She intends to separate herself from her sister "as if [they] had never known each other" (296) and to live in retirement "permanently secured" from the world (295). The fact that Eliza, Georgiana, and Jane do not relate to the past, present, and future in the same way implies that each one's temporal structure is defined individually and cannot be assimilated to some uniform, general system.

Mrs. Reed's time scheme also differs from Jane's and insists even more forcibly on the limitations of Jane's version of the past. With regard to the past, Mrs. Reed remains the same. Her face is as "stern, relentless as ever," and her feelings towards Jane are also unchanged (289). With regard to the future, she has none: eternity lies before her (299). However, Mrs. Reed's apprehension of the past actually achieves what the speaker of "Tintern Abbey" attempts but cannot effect. Her delirium offers her access to the past that bypasses retrospection (although it is not a past conceived as pure sensory perception either). That is to say, in her delirium she also returns to the time of Jane's childhood and relives her old feelings of annoyance and hatred, expressing her animosity unreservedly (290–91). Actually, different times in the past exist simultaneously for her. She abruptly skips from her complaint against Jane to a present-tense expression of her anxiety over her son's financial excesses and his threat to kill himself. She also recounts a prophetic dream in which she envisions John dead (291). (At the time of her illness, John is already dead.) However, this ability to re-experience an unadulterated past does not serve to integrate her identity but to shatter it. This simultaneity destroys the sense of her identity as a continuum as it undermines any principle of mutually relating the separate moments of her life. The past becomes just another hallucination.

Her delirium, then, is a parody of Wordsworth's affective memory and thus of Jane-narrator's project too; it demonstrates through the incoherence of juxtaposition that even the past recaptured cannot guarantee integrity of consciousness. Or, to put it another way, Aunt Reed's delirium problematizes the re-presentation of the past as the symmetrical reverse of the present by representing the past as a mere series of moments. In this way her delirium reveals the contradiction that lies at the heart of the empirical epistemology which underpins both Romanticism and realism: on the one hand, empiricism depends on the continuity of time and its infinite extension to sustain the notion of identity as cumulative. But on the other hand, its notion of identity also depends on the temporal discontinuity between experience and consciousness, which means that the past is always constructed retroactively, *nachträglich*.

Despite the more obvious reference to Wordsworthian autobiographical forms in the two Gateshead sections, the temporality associated with the superimposition of two consciousnesses informs the novel as a whole, although again with a small but telling difference. For *Jane Eyre* represents a departure from the usual tendency of nineteenth-century autobiography to approximate "third-person," omniscient narration (including poems like "Tintern Abbey" which privilege the speaker's perspective) insofar as it adheres more closely to the protagonist's perspective than to the narrator's. But the sense of immediacy thus produced is ultimately undercut through the operation of ironic prefiguration, a structure that insists upon the belated revelation of the double meaning of an event for the reader as well as the characters: it thus retroactively dislocates the event from the temporal continuum. (This complex retrospective structure therefore distinguishes the apparent immediacy of the narrative as a whole from Mrs. Reed's delirium.) More specifically, a seemingly random event, initially placed in relation to other events through chronological order, prefigures another event that occurs subsequently.[15] Yet only in retrospect, when the prophecy is fulfilled, do we recognize that the earlier event was never "random" but always part of a pattern and that it was shaped by the narrator's consciousness as well as young Jane's; the experience, therefore, cannot be located in one moment but oscillates between two scenes. It should be stressed that insofar as ironic prefiguration implicates the reader in the retroactive construction of meaning, prefiguration is enacted, not merely asserted. In other words, ironic prefiguration in *Jane Eyre* dramatizes that causality is the product, not the foundation, of narration.[16]

A good example of ironic prefiguration is provided by the charades which entertain the houseparty at Thornfield and which appear at the time of the event to be designed to register Jane's exclusion from the company, especially Rochester's. Actually, since the incident involves a staged performance and describes Jane's status as outsider through her spectator position, its meaning, even initially, is not simple. For the charades duplicate in miniature the dramatic structure of the entire Thornfield section and transform its theatrical metaphors into literal descriptions, which are reconverted into metaphor once Rochester's team leaves the stage and Jane's attention is "absorbed by the spectators" instead (231; ch. 18). This doubling of levels of reflection, combined with the ease with which one side converts into the other, conflates the two meanings of the word "act" (to do; to pretend) and applies it to both sides of the curtain, thereby insisting on the mediacy of the experience itself. But the specific meaning of each of the dramatizations for Jane's life — the marriage, the offer of jewels, the imprisonment — emerges only subsequently, when the events are repeated with Jane assuming Blanche's role. Thus when we later read of Rochester's courtship, the aborted marriage, and the attempted bigamy, we are forced to revise our interpretation of the charades even as we recognize that the multiple meanings were there, superimposed, all along.

The novel insists on the retroactive construction of meaning through proliferation. Even the many dreams, sympathies, changes in the weather, voices, and visions — the novel's Gothic trappings — are subordinated to the temporal structure articulated through the superimposition of two consciousnesses. Jane's

prophetic dreams imitate the fragmentary form of ordinary dreams and consequently forecast the future through suggestive parallels rather than strict allegory.
Furthermore, not all Jane's premonitions, whether expressed as dreams or other
forms, are consistently interpreted as providential guides. Some turn out to be
just ordinary dreams or false omens. For example, just before returning to
Thornfield from Gateshead, Jane dreams that Blanche Ingram banishes her from
Thornfield while Rochester looks on smiling (304–05; ch. 22). The existence of
these false omens side by side with true prophecies underscores the narrator's
role in identifying supernatural signs. Discrimination between revelation and
superstition, therefore, involves retrospective re-interpretation.

* * *

VILLETTE USES MANY OF THE same structures as *Jane Eyre*. In addition, however,
it denies the protagonist, Lucy Snowe, the same kind of central position that
Jane Eyre, in true Wordsworthian fashion, occupies in her narrative. Consequently, what the earlier novel articulates as an implicit tension between story
and narration becomes a more conspicuous dialectic executed on the level of
narration between incompatible principles of narrative logic (between autobiographical and "third-person" modes). This revision of *Jane Eyre*'s revision of
Wordsworth in turn transforms every aspect of *Villette*: plot, perspective, Gothic
conventions, temporality, and, finally, the very process of reading.

The experiment with double plot which effects this decentering is immediately
obvious in the first four chapters, in which the narrative of childhood focuses
on Polly rather than Lucy. The text resists the logic of autobiography (the
reduction of Polly to the function of a foil or analogue for some aspect of
Lucy — though she is that too), for when Polly turns up again in Villette, the
narrative splits in two, alternates between her and Lucy, to construct a counterplot to Lucy's story that develops concurrently.[17]

On the other hand, the narrative presents Lucy's relationship with M. Paul as
a sequel to her involvement with Dr. John, even though these interrelations
occur simultaneously too. Lucy enjoys Paul's bonbons and books while she
accompanies Dr. John to the galleries, concerts, and theater, but she tells us
about his raid of her desk and gifts afterwards. The text thereby refuses to
apply any single mode consistently. In lieu of counterplot, different perspectives
register the discontinuity between these relationships, offsetting their sequential
presentation. Thus the opposition of Rochester and St. John, which *Jane Eyre*
represents in successive order on the level of the *story*, is here transposed to the
level of *narration* and represented through inconsistent perspectives that offer
divergent versions of the past. More specifically, the narrative adheres to Lucy-
actor's impressions in presenting Dr. John or, more precisely, the narrator's
representation of Lucy-actor's impressions; the text explains that this strategy
accounts for the seeming inconsistencies in his presentation:

Reader, if in the course of this work, you find that my opinion of Dr. John undergoes modification, excuse the seeming inconsistency. I give the feeling as at the time I felt it; I describe the view of character as it appeared when discovered. (273–74; ch. 18)

But it is the narrator's perspective that controls the presentation of Monsieur Paul, which depends significantly on summaries of habitual actions: his habit of leaving presents in Lucy's desk, his chronic suspicion that she knows Greek and Latin. The formal signal for this alternative mode of presentation is the frequent use of the past imperfect tense.

To align such disparity of presentation with a distinction between the protagonist's and the narrator's perspectives on the level of narration exacerbates the discontinuity between the autobiographer's past and present selves to the point of ineradicable difference.[18] The concern here is to interrogate perspective as such. For the imposition of a restricted perspective field is what permits the organization of time around a past/present opposition and its corollary, the subordination of the past. *Villette* underscores the radical alterity of the past insofar as the narrating consciousness refuses the conventional constraints on perspective and produces incompatible versions of the past that cannot be reduced to a symmetrically reverse image of the present, its negative. This inconsistency also undermines the effect of the many references to calendar time which produce the illusion of narrative continuity. Consequently, even though Lucy Snowe at the time of writing is an old lady, her hair "white under a white cap, like snow beneath snow" (61; ch. 5), who can declare authoritatively that "to the end of [their] mutual lives there occurred no repetition of, no allusion to" her showdown with Madame Beck (648; ch. 38), she is far less able to reconcile clashing perspectives — her own as well as others' — than the youthful autobiographer, Jane Eyre.

In this connection, the nun provides a useful point of contrast with the earlier novel. In many ways the nun's function parallels that of Bertha Mason in *Jane Eyre*. It is a Gothic convention that is reversed with the disclosure of De Hamal's disguise; the nun is a projection of Lucy's inner psychological state, symbolizing her temptation to withdraw from life and to suppress her feelings; and certainly, since the nun appears at crucial points of crisis in Lucy's life, it punctuates the stages of her growth. However, Jane's discovery of Bertha clears up all kinds of mysteries: the laughter attributed to Grace Poole, the fires, the rent wedding veil, the mirror vision of the Vampyre, the attack on Mason. As Rochester's deception is laid bare and Jane's presentiments fulfilled, the discovery upholds the authority of Jane's vision.[19]

The same is not true of De Hamal's exposure as the nun. In the first place, De Hamal is pursuing his own love story when he assumes this disguise. Therefore, the meaning of his action is not contained by his function in Lucy's story.

Indeed, his connection to Lucy is accidental, indirect, unlike Bertha's relation to Jane. Secondly, even though each appearance of the nun provides additional evidence that it is no illusion (twice Paul sees it too, and De Hamal's revelation gives final verification of its objective existence), this empirical accumulation of data and corroborative testimony does not add up to a definitive explanation. For instance, it does not render Dr. John's earlier diagnosis completely invalid: Lucy *is* over-wrought as a result of "long-continued mental conflict" (358; ch. 22) and she *is* "in a highly nervous state" over the loss of her letter (356). However, the nun's connection to this condition is not that of a symptom, as Dr. John must believe in his "professional character" because he cannot otherwise conceive of the anxiety which overshadows Lucy's every feeling:

> the atmosphere was stagnant and humid; yet amidst all these deadening influences, my fancy budded fresh and my heart basked in sunshine. These feelings, however, were well kept in check by the secret but ceaseless consciousness of anxiety lying in wait on enjoyment, like a tiger crouched in a jungle. The breathing of that beast of prey was in my ear always; his fierce heart panted close against mine; he never stirred in his lair but I felt him: I knew he waited only for sun-down to bound ravenous from his ambush. (81–82; ch. 7)

The nun makes visible just this split, this sense of "otherness" within consciousness at any given moment, which confounds the distinction between Lucy's past and present selves and eludes assimilation in the mastery of the past through retrospection.[20]

Elsewhere in the text it is presumably a consciousness-altering drug that interferes with the representation of the past as subordinate to the present, that is, as its origin or cause. Lucy's awakening at La Terrasse, for instance, invites comparison with Jane Eyre's return to Gateshead, which is parodied by Aunt Reed's delirium. But as a rhetorical strategy, parody predicates the very dualism of representation that is in question here. Accordingly, in *Villette* it is Lucy herself who fears that she has "passed into an abnormal state of mind" and is "very ill and delirious" (241; ch. 16). However, the narcotic administered by the bonne, which magnifies her sense of temporal and spatial dissociation, only partially accounts for the displacement of retrospection and its implicit temporal order by loss of context and multiple/fractured reflection. For her awakening in the sleeping chamber at La Terrasse duplicates her awakening some hours earlier in the drawing room, prior to swallowing the drug. Furthermore, the furnishings she recognizes are themselves re-presentations (little pictures, pencil-drawn screens, ornaments and relics preserved under glass), which are re-presented in the rooms of La Terrasse and which are in turn reflected in the mirror:

> Bretton! Bretton! and ten years ago shone reflected in that mirror. And why did Bretton and my fourteenth year haunt me thus? Why, if they came at all, did they

not return complete? Why hovered before my distempered vision the mere furniture, while the rooms and the locality were gone? (241; ch. 16)

The passage underscores the fragmentary quality of this return of/to the past (for it is only the furniture that reappears), and the multiple levels of reflection undercut the sense of immediacy suggested by the fact that the furniture actually reappears and is not merely remembered. At the same time, the multiple repetitions focus attention on the context, which keeps changing. As the recovered "origin" (the furniture) is cut loose from a specific moment in the past and becomes subject to a free-floating play shifting from representation to representation, its significance becomes contingent on a process of endless displacement that subverts the very notion of origin.

In the second episode these strategies are expanded and intensified. Lucy wanders out on the night of the festival, which is also in some sense a return to the past insofar as she passes in review the various groups of people she has previously encountered in her history. More precisely, it is a re-vision of Wordsworthian epiphany. Again, Lucy is drugged, but the effect of the strong, consciousness-altering opiate Mme. Beck has ordered for her merely intensifies, does not engender, the endless play of reflections in this episode. The section is so complex that I can only partially describe the numbers and kinds of repetitions that render representation per se suspect. First of all, the intermittent use of the present tense in this part of the narrative undermines the distinction between the time of the writing and the time of the event and signals the narrator's absorption into the re-presented past. Paradoxically, however, this apparent immediacy only makes the past more opaque because other binary oppositions break down along with the past/present distinction. The city of Villette has itself been transformed into a spectacle that confounds the natural and the artificial: "moonlight and heaven are banished" by the blazing flambeaux that illuminate the gaily dressed throngs, many sporting masks (654; ch. 38). The park is "a forest with sparks of purple and ruby and golden fire gemming the foliage," a region teeming, not with trees, but with architectural re-presentations of symbols of Egypt re-produced in timber, paint, and pasteboard (655). This spectacle is part of a fête held every year to commemorate a crisis in the history of Labassecour, but the "original" historical event is itself "of somewhat apocryphal memory" (656).

Among the people gathered at the center of the spectacle to hear music reproduced in concert, Lucy re-cognizes Madame Beck and her entourage. In this encounter still other kinds of duplication proliferate: Madame Beck is re-produced in her daughter, little Désirée. But in the case of Justine Marie and Paul, biological and aesthetic modes of reproduction converge. Justine Marie bears no physical resemblance to Lucy's nun; "she looks, at all points, the bourgeoise belle" (672; ch. 39), and Lucy finally re-cognizes her as a relation of Madame

Beck. But her name re-calls her dead aunt, who was re-presented as "the pictured nun on the panel" in the house of Madame Walravens (671). M. Paul, whose re-semblance to his brother, Josef Emanuel, has been remarked earlier, accompanies Justine Marie and announces that he has taken a berth on the *Paul et Virginie*, a ship whose name re-calls the story by St. Pierre about a heroine who perishes at sea after a long separation from her lover, a fate that M. Paul will perhaps re-peat at the end of the novel. When reproduction proliferates to this extent, the contamination of representational levels makes it impossible to determine an origin or cause for anything. The re-vision thus reveals that the concept of the past as origin is not the ground but the after-effect of the past/present distinction, which functions to conceal the heterogeneity of the past. Against this determinist analysis of time, the text here insists on the non-coincidence of temporal discontinuity with the past/present polarity in order to expose the past as intrinsically duplicitous — precisely not as primal scene, but as "primal deceit," as necessarily exceeding any representation.

The device of reintroduction of characters, associated with the return to Gateshead in *Jane Eyre*, is also greatly transformed in *Villette* so as to draw the reader into the vertigo of duplication that simulates the past for Lucy in the scenes cited above. First, the device is applied to more characters in this novel. Not only characters out of Lucy's childhood but also people she meets later have a way of reappearing unexpectedly. Thus the two men who chase her and make her lose her way to the inn on her first night in Villette turn out to be the two scholars who examine her at the show trial; the priest to whom she makes her confession later appears as Paul's mentor, whom she encounters again when she visits the house of Madame Walravens. Second, the identity of the character who is being reintroduced is not immediately revealed. Consequently, for a while s/he appears as a newly introduced personage. The different names by which a single character is known help to conceal that s/he has appeared before. For example, as a boy Mrs. Bretton's son is called Graham. When he grows up and becomes a doctor in Villette, he is called Dr. John. Dr. John also turns out to be the boorish lover whom Ginevra names Isidore. Third, as the previous example suggests, in *Villette* the device of reintroduction is itself repeatedly duplicated in miniature form for the main characters. Thus in addition to his other appearances as Isidore and Dr. John, Graham Bretton is also the stranger who helps Lucy with her trunk and directs her to an inn on her first night in Villette, and he is the unidentified man among Madame Beck's guests whom Lucy breaks in upon on the occasion of the nun's first appearance. Similarly, before Polly's reappearance as the Countess Paulina de Bassompierre, she is the unnamed girl who is injured during the fire at the theater.

The concealment of the character's identity in the past permits that character to reappear and be apprehended through a fresh perspective uncolored by past associations and impressions. But the device does more than liberate cognition from a priori expectations. It represents identity as radically discontinuous because not recoverable through retrospection. In fact, it might be more accurate to say that it undermines the very notion of identity, which is never immediately present to consciousness but always a product of memory. For the same character appears several times under various guises, but each time s/he is dissociated from the past so that no appearance can be placed in temporal relation to the other appearances. In this iterative process, precisely those contradictions and heterogeneous elements within the personality which retrospection would rationalize are allowed to emerge. At the same time, reintroduction undermines chronology, or any sense of sequence for that matter. When so many characters are reintroduced again and again as if for the first time, the device subjects identity to interminable re-interpretation as it undercuts any notion of first time, of origin, of cause, of center.

The displacement of flashback by this complex form of reintroduction implicates the reader as well as unsettling all the mechanisms of identification, not only the identification of characters (which depends on the temporal co-ordination of disparate impressions) but also the reader's identification with the narrator insofar as reintroduction puts in question the integrity of Lucy's consciousness. In this process, integrity refers to a sense of wholeness or identity rather than honesty, for more is at stake than the narrator's reliability. Indeed, the notion of the unreliable narrator assumes that coherency of vision and controlling knowledge are possible. It supports, albeit negatively, a specular logic which conceives of identity (the narrator's, the reader's) as a precondition for understanding, of identification as the exact coincidence of consciousnesses, and of narrative as a system that reflects rather than produces significance.

But no narrator can know and tell all, and every "reliable" narrator knows more than s/he tells inasmuch as the time of the writing occurs after all the events of the story are over. Consequently, when Lucy admits that Dr. John's identification as Graham Bretton at La Terrasse comes as no surprise to her because she had "first recognized him on that occasion, noted several chapters back," when he caught her staring at him (249; ch. 16), just how much less honest is she than the conventional narrator? More honest in admitting overtly that she did not confide in the reader immediately; no less honest in withholding information. Her "unreliability" consists chiefly in deferring the communication of this information to the reader somewhat beyond the conventional limits and thereby calling attention to the lapse.[21]

Lucy's "integrity," on the other hand, paradoxically comes into question just because of her "honesty," which makes her reticence on other subjects all the more apparent. For the text offers no adequate explanation for her reserve vis-à-vis the reader, even as it frustrates the reader's every inclination to participate in a process of identification conceived on the analogical model.

More specifically, the text explains only Lucy's reasons for keeping the discovery from Dr. John. Her reticence is described as a power play, a calculated lapse in confidence designed to safeguard her privileged insight into his character:

> To *say* anything on the subject, to *hint* at my discovery, had not suited my habits of thought, or assimilated with my system of feeling. On the contrary, I had preferred to keep the matter to myself. I liked entering his presence covered with a cloud he had not seen through, while he stood before me under a ray of special illumination, which shone all partial over his head, trembled about his feet, and cast light no farther. (249–50; ch. 16; emphasis in original)

However, the explanation cannot be extended to the level of narration and applied to the reader because such a reading would imply the reader's identification with this character, which is systematically blocked. In the first place, we share, albeit belatedly, knowledge that is withheld from him: while Lucy does, finally identify herself to Dr. John, she never explains to him what prompted the concealment in the first place. Moreover, this character has all along been presented as singularly unobservant and insensitive in his relations with Lucy, initially "according to [her] presence in the room just that degree of notice and consequence . . . [that] is given to unobtrusive articles of furniture, chairs of ordinary joiner's work, and carpets of no striking pattern" (135; ch. 10). Even on the occasion when recognition dawns upon Lucy, he does not recognize her in return. Actually, he hardly sees her at all: "his notice was arrested" by her intense scrutiny of himself as reflected "in a clear little oval mirror fixed in the side of the window recess" (136).

The reader can readily sympathize with the "perverse" pleasure Lucy derives from Dr. John's misconstruction of the scene. However, the text never offers any such explanation of Lucy's reserve towards the reader. Paradoxically, this very lack of motivation, which impedes our comprehension of and identification with Lucy-narrator, motivates an interrogation of the identification mechanism itself. The text thereby transforms the model of interpretation supported by the traditional notion of identification (a relation of identity between two already-constituted subjects — the narrator, the reader — that serves as a precondition for the exchange of a meaning that is already and always in the text) into a notion of reading as transference (the reader's participation in the textual dynamic by virtue of its illegibility). The term derives from psychoanalytic theory where it designates the dynamics of the analysand-analyst relation. As elaborated in Shoshana Felman's reading of Lacan's reading of Freud, the concept enables us to re-think the reader's implication in the text without reducing that relation to simply the reader's fabrication or "reading into" the text in the sense of projecting a meaning onto the text from outside.

For in transference there is no "objective stance" or outside. In Lacan's description the term designates an entanglement of desires, hence love: "what is there, behind the love known as transference, is the affirmation of the link between the desire of the analyst and the desire of the patient" (*Fundamental Concepts* 254). Nor can this entanglement be conceived simply as a dialectic: "The transference is a phenomenon in which subject and psycho-analyst are both included. To divide it in terms of transference and counter-transference . . . is never more than a way of avoiding the essence of the matter" (*Fundamental Concepts* 231).

Lacan also distinguishes transference from identification:

> How often will you read formulas that associate, for example, the transference with identification, whereas identification is merely a pause, a false termination of the analysis which is very frequently confused with its normal termination. Its relation with the transference is close, but precisely in that by which the transference has not been analysed. (*Fundamental Concepts* 145–46)

If the distinction depends on analysis, what does it mean to analyze the transference?

Not to interpret its *meaning*, for Lacan says that

> what emerges in the transference effect is opposed to revelation. Love intervenes in its function . . . as deception. . . . We are linked together in awaiting this transference effect in order to be able to interpret, and at the same time, we know that it closes the subject off from the effect of our interpretation. (*Fundamental Concepts* 253)

Transference — love — resists interpretation insofar as it catches analyst and patient up in an unconscious repetition, an enactment. Therefore, the analysis must address transference in its performative dimension, not its constative or cognitive level.[22]

At the same time, Lacan takes issue with those who see in transference "no more than the concept of repetition itself" because they disregard the first part of Freud's formulation of transference: "what cannot be remembered is repeated in behaviour" (qtd. in *Fundamental Concepts* 129). Freud's clause indicates that the repetition is caused by a failure of memory due to "the opacity of the trauma — as it was then maintained in its initial function by Freud's thought, that is to say, in [Lacan's] terms, its resistance to signification . . ." (*Fundamental Concepts* 129). As was observed above in connection with *Nachträglichkeit*, trauma refers to an event that does not take place and cannot be located in a single event or moment. Its significance resides not in its meaning but in its structure. Hence its resistance to recollection. Transference, then, is not just repetition but the repetition of a trauma or implication in a temporal structure which functions to interrupt unconscious communication, for it causes the unconscious to close up: "the transference is both an obstacle to remembering, and a making present of the closure of the unconscious, which is the act of missing the right meeting just at the right moment" (*Fundamental Concepts* 145).

Paradoxically, it is just this conjunction of missed encounters or misfires in signification that enables the analysis of transference at the performative level because it makes present the process qua process. We best catch an operation in the act at the moment of interruption or failure. Thus we become aware of the identification mechanism — of identification as a mechanism — in *Villette* precisely where it breaks down. As "making present" also suggests, the analysis of the functioning of repetition can only occur in the present, for the function does not exist apart from the particular intersubjective relation it structures or repeats (i.e., the relation with the analyst is not a substitute for a prior expression whose meaning pre-exists its repetition). And its function is deception. Thus Lacan writes,

> The transference effect is that effect of deception in so far as it is *repeated in the present here and now*.
>   It is repetition of that which passed for such only *because it possesses the same form*. It is not ectopia [displacement of an organ or substance]. It is not a shadow of the former deceptions of love. *It is isolation in the actuality of its pure functioning as deception*. (*Fundamental Concepts* 254, emphasis added)

A question arises at this point because trauma and transference were discovered in relation to work on sexual difference, specifically the construction of the (feminine) subject as hysteric. Furthermore, as we have observed, the trauma of unreadability is a chronic condition in *Villette*, a text both authored and narrated by a woman. At the same time, the transference, as repetition in the here and now, unsettles the notion of sexuality as pre-given. This seeming contradiction compels a return to the question posed at the beginning of the argument: just why and how are the temporality of trauma (deferred action) and its repetition/analysis (transference) particularly feminine concerns? I want to pursue this question by examining the recurrent mirror images in *Villette* because the mirror functions in the novel (as in psychoanalytic theory) to articulate the construction of the subject and the deconstruction of identity.[23]

On the one hand, Lucy functions as the mirror which confirms Dr. John's and M. Paul's self images. With respect to Dr. John, see the mirror image cited above, in which the mirror reflects Lucy's recognition of his identity. As for M. Paul, he sees Lucy simultaneously as his opposite and the same in a passage that could serve as a model for representation according to specular logic, not only in its explicit conversion of difference into sameness, but also in its syntactical arrangements — its parallel structures and carefully balanced antitheses:

You are patient, and I am choleric; you are quiet and pale, and I am tanned and fiery; you are a strict Protestant, and I am a sort of lay Jesuit: but we are alike — there is affinity. Do you see it, mademoiselle, when you look in the glass? Do you observe that your forehead is shaped like mine — that your eyes are cut like mine? Do you hear that you have some of my tones of voice? Do you know that you have many of my looks? (531–32; ch. 31)[24]

In stark contrast to these specular instances is the passage that describes Lucy seeing herself when she accompanies Graham and Mrs. Bretton to the concert. Since she *literally* perceives herself as an *other*, the mirror reflection presents a momentary perception of herself as de-centered or split. But what is even more remarkable is that this vision has a temporal dimension:

> We moved on — I was not at all conscious whither — but at some turn we suddenly encountered another party approaching from the opposite direction. I just now see that group, *as it flashed upon me for one moment.* A handsome middle-aged lady in dark velvet; a gentleman who might be her son — the best face, the finest figure, I thought, I had ever seen; a third person in a pink dress and black lace mantle.
>
> I noted them all — the third person as well as the other two — *and for the fraction of a moment, believed them all strangers,* thus receiving an impartial impression of their appearance. *But the impression was hardly felt and not fixed, before the consciousness that I faced a great mirror, filling a compartment between two pillars, dispelled it*: the party was our own party. Thus for the first, and perhaps only time in my life, I enjoyed the "giftie" of seeing myself as others see me. *No need to dwell on the result. It brought a jar of discord,* a pang of regret; it was not flattering, yet, after all, I ought to be thankful: it might have been worse. (298; ch. 20, emphasis added)

This extraordinary image exposes perception "in the actuality of its pure functioning as deception" to use Lacan's terms. By foregrounding the process rather than the content of the vision, it undermines perception as the guarantee of epistemological security. Perception is thus presented as structured and time-bound (as re-vision), not natural and immediate. More precisely, perception is ruptured through the temporal separation of two components: first the "giftie," in which the eye/I is momentarily taken in and believes that the image is real; then the re-cognition, which neither substantiates nor corrects the first "impartial" impression, but retroactively reveals its status as a mirror reflection by taking notice of the frame, moving attention away from the image to its context. This re-vision, then, depends on the interaction of two moments, neither of which proffers a true image of Lucy's identity. The deferment of knowledge, its temporal separation from belief, makes the discrepancy between the two more apparent. Hence the result: not the reassuring convergence of reflections that confirms the integrity of the masculine image, but "a jar of discord."

This peculiar mirror image, which re-views the incommensurability of self and image, functions in much the same way as the other ex-centric procedures in *Villette*: each mobilizes deferred action to structure the revision of narrative processes — perspective, retrospection, identification — that are supported by and reenforce empirical notions of time and identity. The mirror image, by deconstructing instances of masculine self-reflection, suggests that all these procedures are likewise sexually differentiated, which is to say *only in their functioning*.

For another mirror image works to dispel any notion of this structure of seeing as somehow intrinsically feminine. In this instance Ginevra confirms her superiority to Lucy as she stands by her side and peers at their reflected images:

> just listen to the difference of our positions, and *then see how happy am I*, and how miserable are you. . . .
>   In the first place: I am the *daughter of a gentleman* of family, and though my father is not rich, I have *expectations from an uncle*. . . . I may have as many admirers as I choose. This very night I have been breaking the hearts of two gentlemen, and it is *the dying look I had from one of them* just now, which puts me in such spirits. *I do so like to watch them* turn red and pale, and scowl and *dart fiery glances at each other*, and *languishing ones at me*. (202–03; ch. 14, emphasis added)

Ginevra, like M. Paul, compares herself to Lucy. Like Dr. John, she sees herself being seen. But Ginevra measures her "superiority" to Lucy in relation to a third term, be it father, uncle, admiring male lover. That is to say, when Ginevra looks into the mirror, her image reflects her value and appeal within a system structured by the masculine gaze; it complements that gaze.

As these mirror images resonate against one another to displace sexual difference from an image (content) to the process of looking, they imply a theory of textuality for which the fact of female authorship becomes irrelevant. For deferred action also functions to displace aberrations in narrative form from the author/narrator to the procedures themselves (just as the concept "primal deceit" displaces duplicity from the hysteric to the configuration of circumstances in the case history). From this perspective, narrative conventions and paradigms cannot be regarded as ideologically neutral: in texts by Freud and Wordsworth they operate to shore up and perpetuate the masculine model of identity as the norm. The advantage of this reading is that as these processes are de-naturalized, their foreclosure of the feminine subject is transformed into dis-closure — in both senses: a revelation of a bias and an undoing of closure. For this reading acknowledges the residue of meaning that remains unassimilated to the prevailing phallogocentric narrative logic: the sister's history in "Tintern Abbey," the little girl's sexual difference in the castration scenario, Emma's sexual experience in the hysteria scenario.

But, it may be objected, just what advantage does this association of the feminine with a resistance to assimilation offer? What difference does it make, ultimately, to analyze the processes that either repress or exclude the feminine subject? In reply, I invoke the Heisenberg uncertainty principle, which describes the scientist's implication in his experiment, for it indicates how the act of observation changes the object observed.[25] As another articulation of transference, the principle teaches us that to focus on a particular effect or content (the symptom) is to overlook the lost cause of its production. (As the mirror images in *Villette* demonstrate, looking necessarily involves overlooking or blindness; to look at the image blinds one to its construction.)[26]

To focus on the effect or substance of a scenario commits us to repetition governed by the logic of identity, in other words to perpetuate the same construction of the woman. This is precisely what happens in the castration scenario and in "Tintern Abbey." Each text concludes with the repetition of a specific *content* that represses the prior discovery of repetition of/as *structure.* Thus the little girl and Freud repeat the little boy's misconstruction of castration. Wordsworth's speaker transforms his sister into a re-presentation of his memory, which is to say a re-flection of his present consciousness. By the same token, to focus on the hysteric erects hysteria into the universal meaning of the scenario, an origin that determines all future readings of the scene. In each case the fixation on a single effect conceals its contingency on a specific, time-bound interpretive context, which is open to re-vision precisely because the cause remains indeterminate. In other words, to recognize that meaning depends on context is also to acknowledge the limits of context, to acknowledge that different contexts produce disparate effects: consciousness, repression, trauma, for example. (This is what reintroduction dramatizes in *Villette*: a character's "identity" depends on a specific context; each change in context entails another, different construction of that character.)

Attending to the operating mode, on the other hand, discovers the significance of discontinuities and failures of representation, which allow differences to emerge and come into play. For the absence of a determinate origin or cause means that the subject is not predetermined in some originary moment once and for all, hence not reducible to any particular cultural construction — be it hysteria, castration, femininity, or any other interpretation of sexuality for that matter. To say that the subject remains in question, or subject to repeated re-vision, is rather to insist on the arbitrariness of sexuality (sexuality does not refer to an "identity" that exists outside its construction in a specific representation). Nor is this a regression to sexual indifference. It is a way of articulating the question of sexuality as a question of reading. It is to situate the question of (sexual) difference and the possibility of intervention in the textual movement in the here and now.

Thus attention to the process operative in Freud's and Wordsworth's texts permits a different reading of their crucial discoveries, one at odds with the sexual bias of certain recuperative tactics in their conclusions. It is to re-gard castration as a crisis in vision rather than as an anatomical distinction and the past as an effect of narration rather than its cause or origin.

Attention to the repetition of this temporal structure also enables a re-vision of Wordsworthian procedures in *Jane Eyre* and *Villette* and a reading of the formal transformations in these novels as significant "failures" to make sense in the interest of "making present" the functioning of narrative processes.

Jane Eyre re-views the superimposition of consciousnesses to very different ends or effects than Wordsworth: the text does not posit (sexual) identity as pre-existing representation. At the same time, it insists, by multiplying the number of superimposed consciousnesses, that any representation is open to further revision and that some elements will remain unassimilated to the prevailing system. Moreover, ironic prefiguration transforms the superimposition of consciousnesses into an oscillation between narrative levels that undermines the tendency to privilege the narrator's perspective as it implicates both the reader and the characters in the retroactive construction of the meaning of the past.

Nevertheless, *Jane Eyre* does maintain some sense of hierarchy: the proliferation of superimposed consciousnesses still locates self-difference between distinct moments in the past rather than within a single moment. The elements that resist assimilation to the narrative system are, for the most part, associated with minor characters, whose reintroduction simultaneously preserves chronological order. And insofar as ironic prefiguration only retroactively subverts chronology, it does not overtly call into question the narrator's integrity. In each case the subversive tension occurs between narrative levels.

Villette is a much bolder revision of both Wordsworthian narrative and *Jane Eyre* because deferred action (or repetition of structure), which proves indispensible to the analysis of each narrative process, occurs on the level of narration. The procedures attain new meaning through this repetition with a difference.

Thus the construction of a counterplot disrupts the chronological/causal order of Lucy's story rather than merely resists assimilation to it. The displacement of the superimposition of protagonist's and narrator's consciousnesses by a juxtaposition of perspectives that foregrounds their incompatibility results in an interrogation of perspective per se, specifically its function in the recovery of the past through retrospection. Multiple representations of the narrator's (rather than a character's) past elude recuperation through retrospection and undermine the linear conception of causality it implies. Reintroduction, which is repeated more often and for more characters in this novel, also defers their identification. As a result, the device deconstructs identity as well as undermines the trust in sequence to reveal meaning that is basic to narrative. Finally, the deferral of identification converts the very act of reading from an interpretation of the text's meaning into an analysis of the processes that produce meaning.

Precisely to the extent that *Villette* brings into relief the operation of deferred action on the level of narration, it "makes present" the structuring function of this temporality in disparate signifying practices. By diverting attention from meaning to performance, the text dis-covers the complicity of diverse discourses in reducing sexual difference to a binary opposition (or masculine self-differ-ence). At the same time, this "diversion" demonstrates that meaning is not fixed but subject to a process of displacement, or repetition with a difference (for displacement is governed by a metonymic logic based on contiguity, not resemblance). Thus the transposition of an element from one narrative level to another repeats its form in a different context and thereby radically transforms its meaning. Finally, insofar as the mechanics of each narrative process are laid bare through this "diversion," *Villette* also "makes present" the discontinuities in disparate signifying practices, which allows a mapping of potential sites of local intervention that make room for yet another reading. In short, there is more in *Villette* than "hunger, rebellion and rage" to make it "dis-agree-able"—there is the possibility of re-vision![27]

Pace University

NOTES

1. Jacobus, for example, sets Victorian realism in opposition to Romanticism, which she aligns with the Gothic. In contrast, my argument associates Romanticism with realism because they both assume an epistemology that operates through retrospec-tion, even though Romanticism is not as fully committed to this model of conscious-ness. The temporal dimension is much less significant in the Gothic mode (as defied by Sedgwick and Homans). Consequently, narrative theory is much more crucial to my work than to Jacobus's analysis, which focuses on the function of the Imaginary as elaborated by Lacan. Accordingly, her reading of key aspects of *Villette* differs radically from mine: for example, Lucy's reticence about her recognition of Dr. John as Graham is for Jacobus non-functional and "disconcerting" (45), and all the mirror images are the same in her reading—instances of "representational illusion which denies the lack of absence central to all signification" (51).
2. This distinction of narrative levels depends on the opposition constructed by Benven-iste between discourse and history, which is based on the presence or absence of a narrator. The distinction is, ultimately, a linguistic one made on the basis of tense and person: history uses the aorist tense and third person; discourse is marked by the present, future, and perfect tenses and the use of the pronouns I/you. History suppresses its source, seems to issue from nowhere, no one; its credibility depends on this supposed "objectivity." Discourse, inasmuch as it specifies a source, raises the issue of its credibility by specifying a point of view located in a particular context (Benveniste 208–09).
3. See, for example, the description of Gothic narrative structure in Bayer-Berenbaum (84–87).
4. My argument assumes (1) Ermarth's elaboration of the epistemological premises of empiricism and the conventions used to express them in realistic fiction and (2) de Man's discussion of temporality in Romantic poetry in "The Rhetoric of Temporal-ity" and "Wordsworth and Hölderlin." And my definitions of realism and Romanti-cism suggest a spectrum of positions ranging from a rigorous interrogation to com-plete denial of the temporal predicament underlying empiricism. (No text is a pure

expression of a single mode.) In this scheme Gothic narrative, which grounds knowledge in perception, recognizes no temporal dilemma and therefore ultimately poses no challenge to empiricism. And, as we shall see, insofar as Romantic narrative devices function to conceal the temporal breach, they fail to realize their potential to critique empirical premises and approximate the conventions of realism.

5. The Wordsworth poems referred to are, respectively, "Tintern Abbey," "The Idiot Boy," "Resolution and Independence," "The Old Cumberland Beggar," and "A Slumber Did My Spirit Seal." Having demonstrated that a similar process towards literalization and death is registered in Jane Eyre's Gothic dreams about children, Homans argues that Jane is saved from fatality through various kinds of figuration. Though complementary, my argument shifts the focus to a (temporal) process occurring on a different level (narration).

6. Weber attributes Freud's failure to work out adequately the relation of formal, thematic, and causal factors in his theory of the uncanny to his treatment of castration as merely the content of a representation which succumbs to repression and then returns in identical form instead of as a structure. Weber proceeds to compensate for this inadequacy by himself elaborating a theory of the uncanny as a radical restructuring of experience that involves a certain structure of narration and, though Weber does not say so, the kind of temporal logic elaborated below in connection with the notion of deferred action. See esp. 1111–14 and 1132–33.

7. In a letter to Fliess (21 September 1897) Freud set forth the reasons why he could no longer believe in so many instances of actual seduction by the father, among them "that there is no 'indication of reality' in the unconscious, so that it is impossible to distinguish between truth and emotionally-charged fiction" and "that even in the most deep-reaching psychoses the unconscious memory does not break through, so that the secret of infantile experiences is not revealed even in the most confused states of delirium" (*Origins* 216). My entire discussion of deferred action is greatly indebted to Laplanche's elaboration of the concept, esp. in chapter 2.

8. Repression is thus the after-effect of consciousness conceived as a structure of retrospection and not vice versa.

9. In "Femininity" Freud writes, "it was only later that I was able to recognize in this phantasy of being seduced by the father the expression of the typical Oedipus complex in women" (106).

10. In a letter to Fliess (6 December 1896) Freud described this process of stratification: "The material in the shape of memory traces is from time to time subjected to rearrangement in accordance with fresh circumstances — is, as it were, transcribed. Thus what is essentially new in my theory is the thesis that memory is present not once but several times over, that is registered in various species of 'signs' " (*Origins* 173). Especially noteworthy is the use of the metaphor of rewriting to describe this psychical activity.

11. I have discussed this scenario in somewhat similar terms in "*The Professor*, Charlotte Brontë's Hysterical Text" (358–59) in conjunction with my analysis of Luce Irigaray's reading of the scene in "The Blind Spot of an Old Dream of Symmetry."

12. Although the following argument specifies Wordsworth's "Tintern Abbey" as the model of Romantic autobiographical narrative, this reference need not be applied in a strictly literal sense: I am well aware that Wordsworth did not invent the form (which Abrams has identified and described as "the greater Romantic lyric") and that virtually every Romantic poet attempted it. Therefore, many other poems — for example, Wordsworth's *Prelude*, a number of Coleridge's Conversation poems, Shelley's "Ode to the West Wind" and "Hymn to Intellectual Beauty," Keats's

"Ode on a Grecian Urn" — might have been cited as well insofar as all are concerned with interrogating the possibility of the poet's grounding his representations, that is, his recuperating a privileged origin. But I did choose "Tintern Abbey" because in it childhood experience is designated as the absent origin, it displays the paradigm in miniature form, and it articulates the temporal structure with an explicitness that makes it more readily accessible than in other poems.

13. The issue here is not how old Wordsworth the poet was when he wrote "Tintern Abbey" (he was 28); whatever the poet's chronological age, the speaker's anticipation of his own death in lines 148–49 ("If I should be where I no more can hear/ Thy voice, nor catch from thy wild eyes these gleams") makes him sound as if he were coming to the end of his life. Of course, death itself is an impossible ending in autobiography. Closure must occur at some arbitrarily chosen point and is always somewhat contrived. Hence the capacity of autobiography to call into question the "naturalness" and comprehensiveness of any narrative resolution. However, insofar as Wordsworth's speaker anticipates his own death, he does not exercise this capacity but rather creates an emotional distance from the story level (or past) that approximates the omniscient narration which is characteristic of realism.

14. I am indebted to Kroeber's observation that Brontë often uses this device. But his interpretation of it differs radically from mine: Kroeber argues that the device serves only to preserve narrative continuity (161).

15. Note that the sense of chronology is not simple and straightforward to begin with, for it is determined not by the order in which the events occur, but by the order in which Jane learns of the events.

16. To fully appreciate just what difference this privileging of the protagonist's perspective makes, it is worth comparing ironic prefiguration in *Jane Eyre* with the function of prefiguration in the drowned man episode in Book 5 of Wordsworth's *Prelude*. The closing lines of the passage explain that though Wordsworth was not even nine years old at the time, the sight of the ghastly face suddenly breaking the surface of the water did not strike him with terror because he had been prepared to confront such a spectacle by his reading of fairy tales and romances. Chase argues that these lines serve a recuperative function in that they re-figure the effaced figure of the man in the guise of prefiguration: for when the disfigured face emerges, it initially unsettles the literal/figurative opposition because it reveals that the literal is only *effaced* figure, not some original state that pre-exists figuration. But the closing lines cover up this discovery as they transform the drowned man into a figure of romance, which takes the form of a prefiguration, that is, the product of the boy's reading prior to the episode. Since prefiguration here is merely *asserted* by the mature speaker, not *enacted*, it functions to preserve chronological order and linear causality as it obscures both the speaker's role and the reader's implication in the retroactive construction of such a causal sequence.

17. The construction of a counterplot involves some violations of chronological order. For instance, in chapter 38 Lucy reports an interview with Paul, which Madame Beck and Père Silas interrupt just as he is about to tell her of his intended trip. The interview is described *after* Lucy hears Madame Beck's public announcement of Paul's departure, but it actually took place ten days before. The deferral of the interview enhances its function as a contrast to the account of Paulina's happy reunion with John in chapter 37. In contrast, the strategy in *Jane Eyre* is to underscore the function of characters as foils through the insistence of structure: for instance, the familial configuration of the Reeds is repeated by the Brocklehursts, the Ingrams, and the Riverses. But, as was noted above, the foil characters in *Jane Eyre* are not

equivalent to the sister in "Tintern Abbey" because they are not reduced to mere mirrors of Jane inasmuch as each has a distinct temporal structure that remains unassimilated to Jane's.

18. The refusal to apply a coherent perspective is evident also in those instances where the limitations of autobiographical narrative are transgressed and the narrator renders certain exchanges that suggest omniscience. For example, the secret consultation on the choice of a gift for Madame Beck's fête between Mlle. St. Pierre and Madame is reported by Lucy although she could not have witnessed it. Note that here the extension of the narrator's perspective beyond the conventionally defined "first-person" viewpoint functions not to project continuity of consciousness beyond the ending as in "Tintern Abbey" but to undermine the notion of the narrator's consciousness as fixed or centered.

19. The multiplicity of Jane's superimposed consciousnesses and the diversity of the foil characters' temporal structures do resist assimilation to a uniform system and undermine this authority, but implicitly for the most part. St. John, the East Indian missionary who measures time in terms of eternity, poses the strongest challenge to the authority of Jane's narration: he is given the last words of the novel. Bertha, on the other hand, is the exception among foil characters in that she is never temporally defined and never given a voice: she is incorporated into Rochester's history. (Hence the credibility of Spivak's argument that in this case the function of the foil character takes on a racial significance: the colonial subject's history is effaced in order to make Jane's possible.)

20. It is significant too that this is a cross-dressing nun. For as an effeminate man masquerading as a woman who has renounced her sexuality, s/he perfectly emblematizes what Garber describes as "not just another category crisis, but . . . a crisis of 'category' itself" (32). In other words, the nun makes visible a difference within that exceeds the model of difference organized around a set of paired oppositions, be they past/present, male/female, etc.

21. Reintroduction in *Villette* almost always involves a deferral of identification with respect to the reader, not just here, where it is explicitly acknowledged by the narrator. So what makes this the most flagrant instance of withholding information is that a "seeming inconsistency" in Dr. John's character is not exactly synchronized with a change in Lucy-actor's impressions "as at the time [she] felt it," that is, the strategy explicitly specified by the narrator to account for discrepancies in his presentation. It is worth asking in this connection why readers, who always comment on Lucy's lack of reliability, never seem to impeach Jane Eyre's, despite the fact that ironic prefiguration implicates the reader in a retroactive recognition of Jane-narrator's systematic withholding of information. In the earlier novel, however, the reader's access to knowledge *is* synchronized with Jane-actor's, which fosters a sense of confidence that is enhanced by Jane-narrator's sharing with the reader important information that she withholds even from her beloved Rochester (specifically about the mysterious summons). Moreover, the strategy of adhering to the protagonist's perspective is not spelled out as it is in *Villette*. Precisely because *Jane Eyre* does *not* call attention to this practice, the reader is less aware of any lapse.

22. Thus in her reading of *The Turn of the Screw*, Felman regards the metaphor of the title as a functional metaphor, that is, a metaphor describing the *rhetoric* of the text:

As a performative (and not a cognitive) figure of the ironic textual force of reversal and of chiasmus, of the subversion of the subject by the very irony of language, the "turn of the screw" — or *The Turn of the Screw* — *acts out*, indeed, the very narrative — or tale — of reading, as precisely *the story of the subversion of the reader*. (184; emphasis in original)

See also pp. 119 and 142–43 for other elaborations of transference as reading at the level of rhetoric. Note that this distinction of levels corresponds to the distinction with which my argument began: between the level of discourse or enunciation and the level of history or statement. See note 2.

23. See in this connection Lacan's discussion of the mirror stage (*Écrits* 2–4). In Lacan's analysis the formation of the "I" from an image at a distance makes identification simultaneous with an alienation of the subject from itself.

24. So, too, does Wordsworth's sister serve as his mirror: in "Tintern Abbey" he *sees his past* in her; she displaces his lost past experience (which he "cannot paint"); he thus interiorizes her as *his* memory and assumes she will repeat his experience in the future, which is to say corroborate the universality of *his* experience. In this exemplary poem the appropriation of the woman is accomplished through mirror logic conflated with the past/present polarity. Similarly, we have seen that in Freud's castration scenario the little girl serves as the boy's mirror: she reflects (repeats) his interpretation of castration as *her* deficiency and thereby confirms *his* wholeness and integrity.

25. The Heisenberg principle in quantum mechanics, which is also known as the uncertainty principle, states that it is impossible to ascertain that a particle (for example, an electron) is at the same time at a specified point and also moving with a specified velocity, for the more accurately the velocity is measured, the less accurately can its location be specified and vice versa.

26. In this connection Lacan writes, "the transference, *as operating mode*, cannot be satisfied with being confused with the *efficacity* of repetition, with the restoration of *what* is concealed in the unconscious, even with the *catharsis* of the unconscious *elements*" (*Fundamental Concepts* 143; emphasis added).

27. See Arnold's description of *Villette* in a letter to Mrs. Forster (14 April 1853): "Why is *Villette* disagreeable? Because the writer's mind contains nothing but hunger, rebellion and rage, and therefore that is all she can, in fact put into her book" (qtd. in Allott 201).

WORKS CITED

Abrams, M. H. "Structure and Style in the Greater Romantic Lyric." *From Sensibility to Romanticism: Essays Presented to Frederick A. Pottle*. Ed. Frederick W. Hilles and Harold Bloom. New York: Oxford UP, 1965. 527–60.

Allott, Miriam, ed. *The Brontës: The Critical Heritage*. London: Routledge & Kegan Paul, 1974.

Bayer-Berenbaum, Linda. *The Gothic Imagination: Expansion in Gothic Literature and Art*. Rutherford, NJ: Fairleigh Dickinson UP, 1982.

Benveniste, Emile. *Problems in General Linguistics*. Trans. Mary Elizabeth Meek. Coral Gables: U of Miami P, 1971.

Brontë, Charlotte. *Jane Eyre*. Ed. Jane Jack and Margaret Smith. Oxford: Clarendon P, 1969.

———. *Villette*. Ed. Herbert Rosengarten and Margaret Smith. Oxford: Clarendon P, 1984.

Chase, Cynthia. "The Accidents of Disfiguration: Limits to Literal and Rhetorical Reading in Book V of *The Prelude*." *Studies in Romanticism* 18 (1979): 547–65.

De Man, Paul. "The Rhetoric of Temporality." *Blindness and Insight: Essays in the Rhetoric of Contemporary Criticism*. 1971; 2nd revised ed. Minneapolis: U of Minnesota P, 1983. 187–228.

————. "Wordsworth and Hölderlin." *The Rhetoric of Romanticism*. New York: Columbia UP, 1984. 47–65.

Ermarth, Elizabeth Deeds. *Realism and Consensus in the English Novel*. Princeton: Princeton UP, 1983.

Felman, Shoshana. "Turning the Screw of Interpretation." *Literature and Psychoanalysis, The Question of Reading: Otherwise*. Ed. Shoshana Felman. Baltimore: Johns Hopkins UP, 1982. 94–207.

Freud, Sigmund. "Femininity." *New Introductory Lectures*. Trans. James Strachey. New York: Norton, 1965. 99–119.

————. *The Origins of Psycho-analysis: Letters to Wilhelm Fliess. Drafts and Notes: 1887–1902*. Trans. Eric Mosbacher and James Strachey. New York: Basic Books, 1954.

————. "Some Psychical Consequences of the Anatomical Distinction Between the Sexes" (1925). *The Standard Edition of the Complete Psychological Works of Sigmund Freud*. Trans. and ed. James Strachey, Alex Strachey, and Alan Tyson. London: Hogarth, 1953–74. 19: 248–58.

————. "The 'Uncanny' " (1919). *The Standard Edition of the Complete Psychological Works of Sigmund Freud*. Trans. and ed. James Strachey. London: Hogarth, 1953–74. 17: 217–52.

Garber, Marjorie. *Vested Interests: Cross-Dressing and Cultural Anxiety*. New York: Routledge, 1992.

Homans, Margaret. "Dreaming of Children: Literalization in *Jane Eyre* and *Wuthering Heights*." *The Female Gothic*. Ed. Juliann E. Fleenor. Montréal: Eden P, 1983. 257–79.

Irigaray, Luce. *Speculum of the Other Woman*. 1974. Trans. Gillian C. Gill. Ithaca: Cornell UP, 1985.

Jacobus, Mary. "The Buried Letter: Feminism and Romanticism in *Villette*." *Women Writing and Writing About Women*. Ed. Mary Jacobus. New York: Barnes & Noble, 1979. 42–60.

Johnston, Ruth D. "*The Professor*: Charlotte Brontë's Hysterical Text, or Realistic Narrative and the Ideology of the Subject from a Feminist Perspective." *Dickens Studies Annual* 18 (1989): 353–80.

Kroeber, Karl. *Styles in Fictional Structure: The Art of Jane Austen, Charlotte Brontë, George Eliot*. Princeton: Princeton UP, 1971.

Lacan, Jacques. *Écrits: A Selection*. 1966. Trans. Alan Sheridan. New York: Norton, 1977.

————. *The Four Fundamental Concepts of Psycho-analysis*. 1973. Trans. Alan Sheridan. New York: Norton, 1978.

Laplanche, Jean. *Life and Death in Psychoanalysis*. 1970. Trans. Jeffrey Mehlman. Baltimore: Johns Hopkins UP, 1976.

Sedgwick, Eve Kosofsky. "The Character in the Veil: Imagery of the Surface in the Gothic Novel." *PMLA* 96.2 (1981): 255–70.

Spivak, Gayatri Chakravorty. "Three Women's Texts and a Critique of Imperialism." *Critical Inquiry* 12.1 (1985): 243–61.

Weber, Samuel. "The Sideshow, or: Remarks on a Canny Moment." *MLN* 88 (1973): 1102–33.

Wordsworth, William. *The Pedlar, Tintern Abbey, The Two-Part Prelude*. Ed. Jonathan Wordsworth. Cambridge: Cambridge UP, 1985.

"IN A STATE BETWEEN": A READING OF LIMINALITY IN *JANE EYRE*

By Mark M. Hennelly, Jr.

> Van Gennep has shown that all rites of transition are marked by three phases: separation, margin (or *limen*), and aggregation. The first phase of separation comprises symbolic behavior signifying the detachment of the individual or group either from an earlier fixed point in the social structure or a set of cultural conditions (a "state"); during the intervening liminal period, the state of the ritual subject (the "passenger") is ambiguous; he passes through a realm that has few or none of the attributes of the past or coming state; in the third phase the passage is consummated. The ritual subject, individual or corporate, is in a stable state once more and, by virtue of this, has rights and obligations of a clearly defined and "structural" type, and is expected to behave in accordance with certain customary norms and ethical standards.
> — Victor Turner, "Betwixt and Between: The Liminal Period in *Rites de Passage*"

ALTHOUGH ROCHESTER ASSURES JANE after she spends the night watching over the wounded Richard Mason in *Jane Eyre* (1847) that *he* speaks "without parable" (248; ch. 20), this entire episode, like so many in the text, reads like what the anthropologist Victor Turner calls "the most arcane episodes of the liminal period" ("Betwixt and Between" 107). Before relating Turner's ritualistic theory to the world of *Jane Eyre*, however, we should first simply recall some of the liminal details from chapter 20 to illustrate how semantically appropriate a Turnerian approach might be to the deep structures and antistructures of the novel. This enigmatic episode itself generally describes Jane's night-long vigil with "the stranger, Mason" (238; ch. 20) after his unexplained ordeal while both remain "in the third story, fastened into one of its mystic cells" — in fact, the mysterious threshold to Bertha's "room just above [Jane's own] chamber ceiling." The reader of this strange interlude may first be struck by the sheer number of its thresholds and margins: a "curtain" in the initial sentence, doors, gates, windows, walls, and portals later in the chapter when fifteen such interfaces appear in the space of a page, and finally the "wicket" emphasized at the end of the chapter when Rochester advises Jane to return to the house. The reader may further be impressed by all the haunting references to the "fateful third story" itself, particularly since a web of allusions gradually appears linking the "sequestered mansion" (French *maison*) with Bertha *Mason*, her hysterical "story," and its symbolic relationship to Jane's own ancestral history.[1]

In fact, this portentous threshold to the "mysterious chamber" reads like a metonymic "metacommentary" featuring its twelve panelled cabinet crowned by "an ebon crucifix and a dying Christ" (239; ch. 20). But even more provocatively it poses a teasing relationship: "now St. John's long hair that waved; and anon the devilish face of Judas" in conjunction with the prophetic enigmas of Revelation: "what mystery, that broke out, now in fire and now in blood?" The puns on *eyrie* and *error* also expand the mystery of Jane's self-processing progress through serially panelled boundaries as do the transformative values of the equally reflexive lunar cycle and calendrical round: "a succession of April showers and gleams, followed by a lovely spring morning," which all liminally nurture "a half-blown rose" (245; ch. 20) when Jane rises from Mason's sickbed (and near deathbed). Consequently, and without benefiting from much specific interpretation, this inset piece, like so many in the text, seems to expand physical (if not metaphysical) boundaries, challenge social classifications, test psychological limits, and thus poise Jane (and her reader) precariously on the edge between familiar and alien values. Summarizing this betwixt and between, indeterminate marginality, Rochester notes: "To live, for me, Jane, is to stand on a crater-crust which may crack and spue fire any day." And yet violating norms or "overleaping an obstacle of custom" paradoxically also appears to promise "regeneration of life."

Since such transitional and transformative motifs significantly characterize much of Brontë's text, Turner's applied theory of the *limina* or threshold may uniquely help us identify, interpret, and coordinate such a processual phenomenology. In her general study of some of these concerns in Brontë's fiction, Sarah Gilead has rightly suggested that "*Jane Eyre* is perhaps the paradigmatic liminal novel of the Victorian period" (*Texas* 303), but her broad approach needs to be grounded in a more specific and sustained application of Turner's own metalanguage, particularly as it originates in his seminal essay "Betwixt and Between: The Liminal Period in *Rites de Passage*."[2] And such a task is what I would like to attempt in this essay by paying special attention to the ambiguous, interstructural state of Jane the neophyte, to the related notion of antistructural communitas, to the reflexive value of metatexts like Jane's watercolors and the charades, to sacra or ritualistic symbols (particularly Bertha herself as a personification of sacred *gnoses*, as well as the mirrors and veils which interrelate her and Jane), and finally to a more extended liminal reading of chapter 23, the betrothal scene at Midsummer Eve, which itself profoundly rehearses Jane's liminal conflicts and thus also reflects many of the reading enigmas already introduced in chapter 20.

Before exploring these issues, however, I would like to say a few words about Turner's life and his humanistic, syncretistic, and even belletristic innovations toward what he frequently called "a new processual anthropology." Turner (1920–83) was born in Glasgow, Scotland, and after early training in English literature,[3] he earned his doctorate in Anthropology from the University of Manchester where he was influenced by the dialectic of Marx and the related diachronic or process model of social anthropology developed by Max Gluckman. This early discipleship in the so-called Manchester School of Anthropology quickly led him to break with what he saw as the too confining conventions of British Functionalism and the French Structuralism of Lévi-Strauss. As he later wrote in "The Anthropology of Performance," "For years, I have dreamed of a liberated anthropology" (177), one which recognizes that "structure is always ancillary to, dependent on, secreted from process" (190). His habit of being "prejudiced against system-building" (206) prompted him to pass serially through several different seminal thresholds: the ritualism and comparative symbology of folklorist Arnold van Gennep, the lived-experience philosophy of Wilhelm Dilthey, the fascination with ludic phenomena of Brian Sutton-Smith, the flow theory of the behavioral scientist Mihaly Csikszentmihalyi, the experimental theater and dramatic therapy of performatologist Richard Schechner, and just prior to his death the radically new studies in neurobiology and the bicameral and triune brain. Still, as Turner loved to say, his real passion was "man [and woman] alive" (*From Ritual to Theatre* 46), the town (or field) rather than the gown, whether a given community staged tribal rituals in Zambia, Christian pilgrimages in Western Europe, or carnival inversions in Brazil. To satisfy this passion fully, Turner realized that fieldwork itself symbolized a kind of pilgrimage (*per agros*), that he must borrow freely from these shrines of interest, and that to offer praise to his real ideal, he must maintain a kind of divine madness within his human methodology. As he characteristically and (for me) charismatically suggests, "I am frankly in the exploratory phase just now" (*From Ritual to Theatre* 55). And as we can now trace through *Jane Eyre*, several of these seminal modes are themselves latent in his major contribution to anthropology, his development of liminal or threshold theory.

TO BEGIN, THEN, in "Betwixt and Between" Turner adopts Arnold van Gennep's use of the *liminal* as the starting point for his own diagnosis of *neophytes* or " 'interstructural' human beings" and *rites of passage* or the "interstructural situation" (93). A single excerpt from van Gennep's classic *Rites of Passage* (1909) should suggest its own relevance to the threshold experiences and encounters we have already witnessed in *Jane Eyre*:

it seems important to me that the passage from one social position to another is identified with a *territorial passage*, such as the entrance into a village or a house, the movement from one room to another, or the crossing of streets and squares. This identification explains why the passage from one group to another is so often ritually expressed by passage under a portal, or by an "opening of the doors." (192)

Turner's summary of processual "transitions between states" (93) is cited above; of the three stages comprising the ritual process, he devotes his essay to the second, of "margin or (*limen*)" (94). During liminality, stable structural values are reversed if not subverted as the neophyte tests his or her socially-conditioned value system by challenging its cultural norms in the often corrective context of the *mundus inversus*. From little Jane's immersion into the world of the text at the threshold of Gateshead, she serially passes through such an initiatory process until she finally appears to reenter structured society at the end of the novel.

The idea of such a reentry can itself be challenged, though, by invoking Turner's later theory of the *liminoid*, a concept he developed to account for the existential lifestyles and desacralized, performative genres surviving in industrial or at least post-feudal cultures. In such societies, "perpetual liminality" may be more satisfying to estranged individuals who have lost the security blanket of common cultural norms.[4] Further, Jane's own process of initiation seems played out against the background of what Turner calls "social dramas" or "units of aharmonic or disharmonic process, arising in conflict situations." Such dramas themselves exhibit four stages: *breach*, the "deliberate nonfulfillment of some crucial norm" like Mrs. Reed's rejection of Jane; "a phase of mounting *crisis*" like the "mystery" at Thornfield; "*redressive action*" such as Rochester's courtship of Jane, which may or may not ultimately heal the breach; and finally either the "*reintegration* of the disturbed social group" or "the social recognition and legitimization of irreparable schism between the contesting parties" (*Dramas, Fields, and Metaphors* 37–41), which contingencies can help to explain both the marginalized social opportunities at Ferndean and the problematized "schism" between Jane and (the religion of) St. John. And though further development of the social drama is not within the scope of this essay, such a process may generally be used to clarify the dynastic and kinship interactions within and between the Eyre, Rochester, and Mason clans.

At any rate, the text repeatedly invokes liminal phrasing and marginal figures to describe and diagnose Jane's "transforming process" (116; ch. 10) as she passes through a world "turned topsy-turvey" (417; ch. 34). For instance, when she unconsciously writes "the words 'JANE EYRE' " in "the ravished margin of [her] portrait-cover," while still assuming the "alias" of Jane Elliott, this liminal act marginally "proves [her] identity" (407–08; ch. 33). Or again, before their planned marriage, Rochester pointedly asks Jane, "Are you apprehensive of the new sphere you are about to enter? of the new life into which you are passing?'' (307; ch. 25). And then after she experiences at midnight ''the mystery of that awful visitant'' Bertha, Rochester describes Jane as having entered ''a state between sleeping and waking [when] you noticed her entrance'' (312–13). For Turner, every such entrance *entrances* the ''passenger'' or neophyte, just as Rosamond's ''entrance'' provocatively moves Rivers to reveal that ''my senses are entranced'' (393, 399; ch. 32). And we should remember that according to the dynamics of liminality, no matter how much Jane insists upon the bedrock fixity of her selfhood or ''my unblighted self'' (433; ch. 34), her ''transforming process'' remains a continuous ''flow'' so that her identity is ever in a phase of becoming and never locked in a state of being or what Chase calls her ''illusion of a substantial self'' (75).

In fact, at every entrance and every ''ceremony of parting'' (254; ch. 21), the liminal period and porch seem emphasized — and usually emphasized by the very words *interval* and (especially) *threshold*, which reflects the recurrent ''fascination of the locality'' (376; ch. 30) in *Jane Eyre*. For example, after Jane ''brushed up'' on her ''map of England'' (120; ch. 10) before parting from Lowood and its own ''barriers of separation from the living world'' (131; ch. 11), she intuits that ''A phase of my life was closing to-night, a new one opening to-morrow: impossible to slumber in the interval; I must watch feverishly while the change was being accomplished'' (121; ch. 10). As she approaches Thornfield for the first time, Jane makes a point of emphasizing that ''I stepped over the threshold'' and further remarks at the way the hills seemed ''to embrace Thornfield with a seclusion'' (130–31; ch. 11), which may mark the locale itself as what Turner calls the ritualistic ''seclusion site'' (98). After her near collision with Rochester at twilight on Hay Lane, the entranced Jane muses that '''I did not like re-entering Thornfield. To pass its threshold was to return to stagnation'' (147; ch. 12), which sentiment at this juncture ironically betrays the neophyte's ritualistic innocence. When she flees Rochester and Thornfield, Jane again emphasizes that ''my heart momentarily stopp[ed] its beat at that threshold'' (347; ch. 27). Much later after she reflects upon the value of what we will later term her shared *communitas* with Rochester, it seems clear that she has internalized the significance of passing through *limina* or frontier thresholds and thereby reaping the internal rewards of *antistructural* existence: ''I could never rest in communication with strong, discreet, and refined minds, whether male or female, till I had passed the outworks of conventional reserve, and crossed the threshold of confidence, and won a place by their heart's very hearthstone'' (400; ch. 32).

But we anticipate ourselves. For now we might simply conclude our survey of Brontë and Turner's shared liminal rhetoric by noting, as Turner himself does, that we are not simply plugging values into theoretical circuits — liminal motifs are often as indeterminate for the reader or observer as they are for the participating characters or tribal initiates. For example, a ''Guardian'' Master usually controls each liminal precinct and requires what Turner describes as "complete authority and complete submission" (99) from his or her neophytes. However, during liminality definitive boundaries dissolve, making it profoundly difficult to distinguish between autocratic mentors and tormentors, especially since the threshold itself was originally a place for "threshing" or "thrashing" ripe grain. Rochester and Rivers mutually reflect this kind of crucial confusion in the way that they almost identically deliver the formal pronouncements of ritual Masters, suggesting that both may be tormenting mentors. For instance, Rochester instructs Jane: "you[,] neophyte, . . . have not passed the porch of life, and are absolutely unacquainted with its mysteries" (167; ch. 14), while Rivers similarly demands "a neophyte's respect and submission to his hierophant" (433; ch. 34). And Jane's liminal conflicts, betwixt and between self-submission and self-sovereignty, seem so deeply ingrained that one could even argue that she suffers from a case of "arrested liminality": "I know no medium: I never in my life have known any medium in my dealings with positive, hard characters, antagonistic to my own, between absolute submission and determined revolt" (426; ch. 34). Then again, in *limonoid* (derituralized or "deliminalized") cultures, the rubrics of liminality have so destabilized under institutionalizing pressures — or at least have decayed to such an extent, — that the neophyte discovers the time-honored ritualistic patterns no longer apply, and one must create a private mythology. In fact, in this existential wasteland, it may even be that the third phase of aggregation or return to society must be rejected in favor of the extended if not perpetual outlawry of antistructural alienation and also, paradoxically, of prolonged communitas between neophytes. In this reading, Jane again seems not only right to challenge St. John, her liminoid jailer, and his brand of love and duty, but she must challenge him — just as she and Rochester must ultimately remain on the margin of society to preserve their dearly won communitas, which uniquely allows them to exchange or alternate master/neophyte roles.[5] At any rate, a liminal reading of *Jane Eyre* tends to deconstruct itself by reflexively privileging such undecidable and problematized values.

The correspondences between the concerns of Turner's essay and those of Brontë's text are rather remarkable. And I have tried to paraphrase Turner's process model to account for transformations in the text which seem to me to be quite similar. But Turner's representation of the liminal process may be applied even more specifically. His diagnosis of the neophyte's ambiguous, interstructural statuslessness and role as a socially "invisible" ("Betwixt and Between" 95) non-entity recalls Brocklehurst's notion of Jane as "a little castaway — not a member of the true flock, but evidently an interloper and alien" (98; ch. 7). It is even closer, however, to Jane's own insightful third–person account of her depreciated but now potential selfhood: "She did not exist: she would not be born till to-morrow" (303; ch. 25). Indeed, in this particular instance, Jane is playing with the role possibilities of her future status as Mrs.

Rochester; and, for Turner, liminality is always played out in this subjunctive mood, "a realm of pure possibility" (97), which allows the neophyte the freedom to juggle hypotheses and court antistructural values. And the text is usually very emphatic in its subjunctive displays of liminality. For example, Rivers emphasizes his family's (temporarily) lost inheritance because "it forces rather strongly on the mind the picture of what *might have been* . . . and contrasts it somewhat too vividly with what *is*" (383; ch. 30, Brontë's emphases). Jane similarly toys with "thoughts of what might, could, would, and should be, and that *ere* long" (411; ch. 33, emphasis added) when she reconsiders the effect of the same patrilineal inheritance on herself — just as the reader may consider the potential of one more self-identifying pun in the text and what *ere*'s suggestion of postponed gratification may have to do with Jane's liminal identity. (The reader may even consider the related, suppressed subjunctive possibilities of *eyre* — a tour or pilgrimage through several different stadial precincts.)

During "life-crises" ("Betwixt and Between" 94), the liminal subjunctive does not, then, answer questions so much as it questions answers, and grammatically or even grammatologically, it rewrites the declarations and commands of the indicative and imperative moods. When in a more subtle instance of such subjunctivity Jane responds to Rochester's "mysterious summons" — "near midnight" — as her "soul wandered from its cell," she also begins to echo his *wondering* about the play of his desire: "the alpha and omega of my heart's wishes." When she and Rochester thereafter "entered the wood" (471–73; ch. 38) at Ferndean, they both figuratively or homophonically also enter the *would* (as the Gnat similarly suggests to Alice in *Through the Looking Glass*, Carroll 219–20). This subjunctive modality defies the logic-chopping strictures and structures of courting customs and suggests rather the liminal "wilderness or wood" in Rochester's ballad: "But wide as pathless was the space / That lay our lives between" (300; ch 24).

We should note that near the end of his life, particularly in the essay "Body, Brain, and Culture," Turner discusses the so-called "limbic system" that nurtures such subjunctive and sub-liminal material: "an evolutionarily ancient part of the brain concerned with emotions, cradled in or near the fringes of the cortex." When Turner emphasizes that "the highest and newest portion of the cerebral cortex has by no means detached itself from [this] ancient, 'primitive' region" (252–53), we might infer that the telepathic bonds linking Rochester and Jane throughout the text verify this limbic system. Such bonds are particularly activated during the provocative "mysterious summons,"[6] a kind of subjunctive call to adventure or to the deepest antistructures of liminality. As Turner discovers liminality in the collective Eleusinian Mysteries of the Great Mother in "Betwixt and Between," so too in *Jane Eyre* he might have found that the liminal and "neuronal pathways linking the limbic system of the midbrain (the old mammalian brain) with parietal and frontal areas of the right hemisphere"

("Body, Brain, and Culture" 267) may be associated with the mysterious summons of synchronicity. Turner even associates the "structures of the limbic system" with one of his favorite archetypes, the "milk tree," which invokes a "painful initiation ritual, of separation from the archetypal power of the Great Mother." This kind of rite, symbolically suggested by "the mighty Milky Way" in *Jane Eyre* (351; ch. 28), dramatizes "the relationship between the novice and her own mother" and "the novice's desire to be fully a woman" ("Body, Brain, and Culture" 271). Whether one relates such ideas to the Milky Way, the sacral chestnut tree, or "lunar symbolism" in the text, they do suggest that "the matrilineage of the girl novice," that is, of Jane herself, is as subjunctively represented in *Jane Eyre* as her patrilineage is indicatively and imperatively represented. Moreover, this maternal lineage significantly gives birth to both female and male desire: "the desire of the mature women to add a recruit to their number, the desire of a lineage for replenishment, the future bridegroom's desire for the novice" ("Body, Brain, and Culture" 270). Thus, the cloven halves of the chestnut tree, especially as circumscribed by the full-bodied moon, finally and figuratively "are green and vigorous" again with the certain promise that young "plants will grow about [the] roots" (469; ch. 37) or more subtly with the subjunctive desire for a radical "regeneration of life" (247; ch. 20).

But liminal detachment or death seems a prerequisite for such a rebirth, and for Turner the neophyte's consequent "condition is one of ambiguity and paradox, a confusion of all the customary categories" ("Betwixt and Between" 97). This absence of distinction or even distinctiveness during liminality is initially suggested by the dark or drab color of the neophyte's ceremonial vestments (98), which recalls Jane's usual colorless, grey attire. For Turner, further ambiguity appears in imagery of "tombs and wombs" (99), which recurs throughout *Jane Eyre*, perhaps most crucially in Helen Burns's epitaph *Resurgam* and in Jane's interpretation of dreams of infants as prophecies of death (249; ch. 21). Socially, Jane's liminal ambiguity is evident in her incongruous role as a *governess* who seems to govern almost nothing but initiates, in fact, "*have* nothing" (98), just as Jane, later a mendicant, admits that "poverty for me was synonymous with degradation" (56; ch. 3). And if the neophyte is considered polluted and "unclean" (97) because she defies social classifications, such degradation certainly helps to explain Blanche Ingram's antipathy to the anathematized race of governesses. Psychologically, the neophyte's lack of status is reflected ambiguously in "the symbolism both of androgyny and sexlessness" (98); just so, Jane's "man's vigorous brain" and "woman's heart" (433; ch. 34) may imply androgyny, while her rejection of "feminine" displays can suggest sexlessness. Once again, then, in order to be liminally reborn, one must first die to the old values just as Jane appears "dying at [Rivers's] threshold" (411; ch. 33).

"Deep friendships between novices" are a significant benefit of liminality, and as we have already indicated, Turner later in his career calls such "comradeship" *communitas* (see, for example, *The Ritual Process*). This bond is characterized by "familiarity, ease and . . . mutual outspokenness" (100–01), qualities Jane repeatedly enjoys in her several interstructural relationships. Thus, phrasing like "sympathetic communion" (227; ch. 19), "glimpse of communion" (281; ch. 23), "community of vitality" (304; ch. 25), and "cord of communion" (280; ch. 23) helps articulate communitas in *Jane Eyre*; novices like Jane and Helen Burns can freely be themselves without rehearsing institutionally scripted and structured roles. As Jane insists, "I will be myself" (288; ch. 24). When Jane encounters what Turner would describe as "critical moments of transition" (94), like her entry into Moor House, and moves past the Guardian Elder to the circle of neophytes, here represented by Diana and Mary, she invariably experiences "sympathy" and appears anointed with "balm-like emotion." Further, her ambiguous status liminally forces her to assume the alias of apparent Otherness, Jane Elliott, even though her reflexive, riddling initials (like Currer Bell's) remain the same and translate into her familiar French as an accurate acronym for her selfhood — *J. E.*: "now that I had once crossed the threshold of this house, and once was brought face to face with its owners, I felt no longer outcast, vagrant, and disowned by the wide world. I dared to put off the mendicant — to resume my natural manner and character. I began once more to know myself" (363; ch. 28).

The crucial interplay between institutionalized structures and individualized or gnostic (or even natural) antistructures in *Jane Eyre* is generally clear to most readers because it recurs so insistently, whether staged between Jane's bicameral judgment and feeling (265; ch. 21) or conscience and passion (325; ch. 27) or within Rivers's characteristic conflict: "what struggle there was in him between Nature and Grace in this interval" (438; ch. 35). In the text's "topsy-turvy," dialectical world of liminality, the two passwords which most significantly cue the repeated motif of "Antipodes" (451; ch. 36) or antistructure are *contrast* and *cross*. In fact, "the force of contrast" (437; ch. 35) animates almost every page, and usually it involves an "overwhelming contrast" (466; ch. 37). Jane's own microcosmic "strange contrasts" (340; ch. 27) even seem to reflect the macrocosmic "war of earthly elements" (265; ch. 21), just as Turner finds that liminal transformation "is bound up with biological and meteorological rhythms" (93).

Analogously Jane's "strange contrasts" appear projected on her apparently contrasting suitors — the structure-bound, saintly Rivers and the antistructural rebel Rochester — even though, in a sense, these suitors eventually crisscross values just as Jane seems to integrate her conflicting energies and achieve ritualistic fulfillment. One relevant "passage" even suggests a possible *Rosicrucian* synthesis since it pairs "the standard of the Cross" with "the Rose of the World" (nominally *Rosamond*, 401; ch. 32). But the shifting meanings of *cross*, which word functions as what Turner terms "a semantic molecule" (103), signify both the indeterminacy of the liminal period — "conveying no meaning" (359; ch. 28) like German to uninitiated Jane — and the re-enforced indoctrination of antistructural conflicts. At almost every juncture that Jane "crossed the threshold" (363; ch. 28), such paradoxes challenge her and her reader. And they appear most entrancing after she "crossed" (452; ch. 36) Rochester's offer of an antistructural liaison and flees to and through Whit*cross*, where "four roads meet." It is in passing through this crossroads, as a matter of fact, that Jane seems to reconcile (or does she problematize?) the crucial interstructural conflict between "the universal mother, Nature," here emblematized as "the mighty Milky Way," and "the might and strength of God" as the originary "Source of Life" (349–51; ch. 28). More subtly, the text's allusion to "the etymology of [*Thornfield*'s] designation" (131; ch. 11) may recall the legend that roses did not bear thorns until after the crucifixion, thereby suggesting those primary societies Turner writes about, whose secular and spiritual lives so deeply intermingle and whose antistructural rituals paradoxically confirm, by contesting, "the basic assumptions of their culture" (108).

We come now to the mysterious "communication of the *sacra*, the heart of the liminal matter" but at the same time "the crux of liminality" (Turner 102–03). Each of these "*sacerrima*"or "most sacred things" usually appears as "a multivocal symbol with a fan of referents ranging from life values, ethical ideas, and social norms, to grossly physiological processes and phenomena." Moreover, the sacra always reveal a "*gnosis*, mystical knowledge about the nature of things and how they came to be what they are" (107). In his later writing, Turner further relevantly discusses the sacral nature of performative "metacommentaries" like the Bridewell charades. In "Betwixt and Between," however, he is primarily concerned with specific "pictures and icons representing the journeys of the dead or the adventures of supernatural beings" (102–03) and particularly the (common literary) motifs of Otherness: monsters, mirrors, and masks. Such sacra suggest a significance for Jane's watercolors and their relationship to the Bridewell metaperformance; they also and more especially suggest the ultimate role of that most enigmatic personification of antistructural alterity, Bertha Mason and her own "rich, maternal relations" (405; ch. 33).

My purpose in discussing Jane's watercolors as sacra is not specifically hermeneutic but more generally exploratory. I want to suggest that the dynamics of liminal interstructurality help to clarify the processual values of her expressionistic but finally indeterminate triptych (157–58; ch. 13). Jane painted the pictures during "mid-summer days" when, in Rochester's view, she must have "exist[ed] in a kind of artist's dreamland," one which projects subjunctive shades — "'twilight,'" "half-submerged,'" "blank of meaning." What the reader encounters here is akin to Turner's evaluation of "Jakob Boehme, the German mystic whose obscure writings gave Hegel his celebrated dialectical 'triad,' [and who] liked to say that 'In Yea and Nay all things consist' " (97). If there is a dialectical or dialogic structure interrelating the processual visions of these sacra, it can be said to correspond generally to van Gennep and Turner's three stages of ritual. That is, it unfolds through a series of threshold or transitional moods developing from the death of the "drowned corpse" through the "rising . . . [of the] woman's shape to the bust" to the "shape which shape had none." Such processing could suggest an Hegelian passage through structured, antistructured, and restructured values or a Blakean growth through carnal, cognitive, and celestial stages (Blake's Zoas are one of Turner's favorite metaphors for self-transformation). And yet producing meaning also seems problematized according to whether the interpreter privileges "foreground" or background details, which themselves undecidably posit shifting "polar" or "antipodal" binary relationships.

But the real point of such metareadings if not inevitable misreadings of the watercolors is either that there seems to be no real determinate point, or that the point itself involves a reflexive return to basics, which in liminality and in the watercolors means a return to the body. In other words, the abyssal pictures, like all looking-glass sacra, are cyclically character-reflective and endlessly reader-reflexive. They "look" like so many overlapping Rorschachs for the inquiring, if not consciously self-identifying, textual and extratextual viewer alike. And they finally remind the reader, as Turner also does, that his or her own body mirrors, in fact, a body of knowledge: "the body is regarded as a sort of symbolic template for the communication of *gnosis*, mystical knowledge about the nature of things and how they came to be what they are. The cosmos may in some cases be regarded as a vast human body" in the sacral context of the "human anatomical paradigm" (107).

Such suggestions of interrelated cosmic and personal crises, of chiaroscuro or indeterminate modalities, and of ritualized transition and transformation are more than just insistent. They provide a significant heuristic pattern for other, lesser sacra. They even anticipate Jane's subsequent pictorial contrast of Blanche Ingram (and still later of Rosamond) with herself when she draws both portraits — the first re-presenting society's values, the second more ambiguously projecting antistructural values and implying a relationship between all pictures and mirrors, all portraits and self-portraits: "place the glass before you, and draw in chalk your own picture" (190; ch. 16). The sacral watercolors also provide prophetic value when they portentously preview (and compare and contrast) Rochester's offer of bracelets and rings (287; ch. 24) and Rivers's offer of an "incorruptible crown" (477; ch. 38), both of which are signets for the Guardian/giver and talismanic tests for the neophyte/receiver. And yet again the pictures obviously conceal more than they reveal, particularly in the "mystical power" they derive from being, as Turner would say, " 'painted in blackness' and 'in darkness' " (108–09). Opaque images like the "dark" cormorant,

"dark-blue" sky, "eyes [that] shone dark and wild," and "sable veil" consequently bedevil each canvas and illustrate the seminal chromatic scale Turner
finds associated with "fruitful darkness," the "black" king, and his mysterious
first wife in certain "First Fruits Rituals." Though he is specifically discussing
Swazi rituals here, Turner implies that the King and his Bride are archetypically
universal: "he is unapproachable, dangerous to himself and others. He must
cohabit that night with his first ritual wife (in a kind of 'mystical marriage' —
this ritual wife is, as it were, consecrated for such liminal situations)" (109).
Reflections of this kind lead naturally to considerations of the sacral charades,
of the mysterious and monstrous first wife Bertha and her connection with veils
and mirrors, and finally of chapter 23's own dramatization of a First Fruits
Ritual.

The analogous three "scenes" of the Bridewell charade replay many of the
sacra from the pictures but more clearly suggest a liminal "ceremony" punctuated by "considerable interval[s]" (212–13; ch. 18). Light and dark imagery,
rising and falling postures, bracelets and rings, water, and significant veils,
costumes, and draperies all reappear here. Furthermore, all (in)coherently con-
tribute to the processual "tableau of the whole," a gnostic and reflexive riddle
which spectators are invited to solve but which no one understands as a metacommentary upon the larger or "whole" social drama and psychodrama. Lady
Ingram believes that the neophyte Jane "looks too stupid for any game of [this]
sort," yet Jane's instruction has already begun under her "guardian" Rochester.
Consequently, she can solve the visual allegories quite easily, though she cannot
relate the visionary process of initiation to her own earlier dreamscapes or to
her own future and potentially transformative life crises. Hence the reader is
challenged to solve this narrative puzzle and to coordinate *brides, wells,* and
prisons for her. Marriage, baptism, and penal scapegoating all suggest liminal
rites and thus (though here almost paradoxically) antistructural values. Jane
nearly becomes a bride, which ceremonial charade could imprison Rochester
for bigamy and which would almost certainly imprison her developing selfhood,
just as Rivers's puritanical brand of conjugal "love" would denigrate her body,
or bride's well, and blight her soul.[7] Jane has already poured well water and
"baptized the couch" (180; ch. 15) in Rochester's bedroom during her own
initial *birth* or initiation into the sexual, social, and juridical or redressive values
of *Bertha.* And like the pictures, these charades or *sacerrima* are again further
prophetic of Jane's future love trials besides proleptic of Rochester's later
scorched face and hand at Ferndean. Here he also appears with "the begrimed
face" and "coat hanging loose from one arm" (213; ch. 18). In fact, his "dark
eyes and swarthy skin and Paynim features" further recall Turner's commentary
on the black king and the role of his shadowy first bride or "princess of the
patriarchal days" (212–13; ch. 29). And it is her ultimate gnostic role which
we can now perhaps better appreciate, realizing at the same time that Colonel

Dent's proclamation that "the charade was solved" is not absolutely true in terms of the mystery rites which seem to inform but never logically explain *Jane Eyre*. For Turner, again, such motifs are always "nonrational or nonlogical symbols" (108).

When we hear that "the *mere* name" of *Mason* strikes Rochester like "a thunderbolt" (240; ch. 20, emphasis added), the possibly suppressed pun in French may remind us of Bertha's association with motherhood and suggest that this archetypal madwoman in the attic is even more multifarious than Gilbert and Gubar's influential reading of "Jane's truest and darkest double" (360) indicates. Further, the shock value of the occult name, in a liminal sense, may remind us that Bertha Mason is a mirror of sacra which, reversing those in Masonic rites, reflects a secret sisterhood of inherited values. With her "bloated features" and "corpulent" shape, Bertha seems to provide a grotesque incarnation of somatic sacra. For Turner, such sacra are characteristically disproportionate, monstrous, mysterious, oneiric, and often therianthropic because "Monsters startle neophytes into thinking about objects, persons, relationships, and features of their environment [which] they have hitherto taken for granted" (105). Thus, this "big woman" or "clothed hyena" projects a "purple face" and performs "the gambols of a demon" (321–22; ch. 26) as she seems pregnant with Otherness: with possible antistructural, carnivalesque, and gnostic *différance* for Jane. As Hélène Cixous puts it in "The Laugh of the Medusa" — which seems almost written with Bertha and liminality in mind, though it mentions neither: "In women there is always more or less of the mother who makes everything all right, who nourishes, and who stands up against separation; a force that will not be cut off but will knock the wind out of the codes" (286). This mysterious life force exists "to shatter the framework of institutions, to blow up the law, to break up the 'truth' with laughter" (292) just like Bertha's own telltale "goblin" laugh.

Bertha's mercurial moods, her existential subjunctivity, not only unpredictably transfigure herself but also gradually transform Jane as Rochester's mysterious first wife becomes a "kind of human *prima materia*" (Turner 98) like the alchemical Mercurius or even the *monstrum* itself. Thus, she also becomes the catalyst for Jane's conversion, a mutable mask miming all the mystery elements of feminine creative (birthing) potential, all the gnoses in Jane's initiation process which so resemble those in "Hellenic mystery religions" (98). In *Dramas, Fields, and Metaphors*, Turner further suggests the kind of symbolic communitas fostered by Bertha, which we will also later note in connection with the Philomela-Procne mythology: this community is "the *fons et origo* of all structures and, at the same time, their critique. For its very existence puts all social structural rules in question and suggests new possibilities" (202). In this sense, when Rivers charges Jane with being "violent, unfeminine, and untrue" (438;

ch. 35), he is unwittingly revealing the antistructural matrix of the primordial feminine which Bertha reflects and then recovers in Jane.

Like Turner's "mythical and archetypal midwife" ("Betwixt and Between" 104), then, Bertha ambiguously represents role-possibilities ranging from Jane's suppressed sexual desire for Rochester to her hostility toward the masculine tyranny apparent in Rochester's sexual demands.[8] And her serial appearances seem to provoke and present the significant intervals in Jane's own transforming process. Bertha's sacral role as the "mirror self" and *mère* or mother self reflecting Jane's "mythical history" (103) is most crucial and excruciating right before the end of chapter 25. Here Jane experiences the midnight vision of a "shape" that "had never crossed my eyes within the precincts of Thornfield before" but which now appears conjured as a reflection "in the dark oblong glass" (311; ch. 25). As Turner writes of sacra, "the outstandingly exaggerated feature is made into an object of reflection" (103), and, in fact, "liminality [itself] may be partly described as a stage of reflection" (105). In *From Ritual to Theatre*, he further emphasizes that "mirror distortions of reflection provoke reflexivity" (105). Horrified by her own "object of [self-]reflection," Jane immediately calls out for "Sophie!" and then even thinks of "Grace Poole," but during liminal initiation neither institutionalized female wisdom nor Christian grace can protect against the mysterious summons of nature, the unconscious, or mythologizing matriarchy. Indeed, the "discolored face," "red eyes," and "black inflation of the lineaments" all suggest the momentarily debased chromatic scale of liminality. The "spectre's" obsession with the wedding "veil," her act of rending it in "two parts," and her "close" inspection of Jane's "face" imply much more than just the identity crisis incumbent upon a change in social status from the single to the married state. Such intent behavior also suggests a rupturing of innocence, a self-dividing world view, and even a penetration of the veil of appearances — the "web of mystification" (228; ch. 19) — if not some apparently apocalyptic vision of reality itself, which provokes what Turner calls the "ontological transformation" ("Betwixt and Between" 102) of the inner self.

But is traumatized Jane simply reborn to become another version of mad Bertha? In other words, how terminal and absolute are the implications behind "the mystery of that awful visitant"? Since this vision looks before and after in Jane's transforming process, we must remember that liminality, which Turner (citing J. A. McCulloch) characterizes as "hallucinations, night-terrors and dreams" (104), is ultimately but a prelude to final enlightenment. As Adèle is "the emblem of my past life" (314; ch. 25), Bertha likewise recalls that this is "the second time in [Janet's] life" that she "became insensible from terror" (311–12). The first occurred in the red room when such a "spirit" self also significantly appeared to Jane as she "had to cross before the looking-glass" while laboring under the passionate "mood of [a] revolted slave" like Bertha.

Thereafter, however, "the scapegoat of the nursery" (46–47; ch. 2) under the joint, if different, guardianship of Brocklehurst and Miss Temple and aided by her communitas bond with Helen Burns is able to quell such ancestral voices prophesying internal civil war. Again, on her potential wedding morn, she will wear a similar "veil," "peep" into the "mirror," and portentously behold the apparition of a subjunctive self or "visionary bride" (346; ch. 27): "a robed and veiled figure, so unlike my usual self that it seemed almost the image of a stranger" (315; ch. 26). Turner even suggests a possible relationship between these two ritualized events marking Jane's "developmental stages" (107), that is, "between the statics and dynamics of pollution situations" (97). Specifically, both liminal intervals, symbolically associated with the *mère* name[9] and mirror self, deal with the mysteries of blood and the way that "girls' puberty rites" (101) are "modeled on human biological processes" — here menstruation and sexual intercourse. In both such interstructural situations, the neophyte approximates the condition of Demeter-Persephone because she is deemed "filthy and identified with the earth." She is "stained black" or red because she is "regarded as (ritually) unclean," but since "the unclear is the unclean" (96–97), the liminal context again forcefully conjures *hysterical* Bertha's antistructural and gnostic role in Jane's transforming process.

Significantly, then, the "fateful third story" does not just reflect the historical domain of Bertha, it also houses hysterical (or uterine), maternal matter and the motif of what Dickens in *Dombey and Son* calls the "departed mother" (168; ch. 8), particularly as related to the mirror phase and its haunting importance throughout nineteenth-century fiction — especially *Jane Eyre*'s "unknown world of the departed" (48; ch. 2).[10] Jane's own matrilineal ancestors, as she discovers from the maternal Bessie, have paradoxically tried to ef*face*, but in effect have perpetuated, her link with her own birth mother. Her departed mother's history gives birth to conflicts which Jane seems symbolically (if not actually in the social drama) to inherit and which she attempts ritualistically to solve throughout her own history. Miss Reed had married Jane's father, "a poor clergyman," in an act of antistructural "disobedience," one "against the wishes" of family and friends. Jane's maternal grandfather consequently disinherited his daughter, who soon "caught the typhus fever" from her husband, and both perished from the same "infection" (58; ch. 3), suggesting the familiar link between passion and poison or disease. Then Jane's mother's brother (matrilineal uncle) adopted, for all intents and purposes, the "parentless infant." On his deathbed, Jane's uncle demands that his wife Mrs. Reed "pledge to stand in the stead of a parent to [this] strange child she could not love, and to see an uncongenial alien permanently intruded on her own family group" (48; ch. 2). Obviously, though, Mrs. Reed does not fulfill her promise to become a kind of liminal guardian — even though her husband had assumed what Lévi-Strauss terms *le privilège avunculaire* and acted as a *compère* or godfather to Jane.[11] And this version of the family romance recalls Turner's related discussion of "kinship-dominated societies": "In societies dominantly structured by kinship institutions, sex distinctions have great structural importance. Patrilineal and matrilineal moieties and clans, rules of exogamy, and the like, rest and are built up on these distinctions" (98).

To summarize, in "the secret of the red-room," the liminal chamber or seclusion site where her mother's brother died, hysterical Jane faces her "first recollections of existence" as she confronts not only the projected spectre of her avuncular Guardian but also her first objectified and therefore alienating vision of her face or self within the mirror's haunted limbus:

> I had to cross before the looking-glass; my fascinated glance involuntarily explored the depth it revealed. All looked colder and darker in that visionary hollow than in reality: and the strange little figure there gazing at me with a white face and arms specking the gloom, and glittering eyes of fear moving where all else was still, had the effect of a real spirit: I thought it like one of the tiny phantoms, half fairy, half imp. (45–46; ch. 2)

The half-and-half kind of liminality arrested in this reflected face seems ritualistically conjured by the memory of her matrilineal uncle, and yet no good-enough mother projects a self-clarifying female persona for Jane. And that is why the sacral mirror, at this stage, reflects no clear gnosis or self-compelling, if not self-creating, specular image. Generally, as we age and pass before a reflective surface, those of us familiar with our family's faces (and gestural codes) more and more seem to see the face — or at least family likeness — of the parent of the same sex spectrally appear.[12] For little Jane, however, no such clear ancestral facsimile or even simulacrum is available in what appears to be a reflection of significant Otherness, though the reported and remembered history of her mother's communitas and her related antistructural disobedience and eventual death is significantly available. Moreover, the persecutory gaze mirrored in the not-good-enough mother's (Mrs. Reed's) face certainly reinforces Jane's ontogenetic and even phylogenetic insecurity about the Janus-faced world of mothers and the reflexive feminine matrix of the unconscious.

Interestingly, it is the patrilineal uncle, John Eyre of Madeira, who will "wish to adopt" (267; ch. 21) Jane, whose intervention halts her mock-marriage ceremony, and who does leave her his money or power.[13] The symbolic lack of value in such an exclusive inheritance, however, is signified in her paternal cousin's or "brother's" (St. John's) offer of love, which Jane scorns because his bloodline is too otherworldly, anemic, and light if not because he is no true cross or matrilineal cousin. Rivers is not the dark king with the mysterious first wife Bertha, who, as Jane's later mirror vision suggests, alone can give birth to her true selfhood by, like Demeter, reconnecting the umbilicus to the maternal "Source of Life." Bertha, the big woman, is really pregnant with Jane and then dies so that Jane can be pregnant herself and continue the matrilineal cycle, just as the "mysterious lunatic" participates in and perpetuates past lunar cycles: "Bertha Mason is mad; and she came of a mad family; idiots and maniacs through three generations! Her mother, the Creole, was both a madwoman and a drunkard! . . . Bertha, like a dutiful child, copied her parent in both points" (320; ch. 26).[14] Again, then, Bertha, that sacral "mask" (322), plays a liminal monster incarnating a gnostic truth or Eleusinian mystery for Jane, namely, that the matrilineal bond must be recognized, must be accepted, and must be continued. In Bertha, Jane finally finds her mother and hence her own face, just as Bertha, again like Demeter, finally discovers her daughter in the liminal netherworld of what Angelyn Spignesi suggestively calls "the space of mother-daughter symbiosis" (23) in *Jane Eyre*. With Rochester, the figurative cross cousin who androgynously masquerades as a "sibyl" or "one of the old Mother Bunches" when Jane "crossed the threshold" (220; ch. 18, and 225; ch. 19), Jane finally continues her mother's darkly mysterious cycles.

Jane's courtship ritual at Midsummer Eve (276–85; ch. 23), her own midsummer night's dream, begins at twilight and ends at midnight and provides the most liminally charged interlude in her transforming process. Concluding with a discussion of it not only clarifies many of the general threshold conflicts in the text but also specifically addresses some of the unexplored mysteries from chapter 20, which were introduced at the beginning of this essay. But first a word of caution is necessary regarding the interlude's double liminal focus. Though central and most captivating, this is *not* Jane's ultimate liminal experience. The ironic dialogue (for example, Jane's uninformed insight that "you are a married man" and "your bride stands between us," 281–82; ch. 23), the meteorological imagery projecting bower-of-bliss delusions rather than paradigmatic values, and particularly the role-reversing between Jane and Rochester (who may himself reflect a case of "arrested liminality" here) in terms of the neophyte-Guardian relationship all forecast the need for further transformations. Such hints of what we might call possible counterfeit liminality portend that Jane (and her reader) will not begin to understand the liminal value of this gnostic gospel until the interrupted marriage ceremony, when she undergoes "the awful passage of further suffering" (325; ch. 27) and realizes that "a Christmas frost had come at midsummer" (323; ch. 26). Even in seeing this, we must at the same time discover that what seems to be counterfeit liminality is itself a liminal test. In this sense Brontë becomes the liminal *ludimagister*, or as Turner again suggests of artists in industrial societies, "the solitary artist *creates* the liminoid phenomena" (*From Ritual to Theatre* 52). Even Rochester's courting joke threatening to banish Jane to "Dionysius O'Gall of Bitternutt Lodge, Connaught" (279; ch. 23) connotes authorial play over and above Rochester's twitting, and authorial play may foster a communitas bond with the reader since, in the liminoid context, Master-neophyte polarities are less rigid and more undecidable. In other words, the serious joke reads like one of Turner's gnostic riddles implying that we cannot know anything until we learn that sweet sensationalism proves galling and that bitter spiritualism comes equally to naught: "This coincidence of opposite processes and notions in a single representation characterizes the peculiar unity of the liminal: that which is neither this nor that, and yet is both" (Turner 99) like, as Jane must learn, "the antipodes of the Creole" (338; ch 27).

At any rate, when we read at the end of the chapter that Jane and Rochester "were quite wet before [they] could pass the threshold" of Thornfield, we are reminded that they are leaving one liminal field for another where they will begin to experience the aftermath of the crucial storm, as sacrally represented by the gnostic value of the cloven chestnut tree. Beginning appropriately at twilight, the "splendid Midsummer" interval itself seems quite closely related to what Turner calls "a national First-Fruits ritual, performed in the height of summer when the early crops ripen" (108). In Brontë's words, "the hay was all got in; the fields round Thornfield were green and shorn." Even little Adèle seems part of such puberty rites during which change coincides with biological and meteorological rhythms since "weary with gathering wild strawberries in Hay Lane half the day, [she] had gone to bed with the sun."[15] Resembling her young ward, Jane is also a "ripening fruit," though the context suggests she is much more vulnerable to being "shorn" like the liminally "cleared meadows between." The actual seclusion site here, however, is the "Eden-like" walled-in garden, a *hortus conclusus* that becomes a courting court when Jane "crossed [Rochester's] shadow," thereby bringing her life to "some crisis," like one of what Turner calls "life crises." Indeed, "sunset is thus at meeting with moon-rise" during the process of this love's liminal alchemy, and even at its conclusion "the moon was not yet set, and we were all in shadow." Such imagery repeatedly recalls Turner's contention that "lunar symbolism is prominent in the rites," and he cites Hilda Kuper to detail the "symbolic acts [that] are performed which exemplify the 'darkness' and 'waxing and waning moon' themes" (109). Jane also later makes clear that the moon, dear to Isis, veils and unveils her own maternal "Source of Life," much like her self-reflective watercolors:

> She broke forth as never moon yet burst from cloud: a hand first penetrated the sable folds and waved them away; then, not a moon, but a white human form shone in the azure, inclining a glorious brow eastward. It gazed and gazed on me. It spoke to my spirit: immeasurably distant was the tone, yet so near, it whispered in my heart —
> "My daughter, flee temptation."
> "Mother, I will." (346; ch. 27)[16]

During her dialogue with Rochester, Jane repeatedly stresses her status as a novice or neophyte, that is, her "dependent position" and related "humility";

and her challenge to "get a new situation" (279; ch. 23) recalls that the "first-fruits or a harvest ritual" usually "concern[s] entry into a new achieved status" (Turner 95), whether of "the married or single state" (93). Deluded, Jane even wishes "that I had never been born" and sees herself as "looking on the necessity of death" (280–81; ch. 23), which may remind us of Turner's contention that liminal gaps "are at once tombs and wombs" (99). Moreover, structural norms in Turner's sense of "secular politico-jural systems" (99) always appear to be liminally contingent during the dialogue: "wealth, caste, custom — intervened between me [Jane] and what I naturally and inevitably loved" (280; ch. 23). Thus, antistructural and communitas values also become significant. As Rochester, who clearly "def[ies]" convention here, pleads to his now fellow or comrade passenger, "I ask you to pass through life at my side — to be my second self, and best earthly companion" (282, 284; ch. 23). Or as Jane herself perhaps more profoundly phrases it, "I am not talking to you now through the medium of custom, conventionalities, nor even of mortal flesh; it is my spirit that addressed your spirit; just as if we had both passed through the grave, and we stood at God's feet, equal as we are!" Such extrasensory "communion" or communitas certainly prepares for Jane's later "mysterious summons" from the "limbic system" of emotional recall. In Rochester's words, "it is as if I had a string somewhere under my left ribs, tightly and inextricably knotted to a similar string situated in the corresponding quarter of your little frame" (280; ch. 23).

Moreover, the repeated, verbal emphasis on entranced passing also recurs in the several sacra confronting Jane as she is "roused from the nightmare of parting — called to the paradise of union" (284; ch. 23). In fact, language like *sacred, atone,* and *expiate* lend an insistent ritual tone to the entire interlude. The first of the sacral auguries is "a flock of glorious passenger birds," which prefigures Jane's later liminal self-identification with "the messenger-pigeon flying home" (447; ch. 36) after its aerial-*Eyreial* pilgrimage. This sacral omen is quickly followed by a vision of the transformative "great moth," which Jane identifies as possibly "a West Indian insect; one does not often see so large and gay a night-rover in England" (277; ch. 23). Such a possibility, it seems, becomes a liminal harbinger of the subjunctive "shade" (276; ch. 23) or border patrol of the "mythical and archetypal midwife" (Turner 104) Bertha, that other large, West Indian "night rover" who has so eluded the logocentric nets and colonizing strategies of Anglo and American readers alike.[17] The related nightingale, like Keats's, is just as problematic in its subjunctive, open-ended implications since its "warbling in a wood" helps provoke Jane to "make for the wicket" or liminal *would.* In fact, later its "singing in the wood" even causes Jane to "sob convulsively" and release her "repress[ions]." Thus, it may augur an eventual "full and delightful life" for Jane (as opposed to one with the owlish Rivers), or like Matthew Arnold's nightingale "Philomela," it may recall King

Tereu's act of rape, thereby implicating Rochester, or Rivers, or both. It certainly, however, reminds us that Jane herself is here figuratively transformed into a "wild and frantic bird," but one who as yet cannot sing her own name (much less her ravisher's), who cannot yet "read" her own entrails. In this last sense, like Arnold's bird, it may even mirror "the too clear web, and thy dumb sister's shame" (line 21), in other words, the sacral veil or web of metalanguage between Philomela and Procne, here between Jane and Bertha. Together, such readings reflect Turner's central belief that liminality deconstructs logocentrism because it "is the realm of primitive hypothesis, where there is a certain freedom to juggle with the factors of existence" (106). And such a sense of liminality significantly informs "the ritual and the esoteric teaching which grows girls" (102), for "to 'grow' a girl into a woman is to effect an ontological transformation" (101–02). The repetition of such sacral mysteries in this remarkable chapter suggests that the sustained liminal content of its "evening sacrifice" turns the interlude into a mid-textual microcosm of the transforming process developing throughout *Jane Eyre*.

In conclusion we might cite Frederick Turner's (himself a Professor of Arts and Humanities) tribute to his father as a threshold text for future critical reflection and research:

> Turner would surely approve of the appropriation of his ideas across the disciplinary boundaries that separate the social sciences from the humanities; but we must recognize that he would have been uneasy at the prospect of a system or school of Turnerian literary criticism, especially if it showed signs of turning into orthodoxy. (148)

That is, the liminal field must not be ploughed too well or too wisely lest it fall fallow; its theoretical boundaries must be learned but then bounded over or at least challenged. Only in this way can the reader fully accept Turner's own "invitation" at the end of "Betwixt and Between": "I end this study with an invitation to investigators of ritual to focus their attention on the phenomena and processes of mid-transition. It is these, I hold, that paradoxically expose the basic building blocks of culture just when we pass out of and before we re-enter the structural realm" (110). Turner's liminal model ultimately suggests that all schools of post-structural and antistructural criticism of *Jane Eyre* should likewise remember the value of midday recess from their own class(ifications). Like the text itself, they must remain vigilantly and self-critically, if not self-sacrificially, poised "in a state between," just as Bertha and her ritual avatars guard the crossroads and just as Jane herself continues in eternal fictional time to enjoy her transforming process under the stewardship of each new reader and of each new critical phase of every old reader.

California State University, Sacramento

NOTES

1. Although Monahan does not specifically discuss liminal theory, she does treat Jane's "repeated departures from households" (591) and even "marginal[ized] individuals" (595), while Chase considers "compartments and thresholds" among other "spatial configurations" (91) in the text. Many readers have further noted the specific significance of the third story. Showalter, for instance, sees it *as* Bertha or "the incarnation of the flesh, of female sexuality" (118), while Moglen finds it symbolizing "enlarging stages of Jane's perception" (124). Such references suggest relationships between a liminal reading and other contemporary approaches to *Jane Eyre*. Although there is a great deal of overlap between the two related kinds of approaches, one kind seems generally feminist, that is, concerned with gender-inflected, antistructural "otherness"; besides Showalter (112–24) these critics include Moglen (105–45), Knapp (who calls this the "feminist novel par excellence," 144–64), Christ, Senf, Poovey, and Han. Han's title, "Feminist Literary Criticism: *The Mad Woman* and *Jane Eyre*," recalls, of course, Gilbert and Gubar's by now almost "canonical" treatment in *The Madwoman in the Attic* (336–71), which itself covers topics relevant to a liminal reading like the central roles of Bertha (and madness), the Mother, and the body in the novel. In this context, see also Lerner, Rigney, Griffin, Berg (esp. 81–87), Pickrel, Michie (esp. 23–25, 49–51), Rich, Homans (84–99), Boumelha (esp. 64–73), and finally Spignesi's book-length treatment of "the symbiosis with mother" (23). The second related approach focuses on the motif of the self's "transforming process," especially in terms of what Chase calls "the representation of personality" through the related genres of "romance and *Bildung*" (66) in *Jane Eyre*. (The notion of blurred or mixed genre structures, which Beaty treats, is also a later preoccupation of Turner.) For significant representatives of this second approach, see Maynard's treatment of Jane's "Sexual *Bildung* or prolonged rite of initiation" (117), Merrett, Rowe, Fulton, and Horne.
2. Gilead, in fact, barely mentions Turner in her essay "Liminality and Antiliminality in Charlotte Brontë's Novels," the present study developed independently of Gilead. See my " 'The Force of Contrast': Teaching Structure and Antistructure in *Jane Eyre*" (*Approaches to Teaching* Jane Eyre). See also Gilead's "Liminality, Anti-Liminality, and the Victorian Novel," which makes more specific use of Turner's ideas.
3. See Edith Turner's "The Literary Roots of Victor Turner's Anthropology"; for an almost Turnerian account of "literary anthropology as a paradigm for research," which defines "fictionalizing acts as boundary crossings" (264, 277), see Iser.
4. For Turner's discussion of the *liminoid*, see "Liminal to Liminoid in Play, Flow, and Ritual" in *From Ritual to Theatre* (20–60). For a relevant psychological approach to perpetual or "arrested liminality," see Stein.
5. See Roy for a recent account of Ferndean's role in attempting to reconcile the text's "mixed impulses" (esp. 724–26). See also *Betwixt & Between*, edited by Mahdi, Foster, and Little, for a collection of essays from various viewpoints on relevant ritualistic variations.
6. For an insightful discussion of the summons, see Yeazell.
7. Cowart argues that the "Bridewell" pun "suggests that Rochester is soon to be immured in a vaginal prison" (35).
8. For a development of these extremes and other critical approaches to Bertha, again see Lerner.

9. In fact, as I suggest in "*Jane Eyre*'s Reading Lesson," the French language, whether explicitly from Adèle or tacitly from the narrator's bilingual puns, provides a thematic metacommentary throughout the text.

10. For a discussion of this motif in the novel, see La Belle (137–44). See also Winnicott's theory of the "Good-Enough Mother" and his acknowledged debt to Lacan's "mirror-phase," which focuses on relationships "between the mirror and the mother's face" (117). Winnicott's theories specifically influenced Turner (*From Ritual to Theatre* 121). For Lacan's essay on reflection, see "The Mirror-phase," and for his more general exploration of gazing and gazing back, see "Of The Gaze as *Objet Petit a.*" Finally, for two excellent studies of hysteria, see Hunter and Jacobus.

11. For a relevant treatment of the uncle's role in Dickens, see Levin.

12. I use this fairly common example simply to illustrate general phenomenology. Lacan and Winnicott would insist that for both boys and girls there is a special biological and hence psychological need to refamiliarize themselves with the mother's face.

13. Again, it is as if the patrilineal role is ultimately secondary to the biological primacy of matriarchy, and, at least symbolically or ritualistically in the text, patriarchy serves matriarchy.

14. In "Betwixt and Between" (106) and elsewhere, Turner links Rabelais and liminality. And though *Jane Eyre* is certainly more ambivalent about carnivalesque values than is *Gargantua and Pantagruel*, still Bertha's drunkenness and Jane's craving for creature comforts seem to argue for some version of such values. Bhabha's discussion of "hybridity" in the Colonial (or here Creole) Other (esp. 155–62) seems further relevant to Bertha's antistructural ambiguity: "Hybridity represents that ambivalent 'turn' of the discriminated subject into the terrifying, exorbitant object of paranoid classification — a disturbing questioning of the images and presences of authority" (155). For a provocative analysis of colonialism in the text, see Meyer.

15. For a perceptive account of "the cyclical imagery of the yearly seasons" (45), see Simons. See also Maynard for a discussion of the centrality of the garden scene (119–20).

16. The "rising and solitary star" on Midsummer Eve may suggest the *stella maris* — the star of Isis. Further, Jane's later intended passage to India was also to occur near the midsummer solstice. As Rivers informs her, "I have taken my berth in an East Indiaman which sails on the twentieth of June" (427; ch. 34). In a sacral or symbolic sense, then, it is almost as if Jane's own birth, whether presided over by West Indian or East Indian midwives or matrices, must be processed. If she chooses to "sleep by the Ganges" and learn the "mystic lore" of "Hindustani" (426, 422–23; ch. 34), a fertility cult would still nurture her — though, significantly, there would be neither biological nor epistemological conception through her natural (and by then humbled) dark king.

17. Turner's account of the really universal "Trickster deity of the Crossroads," the two-headed *Exu*, strongly suggests the possibility of Bertha's similar role as a crossroads guardian:

one face is that of Christ, the other, Satan's. *Exu*, whose ritual colors are black and red, is the Lord of the Limen and of Chaos, the full ambiguity of the subjunctive mood of culture, representing the indeterminacy that lurks in the cracks and crevices of all socio-cultural "constructions of reality," the one who must be kept at bay if the framed formal order of the ritual proceedings is to go forward according to protocol. He is the abyss of possibility; hence his two heads, for he is both potential savior and tempter. (*From Ritual to Theatre* 77).

WORKS CITED

Arnold, Matthew. "Philomela." *Matthew Arnold*. Ed. Miriam Allott and Robert H. Super. Oxford UP, 1986. 215–16.

Ashley, Kathleen M., ed. *Victor Turner and the Construction of Cultural Criticism*. Bloomington: Indiana UP, 1990. 86–116.

Beaty, Jerome. "*Jane Eyre* and Genre." *Genre* 10 (1977): 619–54.

Berg, Maggie. *Jane Eyre: Portrait of a Life*. Boston: Twayne, 1987.

Betwixt & Between: Patterns of Masculine and Feminine Initiation. Eds. Louise Carus Mahdi, Steven Foster, and Meredith Little. La Salle, IL: Open Court, 1987.

Bhabha, Homi K. "Signs Taken for Wonders: Questions of Ambivalence and Authority under a Tree Outside Delhi, May 1817." *Critical Inquiry* 12 (1985): 144–65.

Boumelha, Penny. *Charlotte Brontë*. Bloomington: Indiana UP, 1990.

Brontë, Charlotte. *Jane Eyre*. Ed. Q. D. Leavis. London: Penguin, 1966.

Carroll, Lewis. *The Annotated Alice: Alice's Adventures in Wonderland and Through the Looking Glass*. Ed. Martin Gardner. New York: Clarkson Potter, 1960.

Chase, Karen. *Eros & Psyche: The representation of personality in Charlotte Brontë, Charles Dickens, and George Eliot*. New York: Methuen, 1984.

Christ, Carol T. "Imaginative Constraint, Feminine Duty, and the Form of Charlotte Brontë's Fiction." *Women's Studies: An Interdisciplinary Journal* 6 (1979): 287–96.

Cixous, Hélène. "The Laugh of the Medusa." Trans. Keith Cohen and Paula Cohen. *The* Signs *Reader: Women, Gender & Scholarship*. Eds. Elizabeth Abel and Emily K. Abel. Chicago: U of Chicago P, 1983. 279–97.

Cowart, David. "Oedipal Dynamics in *Jane Eyre*." *Literature and Psychology* 31 (1981): 33–38.

Dickens, Charles. *Dombey and Son*. Ed. Peter Fairclough. Intro. Raymond Williams. London: Penguin, 1970.

Fulton, E. Margaret. "Jane Eyre: The Development of a Female Consciousness." *English Studies in Canada* 5 (1979): 432–47.

Gilbert, Sandra M., and Susan Gubar. *The Madwoman in the Attic: The Woman Writer and the Nineteenth-Century Literary Imagination*. New Haven: Yale UP, 1979.

Gilead, Sarah. "Liminality and Antiliminality in Charlotte Brontë's Novels: *Shirley* Reads *Jane Eyre*." *Texas Studies in Literature and Language* 29 (1987): 302–22.

———. "Liminality, Anti-Liminality, and the Victorian Novel." *ELH* 53 (1986): 183–97.

Griffin, Gail B. "Once More to the Attic: Bertha Rochester and the Pattern of Redemption in *Jane Eyre*." *Nineteenth Century Women Writers of the English-Speaking World*. Ed. Rhoda B. Nathan. New York: Greenwood, 1986. 90–97.

Han, Minzhong. "Feminist Literary Criticism: *The Mad Woman* and *Jane Eyre*." *Foreign Literary Studies* 39 (1988): 22–27.

Hennelly, Mark M., Jr. " 'The Force of Contrast': Teaching Structure and Antistructure in *Jane Eyre*." *Approaches to Teaching* Jane Eyre. Eds. Diane Long Hoeveler and Beth Lau. New York: MLA, 1993. 87–96.

———. "*Jane Eyre*'s Reading Lesson." *ELH* 51 (1984): 693–717.

Homans, Margaret. *Bearing the Word: Language and Female Experience in Nineteenth-Century Women's Writing*. Chicago: U of Chicago P, 1986.

Horne, Margot. "From the Window-Seat to the Red Room: Innocence to Experience in *Jane Eyre.*" *Dutch Quarterly Review of Anglo-American Letters* 10 (1980): 199–213.

Hunter, Dianne. "Hysteria, Psychoanalysis, and Feminism: The Case of Anna O." *The (M)other Tongue: Essays in Feminist Psychoanalytic Interpretation.* Eds. Shirley Nelson Garner, Claire Kahane, and Madelon Sprengnether. Ithaca: Cornell UP, 1985. 89–115.

Iser, Wolfgang. "Toward a Literary Anthropology." *Prospecting: From Reader Response to Literary Anthropology.* Baltimore: Johns Hopkins UP, 1989. 262–84.

Jacobus, Mary. *Reading Woman: Essays in Feminist Criticism.* New York: Columbia UP, 1986. 195–274.

Knapp, Bettina L. *The Brontës: Branwell, Anne, Emily, Charlotte.* New York: Continuum, 1991. 144–64.

La Belle, Jenijoy. *Herself Beheld: The Literature of the Looking Glass.* Ithaca: Cornell UP, 1988.

Lacan, Jacques. "The Mirror-phase as Formative of the Function of the I." Trans. Jean Roussel. *New Left Review* 51 (1968): 71–77.

———. "Of The Gaze as *Objet Petit a.*" *The Four Fundamental Concepts of Psycho-Analysis.* Trans. Alan Sheridan. Ed. Jacques-Alain Miller. New York: Norton, 1981. 65–119.

Lerner, Laurence. "Bertha and the Critics." *Nineteenth-Century Literature* 44 (1989): 273–300.

Levin, Harry. "The Uncles of Dickens." *The Worlds of Victorian Fiction.* Ed. Jerome H. Buckley. Harvard English Studies 6. Cambridge, MA: Harvard UP, 1975. 1–35.

Maynard, John. *Charlotte Brontë and Sexuality.* Cambridge: Cambridge UP, 1984.

Merrett, Robert James. "The Conduct of Spiritual Autobiography in *Jane Eyre.*" *Renascence* 37 (1984): 2–15.

Meyer, Susan L. "Colonialism and the Figurative Strategy of *Jane Eyre.*" *Victorian Studies* 33 (1990): 247–68.

Michie, Helena. *The Flesh Made Word: Female Figures and Women's Bodies.* New York: Oxford UP, 1987.

Moglen, Helene. *Charlotte Brontë: The Self Conceived.* New York: Norton, 1976.

Monahan, Melodie. "Heading Out is Not Going Home: *Jane Eyre.*" *Studies in English Literature, 1500–1900* 28 (1988): 589–608.

Pickrel, Paul. "*Jane Eyre*: The Apocalypse of the Body." *ELH* 53 (1986): 165–82.

Poovey, Mary. "The Anathematized Race: The Governess and *Jane Eyre.*" *Feminism and Psychoanalysis.* Eds. Richard Feldstein and Judith Roof. Ithaca: Cornell UP, 1989. 230–54.

Rich, Adrienne. "Jane Eyre: The Temptations of a Motherless Woman." *On Lies, Secrets and Silence.* New York: Norton, 1979. 89–106.

Rigney, Barbara Hill. *Madness and Sexual Politics in the Feminist Novel: Studies in Brontë, Woolf, Lessing, and Atwood.* Madison: U of Wisconsin P, 1978.

Rowe, Karen E. " 'Fairy-born and human-bred': Jane Eyre's Education in Romance." *The Voyage In: Fictions of Female Development.* Ed. Elizabeth Abel, Marianne Hirsch, and Elizabeth Langland. Hanover, NH: UP of New England for Dartmouth College, 1983. 68–89.

Roy, Parama. "Unaccommodated Woman and the Poetics of Property in *Jane Eyre.*" *Studies in English Literature, 1500–1900* 29 (1989): 713–27.

Senf, Carol A. "Jane Eyre and the Evolution of Feminist History." *Victorians Institute Journal* 13 (1985): 67–81.

Showalter, Elaine. *A Literature of Their Own: British Women Novelists From Brontë to Lessing.* Princeton: Princeton UP, 1977.

Simons, Louise. "Authority and *Jane Eyre*: A New Generic Approach." *CEA Critic* 48 (1985): 45–53.

Spignesi, Angelyn. *Lyrical-Analysis: The Unconscious Through* Jane Eyre. Wilmette, IL: Chiron, 1990.

Stein, Murray. *In MidLife: A Jungian Perspective.* Dallas: Spring, 1983.

Turner, Edith. "The Literary Roots of Victor Turner's Anthropology." Ashley, 163–69.

Turner, Frederick. " 'Hyperion to a Satyr': Criticism and Anti-Structure in the Work of Victor Turner." Ashley, 147–62.

Turner, Victor. "The Anthropology of Performance." *On the Edge of the Bush: Anthropology as Experience.* Ed. Edith Turner. Tucson: U of Arizona P, 1985. 177–204.

———. "Betwixt and Between: The Liminal Period in *Rites de Passage.*" *The Forest of Symbols: Aspects of Ndembu Ritual.* Ithaca: Cornell UP, 1967. 93–111.

———. "Body, Brain, and Culture." *On the Edge of the Bush: Anthropology as Experience.* 249–73.

———. *Dramas, Fields, and Metaphors: Symbolic Action in Human Society.* Ithaca: Cornell UP, 1974.

———. "Experience and Performance: Towards a New Processual Anthropology." *On the Edge of the Bush: Anthropology as Experience.* 205–26.

———. *From Ritual to Theatre: The Human Seriousness of Play.* New York: Performing Arts Journal Publications, 1982.

———. *The Ritual Process: Structure and Anti-Structure.* Chicago: Aldine, 1969.

Van Gennep, Arnold. *The Rites of Passage.* Trans. Monika Vizedom and Gabrielle L. Caffee. Intro. Solon T. Kimball. Chicago: U of Chicago P, 1960.

Winnicott, D. W. *Playing and Reality.* London: Tavistock, 1971.

Yeazell, Ruth Bernard. 'More True than Real: Jane Eyre's 'Mysterious Summons.' " *Nineteenth-Century Fiction* 29 (1974): 127–43.

LILY MAIDS AND WATERY RESTS: ELAINE OF ASTOLAT

By Carolyn Hares-Stryker

AS CRITICS ARE OFTEN fond of remarking, a symbiotic relationship existed between the writers and artists of the Victorian period, and chief among those writers who inspired devoted replication was Tennyson. Not surprisingly, therefore, when in 1859 Tennyson offered up a new poetic vision, *Idylls of the Kings*, his choice of subject matter prompted something of a vogue. But the parallel between the verbal image and the painted lay not simply in the match in subject: just as Tennyson would find it necessary to rewrite an old story by expunging aspects of the original, artists too found themselves in a delicate process of revelation and concealment.[1]

As Tennyson began writing "Elaine," he found himself in the position of having to rework the rich cloth that Sir Thomas Malory had left.[2] In the case of the Elaine figure — the lily maid of Astolat who fatally loved Lancelot — Tennyson, while drawn by the poignancy of her tale, nevertheless needed to transform the dangerous, manipulative behavior she exhibited in Malory's text. Thus Tennyson deletes Elaine's gruesome medieval death of self-induced madness, starvation, and dehydration. He presents his readers, instead, with an Elaine of grace and gentleness who meekly listens as "Death, like a friend's voice from a distant field / Approach[es] thro' the darkness" (lines 993–93).

Following Tennyson, artists had also to angelicize Elaine, to disentangle her from her disturbing, disreputable tradition and thereby make her fit for Victorian taste. The image they created, of the dead Elaine floating towards Camelot, was an immensely popular one — as is attested by the number of pale, dead ladies who floated year after year over the walls of the Royal Academy. Like Tennyson, the Victorian artists were able to present Elaine in a way palatable to their audience. By doing so, however, they flew in the face of convention, not because they aestheticized death, which was acceptable, but because the act of suicide was an abhorrence and identified with crime or sin. Suicide, though morbidly fascinating, was not normally equated with sentimentalized death.[3] The Elaine figure was made a case apart, different from the popular image of women who,

129

abandoned by their lovers, threw themselves off the Bridge of Sighs; such were visions epitomized by Frederic Watts's "Found Drowned" (1848) (Figure 1) and Lord Gerald Fitzgerald's "The Bridge of Sighs" (1858) (Figure 2). The viewer can only be horrified and appalled, because the watery deaths of the female subjects are treated with realism, entailing the saturation and bloating of the body and its retrieval by grappling hooks. Though herself a sister suicide, Elaine was perceived quite differently. Although the Elaine paintings were an unrelenting scrutiny of the dead body itself, the artists and the audience were able to reinvent Elaine so that she was not represented as a suicide, a grotesque warning to young women about the dangers of excessive love. In fact, she not only became acceptable but aggressively romantic.[4]

Despite the iconographic echoes of death by drowning, Elaine's death in art is death beautified. This is an image of a boat, draped with golden and silken cloth, gliding over the waters carrying the still beautiful Elaine: "she did not seem as dead / But fast asleep, and lay as tho' she smiled" (1153–54). Very rarely does Victorian art reveal the madness of her despair and the ugliness of self murder. Instead, it submits to its marketplace and offers up to the audience prettified visions of camouflaged death. The artists were able to do so because, just as textually the Elaine figure had been reworked and disguised by layers of sentimentality and religiosity, so too in art layers of allusions to other heroines recreate her and enfold her. The popularity of the Elaine figure was due to fortuitous timing. When one looks to the Victorian art surrounding Elaine, one sees a link between traditions: one that allowed Elaine to be understood as both mad suicide and sleeping woman. Most notably there is the Ophelia tradition in Victorian art, a tradition that began and probably had its heyday in the early 1850s, and there is the pseudo-classical tradition so fond of depicting sleeping women, which began in the 1860s and lasted over a period of fifty years.

It is well to start with Arthur Hughes's "Ophelia" (Figure 3), exhibited as an example of Pre-Raphaelite art at the Royal Academy in 1852, because in this painting one begins to understand not only the fascination with female suicide subjects, but the way such subjects were increasingly made safe by convention (the license of literature-inspired art) and artifice (the inclusion of details overwhelming in their abundance). Hughes bases his depiction of Ophelia on Act IV, scene vii of "Hamlet":

> There is a willow grows aslant a brook
> That shows his hoar leaves in the glassy stream.
> There with fantastic garlands did she come
> Of crow-flowers, nettles, daisies, and long purples,
> That liberal shepherds give a grosser name,
> But our cold maids do dead men's fingers call them.
> . . . Her clothes spread wide
> And, mermaid-like, awhile they bore her up;

Which time she chanted snatches of old tunes,
As one incapable of her own distress,
Or like a creature native and indued
Unto that element; but long it could not be
Till her garments, heavy with their drink,
Pull'd the poor wretch from her melodious lay
To muddy death. (lines 168–73, 177–85)

Instead of showing Ophelia in garb correct for the Renaissance, however, Hughes drapes her in a white sheet; and instead of having her next to a stream, Hughes chooses to place her beside a bog, scum floating on its still waters, a poisonous mushroom near its edges, and a bat flitting over its surface in the background. The composition is shrouded in twilight, eerie and disturbing, and his child-like Ophelia is emaciated, ghostly white but for the dark circles under her eyes. Ophelia here is the only point of attention; here is madness revealed. Not surprisingly, Hughes's painting was not popular and was poorly placed in the Royal Academy exhibition, hung so high on the walls in the octagonal room — commonly known as the "condemned cell" — that to view it closely one had to climb a ladder. Hughes had not made death visually compelling but repulsive and had gravely misjudged the sensibilities and appetites of his audience. Upon entering the bog, Hughes's Ophelia will indeed be pulled down into the suffocating mud to her death.

Another Pre-Raphaelite painter, also exhibiting an "Ophelia" at the Royal Academy in 1852, however, chose to depict his Ophelia ever adrift upon flower-strewn waters, occasioning Ruskin to write that here was "the loveliest English landscape, haunted by sorrow" (*Tate* 55). This is the famous version by Sir John Everett Millais. His "Ophelia" was peaceful and so jewel-like in its detail and attention to the vegetation that surrounded Ophelia that one may forgive Ruskin's omission of the human subject.[5]

How shocked Ruskin might have been if Millais had continued in the vein of his preparatory sketch (Figure 4). It shows a far darker, more disturbing rendition of Shakespeare's subject. In it, one sees Ophelia, her boat (a detail that would suggest that she is both mad Ophelia and mad Elaine) anchored in a pool snarled with branches and weeds. The artist did not choose to remain faithful to his original vision and the finished painting was, of course, much different (Figure 5). Millais employed distancing mechanisms to soften his subject and to beguile his viewer. Nonetheless, a critic of the *Times* still found the juxtaposition of beauty and death disconcerting: "there must be something strangely perverse in an imagination which souses Ophelia in a weedy ditch . . . while it studies every petal of the darnel and anemone floating on the eddy . . ." (Maas 126). Despite such reservations, however, the *Times* critic highlighted what all those who viewed the painting felt: that the attention Millais lavished on the natural details of the scene provided a visual feast. Each flower and weed surrounding the neither fully conscious nor yet dead Ophelia was perfect, and each detail contributed to her sad tale. The willow, the nettle growing amongst its branches, and the daisies near Ophelia's right hand, all taken from Shakespeare, signify love, pain, and innocence. The pansies floating on Ophelia's dress signify chastity and the death of the young. The poppy next to the daisies, of course, is associated with death. Millais even included in the upper left corner a robin, reminding the viewer of the mad song Ophelia sings: "For bonny sweet Robin is all my joy" (*Hamlet* 4.5. 187). And then, to the left of the forget-me-nots (carrying their own meaning in their name) and at the right edge, one may see the vague shape of a skull, a *memento mori* (Warner 96–98). Millais was able to capture in oils a tapestry of lush vegetation and resonant symbolism. The death of Ophelia is made beautiful and fascinating — indeed, it invites study and admiration.

A very different, though contemporary, group of painters, whose work also began in the second half of the nineteenth century and who also invited the audience to scrutinize/enjoy the female subject, were the Neo-Classical painters, of whom Lord Frederick Leighton and Albert Moore were among the best. Paintings like Leighton's "Flaming June" (Figure 6), one of his last works and one for which he is now best known (1895), are, as Jeremy Maas describes them, "luscious . . . essay[s] in voluptuousness, redolent of slumbering warmth" (181). The composition is arresting. The massive, convoluted figure of the sleeping woman fills the entire canvas. The predominant color is a brilliant orange, and the mood exotic, more significantly, sensual. Asleep, covered entirely by the folds of diaphanous robes that wrap tightly about her breasts, hips, and thighs, the woman rests under an awning, while behind her glitters the Mediterranean sea, blue and silver. She has no knowledge of her admirers and slumbers on, both innocent and sexual before our eyes. She will never awaken, and the viewer, made bold, has full (ad)vantage of her body. Bram Dijkstra notes correctly that this is "passive feminine eroticism" (75), the perfection of voyeurism: all of the satisfaction of visual gratification but no risk and no taint of improper action.

The same sexual tension and subject-viewer dynamic occurs in Moore's "The Dreamers" (Figure 7) of the 1880s, although this time with an edge, because one of the three sleeping women gazes out languidly but directly at her admirer, her robe having slipped, seemingly unnoticed, from her right shoulder. Like Millais, however, Moore avoids any discomfiture on the viewer's part by surrounding what would otherwise be a slightly disturbing, confrontational female subject with lavish detail: there are swirls and flowers on the walls, there are lattice windows, pillows, an embroidered couch, a fan, a tiled floor. The colors are rich and the patterns complex and do much to make the composition one dimensional and frieze-like. Though the viewer has a witness, the women will do nothing to cause that viewer to flinch but will rest peacefully and silently, with just the faintest suggestion of sexual exhaustion. It places overbearing emphasis on their physicality but is a decorative, unthreatening treatment of eroticism.

The mid- to late-Victorian Elaine-craze links these two traditions — the fascination with cosmetically displayed suicide and safely displayed sexuality. As Jan Marsh shows, Elaine, lovelorn maiden of Arthurian legend, was one of the most popular of Victorian subjects (145). Gustave Doré, in a gloriously large and impressive book, took up the task of illustrating Tennyson's "Elaine" in the late 1860s. And in his engravings, one sees how Doré re-visions Elaine, eliciting the reader's sympathies for his mild virgin of innocence. In Doré's engraving of the death journey of Elaine, she is shown not as Malory's victim of frenzy and despair but serene (Figure 8). Only the clouds of heaven and Elaine are touched with light. Doré chooses not to depict her holding the letter of reproach; instead, in her left hand she clasps a lily, symbol of the Virgin. The many turrets and darkened windows look down upon her, as does the mute oarsman who gazes in sorrow at her dead, though beautiful, form. Through the moonlight Elaine comes, her hair and her funeral cloths trailing in the cold waters. An object of pity and icon of sacrificial maidens, Elaine nevertheless is still victim of self-willed death, and the black cloth, heavy with water, connects her with the more horrible death of suicide by drowning; indeed, while the oarsman functions as the top of a diagonal, reaching away from the river and toward Camelot and the sky, these cloths pull the viewer's gaze into the black water. Above all, however, Doré's is a tasteful depiction of death on display.

In 1874, American Munich-based painter Toby Rosenthal painted an "Elaine" (Figure 9) that when brought to San Francisco in 1875 caused such a sensation that thieves stole it in the hopes of ransoming it for $25,000, an enormous sum for its day and indicative of the significance and perceived worth of the work (Dijkstra 41). Notice, however, though the black cloths still drag in the waters, how much attention is lavished on making Elaine the fairy princess. Rosenthal's composition occurs in the daylight; Elaine's boat becomes not a solemn funeral barge but a canopy of rich cloths and heraldry, bedecked with garlands of flowers, its prow decorated with filigree carvings and a fairy with feathery wings, holding a tiny golden crown. Flowers float on the water nearby, and swans course across its surface and fly upwards into the sky. Elaine herself is utterly peaceful, utterly beautiful: the Sleeping Beauty, not a corpse. Other safe and prettified paintings of Elaine would follow, mostly as turn-of-the-century models of pseudo-medieval romance heroines. Blair Leighton's "Elaine" of 1899 (Figure 10) and Ernest Normand's "Elaine" of 1904 (Figure 11) are just such examples.

Elaine exists between the eerie and shocking death of Ophelia and the languorous and sexual poses of Olympian girls. As she is depicted and mythologized in Victorian art, Elaine is both a poignant illustration of self-willed death and the representation of lassitude. In her, the artists seem to be able to reflect accurately Tennyson's description of her death due to unrequited love and also to suggest, in the beautiful framing of the body and the sumptuous materials that surround and enfold her, that she is a type of Sleeping Beauty; she is simultaneously a suicide victim and romantic maiden of fairy tale. The popularity of the Elaine vision was precisely because the iconography of the image managed to both terrify and seduce — but never one at the expense of the other, allowing Elaine to be wholly a spectacle of either female suicide or deliciously exhausted femininity. Tennyson would have approved: Elaine was artistically rendered safe.

Few artists dared to discount Victorian sensibilities; few dared to make plain the ugliness and to depict the real fascination the Victorians felt toward the Elaine subject: its danger, its advocacy of the death-wish. Even an artist as daring as Dante Rossetti chose to keep his sketch "Boatsmen and Siren" (Figure 12) a private fantasy of seduction and death.

John Atkinson Grimshaw's "Elaine" of 1877 (Figure 13) illustrates the disturbing undercurrents merely glossed over by depictions like Doré's and Rosenthal's: the intertwining of madness, innocence, and spectacle. Bram Dijkstra writes that in Grimshaw's vision of Elaine one sees Elaine "not so much the victim of self-immolating fervor as the helplessly sacrificial victim of some unspeakable, satanic rite. In this painting, in other words, [is evidenced] the sadistic-aggressive impulses underlying Tennyson's narrative, and his evident delight in Elaine's passionate self-sacrifice" (42). Certainly, Grimshaw's vision seems macabre. As Christopher Wood reveals, Grimshaw owned a copy of Doré's illustration of *Elaine* (133). But if Doré had been content to show the darkened windows of Camelot, Grimshaw gives us a clear linear stretch of background filled with many windowed buildings. Now, a gothic-like cityscape of countless lighted windows watches as Elaine floats by. Again as in Doré's drawing, in Grimshaw's painting only the sky and Elaine are light; the rest of the painting exists in browns and darkness. That she will ascend to the heavens seems unlikely, however, as even the ferocious dragon, its wings outstretched and taut as if for flight, has coils of chain around its neck. At the center of the painting, Elaine smiles enigmatically, and unlike Doré's Elaine, whose funeral cloths were pulled up to her breasts, Grimshaw's Elaine lies exposed to the viewer's eyes: a rich coverlet drapes over her legs and leaves her upper body covered only by a thin, form-hugging silver dress. Instead, Grimshaw chooses to render in crisp detail only Elaine's beauteous form, so that though we may not be able to see the boatman clearly, we can admire Elaine's crown, her bracelet, the sash around her waist, the curves of her body, and the ashen whiteness of her dead flesh. Grimshaw's sinister boatman further contributes to the disturbing atmosphere of the composition because he is strongly suggestive of the underworld. Elaine may be the lily white maid, but her barge is directed by a denizen of hell, perhaps Charon himself who steers the damned over the river Styx.

Finally, in Henry Arthur Payne's "The Enchanted Sea" painted in 1900 (Figure 14), one sees a bizarre and unsettling illustration of the mixing and muddying of the three genres or impulses: the atmosphere of madness (Ophelia), the fetish of undefended sleep, and the beautifully adorned boat of death (Elaine). Here one sees a princess costumed in medieval headdress and ermine coat, yet wearing an oddly Victorian dress with scores of ribbons. She floats in a shell, but this is not the birth of Venus, because no nymphs encircle the woman. One sees instead the floating bodies of seven drowned/fatally-sleeping women. An eagle holds a feather (after all, the shell will soon be its nest, as foreshadowed by the rich cloth dragging in the sea), while the woman stares blindly off the canvas. In one of the last Victorian visions of Elaine, one sees her afloat in waters clogged with dead and dying women: Elaine and her sister suicides.

This study of the Elaine tradition in mid to late nineteenth-century art offers yet another illustration of the Victorian habit of aestheticizing the unpleasant and the potentially dangerous. The Elaine figure highlights, however, the deliberate and always complex negotiations that a Victorian audience had to execute in order for their sensibilities to be soothed and their appetites satisfied. Tennyson's "Elaine" precipitated a new social fashion: the beautiful dead. The Poet Laureate made suicide romantic and the unabashed fascination with the displayed body of a heroine acceptable. The artists simply carried the impulse to its perfection: the visualization of the poetic fantasy. While Tennyson could appropriate his heroine as victim and blessed virgin merely by expunging the sexual nature and anger of Malory's Elaine, the artists shrouded her with the costumes of other women: blameless Ophelia driven to her death by the cruelty and like madness of Hamlet and the unwitting seductresses of Grecian settings. Elaine's self destruction, her suicide, therefore, could be in art excused.

In choosing to die for the love of a man, Elaine appears not vindictive but tragic. The Ophelia iconography mastered by Millais guarantees that Elaine's suicide be understood not as manipulative and violent but as a lamentable action induced by insanity. Elaine did not act deliberately. Rather than accept anything but the pure love of Lancelot, Elaine binds him to her in madness and death. Her logic is distorted, but the sentiment and self sacrifice enacted is, to Victorian tastes, laudable. The second element of layering, the sleeping women, is also a map to rereading Elaine's fate, because in the presence of their iconography one is compelled to view Elaine's decision in a different light: in choosing the manner of her presentation, the barge richly outfitted and her body royally clad, Elaine can be thought of as having not chosen death but cessation. Hers is not the fate of the grave and the worm but of slumbering suspension and of always displayed and never attainable beauty. Moreover, the iconography of the sleeping women, as accented by Leighton and Moore, reinforces what the Victorian audience already knew about the nature and weakness of women: they are snared by their sexuality. In short, Elaine's actions are excused once more, this time by her gender. Not only is Elaine a victim of madness induced by love, and therefore not responsible for her sin, but she is also pitiable because being a woman she is necessarily an easy prey to the carnal demands of the body. Just as the Grecian maidens could not disguise their connectedness to sexuality, the Elaine of Doré and Normand loved Lancelot "overmuch" and, failing to grasp their earthly lover, succumbed to the enticing call of Death, who wooed her in the darkness of her tower.

Marietta College

NOTES

1. This essay began as a paper presented at the Modern Language Association conference held in Chicago, 1990, and was the second of two papers concerned with the means by which Tennyson and Victorian artists negotiated the unattractive, disturbing aspects of Elaine's death — her suicide — for love of Sir Lancelot. My colleague, Mary T. Anderberg, presented a paper on the textual difficulties Tennyson encountered while reworking his material and while creating his Victorian lady of sorrows.
2. Pfordresher describes the changing titles given to this poem. As he was writing it, Tennyson originally called his poem "The Maid of Astolat"; then, when it was first published in the 1859 edition, the poem was titled "Elaine"; but in the 1870 edition the title was changed once more to the now familiar, "Lancelot and Elaine" (31–32, 45).
3. Both Anderson and Gates show that suicide had never been romanticized, particularly the suicide of women.
4. The Elaine tradition stands in marked contrast to the vast majority of English paintings that fall into the "Cult of Death" genre. Most commonly these paintings mitigated the impact of their subject, often by harkening to religious iconography (Henry Wallis's "Chatterton" (1856), for example, invokes the *Pietà*, while Lord Leighton in "And the Sea gave up the Dead which were in it" (1892) draws upon the Apocalypse), by depicting the purity and innocence of those chosen by death (for example, William Lindsay Windus's "Too Late" (1858), in which a young man shields his eyes from the consumptive gaze of his beloved, and Sir Luke Fildes's "The Doctor" (1891), in which a doctor watches over the makeshift bed of a dying child), or by simply removing the victim altogether (for example, Arthur Hughes's "Home From Sea" (1863).
5. Millais paid a price for his myopic vision. He sat on the banks of the River Ewell near Kingston-upon-Thames for eleven hours each day during the summer of 1851, and wrote: "I sit tailor fashion under an umbrella . . . and am also in danger of being blown by the wind into the water, and becoming intimate with the feelings of Ophelia when that lady sank to muddy water" (1: 119–20).

WORKS CITED

Anderson, Olive. *Suicide in Victorian and Edwardian England*. Oxford: Clarendon P, 1987.

Dijkstra, Bram. *Idols of Perversity: Fantasies of Feminine Evil in Fin-de-Siècle Culture*. Oxford: Oxford UP, 1986.

Gates, Barbara. *Victorian Suicide: Mad Crimes and Sad Histories*. Princeton: Princeton UP, 1988.

Maas, Jeremy. *Victorian Painters*. London: Barrie & Jenkins, 1969.

Marsh, Jan. *Pre-Raphaelite Women: Images of Femininity in Pre-Raphaelite Art*. London: Weidenfeld and Nicolson, 1987.

Millais, John Guille. *The Life and Letters of Sir John Everett Millais*. Volume I. New York: Frederick A. Stokes, 1899.

Pfordresher, John, ed. *A Variorum Edition of Tennyson's* Idylls of the King. New York: Columbia UP, 1973.

The Tate Gallery: An Illustrated Companion. London: Tate Gallery Publications, 1983.

Tennyson, Alfred. "Elaine." *The Poetical Works of Alfred Tennyson*. New York: Harper, 1870.

Warner, Malcolm. "Millais's 'Ophelia'." *The Pre-Raphaelites*. Tate Gallery catalogue. London: Penguin Books, 1984. 96–98.

Wood, Christopher. *The Pre-Raphaelites*. New York: Viking, 1981.

1. "Found Drowned." Frederick Watts, 1848 (By permission of the Trustees of the Watts Gallery, Compton)

2. "The Bridge of Sighs." Lord Gerald Fitzgerald, Plate 9 in Junior Etching Club, *Passages from the Poems of Thomas Hood*, 1858 (By permission of the Trustees of the British Museum, London)

3. "Ophelia." Arthur Hughes, 1852 (by permission of the Tate Gallery, London)

4. "Preparatory Sketch." Sir John Everett Millais, 1854 (Private Collection: photograph courtesy of the Walker Art Gallery, Liverpool)

5. "Ophelia." Sir John Everett Millais, 1852 (By permission of the Tate Gallery, London)

6. "Flaming June." Lord Frederick Leighton, 1895 (By permission of Museo de Arte, Ponce, Puerto Rico)

7. "The Dreamers." Albert Moore, 1882 (By permission of the Birmingham City Art Gallery, Birmingham)

8. "The Body of Elaine on Its Way to King Arthur's Palace." Gustave Doré, in Tennyson's *Elaine*, London, 1868 (Photograph courtesy of Shields Library, University of California, Davis)

9. "Elaine." Toby Rosenthal, 1875 (Private Collection: photograph courtesy of the Fine Art Society, London)

10. "Elaine." Blair Leighton, 1899 (Private Collection: photograph courtesy of the Fine Art Society, London)

11. "Elaine." Ernest Normand, 1904 (Private Collection: photograph courtesy of the Fine Art Society, London)

12. "Boatsmen and Siren." Dante Rossetti, 1853 (By permission of City Art Galleries, Manchester)

13. "Elaine." John Atkinson Grimshaw, 1877 (Private Collection: photograph courtesy of the Fine Art Society, London)

14. "The Enchanted Sea." Henry Arthur Payne, 1900 (Private Collection of Charles Cholmondeley: photograph courtesy of the Fine Art Society, London)

"SOMETHING BOTH MORE AND LESS THAN MANLINESS": GENDER AND THE LITERARY RECEPTION OF ANTHONY TROLLOPE

By Nicola Thompson

> "We state our opinion of it [*Barchester Towers*] as decidedly the cleverest novel of the season, and one of the most masculine delineations of modern life . . . that we have seen for many a day"—*Westminster Review* 1857
>
> "My husband, who can seldom get a novel to hold him, has been held by all three [*The Warden, Barchester Towers*, and *The Three Clerks*], and by this [*The Three Clerks*] the strongest. . . . What a thoroughly man's book it is! I much admire it."—Letter from Elizabeth Barrett Browning, 1859, qtd. in Smalley 64
>
> "We may say, on the whole, that Thackeray was written for men and women, and Trollope for women."—*The Literary World*, 1884
>
> "But this prolific author, often dismissed in his own time as a writer for Mudie's and jeunes filles, gradually accepted as a creator of adult books for adult minds . . . seems still in process of being discovered."—Lionel Stevenson 1964

GENDER IS NOT SOMETHING that contemporary twentieth-century critics tend to take into account or consider important when they write about Trollope's literary reputation.[1] And Victorian critical reaction to Anthony Trollope does not at first glance seem structured around preoccupations with gender. A closer examination of commentary on *Barchester Towers* and on Trollope's later works reveals, however, that Victorian critics do employ gendered thinking to assess Trollope's works, and that their overall evaluation of his literary strengths and weaknesses does carry important gender associations and connotations. As the opening quotations indicate, Trollope has in turn, and sometimes even simultaneously, been seen as an intensely masculine writer directing himself toward a male audience, and as a popular writer focusing on young women's love affairs and emotional confusions, writing to a predominantly female circulating library audience. Unlike Charles Reade or Emily Brontë, for example, who respectively conform to

151

or deviate from conventional expectations about gendered writing, Trollope is variously thought to do both. In order to investigate this apparent paradox, this article will examine the role of gender in several aspects of critical discussion about Trollope, including the relation between his social persona and his writing, the subject matter of his novels, his depiction of male and female characters, his popularity, his prolific production of novels, and the nature of his imagination and inspiration. This article will argue that gender considerations influence the seriousness with which Victorian critics take Trollope and that the often pejorative connotations of femininity can also be applied to men in Victorian literary criticism.

There is evidence to suggest that from the 1860s to the end of the nineteenth century the criteria used by Victorian reviewers to judge novels became increasingly polarized according to gender, with "masculine" qualities in writing more strongly valorized, and "feminine" qualities denigrated accordingly. Gaye Tuchman, in *Edging Women Out*, sees this unwritten poetics of gender as evidence of men's desire to wrest control of the economics of the literary marketplace from women. She argues that it was women's success in the genre of novel-writing in the 1840s and 1850s that gave men the provocation and desire to "edge women out": "partly as a reaction to women's prominence as novelists, partly as a reaction against the . . . library-subscribers who crowned the 'queens of the circulating library,' and partly because of the clear economic opportunities that the novel offered writers, men began to define the high-culture novel as a male preserve" (47). Tuchman's argument is supported by, among other things, the archives of the publishing house of Macmillan. Women submitted more novels than men in the 1850s and 1860s and were more likely than men to have novels accepted; by the end of the century men were more likely (and women less likely) to have novels accepted, even though men still submitted fewer novels (7–8). Tuchman's argument views the quest for literary success by authors in the second-half of the nineteenth century as a fight for power between men and women. My study of the decline of Trollope's reputation in this same time period suggests that aesthetic criteria were determined not just by sex but also by gender: as a man, Trollope suffers from being associated with "feminine" literary qualities, and thus the situation is more complicated than a straightforward battle between the sexes.

A survey of literary criticism of Trollope's novels from *Barchester Towers* onwards reveals that Trollope was held in highest critical esteem from the late 1850s through the mid 1860s; during this period he was seen as a possible successor to the literary throne of Dickens and Thackeray, but increasingly, as the 'sixties progressed, Trollope's literary reputation as a serious artist began to decline. Skilton summarizes the tone of critical commentary on Trollope in the 'seventies as one of condescension: "He was no longer thought of as a next-to-great novelist. . . . He clearly retained a fairly large public, but mainly as an author of circulating library fiction'' (32). Related to this loss of critical prestige, in my opinion, is the growing tension that emerges in the same period (1860s to 1870s) between admiration for the "masculine" style and persona critics associate with the author of *Barchester Towers* and disparagement for the increasingly feminized associations made with his writings.[2] As with many other Victorian novelists, masculine associations seem to have some correlation with perceptions of literary merit.

Barchester Towers was the novel that first catapulted Trollope into the literary arena. This novel was only the second in what was to be a lengthy Barchester series, and the intense productivity of Trollope from 1856 until his death in 1884 (he wrote 47 novels in all) demands that any investigation of patterns in Trollope's reception also consider critical commentary on his later work.

Barchester Towers was published in 1857, and was, as Trollope states proudly in his *Autobiography*, "one of the novels which novel readers were called upon to read" (79). It was, in fact, Trollope's fifth novel; the first three had been unequivocally unsuccessful, and the fourth, *The Warden*, had received some, if fairly limited, critical attention.[3] (Probably one of the reasons why *The Warden* did not attract wider attention was the fact that it was not a three-decker.) The appearance of *Barchester Towers*, however, proved to be the turning point in Trollope's writing career, both in critical attention and general popularity. As R. H. Super documents, 750 copies of *Barchester Towers* were published in 1857, of which 200 were bought by Mudie's, and these were followed by a one-volume edition in 1858 (80).[4]

Barchester Towers was reviewed in the following journals: the *Westminster Review*, the *National Review*, the *Times*, the *Saturday Review*, the *Eclectic Review*, the *Examiner*, the *Leader*, the *Spectator*, and the *Athenaeum*. Reviewers were unanimous in singling out Trollope's novel as one of the season's most distinguished offerings. The *Examiner* gives it "unquestionable rank among the few really well-written tales that every season furnishes" (308), while the *Leader* "cannot but describe it as uncommonly graphic and clever" (497). The *National Review* describes *Barchester Towers* as "undeniably one of the cleverest and best-written novels which have been published of late years" (425), and the usually recalcitrant *Saturday Review* devotes an entire article to it, calling it "a very clever book," and admiring "its power and finish" (503). The *Leader* praises "the astonishing energy with which the author writes, the sharpness and concision of his style" (497).

Barchester Towers was thus taken seriously by reviewers, seen as intelligent, powerful, "clever," and "well-written," and in a class apart from ordinary novels. The *Westminster Review* provides the most explicitly gendered assessment, and highlights the implicit gender connotations of terms used in other reviews. In its opinion, *Barchester Towers* is "decidedly the cleverest novel of the season, and one of the most masculine delineations of modern life . . . that we have seen for many a day'' (326). The *Westminster Review* praises Trollope for having written a "novel that men can enjoy" and for his "caustic and vigorous" qualities (327); it concludes by comparing *Barchester Towers* to Mrs. Oliphant's *The Athelings*, which is "in construction and execution altogether feminine" (327); it is perhaps unnecessary to add that Mrs. Oliphant's novel suffers from the comparison. The 1857 reviews of *Barchester Towers* are thus reminiscent of the strongly gendered assessments of Reade's *It Is Never Too Late to Mend*, praised for its "vigour" which was thought to be located in the book's content and style, seen as atypical of conventional novels, contrasted, by the *Spectator*, with "the sentimental woes and drawingroom distresses which form the staple of so much of our circulating library fiction" (877), and juxta-posed, to its credit, with inferior works by women writers.

Critics focus on, and seem to enjoy, what Jane Nardin terms the conservative comedy of *Barchester Towers*: "*Barchester Towers'* comedy of errors begins when a woman tries to think for herself" (33). Nardin argues that "the narrator's tone is . . . consistently misogynistic . . . and there is a lot of rib-digging, anti-feminist humor" (39). Trollope's novelistic persona in this work is clearly that of an orthodox middle-class Victorian gentleman as far as sex roles are con-cerned, as the resolution of the romance between Eleanor and Arabin indicates:

> And now it remained to them each to enjoy the assurance of the other's love. And how great that luxury is. . . . And to a woman's heart how doubly delightful!
> When the ivy has found its tower, when the delicate creeper has found its strong wall, we know how the parasite plants grow and prosper. They were not created to stretch forth their branches alone, and endure without protection the summer's sun and the winter's storm. Alone they but spread themselves upon the ground, and cower unseen in the dingy shade. But when they have found their firm support-ers, how wonderful is their beauty. . . . (239–40)

Many critics single out the characters of Mrs. Proudie and Madeline Vesey-Neroni for attention, the characters who are the source of so much of the novel's humour, along with the despicable clergyman Mr. Slope. The *Westminster Re-view*, for example, is intrigued by the battle for power between the Bishop and Mrs. Proudie, and is paternally anxious for Eleanor's dangerous independence to end in matrimony: "We are anxious for the widow, and long to have her havened out of her perilous widowhood in fast wedlock; man's great ambition to become a Bishop, and woman's wonderful art in ruling one, cannot fail to interest us exceedingly" (327). The *Times* also singles out for attention the conflict between the sexes, clearly identifying with the Bishop:

> Perhaps the scenes between the Bishop and Mrs. Proudie are a little overdrawn, but, although highly coloured, they are not the less amusing delineations of human misery, as experienced by a man who permits himself not only to be henpecked

in his private relations, but also to be in his public capacity under female domination. The poor bishop is not only assailed by his wife in the privacy of his dressing-room, he cannot receive a visitor without her permission. (5)

Critics seem attracted by the treatment of relations between the sexes and by the conservative nature of the humour.

In her book on Victorian novelists, Mrs. Oliphant refers to both Trollope and Reade as "robust and manly figures," writers who "will always stand together in the front of the second rank of Victorian novelists" (471–72). Leaving aside for the moment the vexed question of Trollope's rank among novelists, one of the more interesting aspects of criticism on Trollope is the way it tends to blur the boundaries between Trollope the man and Trollope the writer. Critics viewed Trollope's persona as extremely masculine, and as perfectly congruent with ideas about appropriate masculinity.[5] They frequently compared Trollope's lifestyle, attitudes, persona, or beliefs with the details of his work. This delicate line between Trollope's public image and writing usually functioned to his advantage, giving him credibility and allowing reviewers to identify and sympathize with the writer as "one of us," an educated and somewhat conservative mid-century gentleman.

Time, for example, writes admiringly of the similarities between Trollope's own conversation and the dialogue in his novels, and between his style as a hunter and his style as a writer:

> As it is with the dialogue of Mr. Trollope's literary heroes and heroines, so is it with the conversation of Mr. Trollope himself. In each there is the same definiteness and direction; the same Anglo-Saxon simplicity. . . . As a writer . . . Mr. Trollope is precisely what he is, or used to be, as a rider across country. He sees the exact place at which he wants to arrive. He makes for it; and he determines to reach it as directly as possible. There may be obstacles, but he surmounts them. (627)

David Cecil's remarks on Trollope, written in 1934, still echo Victorian discussion of the author. Like so many Victorian critics, he praises Trollope for being a "sensible man of the world": "Like the other mid-Victorian gentlemen he enjoyed hunting and whist and a good glass of wine, admired gentle, unaffected, modest women, industrious, unaffected, manly men" (228).

Critics praised Trollope for his knowledge and experience of the world, and such compliments are always explicitly or implicitly based on gender. *Time*, for example, admires his "manly imagination" and admires the way Trollope "exemplifies and enforces" his ideas "with whatever suggests itself as suitable in the treasure-house of diversified knowledge and experience which he has assimilated" (632). The *North British Review* is impressed by Trollope as an experienced "man of the world": "His books are the result of the experience of life, not of the studious contemplation of it. . . . While we read them we are made to share . . . the experience of a man who in going through his own daily business, has been brought in contact with an immense variety of people; who has looked at so much of the world as it came in his way to consider, with a great deal of keenness, kindness, and humour'' (370).

While such experience of the world is theoretically open to both sexes, being a ''man of the world'' in Victorian society usually involves being male. Trollope is thought to reap literary advantages from his own experience as a Victorian gentleman. The *North British Review*, for example, believes that Trollope's combination of knowledge of the world with his subtlety allows him to outshine all female writers:

> Mr. Trollope, with the delicate perception which he possesses, seizes upon the distinctive features which underlie so much apparent uniformity, and creates, or rather portrays, a character which is not the less amusing because it is perfectly commonplace. Some female writers have possessed this peculiar subtlety in still greater perfection, but then it is accompanied in Mr. Trollope with a masculine maturity and a knowledge of the world to which there is no kind of parallel in Miss Austen nor in any of her English sisters. (375)

The ease with which critics are able to identify and sympathize with Trollope reveals how his masculine persona enhances his literary credibility. The *Saturday Review* is disarmed by the similarities between Trollope's own profile and that of its own readers and reviewers: ''he always writes like a gentleman, and like an educated, observant, and kindly man'' (1859, 368). The *North British Review* writes that Trollope ''thoroughly understands, because he shares the thoughts and feelings of the majority of educated Englishmen'' (370).

Occasionally, the intensity of Trollope's masculine image or persona creates a feeling of disjunction between the man and his work, as McMaster comments: ''At social gatherings he was a bluff and blustering presence, and people were often astonished at the contrast between the delicacy of his novels and the aggressive assertiveness of their author: 'The books, full of gentleness, grace and refinement; the writer of them bluff, loud, stormy, and contentious,' wrote his friend W. P. Frith'' (qtd. in McMaster 304).

When critics comment specifically on Trollope's writing, their impression of Trollope the man casts a constant shadow over their observations. As David Skilton remarks, ''in general he is socially approved by the critics, even the fastidious *Saturday* naming him as 'one of the few popular writers of the day who always write as a gentleman and a man of sense and principle should write' '' (8). Writing ''as a gentleman and a man of sense'' is seen by most critics as one of Trollope's main talents, if not his central one. Henry James admires Trollope's ''masculine'' thought, stance, and judgment: ''He writes, he feels, he judges like a man, talking plainly and frankly about many things, and is by no means destitute of a certain saving grace of coarseness'' (99). James thus equates Trollope's straightforward lack of prudishness with masculinity.[6]

The clarity and plainness of Trollope's style are also complimented as a masculine trait. Geoffrey Tillotson, writing recently, states that Trollope's style is characterized by "a preference for monosyllables. It likes plain words" (56). It seems to be exactly this aspect of Trollope's style that strikes critics as masculine. *Time*, in 1879, expresses its enjoyment of the "definiteness and direction; the same Anglo-Saxon simplicity" (627) of Trollope's style. Paul Elmer More praises Trollope's "clear, manly, straightforward style" (91).

The *North British Review* admires Trollope's plots, and believes that they conjure up the delights of boyhood confrontations: in an 1864 article it calls them "simply a new version of the old fighting stories of our boyhood transferred to a far more delicate atmosphere; and we watch the struggle between Mrs. Proudie and Archdeacon Grantly with very much the same kind of anxiety as that with which we used to regard the engagements of the Deerslayer with the bloody Mingoes" (378).

The posthumous appearance of Trollope's *An Autobiography* was greeted by Richard Holt Hutton in the *Spectator* within an explicitly gendered framework:

> The absolute frankness of *An Autobiography* is most characteristic of Mr. Trollope; and so is its unequalled — manliness we were going to say;— but we mean something both more and less than manliness, covering more than the daring of manliness and something less than the quietness or equanimity which we are accustomed to include in that term, so we may call it, its unequalled masculineness." (1377)

And David Cecil's reassessment of Trollope admires the "masculine friendliness" of Trollope's "tone of voice," the "genial, leisurely masculinity" of Trollope's "vital and vigorous" humour, and the strength of his satire, which is not weakened "by diluting it in sentimental rosewater" (244–57).

Critics often attributed their enjoyment of Trollope, then, to his "masculine" qualities, and in many respects identification and discussion of Trollope's strengths revolved around male gendered connotations. The volatile nature of Trollope's reception, however, is more complicated and strange than the preceding discussion might imply. Despite critical perceptions of Trollope the man and Trollope the writer as intensely masculine, many critics, paradoxically, also felt that Trollope's writing had many feminine qualities. This perception grew stronger as the 1860s progressed. Occasionally such critics praised Trollope for the versatility and imagination that allowed him to exhibit supposedly feminine writing characteristics; more frequently, just as perceptions of masculine qualities in *Barchester Towers* raised his critical reputation, feminine associations with his later work, are, as I will show, partly responsible for critical attacks on Trollope, ranging from a refusal to take him seriously as a leading and important writer, to an affectionate dismissal as entertaining but slight.

Critics occasionally praised Trollope's juxtaposition of "masculine" and "feminine" qualities, as in the following 1882 remark by the *Saturday Review*:

> He was in the best sense of the word a masculine man and writer, and yet he knew more of the feminine mind and nature than any author of his generation. . . . Among many signal merits of Mr. Trollope's genius was this — that he could handle at will and with equal success the masculine and the feminine nature and bent. (755)

And the *North British Review*, in the 1864 article quoted above, argues that Trollope's ability to combine the "delicate perception" and "subtlety" of feminine writers with masculine strengths puts him in a unique category, one clearly above the reach of women writers.

More usually, however, Trollope's "feminine" qualities caused him to be taken less seriously. As the preceding remarks from the *Saturday Review* and the *North British Review* indicate, Trollope's apparent knowledge of the women and insight into their characters was widely remarked upon and seen as a feminine trait. The *Saturday Review*, praising his "extraordinary insight" into the "working of the feminine . . . mind" (755), recounts a story to this effect: during a dinner conversation, someone posed the following question to Trollope, " 'Mr. Trollope, how do you know what we women say to each other when we get alone in our rooms?' " (755). The *Edinburgh Review* seems perplexed at the apparent paradox in Trollope's ability to identify with young women in the creation of his numerous heroines: "Here we have a middle-aged or elderly gentleman worming himself into the hearts and confidences of young ladies, and identifying himself with the innermost workings of their minds; and a very remarkable phenomenon it is" (qtd. in Helling 81). Henry James, adopting a rather sinister predatorial image, also comments on Trollope's fondness for depicting young English women: "Trollope settled down steadily to the English girl; he took possession of her, and turned her inside out" (qtd. in Helling 82).

But this ambivalent admiration for the attention Trollope devoted to his heroines and the insight he seemed to have into their thoughts and feelings was also frequently the occasion for critical dismissals, as in the following 1869 comment from the *Fortnightly Review*: "[W]e admit Mr. Trollope's power in describing young ladies in love and in doubt. He knows English girls by heart. . . . as the prose laureate of English girls of the better class, why should not Mr. Trollope record something else beside flirtations that end well?" (198)

Unlike Charles Reade, for example, who chose "epic" plots based on theme and action rather than character analysis, Trollope was more attracted to romance-based plots and character. Burns describes Reade as "consciously abjuring the techniques of Trollope and the domestic novelists (whose works he dismissed as 'chronicles of small beer') in an effort to create epic characters equal to what he conceived to be his epic theme" (159). It is quite clear that for Reade, Trollope's "chronicles of small beer" cannot possibly measure up to his "epic themes." Trollope himself was quite candid about the importance of the romantic plot to his fiction. In his lecture on novels, "On English Prose Fiction As A Rational Amusement," Trollope states boldly that novels "not only contain love stories, but they are written for the sake of the love stories" (Parrish 109). As Park Honan stated recently, "Trollope's women remind us that he had immense sentimental energy" (323).

Unfortunately for Trollope, being regarded as a "chronicler of young ladies' thoughts" was not conducive to being taken seriously as a novelist. The *Fortnightly Review*'s praise of Trollope's *Last Chronicle of Barset* reads like a response to such attacks on Trollope's work: "[In his] *Last Chronicle of Barset* [Mr. Trollope] has given us glimpses of a certain tragic and poetic power that place him far above any chronicler of young ladies' thoughts" (190). The implication clearly is that the thoughts of women, young women especially, are by definition frivolous and silly rather than interesting or serious.

One of the ways in which critics classified and evaluated Trollope was by defining his readership. Discussion about the sex of Trollope's readership led inevitably to evaluative statements about his merit as a writer. *Barchester Towers* was greeted by the *Wesminster Review* as "a novel that men can enjoy" (1857, 327), and Elizabeth Barrett Browning praised *The Three Clerks* as "a thoroughly *man's* book," describing how her husband who normally did not like novels was "held" by *Barchester Towers*, *Doctor Thorne*, and *The Three Clerks* (qtd. in Smalley 64). As Trollope became increasingly popular, however, critics began to categorize his audience as both male and female, and, in some cases, as predominantly female. The *Times*, for example, in an 1859 article, argues that Trollope is suitable both for "patrons of Mudies" and for "thoughtful men": "To those who are in the habit of reading novels it is unnecessary to say that Mr. Trollope is one of the most amusing of authors; and to those who in general prefer blue-books, statistics, and telegrams, but now and then indulge in the enormity of romance, we may report . . . that he is a 'safe man' " (109). In a retrospective assessment of Trollope's readership, Michael Sadleir echoes this judgment, calling Trollope "at the same time . . . a novelist for the jeune fille and a most knowledgeable realist" (373).

Trollope himself, writing about the author's relationship to his readers, describes novel readers in primarily female terms, describing how they receive instruction in the ways of the world from the novelist:

> The novelist creeps in closer than the schoolmaster. . . . He is the chosen guide, the tutor whom the young pupil chooses for herself. She retires with him, suspecting no lesson, safe against rebuke, throwing herself head and heart into the narration . . . and there she is taught — how she shall learn to love; how she shall receive the lover when he comes. . . ." (qtd. in Helling 109)[7]

Presumably we can take these remarks as indicative of Trollope's sense of his implied and actual reader. Regardless of Trollope's own assessment of his readership, Trollope's popularity as a writer, and thus his status as a circulating library novelist, seems to be partly responsible for his reputation as a writer for young women.

The *Saturday Review*, for example, writes disparagingly of the popularity of *Framley Parsonage*'s serialization in *Cornhill Magazine*: "[T]he author of *Framley Parsonage* is a writer who is born to make the fortune of circulating libraries. At the beginning of every month the new number of his book has ranked almost as one of the delicacies of the season; and no London belle dared to pretend to consider herself literary who did not know the very latest intelligence about the state of Lucy Robarts' heart and of Griselda Grantley's flounces" (1861, 452).[8] It is perhaps only a small step from this kind of gendered assessment of readership to the pronouncement of the *Literary World* in 1884 that while Thackeray is a writer for men, Trollope is a writer for women. Trollope's view of life is, according to this periodical, "nearer what we may call the female view," and thus, "we may say, on the whole, that Thackeray is written for men and women, and Trollope for women" (275). The *Literary World* goes on to praise Thackeray as "rooted in what is permanent on our nature" whereas Trollope's pictures are destined for only transient popularity.

Trollope's mass popularity and consequent association with circulating libraries constitute (along with his focus on romantic plots and interest in female characters) grounds for many Victorian critics to dismiss him as a serious writer, although it was common for such critics still to express their enjoyment of Trollope. In 1859 the *Times* places Trollope firmly in the category of circulating library writer by virtue of his popularity: "If Mudie were asked who is the greatest of living men, he would without one moment's hesitation say Mr. Anthony Trollope. . . . Trollope is, in fact, the most fertile, the most popular, the most successful author — *that is to say, of the circulating library sort*" (12; my emphasis). For the *Times*, however, Trollope's association with the circulating library raises *its* prestige rather than lowering Trollope's: "These novels are healthy and manly, and so long as Mr. Anthony Trollope is the prince of the circulating library our readers may rest assured that it is a very useful, very pleasant, and very honourable institution" (12). Trollope's continued association with Mudie's, however, eventually led to some critical dismissal. Being "the prince of the circulating library" was a somewhat dubious privilege.

Trollope was also criticized for being unimaginative or for having a mechanical kind of imagination that reproduces rather than creates. Trollope did receive praise for his ability to replicate Victorian society and life, but many Victorian critics saw this as essentially artless. The *Saturday Review*, for example, in 1861, states that "Mr. Trollope himself nowhere pretends to do more than to write down what he sees going on around him. He paints from the outside"

(452). Trollope's reputation for superficiality of imagination, and a prolificacy of production that seemed incompatible with "true" genius or even artistry, had a derogatory influence on Trollope's literary reputation. Both accusations had certain feminine connotations or associations, as I will argue.

The *North British Review* (in 1864) and the *Fortnightly Review* (in 1869) reiterate the complaint of the *Saturday Review* about the apparent absence of imagination in Trollope's brand of realism. The *North British Review* suggests that Trollope disqualifies himself from the ranks of imaginative artists through his emphasis on realism: "he represents ordinary characters, and paints real life as it is, only omitting the poetry. The highest object of imaginative literature he neither attains nor aims at" (401). The *Fortnightly Review* argues that "common-place" life is incompatible with high literary art: "The genteel public of the day may demand portraits of themselves . . . but no amount of skill can make common-place men and common-place incidents and common-place feelings fit subjects of high or true literary art" (196).[9]

These remarks all stem from similar assumptions about the components and attributes of great art: high art should not rely too much on everyday life, but should transcend these particulars by suggesting universals or by dealing only with the heroic or extraordinary. Perhaps inevitably in the divisions and hierarchies of Victorian culture, rigidly schematized according to gender, such critiques and adjectives assume gender associations; the critical objections to Trollope cited above correspond closely to the kind of critical attacks levelled at women's writing. "Masculine" was identified with high-culture, male readers, originality, power and truth, whereas "feminine" was associated with popular culture, female readers, and stereotypically female qualities such as lack of originality, weakness of intellect, and feebleness of ideas. Trollope's literary reputation, from the early 1860s onwards, suffered from being feminized, from being burdened with the kind of critiques that were more usually bestowed upon popular women writers.

In 1867 and 1868, Trollope conducted a literary experiment producing two novels, *Nina Balatka* and *Linda Tressel*, that he published anonymously. The *London Review* responded thus to *Linda Tressel* on May 30, 1868: "We are not aware that *Nina Balatka* was ever said to be the writing of a woman . . . but the appearance of *Linda Tressel* almost settles the point. The heroic fortitude, the simple frankness, and maidenly honor of *Nina Balatka* were the attributes of a creation which might have arisen in the mind of a male artist; but *Linda Tressel* seems to us altogether a woman's woman" (qtd. in Smalley 20). This interesting observation sheds some light on what was perceived as intrinsically yet paradoxically feminine in the character portrayals in Trollope's other novels.

The world of Trollope's novels was a very recognizable one for his readers, focusing as it did primarily on genteel middle-class Victorian relationships in society. And while domestic realism was clearly not the exclusive preserve of women writers, it was, as Showalter reminds us, seen as their most appropriate domain: "By the 1840s women writers had adopted a variety of popular genres, and were specializing in novels of fashionable life, education, religion, and community, which Vineta Colby subsumes under the heading 'domestic realism' " (20). Tuchman argues that women writers were associated "with the least-admired aspects of novels: the details of personal, emotional, and everyday life" ("When the Prevalent" 154).

Women writers were thought to specialize in domestic realism because it required less imaginative and intellectual effort or strength, allowing them to passively regurgitate the details of life they saw around them. Lack of imagination was seen as one of the chief limitations of women writers for many Victorian critics. R. H. Hutton, in an 1858 essay for the *North British Review*, argues this position: "It may seem a harsh and arbitrary dictum that our lady novelists do not usually succeed in the field of imagination. . . . Yet we are fully convinced that this is the main deficiency of feminine genius. It can observe, it can recombine, it can delineate, but it cannot trust itself further; it cannot leave the world of characteristic traits and expressive manner" (qtd. in Helsinger 52–53). G. H. Lewes, in his essay "The Lady Novelists," also argues that women's writing is characterized by a close adherence to domestic experience rather than inspired by intellect or imagination: "The domestic experience which forms the bulk of women's knowledge finds an appropriate form in novels" (*Westminster Review* 133). One writer in 1858 held that women writers gravitated towards unimaginative portraits of everyday life due to their intellectual short-comings:

> In many ways, the natural limitations of feminine power are admirably adapted to the standard of fiction held up as the true model of a feminine novelist in the last century. It was then thought sufficient to present finished sketches of character, just as it appeared under the ordinary restraints of society; while the deeper passions and spiritual impulses, which are the springs of all the higher dramas of real life, were, at most, only allowed so far to suffuse the narrative as to tinge it with the excitement necessary for a novel. (*North British Review* 472–73)

It is apparent that the kind of criticisms directed towards Trollope's supposed lack of imagination and focus on domestic realism were also characteristic criticisms aimed at women's writing. In my judgment, Trollope is taken less seriously as an artist because of his apparently "feminized" attributes as a writer in these respects. As Tuchman argues, "by 1870 men of letters were using the term high culture to set off novels they admired from those they deemed run-of-the-mill" (3). Tuchman analyzes the readers' reports for the publishing house of Macmillan, run by Morley, and believes that the readers viewed "high-culture" in terms of gender:

> As Morley and his successors tried to distinguish and define the high-culture novel through their in-house reviews, they insistently identified men with high culture

and women with mass or popular culture, although they did not use these twentieth-century terms. They identified men with ideas capable of having an impact upon the mind — with activity and the production orientation associated with high culture. Women were identified with mass audiences, passive entertainment, and . . . popular culture. (78)

Trollope, then, is condemned by many Victorian critics for choosing to focus on "common-place incidents and common-place feelings," for ignoring the "highest object of imaginative literature," for being uncomfortably close in popularity and subject-matter to female "circulating-library" novelists, although his skill and wide experience of life make him, for many critics, superior to such "second-rate" writers. An important testimony to these kinds of associations is the *Saturday Review*'s conflation of feminized content, commercial popularity, imaginative weakness, and artistic inferiority in the following 1863 critique of *Rachel Ray*: "There is a brisk market for descriptions of the inner life of young women, and Mr. Trollope is the chief agent in supplying the market. . . . Mr. Trollope . . . has taught himself to turn out a brick that does almost without straw, and is a very good saleable brick of its kind" (qtd. in Skilton 54).

Trollope's precarious position as a serious Victorian writer was also endangered by his productivity. His ability to write so many books, one after the other, was seen as suspicious, tantamout to a rejection of high aesthetic seriousness and to an adoption of a money-motivated and formulaic approach. From 1857 to 1869, twenty reviews of different Trollope works appeared in the *Athenaeum*, twenty-four in the *Saturday Review*, and twenty-four in the *Spectator* (Skilton 12). Of course other Victorian writers such as Dickens, Mrs. Oliphant, or Charlotte Yonge were also prolific, but Trollope is unusual, unique even, not only for the sheer quantity of novels he wrote, but for his own outspoken and gleeful pride in his production. As he put it in his *Autobiography*:

> And so I end the record of my literary performances, — which I think are more in amount that the works of any other living English author. If any English authors not living have written more . . . I do not know who they are. I find that . . . I have published much more than twice as much as Carlyle. I have also published considerably more than Voltaire, even including his letters. . . . I am still living and may add to the pile. . . . It will not, I am sure, be thought that, in making my boast as to quantity, I have endeavoured to lay claim to any literary excellence. . . . But I do lay claim to whatever merit should be accorded to me for persevering diligence in my profession. (253–55)

Although men, such as G. P. R. James and G. W. M. Reynolds, as well as women wrote prolifically and for commercial reasons, women in general were thought to be more susceptible to rapid and unskilled writing, a prejudice that goes back to the eighteenth-century idea of "scribbling women." Greg in his essay "False Morality of Lady Novelists" states that "there are vast numbers of lady novelists, for much the same reason that there are vast numbers of sempstresses": ":Every educated lady can handle a pen *tant bien que mal*: all such, therefore, take to writing — and to novel-writing — as the kind which requires least special qualification and the least severe study, and also as the only kind which will sell" (qtd. in Ewbank 11). Lewes protests in an 1865 essay against the "presumptuous facility" of "indolent novelists," and implies that women novelists are especially guilty (Nadel 361). Dallas felt that "women have a talent for personal discourse and familiar narrative, which, when properly controlled, is a great gift, although too frequently it degenerates into a social nuisance" (qtd. in Showalter 82). Showalter argues that women's writing was seen as effortless, an extension of their natural role and instinct: "Such an approach [i.e., that of Dallas] was particularly attractive because it implied that women's writing was as artless and effortless as birdsong, and therefore not in competition with the more rational male eloquence" (82).

Trollope was vulnerable to similar accusations because of his enormous pro-ductivity. Many critics felt that the sheer volume and rapidity of his literary production meant that the works had to be produced "naturally," without undue intellectual exertion. His notorious statements about writing in his *Autobiography* only served to accentuate existing distrust and disregard for his status as a literary figure.[10] Trollope was perhaps more vocal about the quantity of his work and the financial rewards that followed than any other Victorian figure; Payn writes that "[h]e took almost a savage pleasure in demolishing the theory of 'inspira-tion,' which has caused the world to deny his 'genius' " (167). Trollope was thus dangerously vulnerable to the kinds of critical attacks and associations normally connected with the productivity and literary status of women writers. McMaster attributes negative and ambivalent responses to Trollope to the rate of his literary production: "Trollope's enormous productivity has had much to do with a patronizing dismissal of his work by some critics and a rather apologetic attitude adopted even by his admirers" (317).

Victorian critics were preoccupied with classifying Trollope as a major or second-rate writer. Despite their initial enthusiasm for *Barchester Towers* and its immediate successors in the late 1850s and early 1860s, and despite their own enjoyment of Trollope's work, many had reservations about Trollope's status as a leading novelist who would rank with Dickens or Thackeray. Skilton attributes part of the critical ambivalence to a degree of insecurity about what the "rules" were for excellence in the relatively new genre of novel: "We see the reviewers confronted by the problem of whether or not to regard him as a great novelist, and of how to establish in the first place what constitutes greatness in a genre in which they are still not at home, critically speaking" (xiii). (Dickens and Thackeray were often taken as the two "masters" against whom other contenders were measured (resurrecting the Richardson/Fielding opposition of the previous century), and of course such a preconception or standard tended to somewhat unfairly influence critical vision and judgment, making it harder to see a novelist in terms of his or her unique strengths.)

The *Times* obituary of Trollope had no reservation about placing him in the second-rank of novelists, along with Austen and Gaskell who wrote "realistic studies of English domestic life" (qtd. in MacDonald 113). The *Saturday Review*, however, perhaps remembering their previous partiality to Trollope, rose to Trollope's defense, objecting vehemently to critics who associated him with second-ranked authors like Austen: "it is only 'the stupid critic' that has placed Jane Austen and Trollope 'together in the second rank' " (qtd. in Fielding 434).[11]

Olmsted and Welch suggest that critical ambivalence towards Trollope really began in the 1860s, and argue that the most interesting aspect of Trollope's critical reputation has been the general reader's refusal to be influenced by the often negative remarks of the critics: "Trollope's readers have for the most part been going it alone since the 1860s when writers for the *Athenaeum* and the *Saturday Review* first began to express their irritation at Trollope's 'superstitious adherence to facts' and at what Henry James called 'the inveteracy with which he just eludes being really serious' " (xi).

It is not coincidental that both of the obituaries mentioned above juxtapose Trollope with Jane Austen. It was, in fact, a critical commonplace to compare Trollope with Austen. As Smalley states, "both stopped short of the depth of vision or the high seriousness that were essential to art of a more elevated sort. Both were, however, wonderfully amusing" (14). Smalley's summary conveys the sense that domestic realism was seen as somehow incompatible with high-serious art, as well as the way in which Trollope's popularity was actually detrimental to his stature as an artist. Smalley goes on to imply a similar point when he states that Victorian critics regarded Trollope as "a popular novelist delightful to read" rather than as a "genius" (26).

Implicit in the idea that Trollope was "popular" and that he was "delightful to read" is the reservation that he was too accessible to the ordinary novel-reader to be taken very seriously. Stephen's dismissal of Trollope in 1901 is particularly telling in this respect: "We can see plainly enough what we must renounce in order to enjoy Trollope. We must cease to bother ourselves about art. . . . We must not desire brilliant epigrams suggesting familiarity with aesthetic doctrines or theories of the universe. A brilliant modern novelist is not only clever, but writes for clever readers" (180). Sadleir, in 1927, makes an equally revealing observation with retrospective insight: "The initial obstacle to a sober-minded definition of Trollope's novels is that they provide a sensual rather than an intellectual experience" (366). Again, I would argue that perceptions like these have implicit gender associations — clever, educated, and intellectual were adjectives more commonly associated with male writers and readers in Victorian culture, and even though Stephen and Sadleir's comments are from the early twentieth-century, they sum up the nebulous qualities of Trollope's work and image that complicated the assessment and ranking of Trollope by Victorian critics from the 1860s until his death in 1884.

Frederic Harrison's comparison of Trollope with Austen in 1895 explicitly feminizes Trollope:

> Now Trollope reproduces for us that simplicity, unity, and ease of Jane Austen, whose facile grace flows on like the sprightly talk of a charming woman, mistress of herself and sure of her hearers. This uniform ease, of course, goes with the absence of all the greatest qualities of style; absence of any passion, poetry, mystery, or subtley. He never rises, it is true, to the level of the great masters of language. But, for the ordinary incidents of life amongst well-bred and well-to-do men and women of the world, the form of Trollope's tales is almost as well adapted as the form of Jane Austen. (208)

These remarks demonstrate the association of artlessness so many nineteenth-century critics had with women's writing, the identification of domestic subject-matter as somehow incompatible with the "great masters," and the way Trollope's reputation suffers from being associated with "the sprightly talk" and "facile grace" of a "charming woman." Brophy, writing as late as 1968, reiterates the Trollope/Austen comparison, feminizing Trollope even more strongly than Harrison: "Indeed Trollope is that nice, maundering spinster lady with a poke bonnet and a taste for cottagey gardens whom superficial readers thought they had got hold of when they had in fact got hold of the morally sabre-toothed Jane Austen" (64).

Trollope's so-called "masculine" characteristics were largely responsible for the critical approval he did receive, for *Barchester Towers* for example, and the "feminine" characteristics of his writing (his subject-matter, his interest in and insight into female characters, his imagination or lack thereof, his productivity, his popularity, his readership) are partly responsible for his critical dismissal. In the mid and latter part of his career, Trollope was often associated with the less prestigious feminine qualities and connotations; as I have shown, critical ambivalence began creeping in during the mid 1860s, and was fairly solidly in place from, and after, 1870.

The timing of Trollope's critical fall from grace coincides, then, with the rise of a critical poetics that increasingly desired to distinguish "high art" from "popular art," often along gender lines. Tuchman argues that "[b]y 1870 men of letters were using the term *high culture* to set off novels they admired from those they deemed run-of-the-mill" (3). And in 1880 the *Athenaeum* laments that "Mr. Trollope is not an artist according to the modern school of high art" (qtd. in Skilton 33). As we have seen, the criteria defining "high art" rigorously exclude the feminized qualities so commonly applied to Trollope from the late 1860s onwards, and these gender connotations play a major, even a central role, in Trollope being "edged out."

The volatility of Trollope's reputation has never been satisfactorily accounted for, though critics like Skilton, Smalley, Olmsted, and Welch provide comprehensive surveys of its bizarre twists and turns. Ruth ApRoberts attributes this critical failure to "come to grips with his work" to the inappropriate application of "old theories" of art, such as modernist premises and "new critical" frameworks: "Of all English novelists Trollope seems to be the perfect example of the kind least served by our old theories; and for this very reason, to come to grips with his work may help us towards a new and more workable theory" (11). Contemporary twentieth-century critics overlook the issue of gender in the decline of Trollope's reputation, probably assuming that Trollope's sex guarantees him safety from any sexual double standard that might exist. Ironically though, my argument does not contradict but supplements or complicates conventional accounts of Trollope's fall from "high art," since the very reasons most commonly used to account for this decline — Trollope's productivity and lack of superior imagination, changing literary tastes — themselves have gender connotations which have been ignored in discussions of Trollope. While it would be overstating the case to claim that associations with gender constitute the sole cause of the decline in Trollope's reputation, a "new more workable theory" that would help us understand Trollope should, I think, take into account the previously invisible and overlooked relation of nineteenth-century gender associations with ideas of literary value and high art, as applied to Trollope's novels. Being a "Queen" of the Victorian circulating library was problematic for any writer when popular and high art began to diverge, but particularly problematic if the author happened to be male.

State University of New York — Cortland College

NOTES

1. Nardin's *He Knew She Was Right* is the only explicitly feminist work I am aware of in this field, and it is devoted to textual study rather than to reception considerations.
2. This article argues that gender associations contributed to the deterioration of Trollope's critical reputation. Contemporary twentieth-century critics do not address the issue of gender in this respect; they attribute Trollope's loss of literary prestige to changing literary tastes, to the incompatibility of his productivity with the idea of romantic genius, and to the sense that his subject-matter and his treatment of it were not indicative of superior imagination or profundity, but the gendered connotations of these aesthetic criteria are not discussed. See Macdonald's *Anthony Trollope*, Smalley's "Introduction" in *Anthony Trollope: The Critical Heritage*, and Olmsted and Welch's Introduction in *The Reputation of Trollope* for surveys of the decline of Trollope's reputation. For a general discussion of changes in aesthetic and literary critical ideals from the mid to the late nineteenth century, Stang's *The Theory of the Novel in England* is a helpful source; Skilton's *Anthony Trollope and his*

Contemporaries discusses how Victorian literary critical conventions about imagination, subject-matter, and character depiction affected Trollope's reception and reputation.

3. Trollope's first four novels were as follows: *The Macdermots of Ballycloran* (1847), *The Kellys and the O'Kellys* (1848), *La Vendee* (1850), and *The Warden* (1855).

4. In 1858, Mudie advertised fifty books, but bought most copies of the following four novels: Charles Kingsley's *Two Years Ago* (1200 copies); Charles Reade's *It Is Never Too Late To Mend* (1000 copies); Charlotte Yonge's *Dynevor Terrace* (1000 copies); and 900 copies of Charlotte Yonge's *Heartsease* (Haight 2: 467). Compared to such numbers, Mudie's order for 200 copies of *Barchester Towers* may seem like paltry stuff, but when we remember that the four books above were Mudie's top orders for a year, and that *Barchester Towers* was really the first novel of Trollope's that attracted wide critical notice, 200 seems like a respectable number.

5. Such comments are extremely common in Trollope reviews: a few examples are Dallas's article in the *Times*, May 23, 1859, the June 1864 article in *North British Review*, and the *Saturday Review* article of 1882. The *Times* calls Trollope's writing style "healthy and manly," and "cordially sympathizes" with his "manly aversion to melodramatic art" (12). The *North British Review* finds that "the whole tone and habit of mind implied in these [Trollope's] novels is that of a man of activity and business, rather than of a man of letters" (370). The *Saturday Review* says that he was "a masculine man and writer" (755).

6. Trollope's disagreements with his publisher over the supposed vulgarity of *Barchester Towers*'s language ("fat stomach" was changed to "deep chest," and "foul breathing" was eliminated by Longman's objection) are well known, and are documented with much mischief and wit in the *Autobiography*. In an 1856 letter, Trollope responded thus to Longman's accusations of "indecency" in *Barchester Towers*: "[N]othing would be more painful to me than to be considered an indecent writer. . . . I do not think that I can in utter ignorance have committed a volume of indecencies" (*The Letters of Anthony Trollope* 2: 47). In an 1860 letter to George Smith, Trollope declared ruefully that he would "never forget a terrible and killing correspondence which I had with W. Longman because I would make a clergyman kiss a lady whom he proposed to marry — He, the clergyman I mean; not he W. Longman" (*Letters* 1: 117).

7. This passage proceeds to mention male readers, but devotes more primacy and space to their female counterparts.

8. The sustained and ambivalent attention dedicated to Trollope by the *Saturday Review* is one of the most interesting aspects of Trollope's reception history. Trollope identified the *Saturday Review* in his *Autobiography* as one of the three most important British periodicals for contemporary literary criticism; the other two were The *Times* and the *Spectator*. The particular stance, approach, and readership of the *Saturday Review* self-consciously represented University-educated men, and in fact the *Saturday Review* often interpreted its position as a call to arms to defend elite literary culture against popular invasions. As a result, the tone and content of *Saturday Review* literary criticism is often more predictable and constant than that of other Victorian periodicals. The extent to which the individual perspective of the reviewer or critic became submerged by the journal's persona is evident in a remark by Leslie Stephen, who, going through the *Saturday Review* files years later, is unable to identify his own work: "I had unconsciously adopted the tone of my colleagues, and, like some inferior organisms, taken the colouring of my 'environment' " (qtd. in Smalley 21). The *Saturday Review* found itself in an uncomfortable

predicament over Trollope, however: it identified with Trollope as a fellow middle-to-upper-class educated Victorian man, but objected to Trollope's heretical lapse into behaviour and characteristics which did not accord with its high-culture position, and which, as I argue, had become feminized. Consequently the many *Saturday Review* articles on Trollope show some sign of emotional intensity and conflict, and sometimes contradict each other, as is evident from the excerpts quoted in this chapter, particularly if Trollope's obituary is compared to the journal's earlier commentary on Trollope.

9. The second chapter of Skilton's *Anthony Trollope and His Contemporaries* "Critical Concerns of the Sixties: Tragedy and Imagination" situates criticism of Trollope's supposed lack of imagination in the context of the 1860s: "The better and more favourable of Trollope's contemporary critics . . . found various ways of accounting for why he fell short of artistic greatness. All their explanations amount in effect to the diagnosis that he lacked 'imagination', that his subjects were mundane, his treatment of them plain, and that in short he was an 'observer' or 'photographer' rather than an inventive artist" (45).

10. A. L. Rowse's essay, "Trollope's *Autobiography*" in *Trollope Centenary Essays* (ed. John Halperin) provides more background on how Trollope's *Autobiography* affected his reputation.

11. As Fielding explains in "Trollope and the *Saturday Review*," the *Saturday Review* "liked Trollope because, as they say, he wrote in 'the style of a gentleman' " (431). Fielding goes on to state that "the *Saturday Review* did enjoy Trollope in spite of their apparently hostile criticism, which was sometimes actually hostile" (432). Skilton sees the *Saturday Review* as leaning more towards the critical side of ambivalence, primarily because of Trollope's popularity: "Conscious of their social and intellectual superiority, the university men on the *Saturday* felt a deep scorn for any popular phenomenon, in literature, religion, dress or politics" (53). Skilton summarizes the *Saturday*'s attack on the 1866 *The Belton Estates* thus: "Trollope, says the reviewer, is like an artist who year after year submits to the Royal Academy a painting of a donkey between two bundles of hay. He has published no fewer than three novels in the past twelve months, all concerning someone who is hesitating between two loves, and the only difference between them is that the 'expression of the donkey's eye may vary a little' " (55–56).

WORKS CITED

Anonymous reviews and articles are alphabetized by title of the periodical.

ApRoberts, Ruth. *The Moral Trollope*. Athens, Ohio: Ohio UP, 1971.
Rev. of *Barchester Towers*. *Athenaeum* 1544 (30 May 1857): 689–90.
Brophy, Brigid, Michael Levey, and Charles Osborne. *"The Warden."* In *Fifty Years of English and American Literature We Could Do Without*. London: Stein and Day, 1968.
Burns, Wayne. *Charles Reade: A Study in Victorian Authorship*. New York: Bookman, 1961.
Cecil, David. *Victorian Novelists: Essays in Revaluation*. Chicago: U of Chicago P, 1935.
Rev. of *Barchester Towers*. *Eclectic Review* July 1857: 54–59.
Ewbank, Inga-Stina. *Their Proper Sphere: A Study of the Brontë Sisters As Early-Victorian Female Novelists*. London: Arnold, 1966.

Rev. of *Barchester Towers*. *Examiner* 16 May 1857: 308.

Fielding, K. J. "Trollope and the *Saturday Review.*" *Nineteenth-Century Fiction* 37, 3 (Dec. 1982): 430–42.

"Mr. Anthony Trollope's Novel." *Fortnightly Review* 5, xxvi (1 Feb. 1869): 188–98.

Haight, Gordon, ed. *The George Eliot Letters*. 2 vols. New Haven: Yale UP, 1954.

Halperin, John, ed. *Trollope Centenary Essays*. New York: St. Martin's Press, 1983.

Harrison, Frederic. "Anthony Trollope's Place in Literature." In *Studies In Early Victorian Literature*. London: Arnold, 1895.

Helling, Rafael. *A Century of Trollope Criticism*. 1956. Port Washington, N.Y.: Kennikat Press, 1967.

Helsinger, Elizabeth K., Robin Lauterbach Sheets, and William Veeder, eds. *The Woman Question: Society and Literature in Britain and America, 1837–1883*. Vol. 3. *Literary Issues*. Chicago: U of Chicago P, 1983.

Honan, Park. "Trollope After A Century." *Contemporary Review*. Dec. 1982: 318–23.

Hutton, Richard Holt. "Anthony Trollope's *Autobiography.*" *Spectator* 56, 2887 (27 Oct. 1883): 1377–79.

Irwin, Mary Leslie. *Anthony Trollope: A Bibliography*. New York: Wilson, 1926.

James, Henry. "Anthony Trollope." In *Partial Portraits*. London: Macmillan, 1886, 97–133.

Rev. of *Barchester Towers*. *Leader* 23 May 1857: 497.

"About Novels." *Literary World* 15 (23 Aug. 1884): 275.

Macdonald, Susan Peck. *Anthony Trollope*. Boston: Twayne, 1987.

McMaster, Juliet. "Anthony Trollope." In Nadel, Ira, and William Fredeman, eds. *Dictionary of Literary Biography. Vol. 21. Victorian Novelists Before 1885*. Detroit, Michigan: Gale Research Co., 1983.

More, Paul Elmer. "My Debt To Trollope." In *The Demon of the Absolute*. Princeton: Princeton UP, 1928.

Nadel, Ira, William Fredeman, and John Stasny, eds. *The Victorian Muse: Selected Criticism and Parody of The Period*. New York: Garland, 1986.

Nardin, Jane. "Conservative Comedy and the Women of *Barchester Towers.*" *Studies in the Novel* 18, 4 (Winter 1986): 381–94.

———. *He Knew She Was Right: The Independent Woman in the Novels of Anthony Trollope*. Carbondale: U of Illinois P, 1989.

"Mr. Trollope's Novels." *National Review* 7 (Oct. 1858): 416–35.

"Novels by the Authoress of 'John Halifax.' " *North British Review* 29 (1858): 466–81.

"Mr. Trollope's Novels." *North British Review* 40 (June 1864): 369–401.

Oliphant, Margaret. *The Victorian Age of English Literature*. Philadelphia: David Mckay, 1892.

Omsted, John Charles, and Jeffrey Egan Welch. *The Reputation of Trollope: An Annotated Bibliography, 1925–1975*. New York: Garland, 1978.

Parrish, Morris L., ed. "On English Prose Fiction As A Rational Amusement." In *Four Lectures*. Constable Ltd. 1938. Rpt. Norwood Editions, 1977, 94–124.

Payn, James. *Some Literary Recollections*. New York: Harper, 1884.

Reade, Charles. *It Is Never Too Late To Mend*. 1856. Boston: Grolier, 1943.

Sadleir, Michael. *Trollope: A Commentary*. 1927. Rpt. New York: Farrar, Strauss, and Giroux, 1947.

Rev. of *Barchester Towers*. *Saturday Review* 3 (30 May 1857): 503–04.

Rev. of *The Bertrams*. *Saturday Review* 7 (26 March 1859): 368–69.

"Framley Parsonage." *Saturday Review* 9 (4 May 1861): 451–52.

"Mr. Anthony Trollope." *Saturday Review* 54 (9 Dec. 1882): 755–56.

Showalter, Elaine. *A Literature of Their Own: British Women Novelists From Brontë to Lessing*. Princeton: Princeton UP, 1977.

Skilton, David. *Anthony Trollope and his Contemporaries: A Study in the Theory and Conventions of mid-Victorian Fiction*. London: Longman, 1972.

Smalley, Donald. *Trollope: The Critical Heritage*. London: Routledge & Kegan Paul, 1969.

"Reade's *It Is Never Too Late To Mend.*" *Spectator* 29 (16 Aug. 1856): 877–78.

Rev. of *Barchester Towers*. *Spectator* 30 (16 May 1857): 525–26.

Stang, Richard. *The Theory of the Novel in England, 1850–1870*. New York: Columbia UP, 1959.

Stephen, Leslie. "Anthony Trollope." In *Studies of a Biographer*, Vol. 4. London: Putnam's Sons, 1907, 156–60.

Stevenson, Lionel. *Victorian Fiction: A Guide to Research*. Cambridge: Harvard UP, 1964.

Super, R. H. *The Chronicler of Barsetshire: A Life of Anthony Trollope*. Ann Arbor: U of Michigan P, 1988.

Sutherland, John. *The Longman Companion to Victorian Fiction*. London: Longman, 1988.

Tillotson, Geoffrey, and Kathleen Tillotson. *Mid-Victorian Studies*. London: Athlone, 1965.

"A Novelist of the Day." *Time: A Monthly Magazine* 1, 1879: 626–32.

[E. S Dallas] "Mr. Anthony Trollope." *Times* 23 May 1859: 12.

"New Novels." *Times* 13 Aug. 1857: 5.

Trollope, Anthony. *An Autobiography*. 1883. Gloucester: Alan Sutton, 1987.

———. *Barchester Towers*. 1857. Ed. Michael Sadleir and Frederick Page. Oxford: Oxford UP, 1989.

———. *The Letters of Anthony Trollope*. 2 volumes. Ed. N. John Hall. Stanford, California: Stanford UP, 1983.

———. *The Warden*. Ed. N. John Hall. Oxford: Oxford UP, 1989.

Tuchman, Gaye, and Nina E. Fortin. *Edging Women Out: Victorian Novelists, Publishers, and Social Change*. New Haven: Yale UP, 1989.

———. "When The Prevalent Don't Prevail. Male Hegemony and the Victorian Novel." *Conflict and Consensus*. Ed. Walter W. Powell and Richard Robbins. New York: The Free Press, 1984. 139–58.

[G. H. Lewes] "The Lady Novelists." *Westminster Review*, n.s. ii (1852), 129–41.

"Contemporary Literature: Belles Lettres." *Westminster Review* 68 (Oct. 1857): 326–27.

THE MOTHER'S MISTAKE: SARAH STICKNEY ELLIS AND DREAMS OF EMPIRE

By Randi L. Davenport

A RECURRENT DREAM, ALWAYS experienced on the eve of childbirth, is the mistake which provides the title for Sarah Stickney Ellis's domestic novel, *The Mother's Mistake*.[1] By misunderstanding her dream, Mrs. Clifton, an otherwise admirable woman, becomes "calculating" and "prospective," failing, finally, to procure the "right knowledge of the true character of her child" (3; ch. 1). At the same time, the dream initiates a narrative of maternal neglect which participates in a larger conversation about the condition of England and the future of Empire. The dream itself reflects mid-Victorian concerns about the nature of social hierarchies and the rightful classification — in terms of status, class, gender, and prestige — of the individual.

The Mother's Mistake tells the story of the young middle-class Clifton family, whose rising fortunes suddenly fall. Though the family has been living in a comfortable little villa in Richmond, a short commute from London, Mr. Clifton's business in the financial district — based on speculative investment in "molasses and sugars" and buffeted by "taxes on the colonial produce" (6; ch. 1) falters after a period of early prosperity — and the family's wealth is disastrously eroded. Each child must shoulder, in his or her own way, the burden of providing for the family. The children's activities toward this end are supposed to be fool-proof, based, as they are, on Mrs. Clifton's dream, which draws upon the science of phrenology to help the reader understand the relationship between physical and moral structures. Each dream, in other words, is predictive not only of the child's natural abilities and talents but is an explication of the relationship between middle-class aspirations — figured as the structures of the brain — and a clear moral conscience for both the individual and the society as a whole.

As she dreams, Mrs. Clifton imagines the inner workings of a sleeping infant's brain:

173

as she watched . . . there appeared to be a misty curtain moving slowly over the
head of the little sleeper. Gradually this filmy veil was entirely removed, and
beneath lay the living brain of the future being, all spread out like a map, so
minute in its various and distinctive characteristics and capabilities. . . . Nor was
this spectacle appalling to the beholder, but beautiful . . . for all the inner structure
and the secret office of each portion of the brain was brought distinctly into view —
the very working of energy and life in all displayed — the delicate and mysterious
association, as it were, of soul and body — of nerve and muscle — of will and
act: all these were made manifest so that under the observant gaze might be seen
to grow . . . out of nothingness, the future development of what each portion of
the brain was so constructed as to supply the means of carrying out into actual
and material results. (3–4; ch 1)

The first time Mrs. Clifton has this dream, she sees in her infant's brain a
specially developed section of "elaborate and most complicated" architecture
where all structures seem to be

in the very act of growing, of rising into form and fitness, and placing [themselves]
in some position of utility[:] . . . the graceful bridge was thrown across the river . . . the promontory was pierced by the rapid tunnel . . . the side of the moun-
tain was cleft, and a smooth passage carried over the scattered rocks . . . the very
sea itself was driven out and a proud breastwork of safety planted deep amongst
its raging waves. (4; ch. 1)

When she wakes, Mrs. Clifton is understandably puzzled about the meaning of
this dream so she consults her baby-nurse, who informs her that the dream
means her child will " 'build up the fortunes of his house and family, and great
fortunes they will be. Riches' she said, 'were in store for the son and heir of
the Cliftons; there could be no doubt of that — most likely titles for his descendants; and all through his own energy and skill in putting things together with
a profit in them' " (4; ch. 1).

Delighted, as any striving middle-class mother would be, with the prospect
of riches and titles for her family, Mrs. Clifton sends her first-born to work in
the family business, ignoring the talent for mechanical drawing, engineering,
and architecture that the dream portends. It takes near financial ruin before the
grown child is able to pursue his true abilities and restore financial stability —
but not real affluence — to the faltering family. By sending her five children
off-course, one after the other, each time with disastrous effects, Mrs. Clifton's
actions become the central "mistake" which drives the plot of the novel. The
motion of the plot revolves around the five offspring finding their way back to
their true callings in life and the castigation of Mrs. Clifton for having listened
to her nurse and gotten her plans so wrong. At first glance, then, the novel
seems to be a common Victorian warning against class transgression — the
middle-class mother will find it a very risky business to take the advice of a
member of the working class. Riskier still is the act of listening to a nurse who

uses the science of phrenology — which some Victorians derided as "bumpol-ogy" — to interpret the world.

To the extent that most mid-century domestic novels tended to argue that the tutelage of the "good" mother provided for the appropriate future of the child, neither Mrs. Clifton's dream, nor *The Mother's Mistake*, is particularly remark-able. Yet, when examined as part of a broader cultural dialog about England's colonial mission — with England serving as mother to a host of colonial off-spring — the mid-Victorian concern with rightful placement of the individual within society which Mrs. Clifton's dream conveys appears to be much more urgent. The dream in this domestic novel, in other words, serves not just as prescriptive literature for the mothers of the nation, but as a warning to the nation that would be maternal.

Mrs. Clifton's dream is remarkable, too, in that it reproduces the main princi-ples of phrenology, that science of the late eighteenth and early nineteenth centuries which sought to render not just a theory of character or a theory of the brain but, ultimately, a secular means for assessing the individual's place in society and nature. More importantly, the novel acts as a polemic for "true" phrenology, defending the science while dismissing embarrassing working class appropriations of its principles. In this, Ellis's text accomplishes much of the task set by the early Victorian phrenologists themselves, making respectable through its associations with middle-class literati and intellectuals what was increasingly dismissed as both ridiculous and revolutionary in the mechanics institutes attended by the workers of the lower classes.

Early Victorians were receptive to a theory of human behavior which allowed them to make determinations about the nature of identity and used phrenology to justify and "prove" the inferiority of women, of the non-British, and of those peoples who fell under British colonial rule.[2] In the early part of the ninteenth century, phrenology also "played an important role as a medium by which the ideas of one . . . class were transmitted to another" (McLaren 87) and the narrative of Empire initiated by *The Mother's Mistake* makes this clear. It is a fundamentally exclusionist narrative, claiming for the middle classes the work of building, prospering within, and realizing the dreams of an expanding society. Yet it has ramifications for the upwardly striving working class as well. Like the texts of the phrenologists themselves, Ellis's novel is moving towards a liberal, secular position, offering explanations of the world — and of the individ-ual's place within it — that do not rely on concepts of either original sin or virtue for meaning and consequence.

The dream in Ellis's text thus also becomes a trope of the many tensions and contradictions — especially as these tensions and contradictions speak to the ideology of separate spheres, a public world occupied by men and a private world populated by docile women — woven together in Ellis's work. Probably the best known "idealogue of domesticity" (Davidoff and Hall 182) writing in the second quarter of the nineteenth century, Ellis has been traditionally viewed as a conservative writer who wrote of woman's importance while uncritically supporting her work within the home circle. Her audience, as Leonore Davidoff and Catherine Hall have noted, was comprised of the women in the families of "traders, manufacturers and professionals where there were one to four servants, and where there was no family rank" (182–83). A prolific writer of popular fiction, Ellis is best known today for her books on the condition of women in England. *The Women of England* (1838) was fantastically popular in the 1840s and put Ellis on the literary map, but her books on *The Daughters of England* (1842), *The Mothers of England* (1843), and *The Wives of England* (1843), rapidly published after the success of the first text, were only slightly less popular. Indeed, by 1848, the three books had been collected and published in both England and America under the title *The Family Monitor and Domestic Guide*.

Yet Ellis's use of phrenology to create the dream at the center of *The Mother's Mistake* tends to radicalize her narrative. Instead of drawing a clear division between the public and private spheres, in other words, the mistaken interpretation of the mother's dream, based on the wildly inaccurate musings of the baby-nurse, puts forth the notion that the operations of the private sphere are critical to the function of the public. This is, in and of itself, a powerful and radical critique of the ideology of separate spheres, which Ellis's work has been said to uphold. But it is Ellis's use of phrenology — a field of science that in the nineteenth century belonged to those who were younger, less socially prominent, less professionally advanced, and less likely to have come from a genteel background — that helps to reveal the radical position dueling with the conservative within Ellis's narrative. While the *Medico-Chirurgical Review* maintained that phrenology was "the most intelligent and self-consistent system of mental philosophy that has ever been presented to the contemplation of inquisitive men" ("Review," *Medico-Chirurgical Review* 29), phrenology did not find itself widely accepted among older, wealthier, and more established physicians and scientists. Indeed, as Cooter so rightly points out, what "*by and large* distinguishes those attracted to phrenology was their recently heightened sense of social worth being incommensurate with their place and power in the social process" (47). Certainly Ellis, the daughter of a tenant farmer, born in 1799 and compelled by economic circumstance to make financial contributions to the family from an early age, might have experienced such pressures and contradictions in her own life. Despite her recommendation that all the activities of women be based on Christian principles and faith, seeing women primarily as supportive, loving, uncomplaining wives and mothers, Ellis's writing reveals a strong fellow-feeling for the domestic trials of the Victorian women of the middle-classes. Her polemics, indeed, can take on a nearly plaintive tone as they urge women to educate themselves and not to abandon one another in their servitude: "What should we think of a community of slaves, who betrayed each other's interests? of a little band of ship-wrecked mariners upon a friendless shore who were false to each other? of the inhabitants of a defenceless nation, who would not unite together in earnestness and good faith against a common enemy?" (*The Daughters of England* 90). This is hardly a supple voice calmly enjoining women to take up their "natural" roles; rather, the language of this domestic guide is rich with images of violence: women are metonymically "slaves"; or a species of human cast up out of violent surf who must struggle to survive without friends; or residents of a community so vulnerable to assault that it is virtually without defenses, save for the banding together of the women themselves.

If Ellis is a figure who represents clearly defined domestic values, then the domesticity she decribes names women as vulnerable to the worst kinds of transgressions against the individual; her women, mothers, daughters, and wives are subject to ownership, violation, abandonment, and neglect. Ellis's attention to the problems inherent in women's place in England in the first half of the ninteenth century in fact makes claiming her as the voice of paradigmatic middle-class behavior extremely problematic. Her position is further confounded when she and her work are placed in historical context. When Ellis's world is understood as one that values social reform, especially utilitarian social and political reform — a more secular way of imagining the individual's place in the world — her texts tend to address again and again the problem of woman's power, proclaiming the centrality of her place while quietly acknowledging the difficulty of her position, what Elaine Showalter refers to as a "covert solidarity that sometimes amounted to a genteel conspiracy" (15–16).

Like the phrenologists, then, Ellis seems to reject the reigning philosophical bases to social power. Instead of being secondary, subordinate, and unimportant, in Ellis's texts discussions of women's work and women's lives concomitantly act as discussions of ideas and practices that should be integrated into a reformed society, a society in which would predominate what were obviously more merit-ocratic values. Still, Ellis was no feminist, nor — despite running Rawdon House, a school for girls near her home in Hoddesdon, and writing frequently of the need for better education for women — was she known as an intellectual. Her work was destined for the sewing circle, to whom it may have seemed comforting and familiar, being at once a strongly hinted acknowledgement of the oppressive conditions of most middle-class women's lives, as well as a prescription for the value women felt their positions merited, rather than a simple reflection of the restrictive and exploitive conditions of their lives.

That the sewing circle was assumed to be cognizant of the theories under-girding phrenology is a testament to the importance of phrenology as a social discourse in the first half of the nineteenth century. Phrenology in the late eighteenth and early nineteenth centuries was a combined theory of the brain and, as R. J. Cooter notes, a "science of character" (3) that more or less adhered to the tenets of Franz Joseph Gall, a successful Viennese physician. These tenets, in brief, held that, first, the brain is the organ of the mind; second, that the brain is not a homogeneous unity but an aggregate of mental organs; third, that these mental organs or physical faculties are topographically localized into specific functions; fourth, that other factors being equal, the relative size of any one of the mental organs can be taken as an index to that organ's power of manifestation; and fifth, that since the skull ossifies over the brain during infant development, external craniological means can be used to diagnose the internal state of the mental faculties.[3] From such beliefs sprang notions that one might understand the character of an individual by surveying his or her head. Phrenology was frequently invoked in discussions about criminals and the penal system, with those who argued for punishment rather than rehabilitation fond of buttressing their claims with diagrams of the criminal head.[4]

But phrenology also helped to support the notion of natural divisions between groups of people in the Victorian world, with both gender and race figuring prominently in discussions of qualities that "naturally" inhered in different individuals. In women and indigenous people, for example, the organ of philoprogenitiveness — or love of offspring — was found to be considerably more developed than in the white male. In 1833 Spurzheim recuperated this idea of Gall's in a particularly offensive way, connecting women, monkeys, and a tribe of New Zealanders by noticing that like "negroes and Indoos" (Hindus), each has an over-developed "protuberance," missing in white men, that denotes "love of off-spring" (178–79). Spurzheim includes two discussions to elaborate on this point: in the first, he describes how Gall came to realize that this "protuberance" on the rear of the cranium meant a love of children in general, noticing that while Gall had determined that this was a "regularly occurring protuberance on the back part of the heads of females," as well as "in the skulls of children and of monkeys" (178–79), he had no explanation for its existence. Following a lecture in which he described this puzzling phenomenon, Gall was approached by a clergyman who remarked that "monkeys were very much attached to their young ones" (179). Gall "reflected" on this statement and decided that the protuberance must mean "love of off-spring." It was, after all, impossible to deny the "appeal to observation" (179) of the monkey evidence. In this discussion, Spurzheim clearly slides women and monkeys together so that maternity — the aspect of womanhood that Victorians notoriously believed reduced women to the animal anyway — signifies both their degradation and the reason for their degradation.

Spurzheim's second discussion is worth noting because he feminizes and thus makes inconsequential the chief of a tribe of New Zealanders — a man of "rough and brutal manners" (181) — by noting his overdeveloped philoprogenitiveness, an organ of the mind with which no self-respecting white man, not even a lower-class white man, would be caught dead. Spurzheim, after all, has already noted that "we never hire male servants to take care of our children" (178); to have love of offspring is clearly so degrading that even the British working-class male must be protected from the suggestion of its contamination. In the case of "chief Telora" of New Zealand, however, Spurzheim points out that philoprogenitiveness in the colonized male can greatly improve that man's character. Philoprogenitiveness in the colonized obviously has other desirable effects: to note the chief's fond attachment to his children is to make a woman of him and erase the threat of resistance or corresponding strength. What is particularly interesting about Spurzheim's account of chief Telora is the writer of the travel narrative he cites. A William Ellis, who spent a short time at the Bay of Islands in 1816, provides the account of Telora accidentally stepping on and then comforting his crying child in *The Library of Entertaining Knowledge* (1: 359). This William Ellis traveled throughout the colonies to ascertain the lot of Christian missionaries. When he was not traveling to Australia or New Zealand or Madagascar, he was at home in England writing about his travels. These works were meant to spur interest in missionary life.

William Ellis was also Sarah Stickney Ellis's husband, having married her in 1837, following the death of his first wife in 1835. He introduced her to the problems of the Christian missionary, and she became enormously interested in working on ways to improve their chances of getting their job done. Indeed, *The Mother's Mistake* records this interest in its concluding paragraphs, as two of the Clifton sons — the clergyman and the accidental outlaw of the Australian outback — join forces to create a kind of colonial utopia for themselves and their descendants in Australia. The resolution of the novel thus directs its readers' attention to the extent to which principled individual action could be understood as integral to the colonial mission. Having placed the British citizen — here defined as white, male, and middle class — on a global stage, the novel reassuringly connects colonial initiatives with those ideas about the status of the individual within the social hierarchy of mid-century Britain that were widely accepted at home. In the main, these ideas reflected the ways in which mid-Victorian writers and thinkers increasingly understood individual action to be linked to expanded political responsibility and the concomitant growth of the power of the state. In the case of *The Mother's Mistake*, the activities of the individual which are understood to be the rightful consequences of his inherent immutable characteristics lead to the development of an idealized colonial world that more clearly represented British ideals than the conflicted world at home. That this colonial utopia would be managed by the compleat British citizen — the white, middle-class male — is a message consonant not only with colonial imperatives, which regularly called mid-Victorian men into service, but with the message of the phrenologists, who imagined a social hierarchy organized around individual merit and activities, rather than birth status and titles.

The claims of the phrenologists were hotly debated throughout the teens and twenties. Indeed, even though it was discredited knowledge in its own time, eventually coming to be dismissed as a "pseudoscience," phrenology had its moment in the sun. Phrenology was the nineteenth century's most popular and popularized science, providing a set of claims about the worldwide condition of humanity that were more widely read and accepted than those by Darwin — for example, while phrenologist George Combe's *The Constitution of Man* (1829) sold two thousand copies in ten days the year it was published and was soon found in respectable libraries and mechanics institutes all over Britain, Darwin's *The Origin of the Species* sold sixteen thousand copies in England over the course of fifteen years. Continental phrenologists made rather striking and radical claims about the evolutionary process as well, but British phrenologists tended to distance themselves from such claims, worried that colorful charts depicting man's rise from a mental tadpole-like state might undercut their attempts to be taken seriously by institutions like the Royal College of Physicians.

Phrenology also made strong contributions to Victorian notions of psychology — and hence of the operations of dreams. Indeed, David de Giustino has argued that "one of the areas in which phrenology and medicine could profitably interact was in the explanation of dreams" (44). In 1830, Scottish physician and phrenologist Robert Macnish detailed his theory of "incomplete sleep," in his *Philosophy of Sleep*. This theory held that the supposed activity of one or more organs of the mind produced dreams while the other organs of the mind were at rest. In theory, if one's organ of destructiveness remained awake while the others slept, for example, one might dream of murder or other violence.

Nearly all the major phrenologists addressed the question of dreams, with nearly identical results. Spurzheim wrote that "any particular organ, or even several organs, may be active while the other organs rest; then the particular sensations or ideas which result from this particular activity constitute that which is called *dreams*, which are more or less complicated according to the number of active organs" (qtd. in Grant 257–58; emphasis in original). Andrew Carmichael reiterated this notion in his *Essay on Dreaming; Including Conjectures on the Proximate Cause of Sleep* (1818), but his example is somewhat more colorful:

> If a portion of [the brain] is emancipated, thoughts peculiar to that portion arise, and those thoughts are dreams. The mechanic's imagination may rove among machinery; the mathematician may solve a problem; the orator pour forth unstudied eloquence; the poet, unpremeditated verse; the wit, delectable jests, the musician, unprecedented harmony; yet this does not always occur, only occasionally. (52)

Given these explanations of dreams, one might expect Mrs. Clifton, Sarah Ellis's character in *The Mother's Mistake*, to dream not of the destinies of her children but of her own philoprogenitiveness. What better time to agitate that organ of the mind than on the eve of childbirth? Despite Ellis's own quiet bristling at the constraints imposed by the limitations placed on feminine behavior, the dream of empire that is characterized in phrenological terms in *The Mother's Mistake* is perhaps a dream in which women's collusion in the oppression of other people is prescribed, or even required, as an aspect of the feminine ideal. The dream presents a vision of the world that rests on a broadly liberal and secular appreciation of the individual, but it does not revise Victorian ideas about who the individual was. He — not she — is a builder, an engineer, a thinker, an achiever. He conquers himself in order to conquer others. When Mrs. Clifton dreams of her child's destiny, she is simply reproducing what Jonathan Glance has argued was the predominant physio-psychological paradigm for mental activity in the first part of the nineteenth century; Glance argues that the law of association — which has its roots in Locke's *Essay Concerning Human Understanding* (1700) — proposed that one's waking thoughts will have a hand in the determination of the train of events in one's dreams. Thus, a miser will dream of his money, or a poet will dream of literary activities, or a mother — like Mrs. Clifton — will dream of her child.

Yet the dream that Ellis records is also a version of the prophetic dream, one in which the mother dreams of the actual phrenological structures of her child's mind. For the mid-Victorians, the concept that dreams resulted from the natural structures of the brain promoted by phrenologists was not at all at odds with the notion that dreams served as vehicles for messages from the spirit world or as symbols of events that had not yet — but surely would — come to pass. Even when the newly scientific cast given to studies in psychology is taken into account, such beliefs persisted. Certainly, the *Journal of Psychological Medicine* echoes phrenologists when at mid-century it attempts to explain the prophetic dream. By noting the importance of "waking thoughts" which spring from something inherent and unique to each individual dreamer, the *Journal* is able to claim that prophecies arise from the thoughts that are the "objects of consciousness" (*Journal of Psychological Medicine*, October 1851; qtd. in Grant 191). By claiming that the prophetic dream is the dreamer's "mind in *deed*," the *Journal* is able to suggest that the "nature of our dreams is determined by the gloss or tone of mind which we cultivate, indulge in, abandon ourselves to; so that, whether sleeping, waking, or dreaming, a man's life is nothing else than a dramatic personification of his innate . . . ideas" (*Journal of Psychological Medicine*, July 1849; qtd. in Grant 202–03). Needless to say, those "innate ideas" existed because the organs of the mind regulated each individual's natural and varied powers.

In this, both the *Journal* and Ellis's novel echoed George Combe's *The Constitution of Man Considered in Relation to External Objects* (1829), phrenology's most popular account of the usefulness of attending to the information provided by the map of the brain. Combe's text directly addresses the relation of the science of phrenology to Victorian notions of strong individualism, providing a narrative of the self that is one part utilitarian in its attitudes about self-sufficiency and self-will, one part Christian virtue in its relentless linkages of concepts of the self to the work of God, and one part "scientific" empiricism in its attention to the "fact" of phrenological structures. The story thus told has all the conventions familiar to readers of Victorian fiction, including a smooth and powerful voice which elides its secret inner workings, appealing to common-sense to cover over the contradictions and tensions inherent between and among these various parts. For example, Combe wrote, "If it be true that natural talents and dispositions are connected by the Creator with particular configurations of brain, then it is obviously one of His institutions that, in forming a compact for life, these should be attended to" (99). Here Combe uses a rhetoric of responsibility to the self, which translates into a responsibility both to God and to society, to appeal to what most readers in the first half of the nineteenth century would take to be true in any case. But there is a subtle re-shaping of that same message elsewhere in Combe, especially as he insists that it is the task of the parent to ascertain the child's true abilities and to develop them forthwith. In this, he concludes, parents are not to imagine themselves as abridging natural laws but rather staving off disaster by recognizing early that each individual has a place within a world that is hierarchical by the intention of God. He writes, "these miseries [of ill-developed children] are not legitimate consequences of *observance* of the organic law, but the direct chastisement of their *infringement*" (79; emphasis in original). Indeed, Combe's claims, like Ellis's fictional treatise, address again and again the rightful placement of the individual in a society increasingly fraught with unresolved worries about losing the distinctions between people.

Most Victorian scholars would agree with Raymond Chapman that these unresolved worries were spawned by concerns about class-status and prestige (43). But these worries do not limit themselves to fears about disruptions in a systematic and knowable pattern of class distinctions. Instead, phrenology most persistently reflects distinctions between the self and the other that connect to broader cultural questions about imperialism and empire. Phrenology, as practiced by Combe or Ellis, was primarily an inadvertent form of self-representation, a discourse about the "other" which tells us more about the "subject" than the "object." Combe's text links the knowable future of the individual not just to proper parental identification of the talents of their offspring, but to proper parents; like O. S. Fowler, he is persuaded that some must not reproduce at all, and included among those are the offspring Fowler terms "heathenish" in their neglect of their mothers (*Creative and Sexual Science* 665). At the same time, the "proper" parent is clearly defined. He or she must not be among those who are weak, "feeble, sickly, the exhausted with age, and the incompletely developed" (79). This prescription rules out all but the white European or, in the case of Fowler, the white North American. Tropes of the "other" in the first half of the nineteenth century rested on cultural assumptions about their fitness as people, and it was taken as truth that indigenous peoples — like chief Telora — were weaker, more feeble, and distinctly underdeveloped, the heathens of Fowler's despicable "heathenish."

The examples provided by the phrenologists translate in Ellis's domestic fiction into a narrative that proposes that national identity is predicated on a network of differeces, chief among them the differences between the conqueror and the conquered. When Philip tells his brother that he has a "good mind to start off somewhere to one of these new colonies, and begin a new life" (*The Mother's Mistake* 50; ch. 10), he is responding to his brother Seymour's ideas about the Christian mission of imperialism, in which the false god of the "heathens and barbarians," as wrong as he is, is not mocked or blasphemed in the manner of the Christian God (49), and he is responding to his mother's dream that he is naturally fitted to the task of world-making and Empire-building (50–51). In this, Philip's response rests on the claims of Fowler, who, like Combe, devoted large sections of his work to the fitness of parents, in particular the mother, whose animal nature in the act of reproducing had to be re-written as spiritual, celestial, as being imbued with a version of maternal love that covered over a deeply misogynistic Victorian view of the female body. To give to the mother not the sexual origin of new life but the responsibility for the birth of empire was to draw her into the fold as both the originator of the world and its housekeeper. Certainly this is what Fowler seems to have had in mind when he wrote that the Christian mother was "earth's queen who produces the highest order of children. Voting, legislating, public speaking, swaying the destinies of nations, all else are but baubles in comparison to motherhood; because without it there could be no nations, no anything to sway' (*Creative and Sexual Science* 666). Fowler's Christian mother seems at first glance a far cry from Ellis's Mrs. Clifton, yet Mrs. Clifton is herself defined by her distance from the ideal and thus is relentlessly yoked to a definition of beneficent maternity that suggests both the necessity of the mother's involvement in imperatives about empire and the virtual impossibility of her being able to take up that role, imprisoned as she is within the domestic sphere.

If it is axiomatic that the story of Victorian Britain is a story of growing political responsibility for the individual, coupled with the extension — and the expansion — of the power of the state, then the struggle for representation, both individual and collective, which phrenological discourse seems to reflect and to generate, can be viewed as one of the major issues of the first half of the Victorian age. And Ellis's domestic texts, *The Mother's Mistake* among them, can productively be viewed as participating in that struggle. Yet her use of early and mid-century claims about phrenology also serve as a species of code narrative for the pressures and problems her texts cannot otherwise concede. That is, both scientific claims in the form of phrenology and a seemingly clinical interest in dreams were, along with the domestic fiction that preserves them, part of the cultural mythology surrounding imperialism. Since imperialism as a concept presupposes questions about power relations, it cannot be separated from a broader cultural question — what Spivack has suggested is the question of how and under what conditions the "other" may be appropriated (277–78) — which informs the emergence of mid-century imperialism and supplies the material over which debates about empire might rage. Both phrenology and the fictions of home responded to the growing demand for the work of empire to be located in a particular place, that is, within the confines of a national identity viewed predominantly as moral, Christian, and middle-class.

Alma College

NOTES

1. Date unknown. Ellis published extensively in the late 1830s and throughout the 1840s. *The Mother's Mistake* is one of her least known novels, failing even to be included in the list her nephew prepared for the *Dictionary of National Biography*.
2. For example, Cooter notes that phrenologists maintained that Gall, "had (among other things, such as 'proving' the inferiority of women) perceived the innate sociability of man" (113). See also de Giustino, McLaren.
3. Most contemporary writers on phrenology give this same succinct account of Gall's work; for this discussion I am indebted to Cooter (3).
4. These diagrams and, later, photographs were considered striking evidence in their day, yet all they succeeded in doing is recording the damage done to an individual by successive generations of malnutrition, lack of money, and poor hygiene.

WORKS CITED

Carmichael, Andrew. *Essay on Dreaming; Including Conjectures on the Proximate Cause of Sleep.* 1818.

Chapman, Raymond. *The Victorian Debate: English Literature and Society 1832–1901.* New York: Basic Books, 1968.

Combe, George. *The Constitution of Man Considered in Relation to External Objects.* Boston: Carter and Hendee, 1829.

Cooter, R. J. *The Cultural Meaning of Popular Science: Phrenology and the Organization of Consent in Nineteenth Century Britain.* Cambridge: Cambridge UP, 1984.

Davidoff, Leonore, and Hall, Catherine. *Family Fortunes: Men and Women of the English Middle Class 1780–1850.* Chicago: U of Chicago P, 1987.

de Giustino, David. *Conquest of Mind: Phrenology and Victorian Social Thought.* London: Croom Helm, 1975.

Ellis, Sarah Stickney. *The Daughters of England.* London: Fisher, Son, and Company, 1842.

———. *The Mother's Mistake.* London: Houston and Stoneman, n.d.

Fowler, O. S. *Creative and Sexual Science: or manhood, womanhood, and their mutual interrelations; love, its laws, power, etc.; selection, or mutual adaptation; courtship,*

married life, and perfect children; their generation, endowment, paternity, mater-
nity, bearing, nursing and rearing; together with puberty, boyhood, girlhood, etc,;
sexual impairment restored, male vigor and female health and beauty perpetuated
and augmented, etc. as taught by phrenology and physiology. Philadelphia: National
Publishing, 1875.

Glance, Jonathan. " 'Beyond the Usual Bounds of Reverie': Another Look at Dreams
in *Frankenstein.*" Unpublished essay, 1992.

Grant, Alexander Henley. *The Literature and Curiosities of Dreams. A Commonplace*
Book of Speculations Concerning the Mystery of Dreams and Visions, records of
curious and well-authenticated dreams, and notes on the various modes of interpreta-
tion adopted in ancient and modern times. By Frank Seafield, M.A. [pseudonym].
London: Chapman and Hall, 1865.

Library of Entertaining Knowledge. Vol. 1. London: C. Knight, n.d. 359.

Macnish, Robert. *The Philosophy of Sleep.* [1830].

McLaren, Angus. "Phrenology: Medium and Message." *Journal of Modern History*
46.1 (March 1974): 86–97.

Review of "Observation on Phrenology." *Medico-Chirurgical Review* 4 (March/May
1823): 29.

Showalter, Elaine. *A Literature of Their Own: British Women Novelists From Brontë to*
Lessing. Princeton: Princeton UP, 1977.

Spivack, Gayatri Chakravorty. "Three Women's Texts and a Critique of Imperialism."
"Race," Writing and Difference. Ed. Henry Louis Gates, Jr. Chicago: U of Chicago
P, 1986. 262–80.

Spurzheim, Johann Gaspar. *Phrenology, in connection with the study of physiognomy.*
Illustration of Characters. Boston: Marsh, Capen and Lyon, 1834 [c. 1833].

ANTI-BODIES OF DISEASE AND DEFENSE: SPIRIT-BODY RELATIONS IN NINETEENTH-CENTURY CULTURE AND FICTION

By C. S. Wiesenthal

Desecrated as the body is, a vengeful ghost survives and hovers over it to scare.
— Herman Melville, *Moby-Dick*

The . . . primitive fear of ghosts is still deep in our bones, but it is unconscious. Rationalism and superstition are complementary. It is a psychological rule that the brighter the light, the blacker the shadow; in other words, the more rationalistic we are in our conscious minds, the more alive becomes the spectral world of the unconscious. And it is indeed obvious that rationality is in large measure an apotropaic defence against superstition, which is everpresent and unavoidable.
— C. G. Jung, *Psychology and The Occult*

If we go further and enquire into the origin of . . . anxiety — and of affects in general — we shall be leaving the realm of pure psychology and entering the borderland of physiology.
— Freud, "Inhibitions, Symptoms, and Anxiety"

The conception that antibodies, which should protect against disease, are also responsible for disease, sounds at first absurd.
— Clemens von Pirquet, *Serum Sickness*

The Age of Anti-Bodies

ALTHOUGH THE NINETEENTH CENTURY WAS in fundamental respects the great age of empiricism or of the material body, its collective fascination with spiritualistic phenomena such as ghosts and spectral apparitions certainly presents an antithetical sign of the times, a countercurrent of spiritualism that one might term, in fact, literally anti-body in essence and effect. Indeed, only less grossly than they

187

were with the material realm were Victorians on both sides of the Atlantic engrossed by an occult realm seemingly swarming with spirits and vapory wraiths. As many scholars have shown, Victorian traffic in spiritualism, which peaked in two crescendos of enthusiasm during the decades 1830–40 and 1870–80, precipitated the evolution of a veritable industry in "spirit communication" and spectacle, including such wildly popular forms of private and public entertainment as "materialization seances" and "phantasmagoria" exhibits.[1] Near the century's end, the Victorian penchant for spectral phenomena culminated in the establishment of such prominent intellectual offshoots of the spiritualism movement as the Society for Psychical Research and the International Congress of Experimental Psychology. In literature, too, the period signalled the "heyday of the middle-class ghost" (Finucane 190); indeed, the modern ghost story dates its discovery and development to an all-time "high-water mark" (Briggs 14) through the works of such writers as Edgar Allan Poe, Charles Dickens, Guy de Maupassant, E. T. A. Hoffman, and Henry James, not to mention lesser lights such as Vernon Lee and Sheridan Le Fanu.

Though perhaps most readily evident in the realms of popular culture and fiction, the nineteenth-century captivation with ghosts and apparitions also finds expression in a remarkable array of medical, philosophic, and belletristic treatises on the related phenomena of hallucinations and phantoms. From such largely anecdotal (though influential) works as Mrs. Catherine Steven Crowe's *The Night Side of Nature* (1848) to the SPR's vast compendium of apparition narratives, *The Census of Hallucinations* (1889), and the substantial contributions of such intellectual heavyweights as Henry Maudsley and William James, this varied and extensive literature bears witness to the controversy surrounding much spectral phenomena of the period. Many contemporary medical writers, for example, did not hesitate to link deliberate spiritualistic attempts at ghostly conjurings with an unhealthy predisposition to hysteria or even "spiritualistic madness."[2] Moreover, the inherently ambiguous nature of many individual apparition encounters, as seemingly subjective, psychical experiences involving "ghosts" born of the mind, reinforced the dark associations between the realm of occult phenomena and that of contemporary psychopathology.

As historians of both psychology and the occult have been quick to point out, of course, ghosts have long been associated with forms of morbid mentation: "states of delirium and psychic alienation, hallucination, the sensation of being 'pursued' or possessed by horrifying thoughts" (Castle, "Phantasmagoria' 47). Burton, in *The Anatomy of Melancholy*, associated the seeing of "ghosts, goblins, etc." with a pathologic surplus of melancholy humors, as did Shakespeare before him, in *Hamlet* (329).[3] In 1572, Ludwig Lavater first used the word "hallucination" (from the Latin *alucinato*, meaning "a wandering of the mind, idle talk") to refer specifically to "Ghostes and Spirites Walking by Nyght," revenants attributable to "eyther . . . melancholic, madnesse, weaknesse of the senses, fear or . . . some other perturbation'' (Siegel and West 242; Briggs 142). The conceptual link between ghosts and forms of hallucinatory madness not only persisted into the nineeenth century; by then, the term ''hallucination'' had also expanded to include a more comprehensive range of aberrant perception as well as cognition. According to an influential definition propounded by Esquirol in 1838, ''hallucination'' could now be understood to encompass any perceptual processes which involved ''ascribing a body and actuality to images'' (qtd. in Siegel and West 242). This meant ''all delusive impressions,'' as a British contemporary put it, ''from the wandering mote before the eye, to the tremendous spectre, which are equally destitute of [objective] existence'' (Ferriar 95). From the relatively benign base of spectral illusion or random optical simulacra to more ominous and fully-fleshed phantasms of ''Spectre-work and Demonology,'' apparitions thus came to be more and more subtly implicated with the domains of what, as Carlyle lamented in *Sartor Resartus*, ''we have now named Madness and Diseases of the Nerves'' (Carlyle 195).

In order to explore spectral phenomena as subjective symptoms of ''Madness and Diseases of the Nerves'' in nineteenth-century culture and fiction, this essay will take a bifocal approach. Most immediately, I will seek to recover the essential terms of the contemporary debate over the semiological status and nosological significance of apparitions and hallucinations. Nineteenth-century perspectives on the putative ''pathology'' of spectral phenomena in turn provide the context for exploring the representation of ghosts in *Villette* and *Wuthering Heights*, two well-known mid-century texts instructive to juxtapose because of their evident tendencies toward opposite philosophical ends of the materialist-spiritualist spectrum underlying contemporary theories of apparitions.

At a second remove, my argument shifts to advance a modern perspective on the symptomatic relevance of ghosts in the wider context of the nineteenth-century cultural imagination, offering an interpretation that flows as much from the historical exigencies and psychophysiological nature of Victorian epistemology as it does from certain psychoanalytic precepts, themselves products of the later century. I proceed from the basic premise that the rise of interest in spectral apparitions — whether subjectively- or objectively-based — at this precise historical juncture invites a more detailed psychobiological analysis than it has been hitherto accorded.[4] In particular, I explore the Victorians' pervasive preoccupation with apparitions as a psychoanalyzable symptom of the collective psyche: not as a sign of ''Madness and Diseases of the Nerves'' in the Carlylean sense, to be sure, but as a sign, nonetheless, of a mass nervous dis-ease or ''realistic anxiety'' ultimately (though not exclusively) attributable to frightening new changes in physiological disease and mortality patterns.[5] The resurgent scourge of infectious epidemic diseases throughout most of the nineteenth century is of paramount importance in this respect. For in this case, it is within the contemporary context of the biologically defenseless body that the ghost-ridden Victorian mind may be best understood: that the figure of the spectral apparition, more particularly, discloses its unique significance as a symptom of psychic disease occasioned by the imminent threat of grave bodily disease. At the same time, in its essentially metaphorical function as an imaginary or psychical anti-body, the nineteenth-century ghost also manifests its inherently dualistic nature as a defense mechanism against the very affect of anxiety it signals. In the final analysis, the ghostly anti-bodies which captured the contemporary imagination, and which are, for example, variously embodied in the literary works of Poe, Dickens, James, and Melville, are also seen to prove a prophetic sort of defense mechanism, literally prefiguring the actual discovery, in the late century, of lifesaving new kinds of antibodies.

My eventual objective in this essay, then, will be to trace the permutations and symptomatic expressions of a nineteenth-century dynamic between a spirit-ous species of psychical anti-bodies and serum antibodies of a biological type: a phantom phenomena which I hope to show is based upon something more profound than provocative word play alone. And by thus striking a match in the sepulchral space of "all manner of Spectre-work and Demonology," my larger purpose is to illuminate something of the dynamic intersemiotic relationship between the sphere of the body or soma and the affective realm of the psyche or spirit.

The Semiology of Spectres in the Nineteenth Century

NINETEENTH-CENTURY LITERATURE ON apparitions is voluminous and diverse, of-ten obscure, and almost as often highly eccentric.[6] However, as Terry Castle observes of the "host of polemical treatises on apparitions appear[ing] in En-gland, France, and Germany beginning around 1800,"

> The authors were usually medical men, concerned to eradicate superstition and place all seemingly supernatural phenomena on a solid psychological footing. Their arguments were resolutely Lockean and mechanistic in nature. ("Phantasmagoria" 54)

Heirs of the extreme empiricism of eighteen-century philosophy, contemporary medical writers regarded spectral experiences as intrinsically unreal, preferring to invoke, instead, a "new mentalist concept of hallucination to explain [such] occurrences" (Castle 55).[7] But for them the problem nonetheless remained that nobody could seem to agree as to just what a hallucination was and what it signified. Indeed, bearing in mind the sagacious weight of Galen's ancient apho-rism, that symptoms are apt to follow diseases in the same way that a shadow follows a body, nineteenth-century semiologists were understandably more at a loss when it came to analyzing invisible "shadows" seemingly cast by the mind.

Throughout the century, it is thus largely in the obscure semiological aspect and nosological import of hallucinations that the spectral apparition extended a phantom limb in the form of a not-so-ghostly bone of contention.

On the obverse side, medical arguments were opposed by a heterogeneous coalition of anti-empiricists, themselves united only in a common effort to pluck the mote from the Cyclops's eye of medicine, so to speak, and allow for other, non-pathologic interpretations of the phenomenology of apparitions and hallucinations. Since the countercurrent of Victorian anti-materialism streamed along a continuum running from the muddy waters of a pseudo-scientific material spiritualism to the purer deeps of a more or less genuinely metaphysical and Romantic spiritualism, however, here too, complete consensus proved elusive: even as a non-symptom, the slippery spectre proved a sign of much dispute.

While most medical writers equated ghosts with hallucinations, it is instructive to note the discrepancies that abounded even in regard to the fundamental nature of "the faculty of spectral representation" (Ferriar 100). Some, like John Ferriar, in his influential *An Essay Towards A Theory of Apparitions* (1813), clearly linked hallucination to visual or imagistic modalities of perception: "From recalling images by an art of memory," he stipulates, "the transition is direct to beholding spectral objects, which have been floating in the imagination" (100). Others, however, sought to emphasize the representational nature of the subjective apparition as an essentially cognitive process, more dependent, presumably, upon the symbolic and linguistic components of ideational constructs. Hence, the British surgeon Walter Cooper Dendy concluded in 1841 that a ghost was "nothing more than an *intense idea*"; to see a ghost denoted "an act of thinking" (qtd. in Castle, "Phantasmagoria" 57).[8] Yet again, the language of writers like Samuel Hibbert, in his *Sketches of A Philosophy of Apparitions* (1825), an important early century anti-spiritualist treatise, rather compellingly suggests a contemporary insight into the significance of hallucination as involving an inherently affective realm of "feeling" and "impression." For in contrast to other physicians, Hibbert defined the apparition as "a past feeling, renovated by the aid of morbific agents with a degree of vividness, equalling, or exceeding, an actual impression" (305).

Just as medical opinion differed as to whether hallucinations constituted the externalization of an articulate idea, a vivid but mute image, or even just a power surge of emotion, so too did it vary regarding the diagnostic significance of these enigmatic psychical symptoms. Between "normal" mental processes, such as dreaming, on the one hand, and morbid cases of insane delusion, on the other, where did spectral apparitions fit in? Which end of the scale should be tipped in emphasis, and why? Hibbert, for one, argued that, "a theory of apparitions is inseparably connected with the pathology of the human mind" inasmuch as such phenomena signalled the influence "of certain constitutional and morbid causes" which inevitably prompted "the quality and intensity of

our mental states [to] undergo very remarkable modifications" (14). "[H]allucin-
ations," echoed William Ireland, many decades later in *The Blot Upon the Brain*
(1893), "seem to me to partake of the abnormal, and to be indicative of the
passage of healthy into diseased action" (35).

But though a minority appeared inclined to view hallucinations as veritable
epiphenomena of mental derangement, most medical writers seem more circum-
spect on this point. Ferriar, for instance, deemed spectral visions a form of
"partial affection of the brain," but he stressed that a patient might be "liable
to such imaginary impressions . . . of sight or sound" without necessarily "dis-
ordering his judgement or memory" (14–15). Similarily, while apparitions constituted 'a very near step to insanity" for the influential German psychophysiolo-
gist Wilhelm Griesinger, he also held that they could "not [be] entirely confined
to states of mental disease"; indeed, "nothing would be more erroneous than
to consider a man to be mentally diseased because he had hallucinations" (90).
For both John Conolly and Henry Maudsley, the pre-eminent English authorities
of their respective eras, phantasmical visions, ghost-sightings, or other such
"juggles of starved brains" (Maudsley, *Natural Causes* 189) also did not in
and of themselves signify insanity. It was not the actual experience of spectral
apparitions which spelled madness, Conolly contended, but rather, "the insane
belief" in the objective veracity of such visions which functioned as the criteria
of insanity: "if the hallucination is known to be a hallucination, still there is no
madness; [but] if it is mistaken for reality, the man is mad" (307). Maudsley
agreed with his famous father-in-law but, with characteristic gloominess,
stressed the semiological importance of such manifestations as pretty reliable
indications of a hereditary predisposition to insanity anyway. In Maudsley's
view, spectre-sightings represented a fundamentally delusory "recrudescence"
of or "reversion" to archaic superstition, an atavistic lapse from enlightened
rationalism, or what he confidently termed, "the modern disbelief in ghosts"
(176, 199).[9]

If nineteenth-century medical semiologists were by and large uncertain about
the psychopathological import of the hallucinatory apparition, they became increasingly unanimous over the course of the century in at least one important
respect: their desire to trace spectral phenomena, along with all other signs of
mental disturbance, to an organic substrate in diseases of the nerves. "The
appearance of a ghost" in its "true light" invariably indicates "a symptom of
bodily distemper," as Ferriar declared in 1813, setting the tone for ensuing
decades (138). For indeed, although individual theories as to the precise physiological dysfunctions involved in the production of apparitions varied considerably — from ideas on sensory deprivation, vitiated blood supply, brain exhaustion or irritation, "instability of confederate nerve centres" (Maudsley 180), or
"internal expansion of the optic nerves" (Griesinger 98) — medical writers of
the age increasingly stood united in the general precept that spectral visions,

"though they appear in the mind of man, yet are they bred in the body" (Hibbert 122).

From an opposing perspective, spiritualists and psychical researchers of the late nineteenth century viewed the spectre through different eyes: eyes which sought to vindicate it from the stigma of pathologic stigmata. Their respective positions may be more briefly outlined. The "ghost seers and ghost seekers" (Maudsley 175) that might be called "material spiritualists" of the period consisted of those who sought to refute the alleged pathology of spectral phenomena by demonstrating the objective existence of phantoms and spirits through scientific means. Just as it was possible to extinguish the mind and yet have the body survive in a comatose state, so the material spiritualists believed in the possibility that, after the demise of the mortal frame, the spirit could live on in a "very refined" form — a sort of "nerve ether" or "nerve atmosphere" readily perceptible to the highly attuned sensibilities of the psychic medium (Crosland 105, 108). Interestingly, in its espousal of a paradoxical "new metaphysical cosmology based upon an (albeit rarefied) form of matter" (Owen, preface, n.p.) this group shared as much in its common methodologies, language, and empiricist spirit with the medical materialists whose views they rejected as it did in its common sympathies with other groups.

Conversely, more truly metaphysical spiritualists of the age not only spurned the idea of apparitions as symptomatic of a disordered state of the mind or the nerves but affirmed the possibility of their ontological existence on transcendent or supernatural rather than rationalistic grounds. Into this category could be shepherded not only such Christian spiritualists as typically argued that "the soul perceives that which the bodily eye cannot" (Crowe 2: 380), but also metaphysical philosopher-psychologists such as F. H. Bradley, whose declaration in 1897 that "the more that anything is spiritual, so much the more is it veritably real" signals a direct inversion of empiricist concepts of the "real" (qtd. in Siegel and West 249). The point to be underscored with regard to both material and metaphysical spiritualists, however, is that despite their differences, they remained brethren in the positive value they ascribed to the spectral vision as a consolatory sign: apparitions, after-images of the dead, signified afterlife for the living.

Reflective of a much wider late nineteenth-century cognitive shift to a new subjective epistemology, the theories of the psychical researchers of the time, on the other hand, herald an altogether more critical break with the empiricist mindset that pervaded the thinking of earlier contemporaries. Convinced that hallucinations and spirit-sightings presented primarily paranormal, and not necessarily pathologic, phenomena, British and American researchers such as Frederick Myers, Edward Gurney, and William James attempted to dispel the notion of the spectre as a symptom by providing a psychological foundation for belief not in the objective but in the subjective or intrapsychic reality of the spectral experience. According to Myers's theory, for instance, a ghost could be understood as "a manifestation of persistent personal energy"; not as a material entity, but as a type of "mental projection" from an "agent" to the mind of a percipient (qtd. in Beidler 115). In some cases, the agent and percipient might lodge within the same being, "which meant," as one commentator has noted, "that the person 'seeing' the ghost was seeing something actually in his or her own mind and thus . . . having a subjective, though not necessarily insane, experience" (Beidler 110). William James, similarly, held that the mysteries of spectral apparitions had ultimately to be attributed to secrets of the subliminal self, and wrote of such phenomena as subjective realities "as good and true" as any externally verifiable realm: "*an hallucination is a strictly sensational form of consciousness, as good and true a sensation as if there were a real object there. The object happens not to be there, that is all*" (*Principles* 2: 115). In their ascription of a new phenomenological value to the subjective experience of hallucinations and apparitions, then, late century researchers in effect redeemed the ghost from its empiricist status as — at best — an embarrassingly "unreal" phantom of "unreason."

Pioneer cartographers of inner space in general, psychical researchers studied spectral occurrences in the larger context of altered states of consciousness in general, including somnambulism, hypnotic and hypnagogic trances, spirit possession, and double consciousness (see *William James*). As such, they placed a new importance on the notion of a general semiology of perception, in which perception, thoughts, fantasies, dreams, hallucinations, and so forth could not be sharply distinguished from one another but rather conceived of as on a dynamic continuum, with one state capable of evolving into another.[10] Far from being intrinsically morbid manifestations, hallucinatory visions were viewed instead as "often only *extremes* of the perception process" (James, *Principles* 115). Through similar arguments for a ubiquitous human capacity for such "exceptional" mental and perceptual states, the thrust of the psychical researchers' work might be characterized as an attempt to demorbidify the realm of ghosts, placing them under the new and more neutral terminological aegis of the "paranormal."

The birth of a paranormal realm of the psychical occult, however, by no means presented an unproblematic resolution to the ever-incongruous status of ghosts and apparitions. Indeed, in this respect, the continuing controversy over the semiology of spectres in the late century affords an interesting analogue to that of spiritualistic trance phenomena, which was also hotly contested as a form of ecstasy or insanity (Williams 233). Like the "nerve ether" of the material spiritualists' ghosts, the terms of the debate by the century's end appear only to have been refined. For by then, a new question began to fill the air: how normal, they could now wonder, was the paranormal?[11]

Cross-currents: Villette *and* Wuthering Heights

ALTHOUGH NEITHER VILLETTE (1853) nor *Wuthering Heights* (1847) may in any simple sense be characterized as a ghost tale — for they are, each of them, many wonderful things — they are both good examples of what Julia Briggs calls "the psychological ghost story": a work wherein mental disorder is in some way implicated in the spectral experience, usually by an ambiguous suggestion that apparitions are products of delusion (51, 147). Like Henry James's famous example of this genre in *The Turn of the Screw*, the novels of both Brontë sisters probe the semiological status of spectral visions as potential indications of "Madness or Diseases of the Nerves." But they are also more than just appropriate generic examples. For in their fundamentally antithetical representations of ghosts, the novels of Charlotte and Emily Brontë cast each other into striking relief, managing to encompass between them the entire nineteenth-century dialectic of materialism and spiritualism, of empiricism and subjectivism, and of naturalism and supernaturalism as it has disclosed itself in the debates over the significance of apparitions.

"Say what you will, reader," maintains the beleaguered heroine of *Villette* upon her first sickening encounter with "a figure all black or white" "in the middle of [a] ghostly chamber": "tell me I was nervous or mad; affirm that I was unsettled . . . declare that I dreamed: this I vow — I saw there — in that room — on that night — an image like — a NUN (325; ch. 22). Lucy Snowe's immediate and defensive rebuttal of the reader's assumed scepticism may be forgiven as a well-grounded fear. Even in Brontë's earlier *Jane Eyre* (1846), for example, Rochester attempts to dismiss Jane's nocturnal vision of the white shrouded Bertha — who appears as a "foul German spectre" or "Vampyre" to trample Jane's bridal veil — as merely "the creature of an over-stimulated brain" (286; ch. 25). So also in *Villette* does the physician Dr. John, to whom Lucy describes her experience, promptly declare hers "all a matter of the nerves": "I think it a case of spectral illusion: I fear, following on and resulting from long-continued mental conflict" (330; ch. 22).

The varying responses of Brontë's heroines to such rationalist, materialist explanations of "spectral illusion" are instructive. In the earlier novel, the more spunky Jane Eyre is able to assert unequivocally her conviction of her own lucidity, informing Mr. Rochester: "Sir, depend upon it, my nerves were not in fault; the thing was real: the transaction actually took place" (286; ch. 25). Lucy Snowe, though, is not so confident of her apperception of reality: "I shudder at the thought of being liable to such an illusion! It seemed so real. Is there no cure? — no preventative?" (330; ch. 22). Genuinely shaken, Brontë's later heroine is "left secretly and sadly to wonder, in [her] own mind, whether that strange thing was of this world, or of a realm beyond the grave; or whether indeed it was only the child of malady, and I of that malady the prey" (333;

ch. 22). Later on, however, a calmer Lucy also comes to an outright rejection of Dr. John's diagnosis of "optical illusion — nervous malady, and so on," claiming: "[n]ot one bit did I believe him; but I dared not contradict: doctors are so self-opinionated, so immoveable in their dry, materialist views" (338; ch. 23).

As Sally Shuttleworth has argued, Lucy's equivocal stance reflects one way in which "the constitution of neurosis" in *Villette* "both absorbs and resists the definitions and codifications of female experience offered by the male medical establishment" (313). In the same way, but more specifically, Brontë's novel may be seen both to validate and to gainsay medical theories of the spectral apparition as a morbid manifestation of nervous disease and "a very near step to insanity." Most obviously, of course, insofar as the "phantom" nun of *Villette* is disclosed at the novel's end as a hoax — as a trick perpetrated by the masquerading fop, de Hamal, and thus rationally explained after the manner of Radcliffean natural supernaturalism — Dr. John's medical diagnosis of nervous pathology is ultimately disproven. But the extent to which this diagnosis is also pointedly confirmed by Brontë's text even *before* the advent of the spectral nun bears emphasis. For the self-styled "constitutionally nervous" (456; ch. 31) Lucy has indeed suffered from "a long-continued mental conflict" which has earlier rendered her liable to phantasmagoric hallucinations. Thus, during the Long Vacation, when the heroine's "overstretched" nerves plunge her into "a strange fever of the nerves and blood" and a "peculiarly agonizing depression" (231; ch. 15), she sees the "ghastly white beds" of the empty school dormitory "turning into spectres — the coronal of each became a death's head; huge and sun-bleached" (232). Explicitly identified as symptomatic of a "bodily distemper" of the nerves, this spectral experience recalls Ferriar's theory of a "partial affection of the brain" which does not necessarily impair "judgment or memory." Lucy, at any rate, protests that during his horrific vision, she is "not delirious": "I was in my sane mind" (232). Despite the heroine's clear-headed perspective on her spectral scene, however, it is noteworthy that this episode precipitates a feverish visionary delirium from which her memory and judgment do not immediately emerge unimpaired. After the unconscious spell following her wild confession to a Roman Catholic priest, Lucy regains at first only a most tenuous sense of reality: a vision "distempered" not only because she is confused by what appear to be (and are) the familiar furnishings of her godmother's house at Bretton but because all her eye rests on "struck it as spectral," even her own face in the mirror (237–38; ch. 16). A prelude of sorts to the narcotic, dream-like scene of the final fête night, such earlier episodes establish Lucy's frightful propensity to spectral aberrations and delusions and serve to affirm Dr. John's "dry, materialist views" in almost every context but that of the nun.

In a more comprehensive sense, *Villette* may also be seen as a novel which, in its profound movement towards materialization — materialization both of the self and of the spectral anti-body[12] — reflects the fundamentally empiricist ethos which underpinned the theoretic agendas of nineteenth-century medical men and material spiritualists alike. Mary Jacobus has called attention to the fact that Brontë's spectral nun actually materializes at the end of the novel in dual respects: not only as the figure of de Hamal, that is, but also as a sort of literal "resurrection of the flesh" (*Villette* 563; ch. 39) of the legendary Justine Marie, in the form of the living namesake of the dead nun (53). And in the same way that the "risen ghost" of the mysterious Justine Marie ultimately manifests itself in the form of a "well-nourished, fair and fat of flesh" "bourgeoise belle" (563; ch. 39) so does Brontë's novel as a whole progressively chart the "rising character" of Lucy Snowe (394; ch. 27) from an obscure, timorous, and ghostly creature who lives in "[her] own still, shadow-world" (185; ch. 13) and is deemed by others a "being" as 'inoffensive as a shadow" (403; ch. 27), to a stronger, healthier, and more assertive woman who will not rest content as any "bright lady's shadow" (382; ch. 26) but increasingly claims substance and significance of her own. A direct correlation is developed in the novel between the heroine's sense of corporeality and the notion of "*mens sana in corpore sano*," the healthy mind in the healthy body. It is only once Lucy has progressed from an earlier sense of herself as a shadowy, phantom being that she is able to dispell once and for all the spectres of madness and nervous disease which have haunted her:

> My head reeled, for by the faint night-lamp, I saw stretched on my bed the old phantom — the NUN. . . . I was not overcome. Tempered by late incidents, my nerves disdained hysteria. Warm from illuminations . . . I defied spectra. In a moment, without exclamation, I had rushed on the haunted couch; nothing leaped out, or sprang, or stirred; all the movement was mine, so was all the life, the reality, the substance, the force; as my instinct felt. I tore her up — the, incubus! I held her on high — the goblin! I shook her loose — the mystery! And down she fell — down all round me — down in shreds and fragments — and I trode upon her. (569; ch. 39)

Vindicating her of any lingering suspicion of delusory malady, Lucy's destruction of the nun's effigy comes as an ironic revelation, not only at the expense of supernaturalists in general but also of material spiritualists in particular: for as a "long bolster" of cloth, Brontë's certainly proves to be one phantom of verifiable substance. It is indeed significant that in this mid-century work the reality of the bogus apparition should prove, literally, a swath of material. For the equation of the material with "reality," of course, actually inheres in the word itself, which stems from the Latin root *res*, denoting thing, material, or object. Insofar as the material realm comes to constitute the insuperable index of the real in Charlotte Brontë's novel, Lucy Snowe's action of grasping, ripping, and trampling cloth appears as a clear affirmation of her sanity: she is, as the saying has it, "in touch with reality."[13]

In fact, not only concepts of empirical reality but those of the spiritual and numinous realm, as well, carry the archaic traces of an original sense of material "thingness." The very earliest notions of souls, ghosts, and demons, as Freud was to point out within a few decades, arose upon contemplation of the dead corpse (14: 294). Originally, such spirits were thought of "as [being] very similar to persons": only "in the course of a long development" or evolution did they lose their "material characteristics and become to a high degree 'spiritualized' (13: 76). And that the material root of the spirit should haunt even the word "ghost" is also pertinent in the context of *Villette*'s climactic scene. According to the *Oxford English Dictionary*, the obscure pre-Teutonic origins of our word "ghost" point to senses not only of "fury," "anger," and "ugly" but also of wounding, tearing, and pulling to pieces. As the latent depths of language begin to surface in Lucy Snowe's action of wounding, tearing, and pulling her "ghost" to pieces, a more darkly subversive aspect of this episode perhaps also becomes apparent: for the active exertion that appears an affirmation of the heroine's sanity yet also resembles the passionate excess of maenadic fury.[14]

While *Villette* thus culminates with the materialization or embodiment of spectral anti-bodies, living and "dead," Emily Brontë's *Wuthering Heights*, an anti-body book in a more fundamental sense of the word, flows in an obverse direction toward what Castle has termed the "spectralization" or "ghostifying" of the inner mental self and of the other: a metaphoric internalization or "absorption of ghosts into the world of thought" and perception which coincides with the rise of anti-apparition arguments and scientific rationalism at the end of the eighteenth century ("Phantasmagoria" 29; see also "Spectralization"). Called a Romantic "symphony on the intertwined themes of love and death" (Ariès 443), *Wuthering Heights* most clearly reflects the views and values of the metaphysical spiritualists in its treatment of apparitions as supranatural signs: an essentially consolatory credo most emphatically articulated in the novel by Heathcliff, who feels "unspeakably consoled" by the felt "presence" of his dead love's spirit and who maintains "a strong faith in ghosts," and "a conviction that they can, and do exist, among us!" (2.15: 289–90).

But to observe that the novel depicts a form of transcendent reality which eschews the gross confines of the corporal and earthly — a world in which corpses seem to smile more often than living beings, since fleshly dissolution promises the joy of a higher consummation — is not necessarily to preclude the spectre of mental disorder in Emily Brontë's spiritous realm, either. As in *Villette*, in fact, spectral visions are overtly assigned a status as symptomatic of a nervous pathology which increases through "feverish bewilderment to madness"

(1.12: 122). Indeed, much as Lucy Snowe protests her sanity when she hallucinates the grotesque death's heads, so Emily Brontë's heroine, the elder Catherine, insists to Nelly Dean that she is "not wandering" in mind when she perceives "the black press" and an unrecognizable visage in her sickroom (1.12: 123). While in one sense, Catherine's disordered visions may be regarded as a sort of confused "waking dream," as Nelly suggests, or as a type of spiritual vision in which "the soul," to recall Mrs. Crowe's words, "perceives that which the bodily eye cannot," her delusory perceptions, and particularly her non-recognition of her own haunting image in the mirror she fancies a press, are also manifest signs of a grievous self-alienation: symptoms of a sort of premature disassociation of Catherine's mind and soul from the facades of both her dying bodily self, "this shattered prison" (2.1: 160), and the stultifying confines of "her hated sick-chamber" (1.13: 135). Estranged from the face that stares from the mirror, Catherine in her madness perceives herself as a sort of spectral anti-body. "Don't *you* see that face?" she frets, "gazing earnestly at the mirror." "And say what I could," Nelly Dean narrates, "I was incapable of making her comprehend it to be her own" (1.12: 123).

The heroine of *Wuthering Heights* never fully recovers from "the shock of what was denominated a brain fever" (1.13: 134), and after her demise, it is once again her haunting image which returns to threaten sanity — this time, that of the grieving Heathcliff. Obsessed to the point of "a monomania on the subject of his departed idol," Heathcliff, near the end of the novel, is tormented by the "aspect [of] the ghost of [his] immortal love" which Hareton's uncanny resemblance provokes (2.19: 324). Sufficiently eidetic to obtrude onto his conscious perception of reality, apparitions of Catherine swarm about Heathcliff as earlier in the novel the ghostly "white letters" of her name swarmed about the somnolent Lockwood "as vivid as spectres" (1.3: 17). "[A]nd what does not recall her?" cries Brontë's distracted hero: "I cannot look down to this floor, but her features are shaped on the flags! In every cloud, in every tree—filling the air at night, and caught by glimpses in every object by day, I am surrounded with her image!" (2.19: 324) Brontë's representation of an obsession with a haunting image or "mental apparition" which commands a "potentially *daemonic* hold over [the subject]" is a graphic illustration of the essentially Romantic sensibility which began to manifest itself during the late eighteenth century when "a growing sense of the ghostliness of other people" and a marked preoccupation with the " 'ghost' of [a] dead or absent person, conceived as a kind of visionary image or presence in the mind" began to take on "a new and compelling subjective reality" (Castle, "Spectralization" 237, 249).

To the extent that both Catherine's hallucination and Heathcliff's mental apparitions reflect a spectralization of, respectively, self and other, the ghostly antibodies of *Wuthering Heights* afford a stark contrast to the materialization scenes of sister Charlotte's *Villette*. And although ghosts are implicated with shades of mental disease in both novels, *Wuthering Heights* also differs from *Villette* in the way in which it anticipates the agenda of the late-century psychical researchers by emphasizing the fluid interrelatedness of "pathological" and "normal" spectral experiences. Boundaries between waking and sleeping, conscious and unconscious states, and dreams and apparitions are especially nebulous and ambiguous in this text. Lockwood's ghastly but by no means abnormal nightmare of the importuning ghost child at the window, for instance, is presented as a process closely analogous to Heathcliff's sort of monomaniacal mental visions. Both, that is, are forms of eidetic imagery prompted by an image of Catherine — an image of her face or of her name — which, in Lockwood's words, "personified itself" when the imagination "no longer [was] under control" (1.3: 26). "Only the thinnest line," Terry Castle remarks, speaking of *The Mysteries of Udolpho*, "separates the experience of wishing for (or fearing) the return of the dead and actually seeing them return" ("Spectralization" 241). So indeed does Brontë's text almost erase "the thinnest line" that may separate Heathcliff's monomaniacal and hyperconscious wish for the return of Cathy's ghost and Lockwood's apparently unconscious fear of the same. And while it is true that *Villette* offers, in the end, the dark hint that demystifying the spectral may involve a madness of its own, *Wuthering Heights* with its much stronger emphasis on the essential similarities and blurred continuities between disturbed "waking" visions and "normal" nocturnal phantasms ultimately offers its own unsettling glimpse into the latent irrationalism of everyday perceptual processes.

The Symptom of Neurosis: Repression, Defense, and Dis-ease

GIVEN THAT THE VICTORIANS THEMSELVES so often tended to ascribe a pathologic significance to spectral apparitions in their medical and literary texts, what are we to make of the prominent status of ghosts in the larger context of nineteenth-century thought as a whole? As a sign of the times, the period's veritable fixation on spiritualistic phenomena can be approached from a psychoanalytic perspective which will foreground the inherently dualistic processes involved in symptom-formation: processes of pathological repression and of defense whose dynamic begins to reveal how the fleeting figure of the ghost may be understood as, paradoxically, both a sign of mass anxiety contingent upon an interplay of internal and external threats *and* as an instinctive counter to that dis-ease.

The Freudian conception of the ghost as an external "return" of the repressed unconscious is well-known and perhaps the most obvious point of departure here. In *The Interpretation of Dreams*, Freud offers the following formulation:

> My explanation of hallucinations in hysteria and paranoia and of visions in mentally normal subjects is that they are in fact regressions — that is, thoughts transformed into images — but that the only thoughts that undergo this transformation are those

which are intimately linked with memories that have been suppressed or have remained unconscious. (5: 544)

The process by which Freud theorized that such repressed ideas were "transformed into images" he termed "projection": "An internal perception is suppressed, and, instead, its content, after undergoing a certain kind of distortion, enters consciousness in the form of an external perception (12: 66). Notably, the idea of apparitions as symptomatic projections was, it seems, intuitively grasped by nineeenth-century ghost story writers such as Ambrose Bierce, who defined them as "the outward and visible sign of an inward fear" (113).

If on the one hand, however, repressed anxieties or conflicts may stimulate the genesis of the spectral symptom, then on the other, the phenomenon must also be understood in terms of an essentially dialectical psychic economy — one in which the symptom also, simultaneously, constitutes a defense mechanism. For paradoxically, pathogenic processes of repression and obviating processes of psychical defense are mutually implicated in complex and fascinating ways. The forces of repression activated by anxiety, the "starting point . . . of neurotic processes in general," are also a defensive mechanism in that they provide the human organism with a means of coping with traumas or affects the ego finds unsupportable. Conversely, the concept of the defense mechanism, whose raison d'être is ostensibly to avert danger, also necessarily entails a falsification of "internal perception" which "pave[s] the way for and encourage[s] the outbreak of neurosis" (Freud 23: 237–38). Eventually, it became clear to Freud that "the defensive process is analogous to the flight by means of which the ego removes itself from a danger that threatens it from outside. The defensive process is an attempt at flight from an instinctual danger," (20: 145). In their intrinsically dualistic nature, repression and defense appear as Janus-faced inversions of one another.[15] And viewed specifically in its defensive aspect, the spectral symptom, in particular, discloses its anti-pathologic function as a means of coping with unconscious, intrapsychic anxiety by displacing or externalizing it:

> by means of the whole defensive mechanism . . . set in action[,] a projection outward of the instinctual danger [is] achieved. The ego behaves as if the danger of a development of anxiety threatened it not from the direction of an instinctual impulse but from the direction of a perception, and it is thus enabled to react against this external danger. (14: 184)[16]

E. A. Sheppard, in her study of Henry James, alludes briefly to this defensive function of nineteenth-century spirit phenomena when she speaks of the tantalizing oral tradition of ghost stories, told "in self-defense, as it were, [to] hypostatize . . . fears" (3).

The "affective symbol" or "affective state" of anxiety or fear, however, also constitutes an ambiguous and recondite factor in symptom-formations of the neuroses in general.[17] And what is of most importance for the purposes of my argument is the increasing emphasis eventually placed upon the role of the ego and the perception of *external* dangers in Freud's continuously evolving conception of neurotic dis-ease and its symptomatic manifestations. The earliest psychoanalytic theory of neurotic anxiety as the outcome of repressed libido is succinctly summarized by Rollo May: "the individual experiences libidinal impulses which he interprets as dangerous, the libidinal impulses are repressed, they become automatically converted into anxiety, and they find expression as free-floating anxiety [the unfixed general apprehensiveness of typical anxiety neurosis] or as symptoms which are anxiety-equivalents" (116). In works such as "Inhibitions, Symptoms and Anxiety' (1926) and "Anxiety and Instinctual Life" (1933), however, Freud actually reversed the principal dynamic of this first theory while reviewing the animal phobias of little Hans and the Wolf Man. He now maintains that, "It was anxiety which produced repression and not, as I formerly believed, repression which produced anxiety. . . . It is always the ego's attitude of anxiety which is the primary thing and which sets repression going. Anxiety never arises from repressed libido" (20: 108–09).[18]

It is not only that anxiety is now seen to set symptom formation going as the "primary thing" or "necessary prerequisite" (20: 144). Much to his surprise, Freud also began to appreciate, at this point, the extent to which "neurotic anxiety has changed in our hands into realistic anxiety, into fear of particular external situations of danger" (22: 93). Freud, that is, came to qualify carefully his earlier view that "the danger feared in neurotic anxiety is that simply of inner instinctual impulses" (May 118). For the "anxiety belonging to the animal phobias" of little Hans and the Wolf Man, as Freud now saw it, "was an untransformed fear of castration": "it was therefore a realistic fear, a fear of a danger which was actually impending or was judged to be a real one" (20: 108). Asking himself again, "what sort of anxiety" was crucial to such instances of phobia, Freud writes in "Anxiety and Instinctual Life": "Only [an] anxiety in the face of a threatening external danger — that is to say, a realistic anxiety. . . . [For] above all, it is not a question of whether castration is really carried out; what is decisive is that the danger is one that threatens from the outside and that the child believes in it"(22: 86). As May suggests, the critical point in these later analyses is that "the ego perceives [a] danger," a danger which signals to the analyst a complex "interrelationsip of external and internal factors" (118, 119). With regard to symptom formations of the neuroses, a certain ambiguity of the inside and outside becomes apparent: "in relation to [a] traumatic situation, in which the subject is helpless, external and internal dangers, real dangers and instinctual demands converge" (Freud 20: 168).[19] More particularly, "an instinctual demand," as Freud came to realize, "often only becomes an (internal) danger because its satisfaction would bring on an external danger — that is, because the internal danger represents an external one" (20: 167–68).

Freud's belated insights into the force of "realistic anxiety" as an integral component of the phobic symptom will bear significantly on my theory of the imaginary, ghostly anti-body as a symptom of Victorian dis-ease. For the moment, however, it is worthwhile to underscore some of the basic ramifications of the conceptual trend we have just traced. "What this shift [in Freud's thought] implies," as May contends, "is that anxiety and its symptoms are seen not as merely the outcome of a simple intrapsychic process, but *as arising out of the individual's endeavor to avoid danger situations in his world*," his interpersonal and environmental milieu (124).[20] In terms of the repression-defense dialectic established above, the neurotic symptom can therefore be seen to function "not merely [as] a protection against inner impulses" but also as a defense against "*the anxiety-creating situation*" (May 125, 86). As Freud concludes in "Inhibitions, Symptoms and Anxiety," "It might be said that symptoms are created so as to avoid the generating of anxiety. But this does not go deep enough. It would be truer to say that symptoms are created so as to avoid a *danger-situation* whose presence has been signalled by the generation of anxiety" (20: 129). Creating, in effect, a substitutive satisfaction which serves to circumvent or mitigate a real, external threat, "repressions and symptoms" can, ultimately, "best be viewed as the organism's means of adjusting to a danger situation," the elements of which may straddle conscious and unconscious poles (May 126).

The Imaginary Anti-Bodies of the Nineteenth Century

IN RELATION TO THE NINETEENTH century, however, psychoanalytic conceptions of the spectre would seem to raise at least as many questions as they would answer. Signalling as they do an attempt to negate the terrible finality of death, to sustain the illusion that "the precious dead [are] not really dead" (Castle, "Spectralization" 244), ghosts and ghost-belief can be viewed as the symptomatic expression of an intensely ambivalent attitude toward mortality: an instinctual dis-ease endemic to all of human history.[21] And yet, in what sense can the nineteenth century — of all periods one saturated with elaborate tokens and trappings of mourning and death — be said to reflect such conflicting attitudes? In addition, as both signs of and defenses against a universal and timeless disease, how are the ghosts of this particular period to be distinguished from those of others?

There is no doubt that the nineteenth-century was an era peculiarly conscious of the presence of death in its midst. From the crypts and vaults of Poe's tales, to the pervasive apostrophes and asides on death in such Dickens novels as *Bleak House* or *Our Mutual Friend*, to the mourning rings and rituals, the black crepe, black-bordered stationery, gritted murmurs of "God's will," and, indeed, to the ever-mournful Queen Victoria herself, all indications would seem to suggest more of a fetishization than a denial of mortality. But perhaps all the manifest signs of the nineteenth century's conscious acknowledgement of death need to be set against, or distinguished from, the shadowy traces of a concomitant suppression of it. Perhaps the contradictory split consciousness of the age with regard to attitudes toward death is best understood in terms of Jung's "psychological rule" that "the brighter the light, the blacker the shadow; in other words, the more rationalistic we are in our conscious minds, the more alive becomes the spectral world of the unconscious" (144).

It is, indeed, precisely such an unconscious denial of death that French historian Phillippe Ariès has called attention to in the context of modern industrial culture. In *The Hour of Our Death*, Ariès argues that around the late eighteenth century, more repressive emotional attitudes towards death, caused by a complex variety of demographic, societal, and philosophic factors, subtly begin to manifest themselves in such phenomena as the removal of cemeteries to outlying areas, increased privacy of mourning in middle-class urban life, and, especially, new cosmetic emphases on hiding or denying signs of bodily decay and death. The practise of embalming, he notes, witnessed a resurgence of popularity at this time. Part of the age's obsession with what he calls "the beautiful death" expressed itself in a "Romantic Cult of the Dead" of the sort apparent in a text like *Wuthering Heights*: a fascination with idealized images of the deceased which, Ariès says, directly prefigures the nineteenth-century spiritualist movement and interest in spectral phenomena.[22] The rise of the ghost's popularity in the nineteenth century, then, can be related to a historically-specific wave of romantic sentimentalism, which, seeking to avoid unpleasant reminders of mortality, "exalted death, . . . deified death, . . . and at the same time . . . transformed . . . the [lost] loved one, into an inseparable immortal" (Ariès, 582–83).

The point I want to make, however, is that nineteenth-century ghosts may be understood as symptomatic manifestations not only of a latent dis-ease with mortality generally but of unconscious fears of death by contagious diseases in particular: a response to an insoluable and real, if invisible, external threat or "danger situation." Indeed, the great incidence of infectious epidemics during the nineteenth century, although it is overlooked by Ariès, is one factor which had an undeniably profound impact on the Victorian psyche, especially in terms of anxieties related to death. After a decline in major epidemics during the eighteenth century, the first cholera epidemic of 1831–32 marked an "alarming return to the age of epidemics" (Wohl 118). As a "direct consequence of increased human mobility" during the Industrial Revolution, pandemics of highly communicable diseases swept along the trade routes of the world at fairly regular intervals (Stanley and Joske 555; see also Spink 163), evoking in their wakes the spectre of mass, sudden death to a degree almost unparalleled since the time of the Black Death. Cholera, most especially, "was the classic epidemic disease of the nineteenth century, as plague had been for the fourteenth" (Rosenberg, qtd. in Spink 162). "The very name of cholera," Henri Blanc frankly confessed in a medical treatise of 1873, "inspires a deadly fear" (33).[23] As historian Anthony Wohl writes,

> the possibility of sudden and often painful death from one or other of the many epidemic diseases of the day simply was one of the inescapable facts of nineteenth-century life. . . . [T]he rise . . . of widespread infectious and contagious diseases, and especially of cholera, a disease new to the English experience and the first national epidemic since the seventeenth-century plague, served to remind the Victorians that their society, however progressive, was not immune to the scourges of the past. (117–18)

Of all the major epidemic diseases of the age — cholera, tuberculosis, scarlet fever, diphtheria, typhus, typhoid, influenza, and small pox — only a vaccination against the small pox was available to the Victorians. Cholera, which killed thousands upon thousands in England alone during four major outbreaks, had an "impact out of all proportion to its statistical importance," according to Wohl, exacting a fatality rate of between forty to sixty per cent of those who contracted the disease (118).[24]

Nor was the New World immune to such an alarming "danger situation": Susanna Moodie, in her *Roughing It in the Bush*, recalls with great vividness the quarantine measures implemented at the port of Gross Isle on the St. Lawrence River in 1832, a futile attempt to stem the spread of cholera, which eventually passed from Canada to major American cities such as New York and Philadelphia. Stories of "Typhoid Mary," the New York cook Mary Mallon, who unwittingly infected fifty-four people with fever before being identified as a carrier, have attained the status of a cultural legend. In terms of nineteenth-century epidemiology, Great Britain generally "served as a pattern" for the United States, although as Wesley Spink notes, "the Civil War and the postwar problems added to the deferment of public health concerns" in America (28, 35).

Wohl himself suggests that, through their excessively ritualized conventions of death and mourning, the Victorians helped to "inoculate themselves against [the] shock" of sudden and multiple deaths by infectious diseases. In the same way, however, the period's obsession with ghosts of all types — whether literary, paranormal, or spiritualistic — bears the mark of the same "psychological imperatives" (117). That it may have been in part, at least, precisely the biological defencelessness of the age before a resurgent tide of epidemic diseases that stimulated and heightened the imaginative production of ghosts at this time is suggested, in other words, by the *metaphorical* relevance of the ghost as a psychic agent of defense: as an imaginary anti-body, a protean, mental substitute and compensatory externalization of the very protein antibodies which serve to neutralize pathogenic toxins in the blood and which the populace at large so direly lacked. As a projection of the collective psyche, the imaginary anti-body provided, in essence, a means of instinctual "apotropaic defense" or self-inoculation against the immanent germs of a virulent new dis-ease of death, a dis-ease it at once symptomized and creatively combatted.

In other words, apparitional phenomena of the age may be understood in terms of a defensive response by which "a whole people" sought to "replace an inadequate attitude" or adjust psychologically to the new and deadlier reality of life in an age that raged with epidemic diseases. For "spirits are complexes of the collective unconscious," as Carl Jung put it, "which appear when the individual loses his adaptation to reality, or which seek to replace the inadequate attitude of a whole people by a new one. They are therefore either pathological fantasies or new but as yet unknown ideas" (122). In a very *literal* metaphoric sense, phantom anti-bodies of the era manifest themselves as the fore-shadows of "a new but as yet unknown idea": the idea of biological antibodies against fatal contagious diseases. The imaginary embodiment of a collective hallucinatory wish, as it were, the nineteenth-century anti-body thus figuratively points to its origin as an instinctive immune response to a very real contemporary threat or "danger-situation," revealing in the process its inherently bifacial aspect: the ghost of a deadly dis-ease and an immuno-goblin of the mind.[25]

The Age of Antibody; or, Immuno-goblin Meets Immunoglobulin

TRACING THE INTERPLAY OF ANTIBODIES of serum and anti-bodies of the spirit over the course of the nineteenth century and into our own confirms what has begun to become apparent: that a direct and mutually influential relationship exists between the two. Freud's early formulations of the principle of psychological defense mechanisms in the 1880s and '90s were in fact matched in the late 1870s and beyond by the discovery of the principle of active acquired immunity in the nascent fields of immunology and bacteriology, the achievement of scientists such as Louis Pasteur and Robert Koch.[26] This historical coincidence suggests the broader perspective in which we can view psychological and biological antibodies of the era: namely, as parallel products of a fundamentally psychophysiological heuristic model.

Although it is true that the infectious nature of the biological diseases in question marks a crucial difference from the case of mental diseases, the principle of defense upon which both psychic anti-bodies and their serum counterparts operate is strikingly similar. In biology, acquired immunity denotes the process of inoculation whereby an individual is injected with an attenuated strain of a viral microorganism with a view to prevention. In the same way that a body builds up a resistance to certain pathogens through forms of mild exposure, so, we may note," is "ego modification" or mental resistance to certain pathogenic affects sometimes achieved by an individual's prior exposure to less acutely traumatic disturbances. Moreover, in their unsettling discovery of autotoxins — self-poisoning antibodies of the type responsible for allergies, for example — late nineteenth-century immunologists uncovered a defense-disease mechanism analogous to Freud's repression-defense complex. It is perhaps with a sense of something akin to the "horror autotoxicus"[27] that struck the immunologists that Freud wrote of the potentially self-subverting "defense" mechanisms, whose purpose, like that of serum antibody, was also ostensibly to avert dangers: "It cannot be disputed that they are successful . . . but it is also certain that they may become dangers themselves" (23: 237). And finally, it may be noted that the cellular and cerebral dynamics of both biological and psychological antibody formations hinge upon a similar factor: the ability of the organism to distinguish bodies external or "foreign" to itself. It is telling indeed that Freud employs the immunological metaphor of "a foreign body . . . keeping up a constant succession of stimuli and reactions in the tissue in which it [is] embedded" as an all-time favorite in his descriptions of symptom-formation in the neuroses (20: 98).[28]

Interestingly enough, there is also evidence in the language of the scientific fields of immunology and bacteriology which attests to the subtle link between the occult and psychopathologic realm of spectral manifestations and that of the biological antibody and immunoglobulin. For even today, such discplines echo with traces of imaginary anti-bodies and immuno-goblins, utilizing such suggestive technical terms as "ghost" cells, "toxin spectra," and "chimeras."

Literary Embodiments of the Anti-Body

THE MUTUAL REPERCUSSIONS OF science and psychology in the constitution of the nineteenth-century spectral apparition are anticipated and variously elaborated in a range of contemporary fiction, which, on the whole, not only reconfirms the direct link between ghosts and contagious disease in the contemporary mind but in some cases actually illustrates the function of the ghost as an anti-body of dis-ease and defense. It is in literature of the period, after all, that one finds the most articulate fore-shadowings of truths that science and psychoanalysis had yet to strain toward.

Edgar Allan Poe's 1845 tale, "The Sphinx," for example, traces a clear correlation between mass deaths from infectious disease, mental malaise, and manifestations of an apparitional anti-body. Set "during the dread reign of the cholera in New York" in 1832, Poe's story recounts the hallucinatory experiences of an unnamed narrator who has fallen into a "condition of abnormal gloom" as a result of numerous and sudden bereavements attributable to cholera. "Not a day elapsed which did not bring us news of the decease of some acquaintance," he recalls of the epidemic.

Then, as the fatality increased, we learned to expect daily the loss of some friend. At length we trembled at the approach of every messenger. The very air from the South seemed to us redolent with death. That palsying thought, indeed, took entire possession of my soul. I could neither speak, think, nor dream of anything else. My host was of a less excitable temperament, and, although greatly depressed in spirits, exerted himself to sustain my own. (1246)

Poe's story suggests that, unlike his host, the mentally rattled narrator is "sufficiently alive" to the encroaching "shadows" of death to be "affected by unrealities" (1246).

In this case, the anti-body of the narrator's mental disorder — a monomaniacal obsession with death — discloses itself not as a conventional ghost but as a more grotesque "visionary creature" (1249): a "living monster of [the] hideous conformation" of a gigantic fly (1247). "A terrific animal" of fearful dimensions: "the chief peculiarity of this horrible thing, was the representation of a *Death's Head*, which covered nearly the whole surface of its breast, and which was as accurately traced in glaring white, upon the dark ground of the body, as if it had been there carefully designed by an artist" (1248). When the narrator encounters this monstrous apparition for the second time, he finds it more difficult to succeed "in convincing [himself] that [he] was neither mad nor in a dream" (1247). He calls upon his host to verify his second sighting; the latter, however, "maintained that he saw nothing." "I was now immeasurably alarmed," Poe's narrator confesses at this point, "for I considered the vision either as an omen of my death, or, worse, as the forerunner of an attack of mania" (1249). While the narrator's host, a man of a scientific turn of mind, identifies the "visionary creature" through the narrator's description as a specimen of the insect "genus Sphinx" and dismisses it as an optical illusion — a case of "mere misadmeasurement of [the] propinquity" of an actual insect (1250) — the status of the apparitional fly ultimately remains ambiguous: like the legendary sphinx, it is offered by Poe as a creature of inherently enigmatic nature.

Whether one chooses to credit the host's rationalist explanation or his guest's fears of incipient insanity, the Sphinx fly presents a graphic fictional instance of an immuno-goblin or "monster" born of a mind dis-eased by the imminent — or magnified — prospect of death by cholera. For though it may be sphinx-like in its import as either an optical aberration or as a morbid manufacture of madness, the ghost insect carries an unequivocal and overt significance in relation to communicable diseases such as cholera. That is to say, even before modern germ theories superseded the pythogenic concept of the spontaneous propagation of disease from miasma or effluvia, flies — now of course recognized as notorious air-borne transmitters of cholera — were already linked to epidemics by dint of their omnipresence in the typical "breeding grounds" of disease: cesspools, dung heaps, communal privies, slums (Wohl 88). Cholera, in fact, "was most often spread by water contaminated by the excreta of cholera victims, or by flies which hatched in or fed upon the diseased excrement'' (Wohl 120). It is absolutely appropriate, then, that the spectral fly of Poe's tale should bear the emblazoned crest of the Death's Head, that ghastly *memento mori* also hallucinated by Brontë's Lucy Snowe.

"The Sphinx" conveys a darkly monitory message: it exposed contemporary readers to the *idea* that, in a world in which "the very air" was "redolent with death" invisible to the eye, "cholera" was a term to be reckoned with, a buzz-word of haunting and lethal portentousness. But the interplay of ghostly anti-bodies and the theme of cholera in nineteenth-century fiction is far more pervasive than the example of a single text may indicate; it is an association forged through an entire literary trope of live burial, as well. Pointing to the work of Poe, among others, R. C. Finucane identifies taphephobia — the fear of premature or live burial — as a distinctively Victorian trait and a prominent characteristic of the ghost story (177). One may think again of *Villette* in this context, for example, with its legendary nun "buried alive" under the Methuselah tree. And yet for all its significance as a conventional gothic motif of the "risen ghost," contemporary preoccupations with taphephobia also appear irrevocably attributable to the impact of cholera, an illness whose "apparent symptoms" could include

> violent stomach pains, vomiting, diarrhoea, and total prostration, during which the body turned cold, the pulse became imperceptible, and the skin wizened. During the final stages, the afflicted might well be taken for dead, and gruesome stories circulated of premature burial and the poor victim's anguished attempts to claw free of the coffin. (Wohl 118–19)

Next to actual inoculation against cholera bacilli, shocking stories of the grotesque — like Poe's "Sphinx" or the personal narratives to which Wohl alludes — may have offered the Victorians their only viable alternative: the opportunity to build up the *mental* resistance necessary to cope with the traumas brought on by epidemic diseases and widespread death.[29]

It is also epidemic disease which is seen to produce a spectral anti-body of sorts in *Bleak House* (1853): indeed, " 'haunting' is perhaps the adjective that best describes [Dickens's] novel," Chiara Briganti suggests (211).[30] Critics have often commented on Esther Summerson's spectral aspect in the text, noting that she eventually "becomes," in effect, the ghostly embodiment of Lady Morbury's dying curse on the Dedlock family, when in Chapter 36, she is arrested by the sound of her own "echoing footsteps" along "the Ghost's Walk." It is there that Lady Leicester Dedlock confesses to Esther the tale of her disgraced past, and it is there that Dickens's heroine suddenly realizes "that there was a dreadful truth in the legend of the Ghost's Walk; that it was I who was to bring calamity upon the stately house; and that my warning feet were haunting it even then'' (454; ch. 36).

A detail which seems to have escaped many discussions of ghostly signs in *Bleak House*, however, is that Esther's first self-conscious appearance ''as a figure of the uncanny, [as] that which was once familiar and which has become estranged'' (Briganti 222) comes as a direct result of the ''very bad sort of fever'' carried by the unfortunate crossing-sweep, Jo, and inadvertently passed along to Charley and then Esther (*Bleak House*; 382; ch. 31). What renders Esther's once-familiar face unrecognizable — as ''strange'' as an uncanny spectre before which one ''start[s] back'' in fright, in fact — are precisely the disfiguring traces of a near-fatal contagious disease. ''I was very much changed — O very, very much,'' she laments upon her first glimpse into a mirror after recovery: ''At first, my face was so strange to me, that I think I should have put my hands before it and started back, but for the encouragement I have mentioned'' (444–45; ch. 36).

Esther's markedly estranged appearance as a survivor of small pox fever effectively conveys the uncanny essence of the nineteenth-century dis-ease before contagious diseases — and their deadly breeding grounds, like the ''tumbling tenement'' of ''Tom-all-Alone's'':

> As, on the ruined human wretch, vermin parasites appear, so these ruined shelters have bred a crowd of foul existence that crawls in and out of gaps in walls and boards; and coils itself to sleep, in maggot numbers, where the rain drips in; and comes and goes, fetching and carrying fever, and sowing more evil in its every footprint than . . . all the fine gentlemen in office . . . shall set right in five hundred years. (197; ch. 16)

Dickens's parallel evocations of the ghostly Esther's ''echoing footsteps'' in ''the Ghost's Walk'' and the invisible ''footprints'' of ''foul'' fever in the slum tenement are nice indications of the subtle way in which *Bleak House* figuratively manages to conjure a ''spectre'' of communicable disease: the ''ghost'' of an elusive presence, of an infectious miasma signalled only by the haunting traces it leaves upon ground already trodden.

In Henry James's *The Turn of the Screw* (1898), on the other hand, it is not the abstract concept of infectious disease which is metaphorically prefigured as a spectral entity but the ambiguous apparitions of Miss Jessel and Peter Quint themselves which are conversely presented as contaminating, pathogenic agents of a form of communicable disease. Described by James as ''hovering prowling blighting presences,'' the ghosts of this short novel ''reek with [an] air of Evil'' (*Art of the Novel* 175) which proves as insidious as that ''crowd of foul existence'' bred in the fever slum of Tom-all-Alone's (197; ch. 16). Thus, at Bly, where the Governess presides over her seemingly cherubic charges, Miles and Flora, the advent of the ghosts' appearance is represented as the ''outbreak'' of a "gross" illness or rash of sorts: "after a lull, the grossness broke out," as the Governess states (40; ch. 9). With an ever-deepening conviction of the children's infernal and uncanny communion with the spirits — their "secret precocity — or whatever I might call the poison of an influence that I dared but half-phrase" (63; ch. 17) — the Governess comes to regard Miles and Flora as "sick children": "some wistful patient[s] in a children's hospital," whom she, in the role of a "nurse or sister of charity," must work to "cure"' (63; ch. 17).

Many critics of James's text have rightly suggested that, as the embodiment of a "general vision of evil" (*Art of the Novel* 176), the ghosts need to be interpreted in the Christian context of sin and sickness: as manifestations of inextricably interrelated conditions of moral and physical pollution or corruption. Nevertheless, the connections James weaves between spectral phenomena and contagious disease in particular are so pointed as to be virtually inescapable. That the "wide overwhelming presence" of the ghosts, which at the end of the story "fill[s] the room like the taste of poison" (*Turn*, 88; ch. 24), is a form of noxious pathogen specifically linked to the outbreak of fever is suggested by the fact that, at the crisis of confrontation, both children suddenly succumb to fever fits. Flora becomes so "markedly feverish" (74; ch. 21) after the Governess accuses her of complicit intercourse with the spirit of Miss Jessel that it remains questionable whether her abrupt departure from Bly with Mrs. Gross "will dissipate the influence . . . and carry it off," as the Governess predicts, or, conversely, aggravate her condition, perhaps "carrying off" Flora herself (81; ch. 22). Miles, for his part, is indeed "carried off" at the story's conclusion, by an exorcistic "dispossession" which is accompanied by "a sudden fever of his little body" (88, 85; ch. 24). And James proceeds to draw an explicit link between Miles's "fevered face" (87; ch. 24), the face of contagious disease, and that of the ghost figure when he has the Governess compare the boy's sweaty, pale visage to Quint's "white face of damnation" glaring through the window: "the face that was close to mine," she says of Miles, "was as white as the face against the glass" (85; ch. 24). Images of the ghostly anti-body and the "fevered" body lacking antibodies are here presented as mirror reflections of one another.

The twin outbreaks of ghosts, on the one hand, and of contagion and fever, on the other, point toward an uncanny conjunction that haunts even the substance of James's personal correspondence relating to *The Turn of the Screw*. It is a conceptual association that lurks, for example, in the language of a letter the author wrote to the renowned psychical researcher, F. W. H. Myers, in 1898: "The thing that . . . I most wanted not to fail of doing [in *The Turn of the Screw*] was to give the impression of the communication to the children of the most infernal imaginable evil and danger — the condition, on their part, of being as *exposed* as we can humanly conceive children to be."[31] Even for the late nineteenth century, to imagine "the condition" of children "being as *exposed* as we can humanly imagine children to be" was, axiomatically, to reflect on their exceptional vulnerability to communicable childhood diseases such as measles and scarlet fever — the latter of which "remained a major killer throughout the century," "carry[ing] off" over one thousand children in the city of London alone as late as 1891 (Wohl 129).[32] Children's immature immune systems coupled with the lack of vaccinations for diseases easily preventable today accounted for perhaps the most immediate and real form of "exposure" feared by the majority of nineteenth-century parents; and along with a general Christian ethos of illness as an expression of moral evil, it is this contemporary context of infectious disease which must be seen to inform the imagistic texture of James's work.

While in James's story, ghosts essentially manifest themselves as poisonous anti-bodies of disease, Melville's *Moby-Dick* (1851) presents an intriguing instance of the phantom anti-body in its defensive capacity. Melville's text, despite its preoccupations with anatomy, is also one very much concerned with the interaction of anti-bodies, not only in the form of a ghost of a whale and a white whale of a ghost but in the antithetical figures of the "small black [cabin] boy," Pip, and "the big white God," Ahab (276; ch. 40). Pip, the "crazy loon" who runs about as a shadow of his former self after having been once scared out of his senses, is thus quite literally represented as a shadowy anti-body of madness: an "idiot" boy whose milder strain of lunacy has the potential to neutralize the more vitriolic malady of the insane Captain Ahab (514; ch. 125). Near the end of the novel, for example, Pip offers to shadow Ahab as a sort of phantom limb: "do ye but use poor me for your one lost leg," he pleads (525; ch. 129). In response, Ahab, it seems, intuitively senses something akin to a principle of acquired immunity: the possibility that "the one daft with weakness" may successfully inoculate "the one daft with strength" (515; ch. 125). Perverse madman that he is, he then replies to Pip thus:

> Lad, lad, I tell thee thou must not follow Ahab now. The hour is coming when Ahab would not scare thee from him, yet would not have thee by him. There is that in thee, poor lad, which I feel too curing to my malady. Like cures like; and for this hunt, my malady becomes my most desired health. (525; ch. 129)

The catchphrase "like cures like," a maxim of Victorian homeopathy, suggests the more general influence here of an early nineteenth-century pseudo-science contemporaneous with but eventually undermined by the fledgling fields of bacteriology and immunology.[33] All the same, the notion of Pip's immunizing effect as a "phantom limb" provides an especially valuable counter to those more numerous representations of ghostly anti-bodies as the effects of contagious diseases or vice versa — representations, that is, which more emphatically attest to a pervasive dis-ease in the literary imagination.

Ibsen's Ghosts *and Our Ghosts: A Coda*

ALTHOUGH IT IS A WORK THAT falls beyond the proper purview of this essay, it seems appropriate to turn at last to Henrik Ibsen's *Ghosts* (1881), a play which not only dramatically recapitulates the intimate relationship between spectres and communicable disease in the nineteenth century but one which underscores especially well the way in which "The Age of the Antibody" ultimately speaks in a perhaps unexpectedly direct manner to the late twentieth-century sensibility.

In Ibsen's play, ghostly anti-bodies manifest themselves under the guise of that most Victorian of spooks from the past: hereditary disease. But while the "sins of the fathers" (or mothers) are visited upon countless fictional characters of the age — such as Brontë's Bertha Mason, Thackeray's George Gaunt, Collins's Mad Monkton, or Braddon's Lady Audley, to mention only a few — as cases of insanity, in Ibsen's drama, the dead hand of the past extends its legacy in the form of a crippling infectious disease at once mental and physical. For while the dead father in *Ghosts*, Captain Alving, has left provisions for a "Memorial Home" for orphans to be established in his name, he has left a far more malignant trace flowing in the veins of his son, Oswald, who soon discovers he suffers from syphilis. "There's been something worm-eaten about you since birth," as a physician puts it to the hapless Oswald, who is indeed destined to succumb to a progressive "kind of softening of the brain" (138, 161). Ultimately, Oswald's fate is the syphilitic dementia of general paralysis: a state in which he is left inert, "flaccid," and "expressionless," staring vacantly into space and repeatedly entreating his hysterical and terrified mother: "Mother, give me the sun. . . . The sun. The sun. . . . The sun. . . . The sun" (163–64). "Struck down by this ghastly thing, lying there helpless, like an imbecile child," Oswald is left in Act III by the dramatist "beyond all hope of recovery" (162).

Ghosts, then, may be taken as an apt emblem of nineteenth-century anti-bodies of dis-ease and defense in that Ibsen's wrathful wraiths are essentially psychobiological demons: the anti-bodies of a disease against which no antibodies exist, against which a body is defenceless, and before which a mind becomes dis-eased. And in this singular work of ghosts, madness, and infectious disease, Ibsen's work alights upon a nerve red and sore in contemporary society. For it evokes, perhaps, through the "ghosts" of a deadly sexually transmitted disease a sense of our own newly nervous condition in the age of AIDS, the latest epidemic to have prompted something like a twentieth-century version of the Victorians' "horror autotoxicus." The veritably "oxymoronic" idea of an "immunological disease" (Silverstein 215), an illness in which the immune system that should help defend us against diseases instead sabotages itself, involves an element of particularly perverse pathology, an "exceedingly dysteleologic" state of affairs no less difficult for us to accept than it was for our nineteenth-century forebears (Silverstein 160). And although the experts may keep insisting that there is "still no reason for hysteria,"[34] it may be that the rise of what one popular women's magazine has recently declared our "modern mysticism"[35] is also an index of AIDS-related anxiety, of our collective dread of a disease before which, for all our sophisticated medical technology, we are essentially defenseless. For imaginary anti-body production, it seems, is also on the upswing again, and there are at least some indications that the two phenomena are not entirely unrelated. It is, for example, an extended joke about communicable disease which rapidly empties a crowded elevator in an opening scene of the recent Hollywood movie *Ghost* (1990), an enormous and unexpected box office success.

Accompanying this post-industrial interest in the spirit realm, one may note a modern denial of death and mourning analogous to the "prudery [with which] the sexual impulses were [treated] a century ago" (Gorer, qtd. in Ariès 579). "The denial of death has gone beyond ·the bereaved and the expression of mourning," Phillippe Ariès contends, "[i]t has extended to everything that has to do with death, which has become infectious. Mourning or anything resembling it is [today treated] like a contagious disease (580). Thus, the nineteenth century's increased emphasis on the cosmetic preservation of corpses, for instance, has in our time been taken to outrageous new extremes: to the surgical preservation of the aging, never mind dead, body; to video or gravestone images preserving the faces and voices of the departed for posterity; to the ultimate in "life extension" fantasies, procedures such as cryonics, the high-tech deep-freezing of corpses for thawing and resurrection at some stupendously advanced point in the medical future.

Are changing disease patterns once again finding expression in a dis-eased suppression of death and defensive spectral projections of the psyche? The enigmatic message from the ghosts of our past may be, it's time we asked some bloody antibody.

University of Alberta

NOTES

1. Castle discusses how early phantasmagoria shows, imported to England from France by 1801–02, though "developed as mock exercises in scientific demystification," actually served to heighten the "supernatural effect" of the "*fantomes artificiels*" they produced, enforcing on audiences "a peculiar kind of split consciousness" as to the "reality" of the images before them ("Phantasmagoria" 30, 49). "Even as it supposedly explained apparitions away," she writes, "the spectral technology of phantasmagoria mysteriously re-created the emotional aura of the supernatural," for "clever illusionists were careful never to reveal exactly how their own bizarre, sometimes frightening apparitions were produced" (30). For a thorough discussion of materialization seances in the context of nineteenth-century spiritualism, see Owen.

2. See, for example, J-M. Charcot, "Spiritualism and Hysteria," Lecture XVI in his *Clinical Lectures on the Diseases of the Nervous System*, (198–206). L. Forbes Winslow's highly polemical treatise, *Spiritualistic Madness* (1877), is reviewed by Owen (156–67).

3. A mental sign of melancholy, Burton contends, is that the patient "dare not be alone in the dark, for fear of Hobgoblins and Devils: he suspects everything he hears or sees to be a Devil, or enchanted; and imagineth a thousand chimeras and visions, which to his thinking he certainly sees, bugbears, talks with black men, ghosts, goblins, etc."

4. With the recent exceptions of critics such as Castle and Ariès, historians of spiritualism and literary critics of occult literature, it seems to me, have not focused closely enough on the question of the psychological imperatives behind manifestations of nineteenth-century spiritualism, not to mention biological factors. Most attribute the spiritualist movement, in broad terms, to a general dialectical "reaction" (Briggs 52), "counter-reaction" (Finucane 175), or "antidote to relentless materialism . . . and unfeeling mechanization of modern society" (Reed 103).

5. See Freud, "Anxiety and Instinctual Life" (22: 81). In this essay, I am in other words, presuming neurosis to a large extent as the outcome of a real, external threat, as opposed to the intrapsychic conflicts perhaps more readily associated with neurosis. I will discuss the concept of anxiety and its role in symptom formation in more detail below. I would like to thank the editors of *Victorian Literature and Culture*, particularly John Maynard, for encouraging me to develop this facet of my argument and for referring me to the work of Rollo May.

6. These characteristics apply, for instance, especially to such quasi-theologic treatises as John Neale's *The Unseen World* or Newton Crosland's "new theophisic theory" of apparitions.

7. This is not to suggest, though, that nineteenth-century medical writers necessarily advocated a naive materialistic credo of "seeing is believing." Many were convinced that "matter undoubtably exists in so fine, subtile, and . . . spiritualized a state as to be imperceptible to human sense," and even willing to grant that such invisible matter "may affect us powerfully" (Maudsley, *Natural Causes* 175–76). They were simply unwilling to make the quantum leap from a belief in forms of invisible *matter* to a belief in forms of invisible *spirit*: an entity by definition immaterial. It is a "signal inconsistency," as Maudsley inveighed, with a sharp rap to the knuckles of "ghost seers and ghost seekers" one and all, "to make grossly sensible to eye in ghost form . . . a material agency the essential character of which is a tenuity too fine for the appreciation of the senses" (175–76).

8. As Castle suggests, arguments such as Dendy's, which posited "only a difference of degree," not "essence," between ghosts and mental concepts (Dendy, qtd. in Castle 57), led directly to "the spectralization or 'ghostifying' of mental space" — a metaphor she compellingly traces into the early nineteenth century ("Phantasmagoria" 29). In this respect, she argues, "[t]he rationalists did not so much negate the traditional spirit world as displace it into the realm of psychology. Ghosts were not exorcized — only internalized and reinterpreted as hallucinatory thoughts" (52).

9. In a passage instructive to read in light of Jung's comment on conscious rationality as a form of "apotropaic defense against superstition," Maudsley expounds his theory that any tendency to revert to supernatural beliefs would be "instantly and unconsciously controlled by a silent process of inhibition, owing to the positive knowledge incorporate in the structure of the well-balanced and fairly cultured brain." The "modern day disbelief in ghosts" is attributed to the fact that "as the

region of the positively known increases, the region of the possible and wonderful decreases" (*Natural Causes* 200).

10. In this respect, the late-century researchers appear precursors of modern psychiatric thought, which also advances (among others) a "continuity theory" and a general semiology of perception. See Siegel and West (257–86), and Bernard and Trouve (211–13).

11. For a treatment of this question in the literary context of Henry James's heroine, Verena Tarrant, in *The Bostonians*, see my essay.

12. Sally Shuttleworth notes that in *Villette*, "Brontë offers . . . a thorough materialization of the self" (331), but based on the heroine's temporary hallucinogenic experience during the final fête night, she concludes that the novel ultimately "dissolves the divisions between inner and outer realms" and in this way "suggests an alternative vision to male definitions of the Real" and "male materialism" (332).

13. I am indebted to Theodore R. Sarbin and Joseph B. Juhasz for the following passage on the etymological history of "reality":

[W]here biological survival depended on the ability to differentiate things from shadows, mirages, optical illusions, words, rememberings, dreams, and imaginings, to be "in touch with reality" meant only that the individual did not embrace wood nymphs, or bump into trees, horses, or people. Thus the original use of the word "reality" was in the service of denoting the world of ponderable things. (qtd. in Siegel and West 248)

14. This reading confirms Mary Jacobus's argument that Brontë's realist novel is "formally fissured" by the "buried letter of Romanticism" which manifests itself as a subversive challenge to the claims of empirical reality (41–61).

15. In his early writings, Freud, in fact, used the two terms "indifferently, almost as equivalents," as James Strachey notes (14: 144). On the theoretic permutations of the concepts of repression and defense in Freud's work, see also Ricouer (138–41).

16. It is worthwhile to note that Freud perceived such defensive value not only in occult projections of ghosts and spirits but also in psychotic hallucinations: "the delusional formation, which we take to be the pathological product, is in reality an attempt at recovery, a process of reconstruction" (12: 71).

17. Freud, indeed, called anxiety "the fundamental phenomenon and main problem of neurosis" (20: 144). A useful overview of the direction of Freud's thought on the problem of anxiety is provided by Rollo May (112–27).

18. A similar retraction is voiced in "Anxiety and Instinctual Life": "It was not the repression that created the anxiety; the anxiety was there earlier; it was the anxiety that made the repression" (22: 86).

19. "It must be confessed," Freud admits, "that we were not prepared to find that internal instinctual danger would turn out to be a determinant and preparation for an external, real, situation of danger" (22: 86). A further problematization of the distinction between neurotic and realistic anxiety is provided in the addendum to "Inhibitions, Symptoms, and Anxiety," "Supplementary Remarks on Anxiety" (20: 164–68).

20. "This same trend toward seeing the anxious individual in a struggle with his environment," May continues, ". . . is indicated in the increasing prominence in Freud's later writings of the phrase 'danger situation' rather than merely 'danger' " (125).

21. On the ambivalence of human attitudes towards mortality, see, for example, the latter half of Freud's essay "Thoughts for the Times on War and Death" (1915) (14: 289–300).

22. See Ariès, *The Hour of Our Death*, esp. chaps. 10 and 11 (405–06). Ariès's work was first published in French in 1977 as *L'Homme devant la Mort* and presents a sweeping study of changing attitudes toward death in Western culture since the Middle Ages.

23. Indeed, by inadvertently suggesting just how *un*avoidable this horrific disease was for the Victorians, the very title of Blanc's treatise, *Cholera: How to Avoid It and Treat It*, substantiates the grounds for the "deadly fear" it inspired.

24. The rise of the popular press during the nineteenth century is one factor which distinguishes epidemics of the era from those of preceding ages; all the major cholera outbreaks, in 1831–32, 1848–49, 1853–54, and 1866–67, were well-publicized, resulting in an unprecedented awareness of the high mortality rates (Wohl 118).

25. In addition to their defensive relevance as metaphorical substitutes for biological defenses, nineteenth-century representations of the ghostly anti-body in literature, art, photography, and "phantasmagoria" performances may have served to help "bind" or "contain" a quite literally "free-floating" source of dis-ease. For contagious disease as an essentially amorphous and imperceptible external threat comprises, in a way, a curiously *objectless* objective fear. The ghostly anti-body thus afforded "protection against the anxiety-creating situation" in the same way as does the neurotic symptom:

    When [a] conscious struggle can no longer be tolerated, either because of its increasing severity or because of its lack of success [or resolution], symptomatic changes in the organism take place. These relieve the strain of the conflict and make a quasi- or pseudo-adjustment possible when the conflict cannot actually be solved. Thus it might be said that . . . symptoms are often ways of containing . . . anxiety; they are the anxiety in structuralized form. . . . [We recall] Freud's remark about psychological symptoms: "The symptom is bound anxiety." (May 84)

26. Though the principle of acquired immunity is a discovery of the late nineteenth century, the concept itself dates back even beyond Edward Jenner's discovery of cowpox vaccination in 1798 and the introduction of inoculation against smallpox by the Royal Society's "Experiment on Immunity" in 1721–22. However, the idea and term 'immunity," as Arthur Silverstein notes, did not gain great currency until the 1880s and '90s (1). It was not until 1880 that Pasteur discovered (by chance!) the antibody against chicken cholera; another three years elapsed before Koch succeeded in isolating the disease bacillus (Silverstein 327–28). Even at that late date, the concept of "polluting" immunization was actively resisted by factions of both the lay and scientific communities — with almost as much energy, in fact, as were some of Freud's controversial new theories. See also Wohl (132–35).

27. The recoil of late nineteenth-century scientists from the frightening implications of the concept of autotoxicity is discussed by Silverstein (160–89 and 214–15). Silverstein attributes their resistance to the concept to the offense it gave "the general Darwinian teleological view of a benign immune apparatus" (215).

28. Though Freud seems cognizant of the "danger . . . of exaggerating the importance" of biopsychological parallels in this respect, he cannot help but indulge the fantasy, however improbable, of the "ideal solution" to neurotic disorders, "which medical men no doubt still yearn for": "to discover some bacillus which could be isolated and bred in a pure culture and which, when injected into anyone, would invariably produce the same illness; or, to put it rather less extravagantly, to demonstrate the existence of certain chemical substances the administration of which would bring

about or cure particular neuroses'' (20: 99, 153). In pointing out these parallels, I think it is also worth bearing in mind the generally close interrelationship among the sciences at the time: the immunologists, whose theories were "grounded upon general biological principles derived from other fields," saw "their implications carried over to scientific disciplines well beyond the boundaries of immunology" (Silverstein 305). One of those related "scientific disciplines" was neurophysiology, Freud's early speciality and undoubtedly a formative influence on his thinking.

29. For different perspectives on the subject of taphephobia, see Ariès (396–403); and Freud's comment on fears of premature burial in "The Uncanny"(17: 217–52).

30. Briganti's interesting essay explores Esther's "haunted narrative": just as the heroine's "spectral name" is haunted by the subversive figure of Vashti — the Biblical Esther's predecessor — so is her narrative implicated, through an uncanny "process of feminine filiation" in a web of "guilt and . . . [feminine] desire" that stretches to her through the histories of Lady Leicester Dedlock and Lady Morbury Dedlock (215, 220).

31. James's letter of 19 December 1898 is reprinted in *Turn of the Screw* (112).

32. Ninety-five percent of all cases of scarlet fever, Wohl notes, involved children under ten years of age; see Wohl's ch. 2, pp. 10–42 *passim*, for more on "The Massacre of the Innocents" by contagious disease during the period.

33. Haley has observed that "the practice [of homeopathy] was curiously analogous to inoculation; homeopathic doctors carried with them cases of medicines, from which they would administer minute doses of whatever could produce symptoms resembling those of the disease being treated" (13).

34. Essay subtitle in the popular scientific journal, *Discover*, Sept. 1986 (qtd. in Gilman 259).

35. "Mystics in Our Midst," *Elle*, August 1991: 54.

WORKS CITED

Ariès, Phillippe. *The Hour of Our Death*. Trans. Helen Weaver. 1977; New York: Knopf, 1981.

Beidler, Peter. *Ghosts, Demons, and Henry James: The Turn of the Screw at the Turn of the Century*. Columbia: U of Missouri P, 1989.

Bernard, Paul, and Simone Trouve. *Semiologie Psychiatrique*. Paris: Masson, 1977.

Bierce, Ambrose. *The Enlarged Devil's Dictionary*. Ed. Ernest Jerome Hopkins. Preface by John Myers Myers. Garden City, NY: Doubleday, 1967.

Blanc, Henri. *Cholera: How To Avoid It and Treat It*. London: Henry S. King, 1873.

Briganti, Chiara. "The Monstrous Actress: Esther Summerson's Spectral Name." *Dickens Studies Annual* 19 (1990): 205–30.

Briggs, Julia. *Night Visitors: The Rise and Fall of the English Ghost Story*. London: Faber, 1977.

Brontë, Charlotte. *Jane Eyre*. Afterword by Arthur Zeiger. New York: New American Library, 1982.

———. *Villette*. Ed. Mark Lilly. Intro. Tony Tanner. Harmondsworth: Penguin Books, 1979.

Brontë, Emily. *Wuthering Heights*. Ed. Ian Jack. Oxford: Oxford UP, 1981.

Burton, Robert. *The Anatomy of Melancholy*. (1651). Ed. Floyd Dell and Paul Jordan-Smith. New York: Tudor, 1955.

Carlyle, Thomas. *Sartor Resartus/On Heroes and Hero Worship*. Intro. by W. H. Hudson. London: J. M. Dent, 1908.

Castle, Terry. "Phantasmagoria: Spectral Technology and the Metaphysics of Modern Reverie." *Critical Inquiry* 15.1 (1988): 26–61.

———. "The Spectralization of the Other in *The Mysteries of Udolpho.*" *The New Eighteenth Century: Theory, Politics, English Literature.* Eds. Felicity Nussbaum and Laura Brown. London: Methuen, 1987. 231–53.

Charcot, Jean-Martin. *Clinical Lectures in the Diseases of the Nervous System.* Ed. and intro. Ruth Harris. London: Tavistock/Routledge, 1991.

Conolly, John. *An Inquiry Concerning the Indications of Insanity.* Ed. Richard Hunter and Ida Macalpine. 1830; rpt. London: Dawsons, 1964.

Crosland, Newton. *Apparitions: An Essay Explanatory of Old Facts and A New Theory to which are added Sketches and Adventures.* London: Trubner and Co., 1873.

Crowe, Catherine Stevens. *The Night Side of Nature; or, Ghosts and Ghost Seers.* 2 vols. London: T. C. Newby, 1848.

Dickens, Charles. *Bleak House.* Ed. George Ford and Sylvère Monod. New York: Norton, 1977.

Ferriar, John. *An Essay Towards a Theory of Apparitions.* London: Cadell and Davis, 1813.

Finucane, R. C. *Appearances of the Dead: A Cultural History of Ghosts.* London: Junction Books, 1982.

Freud, Sigmund. *The Standard Edition of the Complete Psychological Works of Sigmund Freud.* Trans. and ed. James Strachey, with the assistance of Anna Freud, Alix Strachey, and Alan Tyson. 24 vols. London: Hogarth and The Institute of Psycho-Analysis. 1953–74.

Griesinger, Wilhelm. *Mental Pathology and Therapeutics.* Trans. C. Lockhart Robertson and James Rutherford. London: The New Sydenham Society, 1867.

Gilman, Sander L. *Disease and Representation: Images of Illness from Madness to AIDS.* Ithaca: Cornell UP, 1988.

Haley, Bruce. *The Healthy Body and Victorian Culture.* Cambridge, MA: Harvard UP, 1978.

Hibbert, Samuel. *Sketches of A Philosophy of Apparitions; or, An Attempt to Trace Such Illusions to Their Physical Causes.* 2nd Ed. Edinburgh: Oliver and Boyd; London: Whittaker, 1825.

Ibsen, Henrik. *Henrik Ibsen: Four Major Plays.* Trans. James McFarlane and Jens Arup. Oxford: Oxford UP, 1981.

Ireland, William. *The Blot Upon the Brain: Studies in History and Psychology.* 2nd ed. Edinburgh: Bell and Bradflute, 1893.

Jacobus, Mary. *Reading Woman: Essays in Feminist Criticism.* New York: Columbia UP, 1986.

James, Henry. *The Turn of the Screw.* Ed. Robert Kimbrough. New York: Norton, 1966.

———. *The Art of the Novel: Critical Prefaces.* Intro. by Richard P. Blackmur. New York: Scribners, 1962.

James, William. *The Principles of Psychology.* 2 vols. 1890; New York: rpt. Dover, 1950.

———. *William James on Exceptional Mental States: The 1896 Lowell Lectures.* Reconstructed and introduced by Eugene Taylor. Amherst: U of Massachusetts P, 1984.

Jung, Carl Gustav. *Psychology and the Occult.* Trans. R. F. C. Hull. Bollingen Series XX. Princeton: Princeton UP, 1977.

Kerr, Howard, *'Mediums, and Spirit-Rappers, and Roaring Radicals': Spiritualism in American Literature, 1850–1900* Urbana: U of Illinois P, 1972.

Maudsley, Henry. *Natural Causes and Supernatural Seemings.* 3rd ed. London: Kegan, Paul, Trench, Trubner, 1897.

————. "Hallucinations of the Senses." *Fortnightly Review* 30 (September, 1878): 370–86.

May, Rollo. *The Meaning of Anxiety*. New York: Ronald P, 1950.

Melville, Herman. *Moby-Dick; or, The Whale*. Eds. Luther Mansfield and Howard P. Vincent. New York: Hendricks, 1962.

Neale, John Mason. *The Unseen World: Communications With It, Real or Imaginary*. 2nd ed. London: J. Masters, 1853.

Owen, Alex. *The Darkened Room: Women, Power, and Spiritualism in Late-Nineteenth Century England*. London: Virago P, 1989.

Poe, Edgar Allan. "The Sphinx." *Collected Works of Edgar Allan Poe: Tales and Sketches 1843–49*. Ed. Thomas Ollive Mabbott. Cambridge, MA: Belknap P, 1978. Vol. 3, 1245–51.

Reed, John. "The Occult in Later Victorian Literature." *Literature of the Occult: A Collection of Critical Essays*. Ed. Peter B. Messent. Englewood Cliffs: Prentice-Hall, 1981. 89–104.

Ricoeur, Paul. *Freud and Philosophy: An Essay on Interpretation*. Trans. Denis Savage. New Haven: Yale UP, 1970.

Sheppard, E. A. *Henry James and The Turn of the Screw*. Oxford: Oxford UP; Auckland: Auckland UP, 1974.

Shuttleworth, Sally. " 'The Surveillance of a Sleepless Eye': The Constitution of Neurosis in *Villette*." *One Culture: Essays in Science and Literature*. Eds. George Levine and Alan Rauch. Madison: U of Wisconsin P, 1987. 313–35.

Siegel, R. K., and L. J. West. *Hallucinations: Behaviour, Experience, and Theory*. New York: John Wiley, 1975.

Silverstein, Arthur. *A History of Immunology*. San Diego: Academic P, 1989.

Spink, Wesley W. *Infectious Diseases: Prevention and Treatment in the Nineteenth and Twentieth Centuries*. Minneapolis: U of Minnesota P, 1978.

Stanley, N. F., and R. A. Joske. *Changing Disease Patterns and Human Behaviour*. London: Academic P, 1980.

Wiesenthal, C. S. "A Jamesian Vision of 'American Nervousness': Masculine Dis-ease and Diseased Femininity in *The Bostonians*." *English Studies in Canada* 15.4 (1989): 478–97.

Williams, J. P. "Psychical Research and Psychiatry in Late Victorian Britain: Trance as Ecstacy or Trance as Insanity." *The Anatomy of Madness: Essays in the History of Psychiatry*. 2 vols. Eds. W. F. Bynum, Roy Porter, and Michael Shepherd. London: Tavistock, 1985. I: 233–54.

Wohl, Anthony. *Endangered Lives: Public Health in Victorian Britain*. Cambridge, MA: Harvard UP, 1983.

WORKS IN PROGRESS

Jerome McGann's essay, "The Complete Writings and Pictures of Dante Gabriel Rossetti: A Hypermedia Research Archive," gives an early description of a long-term project that he began in 1992. The Rossetti Archive is expected to be ready for general use by all students and scholars by 1999.

Ali Behdad's essay, "Colonial Narrative and Its Discontents," is from his book, *Belated Travelers: Orientalism in the Age of Colonial Dissolution*. Duke University Press, published with permission.

David Glover's essay, " 'Our enemy is not merely spiritual': Degeneration and Modernity in Bram Stoker's *Dracula*," is from a forthcoming book on Bram Stoker and the genealogy of popular narrative, tentatively titled Dracula's Children.

James L. Hill's essay, "Joseph's Currants: The Hermeneutic Challenge of *Wuthering Heights*," is part of a project on problems of narrative authority in Victorian fiction.

Patricia Meyer Spacks's essay, "A Dull Book is Easily Renounced," derives from her book entitled *Boredom: The Literary History of a State of Mind*. University of Chicago Press, published with permission.

THE COMPLETE WRITINGS AND PICTURES OF DANTE GABRIEL ROSSETTI: A HYPERMEDIA RESEARCH ARCHIVE

By Jerome McGann

A (Con)Textual Introduction

RECENT YEARS HAVE BROUGHT remarkable developments in electronic storage, management, and analysis of texts. It is difficult to overstate the importance of this technology for the scholarship and teaching of literature. Textual studies is the most fundamental area of literary studies, the subdiscipline upon which all else is based. The new technology revolutionizes textual studies. In doing so, it will eventually bring about profound changes in the way we think about and practise the study and teaching of literature in general.

The changes depend upon a simple fact: book and print technology no longer establish key limiting conditions of textuality. For literary studies, the consequences of this shift in our textual condition appear first and most glaringly in theory of texts and editorial practise.

The technology of the book has developed over many centuries. During this period textual and editorial scholars were important agents who helped to shape, exploit, and modify this technology. Tracing the evolution of codex-based models for critical editing will supply one with a comprehensive survey of the history of the book and its technology: for it was the critical editor and textual scholar who continually reflected upon the possibilities of the book as a tool for defining and transmitting knowledge.

This evolution climaxed in the past two hundred years, when highly sophisticated models for critical editions were developed. These models emerged initially in the eighteenth century as one of the jewels of enlightenment. While textual and editorial scholarship since then has been remarkable, its very successes have exposed the limits of the codex as a tool of information technology. The "information explosion" of the twentieth century has defined those limits even more sharply.

At the same time, however, computer technology has emerged as one way of dealing more effectively with this crisis of knowledge and information. Those of us who work with books and other texts in a professional way have begun to see that this new electronic technology represents an epochal change in our textual condition.

In simplest terms, electronic texts completely redefine our textual limits. Their breakaway from the codex form does not simply involve a power to store far greater quantities of information. It means the discovery of an entirely new textual world and a radical reimagination of textual space.

A Brief Overview of the Present Project

THE MATERIALS OF THE ARCHIVE are the writings and pictures of Dante Gabriel Rossetti (1828–1882). The goals and general structure of the Archive are as follows:

A. Goals

There are two principal goals:
1. to build a dynamic and expandable database (or library) of the written and pictorial works of Dante Gabriel Rossetti. The materials in this library will include an extensive body of related contextual matter (historical, editorial, critical). All the materials are organized for full electronic search and analysis, and all are embedded in a complex hypertextual environment linking the various files and parts of files to related elements in the archive.
2. to use the Rossetti Archive as a model for exploring the theoretical structure of texts in general, and for developing a programmatic approach to the electronic editing of imaginative works that will have wide scholarly application. This model and its related tools incorporates and then reconstructs the traditional models and tools that have descended to us (most immediately) through the textual and editorial breakthroughs begun in the eighteenth century. The new model represents a major innovation not only in textual theory and text management, but (ultimately) in the whole way that the study of literature can be conducted.

This innovation comes partly, as we know, because electronic texts gather enormous amounts of information that can be searched, compared, analyzed, and connected with remarkable speed. In addition, the environment of electronic texts has proved so plastic and flexible that its input data can be represented or transformed to suit the user's specific needs. For textual scholars and editors, this plasticity means that one need not be confined to the customary forms of machine-readable text in order to have the power of machine-readability.

Rossetti has been chosen for this project for the following reasons. First, his work has never been critically edited; all texts center in the series of editions produced right after Rossetti's death by his brother William Michael (culminating in the one volume edition of 1911). Splendid in their day, these editions have long needed to be replaced.

Second, two general aspects of Rossetti's work encourage, and even demand, that the project seek the deepest kind of exploration of the resources of electronic data management. The first is the extreme "nervousness" or "instability" of Rossetti's texts and pictures. Because he worked and reworked everything that he undertook to do, the texts (and even the pictures) rarely have that determinate textual condition — even at some hypothetical level — which traditional editing postulates as an ideal. Rossetti's works exhibit, that is to say, a complex array of "versions" that exist at many different scalar levels. This general feature of his work will force the edition to explore and exploit hypertextual[1] structures in the fullest possible ways.

The other general feature of his work is equally important. Rossetti worked in two media, and he sought to integrate the work of each of these mediums into the other. From the theoretical point of view of this project, Rossetti's dual artistic commitments are extremely useful. This situation does not allow the Archive to depart very far from the documentary state of the original materials. Consequently, the project is called upon to develop its electronic tools with a database of graphic materials. Hitherto no editorial project has laid this demand upon itself. It is a crucial demand, however, if these new electronic engines are to be adapted to the most traditional needs of textual and editorial scholarship.

B. Structure of the Archive

One way of seeing the Archive is as a structure that organizes four interrelated bodies of material: 1. graphic files containing facsimile images of all Rossetti's original manuscripts, proofs, and published texts (one file per page); 2. graphic files of all his drawings and paintings; 3. e-text versions of the original textual documents (B.1. above); 4. e-texts of various other, related materials (contemporary reviews and other records, textual and critical commentaries, notes, etc.).

Or one can view the Archive as a three-level hierarchical structure. Level one comprises all the primary textual and pictorial documents in "facsimile" form (above, B.1. and B.2.). Level two contains electronic models of all the documents in Level one; it is a collection of "virtual" books and pictures — "virtual" because these electronic models are organized as structured sets of tagged descriptions (SGML marked[2]) of the formal features of the Level one documents. These include detailed tagging of the physical features of the documents — typography, page design, etc. — as well as of their substantive characteristics (genre features, iconography, etc.). Level three, which is imbedded within Level two, is a set of e-texts of the Level one documents as well as all the other textual materials in the Archive (see B.4. above). As at Level two, these e-texts are SGML-marked. But whereas the materials at Level two are sets of formal electronic models, the materials at Level three are linguistic: lines of poetry, passages of prose.

The Rossetti Archive means to put at a scholar's disposal, as it were in a single electronic "book," virtual copies (electronic "facsimiles") of all the original documents (manuscripts and printed texts, drawings, and paintings) that scholars and students need. The Archive's various analytic and critical operations are structured in relation to and within this database of graphic files.

General Project Description

A. Relation to Comparable Projects

In recent years literary scholars have begun to exploit the resources of electronic text storage and retrieval processes. Significant projects include, for example, the Dartmouth Dante Project, and Chadwyck-Healey's full-text database of English Poetry and Patrologia Latina. There are many others underway or just starting to be developed. Scholars have also begun to construct hypertext environments for connecting and studying large bodies of related textual materials. Notable here is the Perseus Project and various hypertext editions or teaching tools in different fields: for example the hypertext edition of Thoreau's *Notebooks* now underway, or the Dickens and Tennyson "webs" developed for George Landow's classrooms at Brown.

So far as I am aware, all of these projects organize their materials in relation to a central text or set of texts: *Walden* of Thoreau, the plays of Aeschylus, the *Divina Commedia*, etc. The electronic environment is used as a mechanism for one or all of the following purposes: to help to (re)construct the central text(s) through computerized collation of the textually relevant materials; to facilitate various kinds of search and analysis of the stored texts; to connect the central text(s) to other related texts (for a comparative study of variations) and to a complex body of editorial and contextual materials (for elucidating the central text both critically and historically). The Perseus Project, which epitomizes this last use of computerized tools, represents one of the most sophisticated scholarly deployments to date of computerized text processing.

Organized to perform these functions, the Rossetti Archive has consciously schooled itself in the experience gained by these important scholarly ventures. The Archive departs from its precursors, however, in certain crucial respects. The import of these departures can best be clarified by recalling the key structural features of current electronic editing projects and hypertexts.

Two matters are most important. First, all scholarly electronic editing projects to date are conceptually organized on the model of the book. That is to say, the electronic tools (both software and hardware) are designed to (re)construct, search, and manipulate *a central text*. Second, this central text — the focus of the editorial process — is typically stored as a machine-readable text file or set of files. If any texts (e.g., manuscripts or original printed editions) are stored for retrieval in their original form (as "facsimiles"), these graphic files are not regularly incorporated into the search and analysis operations of the electronic network. They function rather as illustrations of the electronic texts, examples of the originary forms of the e-texts.

The name "Rossetti Archive" indicates how it departs from the traditional model of editing in relation to a central text (whether "primary," "ultimate," or "ideal"). The project is not a critical "edition" but a critical *archive*. It reconstructs a library of all the (historically received) textually relevant states of Rossetti's writings and pictures. For each of the individual "works" in this archive (e.g., the poem known as "The Blessed Damozel," or the picture of the same title), no single state of the work is pre-defined as the critical point of departure or comparison. In terms of traditional textual theory, there is no "base text" or "copy text" or "ideal text," nor even the continuous "process" text pursued by genetic editors. The Archive puts all the relevant documents at the reader's disposal for whatever manipulations are wanted. The user determines the textual point(s) of departure that are adopted for particular acts of reading or study.

Second, on the matter of the use of the graphic materials (the electronic facsimiles of the texts and pictures). These do not function in the Archive as illustrations or adjuncts to a core e-text; the core of the Archive *is* the set of electronic facsimiles. The Archive is at all points structured in relation to the electronic facsimiles. The point of the Archive is to expose as much of the information contained in those original documents to search, analysis, and a hypertextual linking.

B. The Example of "The Blessed Damozel"

A brief example may be useful at this point. "The Blessed Damozel," a key Rossetti poem, exists in a number of finished states, all of them carrying their own special authority. In addition to a fair copy manuscript (made a number of years after the poem was originally composed), key texts were printed in 1850, 1856, and 1870; and the work has a number of other important and authoritative textual states as well. Traditional editorial practise would work to define a text of highest authority and then attach to it a record of the variants from all other known and textually relevant states. In the Rossetti Archive no text of highest authority is postulated (whether empirical, critical, or genetic — to use the common terms of scholarly editing).

The Archive informs the user of the available textual states for each of Rossetti's works. This information guides readers through the Archive's large mass of documents and helps them to determine their critical and editorial points of vantage. Editorial and critical notes are also provided to gloss the texts for the reader and supply other kinds of explanatory materials.

This decentered approach to the textual environment means to exploit to the full the hypertextual organization of the Archive. Every document (and every part of every document) is imbedded in a context of related documents and materials. The most general structure of these relations is defined by the overall hypertext network. Each file in the Archive, however, is its own locus of possible sets of relations. Because the Archive can organize its materials at different scalar levels, the set of possible nested structures can grow quite large. (For example, although the basic file unit in the Archive is a graphic file corresponding to a single document page or picture, these basic units can be made to reveal their various implicit higher levels of organization: e.g., that a manuscript is one face or feature of a poem, that the poem is also part of various possible "higher level" poetical sequences, and that such sequences form parts of different printed works.)

Technical Features and Their Importance

ELECTRONIC EDITIONS are organized as databases of machine-readable text files. These files are then electronically marked up — more or less extensively, depending on the project — for search and analysis by the user. A hypertext network may also be laid on top of the database for further critical operations with the database.

Because the core database of the Rossetti Archive is a set of bitmapped[3] graphic files rather than machine-readable text files, the Archive would seem to have foregone one of the key tools of computerized texts — electronic markup and the analytic power it provides. From the traditional scholar's point of view, of course, the advantages of a "facsimile" database are obvious: editors and scholars ground their work in the original textual materials, and while *any particular* departure from those materials may secure certain critical advantages, *every* departure always involves a loss of critical perspective. So as the demands of traditional editing of literary works draw one away from the radical textual translation involved in the machine-readable text, the call of electronic textuality is exactly toward such a translation and the analytic power it represents.

The Rossetti Archive adopts an unusual approach to its database of graphic files. The approach involves two innovations, one based in a heretofore unexploited feature of electronic graphic files, the other a new tool for manipulating such files.

The Archive will take advantage of an abstract structural feature of electronic databases. This abstract structure (so-to-speak) "points to" and identifies the electronic files irrespective of whether they are textual or graphic. Because the structure is machine-readable, it can be used as a vehicle for electronic markup, including markup of the formal features of the graphic files. We exploit and expand this abstract structure so that the formal, material, and structural features of the file and its original document are SGML-marked for full search and analysis.

There are four specific types of headers, three for the three distinctly different types of text (manuscripts, proofs, printed editions), and one for pictorial materials (drawings and paintings). In the case of the text files, a "ghost" version will also be made, that is, a machine-readable translation of the original textual document. This "ghost text" will lie invisibly behind its original; it can be called into presence as needed, but in any case it too is SGML-marked so that the texts may be manipulated for additional search and analysis.

Further sets of relations with the database files are generated via a tool being designed for the project at the University of Virginia's Institute for Advanced Technology in the Humanities. This is an image annotation tool that allows one to interact with the digitized images that are the core of the archive. With this tool the archive's images can be edited in various ways. Hot buttons and other hypertext nodes can be used to attach other files of information to the graphic file (including other graphic files), and specific areas of the image files or specific features can be isolated for annotation and linked to other defined files or parts of files. An early prototype of this image annotation tool has just been built. This prototype is now being tested and modified on the Rossetti archive.

Hands On: Using the Archive

UPON OPENING THE ARCHIVE, the user will be called to choose one of three *Critical Environments*. Of these three environments, only the third — the "Critical Edition" — gives the user immediate access to the entire hypermedia *Archive*.

Entering the *Archive* through the "Critical Edition" gives the user access to the database via two large bodies of networked information: Rossetti's *Writings* and his *Pictures*. The user may choose to locate a current research session in one of three ways: by choosing a point of departure (basic initial orientation) in the *Writings*, in the *Pictures*, or in both together. In each case the monitor opens to a screen divided into two windows for comparative viewing of materials. Since the *Archive* is completely windowized, this initial double-screen setting can and will be enlarged during the research session to include other windows opened to other materials.

A third set of related information is available to the user as *Research Materials*. The latter is not hypertextually organized, but it is — like the textual information in the *Writings* and *Pictures* — SGML-marked for search and analysis; and the latter contain various specific links to the *Research Materials*. These *Research Materials* may be augmented via the *Extended Research Archive*.

As already noted, both *Writings* and *Pictures* are collections of bitmapped graphic files, each file containing one picture or one page from a MS or printed text. These graphic files are color files as needed (e.g., for Rossetti's paintings). Each of these graphic files is linked automatically to a network of corresponding glosses, notes, and commentaries that elucidate the material in the file. These are the *Research Materials* and they are invoked as needed. In addition, a hypertextual environment connects the database of core materials in various complex ways, and a system of SGML-markup is everywhere applied. (These features of the *Archive* have been described above.)

The foregoing summarizes the basic structure of the *Archive*. The elementary monitor manipulation is a divided screen; the two windows can have (say) just a *Writings* graphic file (plus its e-text overlay transcription[4] in the other window); or a *Writings* graphic file in one window, and a *Pictures* graphic in the second, with the e-text overlay windows in the background to be called as needed (thus running four basic windows, with all attached hypermedia links invokable as needed). Other windows may be opened as needed, to access other materials in the *Archive*, to connect to remote archives, or to perform various analytic operations.

The Extended Archive

THE ARCHIVE IS STRUCTURED so as to be open to as many other electronic textual environments as possible. At the moment these connections are largely parallel in structure and are invoked by opening windows to related materials (e.g., windows to the electronic OED, or to other collections of electronic texts). Libraries and museums are quickly putting their holdings into electronic forms accessible via remote access networks. At the moment the commonest types of institutional remote access connect the user only to catalogues and the like. The *Archive* assumes that such remote networking will expand enormously very soon to include access to electronic holdings.

The *Archive* can be structured so as to permit other individuals or groups of users to work in its environments simultaneously (students, other scholars, etc.).

Note on the Hypermedia Environment:

To date most hypermedia environments used by humanities' projects, and in particular literary projects (e.g., the Brown "Dickens Project"), are fundamentally linear in structure — with minimal recursive features.[5] One does not risk getting "lost" in such environments, but then they do not open themselves to recursive moves. Recursion-structures provide powerful analytic tools to the student, especially in a project like a critical edition of the sort being constructed here. Their danger is the classic one for hypermedia users: "getting lost in hyperspace."

A signal feature of this project will be the development of mediamaps that can be invoked at any point, locating the user (a) at the present nexus of the environment, with buttons to indicate options for further moves; (b) at the present point in the history of the user's current set of moves and operations. A set of buttons will also be available for automatically positioning the user at a number of key environment locations (e.g., returning to the beginning, moving to one of several key crossroads).

Critical Environments

THE ARCHIVE CAN OUTPUT (write) any number of specialized organizations of its material (e.g., an "edition" of DGR's sonnets only, or of the poems that were written for specific pictures, etc.). In this sense it is an indefinitely extendable library. At the moment we imagine it providing the user with three pre-set output options.

The first is the *Archive* itself, the totality of its research materials and tools.

The second is a "book" that might be called *An Introduction to the Works of Dante Gabriel Rossetti*. This will be a relatively brief work designed to introduce students and readers to certain fundamental works: texts and notes appropriate to such a level.

The third is a "book" or set of books that might be called *The Complete Works of Dante Gabriel Rossetti* — the analogy being to, say, an Oxford Authors edition of a poet. In this case, however, the work will be open to the archive of pictures that may be relevant to the literary works.

NOTE ON THE PROJECT. The *Archive* is, from the outset, conceived as a research project rather than as an "edition." That is to say, the project will be carried out as a practical exploration of the possibilities of hypermedia for text management, analysis, and use. We imagine the project as a stimulus for the development of electronic tools that will be useful for storing, accessing, transmitting, and analyzing large bodies of scholarly information.

The immediate aim is to develop models for critical editions of literary works of various kinds.

The exploratory imagination of the project has been adopted because the technology of hypermedia and text computerization, both hardware and software, is developing at such a rapid pace, and because the time needed to construct even the most traditional aspects of this project will insure that those developments will overtake the work of the project. For example, while at present the project is being constructed for color monitors, I strongly suspect that by the time the project is advanced enough to be usable, we will have access to virtual environments, and will be free of the space limitations of the monitor screens. Similarly, the project at present imagines that the *Archive* will be constructed "locally." But it will probably not be too long before various libraries and museums and other depositories are so closely linked electronically that deposited materials can be lent to users across lines, "virtually." In this event the *Rossetti Archive* will function largely as a critical interface environment and data-accessing engine.

April 1993
University of Virginia

NOTES

1. Hypertext and Hypermedia: a technology for nonsequential reading and writing. Hypertext is a tool for connecting large bodies of data in a complex system of relations. The user of the system moves from data "node" to data "node" via a system of "links" that are either preset or that are created "on the fly."
2. SGML Markup: i.e., Standard Generalized Markup Language. This is a text markup system designed for processing by computer applications. It standardizes the markup of electronic text with a set of defined tags that are embedded in the text to denote features of its physical appearance and its substantive content. The text can then be searched and analyzed for its (marked) information. (The searches available in the online OED provide a good example of the power of such standardized markup.)
3. Bitmapped: a term for describing how a graphic electronic file is stored (i.e., by a patterned array of electronic dots or "bits").
4. E-text overlay transcription: this refers to an electronic transcript (in standard machine readable text form) of an electronic graphic image (which, being bitmapped, is not machine readable). The overlay transcription is one tool for allowing the system to search and link its data electronically.
5. Recursive features: "A function which is defined in terms of itself. In hypertext, [recursion] is a method of determining which node to display based on knowledge the hypertext has about itself and about the reader's interaction with it" (from the *Hypertext/Hypermedia Handbook*, ed. Emily Berk and Joseph Devlin (Intertext Publications, McGraw-Hill: New York, 1991).

COLONIAL NARRATIVE AND ITS DISCONTENTS

By Ali Behdad

TRADITIONALLY, CRITICISM OF KIPLING has repeatedly claimed his Anglo-Indian fiction to be a self-assured, direct representation of British imperialism. Whether on the right or on the left, Kipling's critics view his stories as the monolithic, official discourse of the Empire, without any consideration of the possibility of "heteroglossia"[1] and discursive gaps as moments of uncertainty in Kipling's narratives. To read Kipling's fiction merely as an unmediated "picture" of late nineteenth-century Anglo-India by the "prophet of British Imperialism in its expansionist phase . . . and also [by] the unofficial historian of the British army" is not only to dismiss a substantial part of his stories — the gaps, the lapses, the unspoken words, etc. — but to fall back into a pre-Bakhtinian mode of criticism that viewed "realist" fiction as a pure and monologic representation of the real.[2]

I propose, on the contrary, a reading of the colonialist text that takes into account the possibility of a split between the manifest text, which is the scene of what one may call "white" authorial writing (the agency of knowing at work), and the "unconscious" discourse as the site where the unspoken and the unspeakable surface in the manifest text through the speaking subject's lapses and uncertainties (the meaning here being produced through (re)reading and interpreting Kipling's text by a "belated" post-colonial-reader). Reading Kipling's stories as the site of a split mediation involves a kind of perforating or cutting the text to explode the plurality of its messages — because such a text is itself marked by a plurality of subject-positions as opposed to monologic authorial narration (or official discourse). What I read in Kipling is not always the intentional, coded message of the stories, but the subtle beyond, the "sliding signifiers" that escape the text's intentionality and expose its uncertainties, splits, and ambivalences — ambivalences and splits that are ideologically productive in enabling the discriminatory power of cultural colonialism to work. The colonial authority in Kipling, I will argue, is constructed precisely through the mediated function of the unconscious discourse and its effects of splitting.[3]

233

Not surprisingly, my reading of the split in Kipling is itself split. First, on a thematic level, I am concerned with the micro-political effects of the mediated relation of the colonizer to the native: to what extent does the native become the mediator of the colonizer's desire for recognition? How is the colonizer's experience of the Other articulated in the manifest text as "alienation"? Second, on a narrative level, I am interested in how the scene of white writing incorporates the native, thus producing another structure of mediation in which the uncertainties and ambivalences of the colonialist writer become the mediating signs of the unspoken and the unspeakable — whose effects are re-implicated in the relations of colonial power. Is the desire to represent the Other, itself, a mediator for the possible realization of the unrepresented? And, what are the ideological effects and implications of the return of the repressed?

Colonial Alienation

BEFORE I BEGIN discussing the thematic issue of the colonizer's relation to the Other, I must explain my uses of the term "alienation." Is my use of the term a Marxist one that signifies the process through which a group of people (the proletariat) become alienated from the products of their own activity, and with respect to the status of their existence? Or, is it a Lacanian usage which sees the structure of alienation as that of a *vel* with a "dissymmetrical" relation between the subject and the Other?[4] Perhaps both and/or neither. I speak of three kinds of alienation in Kipling's work. First, the colonizer's inability to see the implications of his or her colonial involvement and situation in India. Kipling's colonial figures often remain alien to what they actually *do* in India, and to what they produce in the Empire's machinery of power. Second, there is a cultural alienation that I have called "self-exoticism." The British colonizers spent long periods, or even their entire life, in India, and so they often felt alienated from home (and in that sense, inclined to identify as "Indians") while simultaneously remaining alienated (as "English") with respect to the Indians as "natives." Third, I am speaking of a psychological problem of identifying oneself through a misrecognition (*méconnaissance*) of the native as the Other. Here the alienation renders the relation of the colonialist subject to the colonized object (objectified?) a kind of narcissistic self-acknowledgment: the colonizer mis-identifies himself in the mirror presence of the Other and is thus alien to his own subjectivity. And finally, I use alienation to imply Kipling's own situation with respect to his discursive practice and to the ideological ambivalences of the colonial texts he produces.

Home and the Colony: The Experience of the Uncanny

CENTRAL TO THE production of the colonizer's desire for self-exoticism — that is, the site of a split between the mimetic identification with the Oriental and the differential construction of identity through a disavowal of the Other's subjectivity — in his experience of the uncanny (*Unheimlich*), for exoticism presupposes an unfamiliar, unhomely setting posited against the peaceful security of home. It is for this reason that the field of the Other is often thematized in colonial fiction as the site of the uncanny surrounded with images of foreignness, fear, and horror. Such a frightful encounter with the Other finds its most striking expression in one of Kipling's sketches, "The City of Dreadful Night" (1891).[5] The short sketch describes the narrator's nocturnal ramble through the squalid streets of Lahore, ending with the scene of a woman's corpse being carried to the Moslem burial-ground.

As an account of the narrator's nightmarish experience, the sketch replicates every category of the uncanny he encounters. First, a dreadful sense of claustrophobia is conveyed through the description of "[t]he dense wet heat that hung over the face of the land, like a blanket."[6] Restless in his dark and empty room, the narrator sets out to stroll in the streets but only encounters the uncanny vision of a dead city, exhausted by the stifling heat and invaded by "yelling jackals" and vagrant dogs. Walking in the city proves to be no less eerie than the solitary room, for it too is dark, silent, and deadly. "The long line of the naked dead," the "stifling hot blast from the mouth of the Delhi Gate," and "the stifling silence [that] settles down over the City of Dreadful Night" make Lahore resemble a giant graveyard (LH, pp. 271, 275). The feeling of the uncanny is intensified by a compulsive return to the same horrific scene: "More corpses . . . and again more corpses" (LH, p. 271). The field of the Other, then, becomes an inescapable prison where every turn away from the uncanny brings the subject back to it.

Read as the manifest text, the images of the uncanny in "The City of Dreadful Night" are consistent with the Orientalist stereotypes of the Other: India is portrayed as a primitive, dark, and enigmatic domain devoid of the energy and rigor of a European city, and the Orientals are literally equated with "sheeted corpses," lacking all initiative or desire for change. The negative vision of the Oriental is important to the colonizer's identity because it provides him with an "imaginary" Other onto whom his anxieties and fears are projected. The striking contrast between the restless colonialist narrator, who is stimulated by the heat to stroll and write, and the heatstricken natives pinpoints the colonizer's differential mode of identification. In the context of the colonized's total negation — the sheeted corpses being denied any subjectivity — the colonizer's desire is no longer a desire for recognition by a conscious Other but a narcissistic self-acknowledgment in the frightful mirror. Here the Other is no longer the subject's alter-ego but merely a differential signifier, a medium that produces meaning only for the colonialist subject. The manifest text of the colonizer thus excludes the Other from its semantic field in its very gesture of inclusion: the Other is the locus of non-meaning, of "stifling silence," of death and profound darkness.

And yet, if the uncanny is the return of something familiar and old-established that is transformed by repression into morbid anxiety, the colonizer's narcissistic self-recognition must be viewed also as the expression of his own alienation. In the middle of the sketch, the narrator points out that, of the dreadful spectacle, "Doré might have drawn it! Zola could describe it" (LH, p. 273). In the light of these and the title's intertextual reference to James Thompson's poem, "The City of Dreadful Night" appears as a familiar projection of an earlier sense of disorientation as expressed in Doré's grotesque and dark drawings of London and in Zola's gloomy representations of Paris. The colonialist narrator, as an alienated subject of discourse, even though conscious of his sketch's intertexts, is alien to the implication of their relation to his own discursive production — that is, the effects of mediation projected into the European intertexts which negates his own colonialist vision of the Other as mimetically produced earlier, at "home." Therefore, he fails to realize that the sketch represents not an alien city of ghostly influences, as he seems to think, but the familiar scene of an alienating European city. In this sense, the representation of horror is itself symptomatic of a horror of re-presenting (re-encountering) the earlier sense of alienation.

The colonizer's symptomatic projection of his morbid anxieties and fears onto the Other perpetuates his sense of alienation because such an exteriorization distances him further from the internal predicament of self-identification. In his imaginary (specular?) mode of identification, the colonizer projects his earlier (primordial) sense of loss onto the Other and essentializes his fixation as a "natural" or "real" phenomenon. Instead of recognizing the Other's subjectivity, he objectifies the Other as the source of all his morbid anxieties and fears — the natives in "The City of Dreadful Night" become the incarnation of the colonizer's terror of death, and India appears as the quintessence of his fears of silence, darkness, and solitude.

Colonialist Nostalgia

ONE OF THE EFFECTS that the colonizer's projection of his earlier anxieties onto the Other produces is a regressive longing for home. This occurs in the case of Private Ortheris who, one day, having had some beer with the narrator, feels "sick for London again; sick for the sounds of 'er, an' the sights of 'er, and the stinks of 'er; orange-peel and hasphalte an' gas comin' in over Vaux'all Bridge" (PTH, p. 210). The soldier's experience in the field exposes the absence in him as he compares his present state of nonsatisfaction with the fantasy of a previous state of satisfaction at home. Ortheris describes his pleasant memories of London as a counter-projection of his anxieties in the field: he is sick for the "sights" and "sounds" of London which are the opposite — though similar in their negativity — terms for his Ortheris's homesickness reinforces his sense of alienation because it generates an ideal image that is in fact a counter-projection of the lack he has experienced in the field of the Other.

The treatment of Ortheris's "madness" by Mulvaney and the narrator-reporter confirms the impossibility of recovering the lost object, that is, the mother city/ culture which brings the colonizer to accept his alienated situation as a "Tommy — a bloomin', eight-anna, dog-stealin' Tommy, with a number instead of a decent name" in India (PTH, p. 208). As Mulvaney's attempt to treat Ortheris's madness through physical coercion fails, the narrator suggests a new cure by offering to exchange his civilian clothes with the soldier's uniform and to give him money to help him desert the army — what one may call *disciplinary* cure of alienation. But after the narrator and Mulvaney return, Ortheris has shaken off his "mad" impulse to desert the army: "The devils had departed from Private Stanley Ortheris, No. 22639, B Company. The loneliness, the dusk, and the waiting had driven them out as I had hoped" (PTH, p. 213). The experience of darkness and solitude in civilian clothes helps Ortheris discover the absence of the lost object of desire. Ironically, however, the symbolic journey to London through the mediation of civilian clothes makes the soldier accept his alienated identity as "Private Stanley Ortheris, No. 22639, B Company." For the common soldier, the loss of home leaves him with only one option which is becoming an "insignificant" member of the authoritarian organization of the Imperial army. Ortheris's return to his own clothes is a symbolic return to the alienated space of the colonial army, as he discovers the futility of his fantasy. The irony of the narrator's statement is a duplicitous reaffirmation of the soldier's identity as a number: the discipline works through possible positions for its effects of delinquency — for instance, the ghettoized colonial soldier, the alienated reporter.

Demand for Love, or a Metonymy for Home

BUT IF LONDON and all its images of comfort are lost due to the colonial displacement, being away from home, what can the average colonizer do in India to overcome his morbid anxieties? To turn the site of the uncanny into a comfortable home, some colonizers try to recuperate the most obvious metaphor for the lost object of desire: the mother's affection and love.[7] A young officer's self-delusionary love for a British woman in the field is a recurrent theme in the *Plain Tales from the Hills*. Interestingly, Kipling's fiction contextualizes the demand for love by elaborating on the colonizer's alienating situation in the machinery of the Imperial power. In India, the colonizers are either exiled to a "jungle" or an "out-district, with nobody but natives to talk to and a great deal of work to do," (PHT, "In Error," p. 133) or confined to an office where they are made "to think that there is nothing but their work, and nothing like their work" (PTH, "Wressley of the Foreign Office," p. 224). Therefore, when a civil engineer like Moriarty comes "fresh out of the jungle to a big town," (PTH, "In Error," p. 134) or, say, a Foreign Service officer like Wressley wanders in the streets "between office and office," meets the first woman he encounters, and is "overwhelmed . . . knocked . . . down, and left . . . gasping as though he had been a little schoolboy" (PTH, p. 226).

Yet ironically, the demand for love does not cure his sense of alienation, but replicates it as a new form of social subjection — in other words, to become a slave of the British mistress. The infatuation of Pluffles, a newly-arrived subaltern, with the "cold and hard" Mrs. Reiver is a case in point:

> He learned to fetch and carry like a dog, and to wait like one, too, for a word from Mrs. Reiver. He learned to keep appointments which Mrs. Reiver had no intention of keeping. . . . He learned to shiver for an hour and a quarter on the windward side of Elysium while Mrs. Reiver was making up her mind to come for a ride. He learned to hunt for a 'rickshaw, in a light dress-suit under pelting rain, and to walk by the side of that 'rickshaw when he had found it. He learned what it was to be spoken to like a coolie and ordered about like a cook. (PTH, "The Rescue of Pluffles," p. 44)

Whereas in relation to the natives, the colonizer may appear as a powerful master, the demand for love turns him into a slave. "[B]ound hand and foot to Mrs. Reiver's 'rickshaw wheels," (PTH, p. 43) Pluffles is literally equated with her coolies, a situation that extends his enslaving position as a sub-ordinate officer at the service of the Imperial Army to his private life, and as such consolidates his alienated situation.[8] Needless to say, the demand for love always leads to disillusionment because the colonialist subject who does not take into account the woman's subjectivity demands something from her that she cannot give. Every love story in the *Plain Tales from the Hills* ends with the man feeling "broken, smashed" by the woman who refuses to reciprocate his love (p. 228). As a result, the demand for love is always a lesson in frustration and humiliation, as the search for the lost object of love ends in a discovery of its absence.

Desire for the Other, or Erotic Domination

WHILE SOME COLONIZERS try to master their morbid anxieties through amorous affairs with British women, others are tempted to embrace their phobia by immersing themselves in — or more appropriately "penetrating" — the Other. A familiar theme in Kipling's Anglo-Indian fiction is that of the colonizer who goes native — "going Fantee," as it was termed by the Britishers (PTH, p. 24). Manifestations of the exposure to native life vary from a superficial Orientalist masquerade, as in the case of detective Strickland[9] who gets pleasure from wearing Indian costumes and imitating "Oriental culture," to a more profound search for knowledge by a converted colonizer like Jellaludin McIntosh in "To Be Filed for Reference." But the desire for immersion is most commonly manifested in the form of an erotic relation with a native woman. "Beyond the Pale," "Georgie Porgie," and "Without Benefit of Clergy" are all variations on this familiar theme. What draws the British protagonists of these stories "beyond the pale" of their genteel society and "[d]eep away in the heart of the City" is a transgressive search for the "Oriental passion and impulsiveness," which they have read about in "the old *Arabian Nights*" (PTH, pp. 127, 131). In contrast to the sexually inhibited woman of the club, the native woman is represented as a sexualized figure incapable of resisting her master's desire because of a powerlessness due to racial difference.

As a fantasy of erotic domination, the sexual relation with the native woman appeals to the colonizer's imagination because it combines erotic desire with the desire for mastery. Indeed in every instance, the British protagonist is gratified not only by "endless delight" and "strange things" that happen during the night, but by the woman's acknowledgment of his mastery and dominant power (PTH, pp. 129, 130). In "Without Benefit of Clergy," to give an example, Ameera constantly reminds John Holden that "I know that I am thy servant and thy slave, and the dust under thy feet" (LH, p. 125). The subordination of Ameera makes Holden a "king in his own territory," "the lord of [the] house," allowing him thus to create a little colony of his own (LH, pp. 116, 119).

Although the erotic domination of the native woman by the male colonizer seems ideologically consistent with colonialist mentality, the woman's "low caste" renders such a relationship "an inconsistent affair" (LH, p. 116). Kipling's moralistic narrator reminds the reader in every instance that "[a] man should, whatever happens, keep to his own caste, race, and breed. Let the White go to the White and the Black to the Black" (PTH, p. 127). Since colonial authority is dependent on restricted racial differentiation, the relation with the native woman as a crossing of racial boundaries is considered an act of transgression. As a result, the colonizer's affair with the native woman forces him to live a "double life." Christopher Trejago's situation in "Beyond the Pale" provides an example of this cultural predicament:

> In the day-time, Trejago drove through his routine of office-work, or put on his calling-clothes and called on the ladies of the Station, wondering how long they would know him if they knew of poor Bisesa. At night, when all the City was still, came the walk under the evil-smelling *boorka*, the patrol through Jitha Megji's *bustee*, the quick turn into Amir Nath's Gully between the sleeping cattle and the dead walls, and then, last of all, Bisesa, and the deep, even breathing of the old woman who slept outside the door. . . . (PTL, p. 130)

The contrasting images of day and night, life and death, order and labyrinthine disorder point to the split in the colonizer's identity. While the office and colonial station are identified as the domain of social obligation, respectability, and consciousness, the dead walls and dark room of Bisesa mark the scene of desire, transgression, and the unconscious. Trejago's act of satisfying his transgressive desire for the native woman, intertwined with his desire for mastery, inscribes a gap in his identity, and produces the effect of dividing him between the conscious agent of colonial power and the unconscious subject of a defiant attempt to cross its racial boundaries.

Trejago's predicament is paradigmatic of the contradictions inherent in the colonial identity of Kipling's characters. Inscribed within the economy of desire *and* domination, the colonizer's relation to the Other depends both on recognition and disavowal of the native's subjectivity. The colonizer's narcissistic mode of self-acknowledgment (self-exoticism), mediated through the objectified (or appropriated) presence of the native, produces a split in the colonial identity. To put it somewhat differently, the desire for domination entails and has a place for both identification and alienation, fear as well as desire. Behind the subject's manifest intention to exercise his colonial power are his terrifying sense of alienation and a latent desire to recognize, even identify, with the native, for the Other is after all the site of dreams, fantasies, and desires that are repressed by the colonizer's culture. Here, both the transgressive desire for the native woman and the desire for the colonial power reproduce each other as their effects.

The Other Story-Teller: Narrative Self-Exoticism

THE UNCERTAINTIES AND AMBIVALENCES of colonial identity are not only thematic problems in Kipling's fiction, but they are also embedded and replicated in the micro-politics of narrative economy as parts of the writer's own representational practice. Kipling's narrative is the site of a split between the manifest text of an authorial writing and the excluded discourse that surface the manifest text as noise, as a disturbing figure of its unconscious. I will broach the issue of narrative/textual split — the split between the scene of white authorial writing and the unconscious and repressed expression of the Other's discourse figured as noise — in two ways: first, I consider briefly the general problem of narrative framing as an ambivalent technique; and second, I concentrate more specifically on the micro-politics of Kipling's representational practice as the site of an ontological split between writing and speaking.

Framing, as narrative theory has demonstrated, is by definition a device for splitting the narrative economy, positing at least two positions for the speaking subject. The most obvious narrative ambivalence in Kipling is his use of framing technique. Kipling's narrators are often strange splittings of his duplicitous relation as a colonial writer to the colonialist/Orientalist discourse: while some narrators in his stories are hysterically authoritarian, authoritative, and world weary as colonial experts, some of his ''Other'' storytellers are disempowered, disenfranchised, and marginalized natives. The inclusion of Orientals as story-tellers or speakers of dramatic monologues addressed to sahibs, I want to suggest, expresses a narrative desire for the Other — a desire that ''dialogizes'' the monolithic (authorial) discourse — while it simultaneously points to a hegemonic impulse to appropriate the native voice. To be sure, to adopt a native narrator is an act of discursive appropriation because the colonialist writer takes advantage of a ''voice'' that does not belong to him. The dramatic monologues of the natives are never ''authentic'' representations of the Oriental culture by indige-nous people to which the narrative frames pretend to belong, but narrative masquerades reminiscent of detective Strickland's Orientalist disguises. The sto-ries are usually a series of detached, fragmentary pieces extracted from the ''exotic'' scene surrounding the colonialist writer who has little interest in fully understanding or representing the native's condition. The Oriental storyteller, often reduced to a rhetorical or narrative device, is thus appropriated by the colonialist writer to provide an exotic flavor for his familiar tale while showing his mastery in imitating the Other's speech. In this sense, the inclusion of the native as a narrative frame reaffirms his exteriority in relation to the story's actual illocutionary situation, which is that of ''white'' writing for ''white'' readers. It is not fortuitous that the narratees in all of the dramatic monologues turn out to be sahibs whose silent presence is constantly acknowledged by the Oriental narrators. As self-situating devices, the references to the master's colo-nizer and thus exclude the natives from the stories' system of communication. In short, the natives are excluded as mediators of a white-to-white relation: inclusion is a figure for exclusion here.

And yet, the incorporation of the native speaker in the colonialist text can be also viewed as an instance of what Bakhtin calls heteroglossia. Even though the Other's story serves to express the colonialist writer's own interests and inten-tions, it nonetheless refracts his monolithic discourse because as Bakhtin argues, ''the speech of such narrators is always *another's speech* (as regards the real or potential direct discourse of the author) and in *another's language* (i.e., insofar as it is a particular variant of the literary language that clashes with the language of the narrator)'' (p. 313). To posit a native storyteller as the speaking subject inevitably implies the inclusion of a linguistic, and by extension ideological, system that is different from that of the writer's own. The Other's monologue splits or dialogizes the colonial writer's discourse as an Other point of view, an Other voice subtly insinuates itself in his text. This is not to claim that the Other can or does speak back in the colonialist text — the native is always the excluded third between the colonial writer and his British readers — but the objectified presence of the Oriental storyteller introduces an ''internal bifurcation,'' to bor-row Bakhtin's words again, that undermines the unitary language and monologic style of the colonialist text and makes it an example of discursive self-exoticism — the colonialist text here being attracted to the Other's identity against which it is defining itself. As I will discuss shortly, Kipling's text depends for its narrative economy on the "excluded" presence of the native as a dialogizing background, or as noise, or a kind of elusive resonance that haunts and disturbs the authoritative discourse while mediating the productivity of its colonial authority.

One may sense traces of such elusive voices in "Gemini," for example, where a native begins and ends his story with a critique of the British judicial system in India. Showing his mutilated body to the sahib as evidence, Durga Dass complains that "there is no justice in courts."[10] The victim of mistaken identity, he appropriately identifies the judicial system as inefficient and lacking all regard for the oppressed. Recognizing the power of written statements, the native speaker, who is initially excluded from the scene of white writing, convinces the sahib at the end to "take a pen and write clearly what [he has] said, that the Dipty Sahib may see and reprove the Stunt Sahib" (B&W, p. 231). Similarly, in "At Howli Thana," the native narrator frames his mendacious self-vindication with a brief description of poverty among the natives as he convincingly explains how his "three little children whose stomachs are always empty" will die unless he is employed by the distrustful sahib to whom he addresses the elaborate tale of his dismissal from the police force (B&W, p. 205). Here too the native is able to convince the sahib to employ him and recognize his resourcefulness. Beyond such thematic effects of double-voiced narration, the use of Oriental storytellers is important to Kipling's text for its theoretical implications in the context of the writer's own representational practice. Here the role of Oriental storyteller exposes the ideological *difference* between the art of colonial fiction and the native's oral tradition. Let me explain this issue with the specific example of Kipling's "Preface" to *Life's Handicap* (1890). To contextualize his book for the reader, Kipling recounts his (imaginary?) encounter with Gobind, a one-eyed wandering mendicant, living his last few days of life in the Chubara of Dhunni Bhagat, a multi-religious monastery in northern India. The first conversation with the holy man, who turns out to have been "once a famed teller of stories when [he] was begging on the road between Koshin and Etra," inspires Kipling to write the book (LH, pp. 6–7). Gobind's stories, told "in a voice most like the rumbling of heavy guns over a wooden bridge," mediate Kipling's relation to his own text (LH, p. 6). The identity of the colonial writer, therefore, is produced differentially through the mirror presence of the Oriental storyteller whose function is that of an alter-ego (an Other). Kipling describes to Gobind his profession as "a *kerani* — one who writes with a pen upon paper, not being in the service of the Government," and explains the economic aspect of his practice by pointing out that "the tales are sold and money accrues to me that I may keep alive'' (LH, p. 6). In response, Gobind compares the writer's practice to that of the bazaar storyteller:

> That is the work of the bazar story-teller; but he speaks straight to men and women and does not write anything at all. Only when the tale has aroused expectation, and calamities are about to befall the virtuous, he stops suddenly and demands payment ere he continues the narration. (LH, p. 6)

On the surface, the colonial writer views himself as the modern version of the traditional storyteller. The art of colonial fiction sees itself in the ''mirror'' of the Other's oral tradition and says ''there I am.'' Like the bazaar storyteller, Kipling participates in the political/economical system of his community from the marginal position he occupies — from the position of ''not being in the service of the Government.'' But the Empire's storyteller quickly distinguishes his art from that of bazaar storyteller by reaffirming the difference between writing and speech. Whereas Gobind's tales belong to the ephemeral domain of speech, Kipling's stories mark the domain of monumental writing. Here the colonial artist identifies himself by saying ''I am not the Other'' — the negative containing the appropriation it seeks to negate.

The difference between writing and speech is important because it determines the power structure involved in the mediating relation between the colonialist writer and the Oriental storyteller. In the realm of colonial fiction, it is not speech that is privileged but writing. The native's speech is the external, the nontranscendental against which Kipling defines his representational practice. Speech is also the inferior term that poses a kind of threat to the colonizer's writing. In introducing Gobind, Kipling notes that ''[Gobind's] tales were true, but not one in twenty could be printed in an English book, because the English do not think as natives do'' (LH, p. 6). The native's oral tales are the scene of a potentially disturbing unconscious that must be excluded in the conscious domain of monumental writing for it to produce the order of meaning, the ''higher presence'' that confers upon the white writer the power of representation. Authority in the colonial text is, thus, the authorization to decide what must be written and what should be excluded.

Yet, as every exclusion implies the return of the excluded, the censure of the Other's tale, the Other's speech insinuates itself into the conscious text of the colonizer by leaving the marks of its absence on its surface. Kipling finishes the story of his encounter with Gobind by recounting a final conversation with him in which he promises the old storyteller to inscribe his name in the beginning of the book:

> 'But it is a pity that our book is not born. How shall I know that there is any record of my name?'

'Because I promise, in the forepart of the book, preceding everything else, that it shall be written, Gobind, sadhu, of the island in the river and awaiting God in Dhunni Bhagat's Chubára, first spoke of the book,' said I. (LH, p. 8)

The presence of Gobind's name signifies the absence of his tales, the censure of his words in the sahib's text. Here the desire to include (represent) is the revelation of an absence, the sign of a void, the mark of what cannot be written and must be excluded. Kipling finishes his Preface by acknowledging that "[t]he most remarkable stories are, of course, those which do not appear — for obvious reasons" (LH, p. 9). The native's tales constitute an Other discourse that is outside the scene of white writing. Nonetheless the native tale is beyond closure since it produces the elusive mark of its exclusion on the conscious text — that is the kind of rupture that forces Kipling to see the mediated structure of his fiction and recognize its mode of exclusion. The exclusion of the Other's stories/ speech as the domain of the unconscious in white writing makes the beginning of Kipling's text ambivalent. As an alienated subject of colonial discourse, Kipling situates his text in a split between a kind of narcissistic self-identification mediated through the native's oral tradition and a mode of differentiation from the Other's speech. The beginning of *In Black and White* — the title itself being suggestive of the split mode of representation in the practice of both native black and colonialist white — is literally divided between two kinds of situational self-reference. The book, on the one hand, begins with the writer's "Dedication," which is a pastiche of seventeenth-century dedicatory styles. Offering his third book to his "Moft Deare Father" as part of his "unpayable Debt" to such a great *Vstad* (or *Mafter*), Kipling acknowledges in an archaic, high-falutin' style his filial relation to the European tradition that has furnished him with the power of representation. The dedication confirms that the authority to represent also depends on the authorization derived from the symbolic father to whom the colonialist writer is indebted. Here, the structure of colonial desire to represent sustains the structure of the Law, which binds the colonialist writer to the written tradition. As a self-situating device, the pastiche then defines the context of the book and its addressee as European.

The dedication is followed, however, by an "Introduction" written as a pastiche of the vernacular speech delivered by the writer's native servant who wants to be honored for his task of putting the pages of the book together and for having taken care of the writer. On the first level of its colonial complicity, the Orientalist pastiche is meant to be read as a kind of colonialist humor. Khadir Baksh's exaggerated demand to be recognized as a co-author just for having put the pages in order makes him a comic figure whose ignorance is apt to reaffirm the (colonialist) reader's racial stereotypes of the natives.

The author's appropriation of his native servant as the speaker of his introduction to the stories is also intended to accentuate the demarcation of the writing scene as the sahib's privileged domain. Khadir Baksh begins his speech by reaffirming that the book is written by his master:

> Hazur, — Through your favor this is a book written by my sahib. I know that he wrote it, because it was his custom to write far into the night; . . . I greatly desiring to go to my house. But there was no order; therefore . . . it was my fate to sit without the door until the work was accomplished. Then came I and made shut all the papers in the office-box, and these papers, by the peculiar operation of the Time and owing to the skillful manner in which I picked them up from the floor became such a book as you now see. God alone knows what is written therein, for I am a poor man and the Sahib is my father and my mother, and I have no concern with his writing until he has left his table and gone to bed. (B&W, p. 161)

The scene of writing is white, excluding the black presence of the native. Kept to the side of the master's writing desk, Khadir Baksh can only be a witness to the act of production, never its active agent. As the servant of the white writer, the native enters the scene, symbolically, only when the action is ended and the work accomplished. Therefore, the native's presence on the margin of the writing scene and the appropriation of his speech as a kind of narrative self-exoticism serve the author's own narcissistic mode of identification: "I, the Orientalist/colonialist writer am the producer of the book." On the first level of signification, then, the function of white writing, like the colonialist project itself, is to appropriate the native and his speech and manufacture it as written stories for its English audience.

Yet, if the writer's use of situational self-reference is mediated through the Other, then the introduction can imply a second structure of meaning in which the ironic mode of identification can be itself ironized in the (post-colonial?) act of reading or interpreting. Indeed, it is ironic that the writer who wants to identify the context of his text as white chooses his native servant as the book's "gate-keeper," so to speak. The writer's intentional appropriation of the native speaker manifests a latent recognition of the servant's claim, which is originally repressed in the master's text, that wants to exclude the possibility of an-Other meaning. In this sense, Khadir Baksh's misguided demand for honor can be read as an accurate and justified claim: not only does Khadir Baksh as the head of the sahib's household provide the master with the material necessity for his writing, but the native is also the one who supplies the white writer with the oral tales or "raw material" which the latter manufactures as written stories of the Empire for his own profit, thus reproducing discursively the system of economic exploitation of the Empire. Ironically, *In Black and White* acknowledges the crucial role of Khadir Baksh as the book's "gate-keeper" who introduces the reader to its Indian context without which there would be no stories to tell.

The Productive Function of Colonial Ambivalence

THE POSSIBILITY OF a second order of meaning is crucial to the understanding of the Orientalist/colonialist discourse because it undermines its "polarities of intentionality."[11] The modern mode of colonial representation — the split discourse — in Kipling's fiction is neither a closed structure of meaning nor a coherent system of power, and consequently should *not* be treated as a homogeneous, orderly series of statements, but rather as a practice, comprised of a complex system of irregular, disorderly utterances. The split in Kipling's representational practice articulates the censored discontinuities in the discourse of colonialist fiction which as a discourse of power, depends on producing an effect of order and unity — the order and unity it claims to have. The exclusion of the native from its discursive domain and the censoring of an-Other meaning in its semantic field, on the one hand, inscribe a gap in the colonialist discourse where the excluded third — the native and his voice on the margin — disturbs the certainty surrounding the writing subject. Although the text of the colonial writer is always mediated, as a discourse of power, it represses the phenomenon of mediation because it demonstrates the "constructed" status of its meaning and, particularly, of the discursive subject. But the excluded mediator nevertheless returns to make "noise" in its communicational system or to haunt the discourse as a figure of its unconscious. Kipling's text carries with it a subtle beyond that escapes the intentionality of its author. The colonialist writer, as an alienated subject of discourse, is never in full control of his representational practice, always leaving out or excluding something that traverses and "pricks" the smooth surface of the coded message. In Kipling's fiction, both the gesture of exclusion and the return of the excluded are readable, which illustrates that the discourse of colonial power can only be constituted by means that deflect its coded message and produce "splits" in its apparent unity and confidence. The inclusion of the voice of the excluded native in Kipling has a productive function in that it engenders the effects of splitting which displace the site of racial differentiation inherent in the discriminatory mode of colonial power. The split in Kipling disturbs the mimetic mode of identification — what I have called "self-exoticism" — but its effects are re-implicated in the colonial authority which works precisely through a kind of proliferation of difference — the exclusion in cultural colonialism works through the gesture of inclusion. In Kipling, colonial authority is exercised *not* through the silent repression of the excluded third — the native and his or her voice — but by the mediating effects of the split whereby it produces the "visible" difference that defines the discursive conditions of domination.

University of California, Los Angeles

NOTES

Published with kind permission of Duke University Press.
1. "Discourse in the Novel" in *The Dialogic Imagination: Four Essays*, edited by Michael Holquist, tr. Caryl Emerson and Michael Holquist, (Austin: U of Texas P, 1981). I will discuss the phenomenon of heteroglossia in greater detail later in my essay.
2. The quotations are from George Orwell, but the ideas are expressed by most of Kipling's readers ("Rudyard Kipling" in *Kipling and the Critics*, ed., Elliot Gilbert [New York: New York UP, 1965], p. 76). Indeed, since the late nineteenth century when Oscar Wilde and Max Beerbohm began ridiculing his fiction, Kipling has always been read and condemned in terms of his colonial message. Only recently have such critics as Abdul R. JanMohamed ("The Economy of Manichean Allegory: The Function of Racial Difference in Colonialist Literature" in *"Race," Writing, and Difference*, pp. 78–106, ed. Henry Louis Gates, Jr. [Chicago: U of Chicago P, 1986]), John A. McClure (*Kipling & Conrad: The Colonial Fiction*, [Cambridge: Harvard UP, 1981]), and Zohreh Sullivan ("Kipling the Nightwalker" in *Rudyard Kipling*, ed. Harold Bloom [New York: Chelsea House, 1987]) begun to study the complexities of Kipling's colonialist representation.
3. My discussion of ideological ambivalence as a sign of the productivity of colonial authority is indebted to Homi Bhabha's insightful and provocative discussion of this issue. See, for example, "The Other Question: Difference, Discrimination and the Discourse of Colonialism," in *Literature, Politics, and Theory: Papers from the Essex Conference*, ed. Francis Barker et al. (London: Methuen, 1986), pp. 148–71; also, "Signs Taken for Wonders: Questions of Ambivalence and Authority under a Tree Outside Delhi, May 1817" in *"Race," Writing and Difference*, pp. 163–84.
4. Cf. Lacan's "The Subject and the Other: Alienation," in *The Four Fundamental Concepts of Psycho-Analysis*, ed. Jacques-Alain Miller, tr. Alan Sheridan (New York: W. W. Norton & Co., 1977); [*Le Séminaire de Jacques Lacan, Livre XI*, "*Les quatre concepts fondamentaux de psychanalyse*" (Paris: Editions du Seuil, 1973)].
5. Kipling actually wrote two pieces under this title, one the narrative of his long personal journey to the depth of the city of Calcutta in which he narrates his descent from "A Real Live City" all the way to the lowest circle of "hell," where he visits an opium factory; and the short sketch of Lahore where the more "imaginative" narrator wanders around the town as a *flâneur*. Here I will discuss mostly the second piece, though most of what I say can be traced in the first narrative as well.
6. Rudyard Kipling, *Life's Handicap* (New York: Oxford UP, 1987), p. 270. Unless indicated otherwise, all my references are from this edition. All page references will thereafter be given parenthetically in the text, using the abbreviations, LH (*Life's Handicap*), and PTH (*Plain Tales from the Hills* [New York: Oxford UP, 1987]).
7. The scene of the Simla Club as a whole is symbolic of the colonizer's attempt to overcome his anxieties by regressing into a familiar and comfortable world. The club, as John McClure suggests, is a "little solace," providing the colonizer with a "false security" of home (p. 37).
8. It is suggestive that Pluffles's Colonel "chuckled when he heard of the education of Pluffles [i.e., his affair with Mrs. Reiver] and said it was a good training for the boy" (pp. 44–45). As John McClure has explained, abandonment and humiliation were viewed by the Imperial system as an important part of the colonizer's education because it is precisely the terror of isolation and fear of alienation that makes the

exercise of authority effective. Therefore, the more alienated the colonizer, the better he or she follows authority and the better she or he serves the interests of the Empire.

9. Strickland whose unconventional methods of policing includes disguising himself as a native servant, is a familiar figure in Kipling's Anglo-Indian stories, among which are "Miss Youghal's Sais," "The Bronckhorst Divorce-Case," "The Mark of the Beast," "The Return of Imray," and "A Deal in Cotton."

10. *In Black and White* in *Works of Rudyard Kipling*, volumes 7 and 8 (New York: Aldus Edition De Luxe, 1909), Volume 7, p. 217. All page references for the stories in this collection are from this edition and will be given parenthetically in the text.

11. The words are Bhabha's who uses them to problematize Edward Said's notion of power and knowledge as being possessed only by the colonizer.

"OUR ENEMY IS NOT MERELY SPIRITUAL": DEGENERATION AND MODERNITY IN BRAM STOKER'S *DRACULA*

By David Glover

"[I]N OBEDIENCE TO THE LAW as it then stood, he was buried in the centre of a *quadrivium*, or conflux of four roads (in this case four streets), with a stake driven through his heart. And over him drives for ever the uproar of unresting London!"[1] No, not *Dracula* (1897), but the closing lines of a much earlier nineteenth century work, Thomas De Quincey's bleakly ironic essay "On Murder Considered as One of the Fine Arts" (1854). De Quincey is describing how in 1812 the London populace dealt with the body of one of his prize exhibits, a particularly grisly serial killer who had escaped the gallows by hanging himself in his cell at dead of night. Yet it is difficult for us to read this gleefully chilling passage today without thinking of Bram Stoker's classic vampire novel. The quirky Christian symbolism, the mandatory staking down of the monster to keep it from roaming abroad, the sense of a busily self-absorbed London unaware of its proximity to a murderous presence that haunts its most densely-populated by-ways: together these features seem virtually to define a basic iconography for the vampire Gothic as it achieved canonical status in *Dracula*.

What unites these two otherwise historically distinct writers is their menacing use of the buried past to articulate the present. In the half-century that separated Stoker from De Quincey the punitive assumptions behind the old suicide laws may have become little more than a barbaric memory, but the subsequent attempts to view suicide medically as mental illness, re-defining it as an instance of "moral insanity," offered no easily civilising consolation. So, in Stoker's work the twin poles of past and present make their appearance through a strangely paradoxical trope, that of the modern spectator forced to confront a horror whose very existence seems to compromise any possibility of securing the line between the modern and the pre-modern. This is perhaps especially true of *Dracula*

249

which comes replete with the latest in late Victorian consumer goods: bicycles, phonographs, and portable typewriters. "It is nineteenth century up-to-date with a vengeance," as one of Stoker's characters so aptly puts it.[2] In *Dracula* the accoutrements of the present provide a template for the text's anxieties, so that it can be profoundly "humanising" to gaze upon the lights of London and to hear "the muffled roar that marks the life of a great city" even though that city is simultaneously a site of depravity and danger (251; ch. XVI). However much it might seem to be mired in the past or to invoke a return to a safer, more stable world, I want to argue that in Stoker's novel we find a defence of modernity that looks aggressively towards the future, a defence that is all the more remarkable for its engagement with the uncertainties of the period. These uncertainties hinge upon the question of boundaries: between male and female, animal and human, science and the occult, respectable femininity and the "New Woman," to name just a few of the deceptively simple binaries that are troubled, yet finally reinstated in new ways in *Dracula*.

For some contemporary critics the problem with *Dracula* was that this "clever but cadaverous romance" tried to be too modern for its own good. The *Spectator* wondered whether Stoker's novel would not have been "all the more effective if he had chosen an earlier period" as his setting, particularly given the essentially "medieval methods" by which the vampire is laid to rest.[3] The anonymous reviewer might well have cited the opinion of Jonathan Harker, the first character to fall into Count Dracula's clutches, when he innocently worries that "the old centuries had, and have, powers of their own which mere 'modernity' cannot kill" (49; ch. III). For the mixture of curiosity and fear experienced at the opening of the book by Harker as he makes his journey to Count Dracula's castle in order to finalise the mysterious aristocrat's purchase of property in London is a very modern young Englishman's sense of shock at slipping into a pre-modern world. On his coachride through Transylvania — his first trip abroad — Harker is fascinated by the sight at "every station" of "groups of people, sometimes crowds . . . in all sort of attire." "Some of them" are "just like the peasants at home," while "others were very picturesque" but by no means "prepossessing." "Strangest" of all are the Slovaks, even "more barbarian than the rest, with their big cowboy hats, great baggy dirty-white trousers, white linen shirts, and enormous heavy leather belts, nearly a foot wide, all studded over with brass nails . . . On the stage they would be set down at once as some old Oriental band of brigands" (11; ch. I). Harker's unease is intensified by the "hysterical" reactions that the news of his final destination provokes amongst the local people. When an old lady offers him a crucifix from her own neck, our articled clerk hardly knows "what to do, for, as an English Churchman" he had been "taught to regard such things as . . . idolatrous" (13; ch. I).

This powerful historical pull back into the past becomes even stronger upon Harker's arrival at his final destination. Thomas De Quincey once observed that the gift of total recall "must be the next bad thing to being a vampire," but it is clear that in *Dracula* total recall is partly what defines the vampire.[4] Once ensconced at the castle, the solicitor's clerk hears the Count expatiate with immense pride on his family lineage, tracing it back to Attila the Hun and conceiving time as an endless series of battles and invasions. Harker notes that the Count "spoke as if he had been present at them all," his lyrical nostalgia barely disguising the pure immediacy of the good old days (40; ch. III). At first glance, therefore, *Dracula* seems to present what could be described as a conversion narrative in the face of an occult, not to say truly oscular, dread. It is the story of how Englishmen and Englishwomen come to see that, far from being "idolatrous," "such things" as holy wafers, missals, wild garlic, and the rosary are a vitally necessary means of self-defence — despite their medieval provenance.

Nevertheless, Stoker's novel does insist upon a very different temporality, a continuous present that is jointly constituted through the procedures of law and science. Though *Dracula* is clearly a quasi-legal narrative of the kind pioneered and popularised by Wilkie Collins, it also needs to be read against the background of Stoker's exhaustive compilation of *The Duties of Clerks of Petty Sessions in Ireland* (1879), written with the aim of enhancing bureaucratic effectiveness throughout "the whole British Empire" while the author was still employed as a civil servant in Dublin. There, as part of an ambitious attempt to rationalise the mass of "facts and theories resulting from the operations of the last twenty-seven years," Stoker itemised the formal requirements in preparing evidence for use in court proceedings in words which echo those of the novel's prologue. Thus, "each Information should contain a full and simple statement of all material facts to which the witness can depose" and ". . . should be taken as nearly as possible in the witness's own words, and in the first person."[5] Empirically, therefore, *Dracula* pretends to the status of "simple fact," assembling an impressive variety of sources, predominantly journal or diary entries, but also including newspaper articles, letters, fragments from a ship's log book, and an alienist's case notes. Yet the opening chapters of the novel present us with the law's fallibilities. Not only have the solicitor and his clerk been taken in by Count Dracula, but it takes Jonathan Harker some time to recognise the danger he is in. Deeply impressed by the vampire's business acumen, Harker imagines that Dracula "would have made a wonderful solicitor" (44; ch. III). In a sense, the Count does soon impersonate English law when he dresses in Harker's clothes as a cover for his nocturnal activities, spreading false evidence in his wake. Meanwhile, Harker's Transylvanian journey has placed him beyond any legal redress for he has become "a veritable prisoner, but without that protection of the law which is even a criminal's right" (59; ch. IV). Consequently, human experience is nothing if it is not thoroughly scrutinised by science.

It is science as the rigorously tested accumulation of evidence that ultimately guides the novel's construction, offering a master discourse to order and organise the disparate empirical knowledges and variously inflected voices contributed by the succession of narrator-witnesses. The tension between knowledge and voice is most forcefully exemplified by the alienist Dr. Seward's memoranda on his "life-eating" patient R. M. Renfield, which begin as case notes taken down on phonograph cylinders and develop into the doctor's own personal journal (90; ch. VI). The record of events provided by Seward's "wonderful machine" ring so "cruelly true" that their heart-wringing tones have to be objectified as typescript in order to conceal their suffering (266; ch. XVII). Such all-too-human data must needs be subsumed under some more comprehensive practical explanation if they are to be dispassionately understood. Characteristically, when Jonathan Harker tries to come to terms with the "idolatrous" crucifix, he speculates on whether "there is something in the essence of the thing itself," or whether "it is a medium, a tangible help, in conveying memories of sympathy and comfort" (40; ch. III). In a circular movement, science finally signifies nature brought under the control of the full human subject, relying upon statements "given from the standpoints and within the range of knowledge of those who made them" (epigraph to *Dracula* 8).

This humanistic focus is epitomised by the quizzically encyclopaedic utterances of Professor Van Helsing, "philosopher," "metaphysician," and "one of the most advanced scientists of his day" (137; ch. IX). A kindly though somewhat inscrutable figure, he embodies the uncompromising authority of the scientific voice and is therefore the man best fitted to lead the struggle against Count Dracula. "You reason well, and your wit is bold; but you are too prejudiced," he complains to his former pupil and colleague, the alienist Dr. Seward. "You do not let your eyes see nor your ears hear, and that which is outside your daily life is not of account to you." And he follows this observation with a baffling list of what the puzzled Dr. Seward rather desperately calls "nature's eccentricities and possible impossibilities" (229–31; ch. XIV). Science may run counter to the everyday, but the only significant objects of study are tangible, "positively" or directly ascertainable realities and for Van Helsing — as for the positivist Auguste Comte — scientific theory is rooted in the coordination of observed facts. But *Dracula*'s "possible impossibilities" point to scenarios both of advancement and of backwardness, revealing an unusually close relationship to the aporias and hesitations of late Victorian positivism. Stoker's novel seizes hold of a critical moment in positivism's grand socio-political narrative and weaves a romance around it, turning it into an adventure story.

"BY THE LATE NINETEENTH CENTURY," Josep Llobera has argued, there were an increasing number of European writers who were "expressing serious doubts about the blessings of Western industrial civilisation," doubts that came to be "articulated around the ideas of race, of the crowd, of violence and of selectionism." Often using "perversions of scientific or pseudo-scientific concepts," these discourses parodied or inverted positivism's normative theory of history.[6] While England was hardly the epicentre of this critical movement, it too saw a "sustained and growing pessimism in the 1870s and 1880s about the ramifications of evolution, the efficacy of liberalism, the life in and of the metropolis" and "the future of society" generally.[7] During the 1890s when Stoker was planning and drafting *Dracula* the ruling paradigm in the human sciences, running across medicine and biology into psychology and social theory, was concerned with the pathologies of natural selection — what we might call Darwinism and its discontents — particularly the fear of a slide back down the evolutionary chain. We have already had a foretaste of this discourse in Jonathan Harker's travelogue of Transylvania, that "whirlpool of European races," (41; ch. III) where "thousands" of Szgany or gypsies proliferate throughout the region, "fearless and without religion, save superstition," speaking "only their own varieties of Romany tongue," a breed "almost outside all law" (55–56; ch. IV). Stoker seems to have had a lively sense of the conjectural theorising going on in the sciences of his day and it is remarkable just how thoroughly pervasive the language of degeneration is in *Dracula*, including specific references to well-known writers on the subject like Nordau and Lombroso.[8] Certainly contemporary portraits of the degenerative condition were key referents for Stoker's depiction of the vampire. For example, the list of identifying traits enumerated in Max Nordau's controversial book *Entartung* (1893) seems peculiarly applicable to what we know of the Count. In his morbid mix of energy and lassitude Dracula alternates between *extreme passivity* — that "abhorrence of action" which Nordau likened to a state of reverie — and *over-stimulation*, leading to "love of the strange, bizarre, evil, loathsome, and ugly, and to sexual perversions," a condition tantamount to "moral insanity."[9] Yet it is important to recognise that *all* the characters in *Dracula* are placed in relation to the conceptual field of degeneration theory. Thus if the Count displays his deviant nature anatomically through his "peculiarly arched nostrils," "his eyebrows . . . very massive, almost meeting over the nose," and his "mouth . . . fixed and rather cruel-looking, with peculiarly sharp white teeth" (28; ch. II), Professor Van Helsing can be positioned by his "hard, square chin, . . . large, resolute, mobile mouth . . . [and] good-sized nose, rather straight, but with quick, sensitive nostrils' as Dracula's physiognomic opposite (218–19; ch. XIV).

But while the ideology of degeneration supplies a semantic matrix for much of the novel's characterisation and action, its effects are also complicated by the instabilities inherent in this mode of thinking. "Degeneration" was never a

unitary concept, but instead consisted of a relay of representations unsystemati-
cally inscribed in a whole cluster of professionalised disciplines and cultural
practices. Because its objects were nowhere consistently or satisfactorily defined,
we might best see the various attempts at theorising degeneration as a set of
overlapping hypotheses competing with each other to define the true parameters
of the culture's crisis, its sources and its vicissitudes. Hence their broad and
often uncertain scope, ranging from worries about the dissipation of natural
talent, through narratives of the rise and fall of nations, to moral panics about
disease and infection. Somewhat schematically, these hypotheses can be grouped
into two general categories. The first group perceived a real decline at the upper
end of the social scale especially, though not exclusively, within the ranks of
the aristocracy: "the tainted offspring of forefathers beggared in their bodies by
luxury and riotous living, and of fathers who sapped their manhood in vice,"
as one moralising tract put it.[10] Charles Darwin's cousin, the statistician, eugeni-
cist, and sometime spiritualist Francis Galton provides an exemplary instance
of this tendency. "We know how careless Nature is of the lives of individuals,"
Galton wrote in his 1869 book *Hereditary Genius*; "we have seen how careless
she is of eminent families — how they are built up, flourish, and decay: just
the same may be said of races, and of the world itself."[11] From this postulate
Galton argued that inherited titles were no guarantee of innate ability since this
tended to decline over the course of several generations. In a subsequent study
Natural Inheritance (1889), "prompted by questions about traits of notable
European families," he developed a statistics of decline which he rather combat-
ively referred to as the "regression towards mediocrity," more commonly known
as "regression towards the mean."[12] Like the Manchester economist W. R.
Greg, Galton "used the idea that society could be divided between the 'fit' and
the 'unfit' to attack aristocratic privilege and landed property."[13] And Greg, for
his part, bemoaned a civilisation in which "rank and wealth, however diseased,
enfeebled or unintelligent," triumphed over "larger brains."[14] Symptomatically,
the reduction of Count Dracula to manageable criminological proportions in the
later part of the novel hinges upon the realisation that this decadent European
aristocrat is "not of man-stature as to brain" (406; ch. XXV).

At the same time, Galton also espoused a second perspective on degeneration,
most fully typified by the writings of the psychiatrist Henry Maudsley and the
zoologist E. Ray Lankester, both of whom were chiefly preoccupied with the
threat to the nation emanating from the lower reaches of society. This specifically
urban-industrial focus amounted to a kind of rear-mirror Darwinism in which a
rapid deterioration in the racial stock was believed to result from the pressure
on workers to adapt themselves to a degraded environment, posing formidable
problems of social control as the numbers of criminopathic paupers steadily
grew. Galton wrote of his distress at encountering "the draggled, drudged, mean
look of the mass of individuals, especially of the women, that one meets in

the streets of London," "[t]he conditions of their life . . . crushing them into degeneracy."[15] Not surprisingly, Galton took a keen interest in the developing "science" of criminal anthropology and was one of the few British intellectuals to attend the International Congresses organised by the Italian criminologist Lombroso. In the same year that *Dracula* was published, Galton presented to the fourth (1897) Congress his most enduring contribution to modern policing, a newly devised scheme for classifying fingerprints which was to revolutionise the methods of social control.[16]

Despite the manifest differences between them, the one nervous of the traditionally well-to-do, the other fixing its fears upon the new poor, these two accounts of degeneration do find a point of intersection in the threat they each posed to the security of respectable middle class society, precisely the world of doctors, lawyers and teachers that is under siege in *Dracula*. Stoker's depiction of vampirism draws upon and draws together these twin fears of degeneration, fusing them into a single potent compound. Though the Count incarnates a powerful image of aristocratic decadence, falling into a long line of melodramatic rakes and villains, it is crucial that his preferred theatre of operations is the heart of the Empire, "the crowded streets of your mighty London, . . . in the midst of the whirl and rush of humanity" (31; ch. II). Both Jonathan Harker and his wife Mina speak of the threat to "London, with its teeming millions" (67; ch. IV and 215; ch. XIV), yet it soon becomes apparent that the danger lies not merely in the size of London's population, but in the uneasy coexistence of its social strata, signalled in the novel by the juxtaposition of standard English and demotic or vernacular speech. When the Count's first victim Lucy Westenra has been transformed into a vampire she is known as "the bloofer lady" amongst the "grubby-faced little children" on whom she preys, an indication that established social boundaries are being breached (213; ch. XIII). *Dracula* imagines the Victorian bourgeois family as trapped in a sort of vice (the Count's grip "actually seemed like a steel vice"), under strain from both extremes of the social hierarchy (24; ch. II).[17] Or, transposed into the theoretical idioms of European positivism, the choice of pathologies is between Nordau's "highly-gifted degenerates" and Lombroso's "atavistic criminals."

By vividly dramatising the horrors of degeneration and atavism, the figure of the Count underscores the sexualised threat that lay at their core, the assumption of "a sexual 'instinct' " capable of turning to such perverse or precocious forms as "homosexuality" or "hysteria." Instructively, in his *History of Sexuality* the late Michel Foucault traced "the opening up of the great medico-psychological domain of the "perversions" in the mid-nineteenth century, showing its intrication with new ideas about "heredity" and "degenerescence."[18] His argument suggests that operationalising the distinction between normality and pathology involved working across several different levels.[19] That is to say, the medical expert's attention would move from the minutiae of the sexual act to the classification of various maladies and diseases, and from there to the future disposition of the species, before returning to the sexual act again. In this way the diagnostic treatment of the human body could be connected to a program for administratively regulating hereditary traits, paving the way for the extension of State activity into modern eugenics.

Dracula typically follows the same bio-political trajectory, but in a necessarily more anxious key. Thus Jonathan Harker's temptation in a remote wing of the Castle Dracula — one of the earliest episodes in the book — insistently problematizes his "biological responsibility," his "obligation to preserve a healthy line of descent."[20] Captured and captivated by "three young women," "ladies" of the night who cast "no shadow on the floor," Harker is unnerved but nevertheless consumed with "longing" for the fulfilment of his "wicked, burning desire." This ambivalence is heightened by his feeling that one of the "ladies" seems uncannily familiar to him, though he is unable to bring this elusive memory to consciousness. Yet the racialised contrast which triggers his aborted recollection is familiar enough: the woman Harker thinks he knows is "fair, as fair as fair can be, with great, wavy masses of golden hair and eyes like pale sapphires," while her two companions are "dark" with "high aquiline noses, like the Count's, and great dark, piercing eyes." Significantly, the role of this blonde Aryan woman is to initiate Harker's fatal seduction, attempting to betray him to the corruptions of the flesh and cut him off forever from respectable domesticity. In "delightful anticipation" of other women later in the narrative, she represents "the enemy within," a source of male hysteria and demoralisation, a "dreamy fear" of sexual chaos (51; ch. III).

The progenitive powers of the perverse are also at stake in one of the most dramatic episodes in the novel in which the Count is disturbed while taking possession of *Dracula*'s heroine, Harker's newly-wedded wife Mina. The enormity of this scene is all the more intensely rendered by a double narration: once objectively, as an appalling discovery by the four male protagonists Van Helsing, Dr. Seward, the Hon. Arthur Holmwood, and Quincy Morris; and once subjectively, through Mina's own horrified memory. The Count has broken into the Harker's room and, usurping their marriage bed by reducing the stupefied Jonathan to complete passivity, he has taken Mina by the scruff of her neck, "forcing her face down on his bosom" like "a child forcing a kitten's nose into a saucer of milk to compel it to drink" (336; ch. XXI). The extraordinarily dense web of associations evoked by these descriptions — of castration, rape, fellatio, sadomasochism — are held in place by the vampire's bizarrely composite persona, simultaneously that of rake *and* mother, a patriarch who gives birth to monsters. *Dracula* is a novel which excels in reversals of Victorian convention: men become sexually quiescent, women are transformed into sexual predators who cannibalize children, madness seems ready to overwhelm reason, and all of this is charged by a ceaselessly fluctuating economy of blood. But even so, Mina Harker's violation by the Count signals a remarkable development in the vampire's powers. Certainly this episode explodes once and for all any hierarchically gendered division of the cultural field according to which "[i]n one set of works (Poe, Hoffmann, Baudelaire: 'elite' culture)" vampires "are women," whereas "[i]n another (Polidori, Stoker, the cinema: 'mass' culture) they are men."[21] For it demonstrates once again that in *Dracula* it is matter out of place that matters, the contamination and dissolution of the pure and sacred that counts, the transgression of boundaries and borders that is the ultimate horror, just as in theories of degeneration it was the impulsive, the unstable, the unfixed and the nomadic that were held to be the sign of the savage and the barbarian — those like the gipsies Harker sees at the castle in Transylvania, "almost outside all law" (56; ch. IV).[22] In both cases, anxiety around the question of boundaries is always also a demand that there *be* a boundary.

LONDON IN THE IMAGINARY of the 1890s becomes more than ever the place where boundaries threaten to dissolve. The merest glimpse of Count Dracula in Piccadilly with his eyes on "a very beautiful girl" is enough to turn the convalescing Jonathan Harker "pale and dizzy," precipitating a "relapse" (207–8; ch. XIII). And in much of the contemporary literature on degeneration the city was the site of greatest risk to the proper demarcation both between individuals and between the sexes. It comes as no surprise to learn of Stoker's subsequent affinity for the work of the Viennese philosopher Otto Weininger who claimed that the predominance of feminine qualities in a national culture could be taken as the main index of its degeneracy. In Stoker's appropriation of Weininger in his 1908 novel *Lady Athlyne*, "the great mass of persons" so lacked the biological prerequisites of a fully gendered identity that they "were easily satisfied to mate with anyone," having developed only "a few of the qualities of sex."[23] Stoker's phobic, virtually hysterical, vision of indiscriminate mating presumes a species hierarchy in which degeneration is already the normal condition for the majority and, in this self-fulfilling and self-perpetuating cycle of degradation, sex becomes a type of scavenging. In *Dracula*, when the Count boasts that he already controls the women in the novel and intends to use them as a lure to unman his hapless male opponents, he conjures up a scenario in which they become helplessly undifferentiated vampire subjects, "my creatures, to do my bidding and to be my jackals when I want to feed" (365; ch. XXIII). The first priority of Van Helsing and his associates must therefore be a policy of what was soon to be called *negative eugenics*: to "sterilise" every one of the Count's "lairs" (361; ch. XXIII).

Only truly strong men can rise to such a crisis and on one level *Dracula* charts the struggle to define and defend a resourceful and steadfast masculinity that could be seen to win the day. Despite the general confidence in the ideal of sporting manliness in the last quarter of the nineteenth century, this view was not without its difficulties and complications. One of these quandaries is crystallised through the character of Quincey Morris, the American adventurer who plays a large part in running Count Dracula to ground but who tragically loses his life in the final battle. The Texan's strength and fortitude come in for repeated praise throughout the novel, and he is extolled as "a moral Viking" (209; ch. XIII) by an admiring Dr. Seward. Yet the Viking was a contested figure in English literary culture by the 1890s, and if it conjured up Carlyle's enthusiasm for "the Pagan Norseman" in his book *On Heroes* (1841) or Sir Henry Curtis's "Bersekir" pugnacity in Rider Haggard's *King Solomon's Mines* (1885), it also smacked too much of the pre-civilised conqueror or invader.[24] When Dr. Seward declares that "if America can go on breeding men like that, she will be a power in the world indeed," the corollary is a troubling one, at least in its implications for Britain's position in the league table of nations in the 1890s (209; ch. XIII).[25] Dr. Seward is reminded of this by his patient, the lunatic Renfield, who in an unusually "rational" moment of lucidity tells Quincey that he looks forward to the day "when the Pole and the Tropics may hold allegiance to the Stars and Stripes," and "the Monroe doctrine takes its true place as a political fable" (291; ch. XVIII). Transposed on to the plane of social biology, however, the implicit dangers of inter-imperial rivalry are lifted once Quincey is dead since he leaves no heir (having previously been rejected as Lucy Westenra's suitor, who in any case has died despite receiving transfusions of this "brave man's blood" (180; ch. XII). Instead, the Texan's lineage is commemoratively transferred to British stock, "re-born" in the person of the Harkers' infant son who is named after "all our little band of men together" but is always called "Quincey" (449; ch. XXVII). The story therefore concludes on a resounding counter-note: not only is the vampire's threat to hereditary purity vanquished, but the Harkers' marriage becomes a form of hierogamy which subordinates American energy to the triumphs of British breeding.

Though the late Victorian "code of manly honour . . . echoed evangelical motifs, with its call for self-control and self-sacrifice," it typically "sounded more stoic than spiritual."[26] And in *Dracula* the shoring up of masculinity is partly made possible by the vampire's gradual diminution in which he is secularised and criminalised at one and the same time. At the start of the novel the Count occupies a space that is virtually beyond representation, an unmirrorable image, a force able to assume a multiplicity of forms. But then the inexorable logic of the narrative begins to lay down the conditions of the vampire's increasing legibility, undermining the Count's power by confining him within the categorial boxes of medical and sociological positivism, a phenomenon amenable to calculation and manipulation like any Other.[27] Van Helsing is therefore perfectly right to claim that Dracula is an "enemy" who is "not merely spiritual" (297; ch. XIX). The vampire emerges from a world of "traditions and superstitions" into "the midst of our scientific, sceptical, matter-of-fact nineteenth century" to provide stark confirmation of its known scientific laws (285; ch. XVIII). As the scientist credited with the "discovery of the continuous evolution of brain-matter" (292; ch. XVIII), Van Helsing is well able to appreciate that "this criminal of ours" displays all the predictability of the "imperfectly formed mind" laid down in "the philosophy of crime" or the "study of insanity" (405–6; ch. XXV). It follows that no matter how cunning or physically strong the criminal may be, the forces of law and order will ultimately have the advantage. To mark the turning of the tide the novel's heroes make a "solemn compact," swearing to bring Count Dracula down "in as businesslike a way" as "any other transaction of life," and Van Helsing attempts to stiffen their resolve by spelling out the terms of their superiority, listing their "power of combination," the "resources of science," and their "unfettered" freedom "to act and think" (285; ch. XVIII). In essence this ceremony recapitulates the social contract, but its new association with criminal anthropology shifts the grounds of their "compact" away from spontaneous agreement and places it on a more "objective" footing. Just as eugenics was intended as a science of race improvement, so in Lombroso's new "science" crime could read as the symptom of a nation's weakness. Once rigorously applied, Lombrosian criminology would sharply distinguish the body of truly authentic citizens from those Others whose pathological ineligibility could be revealed with scientific precision, initiating a process of regeneration that would "streamline evolution" and "eliminate the unproductive."[28]

By the same token, the "solemn compact" is also the first step in refurbishing manly virtue, a symbolic occasion for abjuring all forms of personal weakness. Several of the men have already shown themselves to be susceptible to bouts of hysteria, admittedly under extreme pressure, with even Van Helsing breaking down into tears and laughter, "just as a woman does." With the fear of disturbances of gender animating so much of the book it is quite understandable that Van Helsing should subsequently deny "that it was hysterics," and that such moments of breakdown are sublimated into deeds of derring-do (209–10; ch. XIII). But, in the light of the growing belief that "nervous sensitivity was . . . a severe liability in a man," *Dracula* displays a remarkably lenient attitude to male hysteria, reviving the sympathies of an earlier era.[29] Moreover, contrary to received medical wisdom, but in keeping with the narrative penchant for naturalistic explanation, male hysteria is generalized into a gender-free safety-valve, an unconsciously self-produced human mode of "eas[ing] off the strain" (211; ch. XIII). If hysterical outbursts are tolerated and even pardoned in *Dracula*, the heroic alliance against the Count is redolent of the sober and very unheroic tradition of Victorian public service, resembling "a sort of board or committee" which incorporates and directs its members' energies by giving them a new sense of purpose and a new collective identity (282; ch. XVIII).

Another unusual feature of the compact is the way in which it positions Mina Harker as the sole woman amongst "our little band of men" (449; ch. XXVII) and the emblematic weight this unique status forces her to bear complicates her femininity considerably. When Mina first enters the story she is an assistant schoolmistress "overwhelmed with work" (70; ch. V), but her non-traditional appearance of independence is quickly offset by the criticisms she gratuitously lodges against "the New Women" writers for their sexual frankness. Once she has become Jonathan's wife she devotes herself full-time to her husband, while acting as a surrogate "mother-figure to all the other characters in the novel."[30] It might therefore seem as if Stoker was attempting "to show that modern women can combine the best of the traditional and the new" (Senf, 49). However, several factors make Mina extremely hard to place. For example, it is she — rather than the psychiatrist John Seward — who introduces the names of Nordau and Lombroso into Van Helsing's meditations, to the professor's evident delight at the extent of her knowledge. Through the discussion of criminal peculiarities we learn of Dracula's fatal flaw, that "this criminal has not full manbrain," that 'he be of child-brain in much" and so, whatever power he may wield over Mina, he is in reality her inferior (405–6; ch. XXV). The Count is at a considerable disadvantage against "her great brain which is trained like man's brain" and, abandoning her in his haste to escape, he fails to see that in her semi-vampirised state Mina can gain knowledge of his thoughts and thus effectively bring about his downfall (404; ch. XXV). By putting herself in Van Helsing's hands and asking him to hypnotise her, Mina becomes both patient and double-agent, serving as a kind of conductor between vampire and man. She is then a curiously mobile figure, one minute an emblem of "the mother-spirit" (275; ch. XVII), the next mischievously teasing Van Helsing about the record of events leading up to Lucy's death, explaining her "little joke" to herself as "some of the taste of the original apple that remains still in our mouths" (220; ch. XIV). And this instability in her role as heroine reflects a split between her status and her aspirations. For her transition from schoolmistress to transcriber and chronicler of the book's official history is not simply an exchange of teaching for typing: it contains and expresses her aspirations to be a lady journalist, "interviewing and writing descriptions and trying to remember conversations," aspirations which co-exist with her desire to be clerically "useful to Jonathan," even before she is fully implicated in the narrative's events (70; ch. V). Far from seeing Mina's skills solely as an index of the increasing numbers of women teachers and office workers in the lower middle-class sector of the labor force, it is instructive to link her to the exceptional cases of upwardly mobile ladies whose contradictory response to the suffrage movement gave them a strategic position in late Victorian society.[31] One noteworthy example might be that of the influential journalist Flora Shaw, also an Irish Protestant like Stoker, who was at the centre of British imperial politics during this period, rising to the post of colonial editor of *The Times* in 1893 and later becoming the wife of the Governor of Nigeria.[32]

Mina needs to be read as more than one version of the feminine, an unmoored sign of change as well as a firm attempt to hold the line against the New Woman. When Van Helsing pronounces her to be one of those "good women" who "tell all their lives, and by day and by hour and by minute, such things that angels can read' he is in a way providing her with a cover story (221; ch. XIV). His eulogisation deflects attention from Mina's significant break with that model of the Victorian body politic which identified the middle-class man as its head and the middle-class woman as its heart, the "seat of morality and tenderness."[33] But, paradoxically, while Van Helsing ignores Mina's many doubles as a woman, by repeatedly attributing a "man's brain" to her, "a brain that a man should have were he much gifted — and woman's heart," he extends permission for her to double simultaneously as woman *and* as honorary man (281; ch. XVIII). Though *Dracula* enacts a struggle for the possession of women's bodies and ruthlessly punishes the least hint of precocious female sexuality (in the figure of Lucy Westenra), it is a novel which temporarily recruits a woman into a man's place, arming Mina "like the rest" with "a large-bore revolver" as our heroes move in for the final kill (423; ch. XXVI). Ironically, it is only by becoming a man that the woman can ever come to deserve parity of esteem or cease to be other than a problem; but one condition of phallic womanhood is that it is almost immediately abandoned for the over-feminised maternal. Quincey Morris *and* Mina are both described as "brave and gallant" figures, but once she has become the mother of Quincey Harker it is Mina's "sweetness and loving care" that defines her as a woman for whom men would "dare much" including risking their lives (449; ch. XXVII).

With everyone armed to the teeth the campaign against the vampire ends in true imperial style with a paramilitary raid, a search and destroy mission into the heart of Transylvania. Beneath the Gothic wrapping lies a tale of buccaneering, an adventure story to raise the cheer of civilians in which the *unheimlich* terrors of the home are expelled and then quelled on foreign soil. *Dracula* is situated exclusively within the domain of civil society — the household, the private asylum, the countryside, and the open spaces of the city — and its heroes operate directly in and upon these spheres rather than going through official channels. Policemen, for example, are heard but barely seen in the novel, marked only by the flashing of their lanterns and the off-stage sound of their "heavy tramp" (239; ch. XV). But, as highly privatised as this adventure story is, it is intimately connected to the imperialist's dilemma, one which was shortly to be foregrounded as a result of the Boer War. In 1897 Britain was moving into its last brief climactic imperialist phase and the question which faced her was the same one that was jointly posed by *Dracula* and theories of *dégénérescence*, and insistently echoed by later writers like John Buchan: can an advanced civilization continue to produce the heroes it needs? Or is "a mature society . . . being assailed by diseased and vicious children"?[34]

To his undying credit Count Dracula recognises this dilemma from the very beginning. Though his family "can boast a record that mushroom growths like the Hapsburgs and the Romanoffs can never reach," he knows that "in these days of dishonourable peace . . . the glories of the great races are as a tale that is told" (42; ch. III). What is really at stake in *Dracula* is the continuing possibility of racial glory and consequently questions of birth and reproduction are never far away. Hence too the extreme ambivalence concerning those of noble birth so typical of Stoker's texts.[35] Arthur Holmwood, the only true aristocrat on the "board or committee" of heroes is thoroughly bourgeoisified, indistinguishable from the other Victorian clubmen, and does not even accede to a title until half-way through the book (282; ch. XVIII). Even so, with the death of his fiancee he is effectively denied the opportunity to father a child. But it is the mixture of attraction and repulsion provoked by Count Dracula which best exemplifies the unease associated with an aristocratic mien, at times resisting all comprehension. "Ah, sir," says the vampire to the unworldly clerk, "you dwellers in the city cannot enter into the feelings of the hunter" (29; ch. II).

Yet it is, of course, vital that such city-dwellers *do* fully transform themselves into hunters or, perhaps more accurately, into vigilantes — a point made more explicitly in Stoker's draft notes for the novel. There Stoker specifically designates these hunter-citizens as a committee of vigilantes, even making veiled references to lynching which recall both the tacit condonement of this gruesome practice in his 1886 lecture *A Glimpse of America* and the apoplectic racist invective of his last novel *The Lair of the White Worm* (1911). Stoker's work was never quite able to settle with these racial and scientific issues, nor with the closely connected questions of sexual identity, and they flare up in his essays and fiction again and again. In one optimistic flourish "the note of the unity of the Empire" appears to hold everything together as he euphorically describes the special performance at the Lyceum Theatre for the Indian and Colonial troops that was part of the Queen's Diamond Jubilee in June 1897. This great formal gathering "represented every colour and ethnological variety of the human race, from coal black through yellow and brown up to the light type of Anglo-Saxons reared afresh in new realms beyond the seas." As Stoker was to write of stage reception for the 1902 Coronation at the Lyceum Theatre which followed it, this "magnificent sight" could "in type and colour . . . have illustrated a discourse on ethnology, or craniology," harmonised into a sensational imperial tableau with "[t]he great crown and Union Jack seeming to flame over all."[36] Despite its triumphant conclusion, *Dracula* paints a very different picture. Coinciding almost to the month with the Diamond Jubilee, publication in May 1897 offered a kind of shadow-text to this extraordinary moment of public rejoicing. For at a time when "imperialism" was "in the air" and "all classes drunk with sightseeing and hysterical loyalty,'' Stoker revealed a more deadly hysteria about race and selfhood at the heart of national spectacle and jingoistic camaraderie, the shape of things to come.[37]

Rutgers Center for Historical Analysis

NOTES

1. Thomas De Quincey, "On Murder Considered as One of the Fine Arts," in D. Masson (ed.), *The Collected Writings of Thomas De Quincey* (14 vols.), (Adam and Charles Black, Edinburgh, 1890), Vol. XIII, 124.
2. Bram Stoker, *Dracula* (Penguin, Harmondsworth, 1979). All subsequent references are to this edition.
3. The *Spectator*, 31 July 1897, 150–51.
4. Thomas De Quincey, quoted in J. Hillis Miller, *The Disappearance of God: Five Nineteenth-Century Writers* (Harvard University Press, Cambridge, MA, 1963), p. 64.
5. B. Stoker, *The Duties of Clerks of Petty Sessions in Ireland* (John Falconer, Dublin, 1879), pp. v–vi and 27.
6. Josep R. Llobera, 'The dark side of modernity', *Critique of Anthropology*, 8, no. 2 (1988), 71–6.
7. Daniel Pick, *Faces of Degeneration: A European Disorder, c. 1848–c. 1918* (Cambridge University Press, Cambridge, 1989), p. 180.
8. Cesare Lombroso (1835–1909) was the Italian founder of positivistic criminology who originally claimed that crime could largely be explained in terms of evolutionary atavism. Lombroso greatly influenced the German physician and journalist Max Nordau (1849–1923) who helped popularise the concept of degeneration by using it as a critical tool to stigmatise developments in the arts. An English translation of Nordau's *magnum opus Entartung* (1893) was published by William Heinemann (later to become Stoker's publisher) under the title *Degeneration* in 1895. This aspect of Stoker's work has attracted increasing attention in recent years, though few studies go much beyond cataloguing textual affinities. The best analysis to date remains Daniel Pick, " 'Terrors of the night': *Dracula* and 'degeneration' in the late nineteenth century," *Critical Quarterly*, 30, no. 4 (1988), 71–87.
9. Colin Martindale, "Degeneration, Disinhibition, and Genius," *Journal of the History of Behavioral Science*, 7, (1971), 177–82.
10. Albert Wilson (1910) quoted in Richard D. Walter, "What Became of the Degenerate? A Brief History of a Concept," *Journal of the History of Medicine and Allied Sciences*, 11, (1956), 422–29, p. 422.
11. Francis Galton, *Hereditary Genius: An Inquiry into its Laws and Consequences*, repr. (Macmillan, London, 1914), p. 338.
12. See Ian Hacking, "How Should We Do the History of Statistics?," *I&C*, no. 8, (1981), pp. 15–26, p. 21.
13. Greta Jones, *Social Darwinisn and English Thought: The Interaction between Biological and Social Theory* (The Harvester Press, Brighton, 1980), 35.
14. William Rathbone Greg, "On the Failure of 'Natural Selection' in the Case of Man," *Fraser's Magazine*, LXXVIII, (1868), 360.
15. Francis Galton, *Hereditary Genius*, 328–29.

16. See Daniel Pick, *Faces of Degeneration*, 176–79.
17. In an earlier story "The Secret of the Growing Gold" Stoker again explicitly contrasts "the causes of decadence in their aristocratic and . . . their plebeian forms." This story was collected in the posthumous volume *Dracula's Guest* (1914), repr. (Brandon, Dingle Co. Kerry, 1990). See especially 58.
18. Michel Foucault, *The History of Sexuality, Volume 1: An Introduction* (Penguin, Harmondsworth, 1981), 117.
19. Interestingly, part of the challenge the madman R. M. Renfield poses to Dr. Seward's knowledge of the human mind lies in the fact that he is "so unlike the normal lunatic" (78). For an exploration of the replacement of the idea of human nature by "a model of normal people with laws of dispersion," see Ian Hacking, *The Taming of Chance* (Cambridge University Press, 1990).
20. Foucault, *The History of Sexuality*, 118–21.
21. Franco Moretti, *Signs Taken For Wonders: Essays in the Sociology of Literary Forms* (Verso, London, 1983), 103.
22. See Galton's suggestion that "[t]here is a most unusual unanimity in respect to the causes of incapacity of savages for civilization, among writers on those hunting and migratory nations who are brought into contact with advancing colonization, and perish, as they invariably do, by the contact. They tell us that the labour of such men is neither constant nor steady; that the love of a wandering, independent life prevents their settling anywhere to work, except for a short time, when urged by want and encouraged by kind treatment." *Hereditary Genius*, 334.
23. Bram Stoker, *Lady Athlyne* (Heinemann, London, 1908), 81–82.
24. See for example the discussion of the reception of Charles Kingsley's *Hereward the Wake* (1866) in Bruce Haley, *The Healthy Body and Victorian Culture* (Harvard University Press, Cambridge MA, 1978), pp. 216–20. For a description of Sir Henry Curtis in battle, see H. Rider Haggard, *King Solomon's Mines* (1885), Ch. XIV "The Last Stand of the Greys." Note that Count Dracula includes the Berserkers among "the blood of many brave races" that flows in *his* family's veins and that the Norwegian wolf which he appropriates from the London Zoological Gardens is also called "Berserker"; see 41 and 166. Nevertheless, when Arthur Holmwood drives a stake into the heart of his fiancee Lucy, "he looked like a figure of Thor" (259).
25. For a discussion of Britain's world position at this time and contemporary perceptions of it, see Aaron L. Friedberg, *The Weary Titan: Britain and the Experience of Relative Decline, 1895–1905* (Princeton UP, 1988).
26. Janet Oppenheim, *"Shattered Nerves": Doctors, Patients, and Depression in Victorian England* (Oxford UP, 1991), p. 150.
27. On the "scaling down" of the vampire, see David Seed, "The Narrative Method of *Dracula*," *Nineteenth-Century Fiction*, 40 (1985), 61–75.
28. See D. Pick, *Faces of Degeneration*, 126.
29. Janet Oppenheim, *Shattered Nerves*, 148.
30. See Carol A. Senf, "*Dracula*: Stoker's Response to the New Woman," *Victorian Studies*, 26 (1982): 33–49, p. 46. For the perceived links between the New Woman and literary decadence, see Linda Dowling, "The Decadent and the New Woman in the 1890's," *Nineteenth-Century Fiction*, 33 (1979): 434–53.
31. On the growing numbers of women in public services and commerce considered in a literary context, see Peter J. Keating, *The Haunted Study: A Social History of the English Novel, 1875–1914* (Secker & Warburg, London, 1989), 181.
32. Flora Shaw was a key figure in British imperialist politics. A friend of Rhodes and Chamberlain, she was privy to the planning of the Jameson Raid in 1895, keeping

in touch with Rhodes by secret code and publishing premature reports in *The Times*. As described by her husband's biographer Margery Perham, Flora Shaw "always wore black" and "never played the woman as a short cut to her professional objectives." Nevertheless, "[p]ublic men, however cautious, found it surprisingly easy to give away official information to such an interviewer." See Margery Perham, *Lugard: The Years of Authority 1898–1945* (Collins, London, 1960), 54–66.

33. See Leonore Davidoff, "Class and Gender in Victorian England," in Judith L. Newton, Mary P. Ryan and Judith R. Walkowitz (eds.), *Sex and Class in Women's History* (Routledge and Kegan Paul, London, 1983), 17–21.

34. John Buchan, *Memory Hold-the-Door* (1941) quoted in David Stafford *The Silent Game: The Real World of Imaginary Spies* (Lester & Orpen Dennys, Toronto, 1988), 67. Strictly speaking this passage deals with external threats to "the European tradition" but in Buchan's imaginary (as in De Quincey's and Stoker's) the two are inextricably linked. In his 1924 novel *The Three Hostages* the character Dr. Greenslade "theorizes" that "the barriers between the conscious and the subconscious . . . are growing shaky and the two worlds are getting mixed," corroding "the clear psychology of most civilized human beings." See J. Buchan, *The Three Hostages* (Harmondsworth: Penguin, 1953), 14.

35. The early chapters of Stoker's *Lady Athlyne* see its aristomilitary hero languishing in a Boer prisoner-of-war camp, for example. Elsewhere, as in *The Lady of the Shroud* (1909), Stoker preferred to choose his heroes from the disreputable branches of titled families.

36. Bram Stoker, *Personal Reminiscences of Henry Irving* (2 vols.), (Macmillan, New York, 1906), Vol. 1, 251–2 and 339–42.

37. Beatrice Webb's diary, quoted in James Morris, *Pax Britannica: The Climax of an Empire* (Harcourt, Brace & World, New York, 1968), 26.

JOSEPH'S CURRANTS: THE HERMENEUTIC CHALLENGE OF *WUTHERING HEIGHTS*

By James L. Hill

TOWARD THE END OF WUTHERING HEIGHTS, Hareton Earnshaw, at the urging of the second Catherine, uproots the old servant Joseph's gooseberry and currant bushes and creates a flower garden with plants brought from Thrushcross Grange. This episode, together with Catherine's teaching Hareton to read and Heathcliff's strange *accidia*, commonly figures in discussions of the novel as evidence of the triumph of culture over savagery, or as a symbol of the renewal of life after the destructive strife that has marked two generations of Lintons and Earnshaws. But while Hareton's flower garden might well symbolize the triumph of culture, it is difficult to see quite how the replacement of edible by decorative plants points toward a renewal of vitality. The eradication of Joseph's bushes, and their replacement by flowers, is merely one small instance among many in *Wuthering Heights* of occurrences that call out to be read, but where reading may end in contradiction.[1]

Depending on the theoretical basis supporting interpretation of the novel's conclusion, the supplantation and transformation of Wuthering Heights has positive or negative resonance. Gilbert and Gubar (301–2), as well as Eagleton (117–21), read the conclusion negatively, as a reinstitution of a repressive patriarchal hierarchy, while Van Ghent (168–70), Miller (1965: 204–5, 209–10) and Jameson (128), all using radically different critical approaches, read it positively, with varying degrees of a sense of loss as the mundane absorbs or displaces the mythical. All are careful readers, but these opposed readings lead us back to the text, with, at the very least, questions about Brontë's narrative strategy. Gilbert and Gubar invoke an absent Milton as the patriarchal figure behind Brontë's novel, and Stanley Fish has made us aware of the hermeneutic traps Milton springs on his readers (1–22). I suggest that Brontë's extremely sophisticated control of narrative places hermeneutic responsibility on the reader to an extent unprecedented in Victorian novels. Whether or not we read *Wuthering*

Heights as Brontë's "correction" of Milton, as Gilbert and Gubar would have it, the novel's insistence on itself as a text to be interpreted, its emphasis on the perils of misreading (mistaking dead rabbits for live cats, or herbivores for carnivores [Brontë, 13]), and its deliberate, layered opacity, evoke the Miltonic difficulty of "things unattempted yet in prose or rhyme."

Hillis Miller's most recent essay on *Wuthering Heights* makes the point that however we approach the novel, the establishment of a single theoretical framework as a basis for interpretation will lead us into distortions that will, for the sake of the argument, skew interpretation either by omission or obfuscation, (1982: 50–52) a point made somewhat earlier, and for different purposes, by James Kincaid (795–98). The problem, as Miller sees it, is not that the novel is radically flawed, but that it is richly overdetermined, so cunningly constructed that no single critical perspective can hold it to accountability. But this, according to Miller, is not an invitation to open the novel to any and all readings; a responsible reading, perhaps an ideal reading, would conscientiously hold itself to accountability, even more so because, for Miller, *Wuthering Heights* asserts meaning and denies any ground for that meaning simultaneously (1982: 52–53).

If *Wuthering Heights* had presented itself to the reader with even the qualified authority of third-person narration, as we find it in Austen, or with the authorial first-person narrator interposed between reader and narrative, as in *Vanity Fair*, the problem of interpretation might have been as great, but it would obviously have been quite different. Brontë, however, not only chooses the role of author *absconditus*, but also presents the narrative so that events do not occur in and of themselves, but as events already interpreted. So much is explicit in the narratives of Lockwood and Nelly Dean, but it should be clear that virtually all of the characters, even minor figures such as Zillah and Mr. Kenneth, have their own versions of the meaning of the events that form the novel's plot. While *Wuthering Heights* does not develop these different perspectives with the thoroughness of Browning's *The Ring and the Book*, it does, like Browning's monologues, introduce its events already mediated internally by voice or script.

Since the novel presents itself in its first sentence as a mediated narrative, specifying a fictional narrator ordering the materials of its history, we may posit the possibility of an *Urtext* (or a pre-text) for his mediating interpretation. One question, then, would be whether or not that hypothetical text would be capable of producing the generic varieties of Brontë's text. The opening chapters of the novel, concerned with Lockwood's arrival at Thrushcross Grange, and his bewildered and exasperated meeting with Heathcliff and the inhabitants of Wuthering Heights, not only suggest that possibility, but also provide us with a model of text and interpretation. Immured in the first Catherine's bed, that first of the famous Chinese boxes within boxes, Lockwood chooses a Testament for bedtime reading from Catherine's "select" library. He shuts it, unread, and then looks at all her books in turn. When he does begin to read (we are not told in which book), it is not the printed text, but Catherine's marginal writing that catches his interest. The margins of the book are covered with commentary, or "at least, the appearance of one — covering every morsel of blank that the printer had left" (24). What Lockwood reads, however, does not appear to be a commentary on the printed text, but a narrative fragment of Catherine's personal journal, recording the events of an "awful Sunday" from her childhood; a causal relationship between texts now seems to be casual.

Although Lockwood describes Catherine's journal as "faded hieroglyphics," he proceeds to "decypher" it, and reads a narrative of rebellion and punishment. Because it is rainy, the children cannot go to church, and are forced to take up their prayer books and listen to what is apparently a three-hour homily by Joseph. Released from this, they are teased by Hindley and his wife Frances, and then Joseph forces upon them two tracts, "The Helmet of Salvation" and "The Broad Way to Destruction," which they violently spurn, only to be thrown by Hindley into the back kitchen, where Catherine takes up a book and writes her commentary. Lockwood then interprets what he feels must be a break in Catherine's text, for he sees no connection between the sentences: ". . . — we cannot be damper, or colder, in the rain than we are here," and "how little did I dream that Hindley would ever make me cry so!" (27). Between the two sentences he interposes their "scamper on the moors," for which she is punished by her brother. While Catherine's entry identifies a number of texts and commentaries (Joseph's homily, the prayer book, and the two tracts) no specific biblical text appears in the passage, and Lockwood fails to mention even the title of the book where Catherine's journal entry appears. If the Testament should provide the gospel authority for the homiletic procedures of this churchless Sunday, the textual citation for that authority is absent. In its place, instead, is a congeries of texts that draw on, comment on, or depart from an originating text.

Lockwood's eye wanders from Catherine's journal to the book, which we now learn is Jabes Branderham's "Seventy Times Seven, and the First of the Seventy First." Here at last we have a discourse on a New Testament text, Matthew 18.22, and the interpretation of this text, as U. C. Knoepflmacher has pointed out in some detail, is a gross misreading (85). Even the title of Branderham's discourse takes liberties with the Gospel; Jesus limits forgiveness to seventy times seven, while Branderham adds the first of the seventy first. While Knoepflmacher is correct in saying that the reading of Matthew 18 is misconstrued, he is incorrect in saying that Branderham is the misreader. Lockwood gets no further than the title of Branderham's discourse: "And while I was, half consciously, worrying my brain to guess that Jabes Branderham would make of his subject, I sank back in bed, and fell asleep" (27). Lockwood, in the "dream work" that follows, is himself the misreader, projecting a discourse for Branderham in a dream scene that incorporates Joseph (whose caricature presided

over Catherine's journal), Joseph's three hour homily, and the narrative theme
of Sunday rebellion and punishment from Catherine's journal.

In this dream, and the one that follows, the text of Matthew 18 plays a
powerful role (Lockwood, like Brontë, knew his Bible), but it functions in the
"dream work" not so much as an authoritative text, but as one element among
many suspended within the dreams. Indeed, the only direct quotation from
Matthew is the title of Branderham's discourse; other Biblical texts are quoted
(Job 7.10, 2 Samuel 12.7, Genesis 16.12, Isaiah 19.2, Psalms 149.9, Zechariah
8.10) within the dream narrative, and they might or might not figure in the
dream construct as significantly as the passage from Matthew. If the full text of
Matthew 18 serves in some way to adumbrate the fall from innocence to experience, and to indicate the way to salvation through a return to innocence (a
thematic pattern that has been asserted for the novel), the trials of Job as well
as the effacement of names ("that the place which knows him may know him
no more") could also have a thematic relevance, as could Nathan's "thou art
the man," or the story of the descendents of Hagar and Abraham, the generations
that will set their hands against one another.[2]

It is no accident that critics return to Lockwood's entry into the "penetralium"
of Wuthering Heights again and again with the strong intuition that the first
three chapters may hold the key to the deciphering of Brontë's "faded hieroglyphics." In a novel that is insistently repetitive, and in which repetition takes
the form of inversion, revision, and transformation, these chapters appear to
establish patterns and to introduce crucial material for its transformative repetitions. Even apparently casually observed details, such as the repetitions of Catherine's name, written on the windowsill in Lockwood's bed, "Catherine Earnshaw," "Catherine Heathcliff," "Catherine Linton," the changes the first
Catherine rings on her present identity in meditating her future identity, not only
project her possible future, but are also reproduced in the narrative. Catherine
Earnshaw becomes Catherine Linton, and the second Catherine Linton becomes
Catherine Heathcliff and finally, we assume, Catherine Earnshaw.[3]

II

IN HER PREFACE to *Novels of the Eighteen-Forties*, Kathleen Tillotson gives her
reason for excluding *Wuthering Heights* from the novels selected for detailed
discussion: "This novel, which speaks so clearly to our generation, hardly spoke
at all to its own" (vii). Contemporary students of narrative whose approach,
like that of Tillotson, is historically grounded, but whose analytical techniques
draw on theoretical premises developed after her ground breaking study, might
qualify her observation by saying that *Wuthering Heights* perforce spoke to its
readers, but in a language not yet understood. While the first reviews of the
novel, as well as Charlotte Brontë's preface to the 1850 edition, would appear

to support Tillotson's claim for the novel's initial incomprehensibility, the continuing proliferation of critical interpretations suggests that the novel does not speak so clearly now as she infers.

But it is not quite the case that Emily Brontë handed the novel to her readers as a mystery wrapped in an enigma, and did not stay for an answer. While it has been argued that for the intensely private Brontë, publication was in itself a form of self-betrayal or violation, and that she quite consciously employed obfuscating strategies to make betrayal as difficult as possible (Taylor, 72–109), her deployment of her two principal narrators, Lockwood and Nelly Dean, raises another possibility. Neither Lockwood nor Nelly is a member of the two families whose relationships generate the central events of the plot. Lockwood, as a sophisticated, if superficial outsider, functions as the main link between the reader and the narrator; while Nelly, much to Lockwood's surprise, seems more sophisticated than his initial observations of Yorkshire had led him to expect. She explains her acquisition of culture to him as the result of her extensive reading in the Grange library, and he, in turn, validates her claims to literacy by informing the reader that he has set down her prolonged narrative with minimal editorial emendation. Both narrators thus discover that they have a common ground of cultural literacy, and it is this common ground that links them to Brontë's reading audience. Locating her narrators in something like the "real world" of her readers, and then presenting through their narrations a world decidedly different from that world is a strategy that mediates strangeness, just as Swift had grounded Gulliver in a shared culture with his readers before launching him on his voyages. If in both cases narrators are suspect, or unreliable, they are so in terms comprehensible by shared cultural concepts of human behavior. While it may be both Brontë's and Swift's aim to subject such concepts to radical interrogation, their initial strategies of mediation provide their readers with an entrance into the alien in company with the familiar.

Nelly's first person narration, as the tale of the storyteller, with its conventional accoutrements — her sewing by the fire, with the basin of gruel on the hob — evokes the authenticity of a pre-book culture, where stories are not yet published commodities, and she also brings in the detritus of folklore. At the same time, however, her narrative aspires to the authenticity of a new, realistic fiction, in its linear chronology, and its exposition relying on a "scientific" criterion of cause and effect. Both aspects of her performance as storyteller appeal to Lockwood. In his boredom and illness, her story performs the time-filling function of the "winter's tale," while the sustained chronicle of the Lintons and Earnshaws holds the promise of solving the mysteries he has encountered in the Heights world.

Lockwood's affected diction, while it serves a purpose in placing him culturally in relation both to the reader and to the inhabitants of this Yorkshire backwater, also allows Brontë to load these introductory chapters with linguistic pointers. "Penetralium," "hieroglyphics," and "decypher," are verbal markers of Lockwood's sense of his cultural superiority, but they suggest as well that Lockwood, as a modern "profane," finds himself confronting something like a primitive cult, so that his frequent false starts and egregious misreadings of signs take on the semblance of a bumbled rite of initiation, leading up to his spending the night in a version of an inner sanctum, the hieratic bedchamber, where his dreams are dictated by a "sacred" text.

Carol Jacobs reads these initial chapters as Lockwood's initiation into and expulsion, or excommunication from the text of *Wuthering Heights*, or as an assertion of *Wuthering Heights* as fiction against the non-fictional, or "realistic" world of cause and effect that Lockwood represents. Her differentiation between the fictional and the "real" is essentially spatial, in that it asserts that the fictional is "a continual marking of the discrepancy between itself and what claims to lie outside" (80). Jacobs's reading leads to an insight into generic tension in the novel. She assesses Lockwood's problem as that of defining himself in relation to Wuthering Heights either as a "reader" who reduces Wuthering Heights to "a mere formal fiction with a hero and heroine," or as a "reader" who treats it "as a simple, actual history unmenaced by the supernatural" (213), in both cases minimizing the thread of textual possession. Both strategies would require an act of suppression on Lockwood's part, and this the novel will not permit.

If we shift perspectives from the spatial to the temporal, we find another kind of disjunction altogether, that between past and present, which appears to me to be at least as fruitful a means of exploring the relationship of fiction to reality as the distinction between "inner" and "outer" is for Jacobs. While her focus on the novel as text and Lockwood as reader maps out a marking of textual spaces and alternative modes of intertextual representation ("fiction" or "simple, actual history"), it does so at the expense of the novel's own valorization of temporal process. A crucial premise of the nineteenth-century realistic novel is that meaning can be achieved by chronology, an assumption it shares with the developing disciplines of biology, the earth sciences, and history, all of which account for the present state of species, geology, or civilization through the evidences of developmental sequence.

In her discussion of the realistic novel, Elizabeth Ermarth proposes a temporal model that may help us to map the strategy of these opening chapters.[4] In brief, her model is based upon what she takes to be a basic assumption of realistic fiction: the present is a phenomenal field that has been produced by cause and effect over time. If we are to understand that field, we must move backward through time to its origins. Within the temporal dimension of the realistic novel, both characters and plot events are appearances whose meanings must be constructed by an act of memorial retrieval on the part of narrator and reader, a process of abstraction that "solves" the appearance as a phenomenon produced by temporal process. According to Ermarth, such a solution depends upon a cultural consensus that time is homogeneous and continuous, just as the geometric resolution of a figure in space depends on the assumption that space is homogeneous and continuous; in both cases, the abstracting process is possible because of the assumption of a unified field that extends unbroken to temporal or spatial infinity. Ermarth's formulation provides us with a template that allows us to shift the focus from Jacobs's emphasis on the text as privileged and problematized space, to the text as problematized temporal filiation.

Wuthering Heights begins by denying its fictionality, a strategy familiar enough from Defoe forward, if not backward to the *Iliad*, but invoked with particular intensity in realistic fiction. What we meet is a journal, being kept in the present tense of 1801, after which Nelly's remarkale mnemonics construct a past giving Lockwood the chronology of two generations of Earnshaws and Lintons. The function of this chronology is to establish a sequence of cause and effect that will make intelligible to Lockwood the peculiar environment of Wuthering Heights and the web of relationships between its present inhabitants. Lockwood can explain the house as an anachronism, a quaintly common historical survival in Yorkshire, but its inhabitants, particularly Heathcliff and Catherine, seem to him oddly out of place. It is this conjunction of the sophisticated and the primitive that leads him to make the series of misidentifications in the opening chapters, and to request clarification from Nelly. The result is an articulation of the random mutations of Catherine's names on the windowsill into the ordered chronology of Nelly's narrative.

Ermarth's temporal model links the realistic novel with the projects of the modern historian, and with the assumptions of post-Cartesian science, as manifestations of the secularization of space and time characteristic of much post-Renaissance thought. In that light, it is perhaps of some interest to note that Brontë dates the building of Wuthering Heights to 1500, placing it at the beginning of England's Renaissance, just prior to its entry into the Reformation, and that she dates the beginning of Lockwood's journal as 1801, in the midst of England's war with France in the wake of the Revolution, which, among other things, had explicitly secularized Christian time.

One effect of the Reformation had been the placing of sacred texts as a matter of religious principle in the hands of the laity. Each reader then had both the privilege and the responsibility for the interpretation of the text, and while there was certainly no shortage of models of interpretation, either in sermons or written commentary, final responsibility for understanding the text, mediated or not, rested with the individual reader.[5] At least one result of this was the unprecedented proliferation of Protestant sects, all of which insisted on their particular interpretations of scripture. In the opening chapters of *Wuthering Heights* we see a condensed version of the process, not only in Joseph's homily in lieu of a regular service, but also in Lockwood's dream interpretation of Branderham's tract on Matthew 18. Branderham's extension of seventy times seven to the first of the seventy first leads Lockwood to identify him as an extreme example of sectarian Protestantism, and it is in those terms, particularly in the citation of Old Testament texts, that he projects his dream version of Branderham's sermon. The bringing together of citations from disparate books of the Bible for the purpose of authorizing some idiosyncratic moral thesis may also identify Lockwood's Branderham as a practicer of one form of Bibliolatry condemned by Coleridge in *Confessions of an Inquiring Spirit* (59). Nelly brings the same charge against Joseph in her narrative: "He was, and is yet, most likely, the wearisomest, self-righteous pharisee that ever ransacked a Bible to rake the promises to himself and fling the curses on his neighbors" (51).

What is remarkable about Lockwood's dream work is that by the time we get to it we are, in effect, dealing with a layering of at least five texts: Lockwood's journal, Catherine's marginal narrative, Branderham's unread tract, the Bible (both New and Old Testaments), and Lockwood's dream text. To these we might add discarded or unheard texts: Joseph's two tracts and his homily, and the prayer book. Beyond Lockwood's narrative, these layerings proliferate from Catherine's commentary and the title of Branderham's tract, but especially from Catherine's marginal commentary.

Catherine literally enters the novel as marginalia. The permutations of her name are scratched into the paint of the window ledge, naming the space that both divides and connects inside with outside. Lockwood's first drowsing response to her names is spatial, as they swarm to fill up the air in his first dream. Simply as names in space, they are meaningless, enigmatic spectral phenomena, incapable of being construed. Catherine's second entry is temporal, "a date some quarter of a century back" (24) that Lockwood reads on the flyleaf of the Testament. As he opens Branderham's tract and sees her commentary, he identifies it as a "regular diary, scrawled in an unformed, childish hand." The interaction of Catherine's marginal diary and the title of Branderham's tract combine to produce Lockwood's first dream narrative, a Sunday as "awful" and violent as the Sunday described in her diary, but now within the confines of a dissenting chapel.

On one level, Lockwood's dream is an exercise in historical recreation. The chapel he has observed in 1801 in a state of dilapidation is restored in his dream narrative, while Catherine and Heathcliff's rebellion against the patriarchal Joseph is transposed, restored, and replicated in Lockwood's rebellion against the patriarchal Branderham. Catherine and Heathcliff's roughhanded expulsion from the house to the back-kitchen by her brother Hindley, hurrying up from his "paradise on the hearth," is about to be reproduced on Lockwood by Branderham's congregation, when Lockwood is awakened from his dream by the beating of the fir tree branch on the bedroom window, restoring him to the present of 1801.

Catherine's marginal diary stands in playful or ludic antagonism to Branderham's text. Against the authority of the tractarian Joseph and her brother Hindley, she posits the autonomy of the self, enacted not only in her spurning, along with Heathcliff, of Joseph's tracts, but also in her apparent escape with Heathcliff for their "scamper on the moors." What Joseph takes as the repetition of original sin in the children of the next generation, Catherine asserts as originating individuality and rebellious difference. Moreover, she sees her escape to the moors with Heathcliff as a parodic confirmation of Joseph's insistence that the devil would fetch them away for their sinful behavior. Lockwood's dream is similarly ludic, and displays the same assertion of self against communal authority. His self assertion also takes the form of childish impatience: "Oh, how weary I grew. How I writhed, and yawned, and nodded, and revived! How I pinched and pricked myself, and rubbed my eyes, and stood up, and sat down again, and nudged Joseph to inform me if he would *ever* have done!" (28–29).

Branderham's discourse is directed toward Matthew 18.22, and its extension of Jesus's seventy times seven to the first of the seventy first leads Lockwood to denounce him for committing "the sin no Christian need pardon," that is, for tampering with the letter of the Gospel. Matthew 18 begins, however, not with an emphasis on sin, but rather on innocence, a verse that Brontë, Lockwood, and her readers would have known equally well: "Except ye be converted, and become as little children, ye shall not enter the kingdom of heaven" (Matt. 18.3). If Branderham, in his zeal to catalogue the sins of experience in all their detail and variety, has neglected the beginning of Chapter 18, Catherine's marginalia restores it.

Lockwood's second dream, that of the child at the window, recodes the child in terms of the opening verses of Matthew 18, in effect "converting" her to the little child of Christ's admonition. Catherine's return as a child after twenty years of wandering suggests Freud on the uncanny as the familiar we do not wish to recognize, but which is nevertheless brought to light. What is familiar and suppressed might well be the opening of Matthew 18, displaced by Branderham's discourse, restored but not recognized by Lockwood's second dream.[6]

Lockwood's dreams are the first efforts in the novel to uncover the meaning of texts by restoring their historical situations, and the nightmarish results of his dreams come from a struggle between the texts themselves. His reading in Catherine's diary stops with "he has been blaming our father (how dared he?) for treating H. too liberally; and swears he will reduce him to his right place —" (27); then, drowsing, he reads the "red ornamented title" of Branderham's discourse before falling asleep. In his first dream, the authority of Branderham's title acts to suppress Catherine's diary, restoring the "awful Sunday" to its proper location, its "right place," in the chapel, until the pious excess of Branderham's sermon triggers Lockwood's transference of Catherine's rebellion to himself. In his second dream, the child waif suppresses the excess of Branderham's discourse by returning to the omitted verses of the opening of Matthew 18. But Lockwood's refusal to recognize innocence, and his insistence that the child is demonic, shift authority back to the extreme Protestantism of Branderham (and Joseph), and to their shared belief in the radical sinfulness of human nature. One may read the conflicts in Lockwood's nightmares in a number of ways: the authority of community against the autonomy of self, a concept of childhood that stresses innocence against one that sees childish willfulness as the sign of original sin, a return of the repressed, and the subsequent anxiety that seeks to block its recognition. The conflict, however we read it, is a product of a conflict between the irreconcilable texts Lockwood has read, as each attempts to marginalize the other, a struggle to claim textual authority over the reader. In both nightmares, the spatial relationship between texts is refigured in temporal terms, as a historical reconstruction of the originating actions embodied in the texts themselves.

In Matthew 18, textual authority is a different matter. As one of the Gospels, it has, of course, canonical authority as a sacred text. But the more particular authority of Matthew 18 is that it is the first chapter in Matthew after the Transfiguration of Christ, where the Disciples hear the voice of God confirm Christ as His Son. As the first of the Gospels, then, it is the first to proclaim the authority of Christ as the Logos.

Margaret Homans has posited "the unnamed mother" as the figure whose absence generates major narrative tensions in *Wuthering Heights*, tensions between the "literal," which she identifies as female and natural, and the "symbolic," which she identifies as the linguistic construction of the dominant androcentric culture (68–83). Without denying the power of her analysis, which focuses on the difficult problem of authority for the woman writer in a predominantly male culture, and the deeply troubled compromises involved in acquiring such authority, I wish to posit also as an unnamed absence the authority of scriptural text, the revealed Logos whose traces remain merely as disconnected fragments, as in Lockwood's first dream.

When Lockwood reads the names written on the window sill in the closed bed, they appear as random mutations: Catherine Earnshaw, Catherine Heathcliff, Catherine Linton. They may indicate a series in which the first term is always the same, with no particular order implied, they may indicate a progression, they may mean the same thing or something different when read in one direction or another. They may, then, be a code, or an inverted rebus; they are obviously signifiers, but what they signify is missing. When Lockwood begins to read Catherine's marginalia, he records his act in the language of code breaking: "I began, forthwith, to decypher her faded hieroglyphics." "Decipher" can mean both to decode, and to replace meaning from zero. "Hieroglyphics" can mean both an unknown language and a sacred language, and the latter seems confirmed by the first deciphered words of her writing: "An awful Sunday." Catherine's childhood narrative, however, is defiantly secular, located in historical time and place, and her characters are the inhabitants of Wuthering Heights.

Catherine's journal is written in the margin of a printed discourse that is itself marginal, Branderham's commentary on Matthew 18.22. Both Catherine's journal and Branderham's discourse (at least as it is projected in Lockwood's dream) enter into some aspect of the spirit of Matthew 18, and Lockwood himself, in finding what he interprets as an hiatus in Catherine's text, and extrapolating Branderham's endless sermon from the title of his discourse, enters into the spirit of their texts as well. That such an entry into another's text carries danger with it is confirmed by the series of nightmares Lockwood suffers; one risks becoming possessed by the text, the "other," of being violated as the price of entry.

III

THE POWER OF NIGHTMARE, great enough to cause Lockwood to scream in his sleep, comes from its immediacy and its inexplicability: "(why did I think of *Linton*? I had read *Earnshaw* twenty times for Linton)" (31). Recognizable elements of our familiar world remain, but they have become demonized, obeying laws of their own that appear to have little relation to laws that govern our waking world. If the relationships between the inhabitants of Wuthering Heights refuse to conform to Lockwood's familiar social codes, his attempt to decode the hieroglyphics of its inner sanctum, rather than "solving" those relationships, subjects him to forces he can neither understand nor control.

It is left to Nelly Dean to solve the cipher of Wuthering Heights, and she does so in resolutely realistic fashion, using all the devices of realistic narration: chronology, mimesis, diegesis, point of view. Moreover, her memorial retrieval invokes the oldest sanction of mimetic realism, that of the eye-witness. The random permutations of names on the windowsill become a temporal equation encompassing two generations of Earnshaws and Lintons, and by the end of her narrative, Lockwood and the reader understand historically the events that have led to the situation Lockwood encounters when he first visits Wuthering Heights.

The great irony of *Wuthering Heights* is that Nelly's narrative does not finally "decypher" the novel. In spite of her specificity, and the precision of her chronology, one senses that hers is not the full accounting either of the characters at the beginning of Lockwood's journal, so baffling to him, or of their antecedents. The procedures of realistic narration do not solve appearances. For appearances to be resolved completely, they must be capable of representation as the product of a virtually seamless chain of cause and effect, but at crucial points of that chain, data are withheld from Nelly, making resolution hypothetical. Examples of such cruces are the mystery of Heathcliff's origin, left unexplained by Mr. Earnshaw, the bonding between Heathcliff and Catherine, to which Nelly is not privy, and Heathcliff's activities during his three year absence, the results of which are obvious on his return, while their causes are never revealed. Coding these appearances in terms of cause and effect thus leaves a residue that is incommensurate; or, if it can be measured, it can be measured only in the multiplicity of readings, some complementary, some contradictory, that have proliferated as critics have entered (some would say trespassed on) Brontë's text.[7]

Nelly's narration, and Lockwood's as well, have as their coordinates the space-time continuum that is a given for realistic fiction. If, as Ermarth asserts, these coordinates extend to temporal and spatial infinity, and if the laws governing realism are the laws of cause and effect, no single event is repeatable, and the meaning of a specific event is relational, determined by its position in an ongoing sequence; it is the product of prior events, and is causal to succeeding events. On the other hand, as Miller and other critics have insisted, *Wuthering Heights* is constantly repetitious. Hareton Earnshaw is the name of the builder of Wuthering Heights, and at the end of the novel, Hareton Earnshaw is the present owner of the house. Catherine Earnshaw is the first Catherine we meet, and the last as well. Lockwood's sawing of the ghost child's wrist on the broken windowpane in the third chapter is repeated when Heathcliff closes the clasp-knife on Hindley's wrist, Heathcliff hangs Isabella Linton's dog, while Hareton hangs puppies over the back of a chair, Heathcliff nearly succeeds in making Hareton over in his likeness, while the appearance of both Hareton and the second Catherine repeats the appearance of the first Catherine. In her marginal diary, Catherine conjectures that Hindley and Frances have not been reading their Bibles on that "awful Sunday," and Nelly makes the same assertion about Heathcliff in the last chapter of the novel. And the narrative of the second generation of Earnshaws and Lintons rewrites elements from the first generation in a different key.

There is a narrative model for these uncanny repetitions, but it is not to be found in the narratives of realistic novels. It is found instead in the relationship of the Old and New Testaments, where time and space are conceived in radically different terms, and where events have a very different kind of meaning. Here time and space do not stretch into infinity; they have come into existence at the Creation, and will cease to exist with Apocalypse. Events within these coordinates are meaningful as manifestations of God's providence, rather than through their relationship to each other. Their meaning, then, is typical, in that they reveal God as the author of and authority for Christian history.

By the time that Emily Brontë wrote *Wuthering Heights*, efforts to historicize sacred history, and questions as to the precise nature of its authority, had long been launched. And while nothing had been done in England comparable to the development of Biblical hermeneutics in Germany, the Romantic critique of

Biblical and Miltonic narratives of sacred history had taken the form of mythic narrative that corrected, revised, or challenged either Biblical narrative itself, or received traditions for reading Biblical narrative. The most radical challenges, those of Byron, Shelley, and Blake, are made by sympathetic entry into the text, an imaginative projection oddly parallel to that of the early hermeneuticists. Blake's "The Prophets Isaiah and Ezekiel dined with me, and I asked them how they dared so roundly to assert that God spake to them;" (37) is an example both of such sympathetic entry, and correction of received reading, as is Shelley's version of the crucified Christ suffering for the bloodbath of Christian history in *Prometheus Unbound* (I, 539–615) and Byron's recasting of the early chapters of Genesis in *Cain*.[8] But Blake, Byron, and Shelley, however radical their critiques, do not desacralize time, and in all three time is conceived teleologically, rather than as infinitely expanding secular history. Time remains qualified and authorized.

Narrative time in *Wuthering Heights* is precisely quantified (1500, 1801, 1802), as is narrative space: "The distance from the gate to the Grange is two miles: I believe I managed to make it four; what with losing myself among the trees, and sinking up to the neck in snow" (38). Within these coordinates, traditional means of marking become treacherous or useless: "and, as we floundered on, my companion wearied me with constant reproaches that I had not brought a pilgrim's staff: telling me I could never get into the house without one, and boastfully flourishing a heavy-headed cudgel, which I understood to be so denominated" (27). Or they have been reduced, as Jacobs points out, to traces (73): "I had remarked on one side of the road, at intervals of six or seven yards, a line of upright stones . . . these were erected, and daubed with lime on purpose to serve as guides in the dark . . . but, excepting a dirty dot pointing up here and there, all traces of their existence had vanished; and my companion found it necessary to warn me frequently to steer to the right or left, when I imagined I was following, correctly, the windings of the road"(38). Miller reads this passage as an emblem of the difficulties encountered by the reader who enters the text of the novel (57–58), difficulties analogous to those encountered by the reader who enters the hermeneutic circle of the sacred text. How do we find our way into a text such as Matthew 18, which contains both the commandment to become as a little child, and sins to the number of seventy times seven? In Lockwood's two dreams, projected from Branderham's authoritative title and the marginalized authority of a child's handwriting, imaginative response to a text leads to nightmarish violence committed either on the dreamer or by the dreamer.

The superposing of repetition, as elements from Matthew 18 are repeated in Branderham's and Catherine's texts and then projected and repeated in Lockwood's dream, upon the linear narrative of *Wuthering Heights* is a principal source of our sense of the uncanny in the novel. The text seems to be trying to obey two contradictory sets of narrative laws simultaneously.[9] One set of laws has for its ground a conception of meaning that construes characters and events symbolically and mythically, inviting us to read the story of the generations of Wuthering Heights as a repetition of the generations of Hagar and Abraham, condemned again to set their hands against each other, or at least until some form of new dispensation restores the second Catherine and Hareton Earnshaw to their birthrights at their wedding on New Year's Day.

The second set proceeds on the basis of historical analysis, locating the source of its narrative in the introduction of the alien child, Heathcliff, into the closed society of Wuthering Heights, and tracing out a complex pattern of cause and effect as the result of his arrival. From this perspective, the novel looks something like a controlled experiment, as if Heathcliff were an unknown organism introduced into a Petrie dish containing an already known and limited set of organisms, so that one could write the result of that introduction as a nonreversible equation.

What have been identified variously as the metaphysical, the supernatural, and the mythical aspects of *Wuthering Heights* belong to the first set of rules, and if the novel followed only those rules, its meaning would derive from its imitation of sacred history, as it does in *The Faerie Queene*, or, to bring us closer to Brontë, in "The Rime of the Ancient Mariner" and "Michael." As Frye puts it, "polysemous meaning is a feature of all deeply serious writing, and the Bible is the model for serious writing" (221). Seen in that light, the large narrative structure reproduces the tragicomic pattern of the Bible, and the appropriate techniques for reading it would be those developed for reading sacred history, or texts whose authority derives from sacred history, such as *Paradise Lost* or *Pilgrim's Progress*. As Coleridge said, we must read the Bible as we would read any other book, by which he may well have meant that we must read any book as we read the Bible (41, 62). All narratives, however displaced, are reproductions of an *Urtext*.

But, just as Catherine's "An awful Sunday" is immediately followed by a rebellious entry into secular, historical time, so Nelly's narrative historicizes and individualizes the exemplary and typical characters Lockwood meets at Wuthering Heights, gives them psychologies, and sets them in their historically specific socio-economic context. Here, the appropriate reading techiques are those for realistic fiction: attention to reliability of the narrator, psychological analysis of character, analysis of the ideology of form — in short, the repertoire of techniques that allows us to elucidate the text as a diachronic cultural production.

But these techniques themselves, for all their present sophistication, may have at least a part of their origins in interpretive strategies that came into being when the Bible was placed in the hands of the laity. We may note here Matthew Arnold's insistence on the appropriateness of the techniques of literary criticism to the reading of the Bible as a diachronically produced text, a gesture meant to save the Bible as a guiding, but not divinely infallible, text for a laity confused by the Higher Criticism and the findings of contemporary science on the one hand, and the assertions of dogmatic theology on the other. For Arnold's lay reader, the Bible becomes a poetic text that serves, like other poetic texts, as a guide to moral conduct, which is "three fourths of life." If, at this point, Arnold's Bible still has enough authority to keep it from becoming a completely secular text, the thrust of his critical strategy is to make it as available to the non-specialist as other canonical texts that provide the literate layman with "the best that is known and thought in the world" (3: 268).[10]

It would seem virtually inevitable that the shift from a Catholic tradition that located authority within the hierarchical community of the Church, to one that defined authority as the Bible in relation to the individual reader would lead, first, to the problem of understanding as such, then to the epistemological question of how we understand, and finally to the issue of discourse itself, as cultural-linguistic production. To follow this process is to trace the history both of philosophy, as it developed in Protestant Europe from Locke to Kant, Hegel, and Marx, and the development of critical theories brought to bear on sacred and, finally, secular texts.

Hans Frei's history of the development of philological and historical criticism in Germany for the analysis of Biblical narrative points out that the production of narrative theory was not paralleled by the production of a body of German secular fictional narrative. The reverse was true in England, which indeed produced a profusion of fictional narratives, but remained virtually untouched by German textual scholarship until some years after Emily Brontë's death (142). The fictional and critical traditions finally come together in England in George Eliot, whose novels followed her translations of Strauss and Feuerbach, and whose agnostic historicism is conditioned by their texts.

By inviting us simultaneously to apply mutually exclusive techniques of reading to its layered text, *Wuthering Heights* poses the hermeneutic problem in acute form. Are its central figures avatars, or are they historically specific personages, and by what authority can we say they are either the one or the other? Does the novel's textual authority come from its adumbration of a sacred text, such as Matthew 18, and the larger tragicomic pattern of Biblical history? Or does it come from the secular historical conduct of Nelly's narrative, her effort to trace out a pattern of cause and effect that accounts for two generations of Lintons and Earnshaws? Does the novel attempt to save us from a nightmare of freefloating signifiers that seem to be detached from their signifieds by plunging us into history, or is history as mere quantitative duration the nightmare into which we are plunged when signifiers and signified are sundered, when the creating word is no longer the Logos?

We cannot know Brontë's intention. What we can see, however, is that *Wuthering Heights* not only raises the issue of historical transition from an agrarian, hierarchical social order to a newly emerging capitalist economy, as Marxist critics have shown us, or that it challenges androcentric culture, as feminist critics have demonstrated, but also that it forces us to consider the issue of narrative authority itself as narrative moves from a teleologically conceived understanding of history to an attempt to understand historical process realistically and scientifically. This shift is evident in the replacement of the older, typological interpretations of the authoritative text of Europe, the Bible, by philological and hermeneutic criticism.

In *Wuthering Heights*, the narrative itself enacts this shift. Dislocating itself from the authority of the unspoken or unread sacred text, it proposes to read the phenomenal field at the opening of the novel in the terms of historical realism, but it cannot hold its data to strict accountability. The child Catherine, defiantly entering the novel in her own historical voice from the margins of Branderham's discourse, is transformed in Lockwood's second dream both to the archetypal child waif of folklore, and the representative of innocence, the "little child" of Matthew 18, whose destiny is the kingdom of Heaven. So, throughout the novel, the repressed text reveals its traces, refiguring linear chronology as repetition, transformation, and revision. As the novel concludes, Nelly seeks finally to anchor the text in the reality of history, but cannot. She ends her narrative by describing a meeting with another child:

> I was going to the Grange one evening — a dark evening threatening thunder — and, just at the turn of the Heights, I encountered a little boy with a sheep and two lambs before him; he was crying terribly, and I supposed the lambs were skittish, and would not be guided.
>
> "What is the matter, my little man?" I asked.
>
> "They's Heathcliff and a woman, yonder, under t' Nab," he blubbered, "un' Aw durnut pass 'em."
>
> I saw nothing; but neither the sheep nor he would go on, so I bid him take the road lower down.
>
> He probably raised the phantoms from thinking, as he traversed the moors alone, on the nonsense he had heard his parents and companions repeat — yet still, I don't like being out in the dark, now — and I don't like being left by myself in this grim house — (412–413)

The child — and perhaps the sheep and lambs as well — refuse to go on because of ghostly presences, while the strict historical eye of Nelly sees nothing. But the uncanny textual trace surfaces in Nelly's admission of her fear of "being out in the dark." For the historical, or realistic narrative of *Wuthering Heights* to establish itself as authoritative, it would have to demystify the appearance of uncanny repetitions by subjecting them to the scrutiny of analysis, exposing them as anachronistic habits of mind persisting now only at the level of folk-culture — the "nonsense" passed from generation to generation that Nelly hears from the little shepherd. But the atavistic power of signs, dislocated as they are from an initiating text, and persisting as traces, refuses to be reinscribed within the discourse of realism. If, as Jameson asserts, the text is a symbolic act that stages a "polemic and strategic ideological confrontation" (85), *Wuthering Heights* poses that confrontation as a struggle for textual authority between systems of reading that would validate the authority of one text at the cost of the other.

Michigan State University

NOTES

1. Terry Eagleton provides a nice example of the currant/lower crux: "Winnifrith declares himself puzzled by Mrs. Leavis's point that the action of Hareton and Catherine in replacing the Heights' currant-bushes with flowers symbolizes the triumph of capitalist over yeoman, but Mrs. Leavis is surely right: flowers are a form of 'surplus value,' redundant luxuries in the spare Heights world" (117).
2. For an interpretation of the possible significance of these Biblical citations, see Knoepflmacher 85–88. See also Jacobs 76–77 and Davies 130–32.
3. Jacobs (65–67) takes issue with Frank Kermode as to whether or not the varieties of Catherine's names scratched into the paint form a series or are, instead, random.
4. Ermarth's theoretical exposition, focused primarily on one formal aspect of realism, is contained in her initial chapter. "The Premises of Realism," 3–37. For other approaches to the definition of realism in nineteenth-century fiction, see Levine 5; Said 143; Jameson 152; for a nineteenth-century definition, see Masson 253–56.
5. For a detailed survey of the history of the development of strategies for the interpretation of Biblical narrative from the Reformation through Schleiermacher, see Hans Frei.
6. Miller refers to Freud on the uncanny (1982: 69).
7. Catherine's diary, Lockwood's journal, and Nelly's narrative provide enough specific information in the form of dates, weather, and lunar phases to provoke scholars into creating a chronology for the novel, the most detailed of which are Charles Percy Sanger's and A. Stuart Daley's (handily reprinted in the Norton Critical Edition of *Wuthering Heights* (3rd ed. [New York: W. W. Norton, 1990] 331–52). Even here, however, error slips in, and is silently continued in critics who use their work for reference. Somehow, Catherine's diary entry in Chapter III concerning her "scamper on the moors" with Heathcliff is conflated with their excursion to Thrushcross Grange (see, for instance, Jacobs: "The first actual break between the child-lovers occurs at the gap in the diary text, a gap that marks their scamper to Thrushcross Grange" 74). When Nelly recounts the Thrushcross Grange episode in Chapter VI, however, Catherine does not return to Wuthering Heights with Heathcliff. The two scampers cannot be the same, because Catherine's diary records her return to Wuthering Heights with Heathcliff, and their subsequent punishment by Hindley.
8. In his "Preface" to *Cain*, Byron identifies himself as a scrupulous reader of Scripture, in contradistinction to "the Rabbins and the Fathers" on the issue of Eve's temptation. His Eve is tempted by the Serpent, rather than by Satan; thus, Byron "corrects" both a tradition of Scriptural interpretation, and Milton (520–21).

9. Nancy Armstrong makes a similar point: "problems are posed and questions asked in one set of literary conventions that cannot be answered by the other, which is to say what most critical readings strive to deny, that this is an essentially disjunctive novel" (253).
10. The crucial texts are *Literature and Dogma* (6: 139–411) and *God and the Bible* (7: 139–398). Arnold very deliberately makes his plea for the retention of the Bible in government sponsored schools in cultural, historical, and literary terms (6: 499–506).

WORKS CITED

Armstrong, Nancy. "Emily Brontë In and Out of Her Time." *Genre* XV (1982): 243–64.
Arnold, Matthew. *Complete Prose Works.* Ed. R. H. Super. 11 vols. Ann Arbor: U of Michigan P, 1960–77.
Blake, William. *The Poetry and Prose.* Ed. David Erdman. rev. ed. Garden City: Doubleday, 1970.
Brontë, Emily. *Wuthering Heights.* Ed. Hilda Marsden and Ian Jack. Oxford: Clarendon Press, 1976.
Byron, George Gordon. *Poetical Works.* 1904. Ed. Frederick Page. Oxford: Oxford UP, 1970.
Coleridge, Samuel Taylor. *Confessions of an Inquiring Spirit.* Ed. H. StJ. Hart. London: Black, 1956.
Davies, Stevie. *Emily Brontë.* Key Women Writers. New York: Harvester-Wheatsheaf, 1988.
Eagleton, Terry. *Myths of Power: A Marxist Study of the Brontës.* London: Macmillan, 1975.
Ermarth, Elizabeth Deeds. *Realism and Consensus in the English Novel.* Princeton: Princeton UP, 1983.
Fish, Stanley. *Surprised by Sin: The Reader in "Paradise Lost."* London: Macmillan, 1967.
Frei, Hans. *The Eclipse of Biblical Narrative: A Study in Eighteenth and Nineteenth Century Hermeneutics.* New Haven: Yale UP, 1974.
Frye, Northrop. *The Great Code: The Bible and Literature.* New York: Harcourt, 1981.
Gilbert, Sandra, and Susan Gubar. *The Madwoman in the Attic: The Woman Writer and the Nineteenth Century Literary Imagination.* New Haven: Yale UP, 1984.
Homans, Margaret. *Bearing the Word: Language and Female Experience in Ninteenth-Century Women's Writing.* Chicago: U of Chicago P, 1986.
Jacobs, Carol. *Uncontainable Romanticism: Shelley, Brontë, Kleist.* Baltimore: Johns Hopkins UP, 1989.
Jameson, Fredric. *The Political Unconscious: Narrative as a Socially Symbolic Act.* Ithaca: Cornell UP, 1981.
Kincaid, James. "Coherent Readers, Incoherent Texts." *Critical Inquiry* III: 781–802.
Knoepflmacher, U. C. *Emily Brontë: Wuthering Heights.* Cambridge: Cambridge UP, 1989.
Levine, George. *The Realistic Imagination: English Fiction from Frankenstein to Lady Chatterley.* Chicago: U of Chicago P, 1981.
Masson, David. *British Novelists and Their Styles: Being a Critical Sketch of the History of English Prose Style.* Boston: Willard and Small, 1892.
Miller, J. Hillis. *The Disappearance of God: Five Nineteenth-Century Writers.* New York: Schocken, 1965.

————. *Fiction and Repetition: Seven English Novels*. Cambridge: Harvard UP, 1982.

Said, Edward. *Beginnings: Intention and Method*. New York: Columbia UP, 1985.

Shelley, Percy Bysshe. *Complete Poetical Works*. Ed. Thomas Hutchison. London: Oxford UP, 1960.

Taylor, Irene. *Holy Ghosts: The Male Muses of Emily and Charlotte Brontë*. New York: Columbia UP, 1990.

Tillotson, Kathleen. *Novels of the Eighteen-Forties*. 1954. London: Oxford UP, 1961.

Van Ghent, Dorothy. *The English Novel: Form and Function*. New York: Harper, 1961.

"A DULL BOOK IS EASILY
RENOUNCED"

By Patricia Meyer Spacks

AN EVIDENTLY "BORING" BOOK typically attracts little critical attention, except from those who wish to be clever at its expense. When, on the other hand, the right people — not the masses who determine rankings on the bestseller list, but the denizens of New York and Cambridge and Berkeley literary cocktail parties — find a work "interesting," they thereby imply that it justifies serious investigation. *Boring* and *interesting* are not critical adjectives — my freshman English teacher told me that — but the subjective responses that they designate establish a precondition for criticism or make criticism impossible.

The term *boring*, like its converse, comprises an indispensable item in the vocabularies of late-twentieth-century children, adolescents, and adults. More-over, it has acquired critical authority beyond its literal meaning. Applied to books, it possesses a power to damn currently far beyond that of such a phrase as "morally corrupt," once comparably potent. We know, of course, that books, like hula hoops, have their day and disappear. Initially objects of intense and widespread interest, such works as *Sir Charles Grandison* (1753) and *Coelebs in Search of a Wife* (the once immensely popular novel by Hannah More, published in 1809) passed within a half century of their first publication into the limbo of the self-evidently boring. This particular mode of dismissal, however, constitutes a relatively new phenomenon. Although most books have always had a short shelf-life, *boring* has not always been the way to register their loss of immediacy.

The notion of boredom, in fact, is a rather recent invention. According to the *OED*, the word *bore* and its cognates appeared from nowhere "after 1755," with no traceable etymology. *Ennui*, an ancient word in French, had been natu-ralized into English only at the end of the seventeenth century. It appears that English culture in the eighteenth century suddenly required an idea it had not previously needed. I shall not at the moment speculate about why the need arose at precisely this historical moment or attempt a history of how a word initially designating a temporary state of mind gradually turned into a powerful vehicle of denunciation, dismissal, and complaint. Instead, I propose to investigate possible hidden cultural agendas implicit in the shifting levels of interest assigned to a single novel. Mrs. Humphry Ward's *Robert Elsmere* (1888) will constitute my test case.

The mutation in taste by which an interesting work becomes in a precisely equivalent sense boring provides a focus for interrogating the meaning of boredom as a cultural construct. (By "an interesting work" I mean one engaging to so many that "interesting," even in its relatively trivialized modern meaning, appears to constitute objective description.) At its own historical moment, *Robert Elsmere* seemed attractive; now most readers find it dull. What is at stake in such cultural oscillations of interest? How, exactly, *can* an "interesting" book become "boring"?

In the case of *Robert Elsmere*, a ready answer may occur to twentieth-century readers. Ward's novel, narrating a clergyman's intellectual, emotional, and physical career, concerns itself intensively with matters of theological controversy. Once upon a time, we surmise or know, people in general felt interested in that sort of thing. Now they feel the reverse of interest. What further explanation is needed?

The didacticism of *Robert Elsmere*, its employment of fictional devices to inculcate moral and/or theological doctrine, provokes premonitory yawns. J. Paul Hunter, writing of eighteenth-century didactic fiction, observes that

> The difficulty [didactic] focus has caused for modern readers is hard to calculate and almost impossible to exaggerate. The trouble is that readers of our time are not comfortable with such content, such aims, or the tones that support them. . . . All "period" literature — that is, any text that is firmly anchored in some historical present — sooner or later becomes problematic for subsequent readers with different knowledge and different needs, but modern and post-modern contexts of reading present special difficulties for certain traditional modes of writing. (225)

Of course it is by no means true that we automatically deplore the didactic: only such forms of didacticism as Hunter alludes to, those peculiar to distant historical moments. Instructional books fill bestseller lists of the 1990s, telling us how to lose weight, how to make a million dollars in real estate, how to heal our ailments with home remedies, how to become more assertive, how to find love. Not the fact but the nature of old didacticisms offends us. Offends us? These didacticisms *bore* us: we dismiss them.

What bores us never fully engages our attention. Yet boredom, as psychoanalysts have suggested, often contains hidden overtones of aggression. Otto Fenichel, for instance, puzzles over the difficulty of predicting "when a frustrating external world will mobilize aggressiveness in the subject, . . . and when it will be experienced as 'boring' " (301). If one takes seriously the charge that a book is boring — meaning that it bores many of its readers — it would seem appropriate to seek what kind of frustration the book induces, what aggressiveness it might release in those readers.

Such terminology makes no obvious sense in relation to a book like *Robert Elsmere*. What in the detailed record of a minister's moral struggles could possibly provoke aggressive feelings, or more than the most trivial frustration? The novel's utter irrelevance to the modern or postmodern situation seems the obvious reason to label it "boring." But that irrelevance may be more apparent than real, and something genuine is at stake in the dismissal of a work because of the boredom it allegedly generates.

In trying to suggest what may have made this outmoded novel "interesting" to its first readers, I hope simultaneously to discover why later audiences should dismiss it as "boring": to locate ways in which it may challenge our vital assumptions and senses in which its seriousness has become invisible. My argument will engage issues of legibility and of urgency. I shall contend that *Robert Elsmere*, offering covert as well as overt didactic messages, raises questions about how it should be read as well as unanswerable ones about how it *was* read. In what ways has its legibility altered? And finally I shall offer a hypothesis about why the notion of the boring possesses such energy in the late-twentieth-century critical imagination.

First, though, a disclaimer. Boredom implies — indeed, *is* — a refusal to pay attention. The self-cancelling aspect of such an enterprise as mine has become increasingly apparent to me. Books I too considered "boring" when I first read them now bore me no longer. A work that I here declare boring to twentieth-century sensibilities in fact interests me greatly — because I have paid close attention to it. Boredom both causes and is caused by failure or inability to attend. To focus on any work with intense awareness virtually guarantees finding it interesting — not attractive, necessarily, or admirable, but worthy from a historical or sociological or psychological or aesthetic point of view of the consideration one has given it. Yet the question of why people in general don't and won't pay attention to certain books in certain historical periods remains compelling, even though the object of study changes beneath one's eyes. If Adorno is right in characterizing taste as the seismograph of history,[1] shifts of taste that declare books once greatly admired no longer worth notice at all — not bad, exactly, just not interesting — have importance equivalent to that of our choice of "canonized" texts. They tell us what ideas we can no longer afford to admit to consciousness, as well as what forms of literary embodiment have come to seem meaningless. The relevant questions have nothing to do with whether *Robert Elsmere* "is" boring — only with the fact that many more readers now think it so than would have allowed themselves such a judgment in 1888.

Q. D. LEAVIS, contemplating the nature and the function of popular fiction, argues that it serves the important purpose of transmitting "cultural news" from one intellectual level to another. "Such work must be done in order that some kind of communication may be kept up, and only the novel can do it, for . . . the general reading public touches nothing more serious than the novel or newspaper" (71). Leavis alludes here to the state of things when she wrote, in 1932; her description would apply less precisely to the late nineteenth century. But she goes on to make a transhistorical point about the simplification involved in such cultural transmission: "A pertinent objection is that the process necessitates a simplification of the issues that lets slip the essentials and leaves only some unmeaning and often misleading facts. Hence this kind of novel dies as soon as it has begun to date" (71). By this argument, *Elsmere* would become boring as its doctrine no longer manifestly bears on most lives because of the nature not of its doctrine but of that doctrine's formulation — its alleged simplification to the point of meaninglessness. In contrast, *Paradise Lost* and *The Divine Comedy* retain imaginative life for twentieth-century audiences because they communicate doctrine in complex form.

The argument contradicts the more familiar assumption that Milton, for instance, survives by virtue of nondoctrinal attributes: the power of his language and verse, the vigor of his fable and his characters. Leavis suggests that any doctrine that challenges the intellect by its intricacy and energy can hold the interest even of those who do not believe it. She suggests also a snobbish and ahistorical conviction that what fails to interest a reader like herself by that failure declares its inadequacy.

Robert Elsmere, which Leavis cites as a book interesting in its own time but not in hers, seemed to no less a personage than the Prime Minister of England an important work, worthy of extended attention. But William Gladstone, like Leavis, experiences not the slightest doubt of his authority to declare "intolerably dull" works esteemed by his predecessors:

> Those who have systems or hypotheses to recommend in philosophy, conduct, or religion induct them into the costume of romance. . . . When this was done in *Télémaque, Rasselas*, or *Coelebs*, it was not without literary effect. Even the last of these three appears to have been successful with its own generation. It would now be deemed intolerably dull. But a dull book is easily renounced. The more didactic fictions of the present day, so far as I know them, are not dull. We take them up, however, and we find that, when we meant to go to play, we have gone to school. (Gladstone 766)

The writer feels confident that the didactic novels of his own day (he alludes specifically to *Robert Elsmere*, subject of his 22-page review) will not prove vulnerable to repudiation. Less than fifty years later, Leavis would mention Ward's novel as representative of books "long forgotten though they caused mighty reverberations in their day" (71).

Within two months of its first publication, *Robert Elsmere* achieved its fourth edition. Two months later, the seventh full-price edition had appeared (Smith 33–34). The huge library sale of the book meant "that in the large cities of Britain Mrs Humphry Ward had become a cult author" (Sutherland 126). Half a million copies sold in the United States within a year (E. Jones 82). "The popularity of *Robert Elsmere*," Enid Jones writes, "was as sudden and amazing as a tidal wave" (85). John Sutherland alludes with some bewilderment to a "buying and reading mania in Britain, America and even Europe" — adding, rather gratuitously, that *Robert Elsmere* "is not to modern eyes a very readable novel" (130).

"The success of this novel," observes a contemporaneous reviewer in *The Quarterly Review*, "is the most interesting, and in some respects the most instructive, literary event of the present year" ("Robert Elsmere and Christianity" 273). The event's "interest," it seems, derives from the religious controversy the novel dramatizes. "Few persons would be at the trouble to read through so long a novel, for the sake of its romantic episodes, who were not chiefly interested in the religious struggle which it depicts" (274). Although the reviewer finds many novelistic virtues in the fiction, he considers its religious interest fundamental. And he objects intensely to the religious ideas. Early in his long essay, he claims, in patronizing terms, that he will not "censure" the author:

> We refrain, in deference partly to Mrs. Ward's services in other departments of learning, partly to her earnestness and sincerity, and partly to her sex, from expressing the censure which would ordinarily be due to a writer who engaged in an attack upon the received Christian faith with so imperfect a knowledge of the present conditions of the controversy, and consequently with such inevitable misrepresentation. (275)

But the review's subsequent pages consist mainly of detailed quarrels with the religious positions of individual characters in Ward's novel. The reviewer approves only of Robert's pious wife, Catherine, and suggests that Elsmere should simply have consulted her: she would have restored his faith (298). "The victory in this story, to our minds, remains with Catherine," he concludes, praising her for her "instinctive revulsion," her "distrust," and her "loathing" of heterodox positions (302).

The intensity with which the reviewer involves himself in the novel's religious controversy provides direct evidence of how imaginatively and emotionally compelling *Robert Elsmere* appeared to its first readers. Gladstone's sympathetic and perceptive account reveals less immediate involvement but a comparable assumption that one must take this work very seriously indeed. "If it be difficult to persist [in reading *Robert Elsmere*]," he remarks, "it is impossible to stop" (767). He locates the novel's power in its characterization, finding its doctrinal debates unpersuasive. The real battle, he maintains, takes place not about religion but about marriage — "fought in a hundred rounds, between Elsmere and Catherine" (769). (I think he is quite right, and I shall return to this point.) And he summarizes more precisely than does the other reviewer I have quoted the nature of Ward's theological enterprise, saying of the book,

> It may, I think, be fairly described as a devout attempt, made in good faith, to simplify the difficult mission of religion in the world by discarding the supposed lumber of the Christian theology, while retaining and applying, in their undiminished breadth of scope, the whole personal, social, and spiritual morality which has now, as matter of fact, entered into the patrimony of Christendom. (777)

Gladstone's *now* is crucial: Ward's novel belongs peculiarly to its historical moment. As Andrew Lang put it, in another contemporaneous comment, the novel offers "a vast and crowded picture of our distracted age" (814). The word *modern* recurs frequently in *Robert Elsmere*, especially toward the end, to emphasize that the intellectual conflict central to the plot uniquely characterizes the late nineteenth century. Although Elsmere's decline in orthodox Christian faith and his development of a substitute form of theism plus good works derives from personal experience, from accidents of association and of character, it depends heavily, the narrator often points out, on his period's intellectual and religious history. Catherine, clinging to a kind of faith that in her father was already "old-fashioned," refuses to march with the times. But even she, the narrator observes, has changed her views more than she realizes, by virtue of imperceptible pressures felt by all thinking people. In the context Ward predicates for it, *modern* connotes responsiveness to intellectual currents from the Continent, faint skepticism about established truth, awareness of recent scientific discovery, uneasiness about such discovery's religious meaning. The word's significations, for Ward, center on the intellectual, the locus of significance for the novel's protagonist.

"The decisive events of the world take place in the intellect." Robert quotes this line, without attribution, adding that "It is the mission of books that they help one to remember it" (Ward 197). Reader, writer, and thinker, Robert believes himself to have discovered by historical research the illogicality of Christian faith — having learned how cavalierly early writers handled evidence, he can no longer believe in miracles. He must relinquish his role as clergyman, give up the village life he enjoys, and cause his beloved wife immeasurable anguish. His story recapitulates many a Victorian crisis of faith and accords such crises intellectual dignity. Insisting on its own modernity as well as its intellectual seriousness, it presumably attracted at least some of its original readers by just these means, implicitly promising that they would understand their own immediate experience better for reading it.

Although a man fills the title role, two women — Catherine and her sister Rose — share narrative interest. Rose inhabits a conventional romance plot with a difference: she insists against all obstacles on preparing herself as a professional musician. (This vocation, however, in the event serves mainly to make her attractive to London society and to draw two men to her.) Catherine, on the other hand, embodies traditionally female ways of being. She cares for her invalid mother, she ardently performs charitable works, she devotes herself, once married, to husband and child. An old-fashioned woman, a New Woman, a saintly man, and (by way of lover for Rose) an attractive, rich, aristocratic man: the novel offers something for everyone.

Its ostensible plot concerns a clergyman's loss of faith and his simultaneous and subsequent moral exaltation. By the time Robert dies, having exhausted himself in the service of the poor and of his moral vision, he has achieved virtual sainthood. Certainly the reviewers showed some justice in attacking Ward's dangerous theological position. She apotheosizes a man who has systmatically and logically rejected the Christian revelation, offering detailed arguments to support his rejection. The suffering he endures as consequence of his loss of faith only increases his heterodox heroism. No representative of orthodox Christianity in the novel manifests comparable breadth of understanding or energy in good works. The Victorian reader must have felt a thrill of rebelion in the very act of contemplating such a figure as Robert, with such a career.

Yet the novel makes a more complicated claim on our attention than by its exploration of the theologically unorthodox. Its effect, for attentive readers now and presumably for attentive readers always, depends on the coexistence of two other plots. If the action involving Rose clearly constitutes a subplot, the events dependent on Catherine's nature and situation possess importance comparable to that of the Robert-plot. Ward's imagining of Catherine, a devout Christian utterly committed to her father's theology, allows her no rebellion. Her dedication to her husband wavers no more than does her devotion to Christ. She conforms to the standards of the good Victorian woman. Yet the reviewer who thought that Robert should simply allow Catherine to eradicate his religious doubts missed a great deal in this good woman's characterization. Like Robert himself, Catherine is allotted an inner life of some complexity.

Her initial attraction for Robert derives from the sense she conveys of hidden realities. Robert finds her "interesting."

> She had not yet said a direct word to him, and yet he was curiously convinced that here was one of the most interesting persons, and one of the persons most interesting to *him*, that he had ever met. What mingled delicacy and strength in the hand that had lain beside her on the dinner table — what potential depths of feeling in the full dark-fringed eye! (35)

"One of the most interesting persons" (as opposed to "interesting to *him*") suggests the old meaning of *interesting* as "significant." Catherine possesses both moral importance and emotional appeal. And Robert's diagnosis of her proves accurate: "delicacy and strength" indeed characterize the young woman. As for the "potential depths of feeling" in her eye, that Victorian code for erotic appeal — Ward comprehends (although Robert does not) not only erotic potential but the possibility of its transmutation into other forms of energy. Before and after marriage, Catherine specializes in sublimation.

Despite the fact that Catherine seems the very type of the good Victorian woman, tireless in service to others, dedicated to God and to a life of taking care, Ward avoids or reverses many gender stereotypes: another ground of "interest" in her novel. Robert, official representative of the religious establishment, has entered the ministry on the basis not of intellect (despite his and his creator's high evaluation of the intellectual) but of feeling. Although his intellectual brilliance has brought him academic success, he remains — before and after his marriage — largely governed by feeling, particularly tender feeling. Ward makes the point emphatically and repeatedly, analyzing Robert's attitudes toward the squire (a determined and intelligent atheist and a fine historian, whose beliefs and books finally draw Robert away from the Church, but also a pathetic man), toward the squire's steward (bitter and destructive, but a man whose pathos Robert also perceives), toward the poor and the sick, in a rural village and in London. Full of religious, erotic, and filial passion, Elsmere remains a man of integrity, but feeling largely controls his destiny. (Lang suggests that even his loss of faith stems from his pre-existent "fever of unrest, and of anxiety," product of exhaustion [822].) In this respect he conforms more nearly to a conventionally "feminine" than to a "masculine" type. Moreover, from childhood on he suffers spells of illness brought on by the sheer intensity of his feelings and his life. His state intermittently verges on invalidism. He ends the novel, and his life, in a tubercular "decline," like many a fictional heroine. Like a heroine too, he finds himself, in all innocence, the object of attempted sexual seduction. His purity protects him; he escapes the designing female's wiles, but feels, as a maiden might, . . . soiled.

Catherine, on the other hand, despite her orthodox good womanhood, reveals certain stereotypically "masculine" aspects. Most conspicuously, she likes to govern and, in her family of origin, governs well. When we first encounter her, as the angel of her Yorkshire village, she controls her own household (a mother and two sisters), authorized by the dying injunctions of her father. Her determination has prevented Rose from leaving the village to study music abroad. Indeed, she has kept the entire family from abandoning the countryside her father loved. She identifies strongly with her dead father (as Robert identifies with his mother). After her marriage, she happily falls into the role of helpmeet, yet her will and her principles remain powerful. In some ways she appears the stronger of the novel's two central characters. Although she accepts (perforce) Robert's decision to leave the Church and goes with him to London, her silent, steady resistance to him never diminishes. The Angel in the House, in this incarnation, proves not altogether easy to live with.

The marriage of such beings promises — and delivers — drama. Gladstone's perception of that marriage as the novel's center of interest calls attention to difficulties at the heart of the Elsmeres' family relations. Robert and Catherine struggle for control: over systems of belief, over how they shall live. Predictably, the struggle ends in the woman's submission: "white and pure and drooping, her force of nature all dissolved, lost in this new heavenly weakness of love" (531). Robert's "sensitive optimist nature" (528), shocked by a would-be seductress's advances, leads him toward new affirmation of connubial love as the greatest of earthly goods. "One task of all tasks had been set him from the beginning — to keep his wife's love!" (529). Domesticity, that traditional preserve of the feminine, triumphs. But if Robert learns that he must value his wife's love above all else, his wife learns that his way of thinking must be respected as highly as her own. Impossible, finally, that she should be right and he wrong: the reviewer who thought that Robert would regain his faith if he only consulted Catherine must ignore the ideological weight of the conclusion.

The affirmation of marriage by no means constitutes a happy ending, from the "masculine" or the "feminine" point of view. It depends too heavily on compromise, on the tempering of conviction and passion on both sides. Infused with awareness of the necessity of reliquishment, with an almost Johnsonian sense of the emotional insufficiency of human experience, this resolution — the Elsmeres live happily together until Robert's death, which follows with considerable speed — issues from a realism startling in its bleakness. If religion does not create happiness or certitude, neither does romance, parenthood, or family life. Ward's novel proves iconoclastic not only in its challenging of orthodox religious pieties but in its questioning of domestic ones. Happy families are all alike, it suggests, specifically in the compromises they have made to achieve relative contentment.

The Rose story, superficially a predictable romance, reinforces the novel's message that experience inevitably proves painful and flawed. Never imagined as fully as Catherine, Rose seems from the outset morally inadequate in her self-will and her thirst for glamor as well as for music. Her flashes of authenticity appear mainly in her more reprehensible moments, as when she reflects, "Robert has been too successful in his life, I think" (263) — calling herself a "wretch" for thinking it. Her infatuation with Robert's academic friend Langham, quite evidently a misdirected passion, guarantees its own frustration. The rich, aristocratic, intelligent, kind lover Ward finally conjures up for her has rather too much the air of *deus ex machina*: his many virtues appear to guarantee his wife's happiness, but by the time Rose accepts Flaxman, the reader knows that not even rich, aristocratic, intelligent, kind lovers insure contentment. A "loose end" has been built into Rose's character, in her passion for music. Although she has never quite committed herself to a professional career, she has clearly established her longing for more than ordinary social life has to offer. It appears unlikely that Flaxman will gratify such longing. One kind of storybook marriage or another, all will detail the relinquishment of dreams. All demand concessions. All exemplify the radical imperfection of human experience. And, remarkably for a Victorian novel, *Robert Elsmere* holds out little hope that the afterlife will compensate for the insufficiencies of earthly eventualities (although it *does* imagine happy reunions in the hereafter, which presumably offset the specific trials of experienced relationship).

For a reviewer to locate a novel's central struggle in the realm of domestic relations and then pay relatively little attention to it directs attention once more to the problematic of "interest." Gladstone contends that the important conflict in *Robert Elsmere* concerns not religion but marriage, yet the substance of his review focuses on theological rather than domestic problems. The religious could be assumed as self-evidently important; domestic concerns belonged by custom to the conventionally trivialized world of women. Does Gladstone find the struggle between Robert and Catherine "interesting" or consider it a fictional fact with no necessary effect on the reader? And what of the hundreds of thousands of others who composed the original audience? Did the massed attention of those buyers direct itself to the novel's debates over the divinity of Christ or to the drama of marital compromise or to both? Or did they claim to care about the theological while actually interesting themselves in the marital?

Such questions are not only unanswerable but in a sense meaningless, since reading remains an individual act performed by readers with individual characters and histories and consequently individual interests. Yet *Robert Elsmere* in 1888 constituted a cultural event, its popularity a mass phenomenon. To wonder why a fiction now relatively devoid of life should once have seemed so compelling inevitably involves one in speculation about what would have engaged the interests of inhabitants in another culture. And Gladstone's comment about the marital "battle" provides a specific focus for such speculation — although no answer to the questions it implies.

The thematic of interest and boredom sketched within the text of *Robert Elsmere* makes the specific locations of human interest an urgent matter. At the outset, the attitude toward boredom appears altogether predictable. Rose and Agnes, Catherine's other sister, find the rural valley they inhabit dull; so does the vicar's wife, Mrs. Thornburgh, when her plots for arranging marriages seem not to work out well. Boredom implies disengagement. Catherine, deeply engaged in the human life around her, could not possibly feel bored. But her engagement itself irritates and dispirits her sisters, who can joke together about, for instance, Robert as an "interesting stranger" and convey with every word their irksome sense that in fact nothing interesting can be expected to happen where they live. And it's Catherine's fault that they live there.

Robert, as we have already seen, constructs Catherine as "interesting" virtually from the first moment he sees her. He then goes on to take lively interest in all his surroundings, animate and inanimate, and to create for himself a vivid existence by virtue of the vitality of his attention. Catherine, with her intense inner life, also continues to find her experience interesting. But others, lacking the same imaginative and moral capacities, suffer the reiterated fate of boredom. Rose, for instance, considers not only her village but, on occasion, even London tedious. Langham — who fears from Rose the judgment, "You are not interesting — no, not a bit!" (168) — suffers "boredom with the whole proceeding" (177) when he goes to church (although Robert's sermon interests him more than he anticipates), feels conscious that "his friend's social enthusiasms bored him a great deal" (200), and describes his life as one of ever-diminishing interest (218–19). The Squire determines his own course of action often on the basis of his fear of boredom. Flaxman, an epicure of feeling, seeks new experience to avert boredom. Mme. de Netteville, Robert's would-be seductress, gains social position by her "most remarkable power of protecting herself and her neighbours from boredom" (514). (In this as in other nineteenth-century novels, inhabitants of society's upper reaches prove particularly vulnerable to boredom.)

Implicit moral condemnation hovers around boredom's victims, whose disengagement appears to declare their lack of self-discipline — almost an eighteenth-century view of things. But a life rich in interest does not necessarily merit approval. When Robert faces himself and his failings after Madame de Netteville's attempt on his virtue, he concludes that if his wife "had slipped away from him, to the injury and moral lessening of both, on his cowardice, on his clumsiness, be the blame! Above all, on his fatal power of absorbing himself in a hundred outside interests, controversy, literature, society" (529). To designate as a "fatal power" the capacity for large interest reminds the reader of the high moral stakes implicit in every choice. Perhaps it suggests also what is at issue for that reader in responding to the text.

For choice inheres in the reader's locations of interest as in those of the characters. In *Robert Elsmere*, I have claimed two centers of interest: the public, "masculine" sphere of theology and the private, "feminine" locus of domesticity. When Robert goes through his agony of self-realization, his imagination turns from the scene of seduction to "the image of a new-made mother, her child close within her sheltering arm" (529). As Robert lies dying, his watching wife sees a vision of Christ, but the dying man himself, in an "ecstasy of joy," calls out, *"The child's cry! — thank God!"* Catherine realizes "that he stood again on the stairs at Murewell in that September night which gave them their first-born, and that he thanked God because her pain was over" (604). At these crucial junctures, the domestic, in its specificity and emotional energy, takes precedence over the conventionally religious. Indeed, it defines a new realm of spirituality.

The "public" readers of *Robert Elsmere*, the reviewers, treat theology as the novel's central concern, but it is not hard to imagine people (especially female people) reading otherwise. The two fulcrums of interest in effect organize radically different novels. One tells the story of a heroic man who in the course of a self-abnegating career locates for himself a new spiritual center of gravity, whose generosity includes and forgives and accepts the relatively rigid and narrow orientation of the woman he marries. The other focuses on a heroic woman whose considerable gifts realize themselves only in devotion to others. The man she marries, using his intellect to explore uncharted paths, becomes other than she thought him. Unable, emotionally as well as legally, to leave her husband, dependent on him for her work and for her identity, suffering, as Lang puts it, in "silent misery [which] is not a thing to be read about without pain" (823), she realizes that "Her life had been caught and nipped in the great inexorable wheel of things. It would go in some sense maimed to the end" (558). The awkward metaphor, joining the colloquial sharpness of "nipped" with the clichéd vagueness of "the great inexorable wheel," conveys the harshness of Catherine's predicament. But the necessity of religious as well as marital devotion remains. She manages to believe that God can accept more than one way of approaching Him and to acknowledge the sufficiency of a marriage based on compromise.

Catherine's story is sadder than Robert's, and more persuasive. I think it, in fact, more *interesting*.

INSTEAD OF EXPLAINING why *Robert Elsmere* strikes modern readers as boring, I appear to have demonstrated why it does not bore me. My reaction emphasizes the possibility that women might read the novel in different ways from men but also the truth that reading attentively reveals "interesting" things to attend to in more than one aspect of the novel. Many early readers presumably found theological controversy more engaging than most twentieth-century audiences consider it, but we need not assume that interest in the theological necessarily precludes concern with the psychological and social. Widespread modern and postmodern distaste for theology no doubt insures that readers now approach *Robert Elsmere* with considerable skepticism, which may protect them from the impact of the novel's subtext about marriage. The large "public" subject of theological controversy provides a screen for domestic concerns, a screen whose sheer massiveness prevents its being readily set aside.

But the putative interest of Ward's novel and the boredom it allegedly generates bear a close relation to one another. Much depends on the expectations a reader brings to the text; much depends on selectivity. All reading is selective, as everyone knows who has had the experience of rereading a familiar novel and discerning in it altogether new meanings: literally seeing different things. Readers often account for such an experience in terms of their immediate life situation, but cultural pressures also help determine what one notices in a given text. Current readers are unlikely, for instance, to feel the emotional urgency of Elsmere's quandary over the historicity of miracles — partly because they *antici-pate* no genuine urgency in discussion of such matters. Newspaper, talk shows, and magazines reiterate tacit and explicit messages about what interests "us" — that largely fictional collectivity constituted by shared existence in the 1990s. We know in advance that debates over the divinity of Christ won't grab us. Such knowledge contaminates and controls responses to a text. Similar kinds of assumed knowledge enables readers of our era to recognize and dismiss signals of "sentimentality" or simple "romance" — signals abundantly supplied by *Robert Elsmere*. If an early reviewer could remark that few would read the book for its "romantic episodes," later readers can yet more readily judge such episodes worthless. The sources of interest and of boredom in Ward's novel, in short, are not just allied but identical (Robert's problem and its implications, Catherine's dilemma and its meanings): import depends on how you read.

Hunter remarks the tendency of early didactic novels "to pursue readers and pry into their private commitments" (225). This acute observation explains not why such works, when historically distanced, bore us but why once upon a time they bored almost no one. The didactic novelist's pursuit and prying forbid passivity. Soliciting the reader's active response, insisting on how much is at stake for everyone, they allow even repudiation — but not neutrality. Yet Ward's putative prying will no longer trouble most of those few who still pay attention to her: they won't even notice it. By another operation of selectivity, the challenge of *Robert Elsmere* has become inaudible. The sounds of pursuit fade away, the sense of urgency recedes. Failing to recognize Ward's prying into, for instance, the reader's romantic as well as religious faith, his or her belief in the possibilities of connubial bliss, we can adopt a serenely historical perspective and believe that the novel has nothing to do with *us*. We "know" in advance the irrelevance of the book's central concerns. The state of moral passivity implicit in the reader's refusal to engage expresses itself in the judgment that *Robert Elsmere* is boring.

Or does the twentieth-century reader in fact intuit a kind of prying that seems altogether intolerable? Does cultural guilt attend the general abandonment of the faith of our fathers and mothers, so that Ward's implicit interrogation of the grounds of her reader's belief touches a nerve? In an era of widespread marital instability, do reminders and questions about the costs of stability prove especially troubling?

That freshman English teacher of mine forbade us to use *interesting* and *boring* in our essays because such words expressed, he said, only personal feeling, not critical reflection. Yet to call *Robert Elsmere* boring reveals more than personal response even if it fails to convey serious critical contemplation.

Let me reiterate: once almost everyone found "interesting" this book that now bores all but a few. Such a shift of sensibility announces cultural change.

I can make up a story about what has happened here, about what ideas *Robert Elsmere* embodies that, as I put it earlier, we — our culture — can no longer afford to admit to consciousness, about how Ward's old-fashioned novel may still arouse the feelings of frustration and aggression that we conceal with a judgment of "boring." It would go like this. A century ago, a female novelist dramatized the notion that a man's crisis of faith in the divinity of Christ might generate a woman's crisis of faith in her husband ("He for God only, she for God in him . . ."). The fictional treatment of theological issues, although already old-fashioned, in the opinion of some reviewers and presumably some readers, aroused widespread interest testified not only by reviews but by enormous sales of Ward's book. More covertly, the novel's evocation of marital tension and the compromised resolution of that tension, one may surmise, also engaged many. Both subjects, clearly related to one another and presented with barely-concealed didactic purpose, rich in ideological implication, demanded of Victorian readers self-questioning about intimate commitments and intimate doubts. The interest of *Robert Elsmere* would have derived partly from the personal challenges it conveyed.

These challenges have not vanished, but they have become textually obscure and often personally offensive in an era when not everyone can assume or accept a connection between faith in Christ and in a spouse, when a woman's determined fidelity to a self-willed husband will elicit feminist blame more probably than praise, when theological disputes seem as outmoded as female submission to many Western minds, when most people no longer think of theology as part of ideology. *Robert Elsmere* embodies ideas that many, now that a prevailing ethos glorifies "self-fulfillment," feel actively reluctant to think about: for instance, the contention that everyone must bear responsibility for his or her beliefs and failures of belief, and the notion that no conceivable choice will guarantee satisfaction. Such views — we may wish to dismiss them as "Victorian views" — call into question dominant assumptions of our time. To take seriously the implications of *Robert Elsmere* might indeed provoke aggressive feelings. Far easier to declare the book boring: irrelevant.

Robert Elsmere not only does ideological work obviously acceptable at its cultural moment; it also raises questions about standard ideologies. It explores both the theological arguments against the divinity of Christ and the need for women to embrace less than they dream of, the heroism of intellectual exploration and that of domestic acceptance. Its legibility may have differed for men and women; it may differ now. But its high seriousness could still possess the possibility to disturb — if people read it seriously.

That is my story. Ward's novel implies other didacticisms besides those I have mentioned, and other versions of the explanatory story might fit other facts about the book. But if one accepts the insistence of *Robert Elsmere* that something important is at stake in choosing objects of interest, any such story must entertain the possibility that the repudiation implicit in dismissing a work as boring has more than casual meaning. Often the designation *boring* serves to avoid anxieties and antagonisms entailed in acknowledging the interest of complex works.

A sample of one proves nothing. As an interesting/boring novel, *Robert Elsmere* determines little about the vast category of published material that interests large numbers of people at one time and bores most readers later. To hasty or casual readers, the past seems immaterial to a complicated present, especially when evoked in unfamiliar vocabulary with moralistic emphasis and complicated sentence structure. Unless they manifestly demand close attention, promising reward, the import of long-neglected books becomes invisible. The books turn boring.

This category of response (the designation of books as boring) acquires its cultural usefulness and its energy from its capacity to obviate difficulty. It removes the necessity to confront potential challenge, it justifies inertia. Interest is always constructed: literary critics, in the business of creating it, know that. Boredom is constructed too — and a dull book is easily renounced. To try to reconstruct the interest of such a book, however hypothetically, teaches us something about ourselves as well as about our predecessors and reminds us that "boring books" need not bore us.

University of Virginia

NOTES

Reprinted with kind permission of the University of Chicago Press.
1. I owe this allusion to David Kaufmann.

WORKS CITED

Fenichel, Otto. "The Psychology of Boredom." *The Collected Papers of Otto Fenichel.* First Series. 1934. New York: Norton, 1953. 292–302.
Gladstone, W. E. " 'Robert Elsmere' and the Battle of Belief." *Nineteenth Century* 23 (1888): 766–88.
Hunter, J. Paul. *Before Novels: The Cultural Contexts of Eighteenth-Century English Fiction.* New York: Norton, 1990.
Jones, Enid Huws. *Mrs Humphry Ward.* London: Heinemann, 1973.
Lang, Andrew. "Theological Romances." *Contemporary Review* 53 (1888): 814–24.
Leavis, Q. D. *Fiction and the Reading Public.* 1932. London: Chatto & Windus, 1968.
"Robert Elsmere and Christianity." *Quarterly Review* 167 (1888): 273–302.
Smith, Esther Marian Greenwell. *Mrs. Humphry Ward.* Boston: Twayne, 1980.

Sutherland, John. *Mrs Humphry Ward: Eminent Victorian, Preeminent Edwardian*. Oxford: Clarendon, 1990.

Ward, Mrs. Humphry. *Robert Elsmere*. 1888. Ed. Clyde de L. Ryals. Lincoln: U of Nebraska P, 1967.

REVIEW ESSAYS

T'OTHEREST VICTORIANS

By Walter Kendrick

LATE IN CHARLES DICKENS'S *Our Mutual Friend*, Rogue Riderhood encounters a grammatical difficulty. Unaccustomed to conversing with gentlemen, he has devised familiarizing labels for Mortimer Lightwood ("Lawyer Lightwood") and Eugene Wrayburn ("T'other Governor"). But when he meets Bradley Headstone — whom, by a nice touch of irony, he mistakes for a gentleman — Riderhood must overhaul the English language in order to label him. "Why look here," he explains to Bradley:

> "There's two Governors, ain't there? One and one, two — Lawyer Lightwood, my first finger, he's one, ain't he? Well; might you be acquainted with my middle finger, the T'other?"
> "I know quite as much of him," said Bradley, with a frown and a distant look before him, "as I want to know."
> "Hooroar!" cried the man [Riderhood]. "Hooroar T'other T'other Governor. Hooroar T'otherest Governor! I am of your way of thinkin'."

Though Riderhood is no grammarian, "T'other T'other" sounds wrong even to him. Yet standard English seems to furnish only a sort of toggle switch: hit "T'other" twice, and you return to "the one." Ignorance does not prevent Riderhood from seeing that Bradley is other than both Eugene *and* Mortimer, so he coins the superlative of "other." One might say that the evidence of his eyes — abetted by his roguishness — leads him to break out of binary convention into a triangulating system that permits a quantum leap of complexity in the mapping of human relations.

The only actual leap Riderhood makes is into Plashwater Weir, where he drowns, locked in the murderously binary embrace of T'otherest Governor. No such dire fate, I trust, awaits nineteenth-century studies, though recent Victorian scholarship has taken a distinctly Roguish turn, away from binary notions of *these* and *the others*, sometimes beyond threesomes, to discover that even the margins of the margins have margins. Thirty years ago, writing *The Other Victorians* (1964), Steven Marcus found himself "alone in an area where almost none had ever been before"; "a new language or dialect had to be learned," thanks to "the almost total absence of any kind of serious or reliable previous work" (xxi). Since then, the empty field has grown crowded; it has also been cut up into a mosaic of subdistricts, as fresh aspects of Victorian otherness continue to be located and explored. What follows here is a survey — admittedly partial, at times perhaps arbitrary — of some recent Victorian studies that have contributed to our developing sense of how diverse and surprising that age still turns out to be.

Marcus's Victorians owed their otherness chiefly to a strong interest in sex, either as pornographers, as clinical observers like William Acton, or as obsessed participants like the author of *My Secret Life*. Thirty years ago, the prevailing stereotype was that the Victorians owed their formidable energy to intense sublimation, that as for body contact, they all would have preferred to lie back and think of England. The iconic gesture in this regard was the draping of piano legs — referred to, of course, as "limbs" — in order to safeguard the Young Person's cheek from blushes. As Peter Gay remarked in 1984, the Massachusetts headmistress who supposedly performed this quintessentially "Victorian" maneuver "has enjoyed an unwarranted posthumous fame." If she existed at all, she was a marginal figure, "at the most squeamish extreme in the range of permissible behavior" (*The Bourgeois Experience: Victoria to Freud*, vol. 1, *Education of the Senses*, 341). Gay also noted that the headmistress's doubtful reality (she may have been the brainchild of Frederick Marryat) has not prevented twentieth-century writers from repeating the anecdote and extending it to embrace the nonsensical idea that Victorians routinely called a chicken breast a "bosom" (495). Gay's comments should have buried the canard forever, but Peter Brooks has lately dug it up again in *Body Work: Objects of Desire in Modern Narrative* (Cambridge: Harvard UP, 1993). Citing Gay, Brooks adds that those draped limbs, "apocryphal" though they may be, "have gained such currency . . . that they have the cultural authority of myth" (302).

If so, it is a myth of the modern, not the Victorian, an instructive fable that shows how even the most scrupulous critics and historians can be seduced by their own unanalyzed wishes into oversimplifying the subjects they study. One of the twentieth century's fondest dreams is that the Victorians were prudish, squeamish, and hypocritical about sex. Revisionists like Marcus, Gay, and several others have thrown numerous wet blankets on that desire, but at the risk of merely flipping it over into its opposite, the equally crude notion that the Victorians seethed with lust and wasted no time arranging its indulgence, so long as superficial propriety was maintained. This antimyth has also flourished mightily, especially in biographies with a popular slant; a case in point is Dickens's bizarre relationship with Ellen Ternan. Rumors circulated during the novelist's lifetime that he had some sort of connection, probably sexual, with the actress, who was half his age. Rumor first reached print in 1939, but it entered Dickens's standard life story with Edgar Johnson's *Charles Dickens: His Tragedy and Triumph*

(1952). Johnson assumed sexual doings and waxed a bit lurid about them: "Ellen's obduracy had at last given way," he wrote, just after admitting the absence of "undeniable evidence" (1005). The image of Dickens, arch-Victorian and arch-hypocrite, endured for forty years, though Fred Kaplan, in *Dickens: A Biography* (1988), expressed extreme caution: "No conclusive evidence has surfaced to determine whether or not their relationship was sexual. . . . By Victorian private and modern public standards sexual relations would have been likely" (410). It remained for Peter Ackroyd, in his highly unorthodox *Dickens* (1990), to declare the subject "essentially unknowable" (1134) and to make the truly shocking suggestion that Dickens and Ternan did *not* have sex (914–16).

The story of the Dickens-Ternan story is a cautionary tale for scholars; it also reflects the recent turn of scholarship away from old certainties and toward a view of Victorian people that allows them to differ from us in barely thinkable ways. Among the most influential contributions to this revision of the nineteenth century is Eve Kosovsky Sedgwick's *Between Men: English Literature and Male Homosocial Desire* (1985), recently reissued with a new preface by the author (New York: Columbia UP, 1993). Sedgwick ranges from Shakespeare to Walt Whitman, but her most provocative chapters are those on nineteenth-century novels, particularly *Adam Bede, Henry Esmond, Our Mutual Friend*, and *The Mystery of Edwin Drood*. Leaning on René Girard, Claude Lévi-Strauss, and others, she teases out of these "fat rich texts" recurring patterns of "triangular heterosexual desire" that entail "traffic in women" between men (15–16). Often, the "homosocial" bond is far more passionate than any male-female connection; it enables men to consolidate their shared power without compromising the programmatic heterosexuality that keeps them focused on a male erotic object. It is also compatible with an equally kneejerk "homophobia" that allows them to scorn men whose homosociality veers into homosexuality.

The influence of *Between Men* has been enormous, extending far beyond the Victorian field; *Rolling Stone*, an undisputed authority, has praised it as "the text that ignited gay studies" — an unwise metaphor but a fairly accurate one for both good and ill. *Between Men* exhibits several of the most annoying traits of recent academic criticism. Its style wobbles clumsily between polysyllabic abstraction and would-be chummy slang; it repeatedly overreaches itself, claiming (à la Michel Foucault) to trace long-term cultural changes in a mere handful of texts; worst of all, it blithely treats works of literature as if they were unstained windows on the world around them, without regard for the possibility that literature might be different from, say, a census report. *Between Men* did not cause the epidemic of these affectations and misjudgments in contemporary scholarship, but the book's impact has certainly done nothing to discourage them. That impact, however, has been due not so much to Sedgwick's vices as to her virtues, which are numerous. At a stroke, she offered new ways of reading several canonical works about which the last major word seemed to have been said. By applying a feminist perspective to *male* homosocial arrangements, she moved toward a subtler, more complex understanding of relations both within and between the sexes. And despite her yen for grandiose generalizations, she never mistook Victorian society for a cruder version of our own.

At its best, current Victorian scholarship also challenges us to overcome the soothing twentieth-century prejudice that *we* are self-evidently freer, in mind as well as body, than *they* were. The boldest gesture of this kind, which has attracted considerable attention (and not a little outrage) in the popular press, is James R. Kincaid's *Child-Loving: The Erotic Child and Victorian Culture* (New York: Routledge, 1992). Kincaid proposes that, in regard to the sexuality of children and to the sexual component in adults' attitudes toward them, we at the end of the twentieth century are far more confused, constricted, and hypocritical than our forebears were in the middle of the nineteenth. It is we, not they, who suffer from the "eroticization" of childhood, a long, gradual process that began in the late seventeenth century and has reached dire completion in our own time. For the Victorians, the process was still underway; there were gaps in the prison walls, through which the Victorians could escape into greater freedom than we, in our supposedly liberated age, are capable of.

Child-Loving is an unusual book in several respects. It is highly personal: though much of Kincaid's subject matter is scholarly, his style and tone are emphatically not. He frequently invokes his own experience as a late-twentieth-century adult, and he is fond of a sort of jaunty jokiness that many readers may find inappropriate, especially given the solemnity with which children's sexuality is usually discussed. *Child-Loving* is also, despite its subtitle, far more concerned with some problems of contemporary culture than with the relative absence of them 150 years ago. Kincaid's constant theme is that the Victorians were less like us than even most Victorianists suppose, and that we can learn from that difference how to get out of the impasse into which the intervening years have led us. *Child-Loving* accepts the standard proposition that we are more advanced than the Victorians, farther along in a continuous historical development, but Kincaid reverses the standard values, portraying twentieth-century cultural history as something of a primrose path. In his view, the Victorians not only were freer than we are, they also had more common sense.

Kincaid's paradigm of contemporary idiocy is the longest criminal trial in American history, the "McMartin Pre-School Case," which occurred in Los Angeles between April 1987 and January 1990. Raymond Buckley and his mother, Peggy McMartin Buckley, faced sixty-five charges of child molesting, the penultimate stage of a prosecution that had begun in 1983 and had involved the arrest of five other people on over 200 separate charges. On January 18, 1990, the Buckleys were acquitted on fifty-two charges; the jury remained deadlocked on the rest. A "sequel" followed, in which Raymond (who had spent five of the last seven years in prison) stood trial alone on the thirteen remaining charges, later reduced to eight. Finally, on July 27, 1990, a mistrial rang down the curtain on "the Buckley matter," setting free both the last defendant and "those of us who had become experts" on it, Kincaid among them (341–43).

Day after day, along with a few other devotees, he had sat in the courtroom, listening to repetitious claims and counterclaims, most of them horrific as well as boring, in the interest of a book he intended to write. Appropriately enough, he mused: "Who asked me to attend and to write? Who put this event here for the watching and writing — and why?" On June 25, 1990, Prosecutor Pam Ferraro referred the court to "the official Transcript, Page 55,000." Kincaid mused further:

> And after page 55,000, we have not "The End" but page 55,001. We will never have "The End." We will never have "The Truth" either. And that's what the trial is for, I have decided, which is why both the judge and I attend. We are both there to take our parts in a process whereby the end and the truth are centered and held in suspension by being textualized in a way so remarkably sophisticated that our interest will never be exhausted. (344)

The monstrously repellent spectacle of adults molesting children has nevertheless become so compelling that we eagerly squander money, time, even lives, in order to keep it perpetually before our horrified, fascinated eyes.

Endeavoring to show that the Victorians managed these matters better, Kincaid draws on a wide range of sources, most of them extraliterary. His discussion of child-rearing manuals and popular medical guides reveals a refreshing lack of unanimity on many subjects, even masturbation. Several authorities held what has come retrospectively to seem the "Victorian" view, that as George Drysdale wrote in *The Elements of Social Science* (1854), masturbation is a "fatal drain" on those who practice it. But, Kincaid points out, Drysdale waxed equally gloomy about chastity, which "is invariably a great natural sin." In Drysdale's thinking, and in that of many of his contemporaries, Kincaid distinguishes a clash between two conceptions of human physiology, the "exercise model" and the "simple economic one." According to the economic model, "spending" depleted a man's vital powers and coarsened a woman's; the exercise model, meanwhile, proposed that, in John Davenport's words of 1875, "Another cause of impotency is the allowing the parts of generation to remain too long in inaction" (41–43). Very well, the Victorians contradicted themselves; Kincaid delights in spotting blatant instances of their sloppy, even incoherent thinking. But he does so not in order to demonstrate *our* superiority to *them*. For Kincaid, a little incoherence is a healthful thing, far more wholesome than our rigid, unyielding certainties. "To what extent," he asks, "are men like Davenport . . . speaking from within an episteme and to what extent are they being ironic and playful with the very forms of that controlling structure?" He answers: "My money is on deconstruction" (42).

"Episteme," of course, is the ineluctable Foucault's word, while "deconstruction" used to be Jacques Derrida's property, until Paul de Man discovered that he'd always already owned it. All three theorists bob in the brew of Kincaid's method — especially de Man, who frequently sought to demonstrate, as Kincaid also does, that texts had deconstructed themselves before any theorist laid hands on them. At times, Kincaid's method is no more coherent than those of the Victorians he analyzes, but his aim is always clear: to show that, especially where the "erotic child" is concerned, Victorian muddle allowed playfulness, while modern certainty spawns horrors like the McMartin Pre-School Case. Oddly, though, Kincaid is much more convincing when he reads medical or scientific texts than when he turns to literature. His "pedophile" readings of nineteenth-century novels — "Desiring David Copperfield," "Tragic Play with Tess" (306–9, 320–38) — are shrill and rather unpersuasive, as are his discussions of *Dombey and Son* and *The Old Curiosity Shop* under the rubric "The Dead Child" (236–40). Like many other quondam literary critics — he has published book-length studies of Dickens, Tennyson, and Trollope — Kincaid now seems somewhat impatient with the troublesome mediations of art. On the whole, however, *Child-Loving* works in the enlightening direction of complexity, away from monolithic or merely binary assessments of the Victorian age.

Probably the most seductive interpretive duality is that which separates the sexes — or, as they are now too often called, the genders. Feminist scholars have shed a good deal of light on nineteenth-century culture, but sometimes at the cost of perpetuating a simplistic view of gender relations in that age of supposedly impervious patriarchal hegemony. More recent scholarship has, again, favored subtler interpretations that allow room for uncertainties, contradictions, and simple gaps in Victorian power structures. Peter Brooks's *Body Work: Objects of Desire in Modern Narrative*, for instance, goes out from the work of Laura Mulvey, Toril Moi, and others who have studied portrayals of the body in film and literature. The simplistic view would be that, as Mulvey remarks,

> In a world ordered by sexual imbalance, pleasure in looking has been split between active/male and passive/female. The determining male gaze projects its phantasy on to the female figure which is styled accordingly. In their traditional exhibitionist role women are simultaneously looked at and displayed, with their appearance coded for strong visual and erotic impact so that they can be said to connote *to-be-looked-at-ness*. (Quoted in Brooks 101)

Mulvey herself has lately moved away from the absolutist application of this scheme, and other film scholars, like Carol Clover in *Men, Women, and Chain Saws* (1992), have demonstrated that the "gaze" need not be unilaterally male, even in that most apparently sexist of genres, the horror film.

Brooks's eclectic survey of nineteenth-century novels and paintings also seeks to understand their depictions of the female body in a way that transcends the dichotomy of active and passive. In novels by Balzac, Flaubert, Zola, Henry James, and George Eliot, he traces a double process: "Along with the semioticization of the body goes what we might call the somatization of story: the implicit claim that that body is a key sign in narrative and a central nexus of narrative meanings" (25). As the body becomes significant, a bearer of meaning, narrative becomes in a sense bodily, displaying as the century goes on "an increasing preoccupation with bodiliness, and a certain, somewhat sly, shedding of reticence about the erotic body" — at least in France, though in England "a greater weight of social repression affects representation of the body" (20). "Semioticization" is itself an erotic activity, obeying what Freud called the *Wisstrieb*, "epistemophilia" in James Strachey's translation (99). For modern Western culture, to see is to know, and to know is to possess; for the presumptively male gazer, the prime object of sight, knowledge, and therefore possession is the female body: "Man as knowing subject postulates woman's body as the object to be known, by way of an act of visual inspection which claims to reveal the truth — or else makes that object into the ultimate enigma" (97).

The nineteenth-century novel, with its insatiable desire to capture the world in specific detail, might seem to represent the literary triumph of epistemophilia. But the drive to know, as Brooks says, following Freud, "is always inherently frustrated"; "the body can never be wholly grasped as an understandable, representable object" (99). In realistic fiction, the unveiling of the female body must always stop short, at a point determined not by prudishness but by the project of unveiling itself. In an especially provocative discussion of *Nana* (which he puts in the context of kitschy salon paintings as well as of Zola's other novels), Brooks focuses on a scene in which Nana undresses before the apparently possessing eyes of the rich Muffat. Off come her garments one by one, but when the last detail should be made visible, Muffat "closed his eyes in order to see her no more." "When we reach Nana's sex," Brooks comments, ". . . unveiling ultimately encounters a veil, which is here the ultimate veil: the woman's sex as unknowable and unrepresentable" (141).

It is impossible in this limited space to do justice to the richness and subtlety of *Body Work*. The book is, indeed, as intriguing for the questions it does not quite answer as for those it fully explores. Early on, Brooks grapples with the curious fact that in the visual arts, for the Classical age and the Renaissance alike, the ideal nude body was male; only in the nineteenth century did the female body become "the very definition of the nude." At the same time, the erotic potential of the nude male body was repressed or sublimated: "the naked male body, in the art of the Renaissance and thereafter, is supposed to be heroic rather than erotic" (16). Brooks hazards several explanations for these processes, linking them to the biblical story of naked Noah covered by his sons, a myth of "the central scandal of our culture, one that must at all costs be veiled since it reveals the very principle of patriarchal authority" (15). The 1989 furor over

Robert Mapplethorpe's photographs confirms that "the erect penis is virtually the only object still rated obscene in contemporary American society — the very definition of 'hard core' — and subject to restrictions" (15–16).

In the scene of Nana's unveiling, Muffat is presumably aroused by what he sees, yet that arousal is never shown or even directly referred to, although both he and she ought to be reflected in Nana's mirror. Brooks observes that "the censorship of male sexual excitement . . . is of course typical of virtually all artistic representation in the modern Western tradition" (145), and he plausibly connects this instance of it with *Nana*'s larger thematic concerns. Yet the repressed always returns, and all forms of censorship, no matter how thorough, invite evasion. The history (or perhaps nonhistory) of homoeroticism in Western culture remains to be written, though a glancing stab at it has been made by Allen Ellenzweig in *The Homoerotic Photograph: Male Images from Durieu/ Delacroix to Mapplethorpe* (1992), a glossy coffeetable book in Columbia University Press's series "Between Men-Between Women: Lesbian and Gay Studies." Ellenzweig covers the years 1853 to 1989; less than a third of the book is devoted to Victorian photographers, notably Emile Bayard, Frank M. Sutcliffe, and Thomas Eakins. The Victorian section, however, illustrates most clearly the confusion that undermines Ellenzweig's entire project.

The trouble lies with the term "homoerotic": it might adequately describe some of Mapplethorpe's work, but it is of little help with, for example, Sutcliffe's *Water Rats* (1885), his famous picture of naked boys frolicking in Whitby harbor. There is no evidence that Sutcliffe felt any sexual interest in the boys or that he expected the viewer of *Water Rats*, male or female, to be even faintly aroused by it; he undoubtedly intended, Ellenzweig admits, "only an especially picturesque genre scene," and the picture's contemporary commentators seem to have taken it as such (19). A more stylized deployment of naked boys, *Natives* (1890), prompts some ingenious interpretation of props and background that discovers "a heightened degree of eroticism" in the photograph: "However chastely intended, however meditative the scene, Sutcliffe's picture is ripe with phallic suggestion" (21). Whatever phallic suggestion may be, it is hardly the same as homoeroticism, and to dismiss the matter of intention here, while making it pivotal elsewhere, is to blur one's interpretive categories rather hopelessly. *The Homoerotic Photograph* has some value as a visual archive, but Ellenzweig's confusion bears witness to the relative immaturity of gay and lesbian studies, despite the excellent work that has been done in that recently popular field. Publishers are, perhaps, a bit too eager to rush such volumes into print, simply because the topic is a fashionable one.

The older field of feminist studies has meanwhile entered a phase of high specialization, exemplified by a pair of recent essay collections whose narrow focus is made possible by the groundbreaking work of an earlier generation of scholars. *The New Woman and Her Sisters: Feminism and Theatre 1850–1919*, edited by Vivien Gardner and Susan Rutherford (Ann Arbor: U of Michigan P, 1992), prints twelve essays, all by women scholars, that originated in a conference at Manchester University. All concentrate on the intersection between the New Woman — that latchkey-bearing, cigarette-smoking icon of the 1890s — and the theater, where female playwrights, actors, and performers were able to find new ways "to challenge and subvert the prevailing male hegemony," as Gardner says in her introduction (1). The New Woman was, in a sense, herself a theatrical product; though a familiar image long before the opening of Sidney Grundy's comedy *The New Woman*, in September 1894, she thereafter wore in the British public's mind the features of Grundy's Mrs. Sylvester, who feeds her husband cold mutton and fills their house with creatures "of a new gender," her own. The irony is, of course, as Gardner points out, that the "women who played these roles were themselves, in many ways, New Women" (3). They worked outside the home, on the stage indeed, and therefore embodied several of the threatening traits that plays like Grundy's employed them to make fun of.

Ironies multiplied when women appeared on stage in male attire, performances examined in essays by Jill Edmonds and J. S. Bratton. Edmonds discusses the phenomenon of the female Hamlet, numerous incarnations of whom trod British boards from the late eighteenth century through the first decade of the twentieth, after which the melancholy Dane's androgyny went into apparently permanent eclipse. Edmonds's "Princess Hamlet" is predominantly a gathering of names, dates, and contemporary comments, but she also suggests that female Hamlets looked less subversive to Victorian eyes than they might to ours. Such actresses as Alice Marriott, Julia Seaman, and Sarah Bernhardt adopted "costumes modelled on contemporary male Hamlets"; they also adhered to a " 'safe' repertoire of old-fashioned melodrama, pantomime, 'standard plays' and Shakespeare"; they were therefore probably "not seen as breaking new ground." Several among them, however, were managers as well as actors and unabashedly exhibited "the independence and the power of women who earned their own livings" (72). They were, that is, multivalent figures in their own time, and in the brief compass of seventeen illustrated pages, Edmonds nicely captures their variousness.

Bratton tackles the more provocative subject of late-Victorian music-hall women who dressed up in contemporary male clothing; they enjoyed a short but intense wave of popularity between about 1890 and 1910. Little is known about most of these women, even less about exactly how their audiences perceived them; Bratton's essay is therefore appropriately tentative, more of a prolegomenon than a treatment. She is sharply aware of nuance and ambiguity:

What is needed is an analysis of the conventional practice as such, of the assumption of the outward signs of the masculine by women stage performers, by means of various permutations and transformations of male dress, partially or completely covering the signs offered by their female bodies, and interacting with them. Such an analysis needs to accommodate all the shades of political consciousness that might — or might not — be expressed by means of the enactment, reinforcement or subversion *of that convention*. (82)

Bratton herself makes only a halting advance in that direction, but it is a promising one. Noting, for instance, that when newspaper reviewers covered the music halls, they seldom gave male impersonators "more than a blandly appreciative line or two," she speculates:

One is led to ask whether the reticence is because of their unimportance — these are acts chiefly appreciated by women, which the men find dull — or perhaps because of their unhandlability, their potential dangerousness — exciting acts in the hall, but impossible to translate safely into words, to frame within the bland, recuperative discourse of the trade press. (87)

When scholarship ventures on the extreme margins of the cultural record, such delicate caution is a valuable asset.

Like all essay collections, especially those born at conferences, *The New Woman and Her Sisters* is a highly uneven assortment. Its faults are the endemic ones in today's academic criticism: overreliance on frayed buzzwords such as "patriarchal," "hegemony," and "discourse"; niggling quibbling with the pronouncements of prior critics, who would probably seem less egregious in full context; a tendency, when conceptual difficulties arise, to flee into the fog-shrouded embrace of Lacan, Bakhtin, or some other approved pundit. On the whole, however, these essays are more fairly called dense than murky; the weary scholar who clings to the battered belief that lucid writing is an act of courtesy may take heart from even glimmers of lucidity in a volume spawned at a conference. But then, the chill thought comes, these writers are historians, and some lingering devotion to the idea of literal reference still makes history a greater pleasure to read than literary criticism, which long ago renounced that naive faith.

Yet there are some slight signs that the age of deliberate murk may be on the wane even there — giving way, if not to Johnsonian clarity, at least to a nonassaultive stance. Another essay collection, *Famous Last Words: Changes in Gender and Narrative Closure*, edited by Alison Booth (Charlottesville: UP of Virginia, 1993), suggests that younger critics no longer aspire to impenetrability quite so avidly as they did a few years ago. Another conference byproduct, *Famous Last Words* originated in a panel on "novelistic endings" at the 1989 MLA convention (vii); it contains thirteen essays, along with an introduction by Booth and an afterword by U. C. Knoepflmacher. The essays are arranged chronologically by topic, from Lisa Jadwin on *Vanity Fair* to Peter J. Rabinowitz on Sue Grafton's alphabetical thrillers. All are concerned with how novels end, but the nineteenth-century essays (the first seven) devote special attention to the ways in which Victorian women novelists sought to escape from the limited number of endings that seemed possible for women's stories.

Conventionally, fictional women might die at the end, or they might marry — fates that in practice, as Booth remarks, often shared "an uncanny resemblance" (2). Such novels as Harriet Jacobs's *Incidents in the Life of a Slave Girl* (1861), Elizabeth Gaskell's *Sylvia's Lovers* (1863), and George Eliot's *Romola* (1863) and *Daniel Deronda* (1876) maneuvered a "swerve from the foregone destination" (3). It used to be received wisdom about Gaskell that she simply had trouble ending her books, but in "Speaking Like a Woman: How to Have the Last Word on *Sylvia's Lovers*," Christine L. Krueger reinterprets that novel's supposed failure as "structural nonconformity" (136). *Sylvia's Lovers* in fact provides its "last word" six chapters before the end of the novel, when Sylvia tells her own story. Because this story, according to Krueger,

> cannot be pressed into the service of romance closure, it must be excluded from history — the legend of Sylvia with which the novel closes. In order for the romance plot of history to be resolved, the wrongs of woman must be ignored. The effect is to present the wronged woman, and thereby more sweepingly the "wrongs of woman," in inexorable opposition to any ideology or discourse that would figure women as willing or dutiful participants in their own subjection. (138)

This is perhaps overingenious on Krueger's part, but at least it endeavors to rehabilitate a neglected text and to rescue an underappreciated writer from critical patronizing. And Krueger's prose, though hardly luminous, can at least be read.

A third recent essay collection, *Rewriting the Victorians: Theory, History, and the Politics of Gender*, edited by Linda M. Shires (New York and London: Routledge, 1992), did not spring from a conference, though it nevertheless manages to cram three current buzzwords into its seven-word subtitle. Yet the essays it contains are both lucid and, very often, enlightening. They vary enormously in scope and ambition, from Ina Ferris's broad survey of gendered rhetoric in Victorian critical journals ("From Trope to Code: The Novel and the Rhetoric of Gender in Nineteenth-Century Critical Discourse") to Jeff Nunokawa's study of *Tess of the d'Urbervilles* alongside contemporary sightseers' guides ("*Tess*, Tourism, and the Spectacle of the Woman"). In "Excluding Women: The Cult of the Male Genius in Victorian Painting," Susan P. Casteras applies techniques of gender criticism to several pictures that portray the childhood of great men. By selecting these subjects, says Casteras, such artists as Marcus Stone, Edward W. Ward, and William Holman Hunt "serve various cultural imperatives":

> They rely on contemporary philosophical and scientific notions of giftedness as sexed; they soothe contemporary anxieties about the need to regenerate the flagging

state of British art; they create allegories of empire. Returning to the origin of genius, they travel the same road as so many other Victorians who are obsessed with beginnings; those of individuals, those of cultural institutions, and those of civilization itself. (117)

The disparate assortment of topics handled in *Rewriting the Victorians* makes it a far more disjointed volume than Shires's preface would like the reader to suppose. But these ten essays offer some of the best work I have seen lately in the Victorian field. Most of the contributors demonstrate that clear prose and careful scholarship are not, as beleaguered readers have lately feared, necessarily incompatible with theoretical sophistication.

Trends aside, the rarest and most valuable scholarly accomplishment remains what it has always been, the synthesis of precise observation and generalizing insight. Tiny topics can be easily enough exhausted, simply by accounting for all documents relevant to them. Grand theories are easy, too, if one omits recalcitrant facts or glosses them over. But few scholarly books achieve a smooth fusion of exact attention to facts with illuminating general commentary. Judith R. Walkowitz's *City of Dreadful Delight: Narratives of Sexual Danger in Late-Victorian London* (Chicago: U of Chicago P, 1992) is one of those rarities. Walkowitz's first book, *Prostitution and Victorian Society: Women, Class, and the State* (1980), permanently redirected the course of modern thought about the Victorians; it has long since counted as a scholarly classic. In *City of Dreadful Delight*, she expands her focus to take in the whole of inner London, from the East End (where prostitutes prowled) to the West (where respectable women, lately freed from duties at home, went shopping). Both sorts represented the upsetting spectacle of unaccompanied women on the streets, and sometimes they migrated, middle-class philanthropists eastward into Whitechapel and enterprising sex workers westward into the city's respectable retail and theater districts. As the Victorians attempted to understand these and other contemporary urban phenomena, they mapped "a dense cultural grid" of "conflicting and overlapping representations of sexual danger" (5) that possessed as much reality as the actual grid of streets through which these women moved.

Walkowitz begins with a survey of cultural mapping, the figuration of London as a "dark, powerful, and seductive labyrinth" (17) by urban anthropologists like Henry Mayhew and flâneurs like Henry James. An 1888 *Pall Mall Gazette* review of James's essay "London" furnishes Walkowitz's title (251), which (thought she does not mention this) is a play on the title of James Thomson's 1880 poem "The City of Dreadful Night." Night and delight went well together in what James called this "strangely mingled monster" (17), and both could bring dread. Increasingly in the 1880s, London came to be seen as a place whose formerly secure boundaries now were "indiscriminately and dangerously transgressed" (29). In this context, Walkowitz studies two media events: W.

T. Stead's 1885 series in the *Pall Mall Gazette*, "The Maiden Tribute of Modern Babylon," and the explosion of journalism set off by Jack the Ripper's murders three years later. "Media events" is my phrase, and it is not wholly anachronistic. Both episodes involved the interpenetration of real happenings and discourse about them; Stead, indeed, staged his happenings in order to provide an occasion for discourse. Prejudices, misconceptions, and sincere efforts to understand clashed and overlapped in ways that confused contemporaries but, thanks to Walkowitz, can enlighten us.

   City of Dreadful Delight has a few flaws. Parts of it were published earlier as essays, and their combination here has left occasional repetition and disjointedness. And though poor copyediting is rife in all sorts of publication these days, this book is one of the worst examples I have seen. "Misled" appears as *mislead*, "plebeian" as *plebian* (twice), and "multiplies" as *multiples*; there are several other elementary typos. A more complex mistake, however, deserves inclusion in any scrapbook of such things. Discussing the Criminal Law Amendment Act of 1885, Walkowitz no doubt wished to say that it prohibited indecent acts between "consenting male adults." Somehow, this has become *consulting male audits* (82), suggesting hitherto unsuspected depths in the world of Victorian bookkeeping. It is unfortunate that this fine book should have suffered such indignities in its production. *City of Dreadful Delight* is a model of the historian's and interpreter's art, a major contribution to our understanding of the increasingly other, perennially enthralling Victorians.

Fordham University

OF PLOTS, PRISONS, AND ESCAPE ARTISTRY: ISSUES OF POWER IN NINETEENTH-CENTURY NARRATIVE

By Marjorie Stone

"If I were Mr. G oh! heaven, how I would beat her," Dickens said to his editorial assistant Wills, provoked by Elizabeth Gaskell's late and overly long proofs for the serialized version of *North and South* in *Household Words*. His comment epitomizes some of the textual and power relations at the heart of many recent studies of nineteenth-century literary discourse: the relations between those in control of the means of publication and those with little or no control, the relations between men and women, and the relations between masters and the slaves or "hands" they felt free to beat or exploit. Despite their exploration of very different types of writers and works, the three books I will be concerned with here combine a focus on these issues of power with the current interest in narrative plots, the prisons of representation they reflect, and strategic transformations of these plots by enterprising authors. Not surprisingly, each of these studies also sets in motion a plot of its own, as critical paradigms generate familiar narrative patterns. And less surprisingly still, these critical plots divide along gender lines, reflecting the "plausibilities" of a critical revisionism itself in need of revision. Thus, in the two studies concerned with women writers, the critical plots follow the pattern of the captivity narrative and the escape: in each case, the authors considered and the heroines they portray are represented as the protagonists in a struggle for liberation achieved through claiming agency and voice. In the study concerned with a male writer, on the contrary, the underlying narrative represents an author imprisoned within the sexist discourses he deploys, despite occasional textual movements towards illumination and escape. And this author is, ironically, none other than Dickens himself, the nineteenth-century novelist who most explicitly and fully develops the signifier of the prison in novel after novel to represent the "mind-forged manacles" of human perception and systems of representation.

Although Hilary Schor's *Scheherezade in the Marketplace: Elizabeth Gaskell and the Victorian Novel* (New York: Oxford UP, 1992) in some respects follows

317

a pattern familiar in revisionist feminist criticism, it by no means presents a simple parable of entrapment and escape. Schor's book is among the fullest and most illuminating analyses of Gaskell's narrative innovations published to date. As Schor notes, "Gaskell is usually treated as a practitioner of a transparent realism, a naive reporter, an untrained sympathizer," when in fact her handling of novelistic conventions is both "complex and self-conscious" in its participation in larger debates "at play in Victorian fiction" (7). By telling "two parallel stories," the "evolution of the woman novelist, and the 'story' of the heroine across the progress of Gaskell's work," Schor shows how Gaskell's "attempt to write the fiction of those denied a voice within Victorian society led her to an awareness of her own silencing, a sense of the ways literary and cultural plots shape our understanding of the world and limit our ability to describe it" (5).

Schor's careful contextualization of Gaskell's narrative strategies in the material conditions, the literary conventions and the cultural conflicts shaping her writing is one of the strengths of *Scheherezade in the Marketplace*. Another, as its title implies, is its attention to the contradictions and tensions complicating and enriching Gaskell's attempts to politicize and revise the conventional female plots disseminated by writers before her and around her. Gaskell turns the courtship plot so often objected to in the second half of *Mary Barton* into a "critique of received languages and received plots" perpetuating the marginalization "of workers and of women" (14), Schor argues. But this novel's "attention to the politics of representation" as well as to the "representation of politics" (21) derives in part from Gaskell's struggle to construct a public self and voice, a struggle she attempted to resolve by subsuming the necessary egoism of the author within a revisionary "myth of maternal narration" (28). Schor's analysis of the alternate "maternal plot" and "structure of power" Gaskell creates in *Mary Barton* may owe more to the groundbreaking work of Patsy Stoneman's *Elizabeth Gaskell* (Bloomington: Indiana UP, 1987) than she acknowledges. Yet *Scheherezade in the Marketplace* adds significantly to our reading of *Mary Barton*, and even more so, to a fuller appreciation of Gaskell's later works.

Schor's reading of *Ruth* as a revision of Romantic representations of the fallen woman, and as a novel focused on the "forms of perception" constructing the text of female beauty (47), is particularly suggestive, like her reading of *Cranford* as a "female version of *Pickwick*" (113) and an ethnographic "extended commentary on the ways women are taught to read cultural signs" (87). As for *North and South*, Schor turns traditional readings of the novel around in arguing that, rather than moving from the complexities of industrial conflict towards the simplifying mystification of a "marriage plot," Gaskell "in fact moves in the opposite direction: from the 'romance' of the heroine's life . . . into the density of industrial England and its economic and sexual politics" (120). Moreover, as Schor rightly emphasizes, "Margaret Hale's adventure in Milton-Northern is largely linguistic'' as she serves as a ''translator for other characters and for readers'' (129). Whether this makes *North and South* a more innovative text than *Mary Barton*, as she claims, is more debatable. If, in her words, the later industrial novel ''serves as a glossary of industrialization'' (129), employing Margaret as a mediating consciousness, that may make it a capitulation to the middle-class discourses that are more marginalized in the earlier *Mary Barton*, where the reader is plunged into the heteroglot world of working-class voices and perspectives without a ''glossary'' in hand. The ways in which ''capitalism itself is eroticized'' in *North and South* through the interaction of ''the forces of economic power'' with the romance plot (128) is an element also open to different readings than Schor suggests. The emphasis on Margaret's beauty and the property she inherits, along with ''her very specific education into questions of class and labor'' (147), may point to the constraints of that education as well as to its strengths.

Sylvia's Lovers, Gaskell's experiment with the historical novel, is read by Schor as a novel about the confusions ''in the construction of desire itself'' intensified ''in times of violent social change.'' Desire and narrative alike depend on ''culturally assigned'' gender roles. ''*Sylvia's Lovers* suggests that . . . men live in the world of difference, conflict, history; women in the realm of similarity, repetition, myth.'' At the same time, the novel shows how ''the plot of female desire unfixes difference and works its own narrative transformations'' (154–55). Schor concludes with a thought-provoking interpretation of *Wives and Daughters*, Gaskell's novel without an ending, as her most sophisticated exploration of the relativity of knowledge and systems of representation, including the knowledge about origins disseminated by history, Darwinian biology, and the novel. The narrative progress of *Wives and Daughters* ''must be connected with not only the heroine's progress and romance but broader cultural stories: all the stories of origin that offer systems of meaning, a way of reading growth, progress, change, those key elements of Victorian science and Victorian fiction'' (183). Schor's reading of *Wives and Daughters* brings out its affinities with George Eliot's *Daniel Deronda*, another text profoundly concerned with cultural stories and fictions of origins, although this is a relationship she does not explore.

One of the surprising features of Schor's study, in fact, is her relative lack of attention to Gaskell's textual and biographical connections with other women writers, aside from her suggestive comments on the traces of Maria Edgeworth's *Helen* and Charlotte Brontë's *Jane Eyre* in *Wives and Daughters*. The latter connection might have been extended by noting the echoes of Rochester's paternal possessiveness in Mr. Gibson's desire to attach his daughter Molly to him with a tender ''chain'' in a speech Schor cites (188). The number of women writers and poets whom Gaskell draws on for her chapter epigraphs in *Mary Barton* and *North and South* in itself suggests the importance of other women writers in shaping her textual practice. Schor also constructs Gaskell's Romantic heritage largely in terms of Wordsworth, neglecting the traditions Anne Mellor has described as "feminine Romanticism" in *Romanticism and Gender* (New York: Routledge, 1993). Thus, while Schor perceptively analyzes the revision of the "Wordsworthian story of the beautiful lost woman" in *Ruth*, she gives much less attention to the many narratives on the same subject by women writers she briefly alludes to (46). Moreover, her construction of Wordsworth may rely more on gender polarities than is warranted. Is it always true, for instance, that "the consciousness of the woman" remains "unnarrated" in Wordsworth's representations of abandoned women? The assertion may be borne out by "The Thorn" but is it borne out by "The Mad Mother" as well? These are small complaints, however. Schor's consideration of Gaskell's engagement with male precursors and contemporaries from Ruskin to Dickens to Darwin adds greatly to the understanding of her artistry. Her analysis of Gaskell's commercial and textual debates with Dickens is particularly fascinating. These debates left "Mrs. G" cursing in her turn at the assertive editorial interventions of the "Inimitable": "I've been as nearly dazed and crazed with this c——, d—— be h——to it, story as can be," she wrote of her attempts to compress *North and South* into the industrialized, assembly line molds of the serial novel (142).

Schor's ultimate "purpose," as she points out, is to "dispel" the view of Gaskell as "the most easily dismissed of women novelists" (208). Kari J. Winter writes with a similar purpose in *Subjects of Slavery, Agents of Change: Women and Power in Gothic Novels and Slave Narratives 1790–1865* (Athens, Georgia: U of Georgia P, 1992), although the writers she treats have been, in some cases, far more completely "dismissed" than Gaskell. As Winter points out, writers of "slave narratives" like Mary Prince and Harriet Jacobs were subjected to much more complete exclusion from the means of literacy and publication than middle-class women novelists. Moreover, even when their narratives were published, they were subjected to editorial interventions that make Dickens's conflict with Gaskell seem mild by comparison. "For most white readers from the eighteenth century to the present, slave narratives lack credibility unless 'authenticated' by members of the very class that oppressed their authors," Winter points out. Therefore, up to 1865, "the narratives were usually enclosed by white-authored texts" or edited to reflect white abolitionist paradigms and concerns. Ironically, however, this very circumstance then led twentieth-century critics "to doubt the validity or integrity of black-authored texts. These modern critics demand that modern scholars (usually white) once again authenticate the text" (40). Unlike female slave narratives, which had a wide popular appeal before the American Civil war but were "not republished until the 1980s," female Gothic novels by Ann Radcliffe and her many followers have always been "readily available" (12). Yet as Winter emphasizes, both genres have in the past been neglected or completely ignored by academic criticism, the one dismissed as "fantasy or pleasure" and the other as "politics and propaganda"

(13). "Traditional critics of Gothic fiction have focused their attention on Gothic novels by men, either ignoring the existence of Gothic fiction by women or overlooking themes that were central to female writers" (19).

Winter's extended comparison of female Gothic fiction with slave narratives brings out these themes in illuminating ways. "Despite the substantial differences" distinguishing the two genres, both "focus on the sexual politics at the heart of patriarchal culture, and both represent the terrifying aspects of life for women" (13). Reading "both genres as sites of ideological struggle," Winter notes that Gothic writers "were often called 'terrorists' in the eighteenth century," but she stresses that female terrorists "employ the pen to very different ends" than male writers do (18). Whereas "male Gothic novelists from the 1790s to the 1860s lingered over horrible spectacles of sexual violence, gore, and death, locating evil in the 'other' — women, Catholics, Jews, and ultimately the devil," female Gothic novelists "uncovered the terror of the familiar: the routine brutality and injustice of the patriarchal family, conventional religion, and classist social structures" (21). The writers of female slave narratives uncovered far more explicit examples of routine brutality, against far greater obstacles, because they had first to claim their place as human beings "in opposition to the racist, patriarchal ideology that defined black women as chattel" (39). But as Winter shows, "the two genres are remarkably similar in imagery, structure, and social analysis" (13). Both "lament their protagonists' isolation and alienation, and both genres emphasize women's attempts to maintain human connections" (11). The links between the two forms jump out in Harriet Jacobs's observation that "the secrets of slavery are concealed like those of the Inquisition" (47). At the same time, however, this comment in itself calls in question some of the larger gendered distinctions Winter establishes between female and male writers of the Gothic.

Winter traces the narrative paradigm she discerns in female slave narratives and Gothic romances by comparing them to Emily Dickinson's powerful poem, "The Soul has Bandaged moments." "This poem captures precisely the tone of women's Gothic novels and slave narratives. Feelings of horror predominate, punctuated by brief moments of exhilaration and freedom. These moments are essential to female survival and are the birthplace of feminist activity, even though they are followed by times of constriction" (15). After a preliminary chapter concerned with the first step in the struggle for freedom — "Breaking Silence" — the organization of Winter's book reflects the narrative embodied in Dickinson's poem. The parallels established in her second chapter, "Labyrinths of Terror," and in her fourth chapter, "Moments of Escape," are succinctly presented and suggestive. In the former she analyses "three primary sources of terror and horror" represented by female authors of Gothic novels and slave narratives: "the terrifying aspects" of the patriarchal family, in which fathers are "parasites who prey on the sexual, emotional, reproductive, and economic resources of women"; the corruption of *all* of society by the "perverse power inequities" in "intimate family relationships"; and the concerted attempt by those in power "to deprive subjugated peoples of the power to know" (55). "Moments of Escape" analyses the "various methods of resistance" represented in the two genres: self-affirmation, "cross-dressing and 'passing' " (as male, white, and/or wealthy), exploiting male competition, turning to nature as a refuge, and reconstructing a childhood self "free from social constrictions" (115). A final brief but thought-provoking chapter points to the "Problems of Closure" reflected in both female Gothic novels and slave narratives, generated by their struggle against systemic social and psychological sources of terror. "The women who wrote Gothic novels and slave narratives between 1790 and 1865 recognized that they were struggling for a type of liberation that they would never attain in their lifetimes" (148).

Winter's text is most illuminating in the parallels revealed by its conjunction of Gothic novels and slave narratives, in its exploration of slave narratives themselves, and in the light it casts on the union of the two traditions in Toni Morrison's *Beloved*. Its treatment of Radcliffe, Mary Shelley, and Charlotte and Emily Brontë as writers of the female Gothic is a little less satisfying, in part because so much has already been written on the Gothic elements in their texts, and because Winter does not always assimilate that work into her own interpretations. As well, one is left wondering why she did not include some consideration of narratives by white abolitionist writers such as Lydia Maria Child, given that these formed a fertile site for the meeting of the two traditions she explores. *Subjects of Slavery, Agents of Change* is indeed "pathbreaking," as John Sekora suggests in a comment cited on the cover, in Winter's placing of female Gothic romances and slave narratives "side by side." But subsequent criticism may also wish to explore some of the actual lines of historical and textual transmission producing the intermingling of the two traditions.

Less rigid gender polarities than those Winters often reinforces may yield interesting results as well. She argues that unlike "male Gothic novelists," who often "supported slavery" in the eighteenth century at least, "most feminist writers in England and the United States saw the enslavement of African peoples as a brutal case of human oppression that was fundamentally connected to the oppression of white women" (3). But as her chapter "Sisterhood in Slavery?" acknowledges, the appropriations of slavery tropes by white women writers often did not reflect their primary concern with the oppression of African peoples. Moreover, the slave narratives themselves testify to women who were as zealous as the patriarchal masters in beating those whom they subjugated.

Schematic gender oppositions also occasionally undermine the persuasiveness of Patricia Ingham's *Dickens, Women and Language* (Toronto: U of Toronto P, 1992), a study that charts not the woman writer's struggle for liberation from conventional plots and systems of representation, but the imprisonment of one

major male writer within them. Perceptively criticizing the prevailing biographical readings of Dickens's female characters, Ingham systematically analyzes
"Dickens' own sexist 'idiolect' or personal language" for the representation of
women, arguing that he promulgates middle-class stereotypes of femininity that
are often very similar to those disseminated by Sarah Stickney Ellis's didactic
treatises on the "women of England" (4). While this comparison yields interesting insights, Ingham gives much shorter shrift to the many respects in which
Dickens's representation of women and the middle class radically departs from
Ellis's — particularly in his later works. She does succeed, however, in bringing
out some of the darker aspects of Dickens's participation in "prevailing codes
for the representation of women" (4). In an unusual twist, she finds more
troubling elements in his "metonymic and reductive" (136) portrayals of women
than in the less conventional "narrative syntax" (53) constructing his fallen
women — among them, Nancy, the female character whom he beat to death,
at Bill Sykes's hands, in reading after reading.

Ingham identifies five major categories of females in Dickens's novels. First,
she analyses his "nubile girls" — the marriageable and usually middle-class
virgins who seem sexless in their appearance, but who are linguistically constituted as sexual objects through metaphors insistently associating them with food,
and through their fragmentation into isolated body parts. The antithesis of the
nubile girls are the "fallen girls." Ingham suggests the term "girls" rather than
the more usual "fallen women" because characters like Nancy in *Oliver Twist*,
Alice Marwood in *Dombey and Son*, and Martha and Emily in *David Copperfield*
are usually seen as "ruins and wrecks of girls like Rose Maylie" (40). In contrast
to the usual plot emphasizing the evolution or growth of the writer, Ingham
finds Dickens's earlier representations of fallen girls less conventional than his
later ones, identifying Nancy as the most active and autonomous of his fallen
girls (56). What happens to the nubile girl if she does not fall, but marries
instead? That poses many problems for Dickens, according to Ingham, because
married and middle-aged women in Dickens texts usually are represented as
"excessive females" notable for their unregulated femaleness and above all for
their unregulated loquaciousness. The "traditionally misogynistic presentation
of women's speech as characteristically an illogical gush . . . is the main marker
of the voices of married women in many of Dickens' novels," Ingham claims
(72), with the notable exception of some lower-class wives like Polly Toodles
in *Dombey and Son* and Mrs. Plornish in *Little Dorrit*, women praised instead
for their general serviceability.

Ingham finds Dickens's "passionate women" — women associated with
"near-miss adultery" and illicit sexual experience (87) — his most interesting
and least conventional female characters. This group, including Edith Dombey,
Lady Dedlock, and Louisa Bounderby, expresses power and resistance through
"not speaking" in an "ironic reversal of the stereotypical garrulousness that

renders excessive females uniformly undesirable, knowable and despicable"
(103). Ingham's analysis of Dickens's "negative language" to convey the passion of these women leads to one of the most illuminating sections in *Dickens,
Women and Language* (92). Her analysis of the fifth category of female types
in Dickens's novels, "true mothers," is also very interesting, though in my
view less persuasive. Ingham notes that the markers of the "true mother" are
not generally associated with women "who have actually given birth and who
have the societal status of mother" in his texts. On the contrary, "the whole
organisation of signs relating to women serves the purpose of disvaluing biological mothers" (115). Amy Dorrit is the "apotheosis" of all the prepubertal girls
in Dickens's fiction who reach "wifehood" via surrogate motherhood, and who
effect the displacement of biological mothers, according to Ingham. "Amy
Dorrit's speechlessness is the perfection of self-abnegation. It is her womanly
invisibility and silence which allows Dickens to make her the 'heroine' of the
novel, in whom all the desired characteristics of women can be foregrounded
and eulogised" (120–21).

Despite the many insights it leads to, the chief problem with Ingham's systematic critique of Dickens's "idiolect" for representing women is that it often
becomes "metonymic and reductive" itself in its cataloguing approach to various
female types. This approach flattens out any distinctions between early and late
Dickens, and more disturbingly, between Dickens's "idiolect" and the idiolect
of his various characters. Ingham often shifts back and forth between Dickens's
narratorial language and the discourse associated even with his more reprehensible characters without clearly marking the differences, as in her description of
Eugene Wrayburn's perception of Lizzie Hexam and Dickens's, or in her account
of Dombey's, Carker's, and Dickens's itemizing perception of Edith (97). As
a result, she denies to Dickens the very insights into predatory male perceptions
of women that he prompts, even if his novelistic practice does not always itself
consistently embody those insights. Her treatment of Amy Dorrit reflects a
similar flattening out of the complexities of the character and the text she appears
in. In fact, Ingham seems to accept the fictions of a selfless "little mother" that
the Dorrit family creates, and that Dickens shows Amy uneasily participating
in at considerable psychic cost. These are fictions that the narrator himself
caustically anatomizes.

Because Ingham never applies her approach to Dickens's male characters,
one is also left wondering how exclusively female some of the linguistic markers
she itemizes may be. If Dickens's representation of "nubile girls" is often
characterized by the metonymic substitution of people for things and by a technique of "inventory" (21–22), the same might be said about his representation
of many male characters. On the other hand, one often senses an intimate
relation between the most loquacious of his "excessive females" and the novelist
himself, a connection Ingham does not consider in assuming that characters like

Sairey Gamp and Flora Finching are simply negative and misogynist portraits. There is something irrepressible about Sairey Gamp's fictionalizing loquacity that makes her a surrogate of the "inimitable" novelist himself. And Dickens was, after all, very fond of impersonating talkative females like the loquacious landlady of "Mrs. Lirriper's Lodgings."

Generally, Ingham is more successful when she relates her own linguistic inventory to an analysis of "narrative syntax" and what Gillian Beer terms "ghost plots" — that is, plots evoked by the characters' dreams and desires (14). For instance, she presents compelling evidence for a "ghost pornography" in narrative sequences involving the victimization and exchange of nubile girls in Dickens's novels (37) — although, once again, she provides no clear means for differentiating between Dickens's representation of pornographic attitudes and his own participation in them. She is on more certain ground in her "Postscript," where she turns biographical readings of Dickens's female characters on their heads by showing how his fictional representations of women may have shaped his perceptions of the actual women in his life. In showing how the "boundaries between fact and fiction dissolved" for Dickens (133), Ingham demonstrates the pervasiveness and the wiliness of narrative paradigms and representational markers. The fact that such boundaries often dissolve in critical discourse as well, as it enacts its own plots and "ghost plots," is therefore only to be expected. Even the most rigorous critic is, at best, an imperfect escape artist after all.

Dalhousie University

WHEN RUMPELSTILTSKIN RULED: VICTORIAN FAIRY TALES

By Carole Silver

P. L. TRAVERS, the creator of the famous modern children's fantasy *Mary Poppins*, tells the story of a little girl who, assured at bedtime that she need not feel lonely because God was watching her, earnestly begged her mother to ask Him to leave the room. "He makes me nervous," she protested. "I would rather have Rumpelstiltskin" (*About the Sleeping Beauty*, 1977). Like that child, mid-Victorian writers and readers also displayed a decided preference for Rumpelstiltskin. Their fascination with fairy tales resulted in what has since been called "the Golden Age" of literary fairy tales and fantasies, indeed what remains the greatest flowering of writing for children in the history of literature. Victorian England produced many of childhood's major "classics," including Lewis Carroll's Alice books, George MacDonald's Curdie tales, and J. M. Barrie's *Peter Pan*. What explains this extraordinary production? Why did it occur when it did? What special traits characterize Victorian fairy tales?

Three recent anthologies speak to some of the issues mentioned above, while republishing many of the best Victorian children's fantasies: Jack Zipes's *Victorian Fairy Tales: The Revolt of the Fairies and Elves* (New York: Methuen, 1987); Michael Patrick Hearn's *The Victorian Fairy Tale Book* (New York: Pantheon, 1988), and most recently, Nina Auerbach and U. C. Knoepflmacher's slightly more specialized *Forbidden Journeys: Fairy Tales and Fantasies by Victorian Women Writers* (Chicago: U of Chicago P, 1992). All draw directly or indirectly on a fourth, earlier collection, the landmark volume of "Novels, Stories, and Poetry from the Victorian Era" edited by Jonathan Cott, entitled *Beyond the Looking Glass: Extraordinary Works of Fairy Tale and Fantasy* and enriched by Cott's brilliant though fragmented "Notes on Fairy Faith and the Idea of Childhood" (Woodstock, NY: Overlook Press, 1973). The more recent anthologies are available in both hard cover and paperback, and all of them are worth owning.

Yet, while all three works mention the remarkable growth of children's literature during the period, none accounts for its richness and excellence or for its

327

appearing when it did. No one seems able to explain the avid acceptance in the 1860s (by the ostensibly "repressed" Victorian middle classes) of such wildly imaginative literature for the young. Were there connections between this flowering and two phenomena in the realm of adult literature: the rise of the sensation novel and the revival of occult "marvelous romances," at the same point in time? Was the writing and reading of fairy tales connected with the desire to escape from the realities of Victorian life and the forms of realism that encapsulated them, a desire that led to the outburst of fantasy writing for adults in the latter half of the century? Was the same sense of exile that led writers to the recreation of lost worlds and idealizations of them at work in children's fantasies as well? Did Darwin have something to do with this response: was it an attempt to fill the void he had left, to put back some life — albeit fantasy life — in the universe; to create worlds in which there was more than just facts and abstractions?

In the least significant of the collections, one marred by the slightness of its introduction and by its replication of tales by Ruskin, Dickens, and Kenneth Grahame already available in Zipes, Michael Patrick Hearn in *The Victorian Fairy Tale Book* provides essentially negative answers. The Golden Age occurred in the mid-Victorian era, he says, because it could not have occurred before. The persistence of English Puritanism and of English Rationalism (the legacy of the Enlightenment) retarded the revival of literary fairy tales until the 1860s, delaying it from the eighteenth century when it had occurred in France (xvii). In his far more thorough and useful introduction to *Victorian Fairy Tales*, Jack Zipes agrees. Noting that the late blossoming of literary fairy tales in England is puzzling, he comments that fairies were perceived as "enemies of the Enlightenment" (xiii). The Puritan cultural code with its distrust of imagination and emphasis on rational judgment was a guiding principle in England. Thus, didactic tales and instructional, realist stories dominated middle-class children's literature, while the old folk materials (in chapbook and pennybook forms) were thought appropriate only for those who did not matter, that is, the working classes. (They, like the fairies and elves of Zipes's subtitle, had their revenge, for it was working-class servants and nannies who told their middle-class charges the old, subversive folk tales.) Humphrey Carpenter, in *Secret Gardens: The Golden Age of Children's Literature* (Boston: Houghton Mifflin, 1985) — one of the best books on the subject — adds an alternative argument, suggesting that a Golden Age in children's literature occurs when authors feel driven from adult audiences to child readers. Before 1860, he suggests, the world seemed hopeful and inviting, but something happened to make authors reject it and instead court private, childlike responses to reality (11). But, like his successors, Carpenter never identifies the nature of this "something."

Clearly, the recognition of what the Industrial Revolution had done to England's natural and human landscape had something to do with the growth of fantasy. Hatred of urban life becomes a theme in literary fairy tales, as does escape from a machine age, an era in which it has become increasingly difficult to dream dreams and see visions. Such tales as Edith Nesbit's "Fortunatus Rex" with its open attacks on capitalism, land speculation, jerry-built suburban housing, and the destruction of the ecology are clear evidence of this. By the 1870s, at least, economic uncertainty and fears for the future may have helped turn authors away from realism. Then too, the fading of Christianity may have opened the way for alternative forms of belief. It was not, I think, as Gillian Avery contests in her important (and almost unobtainable) book *Nineteenth Century Children: Heroes and Heroines in English Children's Stories, 1780–1900* (London: Hodder and Stoughton, 1965), that fairies became the new guardian angels of children — if they did, the guidance they offered and the morality they taught was, at best, ambiguous — but instead that many literary fairy tales did provide quasi-religious images and vaguely religious "feelings," hints that there was some magic and power still evident in the universe. Perhaps all of these causes — from Darwinism to economic uncertainty — worked together. In any event, by the 1870s, as Jonathan Cott remarks, "men and women could explore their senses of childhood without apologizing for their wishing to do so or having to use alibis" (xlvii).

Certainly the middle-class view of childhood and of the nature of children had changed; children were now considered an appropriate audience — though only one of the audiences — for literary fantasy. Before either primary fairy tales (those of the Brothers Grimm were first translated into English in Taylor's 1819 edition; those of Andersen, already Christianized and moralized, in 1846) or literary versions could have their impact on Victorian culture, notions about what children should read had to alter. Above all, the idea had to be postulated that they could not be corrupted by what they read. From the Romantics had come the idea of the child as "best Philosopher," trailing clouds of glory and hence invulnerable in innocence; the concept gradually took hold. Then too, a lower birthrate and smaller families among the middle class probably led to an increased valuation of the child, to more attention to its needs. It is evident, at least, that Victorians became more child-centered and that, for stability and security, life moved inward to the family unit.

In the earlier part of the period, writers still had to moralize fairy tales or at least suggest their "improving" nature. Taylor, for example, suggested that tales built up "imaginative muscle," something as necessary as the physical and moral varieties; others promoted the value of tales in providing suitable recreation after strenuous intellectual instruction. Some, like Dickens, pleaded the cause on multiple grounds; not only did he declare didactic stories like the tee-totalling distortions of George Cruikshank "Frauds on the Fairies," but he warned in his novels for adults that children who grew up with only the "Facts" were deformed, either emotionally destroyed like Tom and Louisa Gradgrind in

Hard Times or translated into aged monkeys like the infamous Smallweed twins, Bart and Judy, in *Bleak House*. While the Victorians, like our own generation, were aware of the "primitive" qualities of fairy tales, of their bloodthirstiness and frequently unconventional morality, they seemingly accepted the pronouncements of figures like John Ruskin (and Lewis Carroll) that children were naturally "pure" and hence could not be injured by anything in the tales. Thus writers did not have to expunge anger, or the demonic, or even the erotic, provided that the delineation of these elements was sufficiently subtle.

But children were not the only audience for fantasies and fairy tales. The tales had to pass the scrutiny of parents too; they were designed as much for the middle-class adults who selected them and sometimes read them aloud as for the children themselves. Adults were, seemingly, indulgent, perhaps because many of the tales were partially derived from the folklore they themselves had heard as children — passed on to them by rural, working-class nannies or nursery maids. For male readers and writers, fairy tales allowed for the delicious sensation of nostalgia; through one's offspring and their fantasy world, one could recapture the innocence and spirituality of that lost Eden, childhood. For women, as Nina Auerbach and U. C. Knoepflmacher contend in the introduction to their recent *Forbidden Journeys*, the experience was somewhat different. Treated as children legally and socially all their lives, women were less nostalgic about childhood than men.

But what are the hallmarks of the tales the Victorians created? Were they conventional, upholding the virtues of earnestness, caution and work? Or were they essentially amoral, deeply subversive or at least ironic, indirect, and ambiguous? They were all of the above, and one of the most fascinating aspects of reading Victorian fantasy literature for children is examining the wide variety of cultural and literary experience it represents. For it ranges from the utter conformity of Harriet Childe-Pemberton's "All my Doing; or Red Riding-Hood Over Again" — in which talking to a male "wolf" leads to robbery, serious injury, and perpetual spinsterhood — to Maria Molesworth's "Brown Bull of Norrowa," with its praise of an assertive, juggling, show-off princess. Many tales examine social and political abuses, though again, the issues and the attitudes toward them range broadly. Sometimes comment is as overt as in Edith Nesbit's "Fortunatus Rex"; sometimes as sharply pointed as in Mary De Morgan's "A Toy Princess," in which both the king and his kingdom prefer a mechanical doll trained in politeness to a questioning human princess; sometimes it is as subtly embedded in the texture of a tale as in the Apple Woman's comment from Jean Ingelow's "Mopsa and the Fairies" that she, poor and without status on the earth, might as well remain a servant in fairyland. Many can be read as subversive — as subtly contesting gender roles and social attitudes rather than openly preaching revolution.

Jack Zipes is the editor most concerned with the socio-political nature of Victorian fairy tales. In his rather heavy-handed though important introduction to *Victorian Fairy Tales*, he contends that the Victorians consciously reproduced their dreams of better or alternative worlds in the fantasies they wrote; he suggests that, like the Victorian novel itself, fairy tales developed certain discourse and narrative strategies to respond to debates on the Condition of England. The tales question injustice and inequality, progress and rationality, in a world of middle-class hegemony with its tendency towards institutionalization and regimentation in all spheres (xv).

Zipes suggests that from 1840 to 1880, most writers of fairy tales raised social consciousness by writing about the class gap, about problems of poverty, and about the exploitation and deprivation of children (xix). Later in the century, says Zipes, the urge to recapture childhood as an Edenic state — what U. C. Knoepflmacher describes as the regressive tendency in children's literature — fused with utopian beliefs about building a better society on earth. Thus, from the 1860s to 1900, two kinds of tales evolved, the "Conventional" and the "Utopian." In the weakest part of his argument, Zipes identifies most invented tales (including those of Edith Nesbit and Andrew Lang) as conventional, on the grounds that their authors conceive plots to reconcile themselves and their readers to the Victorian status quo. He finds that the virtues promoted by these tales — perseverance, diligence, good sense — are the virtues that build conformist "solid citizens," that the supernatural forces presented are not real threats to established Victorian norms (xxiii), and that magic and nonsense do not truly liberate the participants in the tales.

The Utopians, on the other hand (and they are Zipes's heroes), suggest no reconciliation with the status quo. They question imaginatively the value of existing social relations and rebel against convention and conformity; protagonists in these tales alter their lives and pursue their dreams. In this category, Zipes places the works of MacDonald, Carroll, De Morgan, Ewing, Wilde, Sharp, and Housman. Noting that many of the later fairy-tale writers — including Sharp, Nesbit and Housman — were influenced by Christian Socialist, Fabian and Socialist ideals, he points to their practice of creating alternative worlds to survey conditions in the actual one. The basis of Zipes's judgment is non-literary, and the tales' aesthetic intentions and impact seem unimportant to him. He considers most valuable those stories which deal with social taboos and which lack conventional happy endings — not recognizing that the happy ending, like the marriage plot in novels, is often a "given" of the form. Pushing his thesis too hard, he finds in the stories of Oscar Wilde — tales usually categorized as "aesthetic" or even "precious" and now recognized as homosexually "coded" — a desire for spiritual reformation and an opposition to vulgar materialism, not to mention a plea for the end of class domination and exploitation.

Zipes sees much fairy tale writing as protofeminist and points to the tales' depictions of strong, independent female characters, of equality among children, and of non-gendered quests. He notes that the best of the women writers — De Morgan, Ewing, Molesworth, Sharp and Nesbit — show female characters determining their own destinies or questing for the female self. He notes as well that in feminist Utopian tales, women are the figures who expose oppression and hypocrisy.

Interestingly, Auerbach and Knoepflmacher do not agree with Zipes. With rather more critical sophistication, they contend that while Victorian fairy tales and fantasies written by women differ from those by men, the difference is not what one might expect. Women, unsentimental about childhood, did not paint it as paradisiacal; their subversion of the fairy tale genre was more covert than that of male writers, often taking the form of "ironic indirection." Male writers, these editors argue, could not only be more openly critical in content and experimental in form, but they actually appropriated the woman's plot — the young girl's journey to forbidden countries. Auerbach and Knoepflmacher note that Victorian fantasies by women tend to evoke, comment upon, or repudiate Dickens, MacDonald, and Carroll.

Since women writers' images of childhood are different, so too are their child characters, Auerbach and Knoepflmacher contend. They are less pleasant (downright unpleasant in the case of Christina Rossetti's), less pure, and considerably more angry. Punished rather than tamed, they are repeatedly balked in their search for autonomy and authority. Energies are released within the tales, but children — and the female writers who created them — remain frustrated, leading to tales generally less moving and soothing than those of male contemporaries. *Forbidden Journeys* is divided into sections on the basis of women writers' narrative strategies. It moves from "Refashioning Fairy Tales," the most pleasant section, dealing with female writers' adaptations (and transformations) of traditional materials, to the sourness and rage of Christina Rossetti's strange, grotesque "Speaking Likenesses" — described by the editors as "anti-fantasies."

Again, it is difficult to generalize about the attitudes of writers of either gender toward their female characters. Significantly, however, most of the works reproduced in the three anthologies do not support Karen Rowe's well-known contention in "Feminism and Fairy Tales" (*Women's Studies*, 6 [1979]: 237–57) that fairy tales are not good for women. In Victorian literary tales, for example, woman's power does not always reside in her youth and beauty. Many tales are notable for their portraits of unlikely female heroes and their helpers, middle-aged servants or fairy great-grandmothers. Fairy godmothers (figures not usually found in traditional folklore) abound, and some, at least, suggest images of limited, but nonetheless potent, Earth Mother and Great Goddess archetypes.

Unlike the traditional tales that Rowe attacks, these invented tales do not emphasize women competing with other women for male attention, nor do they promote, through images of the witch or wicked step-mother, female generational conflict. Though they often do suggest that female subordination (through marriage) is a romantically desirable as well as an inevitable fate for women, though they do privilege willing service to the father or the prince, these behaviors are Victorian cultural expectations. And, after all, marriage is the traditional happy ending of fairy tales.

What is unexpected is how lively and articulate the girls and women in these Victorian stories are. Female figures here are not the silent, passive sufferers of the Grimms' tales or of Andersen's; one need only think of Alice. It is true that girls are seldom seen as lovable tricksters (that role is retained by males); and girls are punished more severely for breaking prohibitions than are boys. Yet, the female protagonists in Victorian invented tales are certainly less passive, dependent, obedient, and self-renouncing than in traditional ones (or, for that matter, in conventional novels). Surprisingly too, within the literary tales, female will and female desire are not always suppressed. Girls and women may be punished for what they do and feel, but their needs and desires are at least expressed.

If women in these tales are still not as public as men and are still depicted as leading enclosed and private lives, that too reveals cultural norms. For literary fairy tales, like traditional ones, must make sense within the society that writes or publishes them. They must, as well, focus on (though not necessarily agree with) the goals that middle-class hegemony selects as significant.

The tales themselves reveal three somewhat surprising elements (none of which is extensively recognized in the introductions to any of the anthologies). They are often preoccupied with cruelty and sadism; they contain undertones of adult eroticism; and they are richly connected to the developing study of folklore.

First of all, many of the fantasies manifest what Gillian Avery describes as a "tendency to gloat over the physically grotesque, and a determined insistence on punishment" (48). Of course, the ogres and dwarfs and witches derived from folklore often represented to Victorians the evil that surrounded them; hence they almost had to be rendered as repulsive or shown to be cruel. But the same love of monster-making that creates Quilp is at work in the literary tales. What Avery considers a preoccupation with punishment, we call sadism. The Victorians probably did believe in the moral value of pain, in a sort of salvation by punishment, but in their fantasy and fairy tales, the impulse runs wild. It is not just that in Mary De Morgan, for instance, a Queen goes grotesquely bald and a good man bloodily sacrifices an eye, or that, in Christina Rossetti's "Speaking Likenesses," one child is a grotesque porcupine, another a creature made of slime, and a third a Kafkaesque apparatus composed of hooks, or that they all torment each other and other children; it is the evidence of a cultural fascination with torture and pain. While punishments in the traditional fairy world are always more severe than the crimes that cause them, in these invented tales, the imbalance and excess becomes blatant. Charles Kingsley's *Water Babies* is probably the most obvious example of the expression of sadistic impulses in Victorian children's literature, filled as it is with grotesque tortures and punishments. But the tales reprinted in these collections abound with other instances. Tony, the slothful, dreaming child of Lucy Clifford's "Wooden Tony," is cruelly and permanently transformed into a wooden clock figure that strikes the hour. Amelia, in Juliana Ewing's "Amelia and the Dwarfs," is punched, pinched, abused, and starved; Melisande, in Nesbit's tale of the same name (a sort of revisionist version of "Rapunzel") is victimized and rendered monstrous by her own hair — and for no fault of her own. Victorian fairy tales are certainly not — as Hearn mistakenly suggests — "cleaned up, without ethical ambiguity or devoid of savagery" (xxiii). Instead, they are filled with brutality. Perhaps the authors' intentions are cautionary: to teach children the consequences of transgression or to warn them that the world is truly dangerous or that life is full of pain. But the effect is other than the intention. The same perverse imagination that lies behind the strange tales of Sheridan Le Fanu or Bram Stoker's *Dracula* is present in these works ostensibly for child readers.

The illustrations to the tales are, at times, even more grotesque and sadistic than the narratives on which they comment. The sinister, demonic quality of Housman's goblin men, illustrating Christina Rossetti's poem, the torture of insects and small creatures on the peripheries of Richard Doyle's illustrations for Andrew Lang's "In Fairyland," the hideous children and grotesque hybrids created by Arthur Hughes for "Speaking Likenesses" cannot be overlooked.

The erotic element, present less frequently than the sadistic, is also evident in many of the tales. The relations between Tinykins and the adult fairy Titania (drawn from the figure in Shakespeare's *Midsummer Night's Dream*) in Mark Lemon's "Tinykins Transformed" are frankly sexual. In love with the beautiful child who partially reciprocates, Titania is ragingly jealous of his fascination with an Undine; repeatedly touching and kissing him, she is tormented by a passion that makes her try, but fail, to keep away from him. The Dwarf who wishes to keep Amelia dancing with him is depicted as a diminutive but dirty old man. Housman's "Rooted Lover" dwells on the potent sexual desire of a ploughboy who transforms himself into a flower to win his princess. In an ending that turns the tale into a sort of *Lady Chatterley's Lover* for children, his virile beauty as both a poppy and a man compels his princess to renounce her kingdom for passion in a cottage.

Yet, perhaps, the presence of cruelty and eroticism in these tales is partially explained by their relation to a factor other than either Victorian morality or Victorian psychopathology — their connections to the emerging study of "primitive customs and beliefs." In a letter used as an epigraph to *Beyond the Looking*

Glass, a friend of Cott's remarks on how elemental the Victorians were, how intact their connection was to savage Celtic tradition, and how much the force of the prehistoric world (or at least their vision of prehistoric "savagery") invaded their own ostensibly "civilized" society. This sense of closeness to primal roots was intensified, if not created, by their burgeoning interest in folklore. Victorian readers knew and loved folklore materials and theories about them — made available to them through large numbers of popular books and magazine articles. And perhaps because the British, unlike the Germans, had "lost" most of their Märchen, they freely incorporated ingredients of actual folklore into their own invented works. Ewing's "Amelia and the Dwarfs," for example, is based on Irish folklore, but the author's knowledge of the traditions of fairyland and of changelings far transcends her source. The unpleasant land in which Amelia is confined is the place described in numerous folklore accounts: an underground realm of perpetual twilight, without weather, seasons or time; the Dwarfs' servant (and Amelia's helper) is a traditional underworld inhabitant, the abducted fairy nurse or midwife; even the dwarfs' cruelty is of the conventional folklore variety. As is usual in changeling tales, the Dwarfs replace Amelia with a stock; in reality it is a hairy imp, whose real nature is visible to Amelia only because she has had her eye touched with "fairy ointment."

The view of the "anthropological folklorists," that lore incorporated "survivals" from prehistoric times and enshrined old barbaric morals and practices, gives many of these children's fantasies their dark imaginative power; it also tacitly permits writers to depict violence and sexual passion — these too are vestiges of earlier times. For example, Andrew Lang, a major anthropological folklorist, incorporates into his tale, "Princess Nobody," the folklore motif of the prohibited name (a subject of considerable interest to Victorian theorists) as well as a brief digression on "primitive" peoples' taboo on the use of personal appellations; he interrupts his story to announce that "some nations won't let a wife mention her husband's name" (Zipes 259).

Beyond this, much folklore material that we, though not the Victorians, might think esoteric finds its way into childrens' fantasies. George MacDonald, whose knowledge of Celtic lore is formidable, deals in just one of his tales, "The Golden Key," with the fairies' dislike of dirt and punishment of slovenly housekeepers, with the differences between time in fairyland and on earth (in the former, three earthly years pass in what seems an instant), and with the lore of Elementals (including the relative ages of spirits of Water, Earth, Air, and Fire), so important to Victorian Spiritualists and Theosophists. Mark Lemon's "Tinykins Transformed" and Mary De Morgan's tales are equally laden with lore: Tinykins is a Sunday child and hence can see fairies; bees are elfin messengers; land fairies cannot cross running water; foxgloves (with their powerful digitalis) are fairy bells and fairy medicine. When Tinykins is transformed into various animals, he appears to ordinary mortals to be "Away" (possessed or in a trance), a state repeatedly discussed by folklorists. In De Morgan's "Wanderings of Arasman," the evil fairies are identified as the "dark elves" of Scandinavian legend, while in "Through the Fire," all the major figures except for the protagonist are Elementals. Questions of the size of fairies and of their tribes and species, as well as of elfin relations with gypsies (supposedly traditional enemies), occur throughout Ingelow's "Mopsa and the Fairies," while Elementals, especially evil Gnomes, play their roles in Ford Madox Ford's "Brown Owl." In all, through their use of folklore, the Victorians revitalized and transmitted a cultural inheritance, one that we have lost.

In effect, an examination of Victorian fantasies and fairy tales reveals that the same questions and topics that interested Victorians in general found their way into literature ostensibly for children. Lovingly written for the most part, the stories appealed to the Victorian fascination with the supernatural, a fascination that we share. The powers one has in fairy tale and fantasy — invisibility, flight, knowledge, control of one's environment — as well as the fears — of torture, of abduction, of loss of self and identity — are all richly present. Victorian fairy tales spoke to Victorian daydreams and nightmares; they still seem to speak to ours today.

Yeshiva University

CONNECTIONS AND TRADITIONS IN NINETEENTH-CENTURY WOMEN'S POETRY

By Glennis Stephenson

"NINETEENTH-CENTURY WOMEN'S LITERATURE," as Angela Leighton observes in the opening lines of her *Victorian Women Poets: Writing Against the Heart* (Charlottesville: UP of Virginia and Hemel Hempstead: Harvester Wheatsheaf, 1992), "has attracted considerable critical attention in recent years, but women's poetry, as a distinct genre, has not" (1). The publication of such works as Dolores Rosenblum's *Christina Rossetti: The Poetry of Endurance* in 1986 and Dorothy Mermin's *Elizabeth Barrett Browning: The Origins of a New Poetry* in 1989 certainly encouraged a revival of critical interest in these two particular women, but, on the whole, nineteenth-century British women's poetry has remained a strangely neglected field. American women poets have received far more attention, mainly due to the impressive work of such critics as Alicia Ostriker, in *Stealing the Language: The Emergence of Women's Poetry in America* (1986), and Cheryl Walker, in both *The Nightingale's Burden: Women Poets and American Culture Before 1900* (1982) and her recent anthology of *American Women Poets of the Nineteenth Century* (1992). Over the last three years, however, there have been a number of encouraging signs suggesting a gradual movement towards a more serious engagement with the nineteenth-century female poetic tradition, and Leighton's *Victorian Women Poets*, without a doubt the most important book to have emerged in this field since Kathleen Hickok's ground-breaking *Representations of Women* in 1984, should do much to encourage further research into the works of these poets.

Leighton has three major aims: to offer a useful introduction to the lives and works of eight major women poets; to demonstrate how Victorian women's poetry "grows out of a struggle with and against a highly moralised celebration of women's sensibility" (3); and to tackle the contentious question of the relationship between aesthetics and politics. She begins with chapters on Felicia Hemans and Letitia Elizabeth Landon, not strictly Victorians, but nonetheless the originators of the poetic tradition that she will trace and the two women with whom every subsequent female poet of the nineteenth century, either directly or indirectly, was engaged. Hemans stood "as an example of what was professionally and publicly possible" (16), while Landon "provided a stark reminder of the risks of professional success for women" (45). Both contributed to a general "dissociation of sensibility from the affairs of the world," a dissociation that Leighton persuasively argues is "one of the woman poet's most disabling inheritances. The attempt to overcome that dissociation by writing not from, but against the heart, is an ambition which, although taking different forms, connects all these poets who follow in the wake of Hemans and L.E.L." (3).

In the chapters that follow, Leighton explores this attempt to write "against the heart" in the works of six subsequent poets: Elizabeth Barrett Browning, Christina Rossetti, Augusta Webster, Michael Field (counted as one), Alice Meynell, and Charlotte Mew. Her exemplary readings of their lives and works convincingly argue against the persistent notion of the nineteenth-century woman poet as anomaly by establishing the women's active participation in the ongoing development of a poetic tradition, while at the same time illuminating the highly varied ways in which the women chose to rebel against the suffocating model of sensibility offered by Hemans and Landon.

One of the most interesting chapters of this book is that on Augusta Webster. With the dramatic monologue firmly in place as *the* significant Victorian poetic genre, it is difficult to imagine how a woman who utilized this verse form to such effect should have been so totally forgotten. Webster, Leighton suggests, is "a determined literalist of the imagination" (164). As the work of an "outspoken feminist and social critic," Webster's "verse finds its distance from the 'artificial melancholy' of the heart by turning altogether away from self, and dramatically adopting the voices of others" (164). Leighton shows how Webster uses the split which is typically opened up within the subject speaker of the dramatic monologue, not ironically to expose double standards or double dealings, but to establish her speakers as "victims of historical and social double standards outside themselves"; womanhood comes to appear "self-divided in these poems, not because of disingenuousness within, but because of reflections and myths without" (178).

Part of the reason for the continuing obscurity of such nineteenth-century women poets as Webster must surely be the difficulty of obtaining texts. Until recently, very little advance had been made in this area since the publication of Cora Kaplan's *Salt and Bitter and Good* (1975). While the Women's Press reprint of *Aurora Leigh*, with an introduction by Kaplan, has been available since 1978, there has long been an urgent need for a critically annotated edition, and this need has now been admirably met by Margaret Reynolds (Athens: Ohio UP, 1992). Reynolds's extensive footnotes to her edition of *Aurora Leigh* are a godsend, providing a mine of information about Barrett Browning's references to everything from phalanxes to friezes to false teeth. Just reading these footnotes is both an education and an entertainment in itself. Other features include the most comprehensive bibliography of primary and secondary sources published to date and a complete listing of textual variants supplemented by a reproduction of the opening passages of the first draft manuscript in the Appendix. Reynolds also provides two definitive introductions: one critical, one editorial. The editorial introduction offers invaluable information on the composition, publication, and revision of *Aurora Leigh*; while the critical introduction constitutes the best essay I have yet seen on the poem. Like Leighton, Reynolds believes that "the very best theoretical writing on women and poetry from the nineteenth century is to be found not in the work of the critics, but in the poetry itself, and especially in the poetry written by women, who were often self-consciously and critically aware of their own anomalous position. This is why the work of feminist critics in tracing connections and traditions between women writers is a significant enterprise, with much still to be done" (5).

After detailing both nineteenth and twentieth-century critical attitudes to Barrett Browning, Reynolds sensibly cautions against the "feminist folk-poetics" which would "describe the poem as either effusive autobiography or the recoverable expression of a universal female experience of oppression" (11) and so do no more than provide a "restatement of the classic values relating to women's poetry" (10). Her own reading of *Aurora Leigh* concentrates upon "methods of reading the verse-novel which emphasise the contextual, formalist, and theoretical questions raised by the work" (12). First, she examines the literary context to show how Barrett Browning's theories of poetry grew out of her engagement with Romantic theory and her involvement in topical debates and literary disputes with other writers of the time — most notably Mary Mitford and Robert Browning. Then, she considers "Lady Geraldine's Courtship" and *Casa Guidi Windows* as early models for Barrett Browning's experiment with narrative. And finally, Reynolds offers "a theoretical approach to *Aurora Leigh* as a woman's text which, through its sophisticated narrative construction and challenge to conventional literary form in its methods of diffusion and fragmentation, subverts, at least for the poem's length, the assumptions of the 'liberal humanist' context within which Barrett Browning wrote" (12).

Reynolds's *Aurora Leigh* is, quite simply, an impeccable example of first-class editing, and like Leighton's *Victorian Women Poets*, it is one work that should be in the library of anyone involved in the teaching of Victorian literature. Unfortunately, the cost of this edition will probably make it prohibitive for students. Publishers do, however, finally seem to have caught on to the idea that there is indeed a market for paperback editions of nineteenth-century women's poetry. *Aurora Leigh* has now become a standard text in many Victorian poetry courses, and so, on cue, a Norton edition is forthcoming, and an Oxford edition has already appeared (Oxford: Oxford UP, 1993). It would be unfair to compare Kerry McSweeney's Oxford edition with that of Reynolds, and while it is by no means as complete in its footnotes, McSweeney's *Aurora Leigh* is nevertheless a well annotated and accessible edition. Its usefulness, however, appears to me to be seriously compromised by its introduction.

McSweeney places *Aurora Leigh* within the nineteenth-century literary context by noting the influence of *Corinne, Consuelo, Jane Eyre,* and other novels, and here he does little more than repeat the points already made by Cora Kaplan in her introduction to the Women's Press edition. But unlike Kaplan, who, quoting Ellen Moers, notes that *Aurora Leigh* has become " '*the* feminist poem' radical in its celebration of the centrality of female experience" (11), McSweeney concludes that "the essential context in which *Aurora Leigh* must be placed if it is to be understood and fully savoured is not feminist; it is high Victorian. Like Carlyle and Ruskin, the poet of *Aurora Leigh* is a cultural prophet inscribing a secular scripture" (xxxii). Aligning himself with such critics as Deirdre David and Rachel DuPlessis, who view Aurora's eventual marriage as capitulation, McSweeney repeats that Barrett Browning "did not espouse a feminist ideology and was not a feminist by either Victorian or present-day criteria. *Aurora Leigh* may tell the story of a woman's struggle to free herself from internalized anti-feminist biases and to find vocational fulfilment; but in the end Aurora comes to realize the value of being 'a woman, such / As God made women, to save men by love' " (xxxi). The implication (*but in the end*) that this realization somehow negates all that Aurora learns and achieves is outrageous, and seems to dismiss the central point of the ending — that here, as Margaret Reynolds notes, Barrett Browning "imagines a radical break from the traditions of the nineteenth-century feminine by proposing that a woman's life might contain both love and work and that each might reinforce, rather than contradict, the other" (46). Even so, Reynolds also observes, the success of *Aurora Leigh* "lies not with its resolving, which given the poem's historical context must always be a negotiated compromise, but with the challenge which its 'lived' techniques of fragmentation and disruption present in the process" (11–12). McSweeney is too intent upon imposing cohesion and resolution upon a text which draws its very strength from resistance and disruption.

McSweeney's introduction also unfortunately tends to propagate the mistaken idea that Barrett Browning is some kind of anomaly in the nineteenth century: we are given no sense of her place within a female poetic tradition. On the contrary, after reproducing the much-quoted comment, "I look everywhere for grandmothers and see none," McSweeney instead suggests that while Barrett Browning was a

> sensitive and discriminating reader of the two principal female poets of the next generation, Felicia Hemans (1793–1835) and Letitia Elizabeth Landon (1802–38) . . . [and] while both these writers influenced her thinking about the

distinctive vocational and emotional vicissitudes of the female poet, neither's work was helpful in her attempt to write a long poem of a new class. (xvii–xviii)

One only has to read Landon's *The Improvisatrice*, a direct influence on *Aurora Leigh* (and at points blatantly plagiarized by Barrett Browning) to see just how mistaken McSweeney is in this respect; Leighton's *Victorian Women Poets* provides a necessary corrective in showing how actively Barrett Browning did in fact participate in an ongoing female poetic tradition. My particular irritation with this edition of *Aurora Leigh* stems from my belief that the publishers at Oxford, knowing how widely their texts are used by students, have a certain responsibility to ensure informed and up-to-date analysis of the texts they present: this is not one of the World's Classics series that I will want my students to use.

The establishment of the existence of the women's poetic tradition is one of the most compelling points to emerge in many of the articles and books published on these women poets over the last three years. One of the major strengths of Kathleen Jones's biography, *Learning Not to be First: The Life of Christina Rossetti* (1991), for example, is the way in which Jones identifies the many links between Rossetti and her female contemporaries rather than simply presenting her as yet another aberrant female in the form of the High-Priestess of the Pre-Raphaelites. The sense of community among the women poets of the nineteenth-century seems to have been much stronger than is generally thought.

The case of Letitia Landon, the focus of my own research, provides a striking example of the kind of ongoing dialogue that in fact took place among these women. In 1835 Landon published an essay on Hemans in the *New Monthly Magazine*, and a poem, "Stanzas on the Death of Mrs. Hemans." Both essay and poem, as Leighton points out, insist "on a sentimentalist transparency of life and art, which brings the character of the poet comfortingly within reach" (42):

> With what still hours of calm delight
> Thy songs and image blend;
> I cannot choose but think thou wert
> An old familiar friend.

Barrett Browning soon responded with her "Felicia Hemans: To L.E.L. Referring to her Monody on the Poetess." Simultaneously revealing the influence of, and her struggle with, the tradition of her predecessors, Barrett Browning presses "beyond the narcissistic consciousness of 'woe,' which both Hemans and L.E.L. ostentatiously parade, to the idea of the poem as a separate, impersonal object" (Leighton 43–44). When one of Landon's last poems, "Night at Sea," appeared after her death in 1839, Barrett Browning once again took her to task. Landon, musing on the friends she left behind when she went to Africa, echoes lines from Hemans's "A Parting Song" ("When will ye think of me, my friends? / When will ye think of me") in her mournful refrain: "My friends, my absent friends! / Do you think of me, as I think of you?" Turning the personal into the impersonal, Barrett Browning in "L.E.L.'s Last Question" takes on the larger issues: "what are we that we should / For covenants of long affection sue?" The request for remembrance made by this woman "thirsty for a little love," she observes, is "Not much, and yet too much." But Barrett Browning certainly remembered her — Leighton even makes a convincing argument for Little Ellie of "The Romance of the Swan's Nest" as a thinly disguised L.E.L. No other poet was in fact remembered and reflected upon quite as much as Landon by other women writers of the time. There are also poems about her written by Rossetti (who adapts Barrett Browning's line for her epigraph: "Whose heart was breaking for a little love"); by Alicia Sparrow (who takes Hemans's lines "Now peace the woman's heart hath found / And joy the poet's eye!" for hers); and by Maria Jane Jewsbury, Mrs. Wilson, Camilla Toulmin, and Mary Howitt, among others. Interestingly, many of these poems focus as much upon the woman herself as upon her works; Landon's life and work provided both a warning and a heartening example of the troubles and the triumphs of the woman who also happens to be a poet. It is certainly difficult to imagine this kind of ongoing dialogue taking place among the male poets of the time, to imagine, say, Browning engaging in such ways with the life of Tennyson.

While Leighton sometimes sounds almost apologetic about her inclusion of biographical detail, in the case of nineteenth-century women poets, to reduce the works to abstract textuality — to ignore questions of culture and gender — would surely result in misrepresentation. Certainly, as Barrett Browning reminded Landon, and Margaret Reynolds reminds us, there is always a need to separate the artist and the woman, to avoid reducing the artist's poetry to the woman's self-expression; but, on the other hand, as Leighton's analysis demonstrates, when it comes to the work of the nineteenth-century woman poet, there can be only one answer to Foucault's notorious question, "What difference does it make who is speaking?": it makes a very great difference indeed. How can we, as readers, ignore the historical particularities of the authors of these texts when so often it was their negotiations with these very historical particularities that formed the focal point of their writings?

One recent article that considers two unaccountably neglected poets and succinctly illustrates the potential rewards of considering the circumstances which govern relations between both authors and texts and readers and texts is Christine White's " 'Poets and lovers evermore': Interpreting Female Love in the Poetry and Journals of Michael Field" (*Textual Practice* 4.2: 197–212). As White shows, in "their relationship and their work, Katherine and Edith typify many of the difficulties in deciphering the meaning and nature of love between women'' (197). By identifying the negotiations made by these women within a hostile dominant culture, White begins "the process of mapping out the complicated processes whereby the discourses of lesbianism might have been inscribed in the nineteenth century" (210) and persuasively argues against the influential thesis of Lillian Faderman in *Surpassing the Love of Men* (1981).

Putting White's article and Leighton's book aside, however, it is still the case that the majority of the work done in this field during the last three years has been concerned with Barrett Browning and Rossetti. Barrett Browning studies would seem to have hit a bit of a stumbling block since we are still getting articles on "Gender and Narration in *Aurora Leigh*" (*VP* 29.1: 17–32), a subject which has surely been mined almost to exhaustion. On the other hand, Sandra Donaldson's annotated bibliography of Barrett Browning, due out from G. K. Hall/Macmillan in late 1993, promises to be a very useful addition to the corpus of secondary material, and is a sure sign that this is one woman poet, at least, who has finally arrived. Like Barrett Browning, Christina Rossetti continues to attract much critical attention — the lion's share still going to "Goblin Market." And although Terence Holt, in his " 'Men sell not such in any town': Exchange in Goblin Market," (*VP* 28.1: 51–67), was able to claim in 1990 that "the 'market' of the title has received little attention" (51), this is by no means still the case. The most interesting recent articles on Rossetti all deal to some degree with economics and the commodity culture: Mary Wilson Carpenter's " 'Eat me, drink me, love me': The Consumable Female Body in Christina Rossetti's 'Goblin Market' " (*VP* 29.4: 415–34); Elizabeth Campbell's "Of Mothers and Merchants: Female Economics in Christina Rossetti's 'Goblin Market' " (*VS* 33.3: 393–410); and Elizabeth Helsinger's "Consumer Power and the Utopia of Desire: Christina Rossetti's 'Goblin Market' " (*ELH* 58.4: 903–33). And, of course, one of the highlights of 1990 was the publication of the final volume of Rebecca Crump's three-volume edition of Christina Rossetti's poems (Baton Rouge: Louisiana State UP, 1979–1990).

A number of other useful editions of nineteenth-century women's poetry have also been recently published, including *Women Romantic Poets 1785–1832*, selected and introduced by Jennifer Breen (London: Dent, 1992) and *Emily Jane Brontë: The Complete Poems*, edited and introduced by Janet Gezari (London: Penguin, 1992). Although Breen's *Women Romantic Poets* might have benefitted from more extensive annotation, this is a fascinating collection, reprinting selections from twenty-six poets and ending with a series of biographical notes. One of the most notable features of this anthology, which offers a welcome alternative view of the Romantic period, is that rather than limiting herself to such middle-class women of letters as Felicia Hemans, Joanna Baillie, Jane Taylor, Mary Lamb, and Dorothy Wordsworth, Breen has also included selections from the working-class poets, Elizabeth Bentley, Elizabeth Hands, Christian Milne, Charlotte Richardson, and Ann Yearsley, selections which clearly reveal these women to be much more than simple literary curiosities and certainly deserving of further critical study. The themes and forms of women's poetry during this period, as Breen notes in her brief but incisive introduction, "necessarily emerged from their experience as women in a society which largely ignored them except as wives and mothers who had no legal equality with men nor independent economic status" (xv–xvi). Domesticity as a subject, however, is not necessarily limiting; it allowed "these writers . . . to develop distinctively original female voices. But poets from different classes had different points of view. Middle-class women sometimes wrote from the standpoint of organizers of labour, whereas servant women usually wrote from the perspective of a double subservience to men and women" (xvi). At the same time, working-class women also, as Breen shows, often turned to satire "to expose, among other things, prevailing assumptions about 'suitable' subjects for poetry" (xvii). Elizabeth Hands, a servant, mockingly reveals the pretensions of her employers in a lively satire about their responses to her poetry:

> " 'Tis pity the girl was not bred in high life,"
> Says Mr. Fribello. — "Yes, — then," says his wife,
> "She doubtless might have wrote something worth notice."
> " 'Tis pity," says one — says another, "and so 'tis."
> "O law!", says young Seagram, "I've seen the book, now
> I remember; there's something about a mad cow."
> "A mad cow! — ha, ha, ha, ha," returned half the room;
> "What can y'expect better?", says Madam du Bloom. (xvii)

This is an excellent anthology which will make a racy addition to the usual set texts in Romantic literature courses and will perhaps further stimulate the growing interest in the women Romantics that has followed in the wake of the publication of such works as Marlon Ross's *The Contours of Masculine Desire: Romanticism and the Rise of Women's Poetry* (1990). Another anthology of *Women Romantic Poets*, edited by Andrew Ashfield and due to be published by McClelland and Stewart in 1993, also sounds promising.

Janet Gezari's Penguin edition of *Emily Jane Brontë: The Complete Poems* chronologically reproduces the published texts of the 1846 *Poems* and the most recent manuscript versions of the others. The extensive annotations include commentary on the manuscripts while also placing the publication of the poems in context. This is exactly the kind of edition for which there is now the greatest need — accessible to students, yet also useful for the researcher. In her introduction, Gezari succinctly discusses the publication history of the poems, Brontë's usual process of composition, her choice of copy text and order, and so on. The Gondal story draws only brief mention, and Gezari makes "no effort to reconstruct a coherent narrative in [her] notes to the poems, or to enlarge on a Gondal context for the stories they tell" (xxxii). It is somewhat of a relief to find

Gondal downplayed. As Gezari notes, "the literary interest Gondal has for us . . . depends on the poems that have survived, not on the lost Gondal stories . . . the assumption that the lost pieces of a prose narrative told a coherent story, and that the poems emerged out of it, is anyway open to serious question" (xxxii). Fannie Ratchford's reconstruction of the Gondal narrative, which fails to distinguish between events taken from the poems and events based solely on supposition, has had the unfortunate effect of diverting attention from the poems themselves, and Gezari makes a wise decision in freeing the poetic text from this jumble of conjecture.

Given the questionable centrality of Gondal, it is surprising that most critical studies of Brontë still take this as the primary focus — for example, Teddi Lynn Chichester's "Evading 'Earth's Dungeon Tomb': Emily Brontë, A.G.A. and the Fatally Feminine" (*VP* 29.1: 1–15) and Maureen Peeck-O'Toole's *Aspects of Lyric in the Poetry of Emily Brontë* (Amsterdam: *Costerus*, vol. 70, 1988). Margaret Homans's study of Brontë in *Women Writers and Poetic Identity* (1980), in which she contends that a sequence of non-Gondal poems "forms the core of Brontë's canon," remains the best analysis of the poems to date, and it is surprising that more work has not been done in placing Brontë within her social, historical, and cultural context. Dorothy Mermin has suggested, in her article on "The Damsel, the Knight, and the Victorian Woman Poet" (*Critical Inquiry* 13.1: 64–80), that Brontë at least presents the predicament of the woman poet in much the same way as her female contemporaries; for Brontë, Mermin writes, "the story of the damsel and the knight is the story of the female subject's displacement into the position of the erotic object of male imagination, and she makes poems out of the struggle between them" (77). This struggle can be found in the works of nearly every other woman poet of the time and clearly links Brontë to her contemporaries. I was hoping to find some attempt to identify such links in Gezari's edition, given the current interest in the nineteenth-century female poetic tradition, but her introduction is obviously meant to be editorial rather than critical. While it may therefore be unfair to quibble about a lack of what Gezari does not attempt to provide, her introduction is, as a result, rather unsatisfactory. If Gondal is taken away, how do we place Brontë's poems? As more work has been done on the women's poetic tradition during the nineteenth century, surely we must move away from the idea of Brontë as yet one more female anomaly and reject the implications of Charlotte Brontë's pronouncement, upon the discovery of Emily's poems, that they were not at all like the poetry women generally write. This new edition of Brontë's poems would seem to have provided the ideal opportunity for a reassessment of Brontë's place within the nineteenth-century women's poetic tradition.

The degree to which, as Leighton says, in the case of nineteenth-century women " 'a literature of their own' has tended to overshadow 'a poetry of their own' " (1) promises to be conclusively demonstrated by Isobel Armstrong's anthology, due to be published in late 1993. This anthology, which will include substantial selections from about 100 women poets who were writing between 1800 and 1900, with headnotes, will fill a long-recognized gap. Perhaps the days of spending endless hours putting together photocopied selections of the poems are coming to an end. The teacher interested in mainstreaming these women's work for seminars on Victorian poetry frequently encounters enough problems in trying to convince many students that this material is worthy of serious consideration without having to rely on the photocopied selections which immediately, and inevitably, seem to cast doubt on the authority of the text and insidiously reproduce the marginalization of the woman poet. Armstrong's anthology will not only eliminate this problem, it will also help to generate more critical interest in nineteenth-century women poets. As a larger selection of texts becomes available for study, in the near future, we will no doubt see further work done on such subjects as the cultural and material conditions that influenced women writing poetry in the ninteenth century, on the conventions of female poetics, and, most particularly, on the strikingly dialogic nature of that tradition of women's poetry which, as Leighton observes, is "essentially Victorian, not because it is morbidly sentimental or self-pityingly exposed, as has too often been assumed, but because it has a sense of the constant fret of life against art, truth against beauty, conscience against dream, and thus of the special toll exacted from women for the amoral, objectless pleasures of their imaginations" (298).

University of Stirling

NEW DIRECTIONS IN VICTORIAN PUBLISHING HISTORY

By Bill Bell

WHEN THOMAS CARLYLE FULMINATED in 1829 against the growing mechanization of literature, with "its Trade-dinners, its Editorial conclaves, and huge, subterranean, puffing bellows," he could hardly have anticipated just how pervasive the literary production "machine" would become within a few decades. Nor could he have imagined what fascination that same machine would come to hold for scholars of literature and history over a century later. For what must have seemed in his day like a mundane round of business deals, contracts, and ledgers has in recent years become the object of intense interest for scholars, and particularly for those involved in Victorian studies.

What follows is a brief and by no means comprehensive survey of some of the most recent scholarly offerings to have implications for the future study of Victorian print media. Given the longstanding socio-political focus taken by previous specialists of the period, it is hardly surprising that so much of this recent activity has focused on and around the nineteenth century. It should be recognized, however, that among the most stimulating sources continue to be those whose theoretical concerns give them significance well beyond their immediate historical focus. The study of print history is fast becoming an intellectual space open to a whole host of lively and informative new developments that have implications for reading not only within but also beyond the taxonomies of chronological boundary. "After several decades of growth," announced a recent issue of the *Chronicle of Higher Education*, "book history is now at a point of transition. Researchers are beginning to cross disciplinary and national borders to establish new journals, book projects, centers, and academic programs" ("History of Print Culture," July 14, 1993: 7–8). The majority of the following items have been chosen for the contributions they offer to new theories and methodologies. Taken together, they suggest something of the effect that this interdisciplinary cross-fertilization is beginning to have on our perception not only of the nineteenth century but of print culture in general.

347

As one of the most important public forums for the exchange and the dissemination of ideas in the nineteenth century, the periodical press has always proved an immensely rich resource for the cultural historian. Probably the most self-conscious of recent attempts to address the serial as a genre are to be found in Laurel Brake, Aled Jones, and Lionel Madden's *Investigating Victorian Journalism* (Basingstoke: Macmillan, 1991). While its immediate emphasis throughout is on the press of the Victorian era, of more general interest will be the section entitled "Theorising Journalism," which opens with Lynn Pykett's persuasive contribution, "Reading the Periodical Press: Text and Context" (3–18). Throwing down the gauntlet to more conventional strategies for periodical reading, Pykett argues against the traditional regard for a reflective model in which textual traces of the past are considered as objects unproblematically yielding up their secrets to the modern reader. The notion that periodicals are not, and never have been, passive articulators of cultural value is nothing new, of course, but Pykett's timely reminder that such texts have always functioned as implicit agents of cultural formation as well as articulation is a salutary warning to a scholarly establishment that has too often treated reportage as an unmediated and transparent discourse. The final call for a combined "rhetorical" and "empirical" approach to periodical criticism is undoubtedly more difficult than it sounds. The effect that the cultural critiques of, for example, Gramsci and Althusser are only now beginning to have on theoretical bibliography is long overdue, however, and, as Pykett indicates, should continue to inform some of the most fruitful avenues of inquiry for some time to come.

In an attempt to address the more difficult and fundamental question of what actually constitutes a "periodical," Margaret Beetham, in "Toward a Theory of the Periodical as a Publishing Genre" (19–32), enters on a wide-ranging discussion of some of its more salient formal properties. Here, too, we are offered a welcome departure from the regard for the Victorian serial as "a quarry or mine from which [to] dig isolated articles" (20). Recognizing possible homologies between its origins and its material form, Beetham begins by asserting that a new understanding of the periodical would inevitably emerge from an exploration of the formative influence of its capitalist mode of production. One genuinely original contribution here is Beetham's compelling attempt to engage the terminology of recent literary theory in order to rethink the periodical in terms of a formal bifurcation that she claims as one of its most important definitive features: " 'closed' or 'masculine' forms are seen as those which assert the dominant structures of meaning by closing off alternative options" while "the 'open' form which refuses the closed ending and allows for the possibility of alternative meanings, is associated with the potentially disruptive, the creative, the 'feminine' " (27). The benefits of such a model are obvious, not least for the challenge it offers to the customary treatment of the periodical as a homogenous entity. While she does not exercise herself on how such an oppositional framework might be applied as methodology, it is nevertheless more than possible to see how Beetham's regard for the periodical as a genre and the recognition of its "Janus-like" quality might open up new possibilities for reading serial form.

Other essays in the book fall under two remaining general headings, "The Diversity of Victorian Journalism" and "Directions in Journalism Studies." This is an ambitious collection, whose stated overall purpose is no less than to propose "new directions for the study of media" (xi). Altogether, *Investigating Victorian Journalism* presents probably the most worthwhile source on the subject to appear since Shattock and Wolff's *Victorian Periodical Press: Samplings and Soundings* (1982) and pays testimony to the kind of critical and methodological energy that has been spent on the periodical over the past decade.

With its perennial concern for the material specificity of historical documents, Marxist criticism has over the years exhibited more than a fleeting interest in the production and dissemination of the periodical as an ideological form. Finding a rich provenance, in Britain at least, in the pioneering investigations of Raymond Williams and Richard Hoggart in the 1950s — themselves responses to the Leavises' ill-fated attempt to define the "reading public" a full twenty years before — has been a developing concern for the sociology of the printed word. In recent years a number of contributions to what might be called the "new textual studies" have continued to appear in the form of books and articles, some of the most important of them in the pages of journals like *Literature and History*, where the deployment of such concepts as "audience formation" and "social addressee" has done much to problematize long-held assumptions about ideological relations within Victorian print culture. One of the most thoughtful of recent studies to come out of this critical ferment is Andrew Blake's *Reading Victorian Fiction* (Basingstoke: Macmillan, 1989), which offers a useful synthesis of approach drawing on a by now familiar range of cultural analyses from Althusser to Geertz. Applying "thick description" to the production and consumption of the printed word can yield some interesting results, but Blake is at his most original when he gets away from the explanation of well-worn abstractions and finally comes to grips with the intertextuality of culture. In synchronic readings of three prominent vehicles of 1860s middle-class fiction — the *Cornhill*, *Blackwood's*, and the *Fortnightly* — we are throughout made acutely aware of the extent to which "fiction was a crucial mediating element . . . standing between the private literary production of the letter, the booksellers and publishers, and the lending libraries" (133). The treatment of the periodical as a "point of contact" between bourgeois culture and its correlative audience is a convincing strategy, and as this study shows can open even the most familiar works of fiction to new significances.

Someone who has already made his presence conspicuously felt on the left of publishing history is Norman Feltes, whose *Literary Capital and the Late*

Victorian Novel (Madison: U of Wisconsin P, 1993) provides a substantial addition to inroads already made in *Modes of Production of Victorian Fiction* (1986). Aiming to demystify certain aspects of the fiction-production process, this study covers the relatively neglected last two decades of the century, a period when, so the argument goes, British society underwent a transformation from a "high-capitalist, free enterprise mode of production to the late-capitalist, monopoly-capital mode of production" (4). Covering such topics as the rise of the literary agent, the foundation of the Society of Authors, and attitudes towards women as writers, Feltes sets out to provide an antidote to what he regards as misguided "objectivist" readings of literary history. From an introductory investigation of "Publishing as Capital," Feltes proceeds to uncover some of the assumptions underlying the emergence of "the Literary" as a categorical definition. Following a fascinating reading of the "Hundred Best Books" debate are two final, chronological chapters on the 1880s and 1890s respectively, in which attitudinal developments in the trade are given relentless historical specificity. Though not as ambitious in its scope as *Modes of Production*, this study is underpinned throughout with the kind of rigorous protocol we have come to expect from Feltes. The closely argued sections on the "candour" debate, for instance, and the role of Walter Besant in the battle for literary property, provide genuinely original contributions to the understanding of changing relations within the "profession" at century's end.

One recent critic who takes variance with what she calls the "pessimistic position" of many such contemporary Marxist accounts is Patricia Anderson, who in *The Printed Image and the Transformation of British Culture 1790–1860* (Oxford: Clarendon, 1991) argues against the explanation of mass culture "merely as an instrument of capitalist domination . . . and imposed upon an apathetic working class" (5). In what is a lively methodological introduction, Anderson finds an alternative point of departure in the observation that "the hallmark of a transformed and expanded popular culture was its increasingly pictorial character" (2). Examining runs of the *Penny Magazine, London Journal, Reynolds's Miscellany*, and *Cassell's Illustrated Family Paper*, Anderson sets out to offer what she calls a "nuanced understanding" of the development of pictorial culture over a seventy-year period. The claim that "workers actively chose to buy pictorial magazines and in doing so consented to the various values embodied in these publications" is without doubt a contentious one, as is the claim that "their consent was also a matter of choice and accorded with their individual and collective needs as an emergent class" (6). What, for instance, might "consent" actually mean in this context? And with all that we now know about the complex dynamics of reception, is it simply enough to say that "culture emanates from both producers and consumers" (14)? All in all, Anderson's book raises more questions about the rise of mass culture than it answers, but as the most sustained examination of the magazine illustration and its nineteenth-century audience to date, it provides a more than adequate foundation from which further readings of the popular image will undoubtedly emerge.

Since the publication of Richard Altick's *The English Common Reader* more than thirty years ago, there have been surprisingly few attempts to examine the sociology of readership in any sustained way. Jon Klancher's *The Making of English Reading Audiences, 1790–1832* (Madison: U of Wisconsin P, 1987) is a notable exception in this regard and, while its chronological focus falls outside the Victorian period proper, provides another thought-provoking framework in and around which subsequent discussions of nineteenth-century audiences must surely take place. Chapters on "Cultural Conflict, Ideology, and the Reading Habit in the 1790s" and "Reading the Social Text" are essential reading for anyone interested in the historical study of print consumption, not least for what they suggest about the power of the periodical to "cement an audience previously unrepresented in the universe of public discourse" (24). Finding continuities between contemporary preoccupations with the "reader" and the Romantic legacy that was in part responsible for producing it, Klancher ends with the sobering caveat: "even the foundational texts of British Romanticism acknowledged in the intense friction of their language the pressure of contrary readings and resistant texts" and as such "remind us that there is no comfort in discourse, no refuge in reading, no alternative to the colliding languages of the social text" (177).

A quite different approach to the contrareity of response is offered by Jonathan Rose's article "Rereading the English Common Reader: A Preface to the History of Audiences" in the *Journal of the History of Ideas* (53 [1992]: 47–70). Taking as his starting point Altick's 1957 lament, "If we only had the autobiography of a pork butcher," Rose explores some of the intriguing possbilities that recently rediscovered working-class memoirs might hold for the reconstruction of the "common reader" in history. Unlike Klancher's book, in which "reading cultures" of the past are entities "distinctly opaque insofar as we cannot penetrate the minds of all those readers who left no mark of their understandings" (174), this is a work-in-progress committed to the assertion that such acts of historical recovery are entirely possible. After cataloguing what he identifies as the five cardinal "fallacies of reader response" (48), Rose goes on to suggest that diversity of response can only ever be accounted for by positioning the reader "outside the text" (70). Perhaps the most innovative aspect here is to be found in the uncompromising regard for the importance of the individual reading experience over and above anything that might be asserted about corporate audience identity. When all of the arguments have been rehearsed, however, one troublesome question still remains. How can we even begin to interpret the margins of response? What kind of hermeneutic equipment, in other words, can be best used to forge genuinely helpful observations about the constitution of reading audiences from an otherwise disparate welter of anecdotal information? If, as Klancher maintains, audiences are always "mutually produced as an otherness within one's own discourse" (12), then factual statements about the definition of historical readership can never claim to be entirely innocent. As this and other studies indicate, the reading of reading is always informed by complex and contending assumptions, and at the very least looks set to remain the site of ideological dispute for many years to come.

It was Roland Barthes who suggested that the birth of the reader as a theoretical concept is in some ways concomitant with the death of the author, and it is interesting to consider the consequences that a growing concern with theories of reception within literary studies has had on the more traditional regard for the author as the principal generative locus in the production of texts. Although not primarily concerned with the nineteenth-century novel per se, Maurice Couturier's *Textual Communication: A Print-Based Theory of the Novel* (London: Routledge, 1991) sheds some new light on the concept of authorship within the context of current debates on textual authority. Beginning with the recognition that print always draws attention to itself as a medium, Couturier spends the remainder of his study examining the kinds of strategies that both readers and writers employ in order to circumvent, or even exploit, the limitations of their technology. While the stated aim is to offer an analysis of how novelists have "managed to solve the communications problems they have had to face in each period" (ix), only a disappointing and highly derivative ten pages or so are dedicated to the period that many have come to regard as the "age of fiction." For all that, this is an ambitious book whose substantial introductory chapters on "the printing industry" and "the bookhood of the novel" will offer a number of suggestive ways of rethinking the semiotics of print from Gutenburg to the present.

A more conventional reading of textual relations within the publishing industry is to be found in Peter Shillingsburg's *Pegasus in Harness: Victorian Publishing and W. M. Thackeray* (Charlottesville: U P of Virginia, 1992). Establishing his position with definitive clarity, Shillingsburg early on distances himself from both "the romantic view of the autonomous author" and "the social deterministic interpretation of the writer's function" (13). By far the liveliest section is that which takes on the kind of "social contract theory" which allegedly controls and limits reading to the extent that it paralyzes any possibility of "authorial intentionality" (208). Holding on to what it revealingly calls a "respect for Thackeray's genius" (13), *Pegasus in Harness* despite its introductory qualifications ultimately allows itself to indulge in a traditional kind of literary history that is done with principally the writer in mind. Many there are who will disagree with the assertion that "to admit that the author is one in a line of necessary manufacturers and purveyors of literature . . . is to pursue truth where there seems to be nothing to gain except the miserable satisfaction of knowing it"

(20). For all that, this book is to be commended for helping to identify and define some of the crucial issues surrounding the idea of the writer in the nineteenth-century marketplace, and in its careful rallying of source material it brings some really new light to bear on the difficult question of authorial relations in an increasingly industrial environment.

While much ink continues to be spilt on the question of author-publisher relations, one curiously neglected aspect of the nineteenth-century trade is the often difficult and complex relations between authors and printers, a long overdue study of which is taken up by Allan C. Dooley in *Author and Printer in Victorian England* (Charlottesville: U P of Virginia, 1992). Beginning with the somewhat obvious comment that "printing technology shapes texts," Dooley nevertheless proceeds to demonstrate how "changes in attitudes toward authorship, changing customs in the printing and publishing worlds, different marketing strategies, and advancing technology combined to make it likely that authors — successful authors, at least — would have repeated chances to control their printed texts" (153). Some will be uncomfortable with the use of "authorial control" and other such terms which, while perfectly acceptable to the textual editor, hold dubious significance for the cultural historian and literary theorist alike. To be fair, Dooley does at one stage offer the following preemptive qualifications: "In a broad social sense . . . authors work under restraints (both conscious or unconscious) on what they will write about and how they will express themselves. The history of literary and political tastes, of censorship imposed to enforce those tastes, and of self-limitations by authors serving those tastes, provides ample demonstrations of how a culture's professed values direct and permeate the efforts of its writers" (7). Though it is clearly not the intention of this book to pursue those aspects of print technology which serve to delimit authorial intention, Dooley's casual observation suggests obvious scope for future considerations of the many ways in which the idea of the author became itself a product of the Victorian media and its new technology.

Referring to an emerging scholarly awareness of the importance of "book history" to the understanding of past cultures, one recent commentator has gone so far as to call it "an area of research that has developed so rapidly during the last few years that it seems likely to win a place alongside fields like the history of science and the history of art in the canon of scholarly disciplines." Going on to warn against the dangers of "interdisciplinarity run riot," Robert Darnton maintains in *The Kiss of Lamourette: Reflections in Cultural History* (New York: Norton, 1990) that the subject must resist at all costs becoming "fragmented into esoteric specialization" (107–11). Even a cursory glance at the kind of work being produced these days would suggest that the description of print history as a "field of study" is tenuous to say the least. The use of a metaphor rooted in the notion of fixed boundary in order to describe something whose parameters are as yet more fluid will for many prove imaginatively too limiting.

Ultimately one begins to wonder whether the term "history of the book" has not itself become too restrictive and whether in fact the idea of "media studies" might not profitably be extended to imagine new connections for the study of print culture. Questions about the nature of audiences, the development of production technology, and the dissemination and reception of texts in the broadest sense are, after all, perennial ones and offer no end of possibilities for rethinking aspects of communication well beyond the sometimes artificial limitations of subject and period. To those committed to uncovering the hidden places of negotiation and exchange that over the years have been obscured by ingrained institutional taxonomy, the fear of "interdisciplinarity run riot" will no doubt also ring strange. I, for one, hope that print history will remain a place for disciplines to converge, a space for the exploration of new connections, as well as a revaluation of the old.

University of Edinburgh

REDISCOVERING BY RECONCEIVING: THE DIRECTION OF VICTORIAN ART HISTORY

By Joseph A. Kestner

RECENT DEVELOPMENTS in the exhibition of Victorian art have signaled the advent of powerful reconceptualizations in the philosophy of displaying nineteenth-century British painting. Two directions can be discerned in the practice of the early nineties: one is the very specialized exhibition concentrating on a key and intensely focused element of Victorian art; the other is the inclusion of Victorian painting in contexts which demonstrate both its antecedents and its successors in startling collocations constructed around unusual themes. Certainly most recently, the exhibition has been more aggressive than conventional scholarship in reconceiving new interpretive strategies for Victorian painting. It is of particular note that Ruskin has been the focus of enterprises in both exhibition and academic monographs. Finally and most surprising, several of the key exhibitions were not held in Britain or the United States at all but in Germany, the political inferences of which are several.

The exhibition *London — World City 1800–1840* is one of the most striking of the exhibitions to recontextualize Victorian painting: the show concentrated on the importance of the city of London during the Regency and the early Victorian period, an era marked by the British victory over Napoleon and the rise of political reform, culminating in the 1832 Reform Bill. It is important to remember that the period took its cue about art from the Prince Regent, the future George IV, who was himself a major patron of the arts. The accompanying catalogue *London — World City 1800–1840* (New Haven: Yale UP, 1992) is edited by Celina Fox of the Museum of London. The catalogue includes fourteen essays by scholars, all of which are probing, on such subjects as John Nash, the reigning architect of the 1820s; the role of science; the nature of the London art world; the image of London in Romantic writing; and the role of industrialism in the configuring of the urban landscape. Following the Napoleonic wars, London attained a sense of confidence as it expanded to become the "world city."

The exhibition was presented at the Villa Hugel in Essen, Germany, which in fact is as surprising as the exhibition itself.

London assumed its hegemony for many reasons: the rise of a merchant navy, the "role of London in the marketing of provincial industrial goods" (28), and the "development of the overseas trade" (31). This economic ascendancy was accompanied by crucial architectural and artistic transformations. Andrew Saint argues in his fine essay "The Building Art of the First Industrial Metropolis" that elements such as better docking, provision for safe storage, new bridge crossings, and the transformation of public buildings and churches altered the city to accommodate this new role: the legacy, whether of Regent's Park or Buckingham Palace, endures. Peter Funnell details the nature of the London art world in the early decades of the century, noting that by the 1830s there was "the perception of a larger and socially more diverse art public and of an expanded body of practicing artists" (163), among whom were luminaries such as Turner and Constable as well as watercolorists like Girtin and Cotman. Andrew Wilton in his essay on art in the early nineteenth century specifically cites the "enhanced standing of watercolour" (171) as a key development of the era. The legacy of Joshua Reynolds and his *Discourses* was a major source of contestation, paving the way for the Pre-Raphaelite revolt of mid-century. Single-handedly, David Wilkie reconceived genre painting by emphasizing "virtuoso clarity" (177) and a novelist's sense of setting. Genre painting began to "assume some of the intellectual responsibility of history painting" (178). With Turner, Danby, and Constable, British painting (re-)discovered light.

The exhibition presented an amazing array of objects (nearly 700) to convey the uniqueness of the city: swords, candelabra, medals, portrait busts, court dress, and spectacular art. Thomas Lawrence loomed large in the exhibition, with the inclusion of his portrait of Nash (1824–27) and his group portrait of the partners in Baring Brothers (1806), the latter indicating the power of the merchant class in the imminent ascendancy of London over Amsterdam. The importance of the watercolor was signaled by the presence of Blake, Girtin, Cotman, Scharf, Varley, and Linnell, among others, in the exhibition. In this section, of course, the works of Turner and Palmer remain revelatory, while Constable's rainbows reflect the emergence of the science of light. The oil paintings brought together some of the key canvases of the early nineteenth century: Wilkie's *Chelsea Pensioners* (1822); Danby's *Sunset at Sea after a Storm* (1824) as well as his famous *Disappointed Love* (1821); Constable's *The Leaping Horse* (1825); Landseer's *The Hunting of Chevy Chase* (1826); Haydon's *The Mock Election 1827* (1828); Etty's *Sleeping Nymph and Satyrs* (1828); and several key Turners. The presence of Dyce's *Joash Shooting the Arrow of Deliverance* (1844) was particularly significant: it is presently in the collection of the Kunsthalle, Hamburg, and it also shows the important influence of the German Nazarene artists on British painting. For Victorianists, *London — World*

City documents the careers of these painters, many of whom had considerable influence as the century advanced. The concept of the exhibition, its restricted focus to one city and a four-decade time span, as well as the sumptuous catalogue, set a standard of innovation that marked the exhibitions of the 1992–1993 period.

This exhibition suggested that London was the pre-eminent metropolis of the early nineteenth century. For those unable to view the exhibition in Essen, a hint of this distinction was suggested in *The Great Age of Sail* at the Peabody Museum in Salem, an exhibition of canvases from the National Maritime Museum in Greenwich, accompanied by a catalogue (*The Great Age of Sail* by Peter Kemp and Richard Ormond, published in 1986 by Phaidon, London). The exhibition, which appeared at three venues in 1992–1993, was divided into classifications that clarified the role of the sailing ship in many contexts: exploration, shipbuilding, ceremony, empire, and war at sea. Unlike *London — World City*, which concentrated on four decades, *The Great Age of Sail* spanned British naval enterprises from Tudor times to the end of the nineteenth century. Of greatest interest were the canvases involving Britain during the period of the Napoleonic wars, with the inclusion of such works as Turner's *Battle of Trafalgar* (1823), Devis's *The Death of Nelson* (1809), and West's *Apotheosis of Nelson* (1807). Turner emerges from the conjunction of this exhibition and *London — World City* as an extraordinary amalgam of history painter and visionary, while the construction of a figure such as Nelson by British artists foreshadows Carlyle's fashioning of heroism in print a few decades later. Certainly one develops a new awareness of a novel such as Austen's *Persuasion* from viewing the exhibition and its emphasis on the navy as a transformative agent in British social and economic life. The catalogue essays are incisive, and illustrated by many black and white reproductions, with sixty-five color plates providing the basis for analysis beyond the essays. The rise of steam propulsion early in the century meant the beginning of the end for sailing ships, while the rise of the United States as a sea power suggests the gradual demise of British hegemony in the naval arena. *The Great Age of Sail* takes its impetus from a unique collection. Its concentrated focus on the navy parallels the emphasis on a single city in *London — World City*.

The construction of the hero/heroine through portrait art was the focus of *The Swagger Portrait* at the Tate Gallery (with a sharp catalogue by Andrew Wilton, published by the Tate, 1992). Wilton's idea of organizing such an exhibition, which covers Van Dyck to Augustus John, is clever indeed, as there emerges under the rubric *swagger* a distinct predisposition of portrait painting to aggrandize the human being by flair, dress, bravura, and overstatement. Swagger creates a common denominator for the ordinary and the extraordinary individual, elevating the ordinary to prominence and the extraordinary to heroism/heroinism. As Wilton notes in the brochure to the exhibition, swagger "implies showiness and ostentation . . . Its insolence has become a legitimate social challenge . . . [It is] that class of likeness which puts public display before the more private values" (n.p.). It was Anthony Van Dyck who brought the quality from Antwerp to Counter-Reformation Britain. A key feature is theatricality in the service of self-display: grand gestures and "billowing drapery" (catalogue 17) mark its rhetoric, with the large scale of the canvas itself constituting a stage.

The Victorian and Edwardian canvases in the exhibition emphasize this self-fashioning through theatricality. Thomas Lawrence's work is the great entrée into the style of the early nineteenth century, and his portraits *John Philip Kemble as Hamlet* (1801), *Mrs. Siddons* (1804), and *The Duke of Wellington Mounted on Copenhagen* (1818) incorporate proto-Romantic elements like dark clouds and mysterious landscapes to raise the valence of suggestion and uniqueness in the canvases. Grant's *Queen Victoria* (1841) demonstrates the adaptation of "swagger" to the paintings of the monarch and her consort: Victoria's head is turned away from the spectator to indicate her elevated status, while Winterhalter's *Prince Albert* (1846) silhouettes the Consort between two pillars against a dark and vaguely Turneresque sky to lend him distinction. Tissot's famous *Colonel Frederick Burnaby* (1870) transfers swagger to the quintessential soldier of the empire: Burnaby sits before a map of the world, one hand holding a cigarette, surrounded by the accoutrements of helmet, breastplate, and boots, the red stripe of his trousers elongating the figure, its very diagonal a link between continents. The inclusion of two canvases by Millais re-establishes Millais in a tradition far different from his early Pre-Raphaelitism: *Hearts are Trumps* (1872) and *Mrs. Bischoffsheim* (1873) show how eagerly Millais seized the swagger style to enhance his sitters and enrich himself. The master of the swagger in the late nineteenth century is, of course, Sargent, represented by *Ellen Terry as Lady Macbeth* (1889) and the stunning portrait *W. Graham Robertson* (1894). The former is inevitably theatrical with Terry in costume, while the latter becomes theatrical in an entirely different way as Sargent mutes the tonality of his palette in the manner of Whistler: a detail such as the jade head of Robertson's walking stick is the signature of swagger. The rarely exhibited *Mrs. Patrick Campbell as "Paula Tanqueray"* (1894) by Solomon deploys theatricality to serve the actress and Pinero simultaneously. Orpen's *Mrs. St. George* (1912) carries swagger to the Edwardian era. *The Swagger Portrait* transcends the usual divisions of art history to link painters thought disparate to limn a tendency in British art not often studied in such detail. The exhibition strongly suggests that swagger in Victorian culture must become a component of the "Victorian frame of mind," whether manifest in painting or fiction.

If *London — World City* graced the city of Essen in Germany, the city of Munich was not to be outdone in displays of Victorian art, hosting *Viktorianische*

Malerei von Turner bis Whistler as well as *Viktorianische Photographie 1840–1890* in 1993, both at the Neue Pinakothek and both accompanied by lush catalogues, the former with essays by Christopher Newall, Julian Treuherz and others (Munich: Prestel, 1993) and the latter by Ulrich Pohlmann (Munich: Edition Braus, 1993). Although both exhibitions are marked not by their narrow focus but by their inclusivity, the fact that in 1992–1993 Germany was the venue for three major exhibitions of nineteenth-century British art should have momentous consequences for art history on the continent. If it was the French who during the 1970s exhibited the PRB, then Germany has now assumed a key function in the exhibition of British painting far beyond the scope of the PRB.

Viktorianische Malerei encompasses painters literally from Alma-Tadema to Winterhalter and, as the range of catalogue essays testifies, it purports not only to survey British painting from Romanticism through the end of the century but also to locate British art in the contexts of England's relationship with Germany and Europe in general, or, as Christoph Heilmann entitles his essay, "A Little Rivalry, Much Common Objective." The link, naturally, is Prince Albert, whose own German antecedents already complemented the earlier Hanoverian strain in the British royal line. As Heilmann argues, it was British Romantic literature which began the recognition of things German in the century, with Wordsworth/ Schiller and Byron/Goethe being examples of such cultural transference. One of the most prominent Nazarene painters, Peter von Cornelius, came to London in 1841. An artist like Dyce had strong affiliations with the Nazarene movement, while a German artist like Winterhalter was to paint many portraits of the Queen, Prince Albert, and their family. At a later period, Hubert von Herkomer, born in 1849 at Waal near Munich, was to carry his German background into the arena of the *Graphic* and Victorian realist painting during the 1870s and later. The future president of the Royal Academy, Frederic Leighton, studied under Steinle at Frankfurt. Heilmann's essay and Newall's on "Victorian Painters and Europe" assess these affiliations very well. While the influence of the French and the Japanese on Victorian art has received considerable attention, this catalogue rectifies a gap in its focus on artists' relations between Germany and Britain.

The catalogue emphasizes the importance of Prince Albert in this cross-cultural exchange by including several canvases of him with the Queen, among them Landseer's *Queen Victoria and Prince Albert at the Bal Costumé* (1842–46), Grant's *Prince Albert* (1843–45), and several of Winterhalter's important portraits of the royal family, including the Princess Royal (1856) and the Prince of Wales (1859). The exhibition then included a wide-ranging but comprehensive representative selection of canvases to illustrate the Victorian art achievement: Landseer's *Monarch of the Glen* (1851); several stunning Turners, including his 1842 view of Constance; Danby's great marine *Dead Calm* (1855); typical genre by Mulready, Wilkie, and Cope; Dyce's *Jacob and Rachel* (1853, the Kunsthalle

Hamburg); canvases by Frith, Egley, and Abraham Solomon. The PRB was represented by such key works as Hunt's *The Eve of St. Agnes*, Millais's *The Blind Girl*, Brown's *Waiting*, Burton's *Wounded Cavalier*, Wallis's *The Stonebreaker*, Hunt's *Fairlight Downs*, Rossetti's *Paolo and Francesca*, Hughes's *The Rift in the Lute*, Rossetti's *The Blue Bower*, and Millais's *Souvenir of Velasquez*. While these do not pretend to constitute the PRB achievement, they focus on the major artists, and some of the selections, such as Hunt's *Fairlight Downs*, are especially intriguing. Leighton's *Golden Hours* reveals his strong allegiance to Renaissance artists, while Burne-Jones was represented by a complete *Pygmalion* series as well as *The Doom Fulfilled*, the last of the *Perseus* cycle, now in the collection of the Staatsgalerie in Stuttgart. Waterhouse's *La Belle Dame sans Merci* is included, since it is from the Hessisches Landesmuseum, Darmstadt. Herkomer's *Hard Times* provides a climax to the Germanic emphasis of such items with a German affiliation.

The importance of *Viktorianische Malerei* rests in the areas of new research posed by the exhibition: the role of continental training in the education of nineteenth-century British artists; the major role of William Dyce; the awareness of German culture in art; the fact that major teachers like Leighton and Herkomer were strongly influenced by elements of German artistic practice; and the acquisition of British art by German museums. *Viktorianische Malerei* was presented with a catalogue sumptuously illustrated (both paper and hardback versions available), and the fact that the exhibition moved to the Prado Museum in Madrid after Munich opens yet another continental link. It may be possible to probe the influence of Burne-Jones on the early Picasso, for example. Such an exhibition demonstrates the diversity of product of these artists but also the diversity of their training, with Brown, Leighton, and Dyce exemplifying the power of continental training in their practice. The essays in the catalogue provide bases for the reassessment that *Viktorianische Malerei* compels for art historians.

Viktorianische Photographie 1840–1890 presented an overview of British photography during the era in a show of about seventy photographs. These included major works by Cameron, Prout, and Annan, as well as a range of work by other practitioners. Cameron's portraits and depictions of characters from Tennyson's *Idylls* are famous and were included in sufficient number that her achievement is the eminent one now acknowledged. More surprising were the stunning photographs by Victor Prout, mostly landscapes shot in 1862 and with their attention to shaded areas, reflections in water, and skyscapes to be compared with some of the same subjects in the work of the PRB or British watercolorists. Francis Bedford's photographs of cathedral portraits comprise both documentary-style record and visionary icon, while James Robertson's scenes of Sebastopol are moody compared to Roger Fenton's shots of the Crimea, the latter populated and domesticated. Robert MacPherson's views of Italy are noteworthy, especially his interest in architecture, which parallels Ruskin's equivalent engagement and was probably inspired by it. Francis Bedford's views of Egyptian temples during the 1860s anticipate the role Egypt was to play in the 1880s with the campaigns in the Sudan. The catalogue includes an excellent bibliography and a trenchant essay exploring the manner in which, for example, photography documented the explorations and colonizations of the period. Having *Viktoria-nische Photographie* exhibited at the same time as *Viktorianische Malerei* was indeed astute on the part of the Neue Pinakothek, for the combination of the two exhibitions underscores the diversity of artistic achievement, allowing the viewer to study landscape in both forms.

Exhibitions which concentrate on tightly focused dimensions of Victorian art can naturally achieve different objectives from the sweeping quality of an exhibition like *Viktorianische Malerei. Pocket Cathedrals: Pre-Raphaelite Book Illustration* was presented at the Yale Center for British Art in 1991 (catalogue New Haven: Yale Center for British Art) and proved valuable because the range of essays (by Susan Casteras, Jennifer Ullman and others) concentrates on specific artists like Sandys, Hughes, Millais, and Burne-Jones. Casteras's survey of the nature of illustration during the period is a first-rate comprehensive essay, particularly because it differentiates among the illustrators so precisely, for instance in her focus on the "self-referential element" (21) in Millais. It is particularly valuable to have Jeffrey Collins's assessment of Sandys, with his "Dureresque motifs" (81). The exhibition presented a strong selection of material, grouped by artist, with many major lights (Millais, Hunt, Rossetti, Brown) included with figures less known, like Sandys and William Bell Scott. Since the exhibition was drawn from collections of the Yale Center and the Sterling Library, the catalogue is an important compendium for researchers in the field intending to study the Yale collections. The quality of the reproductions in the catalogue is strong.

The ingenuity of the sharply focused exhibition was demonstrated by *"And When Did You Last See Your Father?"* organized by Edward Morris for the Walker Art Gallery, Liverpool (catalogue National Museums and Galleries on Merseyside, 1992). The Walker owns this famous Victorian narrative canvas by William Frederick Yeames of a young son of a Royalist family being questioned by a group of Puritans who have occupied his parents' country house. Dressed like Gainsborough's *Blue Boy*, the child stands before his interrogators: viewers ever since 1878 have speculated about the boy's reply, wondering if he doomed his family by telling the truth, saved his parents by lying, or baffled his opponents because he knew nothing. Yeames was a member of the St. John's Wood Clique, and the catalogue is an important reassessment of the achievement of Marks, Calderon and others who constituted this group. Artists of this circle were very much concerned with "the lost pages of history" in selecting subject matter, and Morris and his co-author Frank Milner do a deft job of discussing this proclivity, particularly in the chapter devoted to the representation of the Civil Wars during the nineteenth century. To contextualize Yeames's famous canvas, the exhibition included key paintings of the Wars, everything from Brown's *Cromwell on His Farm*, Burton's *Wounded Cavalier*, and Egg's *The Night before Naseby* to Landseer's *Eve of the Battle of Edgehill* and Millais's *The Proscribed Royalist*. The catalogue entries are brief but clear, concluding with Yeames's famous painting and some of its support drawings. The idea of organizing an exhibition around a key painting by judicious loans from other collections and drawing on the Walker's own stores (nine canvases in all came from there) is clever, for such an exhibition enhances the central painting, allows the museum to display other works related to it, and invigorates one's response to a familiar image. The preoccupation of the century with Cromwell, studied by Roy Strong in *Recreating the Past*, is given a new emphasis in the Walker's exhibition. The hero-worship celebrated in *The Swagger Portrait* is here concentrated on a single individual, Cromwell, but the importance of Carlyle is common to both shows. Exhibiting the Yeames with such famous works as the Burton and the Millais reveals the manner in which history is a constant process of construction.

Exhibitions involving constructions of gender or interrogating gendered positions are the focus of several important installations, some of these in small formats. The Tate Gallery has initiated a series of such exhibitions by including canvases from its own collections in carefully curated exhibitions. *The Painted Nude: From Etty to Auerbach*, held in 1992, is a good example of the success of such a practice. Judith Collins, in her short essay in the accompanying brochure, summarizes the trajectory of nude representation from the Greeks, who revered the nude body, through the medieval world, where it was symbolic of evil, to its restoration in the Renaissance. As Collins notes, Puritanism made it difficult for artists to paint the nude in British art, with a few exceptions, until the nineteenth century, when William Etty in particular made it the focus of his career. Etty painted the female more than the male nude, but both are important in his canvases, not only in finished mythological subjects but also in his vast array of studies. The Tate included his *Candaules* of 1830 as well as one study of a female nude. (It is time for a major Etty retrospective.) Etty's nudes were not completely idealized: rather, he transcribed traits of the model before him. The inclusion of Anna Lea Merritt's *Love Locked Out* of 1889, of a naked youth seen from behind, shows that female artists were concentrating on the nude. (The major exemplar was Henrietta Rae, not included in this small show.) Canvases by Gwen John, Vanessa Bell, and Dod Procter carried the tradition of women painting female nudes into the twentieth century. Frederic Leighton's *The Sluggard*, his bronze of a youth stretching himself after sleep, was incorporated into the exhibition as an example of the New Sculpture movement during the nineteenth century, where accuracy of anatomy replaced idealized forms; finished in 1885, the statue now stands at one end of the large gallery devoted to Victorian painting at the Tate.

Another important small exhibition was *Visualising Masculinities*, held between 1992 and 1993 at the Tate. In his brochure for the show, Andrew Stephenson stresses the importance of such imagery in the construction of masculinity, the emphasis on inequality between the male and female, and the inflection of difference. The canvases chosen included the familiar (Millais's *Order of Release*, Watts's *The Minotaur*, Hicks's *Woman's Mission: Companion to Manhood*, Sargent's *Ian Hamilton*) as well as more contemporary works, especially the shock-effect *Sword of the Pig* by Robert Longo, which juxtaposes a muscled torso with missile silos and church steeples to critique phallocratic, macho culture. *Visualising Masculinities*, small though it was, suggests yet another manner of reading a canvas like the Millais or the Hicks, where the male body becomes the site of contestation. The exhibition implied and demonstrated new ways of contextualizing the representation of the male body in Victorian art by linking such depictions with the twentieth century. Also, the male bravura heroism on display in *The Swagger Portrait* in the twentieth century becomes intensely conflicted, as *Visualising Masculinities* revealed.

The visualizing of masculinities is the focus of Allen Ellenzweig's very important monograph *The Homoerotic Photograph: Male Images from Durieu/ Delacroix to Mapplethorpe* (New York: Columbia UP, 1992), part of the Columbia series *Between Men — Between Women* of lesbian and gay studies. The monograph discusses a subject absent from the Munich *Viktorianische Photographie*, as it explores the male nude in the history of photography. Ellenzweig states that his intention is to explore "the nature of cultural attitudes toward male beauty, male sexuality, and homosexuality" (2) through the study of these images. He traces the emergence of the nude male from the academic tradition of painting from the nude model, alluded to in the Tate *The Painted Nude*. This tradition, ultimately inspired by the Greek *kouros*, originates in "the heroic male physique" (7) emphasized by the classical world and the Renaissance. The male model is posed with a staff by Durieu in the 1850s, suggesting the staff or spear which aggrandizes the phallic authority of the male body: "the superb *physique . . .* is an analogue for the perfect penis" (14) in such photographs. It is with Sutcliffe in England and Eakins in America that the nude becomes the focus of studies in the open air, where light on the naked body becomes itself the subject. Ellenzweig notes the intersection of the photographs of Sutcliffe and Eakins with the tradition of male comradeship in the nineteenth century. Sutcliffe's famous *Water Rats* of 1885 shows boys posed in Whitby Harbour, where the sunlight lends a marmoreal element to the bodies. Ellenzweig contends that the boys in Sutcliff's *Natives* are "like classical kuroi [sic]" (21), but in fact the kouros youth was more mature physically than the young boys in Sutcliffe's photo. In America, Eakins posed his male students in classical garb as well as nude in the open, engaged in swimming, boxing, or wrestling, linking his males with the Greek *palaestra*. For Eakins, his nude photographs were preparatory *aides memoires* to his canvases of wrestlers or swimmers, as in the famous *Swimming Hole*.

Ellenzweig does not discuss a key element of the Sutcliffe/Eakins nexus, which is that Sutcliffe always poses his models to conceal the genitals, while Eakins, although showing frontal nudity in his photographs, avoided it in finished oils. This practice demonstrates a decided difference in the treatment of the nude, where photography was willing to accept "nature" in a manner that fine art would not or could not if one were to accommodate patrons. It was in the photographs of the non-English Wilhelm von Gloeden and Wilhelm von Pluschow that the male nude in photography was most manifest during the century, and the youths represented here were Mediterranean, not English. Draped and undraped, frontal or not, these nudes emphasize the erotic basis of Greek culture, often suggested by the nudes posed against classical ruins, but nevertheless "not ancient Greece at all, but a pastiche Hellenism" (42).

The parallel with art, however, is suggested by the fact that several of these nudes have assumed the same pose as the youth in Merritt's *Love Locked Out*: the erotic dimension screened out in paintings can be glossed by such affinities. The key essay on the male nude in Victorian art journalism was "The Nude in Photography" in the first volume of *The Studio* in 1893, which praised "young limbs plashing the waves of a sapphire sea beneath the sun" (106). *The Homoerotic Photograph* is an important work for its exploration of nineteenth-century elements contributing to the ideology of male homosociality now explored by Eve Sedgwick and her successors. The book contains extremely high-quality reproductions of key photographs in this tradition. Ellenzweig's study advances the arguments established in 1988 by Peter Weiermair in *The Hidden Image*. The two books constitute an important archive of material for future research on male sexuality in the nineteenth century.

An exhibition not devoted exclusively to art but relying very much on the symbolic and political force of images was *The Purple, White & Green*, organized and curated by Diane Atkinson at the Museum of London and devoted to the suffragette movement in the Edwardian period. To convey their message to society, the suffragettes deployed a wide range of visual imagery in their processions and literature, including banners, posters, flags, badges, and pins. This installation included an extraordinary range of materials related to the movement, incorporating a film of actual suffragette processions into the exhibition. In addition to the banners women carried in processions, a series of powerful posters conveyed the paradoxical situation of women, revered but unenfranchised. In one image, "Polling Station," the gentry, factory workers and agricultural laborers are shown entering a polling place, while female nurses, academics, and civic dignitaries are left outside. In another poster, "They have a cheek I've never been asked," a female worker stands outside a factory gate, with a sign about factory acts regulating women's labor. This imagery even took the form of Christmas cards, post cards, and playing cards to convey the suffragette message. A game and puzzle of a labyrinth, with Holloway Gaol at its center, was depicted in "Suffragettes in and out of prison," while the cat holding a woman in its mouth became the symbol of protest against the Cat and Mouse Act.

The cover of *The Suffragette*, the weekly edited by Christabel Pankhurst, was an image of armored Joan of Arc carrying a green WSPU banner as the patron saint of the movement. Among the most striking of the banners was one shaped like a shield commemorating the ancient British warrior queen Boadicea. With its 650 exhibits, *The Purple, White & Green* is the most important contemporary account of the suffragette movement to be formed into an exhibition. The opportunity to study this mass of objects provides indisputable demonstration of the political force of imagery. The catalogue accompanying the exhibition (London: Museum of London, 1992) is a valuable compendium of the movement, interspersed with many illustrations and including a list of exhibits and a bibliography. It is unlikely that any American institution could duplicate such an exhibition, so it is regrettable that *The Purple, White & Green* did not travel. One hopes that a video of the exhibition will be circulated as a record of this stunning display.

Gender and art are the focus of several essays included in *Gender and Discourse*, edited by Antony Harrison and Beverly Taylor (Dekalb: Northern Illinois UP, 1992). George Landow explores the sculpture of Margaret Giles, especially her 1896 bronze *Hero*. Landow draws attention to Giles's participation in the New Sculpture, the movement initiated by Frederic Leighton. "The new emphasis on modeling clay, as opposed to stone carving, led directly to the entrance into the field of larger numbers of young women" (245), he notes. Giles demonstrates her originality in the physicality, even musculature, of her sculpture of Hero, in which "she has rejected the basic understanding of feminine beauty commonplace in her time" (247). Landow compares Giles's work with other representations of women during the period to mark its distinction. However, attention to the Hero and Leander theme in painting would have contextualized Giles's achievement, since many Victorian artists painted the subject, from William Etty's famous canvas of 1829 to Leighton's of 1887. This link requires notice because it was Leighton who awarded Giles the sculpture prize. The work also intersects with the theme of woman waiting in literature, as in the poetry of Christina Rossetti. Susan Casteras's " 'The Necessity of a Name': Portrayals and Betrayals of Victorian Women Artists" is more comprehensive in its treatment of subject. Casteras examines a range of imagery dealing with the female and the art world, encompassing the model and the female artist herself. Casteras demonstrates that women "were denied access to the nude in life classes" and were often "lampooned as artists" (213). There is a "dearth of . . . images by female painters of themselves at work" (216), despite the formation of the

Society of Female Artists as early as 1857 as an exhibition venue for women. In her essay, Casteras devotes special emphasis to Emily Osborn, whose *Nameless and Friendless* has emerged as the quintessential image of the plight of the female painter in the nineteenth century: a woman attempts to sell her art to a skeptical dealer as other men leer at her, constructing a powerful indication of the male gaze and its political empowerment. Casteras's essay complements the work of critics like Pamela Gerrish Nunn, Whitney Chadwick, and Lynda Nead in its emphasis on the female artist *qua* artist.

During 1992–1993, there was a significant emphasis on the British watercolor in several extensive assemblages of examples, in particular at the Yale Center for British Art and at the National Gallery in Washington. The Yale Center displayed 125 watercolors from American and British collections in *Victorian Landscape Watercolors*. The catalogue (New York: Hudson Hills, 1992) contains four critical essays, two each by Scott Wilcox and Christopher Newall, which chart the transformation in the practice of watercolor at mid-century after the death of Turner. The authors discuss the development and evolution of the watercolor in four very carefully prepared and scholarly pieces. The work of William Henry Hunt, John Frederick Lewis and others was marked by "the minute touch and brilliant color" (22) of one strand of the tradition, as Wilcox observes, while the followers of David Cox and Peter DeWint worked in "small-scale sketches" (24). Pre-Raphaelite literalism, however, gave way to the more poetic landscape (inspired by Turner) in the work of Albert Goodwin and Alfred Hunt as the century progressed. Christopher Newall traces the influence of Ruskin in the developing importance of watercolor in an excellent essay, in which he notes that Ruskin "was becoming less insistent on meticulous truth to nature in the details of the landscape" (35) as his criticism of the medium evolved. Ruskin's emphasis on the importance of Turner's watercolors impelled Turner's successors to unparalleled achievements.

Every exhibit in *Victorian Landscape Watercolors* received an individual entry in the catalogue, along with beautifully reproduced plates. The emphasis on landscape watercolors concentrated the attention on a particular line of development in the tradition, from works by Palmer and Turner through Ruskin and Cox. The Pre-Raphaelite tradition appears with Seddon's *The Mount of Moab* and *The Well of Enrogel*, where the effects of light on the Palestinian landscape are indelibly apprehended. Some of the exhibits were startling. William Simpson depicted in a dazzling sunset the graves of British dead at Inkerman in his 1854 treatment, a clear indication that Victorian landscape could still intersect with strong political elements. As Wilcox notes, Simpson "endowed his view of the burial ground with a lurid sunset that seems to reflect the recent carnage" (89).

Barbara Leigh Smith Bodichon was represented with a *View of Snowdon* which shows the artist under the influence of Cox but already preparing for PRB involvement. Equally exciting was William Dyce's watercolor version of

Pegwell Bay from 1857, a compositional study for his sensational oil of 1858 at the RA. Edward Poynter's 1859 *Near Argeles* is amazing because it is so unlike anything he achieved in his neo-classical oils: Newall rightly cites its "personal" (102) quality. Major artists like Brett, Boyce, and Walker were well represented in the show. The role of Helen Allingham and Myles Birket Foster in constructing an image of the English countryside (explored by Christopher Wood in his *Paradise Lost* of 1988) is given a fresh treatment in the context of the evolution of the watercolor in the nineteenth century. A work such as Albert Goodwin's *A Sunset in the Manufacturing Districts* of 1883 is a clear form of social protest in watercolor, as the blazing sunset contrasts in its splendor with the ruined landscape. The definite success of *Victorian Landscape Watercolors* rested on the superb selection of examples by Wilcox and Newall, and the strength of their catalogue essays. The exhibition argues strongly that a concentration on the work of British oil painters alone misses the comparable achievement in watercolor, where even the most skilled painters in oil wished to compete. A balanced appraisal of a Poynter or a Walker must confront this dual allegiance.

A fortunate conjunction brought a sweeping exhibition of 250 watercolors from Britain to follow *Victorian Landscape Watercolors*. *The Great Age of British Watercolours 1750–1850* originated at the Royal Academy and is a landmark. It is accompanied by a brilliant catalogue by Andrew Wilton and Anne Lyles (Munich: Prestel, 1993), with every exhibition illustrated by a fine color reproduction and an individual catalogue essay. In some respects the exhibition complements *Victorian Landscape Watercolors*, including some of the same artists of course (Cox, Turner, Dyce, Foster, Goodwin, William Henry Hunt, Ruskin, and DeWint). On the other hand, however, the chronological range of the National Gallery installation of the RA exhibition encompasses the entire spectrum of the origin, growth, and maturity of British watercolor from the eighteenth century through the nineteenth, which entails the inclusion of Alexander Cozens, Gilpin (of picturesque fame), Gainsborough, Paul Sanby, John Robert Cozens, Blake, Bonington, and many others. The founding of the Society of Painters in Water-Colour in 1804 did not initiate the study of watercolor; on the contrary, it had flourished during the eighteenth century.

The Great Age of British Watercolours was organized into six sections: the structure of landscape: eighteenth-century theory; man in the landscape: the art of topography; naturalism; picturesque/antipicturesque: the composition of Romantic landscape; light and atmosphere; and the exhibition watercolor. Because it was a quick-drying, portable medium, watercolor began as a means of recording topographical views; the rise of nationalism transformed this topographical objective into one of "painting," as the name of the Society in 1804 clearly marked. Following the precepts of Reynolds that art should be generalized, early watercolorists permuted scenic elements, no one more so than Alexander Cozens with his idea of "artificial blots" discussed by Wilton in his essay

(36); Gainsborough exhibits the same tendency to idealize nature by combinations of landscape units. However, once one comes to Paul Sanby, everything alters. His *Rocky Coast by Moonlight* (1790) exhibits a new interest in atmosphere and, strikingly, realistic human figures become visible for the first time: his scenes of life in Edinburgh or at Eton College combine studies of light with social recording, a tendency also shared by Turner in his watercolor *Wolverhampton* (1796). By the 1830s, however, Turner's interest in light supersedes any interest in the human figure. The portable nature of the medium also meant that it could record experiences abroad, as with the work of Roberts, Austin, Cox, or Lewis.

Chronicling natural effects for their own sake emerges in the early nineteenth century and reaches a culmination in the work of artists like Constable, Palmer, and then the PRB. Millais was represented by his study of *Ben Nevis*, and he recognized his affinity with the watercolorists when he wrote in 1854: "The sun, with British effulgence, burst out upon the rocky hills . . . and all the distant mountains changed suddenly from David Cox to the Pre-Raphaelites" (137). The visionary drive of Romanticism becomes evident in such works as Martin's *Sunset over a Rocky Bay* of 1830 and Samuel Palmer's *Harvesters by Firelight* of about the same time: here the landscape becomes infused with anthropomorphized sensibility, whether human figures are included or not. Several of Constable's cloud studies are dazzling records of effects, but they too partake of this infused sensibility. Most startling is the realization that some of Whistler's watercolors of the 1880s in their "blots" of color recall the origin of the landscape in Alexander Cozens a century before. A major practitioner like William Henry Hunt was incorporated into the final section on the exhibition watercolor, works intended for display and revealing bravura style, whether in the minute detail beloved by Hunt or the apocalyptic motive espoused by Martin. The National Gallery added its own Hunt, *Interior of Bushey Church*, to the eight paintings by Hunt from Britain, turning this final section of the exhibition into a small retrospective of this astounding artist, even as the National Gallery's *View on the River Wye* supplemented the works from Britain by John Martin. At the end of the century, Alfred William Hunt and Albert Goodwin represent the culmination of the tradition with "mountains plung[ing] dizzyingly from the minutely traced foreground detail . . . to the blur of light and atmosphere across a twilit distance" (264).

The Great Age of British Watercolours was an unparalleled compendium of images and, like the smaller *Victorian Landscape Watercolors*, makes an indisputable case for the extraordinary achievements of artists in this medium during the nineteenth century. The National Gallery installation for *The Great Age of British Watercolours* was outstanding: the rooms were in single tones of grey or blue, permitting the works to display themselves to maximum advantage. In addition, the fact that the Gallery devoted so many rooms to the exhibition meant that pictures were given individual spaces with no crowding of exhibits, essential for a hanging of this kind. The last major exhibition of works by William Henry Hunt was in 1981 at Wolverhampton. *The Great Age of British Watercolours* makes evident the need for another retrospective of this artist, as well as the strong appeal of single-artist shows of the works of Boyce, Danby, and Martin. These two exhibitions should demolish the artificial barriers between oil painting and watercolor in Victorian art history.

John Ruskin, whose endorsement of Turner's watercolors enhanced the confidence of that medium's practitioners, was the focus of the exhibition *John Ruskin and the Victorian Eye* at the Phoenix Art Museum (catalogue New York: Abrams, 1993), which proved to be extremely insightful and provocative. The exhibition essentially showed the education of Ruskin's eye by the inclusion of twenty-five examples of Turner's work (including oils, watercolors, pencil studies), following these with forty watercolors and studies by Ruskin (as well as ten sketches for *The Elements of Drawing*), and then demonstrating the result of this "eye" by the inclusion of an array of famous nineteenth-century canvases which Ruskin had critiqued in his writing. The exhibition was, therefore, a superb "seminar" in Ruskin and Victorian painting from many diverse perspectives. The exhibition had its premise in Ruskin's famous declaration: "The greatest thing a human soul ever does in this world is to *see* something. Hundreds of people can talk for one who can think, but thousands can think for one who can *see*." In toto, the exhibition included about 150 works, extremely well hung at the Phoenix Art Museum, with superb lighting, sufficient space between exhibits, and a natural progression from Turner to Ruskin to Victorian art by others. The co-curators, Susan P. Gordon of the Phoenix Art Museum and Anthony L. Gully of Arizona State University, constructed a challenging and very important exhibition by showing the formation of Ruskin's taste and the canvases about which he wrote.

The effect of the training of the "eye" was displayed in many of the works included, as with the five watercolors by William Henry Hunt; the *Massa, Bay of Naples* by John Brett; and *The Stillness of the Lake at Dawn* by Alfred William Hunt, a superb atmospheric depiction. One of the great pleasures of the exhibition was to see in adjacent positions works by the same artist from different collections. Thus, Dyce's *George Herbert at Bemerton* and *Titian's First Essay*, the former from the Guildhall, London and the latter from Aberdeen, became inter-referential texts, the one about the art of religion and the other about the religion of art. Dyce's dazzling observation of the natural world forcefully demonstrated the influence of the Ruskinian eye. Hunt's *The Light of the World* and *The Shadow of Death* were likewise juxtaposed, becoming a treatise on the trajectory of Victorian religious thought from the idea of Christ as divine to the concept of Christ as human laborer (see Ward's *Robert Elsmere*): in the former, the divinized Christ, in the latter the demythologized figure. One could track

Millais's career from *The Woodman's Daughter* to *The Waterfall* to the demise represented in *Peace Concluded* and *The Escape of a Heretic*. Canvases Ruskin despised, such as Alma-Tadema's *Pyrrhic Dance*, permitted one to test his observations on the spot. The art of watercolor figures most prominently, naturally, with exceptional examples not only by Turner and Ruskin but also by figures such as Boyce, Allingham, Cox, Rooke, and Rossetti, most of whom were included in the two major exhibitions devoted to watercolor discussed previously. The inclusion of other oils supplemented these exhibits, giving a sense of the range of Victorian painting, everything from Eastlake's *Salutation to the Aged Friar*, Frith's *For Better, For Worse*, Collinson's *To Let*, and Redgrave's *The Valleys also Stand Thick with Corn* to Leighton's *A Roman Lady* and Paton's *Bloody Tryst*, the last a superb demonstration of PRB observation in a narrative context. It was an advantage to have Whistler's *Nocturne in Black and Gold: The Falling Rocket* in the exhibition, the basis of the famous trial in 1878 and the ultimate test case about Ruskinian taste.

The catalogue essays concentrate on various dimensions of the formation of Ruskin's taste and its consequences for Victorian painting. George Landow discusses Ruskin as Victorian sage of art; Christopher Newall probes very incisively the significance of drawing for Ruskin; Susan Gordon considers the importance of Ruskin's construction of Turner for other artists; and Susan Casteras in an innovative essay discusses Ruskin's museological theories and their manifestation in the curating of the Saint George's Museum in Sheffield. The exhibition and the catalogue together demonstrate as nothing else could the dimensions of Ruskin's influence, but even more significantly the process of the formation of Ruskin's own "eye" as he evolved into the great critic. The one element unexplored is the opposition to Ruskin's theories raised by other Victorian painters such as Edward Poynter, who lost no opportunity of denouncing Ruskin, as his *Ten Lectures on Art* demonstrates. The inclusion of such a dispute (beyond the Ruskin vs. Whistler fracas) would have lessened the tendency toward hero-worship of Ruskin that implicitly guided the exhibition.

The dimensions of Ruskin's achievement are explored in a very sound collection of essays edited by Michael Wheeler and Nigel Whitely, *The Lamp of Memory: Ruskin, Tradition and Architecture* (Manchester: Manchester UP, 1992). Several of these essays, such as John Illingworth's on Ruskin's ideas about museums and Ray Haslam's on architectural illustration, parallel elements of Ruskin's career and practice demonstrated by *John Ruskin and the Victorian Eye*. J. B. Bullen's "Ruskin and the Tradition of Renaissance Historiography" is a very important piece, showing how Ruskin engaged European ideas about the Renaissance and about the Gothic, examining the role of such figures as Victor Hugo in promulgating the negative view of the Renaissance. This contextualizing of Ruskin's ideas amid those of Rio, Montalembert, and Pugin is essential if one is to grasp the context of Ruskin's denunciation of the Renaissance in *The Stones of Venice*. Michael Wheeler explores in a carefully considered piece the force of Ruskin's religious training on his theorizing about the idea of the temple or ecclesiastical edifice, showing the unique inflection of an idea such as "ruin" in Ruskin's conceptions. Keith Hanley discusses Ruskin's engagement with Romantic discourses of the sublime by exploring the concepts of "the negative sublime" and "the hermeneutics of ruin" (99, 111) prefigured by Wordsworth. This collection is amply illustrated by black and white reproductions, and includes as an appendix "The Lamp of Memory" from *The Seven Lamps of Architecture*. The value of the collection is its location of Ruskin amid the theories and practices of others, like Wordsworth or Hugo; it should serve as a basis for continued study of these components of Ruskin's ideas.

Victorian painting is to be found not only in the major British institutions (Tate, Manchester, Walker, Birmingham, and others) but also in small collections. A very useful guide to one such venue is Alex Kidson's *Sudley: A Guide to the Collection* (Liverpool: National Museums and Galleries on Meryside, 1992). Located in proximity with the outstanding collections at the Walker Art Gallery in Liverpool and the Lady Lever Gallery at Port Sunlight, Sudley is often unacknowledged as a major repository of Victorian painting. It should not be after Kidson's guide, which deftly traces the evolution of the collection by George Holt, who made his fortune in shipping. Sudley includes very important works by Romney, Raeburn, Bonington, Mulready, Turner, Landseer, Holman Hunt, Rossetti, Millais (the famous *Vanessa*), Dyce, Leighton, and Strudwick, among others. Kidson devotes brief essays to each of these painters, making a strong case for Sudley being on anyone's itinerary when in Liverpool. The color reproductions in the guide are excellent, and in its brief compass Kidson's examination of the Holt bequest implies much about the philosophy of collecting during the late Victorian period.

Ruskin's exhortation to *see* cannot be ignored when so many opportunities exist to do so. The elevation of the watercolor, the practice of exhibiting Victorian art on the continent, the recontextualizing of Victorian art under a rubric such as swagger, and the insistent presence of photography all demonstrate that the education of the eye is advancing as much as Ruskin could ever have wished.

University of Tulsa

1. William Holman Hunt, "The Lady of Shalott." Wood engraving from Tennyson's *Poems*, (London: Edward Moxon and Company, 1857).

2. W. F. Yeames, "And When Did You Last See Your Father?" (1878). Courtesy of the Walker Art Gallery, Liverpool.

3. Sir Edward Poynter, "Isola San Guilio, Lago d'Orta." Courtesy of the Yale Center for British Art, New Haven, Connecticut, Paul Mellon Fund.

ROBERT AND ELIZABETH BARRETT BROWNING: AN ANNOTATED BIBLIOGRAPHY FOR 1991

By Sandra M. Donaldson and Catherine Pavlish

The following abbreviations appear in this year's bibliography:

BIS	*Browning Institute Studies*
BSN	*Browning Society Notes*
DAI	*Dissertation Abstracts International*
VIJ	*Victorians Institute Journal*
VLC	*Victorian Literature and Culture*
VP	*Victorian Poetry*
VS	*Victorian Studies*

An asterisk* indicates that we have not seen the item. Cross references with citation numbers between 51 and 70 followed by a colon (e.g., C63:) refer to William S. Peterson's *Robert and Elizabeth Barrett Browning: An Annotated Bibliography, 1951–1970* (New York: The Browning Institute, 1974); higher numbers refer to *Robert Browning: A Bibliography 1830–1950*, compiled by L. N. Broughton, C. S. Northup, and Robert Pearsall (Ithaca: Cornell UP, 1953).

Readers are encouraged to send offprints to Sandra Donaldson, Department of English, Box 7209, University of North Dakota, Grand Forks ND 58202.

A. Primary Works

A91:1. Browning, Elizabeth Barrett. *Sonnets from the Portuguese and Other Love Poems.* New York: Doubleday, 1990. 103 pp. ¶Rev. by Margaret Galloway, *Voices of Youth Advocates* 13 (February 1991): 372.

A91:2. Byatt, A. S., sel. and introduction. *Robert Browning: Dramatic Monologues.* London: Folio Society, 1991. xxxi + 310 pp.

A91:3. Day, Aidan, ed. and introduction. *Robert Browning: Selected Poetry and Prose. Routledge English Texts.* Ed. John Drakakis. London: Routledge, 1991. 230 pp.

A91:4. Harper, J. W., ed. *Men and Women and Other Poems.* London: J. M. Dent & Sons; Rutland, VT: Charles E. Tuttle, 1991. xxi + 244 pp. ¶Reprint of A75:3 and A76:4.

A91:5. Jack, Ian, Rowena Fowler, and Margaret Smith, eds. *The Poetical Works of Robert Browning, Volume 4. Bells and Pomegranates VII–VIII ("Dramatic Romances and Lyrics," "Luria," "A Soul's Tragedy") and "Christmas-Eve and Easter-Day."* Oxford: Clarendon P; New York: Oxford UP, 1991. xxiv + 454 pp. ¶Rev. by Eric Griffiths, *Times Literary Supplement* 22 November 1991: 5–6; G. B. Tennyson and Thomas Wortham, *Nineteenth Century Literature* 46 (1991): 298.

A91:6. Kelley, Philip, and Ronald Hudson, eds. *The Brownings' Correspondence,* volumes 1–8. [See A85:5, A86:5, A87:4, A88:8, A89:7, A90:8.] ¶Rev. by Michael Timko, *Carlyle Annual* 11 (1990): 105–09.

A91:7. Kelley, Philip, and Ronald Hudson, eds. *The Brownings' Correspondence, Volume 8.* [See A90:8.] ¶Rev. by G. B. Tennyson and Thomas Wortham, *Nineteenth Century Literature* 45 (1991): 528–31.

A91:8. Kelley, Philip, and Scott Lewis, eds. *The Brownings' Correspondence, Volume 9: June 1844–December 1844.* Winfield, KS: Wedgestone P, 1991. xiv + 423 pp.

A91:9. King, Roma A., Jr., and Susan Crowl, eds. *The Ring and the Book, Books IX–XII.* Volume 9 of *The Complete Works of Robert Browning with Variant Readings & Annotations.* Ed. Jack W. Herring, et al. [See A89:10.] ¶Rev. by Eric Griffiths, *Times Literary Supplement* 22 November 1991: 5–6.

A91:10. Woolford, John, and Daniel Karlin, eds. *The Poems of Browning, Volume 1: 1826–1840. Longman Annotated English Poets.* Ed. F. W. Bateson and John Barnard. London: Longman, 1991. xxxii + 797 pp. ¶Rev. by Donald Davie, *London Review of Books* 10 October 1991: 20, 22–23; Eric Griffiths, *Times Literary Supplement* 22 November 1991: 5–6.

A91:11. Woolford, John, and Daniel Karlin, eds. *The Poems of Browning, Volume 2: 1841–1846. Longman Annotated English Poets.* Ed. F. W. Bateson and John Barnard. London: Longman, 1991. xv + 518 pp. ¶Rev. by Donald Davie, *London Review of Books* 10 October 1991: 20, 22–23; Eric Griffiths, *Times Literary Supplement* 22 November 1991: 5–6.

B. Reference and Bibliographical Works and Exhibitions

B91:1. Donaldson, Sandra M. "Robert and Elizabeth Barrett Browning: An Annotated Bibliography for 1989." *VLC* 19 (1991): 381–402.

B91:2. Maynard, John. "Guide to the Year's Work in Victorian Poetry: 1990: Robert Browning." *VP* 29 (Autumn 1991): 267–78.

B91:3. Mermin, Dorothy. "Guide to the Year's Work in Victorian Poetry: 1990: Elizabeth Barrett Browning." *VP* 29 (Autumn 1991): 263–67.

B91:4. Thomas, Charles Flint. *Art and Architecture in the Poetry of Robert Browning, An Illustrated Compendium of Sources*. Troy, NY: Whitston Publishing, 1988. xii + 521 pp. ¶Identifies works of art and architecture mentioned or implied in RB's poems, compiles a summary of composite sources (conflations of sources for imaginary works), and includes 260 illustrations. Arranged alphabetically by poem title, it is indexed by artist, source with location, and miscellaneous source. Maps of Florence and Rome are also included.

B91:5. Zorzi, Rosella Mamoli. *Robert Browning a Venezia*. Venice: Fondazione Scientifica Querini Stampalia, 1989. 109 pp. ¶Introduces and catalogues the 141 items of an exhibition held in conjunction with "Browning e Venezia," November 1989 (see below, Perosa); reprinted in part below, C91:86. Translations of "A Toccata of Galuppi's" (by Angelo Righetti) and "Ponte dell' Angelo, Venice" (by Armando Pajalich) are included. In Italian.

C. Biography, Criticism, and Miscellaneous

C91:1. Allison, Alida Louise. "Eurydice: The Lost Voice." *DAI* 51.7 (1991): 2371A. University of California at Riverside, 1990. ¶Discusses versions of the Eurydice myth, including one by RB "Eurydice to Orpheus."

C91:2. Armstrong, Isobel. "The Problem of Representation in *The Ring and the Book*: Politics, Aesthetics, Language." Perosa, *Browning e Venezia* 205–31. ¶Examines RB's poem in terms of "the crisis of democracy, the crisis of representation" in the nineteenth century. Its inheritance plot reveals the "inequality and violence" required to maintain the class structure, challenged at this time

by calls for political representation. The poem is an "enquiry about the signification of the discourse, or discourses, of representation," political, aesthetic, and
linguistic representation all being problematical. "Half Rome" and "Other Half
Rome" pay "allegiance to symbol and phantom proxy respectively," the first
justifying "holistic aristocratic conservatism" and the second "rational bourgeois liberalism and laissez faire individualism." The poem explores "a radical
critique of liberal accounts of democracy" and exposes "its liberal epistemological contradictions," particularly as expressed by Mill. "Browning's text recognises that the meaning of representation is unstable and that a struggle over its
meaning is going on." The task of reading and analyzing is necessarily unfin-
ished and therefore continually renewed.

C91:3. Beatty, Claudius J. P. "Robert Browning and Thomas Hardy: Some
Observations." Perosa, *Browning e Venezia* 155–63. ¶Notes various connections
between RB and Thomas Hardy: an appreciation of art, architecture, and music;
family roots in Dorset; misunderstandings of their philosophies as, respectively,
optimism and pessimism; and admiration for Shelley's poetry. Parallels may be
seen between *The Ring and the Book* and Hardy's *Tess of the d'Urbervilles*.

C91:4. Berardinelli, Daniel Joseph. "Fact on Fancy: A Study of Robert Browning's 'Asolando: Fancies and Facts'." *DAI* 52.3 (1991): 925A. Kent State
University, 1990. ¶Associates the terms "fact" and "fancy" with literary and
philosophical conceptions of the self and describes RB's dialectic between fancy
and fact as "a means of wringing meaning from experience." Speakers of his
poems, and entire cultures, exercise self mystification and self justification.

C91:5. Bolton, Roy E. "Obituary: Edward Richard Moulton-Barrett." *BSN* 21
(1991–92): 68–72. ¶Describes the life and accomplishments of Edward Moulton-
Barrett, the great-grandson of EBB's brother Alfred.

C91:6. Bontempo, Barbara, and Roger Jerome. "The Death of a Duchess:
Teaching Literature Through Drama." *English Record* (New York State English
Council) 40.4 (1990): 14–20. ¶Describes teaching "My Last Duchess" with
drama activities in a high school class in order to engage students with poetry.

C91:7. Brady, Ann P. *Pompilia: A Feminist Reading of Robert Browning's
"The Ring and The Book."* [See C88:8.] ¶Rev. by Helen M. Cooper, *Journal
of English and Germanic Philology* 90 (October 1991): 581–83; Herbert F.
Tucker, *VIJ* 19 (1991): 197–210.

C91:8. Bristow, Joseph. *New Readings: Robert Browning.* London: Harvester
P; New York: St. Martin's, 1991. xi + 178 pp. ¶Revises and expands C87:3.

The structure and style of RB's poems invite re-reading: they constantly seek new beginnings and he "deploys complex techniques of deferral and delay," making his work appealing to the Moderns. But he was a Victorian and sought "to implement ideas about the divine necessity of cultural change." This tension makes for "peculiar scepticism, historical paradoxes, and strange negativities" in his poetry, although he was consistent in the "aesthetic, political and stylistic models" that he followed. Chapters address RB as a post-Romantic; the dramatic monologue; his theory of history and questions of historicism; and his representations of love, sex, and marriage.

C91:9. Bristow, Joseph, ed. *The Victorian Poet: Poetics and Persona.* [See C89:9.] ¶Rev. by Linda K. Hughes, *Victorian Periodicals Review* 24 (Spring 1991): 43–44.

C91:10. Brownlow, F. W. "The Modernity of Chesterton's Browning Criticism." *Chesterton Review* 17 (May 1991): 163–75. ¶Assesses G. K. Chesterton's study, *Robert Browning*, as "one of the first modernist books of literary criticism in English." The book is less about RB than about what RB's works said to Chesterton; it describes his return to RB, whom he saw as being like himself. RB offers "the unexpected romance of being a middle-class Londoner." Chesterton presents him "as simultaneously the father of the modern aesthetic in poetry . . . and as the representative of absolutely normal, optimistic, middle-class Liberalism." What remained unexplained was "either the significance or the source of Browning's grotesquerie and obscurity." In his later *Victorian Age in Literature*, "all those middle-class, provincial qualities that he had praised so highly . . . now appear to him as weaknesses."

C91:11. Bullen, J. B. "Robert Browning, Italian Art, and the Discourse of Art History." Perosa, *Browning e Venezia* 71–83. ¶Explores RB's view of the Renaissance, using Barthes's theories of mythography and historical discourse. Whereas the art and architecture of fifteenth century Italy carry a strong image of Italy's history and culture for the Victorians, conceptions of the period were also formed by "accounts of painters and painting from Vasari onwards," seen in RB's early poetry. Both the substance of the myth and its prevailing ideology underwent a change dating from his Italian tour in 1844: the churches, paintings, and frescoes of the early Christian artists in Pisa and Florence revealed to him the "life energy" of an earlier Italy. In addition, his rejection of the theories of the French art historian A. F. Rio caused him to reexamine his own conceptions. His ideology is political, not religious: great art bears witness to "a people freed from the yoke of political despotism."

C91:12. Campbell, Jane. " 'The somehow may be thishow': Fact, Fiction, and Intertextuality in Antonia Byatt's 'Precipice-Encurled'." *Studies in Short Fiction* 28 (Spring 1991): 115–23. ¶Reveals the "fact" behind Byatt's fiction in her short story "Precipice-Encurled," in which RB is a cental character. Some of the other characters, such as the scholar (Michael Meredith) and Mrs. Bronson, may appear to be fictional but are real, and others may appear to be real, such as the artist Joshua Riddell, but are fictional. The central metaphor in Byatt's collection is of "narration as confecting." Byatt's use of character, plot, RB's line from *The Ring and the Book* ("the somehow may be thishow"), and narrative structure demonstrate that, like RB, she recognizes that "fiction which makes fact alive" is "fact too" or the "somehow" that is also the "thishow."

C91:13. Case, Alison. "Gender and Narration in *Aurora Leigh*." *VP* 29 (Spring 1991): 17–32. ¶Analyzes the dualistic narrative structure in EBB's *Aurora Leigh*, arguing that she does not reconcile Aurora's contradictory roles as female "artist/ hero" and Victorian "perfect woman." The first four books portray the female artist in control of shaping her experiences; in the rest of the work, the romance plot, Aurora is an increasingly unreliable narrator lacking awareness of and authority over her life. EBB does not completely discard marriage as the required telos of a young woman's story because of the age in which she lived, but she did create a "double teleology" for the novel by isolating the plot of poetic ambition from the "undermining influence of the traditional love story."

C91:14. Caughie, Pamela L. "*Flush* and the Literary Canon: Oh where oh where has that little dog gone?" *Tulsa Studies in Women's Literature* 10.1 (1991): 47–66. ¶Notes that EBB defies RB by paying a ransom to save Flush, putting them in different value systems, and that one motive for Virginia Woolf's writing her biography of EBB's dog may have been to help restore *Aurora Leigh* to the literary canon.

C91:15. Cervo, Nathan. "Browning's 'Bishop Blougram's Apology'." *Explicator* 49.3 (Spring 1991): 149–51. ¶Suggests sources and meanings for the name Blougram in RB's poem, one being the cause célèbre of 1820 in which Henry Lord Brougham successfully defended Princess Caroline (Christianity) against divorce from her husband, the Prince of Wales (a sort of madness). The name may also be an anagram for B(ishop) Glamour, suggesting someone, usually the clergy (identified by RB as Nicholas Cardinal Wiseman), versed in the "black art of casting spells by means of written signs." Thus Blougram can be seen as one who casts a spell on Gigadibs in order to "suck his victim's mind and character dry."

C91:16. Cooper, Helen. *Elizabeth Barrett Browning, Woman and Artist.* [See C88:13.] ¶Rev. by Amanda S. Anderson, *Journal of English and Germanic Philology* 90 (October 1991): 577–81.

C91:17. Crowder, Ashby Bland. "Browning and How He Worked in Good Temper." *Victorian Authors and Their Works: Revision Motivations and Modes*, ed. Judith Kennedy. Athens: Ohio UP, 1991. 72–98. ¶Reprint of C89:18.

C91:18. De Angelis, Palmira. "Robert Browning a Roma: La predica agli ebrei nel 'Giorno della Santa Croce'." *Il Veltro* 35.1–2 (January–April 1991): 100–116. ¶Introduces and translates RB's "Holy-Cross Day," including describing the Brownings' life in Rome, the ghetto at the time, and the Catholic Church's former practice of forcing Jews to listen to sermons meant to convert them. In Italian.

C91:19. De Logu, Pietro. "Il tema della morte in *Asolando*." Perosa, *Browning e Venezia* 285–95. ¶Examines the theme of death in the lyric poems in *Asolando*, once intended to be titled *A New Series of Jocoseria*. The poems are his ultimate lesson in existential philosophy. "Rosny," "Now," "White Witchcraft," "Bad Dreams," "The Cardinal and the Dog," "Muckle-Mouth Meg," "Arcades Ambo," "Ponte dell' Angelo, Venice," "Beatrice Signorini," and "Epilogue" are considered. In Italian.

C91:20. Drew, Philip A. "The Critical Fortunes of Browning's Later Poetry." Perosa, *Browning e Venezia* 179–91. ¶Refutes the commonplace that RB's later works were not well received by noting the number of thoughtful reviews that appeared during his lifetime and the sympathetic readership that had developed. His works often received "thorough reading, careful analysis and reasoned argument" from critics. At the turn of the century, critical attention waned, however, and critics have generally disparaged or ignored the later work. Since 1960, some attention has been given to these works by King, Drew, Hassett, Ryals, Priestley, Langbaum, Collins, Kenny, McCusker, Woolford, Siegchrist, and Hair. A fresh evaluation of these poems would be appropriate, especially if accompanied by a "broadening of the definition of poetry."

C91:21. Everett, Glenn S. " 'You'll Not Let Me Speak': Engagement and Detachment in Browning's Monologues." *VLC* 19 (1991): 123–42. ¶Solves the problem of defining the dramatic monologue by focusing not on attributes of the poems but on their "requirements of their readers"; the figure of the auditor is what is new and demanding about RB's poems. We thus "must ask about the speaker's effect upon his listener" and then infer the dramatic situation, which is a process of discovery: first "engagement, then detachment." The question then is whether the dramatic monologue is "essentially lyric, relying on the reader's empathy with the speaker, or truly dramatic." These poems are like objective, modernist poetry because the reader must construct the poem "in a new, more indeterminate fashion" not knowing the author's intentions.

C91:22. Farkas, Ann. "Digging Among the Ruins." *VP* 29 (Spring 1991): 33–45. ¶Asserts that in "Love Among the Ruins" RB did not intend to create an actual ancient city but rather an emblematic one. The poem may be seen in the context of the tradition of emblematic literature, including the writings of Virgil, Plutarch, Ralegh, Spenser, Homer, Layard, Sophocles, and Dante, as well as non-literary sources and other traditions. As an emblem of *Men and Women*, the poem is a complex hieroglyph both guarding and revealing its riches.

C91:23. Findlay, L. M. "Taking the Measure of *Différance*: Deconstruction and *The Ring and the Book*." *VP* (Winter 1991): 401–14. ¶Examines Derridean notions of measure and différance in relation to RB's poem. As a sustained treament of the legal process, much of the work overlaps Derridean différance; however, RB does not privilege writing over speech (or vice-versa) but rather explores the relations between them. RB also pays tribute to the social power of the written word and warns, in the Bishop's advice to Caponsacchi, that phonocentrism is not always positive.

C91:24. Fish, Thomas E. "Be 'Whole and Sole Yourself': The Quest for Self-hood in 'Bishop Blougram's Apology'." *South Atlantic Review* 56.1 (January 1991): 17–34. ¶Asserts that "Bishop Blougram's Apology" dramatizes RB's "faith in the power of the human will that mandates our own willed action." Although the Bishop recognizes the protean nature of the self, he nevertheless consciously chooses, in the end, a stagnant materialism and spiritual complacency over self-revision. The ambiguity of the epilogue forces the reader into the same interpretive role as Blougram. Rather than requiring casuistry, however, this position leads the reader to "the precipice" of a new way of reading, not one that is "detached, objective and self-assured" (like the Bishop's) but rather one that is "engaged, subjective," and the "self-exposing response of a human 'being'."

C91:25. Forster, Margaret. *Lady's Maid.* [See C90:31.] ¶Rev. by Margaret Flannagan, *Booklist* 15 February 1991: 1177; Joanna Kafarowski, *Belles Lettres* 7 (Fall 1991): 30; *New Yorker* 20 May 1991: 108; Coral Lansbury, *New York Times Book Review* 17 March 1991: 14–15; *New York Times Book Review* 9 June 1991: 28; *Publishers Weekly* 11 January 1991: 90; Cynthia Johnson Whealler, *Library Journal* 116 (January 1991): 150.

C91:26. Gee, Karen Richardson. " 'Kins(wo)men of the Shelf': Emily Dickinson's Reading of Women Writers." *DAI* 52.3 (1991): 916A. University of Tennessee, 1990. ¶Examines Dickinson's reading of other women writers and places her in a nineteenth-century literary tradition of women writers which includes EBB.

C91:27. Griffiths, Eric. *The Printed Voice of Victorian Poetry*. [See C89:33.] ¶Rev. by Thomas Wortham and G. B. Tennyson, *Nineteenth Century Literature* 45 (March 1991): 534; J. R. Watson, *Durham University Journal* 51 (July 1990): 280–81.

C91:28. Grube, Alberta Fabris. "Elizabeth Barrett Browning e il Risorgimento italiano." Perosa, *Browning e Venezia* 137–54. ¶Describes EBB's attitudes toward Italians and their efforts towards the unification of Italy, especially as seen in *Casa Guidi Windows, Aurora Leigh, Poems Before Congress*, and *Last Poems*. Woolf noted that her life came to be better known than her works, but feminist critics are now reevaluating the work. Her Italian poems are written with passion but a certain lack of taste deriving from her excessive involvement in the events which she witnessed. Her best verse addresses the trials of her times and has a strong female component, "the sensibility of a woman and mother." In Italian.

C91:29. Hicks, Malcolm. " 'Mystic (and Material) Presences of Power' in the Poetry of Elizabeth Barrett Browning." *New Welsh Review* 3.4 (Spring 1991): 19–23. ¶Analyzes EBB's "The Lost Bower" as being "indicative of her broader evaluation of poetic inspiration and of her future development" and as well of the loss of the visionary gleam. The Romantic malaise of her early poems is seen in the theme of poetic loss and frustration and the desire to "rediscover or reaffirm the revelations" previously enjoyed. "Insufficiency" and Sonnet 29 also reflect these themes and imagery. "High-minded satirical realism" later becomes her route to poetical and social salvation.

C91:30. Hochberg, Shifra. "Male Authority and Female Subversion in Browning's 'My Last Duchess'." *LIT: Literature, Interpretation, Theory* 3.1 (1991): 77–84. ¶Uses a contemporary psychoanalytic approach to examine the portrait of the Duchess in RB's poem as a "countertext of female desire" that subverts the patriarchal authority and control of the Duke's monologue. The Duchess uses several Victorian codes for representing sexual desire (her sexual smile, her active "gaze," her powerful stance) to displace her seeming powerlessness, passivity, even death, becoming the subject or "maker of meaning" of her own silent discourse rather than the object of the Duke's "reading" of her. As a "resisting female discourse that deconstructs, challenges, and ultimately displaces" the Duke's, the portrait thus becomes an emblem for RB's own view of art as self empowering, an idea that links his poetic sensibility with female gender and power.

C91:31. Ingalls, Zoë. "At Wellesley College, Letters that Document a Perfect Love Story." *Chronicle of Higher Education* 13 February 1991: B5. ¶Describes the holdings of Wellesley's Browning Collection, recounting the story of the Brownings' courtship because their love letters are in the library's collection. The collection focuses on EBB because the college's founder regarded her as an exemplary educated woman, symbolizing the college. Other letters, manuscripts, notebooks, photographs, and memorabilia are located there.

C91:32. Ingersoll, Earl G. "Considerations of Gender in the Dramatic Monologue." *Modern Language Review* 86.3 (1991): 545–52. ¶Applies Jane Gallop's literary theories on gender (that metaphor has been linked with Romantic poetry and the phallocentric, whereas metonymy has been associated with realist narrative and the feminine or feminized) to Tennyson's "Ulysses" and RB's "Fra Lippo Lippi" and "Andrea del Sarto." "Ulysses" exemplifies the phallocentric with its lyricism and central metaphor of travel as a way to escape the "feminine" hearth and home. RB uses metonymy in his monologues, which lends them their realism and shows the "feminization" of the poems' speakers who, unlike Ulysses, cannot travel because they "see themselves as powerless to break free."

C91:33.* *Introduction to Modern English and American Literature, Volume 1: The Nineteenth Century.* Santa Barbara, CA: Annenberg/CPB Project, 1990. 30 min. ¶Introduces work of and criticism on RB for a home study course on audiotape. Rev. by Melissa Stearns, *Library Journal* 15 May 1990: 120.

C91:34. Jack, Ian. "Elizabeth Barrett and Browning's *Dramatic Romances and Lyrics* (1845)." Perosa, *Browning e Venezia* 125–35. ¶Suggests that RB's asking EBB to critique his poems before publication was "a brilliant move . . . in the skilful game of chess in which the two of them were engaged for more than twenty months, before it was won by both players and they went off to Italy together." He valued her reading, and she was gratified by the charge. Her comments on "The Flight of the Duchess" have not previously been published and parts are quoted here to demonstrate the "critical dialogue" between them. He revised in response to her comments on rhythm, line length, and meaning.

C91:35. Johnson, Anthony L. "Lyrical Themes and Motifs in Browning's *Asolando.*" Perosa, *Browning e Venezia* 297–323. ¶Demonstrates how in *Asolando*,

RB reinterprets "the experience of Wordsworthian Romanticism" seen in the "Epilogue" as a recognition of the object simply as "Nature to know and name." In the lyrics, woman is "the only actively transforming or transcending principle, in the sense that a loved woman is the ultimate source or origin of sense, and that she alone can make a man transcend his ego-limits and complete his self." At its best this love ethic "is a new, dynamic form of interpersonal Romanticism." In "Now" the poet expresses "The strongest intensity of desire," a "repressed physical desire" it turns out, and sets out a four-term structure of solidity: "Thought and feeling and soul and sense." The "Epilogue" however signals "the failure of his love-quest."

C91:36. Jones, Robert C. "If Mr. Wallace Stevens instead of Mrs. Elizabeth Barrett Browning had written Sonnet #43 from the Portuguese." *English Journal* 80.6 (October 1991): 103. ¶A poem.

C91:37. Karlin, Daniel. " 'Beatrice Signorini': Browning's Last Portrait." Perosa, *Browning e Venezia* 325–37. ¶Considers a relatively-ignored poem from *Asolando*, "Beatrice Signorini." Given the retrospective air of the volume, "Beatrice" may recall the earlier "Andrea del Sarto." The title, however, does not refer to the artist but his wife, who proves to be strong and admirable, as does the artist's lover. The women both are identified with the poet: "with Artemisia by means of the sophistication, awareness, and comic control of the narrative, and with Beatrice, whose gesture is so much more radical and decisive than that of her husband" (she tears up the painting that is his only masterpiece and they discover their mutual love).

C91:38. Kenny, Paul. "*Pauline*: Browning and Romantic Utilitarianism." *BSN* 21 (1991–92): 23–31. ¶Situates RB and *Pauline*, "his intense opening testament," with regard to the period of political reform dominated by the Utilitarians, a "threatening cultural moment." As a poet, he had to detach from political movements despite possible sympathy with them. "Calculated irresponsibility" and an "air of incalculable irrationality" pervade RB's poem, which raises the question of the tension between the psychological hedonism and enlightened reformism of Utilitarianism. In "the persona's case history," RB presents the contradictions and confusions that logically follow; in his *Essay on Shelley*, he does the same, exorcising "the utilitarian Shelley." With *Pauline*, he has internalized "the very spirit of criticism."

C91:39. Laird, Holly A. "*Aurora Leigh*: An Epical *Ars Poetica*." *Writing the Woman Artist: Essays on Poetics, Politics, and Portraiture*, ed. Suzanne W. Jones. Philadelphia: U of Pennsylvania P, 1991. 353–70. ¶Examines EBB's poetics in her verse novel, in which she created a feminist aesthetic, a " 'two-fold' vision of heroism in art and in life, an unironic vision of differences." The alternative poetics which defines women's experience as being victims of men is inadequate; EBB's heroine was not "an abandoned woman speaking of her private woes to a small community" but a triumphant figure who spoke for her age, especially in Book 5. As a hero, the woman writer challenges formulaic positions and systemized thought "for the sake of a lived philosophy": she struggles "through the written word" and engages in epic debates. The critical preference for irony, binarism, and diffeérance leads to detachment; instead, EBB's unironic philosophy of "embrasure" unfolds possibilities, multiplies choices, and permits alternatives — it is a syncretic criticism. Aurora's poetics is not exclusively for women; it is "feminist in that it sees everyone as gendered, and everyone as in need of re-education about women's capacities."

C91:40. Langbaum, Robert. "Browning and Twentieth Century Poetry." Perosa, *Browning e Venezia* 37–55. ¶Traces a line of succession from RB through Hardy's poems to our contemporaries: he replaced "Miltonic resonance and mellifluousness with the rough colloquial diction and rhythms, the fragmented *difficult* music of modern lyricism" as well as modern thought. Hardy reiterates RB's theme of "successful failure," proving ideas about Hardy's pessimism and RB's optimism "oversimple." RB's wit and irony may be seen in Hardy's love poems as well; at his death, Hardy asked his wife to read to him from "Rabbi Ben Ezra." Pound explicitly acknowledged RB as "son père" and *Sordello* as the starting point for the *Cantos*. The dramatic monologue was adapted by Pound, Eliot, Robert Lowell, Theodore Weiss, and Richard Howard.

C91:41. Linguanti, Elsa. " 'Notizie di fatto e di ragione' in Browning's *The Ring and the Book*." Perosa, *Browning e Venezia* 193–203. ¶Views *The Ring and the Book* as a novel of a city "which speaks through many voices," containing "the entire universe of argumentative discourse" through use of the diverse components of the source materials with their various truth claims. RB shapes the legal material carefully, sometimes inventing and sometimes paraphrasing. We might expect Tertium Quid to resolve oppositions, to find the truth through fact and reasoning, but his efforts come to an impasse. Only the concept of relationship provides a "victory over the chaos of fact."

C91:42. Lonardi, Gilberto. "Un padre metafisico per Montale." Perosa, *Browning e Venezia* 57–69. ¶Examines connections between RB's "Two in the Campagna" and "Confessions" and Eugenio Montale's "Due nel crepuscolo," "La casa dei doganieri," and "Dora Markus." The two poets share especially the metaphor of the thread and the idea of the poetic object. The concept of sensuous thought connects them with Baudelaire and Hopkins. Montale writes in a metaphysical tradition that runs from RB to Hardy to Pound and Eliot. In Italian.

C91:43. Lucas, John. *England and Englishness: Ideas of Nationhood in English Poetry, 1688–1900*. Iowa City: U of Iowa P, 1990. 8–9, 165–99. ¶Explores English poets' attempts to identify nationhood; as "the upholders of culture" they were in a position of authority and responsibility. RB's poems are anti-authoritarian, "allowing a range of different voices" and effacing the author. This heteroglossia undercuts his readers' ability to trust any of them; he is a poet "of mass democracy, of city society." *Strafford*, "The Lost Leader," "Cavalier Tunes," and "My Last Duchess" may be seen in the context of the "democratic, republican and feminist" circle of political radicals the young RB knew. In contrast to the Tennyson of the patriotic and chivalric poems, RB in "Childe Roland" shows the absurdity of chivalric heroism, and in "Love Among the Ruins" and "A Lovers' Quarrel," an anti-masculinist stance. The Brownings' move to Italy was a denial of Englishness, as EBB's *Casa Guidi Windows* makes clear. In *Men and Women* especially, RB "unfixes certainty," a "democratic strategy" that is also modern. After EBB's death and his return to England, however, he smoothes away "the problematic readings of Englishness" in his poems.

C91:44. Madden, Lisa Marie. "Diversity Without Discord: The Victorian Writer and Man's Capacity for Integration." *DAI* 51.12 (1991): 4132A. New York University, 1990. ¶Views EBB and other Victorian writers as sages who integrate the conflicts and diversity of an age. EBB seeks to integrate the individual and society and also presents the theme of male/female harmony.

C91:45. Manning, Greg. "Language and Lapsarian States in Browning's 'Soliloquy of the Spanish Cloister': Another Reading of 'Hy, Zy, Hine'." *VP* 29 (Summer 1991): 175–79. ¶Presents various interpretations that, contest-like, have been proclaimed for the line "Hy, Zy, Hine." In trying to establish a definitive interpretation, however, critics participate in the same failure of language as the speaker of RB's poem in his post-lapsarian state as *homo significans*, thus demonstrating "the truly unverifiable, definitely infinite nature of Browning's text."

C91:46. Marucci, Franco. "Fantasie greche, autobiografismo e naturalism nel secondo Browning." Perosa, *Browning e Venezia* 253–71. ¶Considers the relatively neglected poems of RB's mature period, *Balaustion's Adventure* and *Aristophanes' Apology*, the first a Maytime diversion and the second, long and erudite. Both have as their protagonist, Balaustion, an archetypal figure; and both are permeated with aspects of Greek literature, especially the works of Euripides. In Italian.

C91:47. Maynard, John. "Reading the Reader in Robert Browning's Dramatic Monologues." Perosa, *Browning e Venezia* 165–77. ¶Proposes that readers seek "not to define the ideal interpretative position, but to explore the range of responses — experiences — the poem generates." Because of RB's variousness, we might better "see the poem as a system that includes a reading of many readers reporting many experiences." The listeners in his dramatic monologues are often only faintly realized and so interpretations can shift; the poems are three dimensional. For example in "The Bishop Orders His Tomb" we may try to define the listeners, historicize the poem, identify with the speaker, read ourselves as the moral and religious reader, the psychological reader, the deconstructive reader — a continuum of readings emerges.

C91:48. Mazzaro, Jerome. "Mapping Sublimity: Elizabeth Barrett Browning's *Sonnets from the Portuguese*." *Essays in Literature* 18.2 (Fall 1991): 166–79. ¶Answers Heilman (1945) and others who call EBB's *Sonnets* insincere and rhetorical rather than sublime. In her prefaces, EBB explains that her aim is sublimity, which she demonstrates with her "violation" of sonnet form and refusal to "adhere either to the stereotypes of Victorian romance or to most Renaissance love sequences." Sonnets one and two exemplify sublimity in both their violation of form and their mysticism. Subsequent sonnets, "poems of daily life," also contain elements of sublimity: inattention to rhetorical balance and proportion, fluent imagery, use of Biblical allusion, and portrayal of "a wordly divided self." EBB's success as a sublime poet can be seen, therefore, in the very surprise and "Peeping Tom sensations" of which some critics complain.

C91:49. Melchiori, Barbara Arnett. "Browning's Venetian Dream." Perosa, *Browning e Venezia* 109–15. ¶Sees in RB's *Fifine at the Fair*, especially the central dream episode, various escapees like that of the Venetian Carnival: an escape to nonsense, to the ivory tower, to the dangerous and immoral pleasure ground and circus, and to the spiritualists' seances to contact the dead. The mask, as always, serves the purpose of "discreet revelation."

C91:50. Melchiori, Giorgio. "Da Beppo a Pippa e oltre." Perosa, *Browning e Venezia* 95-107. ¶Observes that RB felt so strongly about Italy that he preferred it to England and said so in "De Gustibus —." It was not beautiful, artistic Italy, but Italy oppressed and depressed, recalling "Pippa Passes." He shared this attachment with Byron, whose "Beppo" has thematic, verbal, and stylistic echoes in RB's poem. Other of RB's poems have connections with Byron and

Italy as well. A line may be drawn from Sterne and Byron to RB and Henry James, and even to Joyce. In Italian.

C91:51. Meredith, Michael. "A Fine Distancing: Browning's Debt to Harrison Ainsworth." *BSN* 21 (1991–92): 14–23. ¶Suggests that the popularity of Ainsworth's romances appealed to RB and suggested to him the poems of *Dramatic Romances and Lyrics*. RB adapted incidents, borrowed characters, and distilled period atmosphere from the novels into "poems which were unmistakably his own creations." Ainsworth's melodramas had public approval, which RB sought; they did not, however, have the complex moral viewpoint RB was to develop in his dramatic monologues.

C91:52. Meredith, Michael. "Speaking Out in Venice and London." Perosa, *Browning e Venezia* 85–93. ¶Describes the readings of his poetry that RB gave in the last years of his life as attempts to "demonstrate the accessibility of his poetry, to win over that audience which throughout his life he felt had been denied him." Like Dickens, he read with theatricality, and he emphasized the meaning of the words, rather than their sound. He also favored friendly reviewers with advance copies of poems to forestall unfair criticism and misinterpretation.

C91:53. Mermin, Dorothy. *Elizabeth Barrett Browning: The Origins of a New Poetry.* [See C89:51.] ¶Rev. by Amanda S. Anderson, *Journal of English and Germanic Philology* 90 (October 1991): 577–81; James Fanning, *Zeitschrift fur Anglistik und Amerikanistik* 39 (1991): 76.

C91:54. Miller, J. H. "The Theme of the disappearance of God in Victorian poetry." *Victorian Subjects.* Durham, N.C.: Duke UP, 1991. 49–68. ¶Reprint of C63:34–35.

C91:55. Mollenkott, Marilyn I. " 'An Age-Old Anvil': Theory and Performance in the Sonnets of Gerard Manley Hopkins." *DAI* 51.7 (1991): 2386A. New York University, 1989. ¶Compares the sonnets and sonnet theory of Hopkins to those of EBB, among others.

C91:56. Montevecchi, Massimo. "La camera da letto di Miss Barrett: Riflessioni da una lettura di *Flush* di Virginia Woolf." *Il Lettore di Provincia* 22 (Sept. 1990): 53–61. ¶Describes Woolf's biography of EBB's dog, Flush, as rich in elements both fantastic and polemic. The isolated back bedroom of Wimpole Street reflects the powerlessness of women and also Woolf's own isolation and illness. As EBB knew, illness brings with it a quasi-mystical consciousness. In Italian.

C91:57. Nair, Rama. "Browning's Dramatic Monologue: A Study in 'Interior Stillness'." *Panjab University Research Bulletin (Arts)* 21.2 (October 1990): 39–44. ¶Suggests that RB's dramatic monologues are instead "interior dialogues" in which "the duality of the speaker and the 'unseen listener' is resolved," the unseen listener becoming "an extension of the psychic self" as it attempts to restore order to mental disorder and unity to a fragmented self. The speakers in RB's poems are, thus, also their own listeners as they try to resolve their inner conflicts over power (the Duke in "My Last Duchess"), love (Andrea in "Andrea del Sarto"), and art (Lippi in "Fra Lippo Lippi"). In this sense, these interior dialogues are like meditation because they also attempt to advance an "awareness of mental stillness as a mode of knowledge."

C91:58. Neal, Jean. "The Silverthorne Family." *BSN* 21 (1991–92): 60–65. ¶Describes the family of James Silverthorne, RB's first cousin who was one of the two witnesses at his marriage with EBB.

C91:59. Orr, E. W. *Elizabeth Barrett Browning Undusted, A Complete Study: Poems, Prose, The Critical Heritage.* Eastbourne, East Sussex: Orr, 1987. 263 pp. ¶Describes EBB's life briefly and work extensively, reprinting one of Eliza Ogilvy's memoirs, many of EBB's prefaces and prose pieces, a large part of Alice Meynell's introductions to EBB's work, and a selection from Porter and Clarke's Critical Introduction.

C91:60. Pearce, Brian Louis. "Browning and F. T. Palgrave: Some Notes." *BSN* 21 (1991–92): 65–67, 69. ¶Describes RB's association with Francis Turner Palgrave, editor of *The Golden Treasury of best songs and Lyrical poems in the English language* and professor of poetry at Oxford. Palgrave included fourteen of RB's poems in the second series, published in 1897.

C91:61. Perosa, Sergio. "Browning e le forme del Modernismo." Perosa, *Browning e Venezia* 21–35. ¶Assesses RB's importance in shaping modernist poetry and prose, most notably through the dramatic monologue. Eliot's concept of the dissociation of sensibility is indebted to RB and Tennyson; Pound reflects RB in his theory of the mask or persona; and James acknowledges the influence of *The Ring and the Book* on his narrative style and the idea of the non-existence of truth. Other aspects of modernism influenced by RB may be seen in Conrad, Ford, Joyce, Woolf, Kafka, Pirandello — multiplication and interiorization of point of view, and at the same time a solid sense of place and time, the past and history, and common men and women. In Italian.

C91:62. Perosa, Sergio, ed. *Browning e Venezia.* Florence: Leo S. Olschki Editore, 1991. vi + 340 pp. ¶Collects essays from a conference held 27–29 November 1989 in Venice; some are in Italian and some in English.

C91:63. Phelan, James. *Reading People, Reading Plots: Character, Progression, and the Interpretation of Narrative.* Chicago: U of Chicago P, 1989. 3–14. ¶Uses RB's "My Last Duchess" to exemplify ways of reading character in a text, giving rhetorical and structural analyses and looking at mimetic, thematic, and synthetic elements.

C91:64. Porter, Peter. "Browning's Important Parleying." Perosa, *Browning e Venezia* 1–19. ¶Asserts that RB made poetry interesting again by making it "concern itself with people" as drama does. His new poetry looked back at the old, bringing together the dead and the living — "the single greatest nudge Modernism received." His influence may be seen in John Ashbery's talkativeness, as well as in T. S. Eliot, Ezra Pound, and W. H. Auden. In each of his dramatic monologues talk is the key; in *Parleyings*, however, RB's people are listeners to his autobiography.

C91:65. Porter, Peter. "The Recording Angels: Music and Meaning in the Voices of Poetry." *Times Literary Supplement* 15 March 1991: 3–4. ¶Calls RB "the father of Anglo-American Modernism" and suggests that his dramatic monologues be thought of as "a key speech in a play which doesn't exist but which it creates around itself." Successors have been inspired to fit "analysis and criticism marsupially in their poems." Because of him, poets can write in any voice, can assume readers will not think the world the poet creates is objective reality, and can find material anywhere. RB's characters are opinionated and talkative: "We are born, we talk and we die." Warton Lecture, 26 Febraury 1991.

C91:66. Prins, Johanna Henrica. "Translating Greek Tragedy: Elizabeth Barrett and Robert Browning." *DAI* 52.1 (July 1991): 157A. Princeton University, 1991. ¶Analyzes EBB's and RB's translations of Greek tragedies in terms of the textual tradition of reader as a translator, which blurs the distinction between reading and writing. Neither poet reclaims an original text or proclaims an original voice in their translations. EBB enacts a loss of authorial voice and presents her writing as an effect of translation. In the courtship correspondence, their use of Greek translation presents neither poet as primary author. In later poems, RB views translation as sympathetic reading and also as a confrontation with textuality; his translation of the *Agamemnon* "demonstrates an even more violent disjunction of text and voice." See below.

C91:67. Prins, Yopie. "Elizabeth Barrett, Robert Browning, and the *Différance* of Translation." *VP* 29 (Winter 1991): 435–51. ¶Applies the Derridean concept of différance to the courtship correspondence of EBB and RB. As translators of

Aeschylus, EBB and RB displace themselves as the writing subjects and instead put into practice the "middle voice" hypothesized by Derrida. Through their frequent exchange of quotations and references to *Prometheus Bound*, they use Greek as "a language of desire" to mediate between them, recognizing that they remain untranslatable to each other. The exchange of their letters may also be seen in the context of Derrida's *The Post Card*, the post contributing a kind of "middle voice" that simultaneously brought EBB and RB together and kept them apart. See above.

C91:68. Richter, David H. "Dialogism and Poetry." *Studies in the Literary Imagination* 23 (1990): 9–27. ¶Employs Bakhtin's concepts of polyphony, heteroglossia, and dialogism to analyze poetry which "portrays or represents a speech-act," such as the dramatic monologue. RB's "My Last Duchess" is "cunningly crafted in a doublevoiced style precisely in order to evade the interplay of dialogue, at the time or later." The Duke's speech is neither self-betraying or casually garrulous but rather is a demand of the envoy and, ultimately, of the next duchess.

C91:69. Righetti, Angelo. "Rileggere *Asolando*." Perosa, *Browning e Venezia* 273–83. ¶Rereads *Asolando*, a collection that has a miscellaneous character somewhat like the earlier *Bells and Pomegranates* series. Subtitled "Fancies and Facts," it is a final, cautious homage to the first Romantics, Wordsworth especially. In Italian.

C91:70. Roberts, Adam. "A Source for Browning's *Agamemnon*." *VP* 29 (Summer 1991): 180–83. ¶Suggests that RB drew heavily on F. A. Paley's *The Tragedies of Aeschylus* (3rd edition, London, 1870) for his translation.

C91:71. Roberts, Tony. "An Imaginary Possession." *BSN* 21 (1991–92): 56–59. ¶A poem.

C91:72. Ryals, Clyde de L. "Levity's Rainbow: The Way of Browning's 'Christmas-Eve'." *A World of Possibilities: Romantic Irony in Victorian Literature*. Columbus: Ohio State UP, 1990. 48–59. ¶Considerably revised and expanded from C86:51.

C91:73. St. George, E. A. W. "Browning and Conversation." *Index to Theses with Abstracts Accepted for Higher Degrees by the Universities of Great Britain and Ireland and the Council for National Academic Awards* 38.2 (1989): 531. Dissertation, Oxford University, 1988. ¶Explores Victorians' attitudes toward conversation and links conversational utterance with communication in a poem. RB's own manner of talk is examined, and the ideas are applied to *Red Cotton*

Night-Cap Country, The Inn Album, Pacchiarotto, and *Parleyings with Certain People*.

C91:74. Schoffman, Nachum. *There is No "Truer Truth": The Musical Aspect of Browning's Poetry. Contributions to the Study of World Literature, Number 40*. New York: Greenwood P, 1991. xv + 178 pp. ¶Investigates the effect of RB's musicianship on his poetry, especially his musical ideas and images. A competent keyboard musician, RB used musical concepts in "perceptive and penetrating" ways, and his knowledge of music history and theory was unusual in his time. His use of musical notation in letters indicates that he thought in terms of music, and his poetry contains complex verbal sound effects. A new identification for the piece of music described in "A Toccata of Galuppi's" is proposed: the Sonata-Toccata in F Major. RB's "Parleying With Charles Avison" is unique in ending with music notation and including words set to Avison's melody.

C91:75. Sherwood, Dolly [Delores P.]. " 'The Perfection of All That Is Charming' " and "Womanly Concerns and Girlish Escapades." *Harriet Hosmer, American Sculptor: 1830–1908*. Columbia: U of Missouri P, 1991. 89–114. ¶Describes EBB and RB's association with Hatty Hosmer, whom they knew in Rome and Florence. She sculpted "The Clasped Hands" shortly after they met. They became good friends during the 1850s, but she and RB later quarreled.

C91:76. Slinn, E. Warwick. "Language and Truth in *The Ring and the Book*" and "The Politics of Self in *The Ring and the Book*." *The Discourse of Self in Victorian Poetry*. Charlottesville: U of Virginia P, 1991. 119–48, 149–84. ¶Revised from C89:69. Explores questions of authority and selfhood in RB's poem, looking at what each speaker attaches authority to — social formulas, courtly romance, structures of law and family, class, religion, saintliness, reason, God, nature. The poem is about textualized experience — brutal murder and the discourse that produces its meaning and significance: "the poem produces a challenge to fundamental assumptions about the status of truth and about the production of the self."

C91:77. Smith-Bingham, Richard. "Browning's Subjective Mode." *BSN* 21 (1991–92): 40–55. ¶Examines the contradiction of a poet "so fiercely protective of the author's right to privacy" expressing himself most often through the subjective mode. RB's "objectification of the first person singular" critiques the discourse of Romanticism in its use of the unreliable narrator. Although his vision is "anti-heroic, anti-prophetic, a vision contrary to . . . expansionist optimism" and doubtful of the efficacy of human discourse, he nevertheless uses "the 'machine' of language, 'the process by which thought moves'," "to expound a Christian morality without being dogmatic.'' The dialectic of *The Ring and the Book* does not accomplish this task as well as does that of *Aristophanes' Apology*.

C91:78. Viscusi, Robert, ed. *BIS*, 16 (1988). ¶Rev. by Judith Rosen, *VS* 34 (Spring 1991): 398–400.

C91:79. Vlock-Keyes, Deborah. "Music and Dramatic Voice in Robert Browning and Robert Schumann." *VP* 29 (Autumn 1991): 227–39. ¶Argues that RB found in Schumann a "musical-poetical model," especially in Schumann's notion of music as truth and the key to dramatic voice. Their aesthetics share many similarities: both felt the artist is inextricably bound to the social world, created dramatic personae, used musical syncopation to create character, felt music "captures the soul," and favored imaginative freedom over the formal structuralism of classical symmetry. RB's serious study of Schumann's *Carnival* in *Fifine at the Fair* strongly suggests their relationship is no coincidence.

C91:80. Walsh, Thomas P. "The Frames of Browning's *Men and Women*." *BSN* 21 (1991–92): 32–39. ¶Suggests "Love Among the Ruins" and "Memorabilia" as the frame poems for the first volume of *Men and Women*, and "Andrea del Sarto" and "Misconceptions" for the second. "One Word More" is then an epilogue. The two opening poems may be compared (the second being "a specific instance of the structural suggestions" of the first), as may the two that close the volumes.

C91:81. Wilsey, Mildred. "The Writing of *Aurora Leigh*." *DAI* 52.1 (1991): 172A. Yale University, 1938. ¶Examines influences on EBB during the ten and more years of her writing *Aurora Leigh*. Contemporary poet Alexander Smith influenced her form and manner, some aspects of the poem are autobiographical or based on people she knew, and contemporary fiction contributed conventional story. Swedenborgian thought may be seen in the poem's philosophy. She adopted "reality as the subject of her story" and also retained "attitudes of her romantic heritage." A manuscript and the first edition of the poem are compared in an appendix.

C91:82. Woolford, John. "Browning's 'Flight of the Duchess' and Coleridge." *BSN* 21 (1991–92): 5–14. ¶Asserts that RB's "creative envy" of Coleridge is evident in his "Flight of the Duchess," at once a development of Coleridgean influences and a critique of them. "Kubla Khan" and "Christabel" are intertexts for the ecstacy and sexuality in RB's poem, as "The Rime of the Ancient Mariner" is for its ideas about the "visionary faculty [being] physiological as well as psychological.'' Coleridge's poems reflect poetic deadlock, whereas RB's demonstrate creative release and renewal.

C91:83. Woolford, John. '' 'Life — that's Venice': Browning's Romanticism in *Fifine at the Fair*.'' Perosa, *Browning e Venezia* 233–51. ¶Suggests ways RB revisited — rather than rewrote — *Sordello* in *Fifine at the Fair*, especially in the Venice sequence at the end of the poem. RB makes a ''double reparation'' in the later poem, paying tribute to the power of poetry and remembering ''that the romantics were humanists, and that the fictive or visionary character of poetry does not in itself make poetry illusory or immoral.''

C91:84.* Yeo, Hongsang. ''The Historical Dialogism in Browning's Dramatic Monologues.'' *Journal of English Language and Literature* 37.3 (Autumn 1991): 587–602. ¶In Korean. See below.

C91:85. Yeo, Hongsang. ''Poetry, History, and Utopia: Browning's Social Criticism in 'The Ring and the Book'.'' *DAI* 51.9 (1991): 3088A. University of Wisconsin at Madison, 1990. ¶Applies Jameson's narrative theory, Bakhtin's theory of language, and feminist theory of sexuality to Victorian ideological rewritings of the past in RB's poem and other of his dramatic monologues. RB critiques Utilitarianism and also Victorian sexuality. The poem's discourse is carnivalesque; the ending of history is deferred.

C91:86. Zorzi, Rosella Mamoli. ''Palazzi e personaggi del mondo veneziano di Browning.'' Perosa, *Browning e Venezia* 117–24. ¶Describes people and places associated with RB's visits to Venice from 1878 and after, among others, Katharine Bronson, who owned Casa Alvisi on the Grand Canal and also La Mura in Asolo. The Brownings' son, Pen, and his wife, Fannie Coddington, bought and restored Palazzo Rezzonico, where RB died in 1889. In Italian; reprint in part of B91:5.

BIBLIOGRAPHY INDEX

INDEX